CRAZY HORSE

Crazy Horse

A Lakota Life

Kingsley M. Bray

University of Oklahoma Press : Norman

Library of Congress Cataloging-in-Publication Data

Bray, Kingsley M., 1956–
    Crazy Horse : a Lakota life / Kingsley M. Bray
        p.   cm. — (Civilization of the American Indian series ; v. 254)
    Includes bibliographical references and index.
    ISBN 0-8061-3785-1 (alk. paper)
    1. Crazy Horse, ca. 1842–1877.   2. Oglala Indians—Kings and rulers—
Biography.   3. Oglala Indians—Government relations.   4. Oglala Indians—
Wars.   5. Little Bighorn, Battle of the, Mont., 1876.   I. Title.   II. Series.
    E99.O3B53 2006
    978.004'9752440092—dc22

                                                            2006040261

Crazy Horse: A Lakota Life is Volume 254 of The Civilization
            of the American Indian Series.

The paper in this book meets the guidelines for permanence and
durability of the Committee on Production Guidelines for
Book Longevity of the Council on Library Resources, Inc. ∞

2 3 4 5 6 7 8 9 10

For my mother and father,
Christine Mary and James David Francis Bray

CONTENTS

ILLUSTRATIONS

FIGURES

Following page 286
Crazy Horse, as drawn by Amos Bad Heart Bull
Red Cloud
Spotted Tail
Young Man Afraid of His Horse
He Dog
Little Big Man
Hunts the Enemy (George Sword)
Little Hawk and Lieutenant William P. Clark
General George Crook
Lieutenant Colonel George Armstrong Custer
Colonel Nelson A. Miles
Touch the Clouds
Oglala delegation to Washington
Low Dog
Spotted Eagle
Black Shawl
Crazy Horse's funeral cortege
Crazy Horse's scaffold burial at Camp Sheridan

MAPS

ACKNOWLEDGMENTS

It is a special pleasure to acknowledge the assistance of many members of the Lakota community in North and South Dakota. Several informants requested anonymity, especially in the sensitive matters of Crazy Horse's family life. Many made available private family documents; all have contributed to the deeper background of *Crazy Horse: A Lakota Life*. Especially significant interviews were conducted with the following Lakota people, whose contribution is gratefully acknowledged:

LaDonna Brave Bull Allard, Fort Yates
Emma Chase Alone West, Manderson
Elsie Clown, Eagle Butte
Victor Douville, Sinte Gleska University, Mission
Mario Gonzalez, Black Hawk
Ellen in the Woods, Eagle Butte
Leonard Little Finger, Loneman School, Oglala
Loretta Little Hawk, Pine Ridge
Elaine Quick Bear Quiver, Pine Ridge
Chris and Nita Ravenshead, Custer
Lula Red Cloud and Harry Burk, Hermosa
Evangeline Lucille Runs After, Rapid City
Donovin Sprague, Historian, Crazy Horse Memorial, Crazy Horse Mountain
Alex White Plume, Manderson
Harvey White Woman, Kyle

Jack Meister, of Waleska, Georgia, gave crucial assistance in the interview process. Jack indefatigably tracked down individuals, made calls, and put me in touch with informants. I look forward to more years of cooperation in discovering the Lakota past.

In England, fellow students of the Plains Indians helped at various stages in the process of research and writing. Neil Gilbert, English Westerners' Society, helped crystallize my ideas about the Battle of the Rosebud. Members of the Custer Association of Great Britain, especially Derek Batten, Francis Taunton, and Barry C. Johnson, in inviting me to speak on Crazy Horse, helped me focus my concept of the Battle of the Little Bighorn. Thanks are also due to Barry for his long loan of the Eli S. Ricker Papers microfilm. In many hours of debate in person and on the telephone, I derived knowledge and wisdom from my dear late friend Colin Taylor, dean of American Indian studies.

I owe a special debt to Joseph Balmer, of Erlenbach, Switzerland. A founding member of the English Westerners' Society, Joe was also a prolific correspondent with historians and Indian people. His gift of a large collection of George E. Hyde's research papers helped focus my historical ambitions, and his loans of his extensive correspondence with such reservation contacts as John Colhoff and Eddie Herman are resources that I still consult daily. Without Joe's belief and contribution, this book would be the poorer.

In the United States, the staffs of a number of institutions have been of material assistance. Thanks are due to Barbara Larsen, National Archives–Central Plains Region, Kansas City, Missouri; Michael Musick and Robert E. Kvasnicka, National Archives, Washington, D.C.; Dayton W. Canaday, former director, South Dakota Historical Society. Fellow Indian Wars historians Paul L. Hedren and Jerome A. Greene have helped with encouragement and information. Throughout twenty years of my research, the Nebraska State Historical Society has been an incomparable resource and source of material aid. Through Director Lawrence J. Sommer, the society helped underwrite the costs of research trips. Nebraska Game and Parks Commission helped make accommodations available for my family and me. At the University of Oklahoma Press, I owe thanks to editor-in-chief Charles E. Rankin, acquisitions editor Alessandra E. Jacobi, and manuscript editor Steven B. Baker for bringing this book to fruition. Copyeditor Melanie Mallon helped make the final cuts with enviable grace and meticulous attention to detail.

Colleagues have generously shared knowledge, views, and facts. In particular, I thank Raymond J. DeMallie, Department of Anthropology, University of Indiana, Bloomington; Mike Cowdrey, San Luis Obispo; and Ephriam D. Dickson III, Salt Lake City.

A cluster of friends and their families have been vital contributors to this book and my continuing research into the history of the Lakota people and the Native plains. *Nebraska History* editor Donald B. Cunningham was a gracious host and guide on a memorable trip across the plains—here's hoping for many more! At the Fort Robinson Museum, curator Thomas R. Buecker has been a source of fact, food, and good humor. R. Eli Paul, museum director of the Liberty Memorial Museum of World War One, Kansas City, Missouri, has been generous in sharing documents, views, and knowledge. Gail DeBuse Potter, director of the Museum of the Fur Trade, Chadron, Nebraska, is a constant source of logistical aid and good grace in my trips to the plains. As if that were not enough, she is married to James E. Potter, retired now as editor of *Nebraska History*, who has facilitated research and dispensed wit and wisdom in equal measure. Last but not least, James A. Hanson, editor, *Museum of the Fur Trade Quarterly*, who first invited me to the plains, showed me Fort Laramie, the Powder River country, and one imperishable Wyoming morning, the sunrise over Pumpkin Buttes; he has been for more than twenty years the Prince of Companions.

Finally, no thanks could be complete without acknowledging my family. My father first encouraged my childhood interest in the American West by bringing home from our public library in Yorkshire works by Francis Parkman, Mari Sandoz, and George Hyde. His and my mother's belief in this project is reflected in the dedication. My wife, Ann—lodestone, anchor, and North Star—has been a sounding board for ideas and an indispensable partner in all enterprises. Without her presence, I could not have completed this book. Our children, Ciana, Dubheasa, and David, in not letting me escape from the joyous toils of family life, have contributed more than they can know to my understanding of life in Lakota lodges.

INTRODUCTION

Crazy Horse was the greatest war leader of the Lakota people. Acknowledged by tribal foes as the enemy they most feared, honored by allied tribesmen as the bravest of all warriors, Crazy Horse counted more than two hundred coups, a war record unmatched by any of his peers—Red Cloud, Spotted Tail, Sitting Bull, or any of that remarkable cohort of Lakota leaders growing up during the first half of the nineteenth century. His inspirational courage was a byword, matched by a generosity that won the praise of all his people. Had he been born into an earlier century, his achievements would have been tallied only in the winter counts, the pictographic calendars that recorded Lakota history. Instead, Crazy Horse was born in 1840, just as the presence of Euro-Americans on the Great Plains shifted gears from sporadic trade to a juggernaut of expansion. The Manifest Destiny that transformed the American West from tribal hunting grounds to the agricultural and industrial heartland of modern America provoked inevitable resistance from the Plains Indians.

From youth, Crazy Horse aligned himself with tribal factions that rejected negotiations with the United States. As the buffalo herds, mainstay of the Plains lifeway, shrank, many Lakotas accepted the inevitable and settled on treaty-guaranteed reservations, to be ration fed and educated in the ways of a changing world. Until the last months of his short life, Crazy Horse rejected the reservation system. His tactical leadership in the warfare against the U.S. Army contributed critically to the two greatest defeats for American arms during the Plains wars and ensured him a place in a wider history, high on that honor roll reserved for patriots resisting an overwhelming invader.

Crazy Horse was no brash, unthinking fighting man. Modest, reflective, reserved to the point of introversion, he was inscrutable to many of his own people. His courage was grounded in a profound Lakota piety. To many modern writers, he summed up the romantic ideal of the "mystic warrior of the plains." For a huge constellation of people today, Crazy Horse continues to matter. For modern Lakota people he has remained a compelling symbol of resistance. In darkened rooms and tipis, songs attributed to Crazy Horse continue to be sung, calling for the aid of spirits in healing and in restoring old ways. To Lakota radicals undergoing the vision quest, Crazy Horse has appeared as a guardian spirit, underwriting the continuing legal struggle to regain the Black Hills. The public at large recognizes the name of Crazy Horse as a touchstone of freedom, of integrity and bravery against the odds. In 1999 Viking Penguin Books, ahead of volumes on St. Augustine, Martin Luther King, and the Buddha, chose to lead off their prestigious Penguin Lives series with a profile of Crazy Horse by Pulitzer Prize–winning novelist Larry McMurtry. His elegant essay dwelled on the enigma that was Crazy Horse but also illustrated the need for a new, full life of the greatest Lakota war leader.

For over sixty years Mari Sandoz's *Crazy Horse, the Strange Man of the Oglalas,* has stood as the standard life. A native of the plains, Sandoz commanded a compelling narrative style and an unmatched ability to evoke plains landscapes. Her book resists easy categorization. Characters address each other in direct speech, and motivations are reconstructed and imputed, all in the manner of a typical historical novel, yet Sandoz rooted her fiction in historical research that was groundbreaking for its day. Ahead of any Plains historians, she had examined U.S. Army and Indian Office records at the National Archives in Washington, D.C., explored key regional repositories like the Nebraska State Historical Society, and even conducted her own interviews with Lakota elders to amplify her picture of Crazy Horse and his times. So compelling was her portrait that it helped shift the paradigm in Indian studies, away from the racist stereotyping of the previous century, toward a more empathetic reading of the Lakota world. For over thirty years, no serious attempt was made to replace Sandoz's life. All biographies since Sandoz have built on her book, unconsciously incorporating her assumptions, biases, and reconstructions as fact, even quoting her dialogue verbatim as conversations actually spoken by Crazy Horse and his contemporaries.

In truth, Sandoz forced her materials to fit dramatic unities, not historical objectivity. A historical novel needs its protagonist present at all key events. Consequently, Sandoz's youthful Crazy Horse turns up at the Blue Water Creek battle in 1855, a turning point in Lakota-U.S. relations. Secondary writers have dutifully followed Sandoz, but no contemporary document or Lakota testimony backs up the dramatic reconstruction. To heighten drama, a novelist must simplify the prodigality of real life. Sandoz compresses Crazy Horse's lifelong commitment as a vision seeker into a single vision quest, its chronology placed to ensure maximum drama. Events such as Crazy Horse's investiture as a Shirt Wearer are taken out of historical sequence, the better to maintain drama and, more seriously, to sustain Sandoz's idealized portrayal of Crazy Horse as pure nontreaty Lakota.

Even in a work of fiction, however, characters are permitted conflicting darker sides. Sandoz brushes over blots on Crazy Horse's reputation. His adultery with

Black Buffalo Woman, for instance, was recognized by contemporaries as a potential threat to tribal solidarity. Sandoz invented mitigating circumstances and a childhood romance to explain away the incident. In the closing section of the book, and in private correspondence, her negative reaction to Crazy Horse's last wife, the mixed-blood Nellie Larrabee, suggests that her hero's reality became secondary to the creation of her own idealized supermale—chaste, courageous, and reflective, both warrior and mystic. By contrast, Sandoz casts protreaty Lakotas like Red Cloud as collaborationist villains, reducing the complex reality of the period to a dichotomy of good and evil—and doing no favors to contemporary Lakotas struggling with the reservation inheritance. In writing what remains a compelling historical novel, a beautiful evocation of the plains and a lament for a romanticized Lakota world, Sandoz reconfigured the tragedy of Crazy Horse into a modern saint's life.

Crazy Horse, the Strange Man of the Oglalas remains a literary tour de force, but no one today would attempt to reconstruct the reign of Henry V by reading Shakespeare. For several years, frontier military historians like Robert Utley and Eli Paul have called for a new appraisal of Crazy Horse's life and career. This book returns to the primary sources to construct a life of Crazy Horse grounded in the reality of the nineteenth-century Lakota world. I reassess his achievements in warfare, examine the role he played in the signal victory at the Little Bighorn, and retrace the tragic sequence of misunderstandings, betrayals, and misjudgments that led to his death. I also explore the private tragedies that marred his childhood and shaped his adult life and reassess the evidence for his status as a Lakota visionary, all in hopes of better understanding his role in a momentous chapter of the history of his people and of the wider American nation.

As a historian, I concede that the materials for constructing a life of Crazy Horse are sketchy and fragmentary. The acres of documentation that chart the life of Franklin Delano Roosevelt, or Winston Churchill, or even George Washington simply do not exist for a nineteenth-century Lakota warrior. But, like the biographer pointing out that the sources for Shakespeare's life are insufficient but still infinitely richer than those for any of his peers, I can draw on an unrivaled wealth of interviews, given by Crazy Horse's friends and contemporaries to curious and persistent researchers early in the twentieth century. The Eli S. Ricker and Eleanor H. Hinman interviews, housed at the Nebraska State Historical Society, form the tip of an iceberg of Lakota testimony on the man and his times. Crazy Horse may be a bewitching enigma, but these interviews provide more information about his genealogy, his family background, and his private and spiritual life than exists for any Lakota contemporary. Following Ricker and Hinman, I have interviewed modern Lakotas, filling in vital details on Crazy Horse's childhood and the network of relationships that sustained him. All men and women take secrets to their graves, but I hope to have penetrated far enough beneath the surface to be able to draw in the outline of forces and events that shaped his inner life and determined the course of his career.

The man I was left with was the product of his times. The nineteenth-century Lakotas were as ethnocentric a people as ever walked the earth, assured of their centrality in a world that was about to be transformed beyond recognition. Crazy Horse inherited their sense of exclusiveness, and his adult life was devoted to fighting the enemies of his people. We should not mistake that fight for some high-stakes game or noble martial art: exciting, full of dash and color, it was also a deadly arena in which Crazy Horse, like his peers, killed men and women and routinely mutilated the dead. He was a man profoundly scarred by personal tragedy and loss, his personality marked by melancholy and reticence. Lakotas recognized such traits as the behavior of the *heyoka*, the dreamer of thunder. To them Crazy Horse married the irruptive, unpredictable nature of Thunder power: in war and in peace he moved rapidly to anticipate, trip up, and confound his foes. Crazy Horse's concept of his personal gift of Thunder's power was the central theme of his life, and he strove to refine that power in a mental discipline that, in the last months of his life, opened new vistas for his spiritual growth as a healer in a postwar Lakota world.

Today in Lakota communities, old people remain who recall the affection and respect that the memory of Crazy Horse inspired in those who survived him into the twentieth century and the clipped horizons of reservation life. One old lady recalled as if it were yesterday the visit of the teenage Crazy Horse to his Miniconjou relatives, his training as a scout, his attentive silence before the chiefs and elders. Like that of Genghis Khan in Mongolia, the cult of Crazy Horse is taking on new life, accruing new significance in a changing world: he continues to matter profoundly. Of all my informants, Lucille Runs After, great-granddaughter of Crazy Horse's kinsman Lone Horn, said it best: "My mother and aunts all said that Crazy Horse . . . was an outstanding person; there was something magic about him; he made people happy by his presence."

In a new century of accelerating change and challenge for all people, that memory of magic and presence remains potent as example and inspiration. Honoring it, this is Crazy Horse's story.

CRAZY HORSE

One

CURLY HAIR

1

THE LIGHT-HAIRED BOY

It was fall 1840, the season the people would recall as Stole-One-Hundred-Horses. The short grasses of the high plains were curing yellow. From the pine-covered Black Hills, a web of creeks and gullies snaked east to join the forks of the Cheyenne River. Along one watercourse, horse herds grazed, and buffalo-skin tipis—conical tents supported by an hourglass framework of slender pine lodge-poles—marked a camp of the Lakota people. Family hunting groups were scattered over the plains, hunting small game. Other men were busy at home, grinding arrowheads and repairing hunting gear, while women worked busily at skins for winter clothing. In one particular tipi, a young woman was preparing to give birth.

Twenty-six years old, Rattle Blanket Woman was confident in the impending birth. Already blessed with a daughter of about four, she would soon bear her second child. Moreover, her husband had taken care to ensure her comfort. Most men preferred to have their children born in their own camps, but Crazy Horse—a family name derived from a vision granted his own father—had lingered through the fall with his wife's people, the Miniconjou division of Lakotas.[1]

On the day Rattle Blanket Woman's labor pains began, the family tipi was left to the expectant mother and her kinswomen. Her mother, or some other relative experienced as a midwife, oversaw the birth. A stake decorated with eagle-down plumes was driven into the earth, and near it, a clean deerskin was spread for Rattle Blanket Woman to kneel upon. As the contractions increased, she pressed her hands and knees against the stake. Imperturbably, the midwife fetched water, grease, and swabs of braided sweetgrass until, at last, after unknown struggles, the baby came.[2]

The midwife gently laid the baby on the deerskin, cleared its mouth, and with a sharp knife severed the umbilical cord, nicking the end attached to the afterbirth. Then she wrapped a band of skin around the baby's middle, before cleaning his body and placing him in his mother's arms. As Rattle Blanket Woman held her firstborn son, she was able to examine the tiny form, exclaiming over his light skin and brown-tinged wispy hair.

As mother slept, the baby was fed fruit purees and fitted with a soft tanned diaper lined with cattail down. Over the next few hours, family members quietly visited the new arrival. Among the first were the maternal grandparents, who presented matching charms in the form of beaded pouches representing lizards. Believed to endow health and long life, the lizard charm was the first embodiment of a fundamental concept in Lakota life: *sicun*, a power granted to all animate and inanimate things at birth. A baby had only a small amount, but it was believed that placing the umbilical cord in the pouch would transmit something of the lizard's protective power to the baby. The matching empty pouch was hidden far away to decoy bad spirits from the baby's source of power.[3]

Rattle Blanket Woman's family was prominent among the Miniconjous: their gifts were abundant. Other gifts came from the husband's family. Big Woman, Crazy Horse's married sister, presented elaborate cradles. At length Crazy Horse was permitted into his lodge. Born into a respected Oglala family, Crazy Horse's father Makes the Song was an important holy man. Crazy Horse valued his position among his wife's people. Now his marriage was strengthened by every Lakota man's wish—a son.

Crazy Horse had an elder stripe the baby's face with fine lines of red paint, symbolic of the child's relationship to Wakan Tanka, the Great Holy. Then an honored friend or relative was chosen to ensure the transfer of valued personality traits to the infant. Such a man, renowned for bravery in battle and good nature at home, took the baby in his arms and, gently parting the infant's lips, breathed into his mouth, transmitting the vital life principle *ni*. In the days that followed, Crazy Horse sponsored a feast to honor his wife, and after all had eaten, the village herald stepped into the center of the circle to announce the baby's name.

Whatever name was drawn from the store of honored family titles, it did not stick. Ultimately, the boy would acquire his father's and grandfather's name—Crazy Horse—and make it imperishably famous. But for now, mother or sister coined a nickname. Doting over his comparatively pale skin and the wavy hair inherited from his mother, the black highlighted by a deep brown sheen, the family began to call him by any one of several lovingly ingenious variations on Pehin Yuhaha: Curly Hair.[4]

The 1840 Lakota world that Curly Hair was born into was vigorous, confident, and growing. His Teton people roamed the high plains west of the Missouri River, throughout modern western South Dakota and adjoining parts of Nebraska, Wyoming, and North Dakota. About 11,500 strong in 1840, the Teton divisions accounted for about one-half of the people Euro-Americans knew collectively as Sioux. East of the Missouri ranged relatives and allies who spoke mutually intelligible dialects: Yankton and Yanktonai bands were centered on the long grass prairies of the James River, while in southern Minnesota, the Santees occupied the transition zone between prairie and woodland.[5]

The Tetons comprised seven divisions. Curly Hair's people, the Oglalas, ranged between the Black Hills and the North Platte River in southeast Wyoming. The Brules hunted along the White and Niobrara rivers to the east. North of the Black Hills ranged five smaller divisions, collectively known as Saones: the Miniconjous, his mother's people; Two Kettles; Sans Arcs; Sihasapas; and Hunkpapas.

Lakota domination of the northern plains was implemented by a diplomacy that matched force with intertribal alliance. By definition, all other tribes were considered enemies, except for the Cheyennes and Arapahos, who were accorded an honorary status as part of the great Lakota Alliance.[6]

By the time of Curly Hair's birth, two tribes in particular were emerging as key opponents in the Lakota domination of the plains. Southeast of the Lakota domain, in the lower Platte River valley, the horticultural Pawnee villages lay at the core of extensive hunting ranges on the central plains.

Along the Yellowstone River ranged the Crows, a nomadic tribe, wealthy in horses, that had exchanged long-distance raids with the Lakotas for many decades. As Lakota expansionism fronted Crow hunting ranges in a new war zone along the Powder River, the cycle of raid and reprisal would accelerate during Curly Hair's lifetime. The Crow war would be the arena in which the adult Curly Hair would first prove himself as the greatest of all Lakota warriors.[7]

As young Curly Hair grew into boyhood, his deepest, most sustaining relationships were rooted in the intimacies of family life. Within the embracing circle of the tipi, he lived with his father, mother, and elder sister Looks at Her. His father customarily sat in the honor place, at the rear of the lodge, facing the east entrance. As firstborn son, Curly Hair would sit at his father's left, while his mother and sister busied themselves around the cooking fire, serving food to kinsfolk and visitors.[8]

Even more important than the nuclear family of parents and children was the wider extended family. The *tiyospaye*, or lodge group, was the basic building block of society. A cluster of families, related by blood and marriage, the tiyospaye was typically fifty or a hundred people strong. Curly Hair's large kindred was called Kapozha, meaning lightweight, or "not encumbered with much baggage." The leading family was Curly Hair's own, proudly tracing its descent through a lineage of elders and holy men to his great-grandfather Black Elk I, born in the days before the Lakotas obtained horses. The families of grandfather Makes the Song, his four brothers, and their six adult sons formed the core of the kindred, augmented by those of men who had married in. Ten or fifteen tipis of siblings, cousins, and in-laws made an extended home in which Curly Hair felt the nurturing security of being valued and loved. The proliferation of nicknames affectionately detailing his wavy hair—The Light-Haired Boy, Yellow Fuzzy Hair—reflected the relaxed intimacy of relationships with one's own "band relatives." In his mother's band of Miniconjous, too, Curly Hair enjoyed a warm, reassuring home away from home.[9]

Two other kindreds, identified with the prestigious families of Standing Bull and Yellow Eagle, formed with Kapozha a larger band known collectively as Hunk-patila, or Camp at the Horn, the place in the Oglala tribal circle next to the camp entrance accorded to respected warriors.[10]

A band like Hunkpatila recognized one man as its "chief," or *wicasa itancan*. In Curly Hair's boyhood, Man Afraid of His Horse, a rising war leader and a patron of the Fort Laramie traders, emerged as ranking chief. Elders like Makes the Song sat as an advisory council with Man Afraid of His Horse.[11]

Political organization at band level was more stylized and coercive. Activities like the communal hunt demanded precise coordination, so the council recognized several younger men, proven in war, as *akicita* police, to serve for the duration of the activity.

With the Hunkpatila, two other bands, the True, or Original, Oglala (in theory the senior band within the tribe) and the rather amorphous Spleen band, made up a larger unit, the Oglala Proper. Numbering one hundred lodges, 750 people, when Curly Hair was born, the Oglala Proper camped together for upwards of half the year. After winter dispersals, it re-formed in time for the big buffalo hunts in May, to replenish meat stocks, and again in November, to lay in winter surpluses and supply the traders' demand for thickly haired winter robes. Each June the Oglala Proper gathered with two other bands, the Kiyuksa and Oyuhpe, to offer the tribal ceremony of the Sun Dance, to hunt the great summer buffalo herds, and to make war on tribal enemies.[12]

As Curly Hair grew, he absorbed the deepest values of his society. Four fundamental virtues—generosity, courage, fortitude, and wisdom—animated tribal life. Most basic of all was generosity. It underwrote every aspect of daily life, from the simple sharing of food to the orchestrated giveaways that marked great ceremonials. Family-sponsored feasts celebrated Curly Hair's first tottering steps, his first word. His father presented the poor and infirm with robes, dried meat, and horses in the name of his toddler son. At the 1842 Sun Dance, the parents celebrated Curly Hair's ability to walk and talk by having his ears pierced. Within the dance arbor, families stacked robes, blankets, dried meat, metal knives, and kettles. Curly Hair was laid on a bed of sage. A chosen elder harangued and sang, then took an awl and pierced each of Curly Hair's ears, exhorting the parents to bring up their son according to Lakota customs. As the child squalled, Rattle Blanket Woman took her place at the piles of family wealth, presiding over their distribution to valued allies, respected matrons, and the poor.[13]

The second foundation of Lakota ethics was courage. At his father's side, Curly Hair heard tales of the ancient wars of the Lakota, when warriors fought on foot against the Chippewa. In the boy's family, the greatest living warrior was Male Crow, his father's younger brother. Male Crow was the family's child beloved, in whose name feasts and giveaways were sponsored. He lived the life of the Lakota warrior with the easy poise of a man born to greatness. For young Curly Hair, Male Crow made a dashing role model.[14]

Soon after Curly Hair turned four years old, the security of his infant world was thrown into a turmoil that would radically shape the rest of his life. Male Crow led 160 men, including Crazy Horse, on a horse-stealing raid against the Shoshones.[15] The war party marched afoot through worsening weather, tracking the Shoshone trail north from Wind River into winter ranges shared with the Crows. Nearing their quarry, Male Crow halted the party atop a wooded ridge. After ordering breastworks dug, he detailed his brother-in-law Last Dog, with three other scouts, to reconnoiter from bluffs commanding the Shoshone camp. Last Dog did not reach the camp, which had been augmented by Crow allies. Stumbling on a lone Shoshone, out riding with his young son, the Oglalas opened fire with their muskets. Although his father was killed, the boy and his well-trained pony turned and galloped for home.

The scouts hurried back. Snow was falling thickly, but Last Dog taunted Male Crow to lead an attack. Wiser heads urged caution, but Last Dog continued to brag, and Male Crow's rashness got the better of him. Saying starkly, "I am a man to look for death," Male Crow prepared to march out alone, but four of his five "brothers" and many of their friends and relatives tagged along. One brother—evidently Curly Hair's father—stayed with the main party, anxiously watching the scene in the valley.

Amid thickening snow, hundreds of enemy warriors appeared, encircling the party. Only one Lakota managed to escape. After finishing off Male Crow and his thirty warriors, the Shoshones and Crows raced in pursuit. They stormed the Oglala defenses, where desperate men and youths lobbed rocks down the hillside. Undaunted, the Shoshones and Crows pressed forward until the weather worsened into a blizzard. The enemy disengaged, beating the backs and shoulders of the fleeing Oglalas with bows and whips, and gesturing that they had "killed as many as satisfied them for the time." In panic and disgrace, the 130 Oglalas fled the field, most of them wounded or bearing the welts of enemy quirts.[16]

Several days later the war party reached home, exhausted, hungry, and demoralized. In an ecstasy of grief and mourning, men and women hacked off their hair and slashed their legs and arms with knives so that, visiting trader David Adams wrote, "you cold trak them by the blud whar evr thay went." The horses of the slain were led forward and their tails and manes cut off. Mourners such as Makes the Song harangued, giving away ponies and tipis to war leaders or warrior societies that would pledge vengeance for their relatives.[17]

There was not grief alone, however, but shame. Adams noted that the war party had all but "run therselves to deth becos they was sow badly scert," concluding that "I dont think that thay will get ovr their frit in 10 years."[18] The memory of Male Crow, the happy hero of other fights, was traduced as critics talked up his recklessness. Male Crow at least was dead, but criticism now turned on the survivors. For Crazy Horse, the surviving brother, the agonies of guilt and his family's grief were compounded by insinuations of cowardice. Wracked with shame, Crazy Horse pledged to lead the revenge expedition against the Shoshones.

For three months, he worked steadily to mount a coalition of Lakotas and their allies. "Crazy-Horse says his prayers and goes on the war path," reads the terse mnemonic accompanying one winter count. Scheduling a February rendezvous at the forks of Laramie River, Crazy Horse promised many horses and gifts to those bands that joined him and smoked his war pipe. Hundreds of lodges of Lakotas and their Cheyenne and Arapaho allies pledged their help. A truly massive coalition would avenge Male Crow's death.[19]

The villages gathered late in January 1845, but suddenly the coalition broke apart. Traders with abundant liquor were present, and a drinking session among the Lakota leaders deteriorated into a bloody brawl. The village broke up in acrimony. Many relatives of the warriors lost with Male Crow joined the Kiyuksa Oglalas, confirming the extreme view that Curly Hair's father was to blame for the deaths of his brother and their loved ones.[20]

The powerful weapons of gossip and shame tore at the fabric of Crazy Horse's marriage. It had seemed an ideal match. Crazy Horse was a skilled hunter, and Rattle Blanket Woman, famously beautiful and a magnificent runner, was a fitting bride: as a teenager, she had been chosen to run in ceremonial hunts, leading the game toward the hunters. With her wavy hair plaited in tight braids, in her robe adorned with jingling shells, she had won the heart of the visiting Oglala. Crazy Horse had presented her family with a famous dowry of horses, meat, and pelts.

As happens after many fairy-tale weddings, however, the marriage proved unstable. Gossip linked both partners with adulterous affairs. Because siblings-in-law were potential marriage partners, flirtations between them were accepted behavior in Lakota society, but according to modern descendants, Crazy Horse conducted affairs with Rattle Blanket Woman's sister. The scandal cut two ways, however, when gossips linked Rattle Blanket Woman with Male Crow. Reeling from grief and criticism, Crazy Horse verbally lashed out at his wife. "Why is our son so light-complected?" he demanded, tacitly accusing her of an affair with a *wasicu*, a Euro-American. It was the last straw. Isolated from the sustaining love and support of her own family among the Miniconjous, Rattle Blanket Woman succumbed to despair. Although, as one descendant claims, she was newly pregnant with Crazy Horse's third child, Rattle Blanket Woman left the tipi carrying a rope. Finding a sturdy cottonwood, she hanged herself.[21]

Across all societies, a culture of secrecy frequently surrounds a family suicide. Relatives seek to hide motivations from prurient outsiders and from the most vulnerable victims of loss, children. Unfortunately, children kept from the truth are unable to come to terms with the event: what might be understood and "placed" becomes instead an unhealing wound of enigma, fixation, and doubt.

Fragmentary as they are, all sources suggest that the family tragedy had a traumatic effect on Curly Hair, shaping much of his adult life. Although a classic expression of a Lakota warrior's fatalistic defiance, Male Crow's final words—"I am a man to look for death"—would echo through Curly Hair's life. Passed down in family tradition, they shaped his reaction to the deaths of friends and loved ones. It is easy to picture the growing boy hearing the story of Male Crow's end, brooding over the terse poetry of his words and their prompt, bloody fulfillment.[22]

After losing his mother, Curly Hair became isolated. Winter games like sledding and snow snake occupied most boys, and each spring, girls and boys played together at "moving camp," packing toys and dolls on dog travois. Curly Hair dropped out of these activities and instead often followed grandfather Makes the Song to the council tipi, where he silently observed debate and watched the elders play interminable rounds of the hand game. A child was typically taught to ride in his fifth year. Curly Hair learned quickly, but contemporaries recalled that he often rode into the hills to sit and think alone. A pattern had established itself. Curly Hair clearly remembered this period as a decisive break. Recounting his most famous vision to a young relative, he summarized his own childhood: "When I was born I could know and see and understand for a time, *but afterwards went back to it as a baby*"; he acknowledged the psychological regression. He did not resume "growing up naturally" for three years.[23]

Within months, Crazy Horse married one of Rattle Blanket Woman's kinswomen. Two full sisters survived the dead woman, Good Looking Woman and Looks at Her. One family tradition is that Good Looking Woman left her own husband to offer herself to Crazy Horse and to help raise Curly Hair. But that may have been a scandal too far. Instead, Crazy Horse married Kills Enemy, daughter of the Miniconjou chief Corn. Crazy Horse's relations with his new in-laws were good. As time passed, he took Corn's younger daughter, Iron between Horns, as a second wife. The new marriage consolidated Crazy Horse's Miniconjou links, but through his new wives' maternal connections, he also established important ties with the Brule Lakotas. Through the marriages, a rising Brule warrior named Spotted Tail became another of Curly Hair's uncles.[24]

The family grew. Kills Enemy bore two daughters, and about 1846, Iron between Horns bore a son. Eventually Curly Hair, his father, and his two stepmothers would come to enjoy a relationship of deep and spontaneous affection. For now, though, as his stepmothers doted over the new additions and his father was preoccupied with the fostering of new family ties, Curly Hair suffered a period of transition in his life. Two incidents illustrate these tensions. During the severe winter following Rattle Blanket Woman's death, buffalo could not be found. Crazy Horse, a skillful and diligent hunter, one day brought home two pronghorn antelopes slung across his packsaddle. While his stepmother prepared a family meal, Curly Hair slipped quietly out of the lodge. He rode the length of the snow-drifted camp, calling the old people to come to his tipi for meat.

When they looked out the door flap to find their son, a surprised father and stepmother saw instead a line of old men and women, gratefully holding up dishes. Each of the old folk was served a portion of the antelope, and they left singing praise of Curly Hair's generosity. The next day Curly Hair asked for food, and his stepmother replied that there was none left. "Remember, my son," she advised, "they went home singing praises in your name, not my name or your father's. You must be brave. You must live up to your reputation."[25]

The story smacks a little of a boy trying to prove a point, and perhaps contrasting an idealized mother's uncalculated largesse with the stinting formalism of his stepmother. In another unsettling incident, his father tested Curly Hair's courage. Father and son caught a snapping turtle. As Crazy Horse flipped the struggling reptile over on its shell, he ordered Curly Hair to cut open the animal and eat raw its beating heart. The image, the sensations of fear and revulsion, are said to have remained with the boy the rest of his life.[26]

Moreover, the family tragedy may have caused a withdrawal in Curly Hair's father. In his midthirties, Crazy Horse was at a sensitive stage in life, as warriors sought to make the transition to responsible elder. Typically, an injury or disaster at this stage triggered an introverted man to consider a future as *wicasa wakan*, a holy man. That Crazy Horse, the son of a revered priest, should seek to follow in his father's steps was not unexpected. Already he had secured visions of the Bear and the Thunder, Lakota patrons of warfare. Beginning in these crucial years following the deaths of his brother and wife, he began a long visionary apprenticeship. His new vocation necessarily deprived his family of his presence for lengthy vision quests and ritual training that demanded isolation and sexual abstinence. Preoccupied as he was, something of the spontaneous affection that had animated Crazy Horse's first years with his son must have been withdrawn. Again, a symbolic shift in parent-child behavior may have crystallized Curly Hair's isolation: as he turned six, a son typically relinquished the seat he shared with his father at the honor place of the tipi, underscoring the independence a growing boy must acquire. The birth of his half-brother can only have emphasized the shift in his father's attitude.[27]

It would be misleading to suggest that everything in Curly Hair's life deteriorated in the years after his mother's death. Lakota life was geared to mitigating the impact of unforeseen tragedy on children. Grandparents were typically indulgent and played a full part in child rearing. Children were welcome visitors at the tipis of cousins and other relatives. Friendships made within the band would often last for life. Curly Hair's relative Iron Whiteman was one older playmate who would remain close: at the time of the surrenders in 1877, Iron Whiteman's tipi still stood next to that of his boyhood friend. The son of Man Afraid of His Horse would also remain a respectful friend, even after the polarization of the Oglala tribe over relations with the Americans divided the two men. Little Hawk, a half-brother of Crazy Horse, was only four years older than Curly Hair, but Curly Hair addressed Little Hawk as *atku*, father, and the two would grow up to share similar attitudes toward the Americans, indicative of the close family bond.[28]

An exact contemporary of Curly Hair's was He Dog, nephew of chief Smoke of the Bad Face band, with which the Hunkpatilas often traveled. But most of Curly Hair's closest friendships were with older boys, suggesting something of the precocious maturity the family tragedy forced on him. By the time Curly Hair was about five or six, he had acquired two special friends, who, for the brief weeks of the summer Sun Dance camp or at intertribal gatherings, were famously inseparable. One was Lone Bear, a Bad Face lad with a penchant for getting into scrapes. In the rough games boys engaged in to prepare themselves for adult life as warriors, Lone Bear suffered a relentless flow of accidents. Balls of mud—sometimes with live coals embedded in them—lobbed from springy sticks rarely failed to miss him; and the swing-kicking game usually left him nursing a bloody face. Always Lone Bear got up to do it all over again—an infectiously positive lesson for the brooding, reflective Curly Hair.[29]

Even closer to Curly Hair was High Backbone, a Miniconjou kinsman. Five or so years older than Curly Hair, High Backbone was already husky and broad chested, hulking over the slim figure of his Oglala playmate: adults smiled and gave them a joint name, The Bear and His Cub. In the boisterous wrestling and play fights that boys engaged in, the Miniconjou must have been an invaluable ally. Already ten years old, High Backbone would have begun participating in buffalo hunts, but by all accounts, he was patient and protective of his Oglala friend. As much as Curly Hair's father or uncles, High Backbone was a key tutor in the crucial skills of archery, riding, and combat.[30]

During Rattle Blanket Woman's lifetime, Crazy Horse had begun the habit of a lengthy visit to his Miniconjou in-laws. As Oglala winter camps broke up, the family traveled around the south flank of the Black Hills to join the Miniconjous encamped near the forks of Cheyenne River. Most Miniconjous went east to the Missouri, visiting the great trading center of Fort Pierre during May, when the season's first steamboats brought up American officials to distribute goodwill presents to the Lakotas. Even after his wife's death, Crazy Horse kept up the visits, suggesting that he was at pains to maintain close links with Miniconjou allies. Certainly to his son, the weeks spent with the Miniconjous were a significant part of the year, a valued time when Curly Hair felt the relief of a holiday spent among indulgent grandparents and protective uncles, aunts, and cousins.[31]

Grandfather Corn's sons—Bull Head, Has Horns, Bear Comes Out, and the rest—were already apprentice warriors, mentors in warrior skills who advised Curly Hair how to protect himself in battle. Touch the Clouds, two or three years older than Curly Hair and a son of Rattle Blanket Woman's kinsman Lone Horn, became another close friend. The friendship with High Backbone deepened. Mutual gifts of horses marked each other as comrades, *kola*, who pledged to aid each other in all of life's trials.[32]

The year 1848 was to prove a turning point. Through the spring, the family lingered near Fort Pierre, long enough for seven-year-old Curly Hair to listen intently to a strange visitor to the Miniconjou camps—Jesuit priest Pierre-Jean De Smet.[33] The alien precepts, filtered through halting interpreters, were unlikely spiritual healers, but it was a season of renewal for the boy. To a cousin, Curly Hair remembered it as the end of three years of regression: then "I grew up naturally again—at the age of seven I began to learn."[34]

As his receptivity to Father De Smet's message indicated, questions of the spirit world occupied Curly Hair's mind. From his father and grandfather, Curly Hair absorbed much of the Lakota belief system. He had learned that everything in the natural world was animated by a mysterious force that Lakotas called *wakan*. The totality of all these powers was Wakan Tanka. Human beings were born with the potentiality of wakan power, but to acquire more was essential to personal growth and social advancement. Power might be gained by making oneself pitiable before the wakan beings, through the ritual supplication of the vision quest and the self-torture of the Sun Dance. To interpret the wakan powers' requirements, Lakotas sought the aid of holy men like Curly Hair's father and grandfather, men who had through fasting, vision, and prayer been granted insight into the workings of the universe.[35]

As he approached adolescence, Curly Hair learned how to call on the wakan powers to aid him in his endeavors. Spiritually attuned youths might be expected to show a predisposition for a particular being or constellation of powers. As his teen years neared, Curly Hair had repeated intimations in dreams that Thunder, the most awesome manifestation of Wakan Tanka, had singled him out for especial favor. Dreamers of Thunder, he knew, were granted unmatched powers in warfare. To turn such powers to his people's service entailed drastic lifelong obligations. For now, his father advised him only to be receptive and attentive to his dreams, but by age ten, Curly Hair seemed already an unusually brooding introspective youth.[36]

A lifelong pattern had formed, alternating cycles of brooding inaction with bursts of focused energy. Family tragedy had forced on Curly Hair an outward maturity beyond his years. Most of all, his brief years with his mother—barely long enough for a set of sequential memories—left him with a massive contradiction in expectation: a large capacity for trust, a literal belief in promises that remained childlike throughout his life, was undercut by a matching doubt that could plunge instantly into mistrust and alarm.

At ten years old, Curly Hair cut a strange figure among his playmates. But he was still a Lakota boy. If not built for the rough sports that prepared boys for combat, he had a deceptively wiry strength and friends who clearly felt for him the sort of devotion an unusual child can evoke. One incident indicates something of the affection he evoked. In the evening following a buffalo hunt, Curly Hair and a gang of pals chased a bunch of bawling calves. Dared to ride one of the animals, Curly Hair leapt astride a well-grown bull, managing to keep his seat as it ran over the hills, pursued by his cheering chums. He did not dismount until the calf stopped from exhaustion.[37]

From an early age Curly Hair had loved the thrill of the buffalo hunt. With his playmates, the boy ran after the hunters as they butchered the great beasts, perhaps to be favored by an indulgent uncle with a bite of raw liver, the hunter's morsel. Horsemanship and shooting, under the tutelage of his father, uncles, and friends, became second nature by the time he was ten. To shooting with the bow and, later, the gun, he devoted care and forethought, even leaping from his pony to be sure he hit his mark, the awkward token of lessons hard won from an exacting father.

About the age of ten or eleven, Curly Hair's training paid off as he became a full-fledged provider. His father permitted the boy to accompany him on a buffalo hunt—not just to hold the family packhorses and observe the hunters, but to ride with him in the carefully organized surround. For the Lakota, the buffalo was the staff of life. Women's gathering activities garnered fruits and vegetables crucial to the Lakota diet, but Pte Oyate, the Buffalo Nation, stood in a unique relationship to human beings.

In return for the buffalo's sacrifice of flesh, the Lakotas used every part. In addition to the meat and marrow used in roasts and stews, tongues were eaten in sacred feasts, intestines made into tasty sausages, blood boiled down for pudding. Meat was preserved in wafer-thin sheets of jerky, while fat was mixed with dried fruit to make pemmican and stored for winter surplus. Rawhide was used to make saddles, ropes, riding tack, containers, shields, and hard moccasin soles. Skins were tanned to make tipi covers, robes and clothing, dolls, soft bags, and pouches. Haired winter robes were traded to Americans for manufactured goods. Horns and bones were used to make a variety of tools and implements, hair to provide padding, ropes, and ornaments. Brains furnished a lanolin-like tanning material. Sinew provided threads and bindings; bladders, paunches, and stomach linings served for every type of vessel from cups to kettles. The hooves were made into rattles or boiled down to make glue. A handy switch or hair ornament might be made from the tail, while even the buffalo's dried dung was used for fuel on the timberless plains.

The economic centrality of the buffalo was reflected in ritualized procedures and the supreme value society placed on the communal hunt. Curly Hair observed the return of scouts, understood their signaling by waved robes or maneuvers of their ponies, and watched their reception at the council tipi. There the Deciders— four chiefs nominated each season to oversee the hunt—would offer a pipe to the scouts and, using archaic language and formal gestures, elicit their report. If buffalo were near, the herald rode the circuit of the campground, announcing a hunt and instructing all to repair gear, secure saddles, and sharpen knives and arrows.[38]

Curly Hair's first surround can be reconstructed from typical Lakota practice. The hunters rode out, overseen by akicita—police appointed by the Deciders—so that no premature attack dispersed the buffalo. Once the hunters had taken up positions around the herd, akicita signaled the hunters to charge. With precise coordination, they enveloped both flanks of the herd, circling it into a milling throng. Behind his father, Curly Hair kneed his pony bravely in pursuit of the racing animals. True to his training, he cut out one of the calves, rode up on its righthand side and—after the usual nervously spoiled shots—placed a well-aimed arrow in its flank, angling forward at the heart. The rider's superbly trained pony immediately veered away from the enraged buffalo, but as the wounded animal slowed and then fell, Curly Hair reined in and leapt down to stand breathlessly beside his kill.

After the surround, Crazy Horse and his son roughly butchered the buffalo. Women and elders arrived, leading pack dogs and ponies. Handed the raw liver squirted with gall, Curly Hair swallowed the successful hunter's tidbit before the packhorses were loaded with the quartered joints and hides. As they neared the village, Crazy Horse casually turned over a horse to an elder, who harangued around the campground, announcing Curly Hair's first buffalo kill and calling old folk and unsuccessful hunters to feast at the family tipi. The old man announced a new name to mark the rite of passage: His Horse Stands in Sight. The boy stood uneasily, but for the moment triumphantly, on the edge of the adult Lakota world.[39]

2

YEAR OF THE BIG GIVEAWAY

In the same season as Curly Hair's first buffalo kill, messengers brought long-awaited invitations to Man Afraid of His Horse: Thomas Fitzpatrick, the U.S. agent to the Indians of the Upper Platte and Arkansas, had finally won government approval to hold a grand treaty council that summer of 1851. Across the region, from the upper Arkansas to the upper Missouri, camps and delegations trended toward Fort Laramie on the promise of a big talk and a grand giveaway.[1]

The Plains Indians were rightly proud of their independence and the skill of their hunters and craftswomen in winning a living from an abundant but harsh environment. What made American promises of a new treaty so attractive that upwards of ten thousand people descended on Fort Laramie? What motivated the Hunkpatila band's chief and council to facilitate the treaty?

Understanding the answers to these questions requires putting aside romantic notions, beloved of Hollywood and the latest brand of New Age pulp fiction, that the Lakotas and their neighbors were innocents newly exposed to a rapacious Euro-American culture. In Curly Hair's youth, Lakotas and Europeans had already enjoyed two centuries of direct if sporadic contact. French, English, and Spanish traders brought with them a technology that Indians valued. Firearms and horses transformed native warfare patterns, set communal buffalo hunting on a new, prosperous footing, and became an index of wealth for the nomadic hunting tribes of the plains. Early in the nineteenth century, the Lakotas had won a commanding role in the realignment of plains geopolitics, just as the United States claimed sovereignty of the continental interior.

By the 1820s the Missouri River was dotted with American trading posts that asserted the vitality of the trade alliance between the peoples. In 1825 that alliance was enshrined in a set of treaties concluded between the United States and the Lakotas, pledging each side to peace and mutually profitable trade.

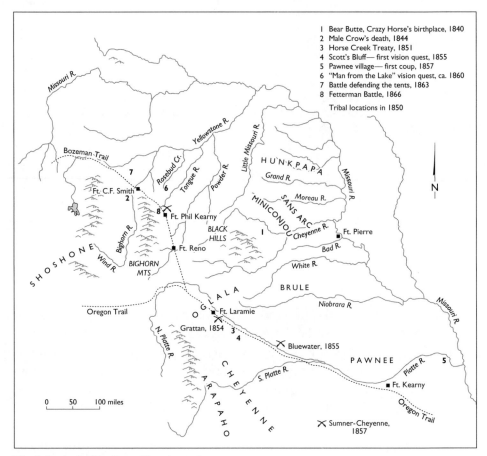

The Lakota world in Crazy Horse's youth

Into Curly Hair's boyhood, the treaty of 1825 held fast Lakota and American interests. Trade, grounded in ceremonial gift exchange, was the guarantee of peace. The trade in winter buffalo robes was maximized by the coming of steamboat traffic to the Missouri after 1832, diversifying the range of trade goods on offer. Intermarriage between traders and Lakota women produced a growing class of bilingual, bicultural children.

Goodwill presents made on the annual visits of Indian Office agents validated American use of trails and waterways through the Lakota domain. In 1831 the value of those presents to all Lakotas just topped one thousand dollars, with exactly two hundred dollars earmarked for Oglala gifts—at best, a handful of guns and blankets, kettles, knives, and tobacco, but such was the solidity of joint interests that Lakotas did not quibble.[2]

The spirit of unquestioning acceptance came under searching review as Curly Hair grew up. The Oglala and Brule advance to dominate the plains of the North Platte River placed those divisions across the path of Manifest Destiny. In the year of Curly Hair's birth, settlers bound for the Oregon Territory followed the Platte west along the route that would become indelible in the national consciousness as the Oregon Trail.

Within five years, the deepening ruts of the settler road had worn away significant reserves of Lakota goodwill. Settler numbers ballooned to one thousand in 1843, and three thousand in 1845. Two years later, the Mormon exodus to Utah swelled the traffic. Settler stock applied critical pressure to summer pasture and transmitted diseases to buffalo populations that environmental historians are only today beginning to understand. Compounded by the midcentury onset of near-drought conditions across the plains, buffalo herds along the Platte perceptibly thinned, pressing hunters into buffer zones contested with the Crows, Shoshones, and Pawnees.

Settler-borne diseases added to the list of Lakota grievances. The 1849 emigration broke all records. Twenty thousand prospectors passed up the Platte valley. For weeks their trains strung across the Lakota domain, destroying pasture and infecting the Indians with the deadly microbes of Asiatic cholera. When the cholera receded, smallpox made its cyclical return. Oglala losses may have been counted in scores, but Curly Hair intimately experienced the horror. As many as four stepsisters, all younger than five years, died in these tragic years. Grief was readily converted to anger. At the reunions of warrior societies, many war leaders concluded that the Americans were malevolently sending diseases among the Lakotas "to cut them off," an explanation readily accepted by an impressionable boy revering warrior idols.[3]

Chiefs like Man Afraid of His Horse argued that only increased spending on Lakota necessities could compensate for depletion of their hunting grounds. Agents like Fitzpatrick knew that Indians must be compensated for resource loss lest their brittle sufferance for the settlers deteriorate into raid and reprisal.

This was why Fitzpatrick's message was so positively received. Curly Hair's father was part of the Hunkpatila council that agreed to facilitate negotiations, and the boy was well positioned to observe the political organization of his people in action. At the Sun Dance, the Oglala tribal council nominated four chiefs to act as Deciders, empowered with coercive authority for the duration of the summer. In turn, the Deciders named four leading warriors to serve as head akicita, policing tribal hunts and removes, and serving as envoys to secure a representative gathering for the treaty talks.[4] Man Afraid of His Horse traveled to the Missouri to secure mass Lakota attendance. In August he returned with camps and delegations of Miniconjous, Two Kettles, Sans Arcs, Sihasapas, and Yanktons. From the western mountains arrived a strong Shoshone deputation. Villages of Oglala and Brule Lakotas, Cheyennes, and Arapahos, filled out a massive gathering of about 1500 lodges.

On September 5, the great council convened at the confluence of Horse Creek and the North Platte. After a weekend of Lakota grandstanding, parades, and intertribal councils, Fitzpatrick and David Mitchell, superintendent of Indian Affairs, opened talks on the eighth. Mitchell stressed that the flow of emigration across the plains was irreversible: Americans needed the right to traverse Indian lands, and the army wished to build posts to protect the settlers. Crucially, he acknowledged that the Great Father was aware of the sufferings of his Indian children and wished to compensate them for the loss of game and resources. Each year for a term of fifty years, fifty thousand dollars would be spent on annuity presents. Indian delegates were invited to accompany Agent Fitzpatrick to Washington. For their part, the Indian tribes were to define tribal territories, establish intertribal peace, and select a head chief in each tribe to control his people and be responsible for their conduct.[5]

As the great expansionist power on the plains, the Lakotas were unhappy with the prospect of rigidly demarcated tribal lands. True to the spirit of the occasion, intertribal truces with the Shoshones and the newly arrived Crow delegation had been effected. The American agenda threatened such agreements, and Lakota speakers contended the proposed boundary between Lakota and Cheyenne and Arapaho lands.

Mitchell conceded that as long as the tribes remained at peace, they might roam at will, regardless of boundaries, but he continued to insist that the tribes select a Lakota head chief. Already, Lakota spokesmen had objected to such an office. The Lakota nation was so large and scattered over so wide a territory, they argued, that "we can't make one chief." Mitchell reminded the restive headmen that, earlier in the summer, treaties had been concluded with the Santee Dakotas of Minnesota. Much closer to the frontier of settlement, the Santees had agreed to sell most of their lands in exchange for subsistence spending and training in agriculture. Lest dissatisfied Santees claim refuge in the Lakota country, Mitchell advised, the Lakota nation should unite behind a single leadership. A quorum of chiefs nominated Man Afraid of His Horse as their candidate for head chief, but the Hunkpatila chief demurred, rejecting the chieftainship as just too contentious.[6]

That evening, two of the Lakota warrior societies staged a dance before the commissioners' headquarters tent, reflecting the crucial support of the akicita. The explicitly political role assumed by the warrior societies sounded a theme that would affect much of Curly Hair's future life. Barely more than temporary dance associations in his father's youth, the societies had grown in influence with Lakota fortunes. Through the succeeding generation, several would assume attitudes toward the American presence that amounted to policies. Some would oppose wasicu encroachment; others would strengthen the American alliance. Although Curly Hair would grow into a classic individualist, instinctively mistrustful of group psychology, the politicization of the warriors was fundamental to his career. His personal response to the societies' decisions to validate the treaty is unknowable, but by his midteens, he would have already acquired a cynicism toward the wasicu alliance that might have been rooted in the treaty and in the family tragedies that had preceded it.[7]

When the talks convened again, speakers announced their failure to agree on a head chief, and Mitchell declared he would nominate candidates. Twenty-four Lakota representatives, chosen pro rata from the tribal divisions, were presented with tally sticks. From their circle, Mitchell led forth Scattering Bear, a headman in the Brule Wazhazha band, and cousin to Curly Hair's stepmothers. Kinswomen loudly acclaimed the selection, but Scattering Bear ordered them silent. Forcefully he outlined his reluctance. "Father, I am not afraid to die, but to be chief of all the Dacotahs, I must be a Big Chief . . . or in a few moons I will be sleeping (dead) on the prairies."

Nevertheless, each of the voting quorum presented his tally stick to Scattering Bear. One elder arose to harangue the young men. He urged them to accept Scattering Bear, and "to have their ears bored, that they might listen to his words, and do what he said." Mitchell then gave a quantity of goods to Scattering Bear. Pointedly reserving nothing for himself or his relatives, the new head chief of the Lakota nation gave everything away.[8]

By the end of the talks, Indians had approved the main points outlined by Mitchell, and Lakotas agreed to a definition of their territory framed by the Missouri, North Platte, and Heart rivers, the western boundary following the divide between the Powder and Cheyenne rivers. On September 17 the treaty was signed. No Oglalas joined the signatories, illustrating the jealousy identified by Scattering Bear. He and five other Brules and Missouri River chiefs were left to touch the pen for the Lakotas—a meaningless formality, once the pipe had been smoked to carry the "visible breath" of the peace to Wakan Tanka.[9]

For three more days the villages awaited their treaty presents, on campgrounds littered with two weeks' worth of domestic waste. Pasture was eaten off, and councils impatiently monitored scout reports of buffalo movements. At last, late on the twentieth, the wagon train pulled in, and on the following day, thousands of people eagerly gathered along Horse Creek. Mitchell and Fitzpatrick first presented military dress uniforms to the chiefs. Scattering Bear was attired in the pantaloons, dress coat, and hat of a major general. Man Afraid of His Horse and his peers were issued brigadiers' uniforms, and so on down the scale. Uniformed akicita aided the chiefs in redistributing the twenty-seven wagonloads of goods. The commissioners had spent Congress's one hundred thousand dollars with a knowing eye for Indian needs and tastes. Bales of blankets, stacks of kettles, cases of knives, tobacco twists, bright rolls of yard goods—unprecedented wealth was borne away by the crowds. So prodigal seemed the Great Father's generosity that it took two days to unpack all the goods.

Lakota winter count keepers would memorialize 1851–52 as Wakpamni Tanka—the Year of the Big Giveaway. Briefly, the sheer scale of the payout seemed to confirm the aspirations of the moderate chiefs who had agitated for redrawn treaty relations. Like the bigger picture of American and Lakota attitudes, however, the treaty of 1851 was riddled with contradictions and inconsistencies. Curly Hair was no preternaturally endowed prophet, but he was a child of his times. He and his peers knew no other life than the post–Oregon Trail Lakota world, with its inheritance of disease, game attrition, and resource loss. Unlike the generation of chiefs and elders celebrating the renewal of the American alliance, they had no idealized memory of a golden age of interethnic relations. A troubled and dissatisfied boy followed his family away from the treaty grounds. Some of his unease was likely grounded in a growing misgiving over the peacemaking on Horse Creek.

3

BECOMING HUNKA

By dusk of September 23, the campgrounds were empty. Across the North Platte lay discarded cloth, windblown piles of baking soda and flour, and bright stacks of copper kettles—all abandoned as just too much of a good thing. Throughout the treaty sessions, village councils had continued monitoring the reports of scouts regarding the prospects for buffalo—the real mainstay of life. Wintering grounds were selected before the villages were struck, and bands departed for all points of the compass.[1]

Through the winter, Curly Hair brooded. Family solidarity was strained by the deaths of his stepsisters, creating a tight focus for the boy's unease about the treaty—an agreement legitimizing the settler traffic that brought disease and death to the Lakota people. New grief reopened old emotional wounds, and Curly Hair was again at odds with his stepmothers—"unable to get along at home," as one tradition has it. His five-year-old half-brother had emerged as the family's darling: doted over as a fragile survivor of the epidemics, he was always dressed in the best clothing, a child beloved in whose name the family gave gifts and sponsored ceremonies. Rattle Blanket Woman's people remained a haven to Curly Hair, where indulgent, protective relatives offered comfort and unconditional love. Now eleven years old, Curly Hair packed a few essentials and rode to the Miniconjou camp, one day's ride east.[2]

Also visiting with the Miniconjous was a fifteen-year-old Oglala youth, a distant cousin to Curly Hair. Horn Chips belonged to a small band of Kiyuksa Oglalas that had decided to winter in the district—disastrously, because buffalo had eluded them and they had survived by trapping badgers, an incident at once seized on to coin a new name: Badger Eaters. Like Curly Hair, Horn Chips had traveled from his band's camp and had been invited to live in the tipi of one of Curly Hair's uncles. As ever, Curly Hair was drawn to an older companion, and the two sensitive youths found each other congenial company.[3]

As they exchanged confidences, Curly Hair appreciated that Horn Chips had an even sorrier tale to tell. Both his parents had died during the epidemics. Living with his grandmother at the edge of camp, Horn Chips had become the butt of his playmates' jibes. At length he had decided to end his life, but in a secluded spot, he heard a voice telling him that Wakan Tanka spoke. He must not kill himself, for he was to grow into a great man. The voice instructed him to fast atop a high mountain in the Black Hills and seek a vision. There a snake appeared to him with instructions as to his future course in life. Horn Chips assured Curly Hair that his vision, promising him a lifetime of spiritual growth to be spent in the service of the people, had convinced him of the worth of his existence. Already he waited impatiently for adulthood and the opportunity to practice the visionary and healing arts.[4]

Curly Hair was immediately affected by Horn Chips' conviction. Still too young to seek his own vision, Curly Hair could identify with his new friend's self-belief. A close and lifelong bond was established between the boys. The new friendship did not go unnoticed by their elders, who prepared to deepen a personal affinity into a profoundly public good. Curly Hair's uncle proposed sponsoring the costly *hunka* ritual for Curly Hair and Horn Chips.

The hunka was the Lakota version of a ceremony found across the plains that fostered peaceful relations and intertribal trade. Leading families adopted each other's children in a ceremony combining elaborate pageantry with profound spiritual truths. The ritual would tightly integrate the participants' families and bands. As visiting "fathers" in the hunka, the Miniconjous would be expected to sponsor massive gift giving to their Oglala hosts.

As host "sons," the Oglalas would have to stage a grand giveaway of ponies to the Miniconjous. Leaders like Man Afraid of His Horse would be at pains to feed presents of food, robes, craftwork, trade goods, and ponies into Curly Hair's family wealth. Horn Chips' poor camp was in an anomalous position, but Oglala leaders enthusiastically fitted them out with presents to ensure that their guests were not shamed in the impending celebrations.[5]

On the morning of the ceremony, inside the preparation lodge, Curly Hair and Horn Chips dressed in shirts, breechclouts, leggings, and moccasins. Outside, singing and the measured beat of drums accompanied a growing procession that made four circuits of the circle. "Where," sang the holy man, "is the tipi of the hunka?"[6]

The voices neared the preparation lodge. Suddenly, a blow struck the tipi skin and a knife slashed open the door flap. The holy man's party swarmed into the lodge, seizing Curly Hair and Horn Chips and dragging them outside like captives.

Oglalas and Miniconjous cheered as the boys approached the open-fronted ceremonial lodge. Men and women ran across the open space with presents of clothing, parfleches stuffed with dried meat, and ponies. Curly Hair and Horn Chips watched the line of singers and drummers form behind two virgins bearing ears of corn, tipped with white down eagle plumes, and two men waving the hunka pipestems in graceful motion above their heads, imitating the easy glide of eagles.

The crowd took up the burden of the victory song as the procession followed its two captives. Approaching the entrance of the ceremonial lodge, the holy man gave the wolf howl of a victorious war party and proclaimed, "We should kill this enemy, but if anyone will take him for *Hunka*, we will not kill him." Curly Hair's uncle stepped forward and announced that he would adopt the two boys as hunka, then led them down an avenue of waist-high screens into the lodge, followed by the attendants, the virgins, and the line of musicians. Their captor seated the boys before an altar centered on a buffalo skull with a blue stripe circling its brow, asserting the hunka relationship between the Buffalo Spirit and the Lakota people.

As the lodge filled and spectators crowded outside, an assistant filled and lighted one of the sacred pipes from a coal of dried buffalo dung. Braids of lighted sweetgrass incensed the lodge. Ceremonial pipes circulated, opening the hours of invocations of the powers and lectures admonishing the candidates of the responsibility placed on them. Each individual in the hunka relationship was bound to the other by ties of allegiance and solidarity stronger than those of blood. Each owed the other a lifetime of mutuality and support. They must assist one another in all undertakings, protect one another in battle, avenge each other's death, and ensure the continued support of their families.

Other speakers stressed the links of obligation that bound the hunka to society. The candidates' names would be constantly before the people as living exemplars of generosity. They must never cease to give food and clothing to the poor. Visitors from other bands and tribes expected to be regaled with presents: as hunka, the candidates should always be first in giving.

As the ceremony climaxed, the holy man waved the hunka pipestems over the heads of the candidates, then placed a piece of meat in each of the candidates' mouths. Then he proclaimed that he was hungry and without food; cold and naked; footsore and without moccasins. At this prompt, Curly Hair and Horn Chips took the meat from their mouths, unfastened their leggings and moccasins, and doffed their shirts, pledges of aid.

The assistants held robes to obscure the candidates from public view. Curly Hair, Horn Chips, and their hunka father were tied together, arm to arm, leg to leg, symbolizing the indissoluble bond between them. White eagle-down plumes were fastened to the left side of each candidate's hair, symbolizing the power of prayer. The holy man painted a blue arch across the candidates' foreheads, then, with sacred red paint, drew a fine line down the side of each face, from forehead to cheek.

At length the robes were drawn back, and the assistants presented each candidate with his own hunka stem and ear of corn. Then, still bound, the candidates slowly rose and filed back into the preparation lodge, where their bonds were removed and they dressed anew in the finest clothing.

Curly Hair and his hunka emerged to cries of joy. Their families drove up horses and spread out gifts of clothing. Curly Hair observed the fine gradations in gift giving. Some presents, made between important families, bound the recipient to a reciprocal gift of at least equal value. In this way, complex networks of affinity and obligation were created, extending across band and tribal divisions. Other gifts, as of horses to the poor, expected no return beyond acclaim. "With this I aid you" was a formula Curly Hair would employ often throughout his life. He absorbed utterly the precepts of the hunka. All accounts agree on his lifelong generosity, and most indicate that his largesse was uncalculating, free from political considerations. So the day progressed with undiminished giving, to climax in a grand feast on the open campground.

Curly Hair's family and band would be prime exponents of the Oglala-Miniconjou alliance, promoting solidarity through gift giving and, as Curly Hair grew into manhood, participating in joint war expeditions. Within the band, any unfortunate could now call on him to share food and clothing. A man fallen on hard times would be outfitted with hunting tools or ponies if he appealed to Curly Hair: family pride would demand that the man's needs be fulfilled.[7] The unstinting generosity Curly Hair associated with the memory of his mother now found formal expression in his deepened relationship with his band relatives.

On the purely personal level, the hunka restored Curly Hair's sense of worth. Within the Hunkpatila band, he had begun to feel dangerously alienated. His father and stepmothers had invested substantial time and labor in their part in the ceremony, an effort not lost on a boy sensitive to nuance. The hunka confirmed his identity and status among his mother's folk at a time when his father's remarriage had undermined Curly Hair's crucial sense of belonging to the community of his uncles, aunts, and cousins.

Supported by both families, the ceremony did more than embody shifting political realities: its profound metaphors of sharing, obligation, and liberation acted with therapeutic good on Curly Hair and his hunka brother, Horn Chips. "You are bound to your *Hunka* as if he were yourself."[8] His adopted brother was no political choice but a companion for life, a spiritual mentor in whom he would place implicit trust, each intuitively attuned to the spiritual capacities they shared. As Curly Hair followed the warrior's path into adulthood, he would seek to excel above all others in the virtue of bravery. Horn Chips made no serious attempt to live the warrior's life to the exclusion of all else: his reflective nature drove him further down the road of spiritual growth. In this way, his and Curly Hair's relationship would remain complementary, untainted by the rivalries that marked friendships among warriors.

Moreover, the shifting of Oglala bands meant that the boys would now be much together. The two friends would not be long separated for the next fifteen years. In Horn Chips' own words, he and Curly Hair were "raised together" in the crucial years between boyhood and adult life.[9]

That fall, several bands located their hunting operations north of a new trading post, the settler stopover of Platte Bridge (modern Casper, Wyoming), where veteran trader

John Richard hoped to corner the lucrative buffalo robe trade of the upper Powder River country. Oglalas, Miniconjous, Cheyennes, and even Crows exploiting the new truces following the Horse Creek Treaty gathered in the vicinity, trading for guns, New Mexican maize and liquor, and colorful Navaho blankets. Richard's expanding trade center may account for a significant event that went far to restore Curly Hair's sense of family well-being. One winter count depicts for 1852–53 a Euro-American, identifiable by his dark clothing and broad-brimmed hat, waving a hunka pipestem over a skull. "A white man made medicine over the skull of Crazy-Horse's brother," reads the mnemonic entry. The bones of Male Crow had at last been reclaimed.[10]

Chronologically, the incident coincides with another important rite of passage for Curly Hair. At age twelve, he recalled to his cousin Flying Hawk, "[I] began to fight enemies."[11] Youths began to join war parties soon after their first buffalo hunt, but such precocious adventures were rarely momentous. Tagging along behind a war party, a boy like Curly Hair was mercilessly joshed but not exposed to real danger. Whether placed in charge of the dog toting the party's spare moccasins, or sent interminably to fetch water for the leaders, boys were quietly protected, and no story indicates that Curly Hair performed any feat of valor. Instead, his role in "fight[ing] enemies" may have been limited to the party, exploiting the Crow truce, sent to locate the remains of Male Crow. After eight years of grief, insinuation, and rumor, the bones of the war leader had been restored to his people. Curly Hair's family could at last draw a line under the memory of Male Crow.

For Curly Hair, the burial of Male Crow's bones confirmed the restorative trend of 1852. Newly secure at home, alive to his responsibilities as a hunka, he at last managed to put his mother's death behind him. Her loss had shaped much of his childhood. The morbid sensitivity to betrayal would never leave him, any more than he would forget Male Crow's fatalistic defiance. But his losses had finally been resolved by the healing force of friendship, ritual, and obligation. From now on, those losses would serve to strengthen Curly Hair's resolve to care for the helpless and to fight bravely for his people. The acceptance permitted him to find a measure of peace in the family home, rebuilding the bond with his father and stepmothers. Reflecting his commitment to the helpless of his band, that bond found especial expression in the relationship with his younger brother, Young Little Hawk.

As Young Little Hawk approached the age of eight, Curly Hair would be expected to shoulder more of the responsibility for his upbringing, devoting himself to instilling the Lakota warrior ethos in the boy. A father's example leaned toward practical skills and the negotiation of social niceties, and an uncle's precepts concentrated on self-preservation in a dangerously competitive world; an elder brother was expected to cultivate the fearless bravado of the warrior. In his brother Curly Hair would find an adept and devoted pupil. Curly Hair loved Young Little Hawk dearly, and people noted that as the older boy grew toward adolescence, he worked diligently to teach the younger all that he had learned.[12]

All these factors were reflected in an incident the following July, the Moon of Red Cherries, 1853. Curly Hair and Young Little Hawk, on the prairie to drive the family horses to water, took time out to rest beside a cluster of cherry bushes, happily munching on the ripe red fruit. A growl startled them, and the horses bolted. The brothers had disturbed a grizzly bear, most fearsome creature of the plains. The boys scrambled up as the lumbering bear put on its deceptive burst of speed. A lone cottonwood offered safety for one boy: without thinking, Curly Hair grabbed Young Little Hawk, boosted him into the lower branches, and in the same movement sprang onto the back of one of the horses. The panicked animal ran out of control until Curly Hair leaned forward along its neck to calm it. Using only the pressure of his knees, Curly Hair managed to turn the horse and urge it into a run toward the bear. The grizzly still growled angrily, dangerously near Young Little Hawk's precarious perch. As Curly Hair's pony closed the distance, he whooped loudly to alarm the bear, unslung the lariat he carried over one shoulder, and swung it over his head, yelling louder. The bear growled and ran at boy and horse, raising itself on its hind legs and baring its yellow fangs. Still Curly Hair rode straight toward a terrible collision, but suddenly the bear turned, flopped onto all fours, and ran.[13]

As he approached his teen years with newfound security, Curly Hair could ponder the future. He was a proven hunter, a skilled horseman, and a fine shot with an arrow, taking care and time to hit his mark. Now his thoughts concentrated on turning these skills along the warrior's path. He had seen warriors returning from raids to the exultant tremolos of the women, driving in stolen horses and waving aloft enemy scalps. He had heard the elders recount their heroic tales of warfare. He was probably determined also to restore his family name. Now, old men gently encouraged his ambitions, remarking that he must have sacred power indeed to rout an angry grizzly and save the life of his brother. They stressed too that before he went to war, he should accumulate more protective power by seeking a vision of guidance, just as Horn Chips had.

In conversations with his hunka brother, Curly Hair left no doubt as to where the future lay. Together they watched the rising warriors of the previous generation emerge into greatness: Red Cloud, of the Bad Face band, and Black Twin, from Horn Chips' own tiyospaye; among the Miniconjous even High Backbone was a tried warrior approaching twenty. "[W]hen we were young," Horn Chips would recall, "all we thought about was going to war with some other nation; all tried to get their names up to the highest, and whoever did so was the principal man in the nation; and [Curly Hair] wanted to get to the highest rank or station."[14] The first halting steps toward achieving that goal would occupy the next four years of Curly Hair's life.

4

FIRST TO MAKE
THE GROUND BLOODY

The same summer of 1853 that witnessed Curly Hair's defiance of the grizzly had already seen tensions between Lakotas and Americans wound to breaking. The flash point proved to be Fort Laramie, the former trading post turned army garrison. In mid-June, eighty to one hundred lodges of Miniconjous were encamped near the post. Large villages of their Oglala and Brule hosts also awaited the arrival of Agent Fitzpatrick and the treaty annuities. Despite the hunka accords, many Brules and Oglalas viewed their Miniconjou guests "as interlopers" and regarded them "with considerable distrust."[1]

Feisty Miniconjou independence was influenced by developments in the northern Lakota zone, beyond the Black Hills. The two northernmost Lakota divisions, the Hunkpapas and Sihasapas, traditionally had the weakest ties to the Americans and were deeply suspicious of the treaty provisions. Members of the Strong Hearts, an increasingly militant warrior society, resented the interference in intertribal hostilities and argued that treaty annuities committed Lakotas to land cessions like those that marked the Eastern Dakota agreements in Minnesota.[2]

Similar misgivings infected the Miniconjous at Fort Laramie. On June 15, Miniconjou warriors started harassing settlers, then seized the ferry over the North Platte, firing on Sergeant Enoch W. Raymond. At Fort Laramie, commander Lieutenant Richard B. Garnett ordered an infantry detachment, led by Second Lieutenant Hugh B. Fleming, to demand the culprit of the Miniconjous, or to secure two or three prisoners in his stead.

The detachment approached the Miniconjou village after dark; finding Chief Little Brave absent and the people unwilling to comply with the arrest order, Fleming posted his command in a defensive formation and led five men into the camp. Some thirty shots were exchanged: three or four Miniconjous lay dead, and two more were taken prisoner before Fleming disengaged. Through the night, the

Miniconjous struck camp and started toward the Black Hills. Garnett hurried a messenger after them, asking Little Brave and his men to return for a talk. When the chief appeared a few days later, he secured the release of the prisoners, but Garnett refused traditional presents to "cover" the deaths.[3]

The incident threatened the fragile peace. Although chiefs assured Garnett of their goodwill, there was much anger at the deaths of fellow Lakotas. The treaty provided for mediating disagreements, not through first-response military action, but by diplomacy between the Lakota leadership and the Indian Office agent. Moreover, Lakotas had welcomed the garrison at Fort Laramie on the grounds that its prime function was to protect Lakotas from settler offenders: such rhetoric seemed thin as the summer progressed, and Miniconjou mourners returned to beg Oglala and Brule relatives to aid them in avenging the deaths. A few reckless threats were made against the troops. Chiefs like Man Afraid of His Horse had to use all their influence to prevent further bloodshed.

For Curly Hair and his relatives, these mourners posed a profound dilemma. Although not yet thirteen, and too young to engage actively in hostilities, Curly Hair's status as hunka to Little Brave's people made his family a first call for Miniconjous seeking vengeance. Curly Hair's father, sitting with the council of elders, uneasily continued to accept Man Afraid of His Horse's advice to maintain peace. The consensus shakily held, but key warriors were increasingly alienated from the peace process. An embryonic faction favoring resistance was emerging throughout the Oglala tribe.

After Agent Fitzpatrick arrived at Fort Laramie on September 10, disagreements were thrown into relief. A cost-cutting Congress had saddled him with securing Lakota signatures to an agreement that reduced the annuity term from fifty years to fifteen. Bitterly, several headmen refused to discuss the amendment, and Fitzpatrick's speech was repeatedly interrupted by war leaders demanding restitution for the killings by Garnett's troops. Only protracted appeals from the agent convinced the chiefs like Man Afraid of His Horse and Smoke to touch the pen, but akicita leader Red Cloud refused to sign. Red Hawk, a warrior closely associated with Curly Hair's family, stalked out of the council in sullen silence and rode across the North Platte, vowing never to return to Fort Laramie.[4]

The signing and distribution was a costly diplomatic victory. Although still small scale, the defections were portents of the future polarization of Lakota society over the issue of accommodation with the Americans. Curly Hair's father was just one band headman who grew increasingly suspicious of the American alliance.

Dangerous portents continued to accumulate through the following winter. Little Brave, the Miniconjou chief, died. His loss left his band more volatile than ever, and the following summer, disgruntled warriors threatened reprisals.[5]

By August 1854, over six hundred Lakota lodges had gathered near Fort Laramie to await the arrival of their agent. Among the small Miniconjou contingent was High Forehead, a grieving nephew of Little Brave. Still mourning relatives from the previous summer, High Forehead announced that "he intended to do something bad."[6]

On August 18 a sick, lame cow strayed from a passing Mormon wagon train. High Forehead shot the animal, which was quickly butchered and eaten. Head chief Scattering Bear rode to Fort Laramie to talk the matter over with Lieutenant Fleming, now commanding the post. Scattering Bear offered to compensate the Mormon with horses from his own herd, but Fleming initially rejected Scattering Bear's efforts at diplomacy, arguing that the offender be handed over for detention. The head chief objected that High Forehead was a guest in his village but conceded that if Fleming sent troops, High Forehead would be given up. At length, persuaded that the matter was one for the civilian agent to decide, Fleming declared that he would not send for the offending Miniconjou on that day. With that, Scattering Bear returned to camp.[7]

On the afternoon of August 19, however, Lieutenant John L. Grattan—a fire-eating West Point graduate with a bottomless contempt for the Indians—insisted to Fleming that he be permitted to secure the arrest of High Forehead. The commander gave in and ordered Grattan to take an infantry detachment with two artillery pieces to the Brule village and secure the offender. Defiant intransigence was about to meet military impetuosity in a tragic turning point for U.S.–Lakota relations.[8]

In the Brule camps, hurried councils convened at news of Grattan's march. The council of elders requested that action be delayed pending the arrival of the agent. Meeting separately, warriors declared that on no account would they permit an arrest. Scattering Bear, donning the brigadier's coat presented to him at Horse Creek, led a group of Brule chiefs to James Bordeaux's trading post, next to the main Brule camp and three hundred yards west of Scattering Bear's Wazhazha camp, which was augmented by fifteen tipis of Miniconjous, including that of offender High Forehead. Pressured by Grattan, the chiefs declined to take action against High Forehead. Instead, they offered Grattan ponies and pressed the elders' suggestion of postponing action until the agent's arrival. As they spoke, a messenger rode up with word that High Forehead categorically "refused to give himself up—he said he would die first."[9]

Grattan ordered his men to march into the camp, where both Scattering Bear and Man Afraid of His Horse vainly tried to defuse the situation. Both High Forehead and Grattan refused to back down from confrontation. As Scattering Bear and Grattan's discussion escalated into argument, and Man Afraid of His Horse tried unsuccessfully to calm the men, High Forehead and five other Miniconjou warriors filed out of his tipi and stood in line outside the lodge, nonchalantly priming their muskets. Brule women hurried their families to cover while men rushed for their weapons.

The lieutenant ordered his men to assume firing positions. A soldier at the extreme right of the line stepped forward and aimed his rifle. The shot rang out and a Lakota fell. In the sudden silence, Man Afraid of His Horse called out to the Lakotas "not to fire; that they had killed one man, and might be satisfied."[10] Other chiefs joined him in calling for restraint. Then a second soldier fired on the left. A momentary pause held, as if by collective shock. The Brules drew back to seek cover, but the Miniconjous remained in a defiant line. Disgustedly, Scattering Bear turned away from Grattan, walking toward his own tipi and casting wary glances backward. Suddenly, the six Miniconjous aimed their muskets and snapped off a ragged volley. A soldier fell. The lieutenant ordered his men to fire at Scattering Bear. A volley rang out, and Scattering Bear fell mortally wounded, shot through the arm, body, and leg. As the black smoke cleared, five other Lakotas lay dead. Man Afraid of His Horse and the Brule chiefs still standing raced for cover.

While the infantry hurried to reload, Grattan ordered the fieldpieces to fire toward the Miniconjou tipi, but the nervous gunners misjudged the range. Before the soldiers completed reloading, Brule warriors overwhelmed Grattan's line, killing the lieutenant and five of the gunners. The soldiers and gunners ran, and hundreds of Brules poured after them, exultantly shooting down stragglers until every man was slain.

Nearby, Man Afraid of His Horse drew up his pony. The line of Oglala warriors, six hundred yards long, was angled across his path. Although he urged them to prevent the Brules from finishing off the soldiers, the warriors quietly refused to intervene, holding their chief's bridle until the last soldier was dead. Then Man Afraid of His Horse led the Oglalas homeward.

The involvement of Oglala warriors, including head akicita Red Cloud, in the closing minutes of the fight demonstrated the volatile nature of the situation. Man Afraid of His Horse worked hard to maintain council consensus around keeping the peace. That night heralds harangued the Oglala village, ordering the restless young men not to leave.[11]

Man Afraid of His Horse sent Lieutenant Fleming word that his people had played no significant part in the affair. He added that the Oglalas "would establish their camp wherever [Fleming] said, and that they were ready to assist him if he desired it." Then the Oglalas crossed the North Platte, heading for buffalo grounds along the south fork of the Cheyenne River.[12]

Disaffected Miniconjous and vengeful relatives of Scattering Bear sponsored a war pipe to unite Lakotas in reprisals against the Americans. Curly Hair's family, related to both groups, once more came under pressure, but the council still rejected all efforts to involve Oglalas in hostilities.[13]

Scattering Bear, who died of his wounds late in August, had pleaded with his relatives not to avenge his death, but his kinsmen led the reprisals. In September, two war parties stole mules from Fort Kearney on the lower Platte. Such raids, with no fatalities, served notice of a break in friendly relations, but on November 13, six kinsmen of Scattering Bear significantly raised the stakes. Four men—Scattering Bear's brother Red Leaf, half-brother Long Chin, cousin Spotted Tail, and Black Heart's Son—with two youths, a nephew, and a second brother of the chief, crossed the North Platte and ambushed a mail coach thirty miles south of Fort Laramie. They killed three men and carried away ten thousand dollars in gold coin.[14]

Later in November the Brules hosted a massive gathering on the Niobrara River. Winter operations were threatened along the Traders' Trail between forts Pierre and Laramie, and the following season, all settler parties on the Overland Trail would be attacked. If the Americans sent troops, they would be repulsed. Brule warrior societies joined the Miniconjous in sponsoring the war pipe that was circulating through the Saone zone.[15]

Through spring and summer, raiders struck the herds of settlers, traders, and Loafer Lakotas along the Overland Trail between Ash Hollow and Platte Bridge. Late in June a Miniconjou war party from north of the Black Hills attacked emigrant trains near Deer Creek, killing three people. The Brule leadership tried to divert summer war efforts, organizing a large raid against the Omaha tribe. Oglala chiefs continued to demonstrate their commitment to peace by returning stock stolen by Miniconjou raiders—Curly Hair and his family once more in the unenviable role of mediators. Man Afraid of His Horse led the Hunkpatila band south to the upper Niobrara. Despite the absence of buffalo herds this near the Overland Trail, Man Afraid of His Horse and his headmen succeeded in "restraining and preventing their young men from joining hostile bands." All Lakotas now awaited the expected military response from the Americans.[16]

Washington had indeed decided to chastise the Lakotas. General William S. Harney took command of a force of six hundred men, but ahead of him, the Indian Office had dispatched a new civilian agent, Thomas S. Twiss, who arrived at Fort Laramie on August 10. He acted quickly to separate peaceful and hostile Lakotas, declaring the North Platte River "the boundary between hostile and friendly Sioux" and ordering all friendly Lakotas to move immediately south of the river.[17]

The Hunkpatilas were divided over the impending war. After a year of enforced peace, Man Afraid of His Horse no longer dared compel his council. Faced with Twiss's ultimatum, headmen were allowed to make their own decisions. Beginning on August 20, family groups began crossing the North Platte at Ward and Guerrier's trading post, eight miles upstream from Fort Laramie. Curly Hair's father at length decided to follow, and for over a week, bands drifted in piecemeal. On August 29 Agent Twiss assigned the Oglalas a campground on Laramie Fork, twenty-five miles west of the fort.[18]

Two-thirds of the Oglala tribe was represented in Twiss's peace party. From the Brules, the response to the agent's summons was less encouraging. Upon news of Harney's march, the Brule village had broken up. Favoring war or simply frightened, more than half the people moved north toward the Black Hills. By September 5 Twiss had located four hundred Oglala and Brule lodges in a united peace party village thirty-five miles west of Fort Laramie. They anxiously awaited news of Harney's march into their country.[19]

On September 2 Harney reached Ash Hollow on the lower North Platte. Three miles across the valley on Blue Water Creek, just within the war zone, stood forty-one lodges of Brules and Wazhazhas. Two miles upstream were eleven lodges of Oglalas, Miniconjous, and Cheyennes. These people represented an uneasy compromise between war and peace factions. Band chiefs like Little Thunder and Iron Shell may have been inclined to heed the warnings from Twiss, but warriors like Spotted Tail, Curly Hair's uncle, were determined not to accede to American demands. Spotted Tail's stance won out when the Brules sent Harney word "that if he wanted peace he could have it, or if he wanted war that he could have that."[20]

Through the small hours of September 3, Harney moved his command across the North Platte. The dragoons cut across country to envelop the Oglala camp, while Harney and the infantry marched up the east side of the Blue Water. The Brules had begun preparations to move as soon as scouts had alerted them to Harney's approach, but when first light disclosed Harney's column a mile downstream, the people broke off their preparations and started up the valley, abandoning tipis and tons of dried meat. Harney secured a parley to delay the village until he knew that the dragoons were in position, then he ordered the infantry to advance. Caught between the two wings of Harney's command, the warriors fought with desperate bravery to cover their families' escape across the Blue Water. The compact body of people made an easy target for infantry fire. Men, women, and children were cut down until, some thirty minutes after the battle opened, the survivors crested the slope east of the creek. From a total of about 350 people in the camps, almost half had been killed or captured—staggering losses to the Lakotas.

At Fort Laramie on September 7, the peace party chiefs conceded to Agent Twiss that Harney's action had been justified. After dividing his captives, sending part under guard to Fort Kearney, Harney marched up the North Platte to Fort Laramie. Twiss arranged a meeting with the peace party chiefs on September 22. Man Afraid of His Horse and Big Partisan "begged piteously" that their people be spared further reprisals. Harney was stern. He announced that he would presently march through the interior of the Lakota country to winter quarters at Fort Pierre. The war was still on, he insisted, and the peace party must remain south of the North Platte deadline, the boundary Twiss had set to demarcate friendly from hostile tribes. His victory at the Blue Water was punishment for the deaths of Grattan's command. Now Harney demanded that the peace party follow up the Blue Water fugitives and secure the surrender of the mail coach war party and the return of all stolen stock. Once these conditions were satisfied, Little Thunder might sue for peace. If he did not, intimated the general, the Blue Water captives would be turned over to the Pawnees—an image that Lakotas would readily interpret as meaning their torture and death.[21]

Harney permitted the anxious chiefs three days to discuss his terms but closed with the warning that "they must do what he asked or fight." The Great Father in Washington had been indulgent of his Lakota children, but now he was angry and demanded reparations. Sustained military action would follow until "their buffalo would be driven away, and . . . the Dacotahs would be no more."[22]

The chiefs returned home, and all adult males quickly agreed to Harney's terms, sending akicita envoys to secure the mail coach raiders.

In the peace party village, the nervous consensus to placate Harney masked much disquiet. On hilltops around the village, scores of red cloth offerings were tied to secure the favor of the spirits and liberate the Brule captives. Curly Hair, a pious youth, doubtless joined in the prayers. For Curly Hair the defeat at Blue Water, the captivity of many of his relatives, and the humiliating terms imposed on his people capped two years of mounting tension between Lakotas and Americans. During those years, his family had come repeatedly under pressure to honor hunka obligations to Miniconjou relatives and join in reprisals against the Americans. After the death of his stepmothers' cousin Scattering Bear, Brule kinsmen like his uncle Spotted Tail added their voices to the demands for vengeance. But a deeper threat, aimed at the Lakota people's independence, registered in the youth's reflections. Curly Hair's unease at the events of 1855, as his band repeatedly moved camp at the whims of Twiss, Harney, and other soldier chiefs, was recalled in oral tradition.[23]

Still only fourteen years old and unproven in war, Curly Hair was in no position to take the warrior's path. Family ties bound him to the same tiyospaye in which Man Afraid of His Horse lived, and his father had warily approved the consensus for peace. But misgivings were natural in a brooding boy whose deepest instincts had been formed in the conservative environment of Kapozha, where his father and grandfather had long embodied a tradition of minimal relations with the wasicu. Those instincts were only confirmed by the youth's deep affinity with Miniconjou comrades like High Backbone and his respect for relatives such as Spotted Tail, now proclaimed a wanted criminal by the U.S. Army.

As for any young person, adolescence brought emotional turbulence into Curly Hair's life. The awkward threshold between childhood and adult life was no easier for nineteenth-century Lakotas to negotiate than it is today: the same conflicts of interest between the sexes and generations were present in Curly Hair's teenage world. For a Lakota youth, it was time to seek resolution of these issues by begging the wakan for a vision of guidance that would clarify his future course and assure him of spiritual protection. It is tempting to believe that the acute inner conflicts triggered by the Lakota political crisis were also fundamental to Curly Hair's state of mind as he told his family that he was ready to "cry for a vision."

Two

THUNDER DREAMER

5

CRYING FOR A VISION

Moon of the Black Calf, September 1855: During the days following news of the Blue Water disaster Curly Hair spoke earnestly to his father about his decision to cry for a vision.[1] Now in his midforties, the older man had gained a reputation over the previous decade as wicasa wakan, a holy man with powers to foresee the future. He stood in an ancient tradition of Lakota spirituality, one that Curly Hair profoundly respected. Moreover, Crazy Horse was a Thunder dreamer, and Curly Hair confided that in dreams he had been told that he too would receive power from the Thunder Beings.[2]

Whatever tensions had marked their relationship since the death of Rattle Blanket Woman, the shared concerns of Curly Hair's new visionary life would foster a renewed intimacy between father and son. Curly Hair would first undergo the purificatory rites of the sweat lodge.

Trusted friends like Horn Chips, another Thunder dreamer, aided Curly Hair in cutting willow saplings and lashing the springy boughs into a dome-shaped framework about six feet across and four feet high. The earth at the center of the sweat lodge was dug out, then carried carefully outside to mark a path ending in a low mound symbolizing Unci, Grandmother Earth. Near the mound, the helpers prepared a ritual fire. First sticks representing the Four Directions were carefully laid, while Curly Hair was instructed to paint red a number of smooth round stones. Then the sticks were capped by the stones, and the fire lit.

Meanwhile buffalo robes were flung over the willow framework. A holy man entered and, after strewing the floor space with sage and tying tobacco offerings to the framework, placed pinches of tobacco around the center hole. He incensed the lodge with lit sweetgrass braids and filled a pipe for Curly Hair. By reverently placing in the bowl pinches of tobacco representing each of the Sacred Directions, the holy man ensured that the totality of wakan powers was present in the pipe, making it a channel of sacred potency. Finally, he sealed the bowl with a plug of buffalo tallow and tied sprigs of sage to each end of the stem. Then the holy man crawled outside and instructed Curly Hair to lean his pipe against the Grandmother Mound, its bowl facing the Thunder Powers of the West. All participants then stripped to breechclouts and followed the holy man back inside. The holy man took his seat at the rear, Curly Hair at his left. A helper passed through another pipe. The rest sat along the inner wall, praying quietly.

An assistant carried four white-hot rocks on a forked stick and placed them in the center hole, marking each of the Sacred Directions. As each stone was laid, the holy man touched to it the foot of his pipe bowl, and the seated men with bowed heads murmured thanks. A pipe was smoked in solemn communion, then the holy man ordered the lodge closed, and the helpers outside pulled down the door flap.

Darkness enveloped the interior. Curly Hair strained to hear the hushed voice of the holy man intoning prayers. As eyes accustomed to darkness, they made out the pulsing glow of the stones. Breaking off his prayers, the holy man ordered Curly Hair to implore the powers for aid. The youth began to cry and pray. Steam hissed as the holy man dashed water onto the stones. "Ho, Grandfather!" cried all as steam released the sacred energies of the stones. Louder, the voices joined in prayer. Briefly, the door opened, and one of the helpers passed through Curly Hair's pipe. Holding its stem to each shoulder, Curly Hair cried to Wakan Tanka, "Be merciful to me! Help me!" before passing the unlit pipe around the circle. The helper then took it outside and leaned it against the Grandmother Mound, pointing east. The door was closed, and the heat mounted again. Sweat pricked the skin, and the men and youths dabbed at their bodies with sprays of sage.

The holy man began to talk to Curly Hair, reiterating the solemnity of the vision quest. He asked how long Curly Hair wished to fast and pray: four days and nights, the youth replied. What guidance did Curly Hair hope to receive? Awkwardly, hinting at his misgivings over the situation of the Lakota people, the youth explained that he wished "for [a] vision and power to serve his tribe."[3] This was unusual: most youths wanted power only to steal enemy horses, to live long, or to charm the village girls.

Four pauses punctuated the prayers and lectures. Helpers threw up the lodge coverings, permitting the group time to relax, changing the mood to broad joking as they gulped water noisily or poured it over their heads. Then new stones were brought from the fire. Each time the holy man imparted practical advice and spiritual counsel, indicating the high place where Curly Hair should go to cry for a vision. Friends who had themselves dreamed of Thunder, like his father and Horn Chips, should accompany him to prepare the sacred place. After the fourth session, ending with the Lakota amen—*mitakuye oyasin*, all my relations!—Curly Hair crawled out the door to sit, wailing, on the sacred path facing the Grandmother Mound. Bodily impurities had been removed by the sweating, and he felt spiritually revitalized by the rite. Curly Hair's helpers placed around his shoulders his buffalo robe, and in his hands the sealed pipe. Then friends led up saddled horses, and a small procession of comrades started out of the camp circle. Bringing up the rear rode Curly Hair, holding his pipe before him.

A fifty-mile ride down the North Platte valley brought the party to the foot of Scott's Bluffs. In summer this was a settler landmark. The twin ruts marking the Overland Trail were visible, but in early fall the road was empty. They rested overnight near the foot of the bluffs, but in the darkness before dawn, his helpers roused Curly Hair and ritually fed him a piece of dried meat and a sip of water. Then the party walked the winding trail to the summit. The helpers cleared away vegetation and dug clean the sides of a shallow pit, long enough for the dreamer to lie in, scattering tobacco over the bottom, lining it with fresh sage, and covering it with brush. Plum bough poles were set up at the four corners of the pit, each representing one of the Sacred Directions. The fifth pole stood at the center of the vision pit, linking earth to the zenith and identifying the pit as the symbolic center of the world, where all powers inhere. A red blanket was cut up to make banners that would stream from the poles as offerings to the powers of each Direction. Strings were tied between the poles and hung with tiny tobacco bundles, wrapped in cloth or in squares of skin cut from Curly Hair's own thighs and forearms, so that the vision pit was bound with a web of sacred offerings. Curly Hair was led to the pit and told to remove his moccasins and breechclout and stand at the eastern pole facing the rising sun, holding his pipe stem toward that greatest manifestation of Wakan Tanka. Then the party left Curly Hair alone as the sun rose over the earth.

Naked, his hair unbound in supplication and his voice raised in a wailing chant for help and guidance, Curly Hair stood alone, humble and pitiful. For the four days of his *hanble-ceya*, he must not eat or drink. Much would come, the holy man had warned, to test his courage. Comrades had advised that many considered the extreme solitude of the vision quest to be a sterner test than even the Sun Dance, but he must hold on to his pipe and not be afraid. As hunger and thirst deepened, he must listen to everything around him: passing birds or animals might carry messages that he should not neglect. Circling eagles, a passing coyote, the hover of a distant hawk—all were to be saluted in prayer, their movement and behavior scrutinized for significance. All day the vision seeker followed the slow progress of the sun, turning at noon to face south, standing at each pole and begging the powers to grant him the clarifying vision. As the sun sank, Curly Hair faced the west, his pipestem tracking below the horizon line until he stood in darkness. Famished and exhausted, he at last crawled beneath the brush to wrap himself in his robe and lie on the sage bed of the pit, his head toward the west. Before sleep took him, he sought to focus through the brush on the wheeling progress of the stars in the massive sky. At dawn Curly Hair rose to address a prayer to the morning star, before he took his place once more to face the rising sun.

So the days passed. His stumbling prayers made the circuit of directions and their powers. At length, as the holy man advised if other prayers failed, he begged power directly from Wakan Tanka, aid to "save his tribe." As exhaustion deepened, he spent more time sitting against the poles, thinking deeply. At night, sounds he had considered familiar took on unsettling clarity: owl hoots, the rushing swoop of night hawks, and the scamper of small animals, all sounded uncannily loud, as if loaded with a significance that lay just beyond the line of consciousness. As the days succeeded, hunger, exhaustion, and dehydration rendered sound itself a tactile presence. Daytime noises like the scurry of ants or the scratching of a grasshopper's legs boomed like thunder; observed movement seemed to slow to a glacial crawl or to accelerate impossibly. Small wonder that a distant roll of thunder roared with revelatory power for Curly Hair; or that flashing forks of lightning seared clarity and the assurance of power into the youth's consciousness. Outside, his nighttime dreams had caused him to fear the destructive power of Thunder, but here, in this sacred space, he stood as if within the Thunder: its power his.

Somewhere late in the four days and nights the vision came, either in sleep or as Curly Hair staggered between the offering poles. We do not know its details: vision seekers spoke openly about their dreams only to the holy men or their most trusted friends, and Curly Hair was more secretive than most. But dreams of Thunder were typically prefaced by a noise in the west and the charge of mounted men, servants of the Thunder Beings. Thunder itself, a huge bird with lightning at its joints, might appear in awesome revelation or speak through one of its envoys, the hawks and bats, horses, dogs, and dragonflies that acted as its akicita. A red-tailed hawk was the messenger of this first vision: this fierce bird of prey would always be Curly Hair's closest guardian spirit. An intense visionary experience followed, and the closing admonition to "Remember what you have seen." Then, finally, the dreamer slept.[4]

As day broke on the fifth day, the holy man led his little party back up the bluff. They took down the string of tobacco offerings and entered the vision pit. The holy man closed Curly Hair's trembling hands over his pipe and led him gently from the pit. His breechclout was put on, and his robe placed over his shoulders before he was helped onto his pony and led down the hill. The offering cloths were left to blow atop the butte, another plea to Wakan Tanka for the liberty of the Blue Water captives. On the plain below, a sweat lodge had been built. The holy man permitted Curly Hair to take a little water, then led him into the lodge where the party underwent the *inipi* again. In slow disconnected phrases, the dreamer sought to recount his vision to his comrades. The holy man unsealed Curly Hair's pipe, and it was smoked in communion to indicate the successful conclusion of his vision quest. At the close, the holy man gave Curly Hair a little dried meat to chew, then ordered the helpers to leave. He arranged Curly Hair for sleep and left him alone within the reassuring womblike shelter of the sweat lodge.

For much of the day and night, the dreamer slept on. On the following day, as Curly Hair's strength returned with food, water, and rest, the inipi was held again as many as three times. Each time the holy man probed at the details of the vision.

He and the helpers, fellow Thunder dreamers, offered their interpretations of its significance, sensitive to the nuance of detail. They were satisfied that Curly Hair had indeed "received the Holy Message,"[5] and assured him that the Thunder Beings would assist him as a warrior in the service of the Lakota people. The holy man then reminded Curly Hair that such visions came at a lifelong price. Lest he incur their disfavor and die by lightning, the dreamer must repeatedly convince the Thunder Beings of his humility and fitness for their blessing. Thunder's protection was one of the greatest gifts the wakan could bestow: Curly Hair must give thanks that would take spiritual humility to the extreme edge of public humiliation. Next spring, after the Thunders ushered in the season of renewal, Curly Hair must pledge to hold the heyoka ceremony in their honor.

While these events unfolded, the eleven-man party deputed to locate the Blue Water fugitives located Little Thunder's camp. When Harney's demands were announced, agreement was soon reached. Iron Shell, whose own mother, son, and three wives were among the captured, addressed Spotted Tail, saying that for the good of the people he should surrender. His own wife and baby daughter in captivity, Spotted Tail replied that he would do as Iron Shell requested.[6]

On October 26, Red Leaf, Long Chin, and Spotted Tail rode into the agency, dressed in their finest war clothes and singing their death songs. Lakotas from the peace party village hosted a feast for the warriors who were ready to throw away their lives for the people. Curly Hair, returned from his vision quest, and his family were likely present. The youth, potent with the Thunder power of his vision, must have watched his uncle closely, eyeing the two bullet wounds and the severe gashes of two dragoon sabers scarring Spotted Tail's body. After two nights spent at the agency, Twiss accompanied the three men to Fort Laramie on the twenty-eighth, where they were turned over to the commanding officer and secured in the guard-house.[7]

On November 5 a slow procession turned out of the Fort Laramie parade ground and down the Oregon Trail. An army ambulance followed by a mounted escort lumbered ahead; a freight wagon loaded with tipis and camping equipment brought up the rear. They were bound for Fort Leavenworth, on the Missouri frontier. In the open ambulance sat Spotted Tail and his comrades, shackled in irons, with their wives and youngest children. As the ambulance passed the Lakotas lining the trail, the three warriors started to chant a song of the Strong Hearts Society. Women sounded the tremolo of praise as for warriors going into battle. Perhaps Curly Hair tracked the progress of his uncle for a while, joining in the high fierce chant for courage. Spotted Tail had shown courage indeed, his nephew knew, but at what price for himself and the people?[8]

Through the winter the nominal state of war continued. General Harney scheduled a grand treaty council at Fort Pierre in March 1856. Convinced that the Lakotas could be controlled by an adequately supported chieftainship, he instructed each tribal division to nominate a head chief and nine subordinate chiefs to represent them at the treaty. To impress their people with their status, these chiefs and a force of akicita leaders would receive regular government subsistence in food and uniform clothing.[9]

The treaty called for the return of all stolen property and the surrender of all warriors guilty of offenses. Once these conditions were satisfied, Harney would free the Blue Water captives. Established trails must be kept open for troops and settlers. To end horse stealing, which threatened settler security, the Lakotas were to extend the 1851 truces to include the Pawnees and, even less realistically, to stop the internal trade in horses entirely. They would consider settling at points near military posts and taking up farming. In return, the Lakotas would have their annuities restored and be protected from abuses by ill-disposed Americans. At Fort Pierre in May, Harney officially announced the end of hostilities, ordering the captives freed and recognizing Bear Ribs, the new Hunkpapa head chief, as Scattering Bear's successor to the nominal chieftainship of all Lakotas.[10]

A new mood favoring consensus and an end to the polarization of the past three years was emerging across the Lakota domain. Hunkpapas and Sihasapas marked the new order by accepting their treaty goods for the first time. During spring 1856 the northern Oglala bands followed Harney's advice to clear the Overland Trail and moved northwest into the Powder River country. At Platte Bridge the local Cheyennes had gotten embroiled with the troops in another petty argument over stock. Fearful of a rerun of the events of 1854, many people were convinced of the need to secure safer hunting grounds, and the Oglala chiefs had organized a season of diplomacy with the Crows.[11]

For Curly Hair, much of the politics surrounding the Harney negotiations probably seemed irrelevant or worse. As spring approached, early thunders reminded him of his pledge to perform the heyoka ceremony. To the Lakotas, the heyoka were sacred clowns. Dreamers of the Thunder, they were expected to ritually display humility reduced to absurdity. Failure to perform these duties would result in certain death by lightning. Some were committed to a lifetime of contrary behavior—dressing in rags, sleeping naked in the snow, willfully performing the opposite of any instruction.[12]

His hair shaved off on one side of the head, carrying a dewclaw rattle and speaking "backwards," Curly Hair had spent the winter being shunned as a bearer of ill luck. As the day of the ceremony approached, Curly Hair's instructors in the vision quest set up a dilapidated tipi, its smoke-blackened skins hung on broken poles. Here the holy man, helpers like Horn Chips, and Curly Hair met in a burlesque of solemn council, dressed in conical caps, shirts trimmed with crow feathers, and winter robes belted at the waist. While the helpers were strangling dogs for the feast, invitations were sent to all the heyoka in the village. Women set to boiling the dogs. Heyoka, dressed in outlandish masks, or sporting phallic false noses, proceeded to impede and obstruct the cooking, neglecting to singe off the dog's hair, hamfisting the butchering. Some adopted obscene postures around the women, reducing the crowd to helpless laughter as they pantomimed ejaculation over the oldest crone, urinated on their own clothing, or began happily hurling excrement across the campground.

Curly Hair had to play a leading part in this performance, scrutinized closely by his instructors. At length, as the heyoka capered madly around the boiling kettles, each singing his own thunder song in glorious discord, Curly Hair's instructors called him aside. They showed him how to rub his hands and cheeks with an ointment made from the chewed leaves of the red false mallow. With this protection, Curly Hair thrust his hands into the bubbling pot and drew out chunks of dog meat, running out to the crowd to serve the laughing press of people by throwing the boiling cuts into their laps. Other heyoka scooped up handfuls of boiling water, hurling it into Curly Hair's face or across each other's backs, to shrieks that the water was too cold. The ceremony ended with full bellies and laughing faces.

The heyoka is commonly viewed simply as a clown to lift the people's spirits, but there were darker aspects to the experience of the Thunder dreamer. After the performance of the ceremony, the fortunate were advised that they had endured enough: the Thunder Beings were satisfied. But a few were told that Thunder demanded of them one more sacrifice: they must kill—like the lightning, with implacable random speed—a man, woman, or child, "in which case he must obey and until he does he is upbraided by the people for not doing what he was advised to do."[13] Although we know little of the details of Curly Hair's heyoka experience, events of the next year suggest that his advisers told him that he must kill a woman.

As summer deepened, messengers from the Platte reported the return of Agent Twiss from the East, the arrival of annuities at Fort Laramie, and the imminent release of Spotted Tail and his comrades from detention in Fort Leavenworth. After petitions from both Twiss and General Harney, the president had issued a pardon for the mail coach raiders.[14]

The Oglalas made their way to rendezvous with the Upper Brules at Rawhide Butte, twenty-five miles north of Fort Laramie, where Twiss had arranged to deliver their treaty goods. According to He Dog's recollection, Curly Hair left the Oglalas and lived for a year with the Brules when they were youths of about seventeen or eighteen. The chronology best fits the year 1856–57, the context of Spotted Tail's return from imprisonment. Perhaps Curly Hair's two stepmothers, keen to see their brother again, and the whole family joined the Brules when, early in October, Spotted Tail and his comrades were released at Fort Laramie.[15]

The men who returned from detention had changed in significant ways. One year before, Red Leaf had been their spokesman, but Spotted Tail returned as the leader. Contrary to all expectations, he explained, the prisoners had been treated well. Many of the officers had proved approachable and friendly: to one, who had carried Spotted Tail's baby from the Blue Water battlefield, he had sworn lifelong friendship. More important than this, Spotted Tail continued, was the sheer number of Americans. Although the prisoners had visited no city, Spotted Tail was an astute observer. Surveying the massive garrison of Fort Leavenworth, observing growing American settlements and the steamboat traffic along the lower Missouri, passing eastern Indian communities marked by farm plots and churches, Spotted Tail accurately saw the shape of the future. Most significant, he understood that Fort Leavenworth, huge compared to the tiny garrisons policing the plains, was only an outlying post in a massive military infrastructure. In public council, warriors' feasts, and family meetings, Spotted Tail reiterated that Lakotas must never contemplate going to war again with the Americans. War could only bring disaster on the people.[16]

Agent Twiss moved to exploit the mood. Although Congress had not yet voted funds to implement the Harney treaty, the agent had been able to secure uniform clothing in the 1856 annuities and used these to outfit a fledgling akicita force, which would keep order at the annuity issue, prevent depredations against Americans, and even seek to regulate intertribal warfare. Members may have been drawn from the Kit Fox warrior society. Unlike the militant Strong Hearts, the Kit Fox leadership was inclined to cooperation with the United States. Among the Brules, the society was the one most commonly called on to act as tribal police, and with a chapter in every Oglala band, the Kit Fox was the strongest of the warrior societies, a potential catalyst for peace.[17]

Sixteen-year-old Curly Hair probably listened with misgivings to these developments, and especially to his uncle's change of heart. Moreover, he heard disturbing reports that the prisoners had served in army reprisals against Cheyenne raiders. In the most serious clash, cavalry attacked without warning a war party sitting out heavy rains on Grand Island, killing six Cheyennes after the warriors threw down their bows in submission.[18]

The Brule Wazhazha band moved to wintering grounds in the Sandhills, trading at Ash Hollow near the Blue Water battlefield. Curly Hair decided to stay on with his stepmothers' people. During the winter, Cheyenne envoys targeted them and other Lakota bands, seeking to win aid for a new war against the Americans. The Wazhazha council repeatedly rejected the Cheyenne tobacco, but Curly Hair was moved by the Cheyenne appeals and began to chafe at the new policy of accommodating Americans. Moreover, he was keen to go to war and test the powers granted him by Thunder. Since his warrior apprenticeship had begun at twelve, the truce with the Crows had narrowed the scope of intertribal warfare: the Brule cooperation with the Americans threatened to foreclose all opportunities for warriors keen to win the battle honors needed in Lakota society.[19]

In May 1857, however, a war party was organized to strike the Pawnee villages in eastern Nebraska. Curly Hair joined the party, leading a mount he had spent patient months training as a war pony. Once the party approached the Pawnee villages, grouped along the south side of the lower Platte River, scouts surveyed the prospect from the hills. Under discipline not to alert the enemy, the war party was ordered forward, and for the first time Curly Hair viewed an enemy village. Below him ran the wide braided channels of the Platte, marked by willowed sandbars snagged with driftwood. Keen eyes could have pointed out the houses of the American settlement of Fremont, Nebraska, across the river—the homes not of fur traders or soldiers but of settlers, proof that this was no longer a world of Indians only.[20]

On the terrace above the river floodplain stood the village of the Skidi Pawnees, earthlodges and tipis strung along the high bank. Below the village clustered the Skidi garden plots, and scouts pointed out the movement within the brush hedges as women, children, and old people worked the fields. Using buffalo shoulderblade hoes, women bent to grub weeds from around the first shoots of corn. Children scampered to shoo off alighting birds; elders intoned age-old prayers for their crops, the inheritance of almost one thousand years of horticulture on the Nebraska prairies.

Their target selected, the Lakota warriors massed for a charge into the fields. Hardly had the war whistles shrilled the signal to attack when a lone rider burst far ahead of the Lakota line, brandishing a light staff. His pony responded instantly to each ounce of pressure he applied through his knees and heels, turning, veering, and clearing obstacles at terrific speed. He was, recalled his cousin Eagle Elk, "making a dash to coup an enemy." The sudden clamor of war whoops alerted the Pawnees to their danger. People began to run down the rows of corn toward the river, women screaming for their children.[21]

Far ahead of the other Lakotas, Curly Hair was already among the Pawnees. A Skidi woman appeared near him. Perhaps mindful of his heyoka pledge, Curly Hair veered toward her. Armed with club, knife, and bow, he could have speedily killed his victim. Instead, he struck her with his staff and the woman fell, momentarily stunned, as Curly Hair counted first coup, most prized of war honors. Without pausing, the youth sped forward, the heady rush of action intoxicating him for the first time. Exultantly, he struck light blows to right and left, counting coup over and over, so that the warriors fanning through the field after him marveled at his precocious courage and skill. By the time the war party disengaged and melted back into the hills, Curly Hair, breathless and triumphant, had decisively stamped his future. "From that time on," remembered Eagle Elk, "he was talked about."[22] With Thunder's power he would strike all Lakota enemies as he had the Pawnees.

Despite the euphoria over his first successful warpath, there remained unfinished business for Curly Hair. Although our culture today is open to the mysticism inherent in the vision quest, it is easy to overlook the central fact that the Lakota vision seeker wished less for enlightenment than for spiritual potency, the transformative power called sicun. To cry for a vision was not to seek the state of disinterested spiritual awareness of Buddhism. All visions demanded for their understanding insight, wisdom, and the exertion of meditative willpower. Older men, and women past the age of childbearing, might acquire profound spiritual awareness and perfect their capacity to live with "all my relatives." Nevertheless, the typical dreamer sought sicun to grant him a spiritual edge, the potential to overcome enemies, misfortune, and illness for his own sake or that of relatives.

To the Lakota, no sicun was more awesome than that granted by the Thunder Beings. In a culture that valued reciprocity, so potent a gift naturally demanded sacrifice. The abject humiliation of the heyoka, for some a lifelong commitment, represented the absolute nature of that undertaking. Heyoka were living lightning conductors, preserving their people from the destructive powers of the Thunder Beings. Instead, they channelled through themselves those staggering energies to strike enemies with the terrible random ferocity of lightning.

The heyoka's total commitment to the warrior ideal outside the tribe was counterbalanced by their domestic role as hapless clowns. Lakota society imposed on all its males a drastic dichotomy: to be a responsible conciliator within the tribe and a cruel implacable enemy beyond it. The heyoka represented the extreme manifestation of the dichotomy, as if society, forced to confront the pathological implications of the warrior ethic, had to resort to mockery—not of the ideals, but of the individuals who most fully lived up to them.

Like figures of carnival licensed to excess, they lived at the far edge of public respect. Small wonder that many a Thunder dreamer "became morose or melancholy and [spent] much of his time alone."[23] This description aptly characterized the adult Curly Hair, whose natural reflectiveness was easily tipped into melancholia. The tragedies of childhood had played a significant part in the formulation of his adult psychology, but the behaviors imposed on him as an active heyoka also shaped and heightened the gloomy reserve that characterized one aspect of his peacetime behavior. Heyoka both gave Curly Hair an accepted public guise for his melancholy and more deeply etched it into his inner being.

If the reconstruction of the heyoka pledges that he warily, reluctantly undertook are accurate, Curly Hair had been ordered by the holy man who interpreted his vision to kill, under pain of Thunder's punishment, a woman. Perhaps this explained his first coup in the attack on the Pawnee village. His dramatic charge, a sixteen-year-old youth outstripping tried Brule warriors, was clearly an extraordinary act of will. There is little room for sentimentality when assessing Plains Indian warfare. Although many fights yielded few casualties as men sought to strike coups—simple blows with the hand or a weapon—steal horses, or engage in daring one-to-one clashes, some were characterized by wholesale killings of noncombatants. Lakota warriors, like their Crow or Pawnee adversaries, sought to terrorize enemy morale by the death or capture of the enemy's women and children.

Undoubtedly, not all men felt easy with such practices. By accident or inner compulsion, Curly Hair spared his victim, striking only a blow for first coup. If act of mercy this was, it did not fulfill the demands of the Thunder Beings. Sometime after the war party returned home, Curly Hair committed his most terrible act. Known only through a terse statement by his friend He Dog seventy-four years later, during the Brule sojourn, Curly Hair "killed a Winnebago woman."[24]

The details of the tragedy are unknown. He Dog was disinclined to expand on the subject to his interviewers, Eleanor Hinman and Mari Sandoz. Perhaps sensing his reluctance, they did not press the matter, but He Dog's own measured statement yields vital clues to understanding the killing. It was certainly no war honor, as Sandoz contended, for Curly Hair made no public statement claiming this as a coup. Instead, recalled He Dog, "I made inquiries about why he had left the Rosebud [Brule] band. I was told *he had to come back* because he had killed a Winnebago woman."[25] The matter was already an enigma, something hidden, only to be solved by "making inquiries" within months of the killing.

The woman involved, significantly, was not a Lakota, but an alien, of marginal status. In circumstances now unknowable, Curly Hair killed her. Curly Hair's relatives succeeded in quickly "covering" the death with whoever called the Winnebago woman a relative. Nevertheless, the act carried enough stigma for Curly Hair to realize that his stay among the Brules was at an end: "[H]e had to come back." Perhaps uniformed Brule akicita implemented Agent Twiss's orders and drove Curly Hair from the village.

It had been an uncomfortable visit, contrasting with Curly Hair's restorative trips to the Miniconjous. Just how much the Brule stay rankled is revealed by the youth's next move. When a number of other young Oglalas proposed a hunting trip into the Cheyenne country, Curly Hair joined them. Curly Hair's flouting of the anti-Cheyenne position taken by Spotted Tail was a considered rejection of the new policy to conciliate Americans, the final act of a strained year.

As Curly Hair left the Brule country for the south, he did not leave behind the moral trauma of killing the Winnebago woman. The historian is free to assign blame, to convict and exonerate or to pronounce a qualified acquittal on the mitigating grounds of psychological disturbance or cultural relativism. The evidence suggests that Curly Hair felt no such comforting cliché. Immediately compensated for by the gift of a few horses, then covered up by enigma, silence, and misdirection, the murder lived on in his mind as an enduring blot.

6

CRAZY HORSE

In July, the Moon of Red Cherries, Curly Hair and his Oglala companions crossed the South Platte River and angled their ponies southeast into the Cheyenne country. Game was scarce. Another hot summer signaled climatic shifts on the plains that incrementally ate at buffalo range, threatening seasonal hardship and the long-term stability of the Plains Indian way of life. Buffalo herds in the region moved east across the shortgrass plains toward the reliable pasture of the lower prairies. As a string of deserted village sites showed, the Cheyennes continued to track the herds downcountry.[1]

Among the group of friends rode the eldest son of Man Afraid of His Horse. Now twenty-one years old and already a leader of war parties, Young Man Afraid of His Horse was good company for Curly Hair. The son of the Hunkpatila chief was himself a Thunder dreamer, thoughtful but with a genial good nature and a spontaneous smile that may have done something to alleviate Curly Hair's mood. As the party rode, they found disturbing signs of new army movements—following the success of the Harney operations, a punitive force had been ordered to chastise the Cheyennes.

Colonel Edwin V. Sumner rode at the head of a command comprising eight companies of the First Cavalry and the Second Dragoons. On July 13 Sumner left his base camp on the South Platte, probing east. Curly Hair's party fanned out scouts to monitor his approach until, after a two-hundred-mile journey, the youths located the Cheyenne village on the Saline River. Curly Hair's party was welcomed to the large white council tipi at the center of the campground, where travelers and visitors were every day debriefed about news of troop movements.[2]

Elders proposed that the village move out of the troops' way, but younger war leaders were determined to fight. Two young holy men, Ice and Dark, believed that their sacred power would render the soldiers' guns harmless. The Cheyennes owned few firearms, mostly smoothbore trade muskets, but Ice and Dark offered to load these weapons with a white powder that would guarantee a hit with every shot. The assurances of spiritual power convinced most warriors that a battle with Sumner could be won. Unlike the Lakotas at the Blue Water, they were actively preparing to choose the place of battle. They agreed that, when the soldiers neared, the warriors should meet them on the south fork of the Solomon.[3]

On the evening of July 28, scouts arrived with word that Sumner's column had gone into camp barely thirty miles north. Into the night, warrior societies paraded around the campground. Inside the lodges men prepared paints, incensing weapons, shields, and battle charms in sacred smoke of sage, sweetgrass, and cedar. Others sharpened arrowheads or heated lead in bullet molds. As Curly Hair watched the preparations, he could only have been impressed by the piety and confidence of the Cheyennes. Before dawn the village was astir. Some mothers, proud and anxious, untethered war ponies and offered sons counsel. Horses were rubbed down with sage, dusted with sacred earth medicines, streaked with paint designs or circles that denoted battle wounds; scalps were tied at bridles and tails bobbed with twists of red cloth. Warriors donned hair-fringed war shirts and feather headdresses. As the sun appeared down the Saline valley, a party of over three hundred men formed behind Ice and Dark and, to the tremolos of the women, headed north toward the Solomon.[4]

Curly Hair and his Oglala friends, after four years of frustration with the Americans, were happy to ride beside their Cheyenne friends. Shortly, the column paused at a small prairie lake, where Ice and Dark ordered the warriors to dip their hands in the water. Now they needed only to hold up their hands toward the soldiers to make the enemy guns useless; then the Cheyennes would charge in and fight the troops at close quarters. The column re-formed and strung out over the plain. About midmorning they crossed the Solomon and dismounted in the thin belt of cottonwoods. Horses were watered and turned out to graze. Curly Hair, still a novice at warfare, would be tense and expectant, but many warriors negligently sat around chatting or gambling, lunching on jerky and pemmican. Midday passed; the day dragged into afternoon.

Suddenly, scouts appeared over a bluff upstream, circling their ponies in wide arcs, the signal that many enemies approached. The warriors formed a well-spaced line, four or five loose rows deep, extending north across the valley floor for almost half a mile. Around the bend two miles upstream, a column of some three hundred mounted soldiers appeared and wheeled into a broad front of three squadrons, four men deep. Before the front rank of blue-coated troops, guidons snapped smartly in the Kansas breeze. The line of blue-coated troops started forward at a trot. War leaders ordered the Cheyennes forward at a lope. War songs started up. On both flanks, warriors were detailed to fan out, crossing the river or scaling the bluffs, and outflank the soldiers. Curly Hair expectantly watched the soldier line, the distance swiftly narrowing to one mile. The soldier chief detached companies to combat the flanking movement. The soldiers on the left quickly ascended the bluffs, forcing the Cheyenne flankers to fall back downhill.

Rifle range neared. Warriors beside Curly Hair shouted battle cries and challenges. A lone figure galloped out from the soldier line and hauled in his pony. Although he wore the soldier's blue jacket, leggings and a bright cloth turban identified him as a Delaware, an army scout from one of the displaced eastern Indian tribes. The Delaware snapped off a shot at the Cheyenne line and wheeled his pony back toward the soldiers. Yelling warriors responded with ragged musketry fire. Through the mounting dust, Curly Hair saw the war leaders wave their lances toward the oncoming troops, turning in their light saddles to urge the warriors onward. Curly Hair and his fellows expected the soldiers to fire a volley from their readied carbines at any moment. Unproven youths flexed hands ready to hold up and stop the bullets.

Suddenly, each soldier simultaneously slung his carbine and drew his saber, the long knives that cavalry carried but rarely used. At sight of the sabers, the Cheyennes hauled in their ponies to a jarring halt. Curly Hair sat in the mill of dust and shouts. Comprehension of the situation was limited for a youth who could not understand the panicked clamor of voices. Up ahead a warrior in a trailer headdress sped along the demoralized line, shouting. Beyond him the relentless front of troops galloped forward, yelling wildly through the dust. The din of hooves and the clink and slap of horse gear added to the confusion of sound. The gap had narrowed to little more than one hundred yards. The Cheyennes seemed stunned by the saber maneuver, milling aimlessly. As the pause lengthened, they responded to insistent shouts by loosing a volley of arrows straight into the juggernaut of troops, then wheeled their ponies away from the field at a dead run. Bewildered and frightened, Curly Hair and his Oglala friends whipped after them, crossing the Solomon and galloping south. Behind them, bugle calls signaled the pursuit.

Here and there across the plain, troopers and Cheyennes clashed in small-scale struggles, in which several warriors and two soldiers were killed. At 3:00 P.M. Sumner ordered recall. While the troops regrouped, the Cheyennes sped south. At news of their defeat, the village began to fall. Some people abandoned lodges, packs and all, in their haste to get away. Most raced south, but the northern Cheyenne bands turned northwest. In hurried conference with Curly Hair and his Oglala friends, they decided to race for the Lodgepole Creek crossing of the South Platte, two hundred miles away. The Oglala friends joined the flight north, valuable intermediaries should the Cheyennes need to seek Lakota aid beyond the Platte.

Riding at horse-killing speed, the vanguard of the fleeing Cheyennes reached the South Platte the next afternoon. A base camp was established to provide food and intelligence for the people following. Through August 5, people continued to filter across the river and over the plains northward. Beyond the North Platte, the flight slowed and scattered. By August 11 one camp of Cheyennes was reported to have reached the south edge of the Black Hills.[5]

Once in the North Platte valley, Curly Hair and his comrades peeled away from the flight. Oglalas and Brules were gathering at Rawhide Butte, and the youths were anxious to be home. Riding along the Overland Trail, they saw the country scarred by many trails. Settler traffic had again been heavy, and thousands of troops bound for a new campaign against the Mormons were moving west. Around Fort Laramie Curly Hair's party found a city of army tents, vivid proof of the American nation's expanding might. A few Brule tipis were pitched around James Bordeaux's trading store. Before riding on to join their own bands, the friends were invited to eat at the lodge of Swift Bear, Bordeaux's brother-in-law, and tell their news. Young Man Afraid of His Horse probably took the lead in speaking, relating the news of their visit with the Cheyennes, while Curly Hair reflected on the events of a momentous summer.[6]

He would remember the central plains as an easy avenue for American travel, traversed by the great thoroughfares of the Overland and Santa Fe trails. Already army topographers were mapping new routes along the tributaries of the Kansas River, bisecting the hunting grounds of the Cheyennes and their allies. The ease with which troops could penetrate the Cheyenne country had been vividly demonstrated by Sumner's march. The Platte country was also tainted by recollections of Curly Hair's uncomfortable visit among the Brules and its abrupt termination. Mistrustful of the new Brule policy of accommodation, Curly Hair would never again travel south of the Platte except as a raider. His future would lie in the north.

The Cheyenne debacle also confirmed other conclusions. Fighting the long-knife soldiers in pitched battle had proved as disastrous as Brule overconfidence at the Blue Water. If warfare continued, a small-scale war of attrition, using Indian tactics of ambush and stock stealing, seemed to offer the best solution. The individualist's distrust of communal panaceas was sharpened in Curly Hair by the farcical failure of the Cheyennes' bulletproof medicine. Although he would continue to seek the personal protective edge offered by *wotawe* charms, all Curly Hair's instincts revolted against the mass manipulation of such power. After 1857 Curly Hair's worldview began to harden: the malleable edges of youth were roughened by what, for such an unworldly man, was probably the healthy abrasion of cynicism.

The sight of the great Oglala camps strung around Rawhide Butte heartened a homesick youth. A herald, using Curly Hair's formal name, circled the campground to announce that His Horse Stands in Sight had returned. Friends called to exchange news and greetings, He Dog among the first. Curly Hair's Bad Face friend told him that he had this same day returned with a war party from the Crows. In another recent incident, Curly Hair's kinsman Iron Whiteman had captured a Crow man. The news revealed that the sporadic Crow truces that had followed the Horse Creek Treaty were finished, which promised a rising warrior renewed scope for war honors in the north.[7]

In August 1857 the great Lakota council proposed in the aftermath of the Harney treaty gathered along the Belle Fourche River, near the landmark of Bear Butte.

Probably all northern Teton tribal divisions were present, with significant numbers of Oglalas and Brules. Logistics of pasturage for the horse herds, of water, fuel, and game, meant that such a massive gathering could have stayed together for only a matter of days. As cosponsors of the gathering, the Hunkpapa and Miniconjou villages raised a huge council tipi and shade. Warrior societies pitched their own meeting lodges on the campgrounds, where colorful society dances, gambling tournaments, and coup-counting contests were held. At the council shade, chiefs and elders held preliminary meetings, but much of the real political action would take place inside private lodges, at feasts hosted by cliques of leaders and society headmen.[8]

Consensus would be a major theme of the talks. Lakota society and politics were habitually volatile, and the most far-sighted leaders understood that the fraught issue of the American alliance held potential for unprecedented factionalism. Increasing dissension had illustrated vividly the threat of generational polarization. Warrior society meetings were still dominated by talk of war. Hearts were made strong, and war leaders declared that in future wars, they would not yield as easily. Warriors questioned General Harney's credentials as a peacemaker, observing that since leaving the Lakota country, the general had gone to war again. Contrasting their own few flintlocks with the weapons of the "great armies" of Harney, Sumner, and the Mormon campaign, war leaders recommended hit-and-run raids by small war parties, running off army horses and beef herds. Here direct input from Curly Hair and his comrades may have been welcomed, as Lakotas concluded that the Cheyenne debacle ruled out pitched battles with the Americans.[9]

On the contentious issue of treaty annuities, chiefs and elders were prepared to give ground, hedging acceptance with qualifications of American intent, as militant Strong Hearts Society spokesmen argued that the goods "scarcely paid for going after them." Debate threw up yet another misunderstanding. Oglalas and Upper Brules understood from Agent Twiss that the 1851 annuities were predicated on Lakota acceptance of the Overland Trail running through their lands; Hunkpapas and other northern Lakotas—their lands still unaffected by the settler routes—understood them to be dependent on preserving peace with the Crows. Bear Ribs won grudging concessions from Hunkpapa warriors that, although they would prefer no annuities and no American interference, as long as they were not committed to ending all intertribal warfare, their people could accept treaty goods.[10]

As the council progressed, speakers identified a central unifying concept—the sanctity of a clearly defined Lakota domain. The Black Hills lay at its heart. As a key wintering ground for the Lakotas and their buffalo, an invaluable resource of timber, water, and small game, a region potent with the elemental energies of Rock and Thunder, and the sacred associations of the vision quest, the Black Hills were defined as the symbolic heart of the Lakota country. "[T]hese Black Hills must be left wholly to themselves," speakers declared. Boundaries would be aggressively maintained against intruders. The Overland Trail and the steamboat route up the Missouri, defining the perimeter, would remain uncontested. Within the interior, only the Traders' Trail linking forts Pierre and Laramie could remain open—a concession clearly pressed by Oglala and Brule moderates. Trade was always a central concern of the elders. They won consensus about the security of the major trading posts but had to concede to hardliners that interior branch posts should be closed. All Americans in the interior could be "whipped out."[11]

Even in these hardline resolutions, however, Lakotas invoked the authority of their treaties through a creative reinterpretation of the Harney accord. Stressing certain aspects of Harney's council agreements and off-the-record remarks, and distinctly downplaying others, moderate leaders could argue that treaty provisions were consistent with militants' aspirations. The point on closing branch posts actually echoed one of Harney's recommendations, that trade be conducted solely at military posts. Speakers ignored the fact that the treaty expressly permitted military parties to cross the Lakota domain. Basing their observations on Harney's informal request that Lakotas cooperate in arresting army deserters, they even declared that persistent intruders could be killed once the ritual four warnings had been served.[12] Wasicu were not the only defined intruders. Yankton visitors from across the Missouri, coming under American pressure to sell their lands, were warned not to seek refuge on Lakota hunting grounds.[13]

Distinctly against the spirit of their treaties, the council turned to consider intertribal relations. Since their brief truce with the Crows had broken down in 1853, Hunkpapa and Sihasapa war parties had infested the lower Yellowstone valley, waging open war on the River Crows, which they categorically refused to give up. Faced with the move to conciliation, hardline Hunkpapa Strong Hearts leaders had formed a feasting club, known as the Midnight Strong Hearts from its late-night meetings, to try to formulate a concerted set of policies. Sitting Bull, eight years Curly Hair's senior, and unlike him an articulate, intensely political man, was recognized as their leader. Such was his renown that he had recently been made a Strong Hearts warbonnet wearer, pledged never to retreat, and invested as a Hunkpapa tribal war leader.[14]

For the first time Curly Hair and Sitting Bull's paths crossed. The Oglala youth could sit only in the outermost arc of the crowded council shade, but as he heard Sitting Bull and other Midnight Strong Hearts argue that on no account would the Crow war be given up, he could recognize a kindred spirit. Proposals to extend hunts into the Crow country, carefully squared with Harney's recommendation that the Lakotas seek hunting grounds remote from the settler trails, met with general approval. Lakota raiders could rationalize westward expansion by citing Crow rejection of joint land-use accords. With key differences adroitly mediated, the great council wound to a close. In summing up the council resolutions, Bear Ribs would tersely state "they had agreed together to hereafter let no one come." For now, chiefs and warriors spoke with one powerful voice.[15]

The Bear Butte resolutions placed the Americans on trial. If they respected the Lakota domain, keeping soldiers and settlers off the hunting grounds, peace might be maintained. If Americans continued to intrude, mechanisms were in place to downgrade diplomatic relations progressively through akicita punishments and rejection of treaty goods to open warfare. In reality, once the tribal divisions moved away for fall hunting operations, each tribe and band was free to interpret the Bear Butte resolutions in light of local conditions. But their spirit would continue to animate Curly Hair's adult life, shaping his responses and strategies to American activity as he grew into manhood. For him the unformed instincts of youth were forged into principles, attitudes, and convictions at the great council of 1857.

Prominent among the Miniconjou warriors at Bear Butte was High Backbone. Curly Hair had made a joyous reunion with his kola, exchanging ponies and, for the first time, being consulted as an equal. Now High Backbone, already a leader of war parties, proposed a raid northward. Soon after the close of the council—if Charles Eastman's account drawn from Oglala contemporaries of Crazy Horse is to be trusted, in the late summer weeks before Curly Hair's seventeenth birthday—he prepared again for war.[16]

High Backbone opened proceedings by sending out invitations to trusted comrades and relatives to eat with him. After he canvassed opinion, they set a date for departure. A day or so before leaving, the war party was formally organized when a handful of the most experienced members of the party were installed as *blotahunka*, the committee of war leaders that would coordinate the expedition under High Backbone's direction. A feast was served, the food being ladled out by the messengers into a single dish with two spoons standing in it. Then the dish was passed around the circle. Each pair of men held the dish as they ate, a practice meant to instill the spirit of implicit trust and comradeship warriors must share. The feast closed with the singing of war songs deep into the night.[17]

The following morning, the party sat shoulder to shoulder on the camp-ground, facing the direction of the enemy's land. As a Thunder dreamer, Curly Hair did not dress in his best regalia but wore only moccasins and a short breechclout. His unbound hair streamed out behind him, the front hair stiffened into a high pompadour symbolizing the strike of lightning. Sprigs of a plant associated with the Thunder were thrust through the pompadour and tied into his horse's bobbed tail. Around his forehead he painted a wavy red line, forked at either end. He dabbed his face and chest with white spots representing hail, then repeated the pattern over the chest and hindquarters of his pony. Then High Backbone led the party north.[18]

As the war party neared enemy country, its progress slowed, and scouts criss-crossed the terrain. After locating the enemy, the party held a night feast at which the blotahunka presided. Around a blazing fire to defy the enemy, officers selected young men, balancing novices and tried warriors, to strike coups in the coming battle. To judge by his conduct, Curly Hair may well have been one of the chosen.[19]

As the party crossed a wide valley, the enemy was sighted—a party of Atsinas, northern kin of the Arapahos, gathered on "a high hill covered with big rocks and near a river."[20] The Atsinas rode tentatively forward, but High Backbone led a fierce charge, and the enemy grouped in a defensive knot on the prairie. High Backbone whipped forward his pony and charged the Atsinas alone, his war gear distinctive—a red cloth turban and matching cape.[21] Such gear identified the "big braves," men whom the enemy recognized and feared, and to whom comrades rallied. Now the line of warriors reined in to observe their leader perform his brave run and empty the enemy guns. Sure enough, a rattle of musketry greeted High Backbone as his charge swung around the Atsina position. Bullets and arrows whistled close to the pipe owner. Suddenly, from the row of Lakotas, a slight figure quirted forward his own pony: Curly Hair had decided to follow his comrade's run.

It was not a moment too soon, for a well-placed shot struck High Backbone's mount, and the pony plunged forward and fell. Its rider, injured and momentarily stunned, lay in the dust. Whoops signaled an Atsina rush to kill the fallen giant, but as the yelling enemy closed on High Backbone, Curly Hair reined back his horse and leapt from the saddle. Arrows struck the earth all around him as he raced to his comrade's side and lifted him up. The superbly trained war pony waited quietly amidst a hail of fire as its owner assisted High Backbone into the saddle, then sprang up behind him. Enemies streamed after the pair, but Curly Hair skillfully effected the escape to rejoin their comrades.

The Lakotas drove the enemy back up the rocky hill, with Curly Hair charging the Atsinas "several times alone."[22] The body of a fallen enemy lay in an exposed spot: none of the Lakotas dared approach to strike coup. To some spectators, Curly Hair's pony "became unmanageable," just as it had in the Pawnee fight. In truth, the pony's mettle was evidence of the months of training it had shared with its rider in his preparation for battle. Now it carried Curly Hair "wildly about" toward the body. Leaning out of the saddle as he careered past, the youth struck first coup.[23]

As the fight turned to rout, Curly Hair laced into the enemy rearguard. Urging his pony to greater efforts, he "rammed his horse into the enemies' horses, knocking the riders off. He did this repeatedly."[24] When the Lakotas disengaged to regroup, Curly Hair rode back bearing two scalps. Although he had also sustained a flesh wound in the arm, Curly Hair's first major fight was another stunning personal victory. As the war party turned for home, High Backbone singled out his protege for praise. The rescue only confirmed the close relationship between the pair. Warrior and youth were now pledged as lifelong comrades, sharing property, food, and booty. In the hunt and warfare, they would assist each other—as Curly Hair had just demonstrated—into the teeth of death.[25]

Several Oglala and Miniconjou bands had established winter camps near one another in the upper Belle Fourche valley.[26] The night before Curly Hair and his comrades returned, they blackened their faces in token of victory. At dawn the leader took his war pipe, wrapped in a wolf-skin cover, and secured it by a cord over the shoulders of the youth who had distinguished himself in the battle. Curly Hair started across the prairie toward the village, the warriors who had won honors striding in line abreast of him, chanting a war song. Other warriors galloped ahead and circled the village, musket shots announcing a victorious return.

As they neared the camp entrance, the line of warriors stopped and sat on the earth. Assistants lit a small fire of buffalo chips, and High Backbone ceremoniously unwrapped the war pipe. Each warrior touched the pipe stem to his lips. At the camp entrance, a crowd of relatives began a song of welcome.

All the warriors mounted to ride into camp, holding aloft their trophies. "I bring a human scalp!" Curly Hair could cry, rearing his pony. Women tremoloed their praise and led the parade of warriors riding abreast in kola pairs, led by High Backbone and Curly Hair. Girls ran up to receive the scalp trophies from triumphant brothers. Youths snatched at the warriors' clothing, carrying away ornaments and weapons for good luck. "Haye, haye," old men chanted their praise as High Backbone trotted over to the council tipi and dismounted, tossing the rein to one of the press of people.

For up to four days, feasting continued. On the final night, as bonfires burned, a tall pole was erected. Painted with a black spiral stripe, scalps and severed hands and feet were fastened to the top. Victorious warriors and their women relatives gathered in a circle around the pole. On the right, the men, handsomely dressed and painted, led the victory dance in song, each beating a hand drum, while the women on the left, carrying brothers' society banners or wearing their warbonnets, shook the scalps and shrilled a high harmony.

Curly Hair, chronically shy, is unlikely to have joined the circle of dancers. On the campground outside the family tipi, however, his father was hosting a feast in his honor. This was the climax of the long years during which Crazy Horse had tried to instill in his son the values of a Lakota warrior: today Curly Hair's triumphant return had more than fulfilled all expectations, matching superb courage with careful judgment and dauntless concern for his comrades. Thirteen years after the Male Crow disaster, Curly Hair had resoundingly reclaimed his family's name. In a single battle, he had counted at least five coups, enough for many men's lifetimes.

Crazy Horse would have sought to secure the presence at the feast of respected elders, prominent warriors, and great chiefs like Man Afraid of His Horse and Lone Horn. At the place of honor with the chiefs sat Curly Hair, his face blackened. A red ring of paint circled his arm wound. Other insignia displayed his deeds: a double cross painted on a legging symbolized his rescue of High Backbone; each of the coups he had struck entitled him to wear a golden eagle plume at the back of his head, one painted red for his wound. As a special token of honor for the conspicuously brave, an elder removed Curly Hair's moccasins and painted his feet red. After the feast and the passing of the pipe, relatives drove up horses fitted with packsaddles, to which Curly Hair's stepmothers fastened stacks of presents and parfleches filled with clothing or dried meat. Curly Hair's father led out a war pony. The chiefs pressed around to assist the youth in mounting, then followed as his father, singing a praise song, led the pony toward the dance circle.

As they neared the victory pole, the crowd opened to allow the family into the circle. The singers fell silent, and a herald announced in a loud high voice that Curly Hair's father and mothers wished to give away presents in honor of their son. Crazy Horse stepped forward and recounted the momentous vision he had received the summer before his son's birth, when the grizzly guardian of the butte "gave to me powers to conquer all earthly beings, including the white men who are coming into our land." He declared that he now transferred his spiritual bear power, and his own name, to his son. The herald picked up the theme, proclaiming that the youth's boyhood names were now thrown away. From this day forward, he would be called by the name of his father and grandfather—Tasunke Witko, Crazy Horse. The career of the Lakota people's greatest warrior had begun.[27]

7

FIGHTING THE CROW PEOPLE

Through the winter of 1857–58, Crazy Horse waited impatiently for the new raiding season. As spring drew on, he and his father—who had assumed the nickname Worm after passing on the family's formal name to his son—repeatedly underwent the sweat-lodge ceremony. Crazy Horse was told to kill a red-tailed hawk, the bird of his first vision quest, and to assemble other materials. Then Worm convened a select gathering of holy men and Thunder dreamers to validate the transfer of sacred power, in what one tradition calls "a ceremony of purification [declaring Crazy Horse] to the deity of the brave."[1]

After the annus mirabilis of 1857, Worm believed implicitly in the unique powers of leadership invested in his son. Like minds assembled, warriors and dreamers from across the northern Oglala and Miniconjou bands, including High Backbone, who declared that Crazy Horse would be the greatest warrior of the coming generation. Red Hawk, an old family friend who had broken with the American alliance five years earlier (see chapter 3), may have been present, bringing holy men from the Wakan family of the Oyuhpe band—a camp that Crazy Horse would come to regard as a second home. The holy men prepared a sacred bundle containing the stuffed skin of the hawk, adding other charms between layers of skin and cloth. Prayer and song imparted the contents with the sacred power of the hawk and other protectors. The bundle would henceforth constitute Crazy Horse's wotawe, or protective war charm. At times of crisis, Crazy Horse reverently opened the bundle, singing prescribed songs and praying to the powers that inhered in the sacred items.[2]

The spirit of the hawk controlled swiftness and endurance, two of the warrior's key attributes. Henceforth he would regard the bird as his spiritual patron, intermediary between him and the greater wakan powers. He was told to "remember" his guardian spirit—a mental and spiritual discipline involving the acute focusing of mind to achieve clarity of thought in which hawk and dreamer became one. Sometimes Crazy Horse would ride into battle wearing the whole body of the hawk tied in his hair; as the years passed and other visionary powers were granted him, he more usually made do with two or three of its feathers fastened at his crown.[3]

The young warrior took seriously the responsibilities such a gift laid on him. The holy men advised him to make himself worthy by studying attentively the ways of hawks. Crazy Horse dutifully observed, noting patterns of behavior, internalizing the hawk's unhurried but focused scanning of opportunity, assessing the movement of its prey in a split-second calculation before descending to strike in its staggering, vertiginous stoop. "He wanted to be sure that he hit what he aimed at," recalled He Dog of his friend's unusual attention to marksmanship, in a striking testimony to Crazy Horse's diligent observation. Throughout his life Crazy Horse would invoke the aid of the hawk, and the evidence indicates that even into the last months of his life, the bird aided him in securing new sicun power.[4]

In May a large interband war party formed and swung west across the Bighorn Basin, tracking Crow camps moving toward the upper Yellowstone. Some Miniconjou relatives of Crazy Horse joined the party, as did the untried Oyuhpe youth Fast Thunder, who called Crazy Horse cousin. Another Oyuhpe boy, eleven-year-old Struck by Crow, tagged along. Already a coterie of youths formed around Crazy Horse, eager to emulate this strangely silent hero, encouraging him to consider a future not simply as a warrior but as a leader in war.[5]

The Crow trail swung north from the Sweetwater. It was a wet spring, and miry travel bogged down in a series of swollen river crossings. The war party repeatedly clashed with other enemies, killing two Nez Perce warriors caught on the prairie, then sweeping through a camp of strange tipis made from grass and brush, a hunting camp of northern Shoshones and Bannocks

Crazy Horse, his hawk wotawe fastened atop his head, joined a knot of riders charging one enemy, but as he struck third coup, a chance shot struck his left calf. Comrades hurried to his side and helped him to the ground as he slumped from the saddle. He passed out, and for a startled instant, the warriors glanced at each other as his body sank in their arms with the dead weight of Rock.[6]

Revived and undaunted by the flesh wound, Crazy Horse remounted and galloped on at the leading edge of the Lakota line. Suddenly, another shot brought down his mount—the first of a long line of luckless war ponies he would lose over the next nineteen years. Crazy Horse toppled forward into the dust and rose unsteadily on his wounded leg to find himself cut off. The Grass House warriors had begun to hold their position, screening their people's retreat and pinning down the Lakota line. Unlike Crazy Horse's daredevil rescue of High Backbone, no one raced forward to rescue the young Oglala. Crazy Horse began a hobbling run back to his comrades, but a mounted enemy galloped forward to head him off. Instead of retreating, Crazy Horse lurched forward, unhorsed the warrior, killed him, and dragged himself astride the enemy pony. With a whoop of defiance, he clapped his right heel to the animal's flanks and galloped to the safety of the Lakota line.[7]

When the Lakotas disengaged, they could count a significant victory. A number of the enemy had been killed, including visiting Crows: one contemporary account indicates that Big Robber, architect of the Crow-Lakota truces of 1851–57, may have been among the dead. The fight with the Grass House People signaled an end to the western truces the Lakotas had agreed to in the wake of the 1851 treaty, ushering in a new period of concerted aggression against the Crows, Shoshones, and other western tribes.

Many who saw the skirmishing declared that Crazy Horse's personal combat was the bravest of all his deeds. It marked the culmination of a defining year, in which the latent promise of adolescence bore fruit in imperishable achievement. As if aware of these patterns, Crazy Horse chose to mark the transition into manhood as he had done that from boyhood almost seven years earlier: he accepted an invitation by High Backbone to make a protracted visit among his mother's people. Together the comrades trekked north to the Miniconjou hoop. There, Crazy Horse's kinsman, the head chief Lone Horn, was concluding his yearlong Ghost Owning with the White Buffalo ceremony—a massive giveaway in which Lone Horn validated his new status through heroic generosity, binding to him in the complex calculus of obligation a network of rivals and allies. This lesson was not lost on the young Oglala, who (Miniconjou elders recalled over half a century later) assumed his peacetime reserve throughout the stay. Contrasting with the troubled Brule visit, he was attentive and respectful among his elders. With peers, Crazy Horse had nothing of the brash young warrior about him, adopting instead an air of unassuming modesty amid the praise songs celebrating his deeds.[8]

True friends alert us to our weaknesses and consolidate our strengths: so High Backbone intuited his comrade's tendency to isolation. The nervy heyoka energies of Thunder power had to be grounded with the generative maturity that Lakotas identified with the buffalo bull. Himself a famous scout, High Backbone inducted Crazy Horse through a master class in the craft. Less glorified than the warrior, scouts performed services that benefited the whole tribe—locating game, alerting to the presence of enemies, guiding tribal migrations. Crazy Horse refined his knowledge of animal behavior, sharpened his observations of natural phenomena, and honed his powers of endurance as High Backbone led him across the trackless plains. He was taught to run at night, feeling the earth to locate game trails, detecting water by the minute changes in air currents. At the council tipi, he knelt before the Deciders who coordinated hunts and reported facts of game location, prospects for the tribe's meat supply. As High Backbone predicted, Crazy Horse found scouting congenial, turning his self-sufficiency to the people's good: to leap ahead in the story, one indicator of his commitment to the 1877 peace with the Americans was his kneeling before General Crook (see chapter 21)—the stylized gesture of a returning scout.[9]

The following year Crazy Horse had the opportunity to exercise his new skills. In early spring 1859, two sons of Miniconjou chief Black Shield were killed by Crow raiders. Crow negotiations had continued fitfully, but these deaths sealed the end of the Horse Creek truces. Black Shield sponsored a war pipe that brought together Lakota bands in a great gathering north of the Black Hills.[10]

Crazy Horse made a glad reunion with Oglala comrades like He Dog. Early in June Black Shield's party, leaving a trail of eighty campfires, sliced toward the Bighorn valley in search of Crows. Black Shield, an experienced war leader, fostered a spirit of camaraderie among his diverse followers. His careful assignments perhaps numbered High Backbone and Crazy Horse among the scouts. They reported Crow bands gravitating around Fort Sarpy, the Crow trade center on the Yellowstone River, but keen eyes spotted a small party moving down the Little Bighorn. On June 12, with Thunder-like ferocity, the Lakotas struck, killing eleven young men and a woman, forcing the Crows north and west of the Yellowstone and Bighorn rivers.[11]

When Black Shield's coalition broke up, Crazy Horse turned homeward with the Oglala contingent. The cycle of adolescence, begun in another Miniconjou sojourn, was ended as Worm and his stepmothers welcomed him in the family tipi. Worm too had completed a circle. In the endgame of his tragic first marriage, he had bitterly accused Rattle Blanket Woman of adultery with a wasicu, a slur that the light-haired son surely registered intimately. Since the tragedy, Worm had patiently followed the holy man's path. As a captive of the sacred powers, bound head and foot in a darkened tipi, he had acquired the gift of prophecy—a gift that convinced him of his son's unique ability to defeat the enemies of the Lakota.[12] If this smacks of overcompensation, it nevertheless sealed the renewed bond between father and son. Crazy Horse took over as the family's main provider—a role in which, Worm acknowledged, he never failed.

The following winter, Crazy Horse joined the Oglala hunters on a famously successful buffalo hunt. As scouts signaled the herd, Deciders ordered forward men with good horses to hunt for the poor and infirm. Crazy Horse acted as if born to such duty. Darting in and out of the milling buffalo as bravely as he charged the enemy, Crazy Horse was able to fell ten cows.

Even before the return to camp, Crazy Horse called over unsuccessful hunters as he tracked through bloodied grass and snow after his kills. Worm was still an able hunter, well able to provide for the family tipi, so Crazy Horse gave away all the meat, reserving only the ten tongues. It was an echo of the boy who had blithely promised the family's food to the hungry elders. As the line of hunters and laden ponies approached home, they struck up a song of thanks to the slender youth whose uncommon skills seemed matched by his generosity. That evening, as the elders gathered in the council tipi, Crazy Horse had the tongues sent over for their feast, causing the old men to rise and chant their thanks. Besides proving his generosity, the event confirmed that Crazy Horse excelled as a hunter as well as a warrior and a scout.[13]

It also signaled the onset of a decade in which Crazy Horse and the tribal leadership of civil chiefs and elders were most at ease, as a revived spirit of national wellbeing swept the Lakota world. The revival was rooted in the abundant gamelands they had won. Until the intertribal agreements of 1851, much of the Powder River valley had formed a war zone between the Crows and their enemies. For decades its game reserves had been underexploited. After Black Shield's victory, the Lakotas made the broad swathe of territory between the Black Hills and the Bighorn Mountains their last great hunting ground. Years of insecure hunts, of military stalemate in the Crow war, and shame in their capitulation to Harney were quickly forgotten in an upswelling of tribal pride.

The Powder River country was a rich and varied habitat for game and people. The high shortgrass plains were watered by major rivers rising in the pine-clad flanks of the Bighorns. Abundant buffalo were matched by antelope herds and high-country game such as elk and bighorn sheep. Crazy Horse felt deep affection for these lands wrested from the enemy. The Powder River country would remain his true home. In 1877, as Lakotas faced capitulation to the Americans, Crazy Horse resisted the alternative of flight to Canada: more than anywhere else, the Powder River country elicited from him the fierce sentiment of belonging.

Crazy Horse continued to seek spiritual power. Most men endured the physical sacrifice of the Sun Dance in their early twenties, hanging from the center pole by stakes cut through their chests. Crazy Horse is not known to have undergone the ceremony: perhaps the flashy exhibitionism of many peers, their Sun Dance scars circled in vermilion, violated his sense of private spirituality. Nevertheless, some men offered their sacrifices alone, suffering the weight of buffalo skulls hung from their backs, or hanging from stout saplings in a remote spot. In visions of the Shadow, the Badger, and the Day, he successfully accumulated sicun power. But most of his visions remained within the ambit of his first revelation from Thunder. The prancing horse that appeared in one vision and confirmed his name was a servant of Thunder. Under the tutelage of Horn Chips, Worm, and the older holy men, Crazy Horse would be able to interpret his visions as gifts from the world of the Thunder Beings.[14]

During the inactivity of winter, conversations with his father widened into profound philosophical debates. Constantly Worm advised Crazy Horse to apply clarity of thought and attentiveness of mind to the revelations of his guardian spirits. Visions were not only for the moment but should be afforded lifelong contemplation. Much as we today may ponder a favorite text or work of art, establishing an interactive relationship that will continue to develop through life, recurrent contemplation established the vision as a locus of evolving regenerative thought.

One theme Crazy Horse may have traced was movement. Thunder's envoys shared an unpredictability of motion that a contemplative warrior might well devote "effort and study" to comprehend. The jagged line of lightning; the sudden fall and climb of a dragonfly; the tipped swoop of a flock of swallows ahead of thunder; the squeaking night flight of bats; a horse's sudden run or the awesome drop to the kill of Crazy Horse's own guardian, the red-tailed hawk—all were characterized by suddenness, unpredictability. *Kicamnayan*, Lakotas called this erratic motion, recognizing it as a property of the Thunder Beings and their messengers.[15]

Such motion was of inestimable value to a warrior. Crazy Horse worked hard to assimilate Thunder's message, fronting charges to act as the leading edge of an unpredictable lightninglike strike. Against the Crows, and later in such large-scale clashes with the Americans as the Battle of the Rosebud, he led long oblique lines of charging horsemen that rippled across the terrain like lightning. He placed himself always thirty or forty yards ahead of the line, ordering his men not "to close up on him."[16]

Pondering the erratic motion of his guardian spirits had deeper lessons too. His adult behavior, veering between passivity and fierce action, was clearly grounded in the emotional traumas of childhood. A lesser man, without the compelling assurance of Crazy Horse's visions, might have stultified in impotent mood swings. Beyond their promises of protection in battle, the Thunder Beings gave Crazy Horse a way of turning trauma to advantage, locating an energy that permitted him to shift with bewildering speed from inactivity to defiance, diffidence to assertiveness. That energy could trip up political opponents as well as battle adversaries: in assessing the power plays with Lieutenant William P. Clark or agent James S. Irwin during the final weeks of Crazy Horse's life, one may detect the unpredictable contours of kicamnayan.

As was customary, the enigmatic Crazy Horse revealed little of his own dreams and guardian spirits. Warriors speculated with affectionate irony about their leader's power, joking about the unfortunate record of his war ponies, and concluding that he had dreamed of Rock so "that he was as heavy as a rock. That's why no horse could pack him."[17]

The most famous vision of all, misrepresented by earlier biographers, probably took place about 1860–61, because Crazy Horse gave the locale as near Rosebud Creek, in the heart of the old Crow domain. According to the account Crazy Horse told his cousin Flying Hawk, he had endured the vigil of starvation long enough to begin hallucinating. A stalk of slough grass blew against his head: "I took it to look at," recalled Crazy Horse. In the abrupt juxtapositions of dream, the stem appeared to overlay a trail down the hillside. Tottering, Crazy Horse followed it down to the shore of a small lake, staggering into the shallows where the trail abruptly ended: "I sat down in the water; I was nearly out of breath; [then] I started to rise out of the water."[18] As he waded toward shore,

> A man on horseback came out of the lake and talked with him. He told Crazy Horse not to wear a War Bonnet; not to tie up his horse's tail. (The Indians invariably tie up their horses' tails in a knot [when going to war].) This man from the lake told him that a horse needed his tail for use; when

he jumped a stream he used his tail and at other times, and as Crazy Horse remarked in telling this, he needs his tail in summer time to brush flies. So Crazy Horse never tied his horse's tail, never wore a warbonnet. It is said he did not paint his face like other Indians.

The man from the lake told him he would never be killed by a bullet, but his death would come by being held and stabbed.

The rider from the lake showed Crazy Horse how to take "dirt thrown up by the pocket gophers" and sprinkle it over himself and his pony before going into battle. He also told him to take "two or three straws of grass 2 or 3 inches long" and wear them in his hair.[19]

To his kinsman Flying Hawk, Crazy Horse disclosed that he waded to shore, feeling a sense of renewal too intense to be described in clichés of rebirth. "[W]hen I came out," he said, "*I was born by my mother.*" The essence of his past, including the jagged hiatus following his mother's death, was relived and finally "placed," liberating the warrior to a life of full adulthood. Two generations of historians have misrepresented this crucial vision. It is time to unravel the true significance of the rider and his message.

Billy Garnett, who personally heard Crazy Horse's account of the vision, repeatedly identifies the mysterious rider as the "man from the lake." In her influential rendering, Mari Sandoz jettisoned the crucial context of water. Knowing that Crazy Horse derived many of his powers from the Thunder Beings, and dramatically compressing his long visionary career, she sought to press Garnett's bare account into the context of a Thunder dream. Crazy Horse's brother-in-law Iron Horse established that the grass Crazy Horse was told to wear was a water grass that grows in prairie sloughs, underlining the water connection. Moreover, the pocket gopher burrows beneath the earth and was believed to cause scrofulous sores: only a wakan person would dare to handle the dangerous dust thrown up by its digging. Instead of a Thunder Being, the rider from beneath the lake was a Water Spirit representing the Unktehi, the Underground Powers that live beneath the earth and waters. Throughout North American mythology, the Underground Powers range in eternal enmity against the Thunder Powers of the Upper World. Lakotas believed that firearms were empowered by the Thunder. In promising him invulnerability to bullets, the man from the lake was neutralizing Thunder's potential to harm Crazy Horse.[20]

The true significance of the vision was that it completed the cosmic empowerment of Crazy Horse. Through prayer he could call on the powers of Upper and Lower Worlds to aid him: in sacral contexts he embodied the totality of their strength. When he rode into battle, Crazy Horse was not simply a naked warrior with a curious paint design: his being crackled with the awesome destructive powers of the total cosmos. At twenty, an established warrior with an unlimited future, that power must have seemed supremely liberating. Since boyhood he had dreamed of "get[ting] his name up to the highest."[21] For now, he could be forgiven for slighting the costs of such power, unaware that a day might come when the universe would war within him, and tear his being apart.

As the onset of cold weather curtailed raiding in fall 1862, Crazy Horse confided in Horn Chips about another new vision. This time he had dreamed of the Rock. Perceived as the primal element of the universe, the oldest of the four manifestations of Wakan Tanka, Rock was unique—the only thing in nature that is not round, a manifestation not of the generative assurance of the circle, but jagged, irruptive, of fearsome strength and eternal endurance. Crazy Horse guardedly revealed something of his anxieties to Horn Chips. Although unwounded since the fight with the Grass House People, Crazy Horse had brooded over the words of the man from the lake: that, although invulnerable to bullets, he would be killed by being stabbed. Horn Chips sought the advice of his own visionary guardians.

After his vision quest, Horn Chips invited Crazy Horse to join him in the purification rite of the sweat lodge. Horn Chips produced a round white stone, as big as "a good-sized marble," one of the translucent hemispherical rocks found near anthills, that offered more comprehensive protection than any previous charm. He told Crazy Horse to drill a hole through the stone and pass a thong of braided buckskin through the hole. Invested with Horn Chips' Rock power, the stone was made a spirit rock, *tunkan wasicun*. Horn Chips then wrapped it in a *wopiye* pouch of buckskin, and secured it to the thong.[22]

Besides the snake, Thunder, and Rock, Horn Chips had dreamed of the eagle. He possessed a powder made from the dried heart of the spotted eagle, mixed with the seeds of the wild aster, to be rubbed over the body before going into battle. Some of the powder he now placed in Crazy Horse's wopiye. Next he took the two identical feathers at the center of the spotted eagle's tail. One he attached to the wopiye, the other he directed Crazy Horse to wear in battle, hanging down from his scalp lock. Into the pouch he placed the eagle's claws, then from the wing bone, Horn Chips fashioned a war whistle. If these medicines were used before battle, Horn Chips recalled telling his friend, "no bullet would touch him." Then, addressing Crazy Horse's anxiety about death by stabbing, he added that the stone "would protect him against the knife if his arm was not held; but if it was held," he concluded gravely, "he would not be protected."[23]

"Crazy Horse put great confidence in his medicine," Horn Chips recollected. "He seemed to bear a charmed life, and no matter how near he got to his enemy they could not hit him."[24] This was true, and Crazy Horse was never wounded again in battle. But his hunka's confirmation of the man from the lake's warning, that if his arm was held, he was vulnerable to a knife, remained with the warrior, an unsettling quibble amid the wakan powers' assurances of total protection.

Midsummer, Moon of Making Fat, 1863: As daylight spread over the Pryor Creek valley of southern Montana, a great war party of Oglalas and Cheyennes, augmented by Miniconjous and a few Arapahos, approached the main Crow village. Below them the creek swung in a wide curve, and downstream many Lakota women and older men dismounted atop a bluff that afforded a commanding view of the valley. Behind the bluffs, the warriors paused to put on their war gear and prepare their horses.

After stripping to breechclout and moccasins, Crazy Horse rubbed his pony down with sprigs of sage, murmuring words of encouragement. Then, following the instructions of the man from the lake, he took a pinch of dust from a pocket gopher burrow and rubbed it between the war pony's ears. He scattered a handful of the dust over the horse's head, then threw another handful over its rump. After brushing off the excess, he rubbed the dust gently into the horse's skin in streaky lines. He tipped out a little more of the dust and spat into his palm, dabbing one or two spots into his hair.

Perhaps he favored Kicking Bear, a fifteen-year-old Oyuhpe cousin who stood worshipfully at his side, with a portion of the bulletproof medicine: certainly he would give quiet words of support for the youth's first serious battle as he concluded his preparations. At his throat, he hung the eagle wing-bone whistle Horn Chips had given him. Over his right shoulder, he looped the thong of braided buckskin, securing the round stone wotawe in its pouch high up under his left arm. He unfastened his braids but tied up his front hair in a stiff war knot, thrusting through the pompadour two or three stems of the slough grass the man from the lake had identified. At his crown were fastened two or three hawk feathers from his war bundle, and the eagle tail feather pointing downward. He dabbed his fingertips with white paint and dotted hailstones over his face. Down his left cheek, his finger trailed a wavy red line. Over his body he rubbed a little of the eagle's heart medicine. His preparations complete, Crazy Horse briefly pondered the elemental powers of Thunder, Rock, and the Underground Powers now at his command. Murmuring a final prayer, he leapt astride his war pony and kneed it forward to join the warriors fanning out to crest the valley bluffs. The column began filtering upstream to a point where the creek could be easily crossed.

Scrutinizing the Crow village in the rising sunlight, the Lakotas and Cheyennes could see that all was activity. On the plain beyond the creek, the Crows hurriedly took down and repitched their lodges in a tighter circle that left no gap for the attackers. Outside the circle, hundreds of mounted Crow warriors were gathering. Under unusually tight discipline, they formed a densely packed rank protecting the village.

Suddenly, ten Crow warriors raced forward to challenge the enemy. A few arrows were exchanged, and a string of Cheyennes pursued them back toward their line. One Crow struggling to keep up was brought down. A lone Cheyenne, Brave Wolf, rode right into the Crow ranks. Awestruck, the Oglalas watched their comrade's suicidal bravery. Circling his horse, Brave Wolf began to ride back, arrowshafts bristling from his body.

One hundred whooping Crows followed the wounded Cheyenne as far as the creek, where Brave Wolf at last slipped from his saddle and fell into the water. One Crow leapt from his pony and splashed into the creek. Kneeling to take Brave Wolf's scalp, he gestured that this would be the first of many that day. To the shrill tremolos of the watching women, the Lakotas and Cheyennes charged across the creek, spreading out in a long line to outflank the Crow defensive line.

Crow leaders ordered forward men noted for their marksmanship. Armed with bows and muskets, these warriors were rushed to a point forward of their vulnerable flank. As Crazy Horse and other leaders formed the Lakota line for a charge, a loud command was heard from the enemy line, and the Crow marksmen opened a concerted fire, emptying several saddles. Regrouping, the Lakotas and Cheyennes charged again in a dense rank that folded the Crow countercharge and pressed it against the circle of tipis.

Along a broad front, individual warriors clashed in daring combat. Young Man Afraid of His Horse, his pony shot twice in the breast, pursued one dismounted Crow almost to the lodges. Elsewhere He Dog overhauled a fleeing Crow, counting coup with the Crow's own saber. But no warrior outshone Crazy Horse. At the head of the charge, he galloped through a hail of arrows and lead, shadowed by young Kicking Bear. A dismounted Crow fleeing for the tipis attracted his attention, and he heeled his pony forward. In the melee, his pony was struck, and Crazy Horse vaulted from the saddle to pursue his foe on foot. Right up against the lodges he caught the Crow, and in single combat killed him, scalped him, and threw the lifeless body against a tipi. With a whoop of triumph, he withdrew, still unharmed, to join his men. They gathered around him in a protective cluster, crying out his name in tribal pride.

Pressed up against their camp, the Crows at last remustered their strength. Charge and countercharge followed, but neither side could dislodge the other, raising the casualties to five Oglalas and five Cheyennes. Distant dust portended Crow reinforcements, and Crazy Horse and the other leaders ordered a disengagement.[25]

If hardly the battle to end all battles with the Crow people, it had been a day of glorious action. The Battle Defending the Tents would go down in Lakota and Crow annals as a memorable encounter of the war years 1858–65. To some outside Crazy Horse's band, the battle marked the beginning of his rise to greatness, when his name was on every tongue. By the mid-1860s, the Crow war had seen Crazy Horse rise among his people to a revered status as an inspirational warrior. Courageous yet never foolhardy, he had completed the rehabilitation of his family name. The recklessness that characterized Male Crow was not a feature of Crazy Horse's war ethos. Although he made a point of never being outstripped in a charge, he fought with careful forethought. Unlike those who wished to die in battle, he never threw aside his gun to charge with quirt or club: "Crazy Horse always stuck close to his rifle," remarked He Dog. Moreover, he tried to instill the same cautious ethic in his followers. "He always tried to kill as many as possible of the enemy without losing his own men."[26]

By 1865 those followers were growing in number. The least sociable of men had a clique of warriors convinced of his invulnerability, his luck, and his power. His war parties were doubtless the most informal affairs, trailed by a quiet feast and rapid word-of-mouth. Logistical preparation is unlikely to have devolved on Crazy Horse himself, but he had friends aplenty on whom he could call for practical help. Moreover, these comrades were not confined to his own band. Close comrades like Lone Bear, Good Weasel, and He Dog formed a significant core of support in the important Bad Face band. As a regular visitor among the Oyuhpes, Crazy Horse could always rely on key friends within that band, including such coming men as his cousins Fast Thunder, Black Fox, and Kicking Bear, or the grimly redoubtable Low Dog. Miniconjous like his kola High Backbone maximized Crazy Horse's reputation among his mother's people. Although he had no ambitions to be a chief, Crazy Horse had built the sort of interband support fundamental to tribal leadership.

When Crazy Horse led a war party, his followers felt an easy confidence in their success and safety. If he felt unsure of a coming fight, he would call it off, regardless of the ribbing he received from less cautious comrades. Leading a party against the Shoshones with High Backbone among his followers, Crazy Horse concluded that defeat was likely, and he simply turned home. "He didn't like to start a battle," recalled He Dog, "unless he had it all planned out in his head and knew he was going to win. He always used judgment and played safe." The same ethic of careful preparation was carried into the heat of battle. "All the time [He Dog] was in fights with Crazy Horse[,] in critical moments of the fight Crazy Horse would always jump off his horse to fire. He is the only Indian I knew who did that often. He wanted to be sure that he hit what he aimed at. That is the kind of a fighter he was."[27]

As well as possessing supreme courage tempered with calculation and caution, Crazy Horse was uncommonly generous as a war leader. A guiding principle of Lakota life was the adult's careful mentoring of the next generation. Crazy Horse possessed this virtue in full measure. About 1862 Crazy Horse's brother Young Little Hawk joined his first war party in a raid against the Utes of the northern Colorado Rockies. As his tribesmen fought a stiff defensive action, one Ute marksman "came forward and no one could go up against him. Then Crazy Horse went for him and shot down the Ute. He rode right up to him. The Ute fell, and Crazy Horse called for his younger brother to come and get his first coup."

By the mid-1860s such behavior was commonplace. Crazy Horse delighted in setting up situations where youthful comrades could gain war honors: "He does not count many coups," expanded Eagle Elk, "He is in front and attacks the enemy. If he shoots down an enemy, he does not count coup. He drops behind and let others count three or four coup counts. He takes the last coup . . . I often wondered why he did that. He had such a reputation that he did not have to get more of that."[28]

No wonder Crazy Horse inspired such loyalty among the young. He remained fiercely protective of his younger brother. In a skirmish soon after the Battle

Defending the Tent, Crow pursuers caught up with the Oglala war party. Crazy Horse's pony, the latest in a long series, was shot from under him, and two Crows cut off Young Little Hawk and another "younger brother." Leaping astride a new mount, Crazy Horse charged at the Crows, killing and scalping one and single-handedly driving back the enemy.[29]

At home he won the accolades of the old as well. His generosity was a byword. He made it a point of honor to retain no battle spoils except weapons. Horses and other booty were distributed among the old and the poor, in exhibitions of the sort of spontaneous generosity that expected no return.[30]

By his early twenties, Crazy Horse had acquired the stature, physical appearance, and mannerisms that would characterize him throughout life. Standing at about five feet eight or nine inches, Crazy Horse just topped medium height among the Lakotas. To many he still seemed slender, even slight, compared to the run of his tribesmen. His fine waist-length hair, at home usually plaited in two braids, still hung in a lightly colored wave. Like his hair, his skin was comparatively light, "much lighter than the other Indians." Most people thought his face was narrower than the norm: "His features were not like those of the rest of us," summed up He Dog's younger brother Short Bull. By Lakota standards his nose was small and finely made, "sharp [and] aquiline" according to one acquaintance, "sharp and high" and "straight and thin" to two others.[31]

His eyes were remarkable, characterized by a sidelong glance "that hardly ever looked straight at a man, but they didn't miss much that was going on all the same." Noted as the generic Indian black in the records of his brief enlistment as an army scout, they too might have been lighter than most Lakotas': vividly describing her one meeting with the man, Susan Bordeaux Bettelyoun recalled them as hazel. To a newspaperman in 1877, Crazy Horse's eyes were "exceedingly restless and [they] impress the beholder fully as much as does his general demeanor" of unusual dignity. Perhaps they contributed to an overall impression of youth that stripped years off many estimates of his age. They lent an androgynous quality—testimony to his mother's famous beauty—reflected in Agent Irwin's initial impression of the thirty-six-year-old Crazy Horse as a "bashful girlish looking boy."[32]

He dressed plainly. Following the instructions of the man from the lake, he never wore a warbonnet, and he restricted his body paint to the hailstones and lightning streak of his heyoka vision. Habitually he fought naked, again like a heyoka, except for breechclout and moccasins. At home he usually donned a plain shirt, leggings, and blanket, while his single item of ornament was a plain necklace of "Iroquois" dentalium shells. After 1859 he, with pals like He Dog, began that other preoccupation of young Oglala men: courting the girls. Riding around the camp circle, plying a nonchalant eagle-wing fan, potential beaus spent summer downtime conducting affairs and intrigues, idling outside the tipis of the fair to snatch minutes of whispered conversation before chaperones interrupted. The lovelorn might play plangent melodies on their flutes, or approach Elk dreamers for

love philters, but Crazy Horse's attitude to girls remained, thankfully, uncompli-
cated. He Dog's memory indicates that in this sphere at least, Crazy Horse was simply a healthy young man.[33]

Similar to his kicamnayan tactics in battle, his taciturn manner could be off-
putting and contradictory, a mixture of the diffident, the off-hand, and probably on
occasion the studiedly enigmatic. "Never was excited" was Black Elk's curt assessment. Reflecting another conscious switch in mental energies, Black Elk noted that
in private gatherings at home, his cousin was reasonably sociable, but in formal situations, as when leading a war party, "not at all" so. Even at home he was hardly
talkative; doubtless his silence and that sidelong scrutiny could be unsettling to an
unfamiliar visitor. "He was a very quiet man except when there was fighting," summarized He Dog. Around the camp he always seemed alert and self-possessed, on
his guard "even with his own people," according to statements given interpreter
John Colhoff. Although eligible to attend councils, Crazy Horse had no interest in
politics. The day-to-day logistics of camp life, where Deciders and elders debated
the problems of pasture, wood, and water; the availability of game; and the next
remove—these held no interest for him. At this stage he also stayed away from more
momentous talks—about Lakota relations with the Americans, say, or akicita assemblies to declare hunt edicts and lay down disciplinary guidelines for tribal events.
Consequently, he attended few councils. When he did, he was usually seen to listen
attentively, but he hardly ever spoke.[34]

"He had no ambition to be a chief," stated Billy Garnett. Of all the duties and
roles he fulfilled, that of simple scout was probably the most satisfying. Self-reliant,
solitary, but of vital value to his community—such was Crazy Horse's own idealized self-image. When moving camp, Crazy Horse usually rode alone, off to one
side of the column, as if he had profoundly internalized the role. Lakota society recognized three emblematic roles for younger men: hunter, warrior, and scout. Few
excelled in more than one, but Crazy Horse, together with his kola High Backbone, was said to be superb in each role.[35]

"Queer in his ways"; "He was a queer man." Such were some of the off-the-
cuff recollections by friends and relatives of Crazy Horse's habitual peacetime manner. Enemies, like the Crows and Shoshones he fought every summer for most of
his adult life, did not see this side to the man's character. To them, even more than
to his own people, the awesome power he assumed on the battlefield suggested a
man truly granted Thunder's aid. By the mid-1860s, as the Crow war was about to
be superseded as Crazy Horse's prime military concern by renewed conflict with
the Americans, the Crows had already concluded, "We know Crazy Horse better
than we do you other Sioux. Whenever we have a fight, he is closer to us than he
is to you."[36]

8

TILL THE ROAD WAS OPENED

On Monday morning, July 20, 1863, barely a month after the Battle Defending the Tents, Lakota scouts posted on the pine-studded foothills of the Bighorn Mountains watched a civilian wagon train form a defensive circle at the crossing of Little Piney Creek. A large party of chiefs and warriors hurried forward and, through train guide Rafael Gallegos, indicated that they wished to speak to the "Captain." John Bozeman stepped forward and stated that he was pioneering a route linking the Overland Trail to the new gold diggings in western Montana: his route sliced north from the North Platte to the valley of the upper Yellowstone, crossing the rich new Lakota hunting grounds of the Powder River country.

Settlers later recalled that the chiefs had come "to warn us not to proceed farther through their country, that they were combined to prevent a road being opened through there." Bozeman's party turned back to the Platte and followed instead the uncontested route to the mines through Crow country, west of the mountains.

Within three years, the trail blazed by Bozeman would complete the degradation of the uneasy peace that descended on the northern plains after the Harney campaign and the great council of 1857. The Crow war would be sidelined as Lakotas combined to oppose a new American advance. And Crazy Horse would play a significant part in the war to come.[1]

In the same years that northern Oglala warriors were preoccupied with the war to dispossess the Crows, Lakota relations with the United States came under new and unprecedented pressures. An intractable knot of problems centered on the twin issues of land and treaty rights. These were first highlighted early in 1858 when, just as Lakota speakers at Bear Butte had feared, their Yankton relatives ceded their lands east of the Missouri, retaining only a small reservation. Northern Lakotas reacted angrily to the sale, threatening a renewed boycott of treaty relations with the United States. Chiefs like Bear Ribs, returning with treaty goods to the hunting grounds, had their horses killed by disillusioned warriors. The Strong Hearts ideology of separatism, increasingly identified with Sitting Bull, took deeper root. On August 22, 1860, Hunkpapas served notice of the switch in tribal policy by unleashing an all-out attack on Fort Union, the main trading post on the upper Missouri. In the weeks that followed, Hunkpapa raiders, augmented by Sihasapas and Sans Arcs, swung south along Powder River, striking the stretch of the Overland Trail west of the Upper Platte Agency. In a pointed affront to Oglala tribal authority, they stole horses from the trading community and killed stragglers.[2]

In the Platte zone, the Oglalas continued to enjoy a reputation as the most tractable of the Lakota divisions, but here too loss of Indian lands was a rising issue. Also in 1858, gold was discovered high up the South Platte River. The following year, massive emigration poured into Colorado Territory: one hundred thousand miners and assorted entrepreneurs—their numbers exceeding all the Indians on the plains—founded Denver and a cluster of other boomtowns along the front range of the Rockies. The influx swamped Cheyenne and Arapaho hunting range between the forks of the Platte, and during spring 1859, large numbers of Arapahos filtered north. They appealed to Lakota leaders for permission to join their hunting operations in the Powder River country.[3] The appalling situation of the Arapahos—who had effectively lost their lands to the mining frontier without prospect of compensation—focused many Lakota minds on the issue of adequate treaty payments, but to Crazy Horse and a cohort of warriors who were winning their people rich hunting grounds from old tribal enemies like the Crows, the issue of a few more sacks of moldy flour or the arrival of plows and seed corn was at best irrelevant.[4]

In these years, Crazy Horse was invited to join the Strong Hearts, surely courted by the inner elite and invited to the private feasts at which the isolationist members sought to forge society consensus on their agenda. Crazy Horse sympathized with their position. All his instincts were to reduce the disturbing level of dependency Lakotas were acquiring. In intertribal relations, such systems helped all participants to weather bad seasons. But the relation with the Americans seemed badly out of balance. As the emergence of bands like the Loafers testified, significant sections of the people were becoming dependent on American largesse. Foodstuffs like flour and bacon were no longer novelties to the Loafers, but a vital part of their diet. Manufactured cloth and garments had become essential handouts to a people without access to buffalo herds. Against such developments, Crazy Horse had a lifelong aversion. But he was never the tool of political cliques, and he felt uncomfortable with the sort of plotting Lakota pressure groups engaged in. Ingrained respect for the elders also played its part in keeping Crazy Horse out of politics.

In 1861, however, new strains were placed on Crazy Horse as conflicting loyalties impinged on the issues of land and treaty rights. Stoking Lakota fears of land loss, an unrepresentative body of southern Cheyenne and Arapaho leaders, dismayed at the failure of game and tempted by the promise of increased subsistence spending, had signed an agreement ceding all tribal lands except a small Colorado reserve. The agreement remained a bitterly divisive issue in Cheyenne society. As a reminder of the Cheyennes' loss, thousands of American cattle, the herds of freight companies and private ranchers serving military posts and Colorado boomtowns, now grazed the plains between the North and South Platte rivers. Buffalo in the region were virtually extinct.[5]

Treaty issues were just as divisive as those of land. In August, when Man Afraid of His Horse led the Hunkpatila and associated bands toward Deer Creek to receive their annuities, they met a stronger village of Miniconjous who forbade the Hunkpatilas to continue, telling them that accepting annuities would result in open warfare.

Sections of Oglala opinion began to swing behind the Miniconjou position. Reports reaching the agent claimed that these Oglalas were "overawed" and intimidated by the Miniconjous.[6] While such factors played a part, the Miniconjou example likely fired the Oglala Strong Hearts to adopt wholesale the ideology of separatism. Strong Hearts pointedly feasted only on traditional Lakota dishes, enthusiastically consuming buffalo broth and rejecting novelties like bacon and coffee. The Strong Hearts set deadlines preventing Oglala movement to the agency. Offenders would have their horses killed.[7]

As winter deepened, visitors arrived, Hunkpapas, Miniconjous, and even Yanktonais trekking down the west side of the Black Hills. Strong Hearts chapters feasted and intensified pressure to break off all diplomatic relations with the United States. They ordered trade closed and sponsored a war pipe to build an anti-American coalition. The situation starkly highlighted the generational differences between warriors and elders. For most Lakota men born before about 1835, the buffalo robe trade was their fundamental economic activity. They had grown up in a world with few wasicu. The exchange of surplus robes for valued manufactured goods seemed unproblematic and represented a golden age status quo. Chiefs like Man Afraid of His Horse viewed the equation of trade and peaceful relations as fundamental to Lakota well-being. For the rising men of Crazy Horse's generation, the equation seemed less compelling. After 1862, trade declined, not just from Strong Hearts edicts, but from the meddling of corrupt Indian Office agents and, increasingly, from army-driven bans targeting ammunition sales and tribal wealth. Crazy Horse's generation grew into responsible adulthood, marrying and establishing households, in a world without the robe trade. And, haltingly, some Lakotas recognized that the trade itself, targeting as it did adult female animals, threatened the long-term stability of buffalo populations. Small wonder that they, unlike their fathers, could easily imagine a world in which the absence of Americans was an unmitigated good.

The bitterness and hostility of northern Lakotas only deepened against the Americans. In Minnesota, years of mounting tension between Santee Dakotas and the growing American population erupted in open warfare. Early Dakota victories were soon reversed, and flight and capitulation spelled the de facto loss of the

Santee reservation. By 1863 Minnesota, the ancient homeland of all Lakotas, was exclusively wasicu land.[8]

In 1862, gold discoveries in western Montana had fueled a wartime bonanza on the northern plains. Steamboat traffic on the Missouri and civilian wagon trains pioneering new routes like John Bozeman's trail threatened what remained of Lakota goodwill. Late in 1863 the northern Oglalas established winter camp near the forks of Powder River. Upstream the northern Cheyennes and Arapahos located their camps; south of the forks were the Miniconjous; while at the junction of the river with the Yellowstone, a large village of Hunkpapas and other northern Lakotas, hosting a contingent of Santee refugees, pitched their tipis. Such close proximity dictated a season of talks and councils. Through the winter, these talks refocused Oglala minds on the need to address radically the issue of American access to their lands.

In January, Red Dog, a war leader in the Oyuhpe band, arrived in the Oglala Proper village and told a general council that the Lakotas to the north, including Miniconjous and Hunkpapas, had agreed to fight the Americans. They had appointed Red Dog to treat with the Oglalas and secure a final decision. In a large bundle he carried a black-stemmed war pipe with which to cement an offensive alliance. A deputation of Minnesota Santees added their weight to Red Dog's oratory.

Crazy Horse must have been in these councils, listening attentively to the debate and quietly registering his approval of the call to war. He curiously inspected these strange Santee relatives. Many wore manufactured clothes, the threadbare relics of their prewar annuities; some, educated at mission schools, spoke English; a few had even been Cut Hairs, ultra "progressives" who had hacked off their braids in deference to American hairstyles. Embittered beyond conciliation, they made persuasive and articulate speakers, arguing that Santees and Lakotas unite to "drive the Whites away from the Platte, & block the Overland & mail route." With regular troops replaced by skeleton militias, the Santees reasoned that the time was propitious to roll back the frontier.[9]

Making much of their refugee status and the wartime tension between the United States and Great Britain, some speakers claimed that Canadian officials sympathized with the Lakota cause and in the future might weigh in against the Americans. Safe haven in the British possessions was a theme that would occupy Crazy Horse in years to come. Santee access to Canadian Métis traders with large ammunition stocks was doubly significant, although this probably did not carry much weight now. Most important, the loss of Santee lands convinced many Lakota warriors that a preemptive strike against the Americans was necessary. "The white men have come to take over the entire land," agreed Oglala war leaders, "so in this manner they press on . . . [until] they will completely annihilate the Lakota people!"[10]

No speaker himself, Crazy Horse was not involved in the responses. Instead, three Oglala speakers dominated the debate. For the warriors, forty-three-year-old

Red Cloud rose to speak in support of Red Dog, his brother-in-law. Red Cloud, the greatest Oglala warrior of his generation, proved a forceful and direct spokesman. From the arc of chiefs, Brave Bear—coincidentally another brother-in-law of Red Cloud's—urged peace. War, he argued, risked the loss of their home-land. Warriors noisily dissented. Lest tribal solidarity be shattered, the chiefs withdrew their opposition, and Red Dog's war pipe was unwrapped and smoked. Crazy Horse was among the warriors who passed the pipe around the great circle, smoking a few whiffs in solemn undertaking of war. Heralds announced the decision, declaring open war on the Americans.

In this radical realignment of Lakota-U.S. relations, for the first time Americans were defined as enemies. Crazy Horse wasted little time in putting the new policy into effect. There was little in the way of a concerted strategy. A loose agreement was made to launch a major offensive against settlers and other wasicu along the Overland Trail in July. But as soon as the grass was up, small war parties would harry the trail. Such raids were second nature to Crazy Horse now. Moreover, as an Oglala familiar with conditions along the North Platte, Crazy Horse was vital to the plans of northern Lakota and Santee warriors. He could lead war parties directly to posts, stage stations, and settler stopovers, mapping tactics onto familiar terrain.

Crazy Horse formed a partnership for raiding along the Platte with Little Big Man, named for his distinctive build: scarcely five foot, five inches tall but with a powerful physique and Sun Dance scars on his heavily muscled chest, habitually ringed in red. The two made a strange pairing, but Little Big Man's blowhard manner may have been a necessary corrective to Crazy Horse's quietism. Someone had to deliver disciplinary talks to unruly followers—a proactive leadership not congenial to Crazy Horse. The indications are that they worked well as a team, regularly returning from the Platte with stolen stock right through the war years of the 1860s. Billy Garnett remembered their enterprise as "a lively business," suggesting that the partners often traded on stock northward.[11]

From April through June, small raiding parties laced across the North Platte, striking at trading posts, ranches, and garrisons, and harrying the early settler traffic. They came from a cluster of villages, chiefly Miniconjou, but including Oglalas, Hunkpapas, and Two Kettles, strung along the Yellowstone near the mouth of Powder River. Most parties were less than ten men strong, concealing themselves near the Overland Trail until an opportunity arose to "run off stock without danger." The raiders melted into the north, killing a few straggling settlers and looting their wagons.[12]

The initial military response was to close all trade in ammunition. As raiding continued, Lieutenant Colonel Collins ordered a total closure of trade except for those Lakota bands living permanently near the agency. Crazy Horse continued to visit relatives there occasionally, though now he had a double purpose in assessing prospects for raiding. Visiting in spring 1864, he found the agency relocated to a site twenty-eight miles south of Fort Laramie. Agent Loree had already erected a stone agency building and a log warehouse. As spring opened, employees had dug an irrigation ditch and plowed fifteen acres of bottomland; Lakota women dutifully planted a crop of corn. Crazy Horse probably observed this development with wary skepticism. July hailstorms destroyed one part of the fields, and loutish settlers drove their cattle through another: an August plague of grasshoppers consumed what remained. Crazy Horse found the chiefs and headmen, including Smoke and Swift Bear, nervous about a northern Lakota threat to "kill all the Laramie Sioux that stay among white men."[13]

Midsummer brought new traffic along the Bozeman Trail, and Oglala warriors were concerned to close this unnegotiated route through their hunting grounds. One wagon train bound for the Montana diggings was met beyond Richard's Bridge by a party of fifteen painted Oglala warriors. In sign language, they persuaded the train leaders to switch their route to the uncontested trail pioneered by Jim Bridger, passing west of the Bighorn Mountains. Other settlers were more determined, and several trains pressed up the Bozeman Trail, resulting in some desultory raiding.[14]

As the settler season passed, northern Oglala chiefs tried to restore the policy of peace, but emigrants and militia garrisons alike were trigger-happy, and at the agency, the goods were few and poor. On Powder River, news of the derisory goods did nothing to help the position of the Northern Oglala chiefs, and diplomacy fizzled out.[15]

Events on the central plains transformed this uneasy limbo into irretrievable crisis. There, southern Cheyenne and Arapaho councils had rejected the Lakota war pipe circulating in early 1864, but Colorado territorial authorities, determined to extinguish all Indian title east of the Rockies, had pushed the tribes to war.

After a September truce between the territorial officials and the Cheyenne chiefs, one hundred lodges of the friendliest Cheyennes settled for the winter at Sand Creek. The Colorado militia, led by Colonel John M. Chivington, a Methodist lay preacher with a self-proclaimed mission to annihilate the Indians, decided to strike Sand Creek on November 29. In the massacre that followed, some 150 Cheyennes, mostly women, children, and the tribal elders who had earnestly tried to maintain peace, were killed. The jubilant militia in mob frenzy mutilated the dead, hacking off men's private parts to make tobacco pouches, and dismembering women to adorn saddles and hats with female genitalia. Cheyenne survivors, half-naked on the frozen Colorado plains, fled to join the militant Dog Soldiers.[16]

Sand Creek was a true turning point. Moderates were alienated, and the most intransigent rhetoric of Strong Hearts and Dog Soldiers seemed vindicated. Southern Oglala and Brule leaders smoked the inevitable Cheyenne war pipe, approving a move from the war zone to the refuge of the country north of the Platte.

Since the fall, Man Afraid of His Horse had worked to restore peaceful relations. Among the northern Cheyennes, chief Gray Hair was trying to keep his people out of the war. Farther down the Powder, Lone Horn had a following of fifty

Miniconjou lodges that he too had sought to keep peaceful. The work of these moderate men was undermined by the arrival in March 1865 of the Sand Creek fugitives. Tales of American betrayal and brutality were vividly brought home by maimed survivors. Ragged widows and bewildered orphans were led onto the Oglala campground, where chiefs had their wives hurry forward with steaming kettles and stacks of robes, blankets, and clothing. Wailing Cheyenne mourners, their hair hacked short and legs gashed and bloody, placed their hands on the heads of chiefs and warrior society leaders, begging piteously for vengeance.[17]

Crazy Horse was a man of keen sympathies. Listening to the Cheyenne tales, he must have felt all his instincts harden against the Americans. In this reaction, he was no more than typical of his generation. A defining moment had been reached. After 1865 the Oglalas would never again enjoy the reputation among Americans as being the most compliant and reliable of the Lakota divisions.

For the chiefs who had fought so long for peace, it was a grim period. Turning away the Cheyenne fugitives would have been unthinkable. "The first start of the War of 1864 [was] with the Cheyennes & [Santee] Sioux," the Oglala chiefs would later state, "The Cheyennes staid south—the Sante[e] Sioux were on the Missouri & we in the middle—& they kept crowding us until we had to fight." For two months, the chiefs resisted urgings to accept the Cheyenne war pipe. In early May, on the headwaters of Tongue River, a united Oglala village met to choose the Deciders and akicita to coordinate summer activities. The Cheyennes had already nominated the Crazy Dog Society as police, and it is likely that the Oglalas named their counterpart society, the militant Strong Hearts, to control their village.[18]

One year earlier, the chiefs and elders had withdrawn their opposition to the calls for war, and in 1865, they took the situation a stage further. Lest society be irretrievably polarized, the chiefs assisted in actively coordinating a second season of attacks along the Overland Trail.

The war the chiefs were prepared to sanction was clearly a limited one. Once Cheyenne vengeance was satisfied, it was hoped that renewed diplomacy could restore peace—a peace dependent on the securing of land rights. The Oglalas decided to cut their losses. Relinquishing all claims to the central plains, they asserted the line of the south fork of Cheyenne River as a deadline dividing American from Indian domains. North of the Cheyenne, in the Powder River country hunting grounds wrested from the Crows, the land was still "filled with buffalo." The Americans had no treaty rights to travel there, and Lakotas would sanction no more joint-use rights-of-way. Crazy Horse, who would respect this boundary for the rest of his life, surely voiced his acclaim.[19]

In mid-May, war parties started south, and for two weeks, raiders laced through the Overland Trail from Fort Laramie west to the Sweetwater, tearing up the telegraph line, driving off stock, and generally outfighting the tiny detachments sent in pursuit. As quickly as the raids began, however, they ended, war parties melting back into the north during the first week of June.

During these spring weeks of preparation, Crazy Horse paid what would be his last friendly visit to the Fort Laramie district. He found agency relatives more fearful than ever. The Fort Laramie authorities had ordered the friendly Lakotas to concentrate along the five-mile stretch of the North Platte between the trading houses of Bordeaux and G. P. Beauvais. Collins oversaw the rationing of the community on condemned provisions, and the distribution of army-surplus clothing. An akicita force headed by Loafer headman Big Mouth was appointed to keep order and pass on intelligence.

By April the one hundred–lodge village was augmented by the surrender of some 185 lodges of Brules and other Lakotas, but army high command ordered that the friendly village be forcibly relocated to Fort Kearney—in the midst of Pawnee enemies—and compelled to plant corn. Collins's successor as commander, Colonel Thomas Moonlight, lacked sensitivity in dealing with Indians. On April 23 he ordered hanged a Cheyenne headman implicated in the capture of an American woman the previous summer. In May a small Oglala camp opened talks with the agency camp, but when Moonlight learned that they held another captive, he ordered the camp brought in under guard. The men were imprisoned, and on May 26 Moonlight had headmen Two Face and Blackfoot hanged also. Still manacled in artillery trace chains, the three bodies were left to rot on the gallows, a stark image of the breakdown in interethnic relations.[20]

The executions were not the only Lakota casualties. Nervous settlers were quick to respond with lead. In one incident, a troop patrol reconnoitering opposite the agency camp stumbled on a sleeping Miniconjou youth. The soldiers shot and scalped the lad. When the patrol clattered into Bordeaux's, Lakota women were horrified to see the boy's scalp hanging from a sergeant's bridle. Across the river, the youth's lamenting comrades bundled the body in robes and lashed it to the boughs of a cottonwood, making "a great landmark for many years."[21]

Such incidents were commonplace. And in one like it, the indiscriminate horror of the war was vividly brought home to Crazy Horse. Details are unclear, but during his stay near the post in early 1865, a "brother" of Crazy Horse was murdered at Fort Laramie. The identity of the brother is unknown: it was not Young Little Hawk but may have been one of the sons of his father's brothers or of his mother's female relatives. Conceivably, it could even have been that Miniconjou youth so cowardly shot as he slept. Whatever the exact situation, the killing ended Crazy Horse's stay in the friendly village. One spring day he rode across the sandy braided channel of the North Platte and struck into the north. It was a final departure. He would not visit an agency again until surrender was forced on him twelve years later. Nor would he return to Fort Laramie except as a raider. Crazy Horse's anger at American encroachments had gained a vividly personal dimension. Hitherto, he had raided along the North Platte for recreation and profit. Now vengeance too must be satisfied.[22]

Three

SHIRT WEARER

9

FIGHTING FOR THE ROAD

For Crazy Horse and for the Lakota people, the war against the Americans would change in character after the spring of 1865. A new motive—profit—underwrote the stock raiding he and Little Big Man had led for the past twelve months. Now, outrage at the Sand Creek atrocity, and solidarity with vengeful Cheyennes, had been matched by the personal loss of a kinsman. Warfare assumed the character of blood revenge, fired by a purposeful anger against Americans that would characterize Crazy Horse's attitudes and actions for the next twelve years, determining his political sympathies, allegiances, and agendas until the last months of his life.

This deepening anger animated many men of his generation, too old to have participated in the heyday of the buffalo robe trade and its ideology of interethnic cooperation. But the spirit of resistance took root across generational divides. "The band I was in," recalled one Oyuhpe youth of the day, "got together and said they were not going to let the white men run over them." Some elders also, like Worm, had come to question the whole concept of interethnic relations. Youths who formed boyhood chapters of recognized warrior societies echoed the rhetoric of resistance: "At the age of ten or eleven," remembered Holy Blacktail Deer, "I had a six-shooter and a quiver full of arrows to defend my nation."[1]

Although many capable war chiefs emerged in these years, none outshone Crazy Horse as a tactical leader of warriors. Always mindful of the coming generation, he was a popular mentor of those youths determined to "defend their nation." Crazy Horse's courage and an indefinable panache in action inspired confidence, loyalty, and a wry affection for the gauche young man. By the end of the Bozeman Trail War, none was more acclaimed than Crazy Horse. In the apt phrase of historian Robert M. Utley, by 1868 Crazy Horse was already "the greatest Lakota warrior."[2]

The years of warfare provide only sporadic glimpses of the man, and then only in action, fighting with inspirational courage. It is as if the insecurities of youth and the visionary period of young manhood had been put behind him. In action, fighting the enemies of his people, he successfully projected a self-image purely as a fighting man. "Crazy Horse was good for nothing but to be a warrior," observed Billy Garnett, who got to know him late in the Bozeman Trail War: "[He] considered himself cut out for warfare [alone]," and resisted the attempts of civil leaders to engage him in "affairs political." Such was his fame, however, that he would become a silent shaper of the political agendas that would secure victory in the Bozeman Trail War.[3]

Moon of Making Fat, early June 1865: Oglala and Cheyenne villages gathered along the Clear Fork of Powder River. Warriors and scouts like Crazy Horse returned from the raids along the Overland Trail. Chiefs and warrior societies debated the target for the major assault of the season. Opinion came to favor a blow against the garrison overseeing the Platte Bridge crossing, formerly the location of Richard's trading post. Platte Bridge Station, 130 miles upstream of Fort Laramie, was a key link in the Overland chain: a cluster of log and adobe buildings manned by one hundred officers and men of the Eleventh Kansas Cavalry. A decisive blow here could open a wedge on the Overland Trail like that made by Cheyenne raiders along the South Platte the previous year—arresting traffic for weeks and forcing settlers and miners from the Lakota domain. Success there, and the warriors would overwhelm other small outposts along the Overland before pressing south to cut off once more the Colorado capital from the road to the States.

Band chiefs like Man Afraid of His Horse and his Cheyenne counterpart Dull Knife sat on the blotahunka, beside warrior society headmen such as Red Cloud. The participation of the chiefs underscored the fact that this was a tribal undertaking, a formal revenge expedition for Sand Creek. As plans advanced in mid-June, the news from Fort Laramie about the order to remove friendly Lakotas to Fort Kearney raised the stakes. Almost three hundred lodges of people, led off by the wagons and carts of the inmarried trading community, started down the Overland, escorted by 135 soldiers of the Seventh Iowa Cavalry. Big Mouth's akicita force patrolled the line, but in night meetings, they plotted a breakout with Spotted Tail and other war leaders. At Horse Creek on the morning of June 14, the leaders implemented the plan, repulsing the pursuit and supervising the safe crossing of the North Platte. Fleeing north, the fugitives met a late war party led by He Dog, Crazy Horse's close comrade, and on June 17, the warriors dashed down on Colonel Moonlight's breakfasting pursuit column and drove off seventy-four head of his carelessly guarded horses. Then, still reluctant to be drawn into the war, most swung up the east side of the Black Hills.[4]

On July 21 the massive war party departed the villages at the mouth of Crazy Woman Creek. At the head of the column rode a line of chiefs and headmen, each cradling a black-stemmed pipe in the crook of his left arm. Behind them a rank of Strong Hearts and Crazy Dog warriors fronted the tightly disciplined body of at least one thousand warriors. Eager to be avenged for the death of his brother, Crazy

Horse rode with the column, probably fanned out ahead with the scouts. Cheyenne Dog Soldiers and their Lakota counterparts, the Miwatani Society, patrolled the rear of the column. The war party reached the hills overlooking Platte Bridge on the twenty-fourth, and after dispatching scouts made an early camp. The following morning Man Afraid of His Horse and the other pipe owners deputed ten or twenty men to act as decoys in drawing out the soldiers. Although his actions in the battle are not known, it is possible that Crazy Horse was one of the decoys—certainly the top-class operation he led eighteen months later had its dry run somewhere in the fighting of 1865. Strong Hearts and other akicita took up positions on each side of the compact mass of warriors and, at a signal from the pipe owners, began pressing them forward toward the river bluffs. There the chiefs and war leaders scrambled forward to view the valley. They passed a set of field glasses along the line to survey the decoys and their pursuers, a company of cavalry followed by an artillery unit. At the sound of gunshots from the valley, warriors surged forward to crest the blufftops. Whip-wielding akicita pressed the warriors out of sight lest the element of surprise be lost. The first day's action proved abortive in any case, but that night decoys were sent out once more.

At daybreak on the twenty-sixth, they began riding back and forth along the valley floor opposite the post. Up in the hills, the pipe owners implemented a more flexible strategy, detailing three distinct bodies of warriors to cover the valley. While one group infiltrated the brush and timber immediately below the bridge, another took position behind the bluffs fronting the crossing. The largest body moved behind the higher bluffs a half-mile above the bridge. About 9:00 A.M. a detail of twenty-four troopers turned smartly out of the post and clattered across the bridge. Led by Lieutenant Caspar Collins, this detachment was actually riding to escort an eastbound supply train, but exultant warriors cocked muskets and nocked arrows to bowstrings.

As the troopers angled left up the North Platte valley, warriors on the bluffs signaled upstream and down. A party of warriors moved down to the telegraph line. Shinning up the poles, they began cutting the wires but at sight of Collins feigned alarm, dropped onto their ponies, and galloped toward the bluffs. As Collins pressed forward, half the body of warriors in the valley bottom filtered out of the brush to fan out toward the bridge. The shrill blasts of war whistles alerted Collins to the danger in his rear. Faced with a charge to cut him off from the bridge, he ordered a retreat. A second charge from the bluffs threatened to intercept him, and Collins ordered a headlong charge for the bridge. From the post, infantry poured out over the bridge, opening a covering fire for their comrades. A fieldpiece also opened fire, but the gunners failed to find the range. As Collins's men streaked for the bridge, a heavy charge was driven into their left flank. Inside an impenetrable dust cloud, warriors and troopers clashed in a collision of horseflesh shrill with whoops, shouted orders, and gunfire. Such was the chaos that warriors rained bullets and arrows into one another, and war leaders shouted to use only hatchets and clubs.

Five soldiers, including the gallant Collins, were cut down before the troopers smashed through the reeling warriors. Infantry fanned forward to cover their comrades' retreat over the bridge. The howitzer finally found its range, and the warriors fell back. About 11:30 scouts sighted the unsuspecting supply train winding down the valley. Hundreds of warriors galloped upstream. Sergeant Amos Custard circled his five wagons and deployed his small escort well, but after four hours of stealthy attrition tactics, the warriors overwhelmed the train, killing all and burning the wagons.[5]

On the morning of July 27, the great war party filed along the valley in sight of Platte Bridge Station, then swung back into the hills. The bid to crush Platte Bridge had failed, though some twenty-eight soldiers lay dead. Military estimates indicated that up to sixty warriors had fallen; even if inflated, a significant toll had been exacted. As far as the chiefs were concerned, vengeance had been satisfied, and diplomacy should be reinstated. The villages dispersed, scheduling a Sun Dance reunion near Powder River forks for late August.

Unknown to the Indians, the army had moved speedily to implement a major campaign against them. Coordinating strategy was General Patrick E. Connor, commanding the newly established Department of the Plains from headquarters at Fort Laramie. The end of the Civil War freed huge numbers of troops to serve on the frontier, and Connor worked speedily to coordinate a campaign that would clear the northern plains of hostile Indians. While General Sully was expected to tackle the Hunkpapas and their allies in the upper Missouri arena, Connor readied columns to attack Indians in three regional blocs. Most elusive would prove the Fort Laramie fugitives, believed to be in the Bear Butte district east of the Black Hills. In the valley of the middle Yellowstone, Miniconjous had gathered. The bloc of Oglalas and Cheyennes was known to be in the valley of Powder River.[6]

Connor's orders were bluntly genocidal: the troops were to accept no overtures of peace but were to locate, attack, and kill every male Indian over the age of twelve. He first ordered the column of Colonel Nelson Cole to strike the Bear Butte concentration from the east. Departing Omaha on July 1, Cole's fourteen hundred men were to trek around the north edge of the Black Hills, then angle west to unite with the other columns on Rosebud Creek by September 1. From Fort Laramie on August 5 Lieutenant Colonel Samuel Walker's six hundred men marched due north. Connor commanded the third column, over five hundred troops augmented by 179 Pawnee and Winnebago Indian scouts and a complement of civilian guides. Connor marched from Fort Laramie on July 30 and struck north along the trail pioneered by John Bozeman. On August 11 he reached the upper crossing of Powder River where, three days later, his men began hauling wood to erect a hasty quadrangle of log buildings dubbed Camp Connor.

Barely fifty miles north, the Oglalas and Cheyennes were unaware of Connor's march. Hunkpatila warriors had scattered widely, joining Miniconjou and Cheyenne raiders, targeting Americans and Indian foes. On August 16 one party of twenty-seven warriors was annihilated by Connor's Pawnees. Clashing with a civilian wagon train bound for the Montana goldfields, Hunkpatila warriors parleyed with train master James A. Sawyers and learned of Connor's march.[7]

As the Oglalas gathered at Powder River forks, a tribal emergency was declared. Scouts like Crazy Horse investigated the reports of Connor's march, monitoring the construction of Camp Connor and the August 22 departure of the main command to rendezvous with Cole and Walker. They located the remains of the party cut off by Connor's Pawnees. Messengers, including nineteen-year-old Young Little Hawk, were sent to warn the Miniconjous. Responding immediately to his kola's call, High Backbone led out a war party against Camp Connor, Young Little Hawk striking second coup on one of the Winnebago scouts. Crazy Horse led another war party against the garrison, harrying stragglers and stealing stock: eleven-year-old Red Hawk, son of the intransigent warrior who had deserted the Hunkpatilas in 1853, served as water-boy apprentice and proudly recalled his first war party under Crazy Horse's leadership.

For the next three years, Crazy Horse's band repeatedly targeted Camp Connor (renamed Fort Reno in 1866). Even when other Oglala bands restricted their attacks to troops stationed north along the Bozeman Trail, Crazy Horse and his kinsmen refused to abandon the offensive against the post at the head of Powder River. Clearly, a family member was killed (probably by the Winnebago contingent) in the first skirmishes around the post, opening a raiding cycle that persisted until the army abandoned the Powder River country in 1868.[8]

Both Oglalas and Cheyennes began their separate Sun Dance celebrations about September 2, but late on the fourth—immediately prior to the climactic final day of self-torture—Miniconjou messengers from downstream raced into the villages. High Backbone reciprocated the warning sent by the Oglalas, announcing that some two thousand American soldiers—Cole and Walker's united columns—were barely a day's journey downstream and marching toward the Sun Dance camps. United with Hunkpapa, Sihasapa, and Sans Arc warriors from the Little Missouri, the Miniconjous had repeatedly clashed with Cole and Walker over the past four days. Connor's search-and-destroy commands were proving woefully inept, hampered by morale problems and issues of command seniority, but the plains weather did the direst work. Weeks of baking drought ended on the night of September 2, when temperatures plummeted during a storm of driving sleet. Over the next twenty-four hours, 225 exhausted horses and mules died, struck down by the sudden reversals of heat and cold. Nevertheless, the bedraggled troops were moving toward the Oglalas and Cheyennes.[9]

The warriors first came upon Walker's smaller command, but when Walker halted his progress and moved part of his column downstream to support Cole, the warriors were content to mount a holding operation from the blufftops. Most rode on toward the sound of gunfire and cannonades. Fifteen miles south of Walker, in a flat bend of the valley, Cole had formed his command into a hollow square to guard the corral of wagons. A single company fronted the riverbank, but stronger units sketched the other three sides, and Cole had his artillery drawn up on the flank opposite the river. Along the west side of the valley, Indians were visible massing atop hills or filtering downstream to surround Cole's position. One hill in particular hosted a gathering of war leaders. There, Crazy Horse, High Backbone, the Cheyenne Roman Nose, and other leaders conferred.

"Let's draw them out of that country by making them believe we are ready to run away," suggested High Backbone.[10] Signaling with mirrors, warriors formed in groups from ten to one hundred strong, then drove in charges to within 250 yards of Cole's perimeter. Suddenly veering away, they tried to lure units of defenders in pursuit, but Cole's defense was stern. The new seven-shot Spencer repeating carbine kept up a rapid fire that repelled all but the boldest warriors.

After almost three hours of inconsequential action, Crazy Horse rode to the front. "Just keep away for a little while," he ordered the warriors. "These soldiers like to shoot. I am going to give them a chance to do all the shooting they want to do. You draw back and I will make them shoot. If I fall off, then you can do something if you feel like it; but don't do anything until I have run by them." With that, he kneed forward his pony and galloped the length of Cole's defensive square. Firing at will, the troopers snapped off shot after futile shot at the slim figure leaning low over his pony's neck. Opposite the end of their line, Crazy Horse drew rein and briefly rested his mount, still in clear range. Then he galloped back, veering closer to the line of barking Spencers. Still no bullet touched him. A third time he charged, nearer again to the soldier line. A few ragged shots tracked his run, but presently the firing stopped. Even when he made a direct dash toward the line, the guns remained silent, and Crazy Horse swung back to rejoin his stunned comrades. His disarming, wry modesty surfaced: "Now my friends, don't worry," he grinned as they pressed forward to reassure themselves of his safety.[11]

Action shifted across the river as Cheyenne warriors led by Roman Nose accessed the field from the east. Not to be outdone, Roman Nose repeated Crazy Horse's brave run as reinforcing warriors forded the Powder, increasing the pressure all around Cole. The commander ordered his howitzers to open up, and several horses fell screaming as grapeshot exploded across the field. The warriors fell back. Now Cole trained his artillery on the hilltops bristling with warriors. Crazy Horse and the cluster of leaders grouped around a red flag made a distinctive target, and presently a screeching shell exploded on the hillside, dispersing the war chiefs. To the desultory roar of cannon shells, the battle closed as warriors withdrew toward their villages.

While Cole and Walker trudged upstream, the Cheyennes decamped for the Black Hills. On September 8, as the troops neared the Oglala village, Red Cloud and other leaders coordinated a dogged holding action in driving rain. Women worked hard to pack and strike tipis, and the Oglalas too tracked east, leaving the Sun Dance lodge standing in the middle of the deserted circle. Although they withdrew before

Cole and Walker, Crazy Horse and his fellow war leaders could congratulate themselves that these soldiers were neutralized as a fighting force. The deteriorating
weather finished off another four hundred of the troops' stock in a single night, and
the command limped slowly upstream. The charred remains of their wagons, har-
ness, and other discarded materiel would make a landmark on Powder River for
years to come. General Connor, returning from his campaign's one clear victory—
surprising an Arapaho village on Tongue River on August 29—ordered the expedition wound up and marched his men back to Fort Laramie early in October. Except
for the skeleton garrison and seventy Winnebago scouts left to winter at Fort Reno,
Connor could point to no lasting achievement.[12]

As their foes slunk south, the Lakotas and Cheyennes could dance in triumph.
In mid-September the Oglalas regrouped high up the Little Missouri. After successful defense against a surprise attack on the village, warrior societies commonly
nominated a body of blotahunka from the warriors who most distinguished themselves. They would hold the seats of honor at the feasts celebrating victory and be
temporarily accorded significant political influence. Honored for his strategic contribution to the events of the summer, Red Cloud "was ranked first," but Crazy
Horse too was invited to attend the councils. Miniconjous High Backbone and
Spotted Elk, as well as prominent visitors like Little Wound, a southern Oglala
refugee from the central plains, and the Brule chief Iron Shell, joined the conclave.
No Water, a Bad Face warrior who had served as an akicita under the Harney
regime, completed the roll.[13]

For the man accustomed to sitting silently through the few councils he had
attended, the season promised to be an uncomfortable novelty. Connor's retreat signaled that the Americans had put the war "back in the bag," and chiefs and elders
hastened to retrack the peace process. Red Cloud declared the raiding season over.
Lakota messengers from the Missouri and the North Platte soon brought news of
a major American peace initiative. Initial talks were scheduled at Fort Sully—a new
post near the site of the old Fort Pierre—for October.[14]

Red Cloud's war council refused to attend both the Fort Sully talks and the
follow-up councils at Fort Laramie. Reports of the treaty, concluded with friendly
bands along the Missouri River, angered Oglala war leaders like Crazy Horse. Aid in
agriculture was promised, with guarantees of government protection of Lakotas who
took up farming. Potential signatories were reminded that annuities under the Horse
Creek Treaty were due to expire. The scale of the promised twenty-year annuity
increased about fourfold the annual per capita spending on the Lakotas—a significant
inducement to accept the most sinister clause of all: signatory bands must withdraw
from all routes of travel through their country, guaranteeing not to molest settlers.

Warrior society meetings nominated Red Cloud to speak for the tribe in subsequent negotiations, empowering him to reject any proposal that legitimized the
Bozeman Trail. Runners were sent to other villages to forge a consensus on continuing the war until all troops were removed from north of the Platte.[15]

An uncommonly hard winter placed strains on the hardliners' position. Amid howling blizzards, droves of horses starved to death in the drifts. Mothers hacked at the animals' frozen flanks to feed their hungry families. Resolve wavered. Upper Platte agent Vital Jarrot sent out more messengers, and Man Afraid of His Horse tried to build a new consensus on their proposals. The Hunkpatila chief was surely dismayed at Red Cloud's usurpation of his diplomatic seniority. Despite its short-comings, the Fort Sully accord did address the issues that had preoccupied him for the past six years. Not only would Lakotas who engaged in farming receive aid in making the transition from the hunting life, their territorial rights would be guaranteed by the government. If the controversial clause about withdrawal from settler routes could be finessed, the treaty might be sold as providing to the Lakotas the best of both worlds.[16]

In a high-risk strategy that compromised his authority with his young men, Man Afraid of His Horse, late in January 1866, sent word that one hundred lodges of northern Oglalas wished to plant near Fort Laramie that spring. According to the treaty, such a unit could select its own farming location and receive assistance in plowing, as well as a dedicated blacksmith—always in demand for gun repair and maintenance. Man Afraid of His Horse's messengers urged Jarrot to ensure a rapid resolution of that issue, lest war resume once good weather fattened stock and refilled meat parfleches.

Even within Man Afraid of His Horse's own Hunkpatila band, many leaders were disinclined to follow him. Worm began to distance himself from the counsel of the older chief. Worm's younger half-brother Little Hawk, who at thirty was only four years Crazy Horse's senior, had emerged as a key war leader in the old Standing Bull tiyospaye. He even more vigorously upheld the antitreaty line. Crazy Horse silently endorsed the skepticism of his "fathers" on the issue. Almost imperceptibly, Crazy Horse's family was shifting away from the consensus that Man Afraid of His Horse had imposed on Hunkpatila politics for the past generation.[17]

But hunger bit deep. More messengers from Fort Laramie appeared. At talks on Powder River, even Red Cloud conceded he would visit Fort Laramie early in March. Hou's of acclaim from the hungry, the old, and the uncommitted met the speech, marking Red Cloud's bid to extend his zone of influence beyond the irreconcilable. Spotted Tail, nominated by Brule chiefs and warriors as their tribal spokesman, also moved down to the fort, determined to forge a consensus around accommodation. Agent Jarrot urged the treaty commissioners to hurry west, lest a unique window of opportunity close.[18]

When he arrived at Fort Laramie, on March 12, Red Cloud undermined the urgency of Man Afraid of His Horse and Agent Jarrot. The people were hungry and the stock poor, he assured treaty commissioners; it would take until late May to gather the bands. In the meantime he would guarantee the de facto truce that had held since the fall. A late spring conclave ensured that Lakotas and officials met on equal terms: replenished stores meant less chance of hungry chiefs signing agreements in return for handouts. Chairman of the commissioners Edward B. Taylor agreed to proceedings opening June 1. Red Cloud rode home in triumph. Without committing the Oglalas to anything, he brought presents of tobacco and provisions to prime his own status networks.[19]

Sensing the limitations of his position, Man Afraid of His Horse moved his stance closer to Red Cloud's, but the Bad Face leader shifted gear too as bands regathered along the upper Belle Fourche. When a war party of Oglalas and Miniconjous formed to break the truce, Red Cloud led a line of chiefs and akicita to intercept the warriors, killing their ponies and slashing their tipi covers. The objective of the raiders is not known, but Fort Reno was the most likely target. As such, the warriors might have included Crazy Horse. The incident ended Red Cloud's honeymoon period as warrior spokesman.[20]

During May, as Jarrot had predicted, the greening grass hardened warrior opinion. War leaders, including Crazy Horse, refused to travel to Fort Laramie. Instead, a deputation of chiefs and akicita was sent to meet the commissioners, assess their terms, and report. The ranking Oglalas were Red Cloud, retaining his status as tribal spokesman, chiefs Man Afraid of His Horse and Sitting Bear, and Bad Face war chief Trunk and his Hunkpatila counterpart Buffalo Tongue. Red Leaf and Iron Shell represented the Brule bands that hunted in the Powder River country. At Fort Laramie they found two thousand tractable southern Brules, southern Oglalas, and Loafers. Their leaders, including the new Brule head chief Spotted Tail, had no interest in the Powder River hunting grounds and were viewed with skepticism by the war councils.[21]

Talks finally opened on June 5. The emollient Taylor read a prepared address explaining that the government desired not to buy Lakota lands but simply to secure a right-of-way through the hunting grounds to the Montana goldfields. Amid promises of generous compensation for the loss of game resources, Taylor let slip that the "Great Father does not wish to keep *many* soldiers in this country," a tacit acknowledgement that the garrisoning of the Powder River country was under consideration.[22]

The following day the council was suspended with a series of short statements—nuanced in various grades of reluctance—by which Spotted Tail, Red Leaf, and Man Afraid of His Horse each joined Red Cloud in stating that "a treaty could and would be made" to permit the controversial right-of-way.[23] Such an outcome, however, needed the presence of all. Speeches closed with a request that messengers be sent with presents to the villages on White River, inviting them to attend a second round of talks. Agreement could then be validated by a full and open council.

On June 8 the chiefs departed for White River with a packtrain of provisions, assuring Taylor they would return in four days' time, ready to restart talks on the thirteenth. The two-day hiatus and the deployment of the key chiefs indicate that initial messengers had met a stony reception. This was made clear when Bad Face warriors intercepted a commission messenger bound for the Cheyenne village on

Powder River: they quirted him soundly and sent him packing back to Fort Laramie. Their words of warning revealed clearly the hardening of public attitudes. While the elders and most band chiefs stood for peace, warrior society meetings favored resuming the war. Most significant, the general mood in private lodges was moving against concessions: "[T]here was no desire for peace" among the people at large. Crazy Horse and like-minded warriors acclaimed the move away from accommodation.[24]

A couple of days of hard debate followed the chiefs' return to White River. Red Cloud and Man Afraid of His Horse were confirmed as tribal negotiators, but Crazy Horse and the other war leaders still refused to permit the village to join the treaty conclave. Band-level distinctions are detectable, with Bad Face speakers declaring Crazy Woman Creek a deadline beyond which intruders would face reprisals. Crazy Horse and the Hunkpatila warriors made an unexpected concession, acknowledging that Fort Reno might remain as long as traffic was routed from there west of the Bighorn Mountains, and only if the contingent of Winnebago scouts at the post be removed. Red Cloud and Man Afraid of His Horse were instructed to participate in no further treaty sessions until they had secured total agreement to this agenda from the friendly Lakotas around the fort.[25]

Returning on schedule, Red Cloud and Man Afraid of His Horse cooperated closely, seeking to secure support from Spotted Tail and the protreaty faction in long talks and feasts through June 12 and 13. Both leaders consistently refused goodwill presents from the commissioners. As the afternoon of the thirteenth lengthened, a completely unforeseen turn of events created an irretrievable crisis. Seven hundred soldiers of the Eighteenth Infantry marched up the Overland Trail and went into camp south of the fort. Their commander, Colonel Henry B. Carrington, with disarming frankness told a Brule visitor that the troops were bound to garrison the Bozeman Trail. Conceding that Spotted Tail's southern Brules would sign the agreement, Standing Elk warned Carrington that the "fighting men in that country have not come to Laramie, and you will have to fight them."[26]

New messengers were dispatched to ask the war councils on White River to attend the talks, again to no effect. Both Man Afraid of His Horse and Red Cloud made speeches openly opposing Carrington's mission. The Hunkpatila chief was mortified by the crass timing of Carrington's arrival, compounded by the colonel's naive wish to act as a facilitator in the treaty talks.

Red Cloud's response was more robust. On the fourteenth he delivered a stirring harangue, urging the protreaty faction to boycott talks. Red Cloud argued that the commissioners were treating the Lakotas like children, "pretending to negotiate for a country which they had already taken by Conquest." For years the Americans had crowded the Lakotas onto smaller hunting grounds, he contended, but now all bands must unite and fight to preserve what land they retained. The war might be long, but Lakota unity and the justness of their cause would guarantee the ultimate victory. Spotted Tail and his supporters were unimpressed by Red Cloud's rhetoric. At length, Red Cloud and his retinue of warriors withdrew, declaring that they would hold no further talks with the peace party.[27]

Man Afraid of His Horse stayed to hear out the day's debate but was careful not to undermine Red Cloud's position. On the following day an unscheduled meeting with Carrington and his officers resulted in angry words. "Great Father sends us presents and wants new road," succinctly observed one speaker, "but white chief goes with soldiers to *steal* road before Indian say yes or no!" Both leaders warned the officers that to march north of Fort Reno meant war; Buffalo Tongue, speaking for the Hunkpatila akicita, assented. Restricting threats to a war of stock theft— still a stage down from blood reprisals—the Oglala leaders warned that "in two moons the command would not have a hoof left." Outside the fort, the two chiefs were observed ordering their followers to strike tipis. Overnight the Oglalas and northern Brules hurried across the North Platte to join their villages. By morning of the sixteenth, only the peace party remained at the fort.[28]

In early July, the northern Oglalas gathered for the tribal Sun Dance high up Tongue River. Arrivals from Fort Laramie brought news that a second round of talks had resulted in a treaty signed by Spotted Tail, his Brule headmen, and an Oglala contingent headed by Big Mouth. Warriors were enraged at the news and quarreled fiercely with one incoming party packing treaty presents.[29]

The atmosphere only deepened divisions between war proponents and the civil leadership. These divisions were readily apparent to a party of Cheyenne chiefs invited to attend the Sun Dance holy days. Away from the reverential hush of the dance arbor, the Cheyennes learned of deep splits. "[N]early all the old men oppose any contests with the whites," they observed, reflecting the elders' continued commitment to peace. Warrior society meetings had openly flouted the chiefs' claim to tribal authority and had vetoed them as candidates for the year's appointment of Deciders. The war council assumed control of the village. Older war leaders such as Black Twin, of the Bad Faces, the Hunkpatila Buffalo Tongue, and the Oyuhpe Big Road, were invested in the seats of honor at the back of the council shade. First among equals was Red Cloud, recognized as supreme war chief, *blotahunka ataya*.[30]

On July 13, scouts reported that Carrington had halted at Little Piney Creek and had begun construction of a major post, Fort Phil Kearny. "White man lies and steals," Red Cloud fulminated to the Cheyennes, "My lodges were many, but now they are few. The white man wants all. The white man must fight, and the Indian will die where his fathers died." Only if Carrington withdrew to Fort Reno would the Lakotas concede peace. Red Cloud closed his speech with a veiled threat: the Cheyennes must join the Lakotas in fighting the intruders and preventing any extension of the chain of forts.[31]

The war council was keen to widen the scope of hostilities. Man Afraid of His Horse moved to distance himself from Red Cloud, taking a position that a negotiated solution must be found to the new crisis. As soon as the Sun Dance ended, he led his camp a day's journey down Tongue River, the better to formulate an

independent policy. Carrington's rising stockade ruptured Hunkpatila band solidarity. The ranking akicita Buffalo Tongue gathered a faction of war supporters,
including Crazy Horse, Little Hawk, and the band chief's nominated heir, Young
Man Afraid of His Horse. Reflecting their commitment to terminating Fort Reno,
the dissidents formed a war camp along the middle Powder, scouting parties infest-
ing the Bozeman Trail. Buffalo Tongue declared that his party would "cut off further approach of travel" by troops and civilian trains.[32]

Red Cloud led a party to the Bighorn crossing of the Bozeman. An Arapaho
village, hitherto peaceful, was prevailed on to join in harrying the wagon train laying over at the ferry. Red Cloud personally led a charge that ran off most of the
ferry's herd on July 17. On the same day, Oglala warriors first struck the soldiers'
stock at the new fort rising beside the Little Piney. In Red Cloud's absence, Bad
Face leaders at the village also bullied the Cheyenne chiefs, striking them with
bows and forcing the Cheyenne village to move south, out of the war zone.[33]

Simultaneously, on July 22, raiders struck forts Reno and Phil Kearny, driving
off stock in a choreographed opening of hostilities. On the following day, Crazy
Horse's party intercepted a military train as it approached Crazy Woman Creek,
killing a lieutenant in the first seconds of surprise. The small troop escort managed
to corral the wagons atop a knoll, and for the rest of the day the warriors circled
the defenses in headlong charges—a textbook Hollywood Indian fight, but rare in
reality. The train remained pinned down through the night, but on the twenty-
fourth, relief squads from both posts dispersed the attackers. Crazy Horse's party fell
back to harry traffic south of Fort Reno.[34]

Early in August Carrington detached another two companies to establish Fort C.
F. Smith at the Bighorn crossing. Red Cloud immediately sponsored a formal war
pipe and proposed major offensives against the two new forts once winter closed military communications. A war pipe meant a formal tribal war, committing large forces
to extermination of the enemy—a far cry from the stock-theft "half-war" threatened
two months earlier. Man Afraid of His Horse received Loafer messengers inviting him
to attend new talks at Fort Laramie. He won tentative approval of the moderate
Hunkpatila young men, but a new flurry of raids around Fort Reno in mid-August
was Crazy Horse's unfavorable response to the news. On the seventeenth, warriors
boldly entered the post corral and drove out seventeen mules and seven horses.
Wealth and war honors continued to accumulate for the hostile Hunkpatilas.[35]

Intertribal diplomacy took a new turn late in August. Red Cloud and Man
Afraid of His Horse jointly led a one hundred-man Oglala deputation across the
Bighorn to the main Crow village on Clark's Fork. Red Dog, the finest Oglala orator, was on hand to present Red Cloud's case. Crazy Horse accepted the invitation
to attend and won the accolade of the Crow chiefs as the bravest Lakota they knew.
In hard-nosed councils, between the feasting, Red Cloud proposed that Crow warriors join the offensive against the new posts: in return, he promised that part of the
old Crow hunting grounds east of the Bighorn would revert to a joint-use zone.

The Crow leaders were discomfited when some of their young men seemed disposed to accept Red Cloud's terms. Then Man Afraid of His Horse quietly defused the situation by announcing the offer of new talks at Fort Laramie. Any decision on so momentous a matter as a war pipe should wait until diplomatic channels were exhausted, he contended. Promising a return visit to the Lakota villages, the Crow chiefs declared that their response to Red Cloud's proposal would wait.[36]

By September some five hundred Lakota lodges were pitched within half a day's ride along the Tongue. The Miniconjous encamped on the Bighorn were also about to enter the war. A tribal war council had named High Backbone as principal chief for the season. Smoking Red Cloud's war pipe, High Backbone sanctioned small-scale raiding around Fort C. F. Smith in mid-September; late in the month, his warriors joined Red Cloud's in operations around Fort Phil Kearny. Soon almost one hundred Miniconjou lodges had augmented the Tongue River villages.[37]

In October, Crazy Horse accompanied Buffalo Tongue's camp back from the Powder, satisfied that with civilian traffic closing for winter, they had stolen all available stock along the southern stretch of the Bozeman. Indicating their distance from their own band chief, the Hunkpatila war leaders clustered closer to Red Cloud. The Bad Face leader cultivated them, inviting the younger Yellow Eagle, a close comrade of Crazy Horse, to plan a major raid on Fort Phil Kearny. Young Man Afraid of His Horse also joined the Bad Face war talks; however, Crazy Horse was signally honored to sit on Red Cloud's left at the honor place in feasts and councils. Some observers viewed Crazy Horse as a key aide or lieutenant to Red Cloud.[38]

During these fall weeks, Crazy Horse and Red Cloud were closer than they ever would be again. Nineteen years older than Crazy Horse, Red Cloud had been the greatest Oglala warrior of his generation. Possessed of a powerful physical presence, and an astute political operator, Red Cloud probably viewed the slight Hunkpatila with bemused curiosity. Crazy Horse would have seen that Red Cloud was not personally engaged in combat operations but fulfilled the role of a strategic war leader. Raiding was carefully coordinated with buffalo surrounds so that hunters were able to lay up vital surpluses. Meat was supplemented from the hundreds of oxen and cows seized by raiders along the Bozeman. Although diplomacy was officially off the agenda, Red Cloud encouraged visits by Loafers to secure intelligence and to trade robes for firearms and ammunition. Besides bows and lances, most warriors were still armed with Northwest muskets and percussion Hawkens. Repeating rifles were an unknown quantity, but revolvers were becoming a common sidearm. Red Cloud also sourced new lines of supply. Through fall, a series of one-day truce-and-trades was held with the Crows along the Bighorn. Another vital new channel was to the Canadian Métis traders, directly or through Santee and Hunkpapa visitors like Inkpaduta and Sitting Bull.[39]

During the crisp weeks of fall, Crazy Horse and his comrades joined the Bad Faces in harrying Fort Phil Kearny. Repeatedly, they targeted horse herds, straggling pickets, guards, and the watchmen atop Carrington's lookout tower on Pilot

Hill. As haying details were succeeded by woodcutters laying up winter fuel, Indian attacks focused on the trail between the post and the pinery, in the foothills upstream of the post. The attacks, though small scale, kept Carrington on the defensive. As the state-of-the-art defenses of Fort Phil Kearny testified, its commander was a meticulous designer of fortifications but temperamentally unsuited to aggressive operations. To do him justice, even the modest reinforcements he received in November, raising his strength to some four hundred effective troops, could not have implemented the search-and-destroy missions urged by superiors and subordinates alike.

By the beginning of December, the plans of Red Cloud and High Backbone had matured. Taking advice from Crazy Horse and his fellow tactical leaders, they decided that a single blow should be delivered at Fort Phil Kearny. On December 6 Yellow Eagle led a dry run. The strategy would be to send decoy warriors to lure Carrington's troops out of the fort, over Lodge Trail Ridge into the Tongue River drainage. Beyond support of reinforcements, the pursuit would be overwhelmed, and the Indian forces would move to invest the fort.[40]

Yellow Eagle's attempt was foiled when the cautious Carrington called off pursuit of the decoys. During the second week of December, however, all Lakota camps consolidated on the Tongue, seventy miles north of the fort. High Backbone and the other war chiefs met and sent messengers to summon key warriors to join them as blotahunka. Crazy Horse was so honored and was treated with conspicuous favor by his Miniconjou kola. The war council decided on an attack at the time of the new moon.

On December 19 the massive procession, joined by the Cheyenne Crazy Dog Society and some seventy-five Arapaho warriors, moved up Tongue River to Prairie Dog Creek, straddling the modern Montana-Wyoming boundary. Leading the column, High Backbone bore in his arms the wolf-skin bundle containing the war pipe. A row of blotahunka including Red Cloud flanked the pipe bearer, while immediately behind rode the Miniconjou contingent fronted by Black Shield.[41]

Between the Miniconjous and the Cheyenne contingent at the rear rode the Oglalas, led by Crazy Horse, who was flanked by his comrades Long Man and He Dog. Determined to win battle honors, Crazy Horse had selected his war pony wisely, borrowing his brother's famous bay racer, distinguished by its white face and stockings. Young Little Hawk had gladly turned over the bay to honor his elder brother. Now Crazy Horse rode an ordinary traveling horse, leading the prized war pony on a short rein to preserve its strength.[42]

After making camp, many warriors rode to the vicinity of the fort and made a rousing attack on the wood train. Relief troops appeared and the warriors, drilling maneuvers, speedily disengaged. As on the sixth, the troops were cautious, and the blotahunka discussed the need to lure a large force beyond hope of support from the fort.

On the morning of the twentieth, the whole war party left the village and rode up Prairie Dog Creek to a wide flat at its forks. Perhaps fifteen hundred strong, they huddled in blanket coats or winter robes, fanned out in a long line across the bleak valley. The blotahunka ordered forth their chosen war prophet. Astride a sorrel pony that zigzagged over the hills rode a *winkte*, a male instructed in a vision to live as a woman. All sat in hushed expectation as he rode back and forth between the war chiefs and the distant hills. Each time he returned, his fingers clutched more convulsively, and he leaned this way and that in the saddle, first declaring he held in his hands ten soldiers; then twenty; then fifty—to be dismissed as bringing too few enemies for such a massive war party. On the sacred fourth try, the winkte hauled in his pony only to fall from the saddle as if balancing an impossible load. He struck the earth with both hands and, looking up at High Backbone and his comrades, cried in his fluting voice, "Answer me quickly, I have a hundred or more." Down the line, Crazy Horse joined the others in a shrill yell of triumph. They kneed forward their ponies and, leaning in the saddle, struck the ground all around the winkte's hands, as if counting coup on enemies whose fates were already sealed.[43]

The war party moved up the valley, now lightly blanketed in snow, through a bracing winter day. At a point ten miles north of the fort, the blotahunka announced camp would be made on a wide flat dotted with small timber. First, however, the warriors were ordered once more into line. Two chiefs turned out and rode along the line to select the decoy warriors for the next day's battle. Heads craned to observe the selection, knowing that only the coolest warriors, the best riders with the swiftest ponies, would be chosen for this essential task. Pausing before a candidate, the two chiefs leaned forward in their saddles, took hold of the warrior's bridle, and led horse and rider out of the line. Two Cheyenne, two Arapaho, and six Lakota warriors were chosen and turned to face their comrades. Three of these were Oglalas: American Horse, the son of the True Oglala chief Sitting Bear; Sword Owner, a nephew of Red Cloud's; and Crazy Horse, proudly sitting on his brother's bay. The blotahunka named Crazy Horse leader of the decoy party, and Sword Owner his assistant in ensuring the precise coordination of the operation.[44]

The ten warriors would lure the soldiers from the fort, over the ridge north of Big Piney, and down the slope toward the headwaters of Prairie Dog Creek, where the war party would lay an ambush and overwhelm the troops. The decoys would prepare themselves and their ponies and start before dawn to be in place for a morning attack. The whole war party would follow at sunrise. Instructions imparted, individual war leaders might ride forward and present to the decoys weapons, staffs, or coup sticks.

As the rising sun lit an infinite barren December plain, Crazy Horse rode out at the head of his little column. West, a jumble of low ridges climbed toward the dark shoulders of the snow-capped Bighorn Mountains. Icy hollows pocked the boulder-strewn hillside that topped out on a high saddle overlooking the Big Piney. The Bozeman Trail descended to the creek three miles southeast. On the flat beyond stood the formidable stockade of Fort Phil Kearny. Despite the tight discipline of the akicita, almost thirty warriors slipped past the decoys and descended into the bottomland brush facing the stockade. Immediately before the decoys, the ground fell steeply away down Lodge Trail Ridge. Crazy Horse's men dismounted and silently took up positions near the eastern end of the ridge.

High Backbone's plan called for the troops to be lured over this upland, and Crazy Horse examined the landscape minutely. Broken by draws and studded with scrubby pine, Lodge Trail Ridge fronted the north bank of Big Piney Creek for over three miles. Below them the frozen course of the creek glittered through a straggle of bare cottonwoods. Scanning the back trail, the warriors would see the main war party halting at the foot of the narrow ridge they had ascended. Blotahunka made assignments and the force divided, some led by Red Cloud, filtering along the draws framing the west side of the ridge, taking cover in the bare clusters of ash and box elder timber. Warriors without horses hid in the long yellow grass along the course of Peno Creek, in position to block any troop advance. Miniconjou warriors were assigned places in the draws down the east side of the ridge.[45]

When the morning wood train started for the pinery, accompanied by a strong escort, signals were passed to alert the war party, and a contingent of warriors was dispatched around the western end of Lodge Trail Ridge. As Crazy Horse continued scanning the valley, these warriors launched an attack that forced the train to stop and form a defensive corral two and one-half miles west of the fort. Now Crazy Horse keenly scanned the stockade for signs of a response. To ensure the bait was taken, he and a scatter of warriors rode along the ridge. After several anxious minutes, Crazy Horse made out the watchmen in Carrington's lookout tower signaling the wood train's plight. Finally, the fort's gate swung open and a force of some fifty infantry marched out of the stockade, commanded by Captain William J. Fetterman, a brash fire-eater with as low an opinion of Indians as Grattan's twelve years before. Carrington issued strict orders for Fetterman to relieve the wood train and on no account to follow Indians beyond the summit of Lodge Trail Ridge. Instead of following the wood trail, Fetterman angled toward the Big Piney, as if to follow upstream and cut off the attackers' retreat.

The decoys defiled down the ridge as Fetterman approached the crossing. One man dismounted in plain view of the fort and sat against a tree, his red blanket making a bright target. Before Fetterman could reach the ford, Carrington ordered his gunners to drop a case shot squarely in the bottomland brush, unhorsing one warrior and flushing the hidden thirty, who fled up the gullies of Lodge Trail Ridge. To the west the firing on the wood train ceased, evidence of the tight choreography deployed by High Backbone and Crazy Horse. A force of twenty-seven cavalrymen led by Lieutenant George W. Grummond followed Fetterman. A clutch of volunteers and civilians made the total force leaving the fort to be eighty-one effective men. After Grummond united with Fetterman's infantry, the command moved in skirmish formation up the creek. Decoys, scouts, and war leaders signaled each other to synchronize minutely the next few minutes' crucial action. First, the warriors disengaged from the wood train, having lured out a significant proportion of the garrison. High Backbone's plan did not entail a costly running fight. Feigning alarm, the warriors strung back northward, leaving the wood train free to press forward.

Here was the critical moment for Crazy Horse, and without pause, he mounted and led the decoys out along the lower slopes of Lodge Trail Ridge. With shrill whoops, the warriors strung west along the ridge, keeping just beyond rifle range. Fetterman ordered his men in pursuit, crossing the frozen creek and deploying his infantry as skirmishers as they climbed. A bugle sounded, and the cavalry charged after the decoys, who quirted their ponies up the slope. The pursuit opened fire, raining lead around the warriors, but then suddenly halted: to the warriors, it looked as if they would follow no more. The last warriors retreating from the wood train were visible, climbing the west end of the ridge two miles away. Perhaps alarm bells briefly rang in cooler heads. Then, greatly daring, decoys charged again, forcing the cavalry to resume the pursuit. As bullets struck around them, they held in their ponies, slowly climbing the slope.

Knowing that these soldiers had many times faced the timeworn decoy tactic, Crazy Horse's men played virtuosic variations on the theme as they neared the crest. Here a man dismounted as if his pony were lame, causing the foot soldiers to run in pursuit. Topping the ridge one by one, warriors galloped along the summit, turning to shoot downslope and braving the return fire, yelling taunts. Others dismounted and tugged at the bridles as if their ponies were played out. As Fetterman's command topped the ridge and halted where the Bozeman Trail cut the icy summit, the decoys were stringing down the ambush ridge. To their practiced eyes, telltale signs indicated that the trap was set. In every gully, warriors flexed bowstrings or eared back musket hammers, pinching their ponies' nostrils to keep them from whinnying an alarm.

Big Nose, the Cheyenne rearguard warrior, rode right at the soldiers, lacing around the cavalry before galloping after his comrades, making an irresistible target. Fetterman ordered his whole command in pursuit. The cavalry took the lead, while the civilian sharpshooters picked off shots at the decoys. With the troops within the jaws of the trap, Crazy Horse picked up speed, stretching his party's lead to three-quarters of a mile as the trail flattened out. Behind the party, the troops were strung along the length of the ridge, the cavalry outpacing Fetterman's slow-moving foot soldiers. Out on the flat, the decoys divided into two diverging lines, then turned their ponies and began to ride back the way they had come. The maneuver happened with appalling swiftness. If the cavalry registered it at all, they had no time to respond. The two lines of decoys recrossed. The instant of intersection was the signal. "Hopo! Hokahe!" Leaders yelled the war cry to shrill yammers of response. A rank of dismounted warriors rose from the creek bottom and poured a volley of arrows into the vanguard, felling an officer's horse, its rider scurrying uphill. Down each side of the ridge, warriors sprang into their saddles and clapped heels against their ponies' flanks, their charge engulfing the trail.

In the lead, the civilian volunteers and a handful of troopers dismounted and opened heavy fire from the cover of a few boulders. This was the theater of action

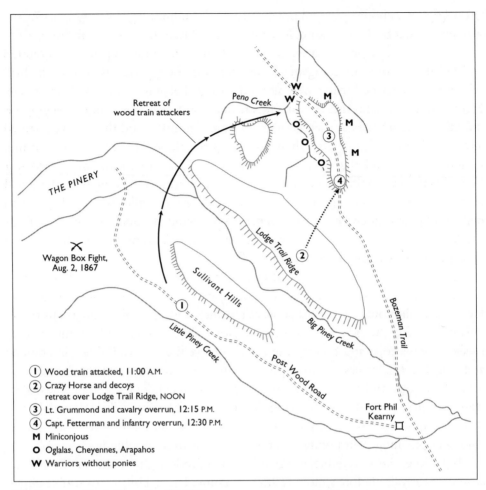

Key on map:
- (1) Wood train attacked, 11:00 A.M.
- (2) Crazy Horse and decoys retreat over Lodge Trail Ridge, NOON
- (3) Lt. Grummond and cavalry overrun, 12:15 P.M.
- (4) Capt. Fetterman and infantry overrun, 12:30 P.M.
- M Miniconjous
- O Oglalas, Cheyennes, Arapahos
- W Warriors without ponies

The Fetterman Battle, December 21, 1866

closest to Crazy Horse. Fittingly, it was where the Indians met the stiffest resistance. The civilians laid down a blistering fire, levering shells from their sixteen-shot Henry repeating rifles, augmented by single-shot Springfields. Warriors circled the position, leaning behind their ponies' necks to snap off shots at these cool fighters. The civilians felled many ponies, driving off the initial charge, and behind them the cavalry withdrew up the slope after opening heavy fire from their seven-shot Spencer repeaters. If a late oral tradition is to be trusted, Crazy Horse led the charge into the cavalry, hacking around him with a hatchet as he repeatedly rode among the troopers, braving sustained and deadly fire.[46]

Trying to prevent precipitate flight, Lieutenant Grummond covered his men, slicing off a warrior's head with his saber before falling from his white horse. At Grummond's death, his men broke and fled up the ridge. Crazy Horse's followers streamed after them to join comrades surrounding the position of Fetterman's infantry.

Fetterman managed to maintain tactical cohesion as he withdrew his men as far as a cluster of large boulders. Here he formed a line fronting both ways and ordered concerted firing into the swarming Indians. As the foot soldiers held their ground, the demoralized cavalry fled past them to a position one hundred yards above.

Downslope the infantry faced the main brunt of the Indian attack. After the first general charge, the fighting slowed, and warriors resumed positions in the gullies. Occasionally a lone warrior would make a brave run through the infantry position, usually to be shot down by the disciplined fire. To break down enemy defenses for a fresh assault, war leaders ordered a volley of arrows from both sides of the ridge. Aiming high, they rained shafts over the ridge, taking a deadly toll among friends as well as foes. Red Dog was just one Lakota wounded by an overshot arrow; a luckless comrade was killed when his forehead blocked another shaft.

Giving the troops no time to recover from the shock, the cry to charge was called, and Lakotas and Cheyennes overran the infantry position, grappling in hand-to-hand combat with the desperate soldiers. Fetterman remained mounted, exhorting his men, until American Horse smashed his pony into the officer's mount and dealt a staggering blow to Fetterman's head, unhorsing the commander. Dazed, Fetterman put up no fight as American Horse leapt from his saddle and slashed open his throat. Exultant warriors poured up the slope toward the cavalry.[47]

Overhead the air, palled in powder smoke, was darkening with approaching snow. The temperature continued to drop, freezing bloody wounds and skimming hard the trampled snow. Chiefs ordered the warriors to dismount and fight afoot. The cavalry fell back, struggling to lead their mounts amid a renewed hail of arrows. Some mounts fell dead; others plunged and broke away. The soldiers started to run for a new defensive position at the head of the ridge, letting their remaining horses go in a bid to deter the pursuit. Barely forty-five minutes after the opening charge, the last of the cavalry was overrun. One or two pockets of resistance along the ridge remained to be mopped up: the civilians at the lower end may have been among the last to fall, a litter of Henry cases at their position attesting to their grim defense. Of twelve ponies killed outright on the field, ten lay around the civilian position. By 12:45, as an appalled relief unit topped the ridge to view the scene of carnage, the battle was over. Warriors were moving down the ridge, stripping, scalping, and mutilating; looting clothing, guns, and ammunition; firing arrows to bristle from frozen naked bodies.

All eighty-one men were dead. Of the Indians, as few as eleven might have died on the field. About sixty were wounded, some fatally: many more, like Crazy Horse's uncle Black Elk, who had sustained a crippling leg wound, were maimed for life. Dead and wounded alike were removed on makeshift travois from the field, but if a later reminiscence by frontier scout Frank Grouard is to be trusted, it was not until after the battle that one casualty was missed. Crazy Horse and High Backbone did not long savor their triumph, for on the march home, they learned that their comrade Lone Bear was not with the column. The two friends rode back toward the battlefield. It may have been dark before Crazy Horse and High Back-bone were able to locate Lone Bear. He had sustained a terrible wound in the leg, and blood poisoning had set in. Already his limbs and extremities were badly frozen, and the luckless warrior clearly would not live. The friends did all they could to ease Lone Bear's passing, and at the end, Crazy Horse crouched down to cradle him in his arms. High Backbone towered over the prostrate form, weeping. With a vicious norther threatening, the comrades finally mounted and struck down the barren valley toward home.[48]

There, four days later, the victory dances began once the blizzard and the grief of mourners were blown out. At celebrations in the Oglala village, political rivals sat together: Man Afraid of His Horse ate beside Red Cloud and Red Dog in feasts to honor the victorious blotahunka and warriors. As the ranking Oglala war chief, Red Cloud "had all the honor" of the battle, according to one eyewitness.[49] The victory indeed seemed to bear out all that Red Cloud had predicted at Fort Laramie six months earlier: with the unity of the Lakota people and the justness of their cause, the wasicu intruders could be destroyed.

In the songs and coup-counting contests, the decoy warriors were picked out for special praise. Sword Owner, American Horse—these were the sons of chiefs, born to greatness; their courage on the Fetterman battlefield could only enhance their prospects of political leadership. For Crazy Horse, the diffident son of a holy man, such prospects had never been his goal. But unrivaled bravery and generosity were themselves qualifications for civil leadership. Now, in his precision coordination of the decoy party, he had displayed a gift for inspirational leadership that sympathetic elders might read as another of the four key Lakota virtues—fortitude, the moral courage that is an example to all. Old men singing in praise of Crazy Horse recognized his bravery but talked also of his wakan power in battle. For the first time he was regarded as a future leader of the people. Even Cheyennes began to look to Crazy Horse as a warrior they would follow into the heat of battle. His role as the chief tactical leader in the Fetterman fight meant that Crazy Horse would never return to the world of the plain warrior, sitting dutifully silent through the councils of his elders. Chiefs now would consult him, seek his support to secure warrior opinion around their positions, feast and groom him for a political life. Celebrating the greatest victory of his young manhood, Crazy Horse was at another turning point in his life.

10

CLOSING THE ROAD

For four days and nights, victory dances continued throughout the villages on Tongue River. Then, with surpluses depleted and winter closing in, the bands broke up. Red Cloud's Bad Face camp moved west into the valley of the Little Bighorn, others gravitated downcountry into the valley of the Yellowstone. In the wake of the Fetterman disaster, the army sought to respond as quickly as a Wyoming winter permitted, and troops were soon on the march to reinforce the Bozeman Trail garrisons. Rumors of larger troop movements were rife, and the Indians remained strung along the Yellowstone throughout the winter.

After the worst blizzards had blown themselves out, the hostile Hunkpatila leadership reassessed strategy. Rejecting Man Afraid of His Horse's continued search for a negotiated solution, they shared Red Cloud's militancy but were alienated by his arrogance in appropriating "all the honor" for the victory of One Hundred in the Hands. Camp leadership devolved on Little Hawk, but the battlefield charisma of his nephew Crazy Horse won new adherents from the Bad Faces and Oyuhpes. Straggling Cheyennes, following holy man Ice, were also drawn by Crazy Horse's battlefield genius. As many as seventy lodges followed Little Hawk and Crazy Horse up Powder River.[1]

After establishing camp downstream from Fort Reno, Crazy Horse's warriors repeated the pattern of the previous summer. On February 27 they struck a detachment of Companies B and I, Twenty-seventh Infantry. Three soldiers were swiftly killed, but the war party disengaged before the troops could inflict casualties. Although no follow-up attack transpired, Crazy Horse's men infested the Bozeman Trail, monitoring the movement of troops filtering up the Bozeman to reinforce Carrington's garrison; by July, nine hundred effective troops garrisoned the three posts.[2]

The influx of troops masked two significant facts. First, settler and freight traffic did not resume along the Bozeman Trail. Virtually the only civilian entrepreneurs using the bitterly contested road were military contractors. Second, the army high command had lost the diplomatic war in Washington. The clamor for reprisal immediately after the Fetterman disaster had moderated: initial plans for a punitive expedition were put on hold and a new commission was ordered to investigate the causes of Indian hostility. Chaired by John B. Sanborn, a Minnesota lawyer who would figure large in Lakota-U.S. relations, the commission convened in Omaha in March.[3]

Word of the commission was telegraphed west and carried onto the hunting grounds by Loafer messengers. It arrived at an opportune moment, just as the scattered bands began to regather. Late in March the main Bad Face and Hunkpatila camps collected at the mouth of the Rosebud.[4]

Little Hawk and Crazy Horse resumed their place in the tribal circle. With winter meat packs exhausted, peace proponents won consensus on attending talks at Fort Laramie. Negotiations ensured liberal rationing for Indian participants. With rumors of punitive marches still current, the continuing crisis in ammunition supply did nothing to recommend an entrenched hardline position: besides presents, dialogue that might reopen trade on the Platte was another reason for the public mood to favor negotiations. Ready at last to secure a consensus, Man Afraid of His Horse moved to reassert his seniority in the village.

The elders staged feasts and dances, inviting new members to sit with the council. Members donned buffalo horn headdresses, their naked bodies painted white, and danced the buffalo dance as a plea for a season of plenty. They moved to recruit key war leaders who had helped secure the victory against Fetterman: American Horse and Sword Owner were among the intake. Although surely invited to feast and confer with Man Afraid of His Horse, Crazy Horse was not among the intake, hinting that he remained unwilling to come on board a revived peace process.

Red Cloud was deeply dissatisfied with the political reversal. He united around him a following of sixty lodges, chiefly Bad Faces, and withdrew to join the Oyuhpes and Miniconjous, where no peace movement had taken hold. Rejecting the authority of the chiefs and elders, Red Cloud's faction recognized a new council comprising younger war leaders, the Ska Yuha, or White Horse Owners. About 135 lodges remained with Man Afraid of His Horse.[5] The fragile restoration of Hunkpatila band unity also held. That Little Hawk and Crazy Horse, committed to an even more radically militant policy than Red Cloud's, chose to remain in the main village speaks to the profound mistrust and jealousy that already existed between their faction and the Bad Face war chief.

Late in April, the village contacted Red Leaf's Wazhazha camp and Lone Horn's Miniconjous, both eager to settle the Bozeman Trail issue and resume the status quo. Runners arrived from Fort Laramie with the first formal invitation from the peace commissioners.

Even as the chiefs were conferring, however, a new arrival from Fort Laramie brought unsettling news. Far to the south, on the plains of western Kansas, General

Winfield S. Hancock's command was not constrained by the Sanborn commission's truce. Hancock had marched on the combined southern Oglala–Dog Soldier Cheyenne village. Frightened of another Sand Creek, the people had deserted their lodges on April 14, fleeing north. Five days later Hancock ordered the tipis and camp equipment burned, signaling a new war on the central plains. In Indian country, rumor and fact usually tangled in an intransigent knot: even as Man Afraid of His Horse's tipis were being struck and people mounted, ready for the Deciders' order, a Loafer named Smells the Ground brought sensational word that "the whites were all going to war" along the Overland Trail.[6]

The fragile consensus was shattered, and the village broke up. Scouting parties were ordered to watch the Bozeman Trail. Crazy Horse and his party returned to Fort Reno, where they served notice of their outrage by attacking detachments from the post on April 26 and 27, killing one soldier and escaping again without casualties.[7]

The sudden switch in mood seems to have convinced militant leaders to respond to a new invitation. North of Powder River forks, a massive gathering of northern Lakotas was planning summer operations. Besides Miniconjous and Sans Arcs, the main Hunkpapa village had arrived to coordinate strategy. Word had it that the Hunkpapa warrior societies would nominate a principal war chief, a northern Lakota counterpart to Red Cloud.

Crazy Horse and his followers brought their camps into the gathering, forming a smaller Oglala circle, adjoined by Ice's Cheyenne camp, upstream of the three host villages. Two Kettle, Sihasapa, and Yanktonai visitors clustered around the larger circles. Councils were dominated by the issue of war. Sans Arc leaders pledged to assist the Miniconjous in operations against the Bozeman Trail posts: Crazy Horse's campaign against Fort Reno was promised aid. Hunkpapa speakers undoubtedly dwelled on new forts in their own country. Fort Buford, at the mouth of the Yellowstone, had been besieged through the winter, much as the Oglalas had assailed Fort Phil Kearny.

The gathering climaxed with the nomination of a titular national war chief. Crazy Horse was invited to sit with the host chiefs in the great council shade. The four Hunkpapa Shirt Wearers carried their nominee on a buffalo robe and seated him in the honor place. It was Sitting Bull, the Strong Hearts leader Crazy Horse had met ten years earlier at the Bear Butte council. Now thirty-five, a stocky broad-chested man with an expression that moved easily from dour to playful, Sitting Bull had matured into a reverent but unpretentious Lakota. The envious might question his war record, but his generosity was as famous as Crazy Horse's, and though an accomplished political operator, Sitting Bull viewed the play of interest and faction with a wry detachment. He made an unconventional leader, imbued with a charisma all the stronger for his commonplace unpretentious manner.[8]

Hunkpapa speakers harangued, investing Sitting Bull with the power to decide on peace or war: "When you say 'fight,' we shall fight: when you say 'make peace,' we shall make peace." Indicating the validating presence of Crazy Horse and other guests, they told Sitting Bull he was made head war chief of the Lakota nation. After being presented with a magnificent calumet, a bow and arrows, a flintlock musket, and a superb trailer headdress, Sitting Bull was led out of the council tipi to where a fine white horse was held. A Shirt Wearer and an akicita leader lifted him into the saddle. Then Sitting Bull led a warrior society parade around the campground.

The show of solidarity could not mask the divisions that characterized Oglala politics. A significant minority of Hunkpapas favored treating with the Sanborn commission. Outside the Hunkpapa sphere, many northern Lakota leaders articulated a similar but independent line to Sitting Bull's. What the investiture did was dramatically focus and personalize issues, creating a symbolic leadership for Lakotas who sought a minimalist peace with Americans. Crazy Horse's visit was brief, but he established a good working relationship with the Hunkpapa war chief. To the introspective Crazy Horse, the more expansive Sitting Bull may have articulated key ideals for the future of their people, rooted in older northern Lakota attitudes that favored wasicu noninterference in Lakota affairs.

Crazy Horse and his Oglala followers left the gathering in early May, trekking up the Powder River valley to pitch their tipis on Clear Fork. Clearly, Crazy Horse and Little Hawk resisted any resumption of diplomacy. Their warriors, augmented by some of Ice's Cheyennes, besieged the district south of Fort Reno. At Bridger's Ferry they mounted an attack on the first supply train of the season, driving off the cattle of Jules Ecoffey, a trader turned army contractor. The train's cavalry escort promptly recaptured Ecoffey's animals, but on Sage Creek a couple of days later, Crazy Horse's warriors targeted the train again. Hovering around the camp, they sought to drive off more stock, withdrawing when escort commander Captain John Green led a fifty-man detachment in pursuit. For two miles the cavalry followed the war party, killing one warrior and one pony, before the Oglalas mustered enough fire to fell two cavalry horses. Both sides were happy to disengage, and the train continued past Fort Reno to arrive at Fort Phil Kearny on May 31.[9]

Responding to the growing traffic along the Bozeman, the war party returned to Bridger's Ferry and attacked a detachment of Troop E, Second Cavalry, on May 23. Having honed their tactics they managed to kill two soldiers before withdrawing. Around Fort Phil Kearny, Red Cloud's followers were also opening the raiding season.[10]

Meanwhile Man Afraid of His Horse and the other Deciders had reasserted their control and laid down strict prohibitions on further raiding: all war parties were ordered in as the village prepared to attend talks at Fort Laramie. Crazy Horse's war party would be the stiffest test of the Deciders' resolve. Crazy Horse's warriors warily authorized Man Afraid of His Horse to attend peace talks at Fort Laramie. The chiefs impressed on them that the commissioners might recommend the closure of the Bozeman Trail posts. Some warriors joined the village movement south; others, like Crazy Horse, who still refused to travel to Fort Laramie, agreed to observe a new truce pending negotiations.

At the village, the warriors met in council and formally transferred to the chiefs and elders control of negotiations. All would support a central line: closure of the posts, restoration of peace, and reinstatement of trade. Other topics—land cessions, farming, even the restoration of annuities—were not up for discussion. Finally, as proof of American goodwill, the chiefs must secure substantial presents of ammunition. Through his mouthpiece Little Hawk, Crazy Horse may well have been one of the warriors articulating the tenets of this minimalist peace.[11]

The crestfallen delegates returned two weeks later with nothing achieved. The commissioners had conceded merely that the Bozeman Trail might constitute a just grievance. Insisting that their agenda was purely investigative, they had refused even to dispense ammunition. Foreseeing a troubled summer, Man Afraid of His Horse had bleakly observed, "The powder must be very strong, if you are afraid to give us [even] that much." Hoping to secure desertions to Spotted Tail's friendly village, at the Platte forks, the commissioners finally turned a blind eye while traders exchanged stockpiled buffalo robes for powder and lead.[12]

To Crazy Horse and Little Hawk, none of their objectives had been met. Not only had the commissioners failed to close the Bozeman, reinforcements continued to pass up the trail. As if that were not enough, another five hundred soldiers were locating a fourth post, dubbed Fort Fetterman, to anchor the trail on the upper North Platte. News of this development forced a crisis in the village. Forty years later, Horn Chips recalled that this was the only time he and his hunka were separated: "Crazy Horse went north and [Horn] Chips came with the white people." Forty lodges, the personal kindreds of Man Afraid of His Horse and Red Leaf, started for the Platte forks. A single tipi—possibly Horn Chips' family—hurried south, to arrive in Spotted Tail's village on July 8 and announce the imminent arrival of the two chiefs.[13]

The news was premature. Although sources fall silent, it is clear that akicita deployed to prevent their chief's departure. Crazy Horse and Little Hawk were doubtless prime articulators of a movement to discredit the peace faction; after the diplomatic disaster, the mood of the village swung again behind them. Everywhere grass was up and the horses fattening. News from Red Cloud hastened the drift back to hostilities. His village was moving up Tongue River toward the Sun Dance rendezvous. After a month of desultory raids, a larger war party led by Yellow Hand reopened hostilities against Fort Phil Kearny on June 12, pointedly the day Man Afraid of His Horse met the commissioners. Again, on the eighteenth, the war party clashed with a cavalry patrol. Yellow Hand revived the decoy tactic but found the troops reluctant to bite. A final blow in this minicampaign was struck on June 30. The war party turned homeward to prepare for the Sun Dance.[14]

During the first days of July, the Man Afraid of His Horse village opened a cautious dialogue with Red Cloud. Mutual suspicion ran deep, and recriminations deteriorated into an ugly brawl when Bad Face warriors rode into the Hunkpatila camp. Elders intervened to prevent bloodshed. Crazy Horse and his comrades had a part to play, too, and things were patched up after Man Afraid of His Horse and the other chiefs produced the ammunition they had received through trade. In giveaways on the campground, they tried to create obligations among their Bad Face counterparts, presents of powder and ball committing the recipients to restoring reciprocity.[15]

Nevertheless, the chiefs favoring negotiations were marginalized again. Hunkpatila warriors forbade further talks, flatly declaring their chiefs to be fools. "The chiefs took the part of the whites," they rebuked, "they got the whites into our country, now the Buffalo are scarce and we can hardly live."[16]

The evidence indicates that Crazy Horse and Young Man Afraid of His Horse, as the band's ranking war leaders, represented the Hunkpatilas in the war councils to plan an offensive after the Sun Dance. Oglalas, Miniconjous, northern Brules—all agreed on a new principle articulated by Red Cloud: resumption of negotiations was impossible until the Bozeman Trail posts were abandoned. Crazy Horse acclaimed the new diplomatic bottom line. Tribal speakers declared that the Oglalas "were all determined to make war this summer [even] more actively than last." Akicita announced that no one would be permitted to travel to the Platte. Miniconjous, Sans Arcs, and Cheyennes joined the Oglalas, and a massive warrior party rode into the Bighorn foothills to force a trade for horses with the nervous Crows.[17]

For the Sun Dance, the gathering moved to the Little Bighorn, only forty miles from Fort C. F. Smith. Confident of victory, war leaders met to discuss strategy. Oglalas favored another attack on Fort Phil Kearny; most Cheyennes wanted to attack the Bighorn post. On the morning of July 31, a final council was held. Red Cloud forcefully argued that the first blow fall on Fort Phil Kearny: after it was destroyed, the alliance might take out the post on the Bighorn. Several Cheyennes and Miniconjous disagreed, and after a bitter quarrel, the leaders decided to split their force. Most Cheyennes rode to Fort C. F. Smith, while the Oglalas, Sans Arcs, and some straggling Miniconjous and Cheyennes would ride the one hundred miles to attack the fort on Little Piney Creek.[18]

The war party immediately set out, but hasty preparations showed in a lack of coordination. This operation would not be conducted with the precision and control High Backbone had demonstrated the previous winter. No blotahunka led the expedition; instead, knots of warriors formed around the "big braves" like Red Cloud, High Backbone, the Sans Arc Thunder Hawk, and Fast Thunder of the Oyuhpes. The largest group strung behind Crazy Horse, flanked by Young Man Afraid of His Horse. Their strength showed the solidarity of the Hunkpatila band in its new war front. The fifty or so Cheyennes led by Ice also clustered around Crazy Horse, fired by the inspirational example the Hunkpatila warrior now represented even to non-Lakotas.

Late on August 1, the war party climbed out of the Peno Creek valley to survey the environs of Fort Phil Kearny. Wood trains were once more busy in the pine-wooded foothills, and the party quickly agreed to attack first the woodcutters' camp six miles west of the fort. Between the big and little forks of Piney Creek lay a high meadow a mile or so square. Near the center, the wood party's escort, Company C, Twenty-seventh Infantry, had formed a corral of fourteen wagon boxes stripped of their running gear and laid in an oval to provide nighttime security for the wood train's livestock. On the south side of the corral was pitched a line of wall tents. The woodcutters were working the lower pinery, a mile south across Little Piney Creek, guarded by four soldiers. At the creek crossing, three more sentries manned a picket post.

In the early hours of August 2, the war party, at least six hundred strong, got into position, then filtered west along the hills north of Big Piney. Parties of warriors were still arriving, and smoke signals plumed the foothills soon after daybreak. Strategy called for the meadow to be surrounded, and before daylight, Crazy Horse led about half the force in a wide detour upstream, fording the creek and striking across the valley to enter the woods beyond Little Piney. Silently they approached the woodcutters' camp deep in the timber, finding a clearing dotted with sawyers' gear, tents, wagons, and smoking breakfast fires. One train had already started for the fort, and men had unhitched oxen and mules to load the second train with cordwood. Briefly, the warriors waited for the signal to attack, an assault to be synchronized with a rush on the mule herd and a charge on the corral from beyond the Big Piney.

Seven scouts led by High Backbone made the bid for the herd. Whipping their ponies into a dead run, they charged over the meadow. Sleepy sentries at the picket post sprang to life and at seven hundred yards opened fire, dropping the lead warrior's pony. Its rider scrambled up behind a comrade, and the charge continued. At sound of the shot, action broke out everywhere. Parties of warriors converged on the meadow, darting for the mule herd. A large force of dismounted warriors failed to drive off the animals, but sixty mounted braves galloped in, dispersing the herders and stampeding the mules behind Indian lines.

In the woods Crazy Horse led a charge that sliced into the woodcutters' camp. Alerted by the shots, most of the civilians and their escort had broken for the hills. An unfortunate four woodcutters were caught in the camp and killed by Crazy Horse's party. Two soldiers were also killed in the retreat. The warriors looted the camp, burning the tents and wagons and carrying off arms and foodstuffs. Some warriors seemed more intent on eating than on fighting. Crazy Horse's fifteen-year-old cousin, Eagle Elk, tried driving away a yoke of oxen. Most strung out in pursuit of the sentries who fled from the picket post toward the wagon boxes. The soldiers withdrew well, covering their retreat with a steady fire that felled Paints Yellow, an Oglala, and dropped the pony of Few Tails. In the timber Eagle Elk momentarily forgot the oxen and dashed across the meadow to rescue his cousin. From the corral, a sergeant raced out to lay down a covering fire for the sentries. Lead rained around Eagle Elk as he hauled back his pony and dashed for cover, Few Tails clinging behind him.

Inside the corral, Captain James W. Powell commanded a force of thirty-two men, including four civilians. Powell coolly watched the parties of warriors converging near the Little Piney. Riding in a circle formation that buzz-sawed closer with each pass, individual warriors charged to within yards of the corral—none nearer than Crazy Horse's cousin Fast Thunder, reckoned the bravest warrior in the battle. The command hunkered under cover, but they had an advantage unsuspected by the Indians. The warriors were used to the infantry being armed with single-shot muzzle-loading rifles, but in July, the garrison had been issued the new Springfield 1866 model breechloader. Although still single shot, the weapon was rapidly reloaded and reliable. Seven thousand rounds of ammunition lay at the defenders' disposal. Now they faced hundreds of warriors streaming along the south side of the corral, leaning low behind their ponies' necks as the soldiers dared the first volley.

Shots crashed out, felling ponies, unhorsing many warriors and wounding several more. Here lay the pause where determined warriors might overwhelm the wagons, but a fresh volley barked, dropping more ponies. The warriors fell away to regroup beyond rifle range. The soldiers observed many strip to the breechclout, as if for close combat. A few warriors lost all interest in the fight and fell to feasting on captured oxen before leaving the field. On a hill one half-mile east of the corral, a group of older war leaders including Red Cloud conferred. They pointed out that the curving bank of the Big Piney afforded cover within one hundred yards of the northwest side of the corral. A dry gully feeding the creek offered access for a foot charge below the soldiers' field of fire. Action shifted to this sector of the field. Gun-armed marksmen leveled a dangerous fire into the corral, killing Lieutenant John C. Jenness and two privates. Bowmen lobbed fire arrows that ignited hay and a month's accumulation of dried dung. During the lull, Powell's command worked tirelessly, dowsing fires, pooling scanty water supplies, and downing the tents that offered warrior cover. Scores of warriors were visible watching from the low hills or idling their ponies over the meadow.

As the baking morning drew toward noon, hundreds of warriors dismounted in the creek bottom and advanced in regular formation up the gully, voices raised in a low chant. At their head marched Red Cloud's nephew Lone Man, distinguished by a magnificent headdress. Within one hundred yards of the corral, they broke from the swale and charged forward in a wedge formation. Lone Man made a perfect target for the soldiers and fell dead, but the warriors advanced in broad line, only buckling when concentrated fire poured into their right flank. The warriors melted back into the swales, mounting little sallies that zigzagged from gully to gully, trying to drag away their dead and wounded. Two or three smaller charges on foot failed to carry the position, and four Miniconjous lost their lives in dashes to within feet of the corral.

As Indian will was sapped, the warriors regrouped below Red Cloud's position, summoned by mirror flashes and galloping messengers. Powell anxiously observed the knots of spectators dissolve to join the massing throng. A last mounted charge was driven in from the Little Piney, for the loss of one Cheyenne. Half-heartedly, warriors tried setting fire to the grass. Powell's sharpshooters targeted the hilltop conference of war leaders, and Red Cloud's group rapidly dispersed as the Springfields threw up dust around their horses' hooves. Down the trail, the tardy relief column appeared and lobbed a howitzer shell among the warriors. After four hours of action, it was time to leave the field. Crazy Horse, High Backbone, and Thunder Hawk each called to their followers that the fight was over. The warriors mounted and withdrew northward, leaving the field to Powell's doughty fighters and the welcome reinforcements. The Wagon Box Fight was over.[19]

It was time to take stock when the villages regrouped on the Rosebud. Cheyennes returning from the August 1 assault on Fort C. F. Smith could report a nearly identical repulse. Undoubtedly, warriors were concerned about the improved firepower of their foes, but the Lakotas and Cheyennes were not demoralized. Their losses were far from the hundreds soon claimed by Americans keen to expunge the memory of the Fetterman disaster, and their tally of stolen stock had risen again. Moreover, Red Cloud's strategic aims had been met. The Bozeman Trail had been closed to civilian traffic, and its strengthened garrisons forced onto the defensive. Supply trains were harried between the North Platte and the Bighorn, forcing the government to contemplate the unthinkable: closing the trail and removing the contentious garrisons.

Nevertheless, disappointment at a wasted opportunity may have been uppermost in Crazy Horse's mind as the villages prepared to scatter. Dissension and hasty rethinking of strategy had spoiled what should have been a victory as well timed as that over Fetterman. The failure to implement the clear command structure mastered by High Backbone in December had led to a bewildering spinoff of mini-battles as warriors chased stock, pursued stragglers, or simply sat out the fight. Crazy Horse had fallen on the woodcamp in good time, but when his force should have joined in overwhelming the wagon box corral, it was occupied in looting. Fifteen crucial minutes between the first shots and the massed charge on the corral were lost, and the battle with it. Behind their defenses, Powell's men were able to deploy their superior firepower and repeatedly repulse the most spirited charges.

Although five years would pass before he fought another large-scale action against troops, the Wagon Box Fight was a lesson not lost on Crazy Horse. Weaponry was a clear issue. Judging from the random sampling of bullet wounds sustained by Fetterman's men, less than 10 percent of warriors were equipped with firearms—and most of them were still the smoothbore flintlocks of the robe trade era. In the following decade, Lakotas would systematically seek to upgrade their firearms, so that at surrender in 1877, more than 50 percent of Crazy Horse's warriors would turn in a gun—a figure discounting the weapons they were able to cache. Moreover, although flintlock trade guns remained the core of their armory, more warriors tried to keep up with technological developments. Crazy Horse paid tribute to the weapon that won the Wagon Box Fight: by the early 1870s he owned a Springfield breechloader. Improved repeating rifles were also desirable, commanding the price of a good horse or a mule from traders operating without benefit of a license. By the Sioux War of 1876, about one in ten Lakota warriors was armed with a repeater. Crazy Horse would turn in no fewer than three Winchesters upon surrender.

The fighting around Fort Phil Kearny taught wider lessons too. Crazy Horse was temperamentally unsuited to the kind of fixed-position strategy that High Backbone had so devastatingly implemented against Fetterman—a victory reminiscent of woodland Indian warfare against colonial period troops. Massed foot charges, another standard tactic in prehorse Lakota warfare, were employed at the Wagon Box Fight—with disastrous results against improved firepower. All Crazy Horse's instincts lay in open action, the rapid deployment of mounted warriors against a moving foe. The kicamnayan tactic of mastering the moment of maximum instability favored fluid fighting in open terrain. In future battles he knew that he must keep the combat open and mobile, keep the soldiers on the run, and prevent them from securing a permanent defensive position. He would be prepared to risk much to dislodge the enemy from an unsatisfactory position, but would as quickly drop a costly assault on an impregnable defense. In a fluid fight, mounted warriors might count on their better riding skills, their shock and rapid-response capabilities, to isolate troop units. Deprived of the soldiers' greatest advantage—a coordinated command structure that overrode all sectional interests—the troops could be defeated piecemeal; of that Crazy Horse had been convinced in the Fetterman battle. In such fighting, the individualistic ethos of the Plains Indian warrior could better be deployed, turned to advantage against a foe prone to panic if prescribed tactical situations broke down. When full-scale warfare returned to the Powder River country, in 1876, Crazy Horse would have had time to digest these lessons.

As Crazy Horse's summer activities climaxed in the weeks following the Sun Dance, high diplomacy one thousand miles east was shaping the contours of the Lakota future. Washington policymakers turned to address the issue of Indian affairs with a renewed zeal following the end of the Civil War. Hawkish army chiefs and social improvers agreed that Indians should be excluded from a wide belt of the central plains. Two massive tracts of land were proposed, one north of Nebraska, the other south of Kansas, as reservations for the tribes of the northern and southern plains. Such a scheme isolated the crucial transcontinental routes along the Platte and Arkansas rivers from Indian interference, making the job of the army easier by separating the warlike nomads of the high plains into distinct regional blocs, and defining a swath of territory off-limits to Indians and subject to army jurisdiction.

The proposal satisfied Indian policy radicals by securing legally guaranteed reservations where the Indians could be protected from the worst effects of American civilization. The tribes would be culturally debriefed, and reeducated in the prevailing Christian, agrarian ethos to become yeoman homesteaders tilling the soil. Supported in the crucial transition years by increased subsistence spending on food, clothing, and hardware, Indians were expected to react with simple gratitude and be fully absorbed into the national mainstream within a decade. Thankless recalcitrants might regretfully be turned over to the military.

Such was the paradigm underlying the Indian policy review in the summer of 1867. On July 20 an act empowered the creation of a new Indian Peace Commission. Comprising a cross-section of military and civilian opinion, the commission was instructed to review once more the causes of Indian hostility, but this time their remit was extended to remove those causes, a concession that might have startling consequences for the Bozeman Trail garrisons. Army chiefs were loath to sacrifice the route, but Indian resistance had rendered it not a route to Manifest Destiny but an economic liability. And every westward mile of the transcontinental railroad being built across Nebraska reduced the significance of other routes over the plains. The generals were reluctantly prepared to pull back their posts and pour men and materiel into holding the Union Pacific line.[20]

Convening in St. Louis in August, the commissioners wasted no time in preparing the way for their progress. Loafer messengers were once more recruited, inviting the Oglala and Brule chiefs to meet the commission at Fort Laramie at the next full moon, September 13.[21]

Immediately following the Wagon Box Fight, the villages had scattered. The Man Afraid of His Horse village had returned to the middle Powder valley, where the peace chiefs remained discredited. Authority was recalled from the Deciders and vested in a thirty-man akicita force. Crazy Horse was among its leaders, with Little Hawk one of the leading speakers. The war council approved a new round of attacks along the southern Bozeman. On August 14 and 16 skirmishing resumed around Fort Reno, and over the next week Crazy Horse's raiders began targeting work details building Fort Fetterman on the North Platte.[22]

Early in September, the messengers from Fort Laramie entered the village. The initial response was muted. Akicita spokesmen reiterated that no negotiations were possible until the Bozeman Trail was abandoned. Man Afraid of His Horse would not publicly depart from this line, but he questioned the messengers closely and readily detected the shift in American opinion: closure of the contentious road was finally negotiable. The war council conceded that a party of five Oglalas and one Brule should accompany the messengers to Fort Laramie. They should remain there four nights, check the veracity of the messengers' news, and report back. Meanwhile envoys were sent to invite Bad Faces and Miniconjous to attend talks at the village. Black Twin hurried down to counsel; Lone Horn appeared with some Crow guests; and a Cheyenne camp arrived, so that by late September the village numbered three hundred lodges.[23]

Despite initial optimism, the latest round of talks was repeatedly postponed and finally foundered. The commissioners were delayed in dealing with the southern Plains tribes. At Fort Laramie, Lakota messengers were badly treated. Moreover, the real possibility of post closure convinced some that this was no time to quit the armed struggle. Crazy Horse and the Hunkpatila militants once more prevented

Man Afraid of His Horse from attending talks, delivering a flat rejection of negotiation: "[T]he whites have always deceived them and they no longer wish to come at their call."[24]

Late in October, the Red Cloud and Man Afraid of His Horse villages reunited for fall hunts. The war councils approved a new round of raids along the seventy-mile stretch of the Bozeman Trail, centering on Fort Phil Kearny. No large-scale campaign like the previous winter's was planned, and Fort Reno was dropped as a target. Instead, small war parties were permitted to target details patrolling the trail. Warriors first struck at the Crazy Woman crossing on October 20, losing one man; six days later, they attacked a cavalry patrol north of the fort. Early in November a supply train started for Fort C. F. Smith, escorted by a detachment of the Twenty-seventh Infantry under command of Lieutenant E. R. P. Shurley. On the fourth, the train wound along the course of Goose Creek a few miles north of modern Sheridan, Wyoming. The village was nearby, but with most of the warriors absent, a party of old men and boys rode over to investigate. Crazy Horse was present with a handful of fighting men, and as they scanned the line of covered wagons, they sketched out a strategy. Skylined atop a ridge, two outriders made a handsome target. A well-concerted fire tore into the escort, killing one soldier and wounding four more, including Lieutenant Shurley. Teamsters whipped up their mules, and the train hurried northward, abandoning two sutler's wagons. Satisfied with their coup, the ad hoc war party looted the wagons and drove one home. A rich stock of army blankets was among the booty. Crazy Horse is said to have selected a fine scarlet blanket for himself, and to have worn it until his death.[25]

Later in the month, after fall hunting closed, Red Cloud's village remained in the Tongue River drainage, but Man Afraid of His Horse moved east to the Powder south of Clear Fork. The two men remained in dialogue. Further raids followed, hitting patrols at Crazy Woman again on November 13, and at Lake De Smet on the 22nd. At this point, with war parties still in the field, a new peace initiative took hold. The commissioners outlined a new round of talks early the following summer to be held either at Fort Rice or at Fort Phil Kearny. They stated that a final decision on the future of the Bozeman Trail could not be made yet but proposed a truce, asking that Red Cloud and other chiefs accept a ceasefire until negotiations started. Finally, they were leaving a special agent at Fort Laramie to oversee preliminary negotiations through the winter: he would be happy to receive visits from the Lakota chiefs.[26]

A party of Bad Face scouts met the messengers and led them into Man Afraid of His Horse's village. Sensing a final breakthrough, the Hunkpatila chief moved firmly to consolidate village opinion. His brother Yellow Eagle, brother-in-law Blue Handle, Worm, and Little Hawk represented the other Hunkpatila tiyospaye. Crazy Horse was prominent among the war leaders the chief would have been careful to cultivate. A prized gift, or the pledge of a famous pony, may have accompanied the wand inviting Crazy Horse to feast with the band council. Man Afraid of His Horse forcefully presented the case for accepting the ceasefire proposal—the simple fact that, with winter approaching, the Bozeman Trail would be closed to all traffic. By spring, Lakota negotiators would have gauged the sincerity of the peace commission and could recommend a full peace or resumption of hostilities.

The chief quickly convinced the council that they had nothing to lose by agreeing to the truce. One by one, Worm and the other headmen assented and the pipe was passed, pledging each to the ceasefire. Crazy Horse's words were doubtless few and marked by a wary caution: oral tradition indicates "he decided to remain aloof" from the whole peace process, but he did not attempt to thwart negotiations. He would honor the truce, he tacitly agreed, until next spring; accepting the pipe, he drew a whiff and passed it along the arc of headmen.[27]

With his key war leader at least tentatively on board, Man Afraid of His Horse wasted no time in preparing a message for Red Cloud. Red Cloud saw the logic in the ceasefire proposal. Red Cloud was in the true sense a strategic war chief: he was fighting not a war of race hatred, but a contest for a set of explicit objectives. He saw those objectives now within his grasp. Once all the war parties were in, no more would be permitted out, Red Cloud promised. Tell the special agent, Red Cloud concluded, "I will come in and see him" once all was arranged.[28]

At the very end of November, 150 lodges met in general council. A party of fourteen young men and four women was deputed to meet the special agent. The party was led by Buffalo Tongue and by Crazy Horse's comrade Yellow Eagle III, son of the Hunkpatila second chief. Since the numbers exactly match the officers and female singers of the White Packstrap Society, this warrior club was probably prepared to support its founder's bid to negotiate a new peace treaty. Sounding out the special agent, the envoys were to assure him that Man Afraid of His Horse and Red Leaf would visit the fort before midwinter. Red Cloud too hoped to make the trip if his schedule permitted; if not, Black Twin might represent the Bad Face council.[29]

A new spirit of reconciliation marked relationships between the Oglala bands. Diplomacy was synchronized, both villages ordering the suspension of war parties. Messengers kept each informed of developments in their respective spheres. Once more spokesmen stressed the unity of Man Afraid of His Horse and Red Cloud in the round of preliminary talks with commission special agent A. T. Chamblin at Fort Laramie, and his counterpart H. M. Mathews at Fort Phil Kearny.[30]

On the Platte, diplomacy opened when the White Packstrap officers met Chamblin on December 6–8. Two larger deputations followed over the next month. They stated that they would seek to secure a general agreement for a treaty council at Fort Laramie. As he had done two years earlier, Man Afraid of His Horse argued for a tight schedule, proposing mid-April as the date.[31]

On Rosebud Creek the White Horse Owners deputed Red Cloud's brother Spider as its principal negotiator for the winter. Meeting with Mathews at Fort Phil Kearny early in January, Spider stipulated the closure of all three posts. It was the first time a Bad Face representative had included Fort Reno in his demands. The move assured Crazy Horse and Little Hawk that their agenda was being addressed, keeping intact the fragile consensus for peace.[32]

In March the two northern Oglala villages reunited high up the Little Powder. Almost immediately, positive word arrived that the War Department had ordered the Bozeman Trail posts abandoned. It was left to warrior societies to debate the parameters of a new modus vivendi with the United States. As one of the new generation of war leaders whose victories had forced the Americans to terms, Crazy Horse was a key player in these debates. Political engagement was still anathema to him, but the time spent with Sitting Bull had helped Crazy Horse shape instinctive beliefs into a consistent set of policies. Reflecting renewed harmony between chiefs and warriors, peace was to be restored with the Americans. Assuming the Bozeman Trail was closed, and no further trespass occurred in the interior of the Lakota domain, hostilities would permanently end. Trade, as the guarantor of interethnic cooperation, should be reinstated immediately.

So much reflected the restoration of the status quo. Other measures the warriors insisted on were more radical. Drastically redrawing the diplomatic paradigm established by the treaty of 1851, they demanded a minimalist peace, one without annuity goods in exchange for rights-of-way. Treaty presents, distinguished as "peace goods," were acceptable in the spirit of goodwill gifts "on the prairie." In return, the northern Oglalas and northern Brules were willing to concede all routes south of the North Platte. The warriors wished no more goods: they expected to trade for their necessities as of old—"not to get goods," they emphasized, "without trading for them." They specifically named Fort Laramie as their favored place of trading: the very term "agency"—*owakpamni*, referring to the distribution of annuities—was dropped in favor of the less divisive "trading post." Finally, the warriors accorded Red Cloud and Man Afraid of His Horse the roles of joint negotiators with the commission. Messengers were sent to announce that the northern Oglalas would arrive at Fort Laramie late in April.[33]

Meanwhile in Washington, the commission was putting the finishing touches to the treaty it would offer to the northern plains tribes. Its central clauses established the Great Sioux Reservation, bounded on the east by the Missouri River, on the south by the northern border of Nebraska, on the west by the 104th degree of longitude, and on the north by the 46th parallel. Comprising the western half of the present state of South Dakota, the reservation embraced the old Lakota heartland between the Missouri and the Black Hills. Elaborate clauses provided for the rapid transformation of the Lakotas from hunters to homesteaders. From the common pool of reservation land, every head of family would be guaranteed exclusive ownership of up to 320 acres suitable for agriculture. For variable terms, cooperating Indians would receive free seeds, cattle, agricultural implements, and comprehensive training in modern farming techniques.

Education was a priority of the document, with the government pledged to provide a schoolhouse with resident teacher for every thirty children enrolled.

Physicians, farmers, carpenters, and other craftsmen would also be payrolled by the Interior Department to serve the Indian community. For a term of thirty years, the United States agreed to supply annually clothing for every man, woman, and child. The commissioners were unwarrantedly optimistic about the time it would take for Lakota farmers to become self-sufficient. To fill the gap, subsistence rations of meat and flour were pledged for every person over the age of four for four years from date of enrollment on the reservation.[34]

These clauses satisfied the aspirations of radicals and reformers on and outside the commission and went some way toward fulfilling the needs of Indians not wedded to the old nomadic life. Many bands living along the Missouri no longer had access to rich hunting grounds: they knew that a new economic solution was imperative to the Lakota future. Meeting the westbound commissioners in early April, Spotted Tail also extended personal support for the reservation scheme.

The commissioners finally arrived at Fort Laramie on April 10. Immediately they dispatched runners to hurry in those bands still in the north. The northern Oglalas had grouped in four camps totalling 315 lodges along the northwest edge of the Black Hills: reflecting their renewed ideology of cooperation, Red Cloud and Man Afraid of His Horse remained in a single camp. Crazy Horse was probably also in the camp, ninety lodges strong on Bear Lodge Creek. Councils debated the news from Fort Laramie.[35]

The elaborate plans for a farming future held little attraction for Crazy Horse and his peers, but the runners indicated that the commissioners had approved territorial concessions that went some way toward addressing the warrior society terms. Two zones of hunting range, distinct from the reservation, had been agreed to, "so long as the buffalo may range thereon in such numbers as to justify the chase." In response to the demands of Spotted Tail and others, the commissioners extended one zone south, across western Nebraska to the Republican River. The second would comprise the region immediately west of the reservation, "north of the North Platte River and east of the summits of the Big Horn Mountains." The northern boundary of this "unceded Indian territory" was left tantalizingly vague, but the concession meant that the Powder River country was exempt from American occupation and trespass. In a bid to hasten in the northern chiefs, the commissioners guaranteed the abandonment of the Bozeman Trail and its garrisons "within ninety days after the conclusion of peace with all the bands of the Sioux Nation."[36]

Testing the commission's good faith, a deputation of chiefs and warriors parleyed at Fort Phil Kearny on April 8. The garrison seemed in no hurry to leave, and new unease gripped the Oglala camps. The Oyuhpes were the first to oppose going to Fort Laramie. The band council made a vague undertaking to join Miniconjou relatives in a second round of talks on the Missouri, scheduled to start in early June. Capitalizing on the uncertainty, Hunkpapa envoys from Sitting Bull were drawing Sans Arcs and Miniconjous out of the peace camps, and several small war parties were launched into the peace zone south of the Platte. As messengers from Red Cloud and Man Afraid of His Horse repeatedly warned of delays in the schedule, consensus began to unravel.[37]

Late in April, warrior society meetings withdrew all support for negotiations until the Bozeman Trail posts were physically abandoned. In traditions probably recalling these events, Crazy Horse is said to have rejected further negotiations over "False Papers."[38] Red Cloud and most Bad Faces and Oyuhpes ordered their camps moved west to the upper Tongue to monitor developments along the Bozeman. The Hunkpatilas were again divided. Frustrated, Man Afraid of His Horse remained committed to the treaty, but forty-five lodges of his band followed Yellow Eagle and Little Hawk west. Crazy Horse rode with his relatives. Early in May, Red Cloud sent the commissioners a message: "We are on the mountains looking down on the soldiers and the forts. When we see the soldiers moving away and the forts abandoned, then I will come down and talk."[39]

Red Cloud's son formed a war party to raid the Shoshones; chafing after months of idleness, Crazy Horse may well have joined it. In the Wind River valley, the Oglalas clashed with the enemy, but Red Cloud's son was killed, and the warriors withdrew. By the time they returned to the Oglala camps, political events had taken a new turn. Messengers had brought news that the Brules had signed the treaty and that Man Afraid of His Horse had finally gone in to open talks with the peace commission. Reassurances had convinced the Hunkpatila leaders to follow their chief to Fort Laramie. Even Red Cloud agreed that he would soon follow. But the news of his son's loss committed the Bad Face leader to sponsoring a war pipe against the Shoshones.[40]

Crazy Horse, still resisting any visit to Fort Laramie, remained on Tongue River, but in mid-June word from Little Hawk arrived of his reception at Fort Laramie. The post commander had approved issuing the Hunkpatila camp twenty-five beef cattle, while interpreter Charles E. Gueru handled the distribution of "peace goods"—"blankets, cloth, cooking utensils, butchers' knives, and some guns and ammunition." Convinced by Man Afraid of His Horse that the peace was a fair one, and with the clear impression that they were under no compulsion to settle on the reservation, Yellow Eagle and Little Hawk touched the pen. Their message concluded with a request that all war parties terminate operations.[41]

The report meshed with the warrior society demands for a minimalist peace—closely enough to convince Crazy Horse to rejoin his relatives. Red Cloud's people determined to remain in the north until the posts were visibly abandoned, but Crazy Horse hurried south. Man Afraid of His Horse impatiently laid plans for a separate Sun Dance southwest of the Black Hills. Pointedly, he issued no further invitations to Red Cloud. With the Bozeman Trail garrisons visibly gearing for abandonment, it was time at last to celebrate the victory of diplomacy.[42]

11

SHIRT OF HONOR

Summer had lengthened before the bands gathered in a single circle to offer the Sun Dance. At a spot high up the valley of the south fork of Cheyenne River, the *cangleska wakan*, or sacred hoop of tipis, stood on a wide flat of yellowing grass. Red Cloud's people would remain in the north, but the circle still comprised as many as two hundred lodges, fronting a campground a half mile in diameter. The northeast quadrant of the hoop, abutting the camp entrance facing east toward the Black Hills, was occupied by the fifty-five tipis of the reunited Hunkpatila band. Still living in the unpretentious lodge of his father and stepmothers, Crazy Horse had no household of his own; but as ever, the poor and infirm knew that this family's eldest son stinted no one in gifts from his herd and the bulging meat parfleches of Sun Dance time.[1]

In the center of the campground stood a large council tipi. For days the people had awaited a significant spectacle here. Ceremonial shirts were being made ahead of an investiture of a new generation of leaders. Fashioned from two whole mountain sheepskins, the shirts were painted in the sacred colors of the primary manifestations of Wakan Tanka: blue and yellow for the powers of Sky and Rock; red and green for Sun and Earth. Each was trimmed with quill-worked bands and fringed with locks of human hair donated for the purpose or taken from preserved enemy scalps. Some of an individual's spiritual essence, or *nagila*, was believed to inhere in the hair, so that to own another's hair was to exert a measure of control over him. Now the senior generation of Shirt Wearers was ready to step down and nominate successors. In investing leaders with the honor shirts, the council recognized them as Owners of the Tribe, able to bind the tribe to those decisions entrusted to them. By characteristic Lakota balance, that power was discretionary and might be withheld by the council. The shirts were "owned by the tribe," and, like their wearers' authority, might be recalled for due cause.[2]

For days holy men had prepared the shirts to the accompaniment of sacred chants and the reverent burning of sweetgrass incense. Now speculation was turning on the council's choice for the four Shirt Wearers who would replace the outgoing generation. With the elevation of Red Cloud, Sitting Bull, and High Backbone, the war years had seen a concentration of authority and status in the hands of new tribal-level war chiefs, as Lakota divisions sought to streamline their capacity for decisive leadership.

By contrast, the ceremony being so carefully stage managed asserted significant continuities with the prewar Oglala world. Leadership would be vested not in a single chief, but in the traditional four equals. Moreover, the ceremony affirmed and validated the new treaty. On the Missouri, northern Lakotas had confirmed the agreement—even Sitting Bull had indicated qualified approval by nominating a delegation to attend the Fort Rice talks. August would see the final closure of the three Bozeman Trail posts, a triumphant vindication of Man Afraid of His Horse's pursuit of a negotiated solution to the crisis on the hunting grounds.

The ceremony would celebrate the restoration of stability in American relations even as it honored the new generation of leaders who emerged in the war years. The candidates, chosen from the village's akicita leaders, were expected to retain their positions in the warrior societies, a bid to minimize the friction between chiefs and fighting men. The chosen four were men whose bravery and fortitude had won the war for the Oglalas. Now, to complete the Lakota virtues, the nominees must exercise generosity within the circle and acquire wisdom to lead the people.[3]

On the day of the ceremony, akicita opened the front of the tipi and rolled up the covers for the people to see the performance. A herald called the council members, and chiefs and headmen made their way across the circle to take their seats.

The loud proclamations drew people from work and play. Women laid aside craftwork, grandmothers gladly unbending from scraping hides or the laborious task of tanning. Youths ran in from the pasture, and gangs of boys gradually ceased their noisy games. The four honor shirts hung on racks before band chiefs and principal men. Akicita took command of proceedings. They spread four fine buffalo robes near the center of the floor space and led up painted ponies, their tails bobbed as if for war. Over the campground a group of women approached, carrying kettles. The akicita servants had kindled a fire near the entrance and took charge of the food. One kettle contained buffalo meat, symbolic of the people's staff of life; another, cuts of dog, a dish for honoring. A third kettle contained beef, issued at Fort Laramie, carefully chosen to symbolize the new relationship with the wasicu.[4]

From his seat with the chiefs, a herald rose to issue orders to the akicita. Several of the officers marched to the entrance and leapt astride their ponies. People were now agog, pushing toward the center and straining to see. Spectators fell aside as the akicita rode in pairs, scanning the crowd as if for game or enemies. Simultaneously they drew rein at the four semicardinal points of the circle and dismounted, hefting their whips as they marched into the crowd. Each pair seized the arm of a chosen young man and led him forward, as one might a captive. Then they firmly helped the warrior to mount, and seizing the bridle, led the pony toward the council tipi. Strings of whooping boys and youths tracked their progress, but the press was such that few could make out the riders until the horses drew up outside the entrance.

Throngs of women and children parted to see the four mounted men, stripped to breechclout and moccasins, their hands held aloft in supplication to Wakan Tanka. The akicita helped them dismount, then led them singly to sit on the robes facing the row of chiefs. First was American Horse, whose True Oglala band was the nominal parent band of the tribe. Twenty-eight years old, his courage as a war leader had been more than matched by his oratorical and negotiating skills in winning concessions from the peace commission. His father, Sitting Bear, sat in the arc of chiefs, one of the four Shirt Wearers of the previous generation. American Horse's selection was confidently expected. Women trilled the tremolo cry of praise.

Now a second candidate was led forward. Thirty-two-year-old Young Man Afraid of His Horse was the favored son of the head chief. A courageous fighter in the early stages of the war, he was already a trusted envoy for his father. Modest, unassuming, kind, and generous, to many he would remain the very model of the Lakota virtues. As he sat next to American Horse, eyes turned to the two remaining candidates. Seated on the rear pony, Sword Owner was another unsurprising candidate. His father was Brave Bear, another former Shirt Wearer. The chiefs and elders were plainly driving home an ideology of continuity in leadership.

As Sword Owner awaited his own cue, the third candidate dismounted. Officers led him onto the floor space, and people craned to make out his identity. If the pattern of other candidatures held, this should be one of the sons of the last of the old Shirt Wearers, the late chief Smoke. Such sons there were in plenty—here, visiting with the Loafers, and more up north in Red Cloud's village. According to one oral tradition, another mooted candidate was No Water, formerly a Harney treaty akicita and related by marriage to Smoke. But the slim figure being seated was none of these: to cries of recognition and acclaim, Crazy Horse sat in the row of candidates and modestly bowed his head.[5]

The crowd hushed as a sacred pipe was lighted and passed around the circle of elders. Each of the candidates drew a whiff, then the oldest of the chiefs stood and lectured them in their duties. As elders slipped the ceremonial shirts over the candidates' heads, he began, "Though you now wear the shirt, be a big-hearted man." His arm took in the arc of elders, then the steaming kettles, as he continued. "Do not think ill of other members. The food they eat is the vital element [that gives life to the people]."[6] Now his words stressed their responsibilities within the tribe. The Oglala people were given into their care, he explained. To the Shirt Wearers fell the ultimate responsibility of selecting campsites and hunting grounds. The tribe might call on them to decide any issue, resolve feuds, and conduct diplomacy. No longer could they be satisfied with the life of a simple warrior: each must shoulder the responsibilities of a chief. Generosity must be extended to the poor especially, he observed, gesturing to the widows and orphans of the post-ward camp. In a telling reference to the territorial concessions they had won from the peace commission, the old man enjoined the four to "look after the land."[7]

Turning to issues of tribal solidarity, he exhorted strength, forbearance, and harmony. "[T]here are many kinds of timber in this territory, some are weak, others stronger, only one is firm, sound, and stronger than all others[;] you are like this one"—he gestured toward the ashwood wand each councillor owned, the ash clubs and quirt handles of the akicita—"firm, sound, strong. Keep so, and do not get weak, the trail you are to lead your people [on] is narrow and full of thorns and cactus."[8] Intratribal feuding, sexual jealousy—these must be put aside. "[E]ven when your own brother falls at your feet mortally wounded," the candidate must remain calm. Should men seduce his wives, he must pay no more attention than if a dog urinated against his tipi. Never forget you are now a big heart, the orator concluded. To underline their role as mediators, pipes with quilled bags tied at their stems were placed in the candidates' hands: "Always remember your sacred Pipe," instructed the speaker.[9]

"These rules are hard to comply with, but we have given you this shirt. If you are to meet enemies, go right up to them; it is better to lie naked in death than to be wrapped up to harbor corruption."[10] To enshrine the candidates' warrior status, an eagle feather was tied at each man's crown, positioned to hang horizontally. Finally, akicita lighted the new Shirt Wearers' pipes, and each man smoked meditatively. Society headmen dished out portions of meat and offered a spoonful to each of the four, before bowls were filled for the whole assembly and the public ceremony closed with a grand feast. Crazy Horse and his comrades had been consecrated to the tribal good.

"Look after the land," Crazy Horse and his fellow Shirt Wearers had been enjoined. Within weeks of their appointments, events tested their commitment. Throughout the treaty proceedings, commissioner General W. T. Sherman had fretted at the concessions made to the Indians. As the commission wound down its operations, the hawkish commander of the Military Division of the Missouri was determined to secure control of Indian affairs from the Interior Department. On August 10 Sherman issued an order making the Great Sioux Reservation into a separate military district under command of General Harney. The army would control the reservation, while Indians remaining in the unceded territory would fall under the jurisdiction of local commanders. In instructions to Fort Laramie's General A. J. Slemmer, Sherman outlined a minimalist role for these de facto agents, whose main function would be to urge removal to the reservation. The arrival of a new peace commission special agent at the fort put these new undertakings to the test. Slemmer refused to cooperate with him, stating that Sherman's order left him in charge of local Indian affairs.[11]

On August 26 messengers from Red Leaf's camp arrived to ask permission to visit and trade. Slemmer was curt, telling the messengers that their people could

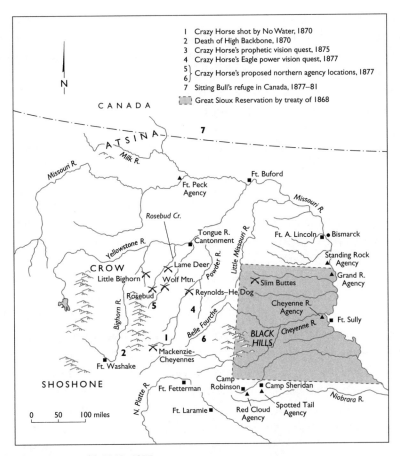

The Lakota world, 1868–1877

only trade on the reservation. Provisions were not available for them, and Indians were not welcome at the fort. Messengers apprised the Man Afraid of His Horse village, moving down Powder River, of the startling shift in army attitudes. Sherman and his subordinates had abrogated explicit verbal agreements reached with the commissioners. Military intransigence called into question the status of the unceded territory, threatening to unravel the whole accord.[12]

Crazy Horse and the other Shirt Wearers focused the debate in the council tipi. They came to a rapid decision to match Sherman's upping of the stakes. Hitherto, the Oglalas had evinced a relaxed attitude toward tribespeople going on the reservation. Besides the Loafers, Spotted Tail had led some two hundred lodges of peace party Brules and southern Oglalas from the Republican River hunting grounds onto the reservation. Grass had already detached his tiyospaye from the northern Oglala village, ready to start for the Missouri. In an edict soon matched by Red Leaf's village, the Oglala Shirt Wearers announced that the reservation was off-limits. If necessary, they declared, they would prevent further removal to the Missouri.[13]

A clamor by war leaders to mount raiding parties was sympathetically heard. Village composure had already been shaken by news of new hostilities breaking on the central plains, after southern Cheyenne warriors attacked settlements in western Kansas. The Shirt Wearers approved a limited number of war parties, doubling as fact finders, to target the zone south of the Platte. One, led by High Wolf, seized fifteen mules from an American party trespassing in the southern Bighorns, then, slicing southeast, lifted ten more at the military sawmill on Laramie Peak. Other raiders targeted herders and stragglers near Fort Halleck and the Union Pacific line. All served notice that the Lakotas could as readily abandon goodwill concessions as the army had.[14]

The cycle of raids was well disciplined, winding down quickly by mid-September. The village had swung north to Bear Lodge Butte and finally reopened dialogue with Red Cloud on the Yellowstone. An October rendezvous was arranged to discuss the latest developments. After three months of being in the public eye, Crazy Horse was keen to return to the relative anonymity of the warpath. The restoration of relations with the Red Cloud village offered an opportunity for adventure. Having discharged his functions as envoy, he visited with his old friend He Dog and quickly formed a war party to cross the Bighorns and raid the Crows or Shoshones. Rapid preparations notwithstanding, Crazy Horse had time to observe political developments in the village. Earlier in the summer, He Dog and the Oyuhpe Big Road had been named by the White Horse Owners as Shirt Wearers; after the withdrawal of the Bozeman garrisons, both Red Cloud and Black Twin were similarly honored for their strategic contributions. As the senior Shirt Wearer, Red Cloud was now pipe owner for a major expedition being planned against the Crows once the villages were reunited.[15]

Early in October the Man Afraid of His Horse, Red Cloud, and Red Leaf villages gathered to complete their fall hunts high up the Belle Fourche and Powder rivers. Visiting Sans Arcs, Sihasapas, and Hunkpapas came to weigh the diplomatic dividends of the season. It was decided that Red Cloud would travel to Fort Laramie and sign the treaty. The winter trade had to be finalized, and the Oglalas were determined to have their full share of the powder and ball that had been made available to their Crow foes. Moreover, Red Cloud could use the talks to express dissatisfaction with events. Late in the month, he led a deputation of some 130 headmen and arrived at the fort on the morning of November 4.[16]

Apprised of Red Cloud's approach, Slemmer's successor Major William M. Dye had requested instructions from headquarters in Omaha. Department of the Platte senior commander Christopher C. Augur acted on new guidelines from Sherman. On November 4, even as Red Cloud opened dialogue with Dye at Fort Laramie, General Augur readied a wire that reflected a further hardening of army resolve, ordering Dye to forbid any trade with Red Cloud's people, to instruct the Oglalas they could trade only at approved sites *on* the reservation, and to issue provisions expressly to expedite their journey to the Missouri.[17]

Had Augur's wire been read to Red Cloud, the Bad Face chief probably would not have signed the treaty. As luck would have it, however, the telegraph line along the North Platte was down, and Dye opened talks armed only with a copy of the treaty. In three days of debate, Red Cloud was by turns forceful, lordly, and blasé. He advised Dye that his mark on the treaty signified peace alone, and he blandly enumerated a string of provisos.[18]

Red Cloud pressed his own agenda. Where were the powder and lead? How extensive was the unceded territory? What were the exact provisions excluding Americans from it? Warily satisfied with those safeguards, convinced by his off-the-record talks that trade would be restored, Red Cloud "with a show of reluctance and tremulousness washed his hands with the dust of the floor" and placed his mark on the treaty on November 6.

Presents of powder and lead were not forthcoming, but overall, the Lakotas were satisfied with their reception. Perhaps the summer's setbacks had been but the whim of an ill-tempered soldier chief. With the American menace removed, successful winter hunts were predicted, and warriors readied horses, gear, and weapons for the renewed conflict with the Crows. Red Cloud moved easily from his role as diplomat to chairing the tribal war council, consulting war leaders, and strategizing. The Oglala Shirt Wearers yielded seniority to him, but as the Moon of Falling Leaves deepened, eyes turned west over the Bighorn passes to await the return of their greatest warrior.

12

STAYING SINGLE

The wide plain between the forks of Piney Creek lay fall brown. Barely three months before, the hated walls of Fort Phil Kearny had stood beside the wheel-rutted trail; now five hundred Lakota tipis rose from the flat. The pine stockades were blackened stumps, buildings charred shells that thrifty matrons looted for firewood. Here, Crazy Horse and He Dog returned from their fall warpath over the Bighorns. The pair had timed their arrival well. On the campground, hundreds of warriors were milling as the blotahunka made its final dispositions for the Crow campaign. When outriders announced Crazy Horse's return, an ecstatic crowd surged from the circle to welcome their hero.

It was a sight to make a warrior's heart swell. As many as three thousand people chanted acclaim, the crowd breaking apart to let the riders pass through the entrance onto the campground. Before a fire of dried buffalo dung, an arc of war leaders centered on Red Cloud rose to offer the pipe and welcome the returning warriors. As the day drew on, it was plain that a strain had been placed on tribal solidarity by the latest round of treaty talks. Wartime distrust between the Hunkpatila and Bad Face bands was rekindled, so responsible men looked with favor on the comradeship of Crazy Horse and He Dog.

That night, as bonfires blazed, blotahunka officers presented regalia—rattles, banners, and lances—to warriors selected to count coup in the coming battle. Two staffs bent like shepherd's crooks and wrapped in ancient wolf skin were the prime weapons of honor. Said to be three or four hundred years old, these tribal war lances dated from a time when the Oglalas and other Lakotas still lived in the lake country of Minnesota: the lances carried the aura of generations of Lakota victories. Now, proclaimed a herald, they were "the gift of the whole tribe . . . given by the older generation to those in the younger generation who had best lived the life of a warrior." To renewed acclaim, Crazy Horse and He Dog were led forward to accept the lances, each charged to kill an enemy in the battle ahead. Scarcely less important, their friendship was invoked to promote tribal solidarity in a time of fragile accord.[1]

The battle with the Crows proved joyfully inconclusive. Neither disaster nor victory, it whetted the appetite for warm weather and the resumption of full-scale raiding. In late November, active hunters began to plan surrounds for the winter hunt. Buffalo fur had thickened to a serviceable pelt, and many hunters expectantly awaited the arrival of traders from Fort Laramie. Another kind of planning seems to have been under way in Crazy Horse's tipi. By their midtwenties, most men settled down to family life: now twenty-eight, Crazy Horse had remained single longer than most of his contemporaries. Like parents the world over, Worm and Crazy Horse's stepmothers were concerned at this state of affairs. They wanted for their son the deep stability a good marriage offered; and, once tipis rose on the wintering ground, they opened dialogue with a suitable family.

The woman they wanted as daughter-in-law was Black Shawl.[2] At twenty-four years old, Black Shawl herself had "stayed single much longer than is usual among our people"—as her younger brother Red Feather observed. Most girls married in their early twenties, bearing their first child by twenty-two. Black Shawl was attractive and had the right family connections, living with her mother Red Elk Woman in the Oyuhpe band. The leader of their tiyospaye was the Shirt Wearer Big Road, instinctively committed to the hunting life away from the reservation. In family background, therefore, Worm and his wives showed real sensitivity in selecting a partner for their son.[3]

In marriage negotiations of this kind, a leading part devolved on the wooer's brother and close male kin. For Young Little Hawk, the reckless brother, this was a task of unwonted finesse. He paid a series of formal visits to Black Shawl's family, who hosted a feast for relatives, redistributing Young Little Hawk's gifts among the guests as the untried negotiator sought to close the deal. The *hakataku*, or older brothers of the prospective bride, in theory controlled her disposal in marriage. They presided at the feast and led family discussion. Marriage was in every sense an exchange, and a bride price had to be agreed on. Gifts were concrete metaphors for the obligations that bound families in kinship. Six buffalo robes or their equivalent was the standard price, but any hakataku worth his salt would talk up his sister's beauty, industry, and modesty to raise the price indefinitely.[4]

At length Young Little Hawk could report to his parents the desired outcome. The two families looked forward to an early wedding, but the happy prospect was blighted by two factors. First was Crazy Horse's attitude to the match. Normally, family negotiations paralleled an active courtship. As a young man, He Dog remembered, Crazy Horse had courted the girls, but during the war years in the Powder River country, he showed little interest in affairs of the heart. His parents and relatives had canvassed several prospective brides, but Crazy Horse had turned down the matches. Now, with war settling into the old cycle of raids against the Crows, he at last gave in and told Worm that he would marry Black Shawl. Although Black Shawl was an attractive young woman, the courtship seems to have been perfunctory and passionless, perhaps defused by the very familiarity Worm seized on as the key to a good marriage.[5]

The courtship climaxed with Black Shawl's brothers inviting Crazy Horse to join them in the family tipi. He was shown to a seat next to the bride-to-be, and she signified her own happiness at the match by smiling on him and fetching him water, food, and a pair of beaded moccasins she had made for this moment. To indicate his acceptance and announce a betrothal, Crazy Horse put on the moccasins.[6]

Black Shawl's health was the second factor in turning impending marriage into indefinite betrothal. Although she would live into her eighties, Black Shawl was a sickly young woman, prone to recurring respiratory illnesses. Winter brought on a new bout of sickness and bloody coughing, and her family now sought to postpone the marriage to keep their daughter in the nurturing care of home. Crazy Horse approved the deferral and sent word to Black Shawl's parents that "perhaps it was the best thing for her to do."[7]

Politics now raised its head, introducing a second theme that would dominate much of Crazy Horse's life for the next eighteen months: the question of the significance of the treaty signed at Fort Laramie. After the raid against the Crows, factionalism broke out anew between adherents of Red Cloud and those of Man Afraid of His Horse. At Fort Laramie, the repaired telegraph line had tapped in General Augur's order to ban all off-reservation trade. When word trickled north, some Bad Face warriors flatly disowned the treaty and wished to resume raiding. Tensions resurfaced with the Hunkpatilas when they threatened "to kill 'Man afraid of his horses' in consequence of his efforts for peace."[8]

Hunkpatila partisans were incensed by Red Cloud's continued dominance of tribal council proceedings. A further element in the escalation of tensions was an unexpected one: scarcity of game. For three years, warriors and holy men had ascribed poor hunts to the American occupation of the hunting grounds, but this winter was shaping into another hungry season. The Piney Creek district was an ideal site, a winter haven for buffalo and elk, but game was unaccountably scarce.

A big council was held in December at which these issues came to a head. To forestall dangerous factionalism, the village split. Man Afraid of His Horse and his followers, about two hundred lodges, moved south. The split probably divided Crazy Horse's and Black Shawl's families. Man Afraid of His Horse led his camp to new winter quarters on Lance Creek sixty miles north of Fort Laramie. Red Leaf's Wazhazhas went south also.[9]

Game was no plentier on Lance Creek, and the village was soon augmented by seventy-five lodges of southern Oglalas. Wary of military reprisals after a season of warfare on the Republican, headmen Whistler and Pawnee Killer reported that the rest of their band had joined the trek to the Missouri River. As the year turned, removal to the reservation became a live issue. The chiefs and Shirt Wearers debated a visit, but news from the Missouri was discouraging. They learned that an agency had been established for the Brules and Oglalas at the mouth of Whetstone Creek, but provisioning was inadequate and game virtually nonexistent. Man Afraid of His Horse, Red Leaf, and Grass declared again that they would not go to the Missouri River.[10]

Further discouraging news came regarding trade. Grass visited Fort Fetterman in mid-January to seek traders but was told flatly that all trade must be conducted on the Missouri reservation. Spider, Red Cloud's regular envoy, appeared late in January to debate with his father-in-law Man Afraid of His Horse. Visiting Fort Laramie, Spider declared that Red Cloud would come to the post in the spring, expecting to trade: closing commerce on the North Platte would threaten the fragile peace won by the treaty.[11]

In March Red Cloud and Man Afraid of His Horse reunited and swung south to Rawhide Creek to appeal at Fort Laramie for provisions. An inconclusive parley at the fort, in which both sides attempted to cow the other, concluded with commander Dye issuing limited rations. Faced with another rejection of the reservation, he advised the chiefs "to go north at once, where they can find game."[12]

The northern Oglalas returned to upper Powder River, where Red Cloud, who had continued to plan a vengeance raid against the Shoshones, reasserted his status as tribal war chief. Oglala war parties operated in the Wind River country from April through September. A tribal policy of opening the Shoshone ranges to Lakotas is detectable, surely acclaimed by Crazy Horse and the Shirt Wearers. Loosely cooperating with the northern Arapahos, whose chiefs were pursuing a negotiated joint-use zone on Wind River, the Oglalas pressed raids against the Shoshones. They also harried new American mining settlements near South Pass, as well as Camp Augur, a military post established to oversee the Shoshone reservation. Crazy Horse was undoubtedly involved in this warfare, stealing stock and killing outlying enemies both Shoshone and American.[13]

The raiding season would be the last carefree summer of Crazy Horse's life. Raid and counterraid against the Shoshones made a relaxed coda to the war on the Bozeman Trail. Both Crazy Horse and his brother distinguished themselves in the fighting. They made an incongruous looking pair. The elder brother remained plainly dressed, but Young Little Hawk, at twenty-three still the family pride, was always turned out in fine clothing, riding a mettlesome pony hung with fancy saddle trappings. The boundless confidence instilled in him as a child beloved was reflected in a recklessness that lent a dangerous edge to his courage. Some elders already opined that his bravery would make him a greater warrior than even his elder brother; fighting men like He Dog concluded that Young Little Hawk was too reckless, exposing himself to any danger regardless of tactical considerations.[14]

A skirmish recalled by Short Bull may have taken place this summer. The Oglala war party was pursued down Little Wind River by an outnumbering

Shoshone force. Crazy Horse and Young Little Hawk formed the rearguard, making crisscross maneuvers across the retreat to hold off the Shoshones. At length, Crazy Horse's pony played out, and he turned the exhausted animal loose. Young Little Hawk dismounted and drove off his own mount. In set-piece combat, the pursuers reined in and two Shoshone warriors rode out to fight hand to hand. Dismounting, the warriors closed on the Oglala brothers for a fair fight.

"Take care of yourself," Crazy Horse told Young Little Hawk; "I'll do the fancy stunt." Crazy Horse ran at the first Shoshone in his characteristic rush—blindingly quick, seemingly without any forethought; it was his most obvious use of the kicamnayan tactic, tripping up one's foe by sheer speed, wresting the initiative from the situation. The two men grappled, but in the struggle, Crazy Horse got the better of his foe. The second Shoshone showed a clean pair of heels, and Young Little Hawk joined his brother. Mounting the two enemy horses, they shook the Shoshone scalp in defiance and watched the pursuit melt away. The exultant brothers galloped after their comrades.[15]

Another strand in Crazy Horse's life surfaced in the carefree aftermath of the Shoshone summer. Already he had begun a clandestine relationship with a married woman: by fall, it had become public knowledge—and "trouble" for the Shirt Wearer. Famously beautiful, near Crazy Horse's age, Black Buffalo Woman was Red Cloud's niece. Moreover, her husband was No Water, the brother of Black Twin. Now thirty-seven, No Water was associated with the pro-American factions: he had been one of the akicita recognized under the Harney agreement of 1856. More recently, he was allegedly passed over as candidate for Shirt Wearer in favor of Crazy Horse. Bad blood might have existed between the men since the ceremony; certainly the Hunkpatila–Bad Face dimension of the affair carried potential for a dangerous feud.

Mari Sandoz decided that the couple had been childhood sweethearts separated by a cruel ruse of Red Cloud's, and that Black Buffalo Woman had yearned for Crazy Horse through years of unhappy marriage. Sandoz's romantic, hugely influential reconstruction may possibly have roots in Pine Ridge gossip, but the major sources she consulted are entirely silent on the matter. The single most important source, He Dog, simply remarked that Crazy Horse "had been paying open attention to the woman for a long time" when the affair climaxed in May 1870.[16]

"Paying open attention to the woman" hardly amounted to a full-blooded adulterous affair, brazenly carried on in the open spaces around camp—such were many liaisons. Rather, it suggests the kind of transparent solicitousness that begins in uncharacteristic meetings, unscheduled visits, halting words. To talk to a woman was one Lakota idiom for courting, and talking, communication, may have been important in Crazy Horse's emotional makeup. Certainly, in the last love affair of his life, the passionate relationship with Nellie Larrabee, was an unusual level of trust and communicativeness, a willingness to accept her words unprecedented in Crazy Horse's dealings with anyone other than the holy men he revered (see chapter 23). This need for communication, like so much else in Crazy Horse's life, may be rooted in the loss of his mother. Certain women were able to cut through the defenses of withdrawal and reserve, the heyoka melancholia, and speak with the living man.

Crazy Horse may have openly courted Black Buffalo Woman, stopping to talk intimately as she labored over scraping hides or in the bustle of moving camp. Perhaps during No Water's absences, Crazy Horse haunted the spaces in back of her tipi, attempting the plangent minor-key themes of the Lakota love flute. Certainly, gossip credited him with securing love philters to seduce Black Buffalo Woman. Such images contrast with the perfunctory courtship of Black Shawl, suggesting that the affair had its origin in the months before his family opened marital negotiations on his behalf.

"No Water did not want to let the woman go," recalled He Dog, which suggests that the possibility of a divorce was openly discussed and dismissed by No Water. Marriage was essentially a civil matter, contracted between individuals and families. Adultery, laziness, incompatibility—all were reasonable grounds for either husband or wife to initiate divorce. Although lifelong fidelity and successful marriage represented an ideal, Lakotas were realistic about personal happiness—divorce was reasonably common and carried little opprobrium, the security of children being cushioned by the deeper continuities of the extended family. No Water's measured response also suggests that his reactions were constrained by the lack of evidence for sexual infidelity. A cuckolded husband might avenge himself on the lover and inflict punishment on his wife, to the extent of cutting off the tip of her nose before publicly throwing her away. No Water did not take this course. The fragmentary evidence indicates that though everyone knew of the emotional attachment, no one knew for certain if sexual intimacy had taken place.

By late 1869 the affair was becoming a talking point. Horn Chips was one of the disillusioned Oglalas who drifted west from the reservation that fall, and living in Black Twin's tiyospaye, he was well placed to observe the intrigue. As a Shirt Wearer, of course, Crazy Horse had pledged a life of self-denial for the people's good. The affair sat uneasily with that pledge, carrying potential for an explosive feud in the already strained relations between the Hunkpatila and Bad Face bands. That it continued for so long without an obvious resolution may reflect the pressure on Crazy Horse of elder opinion and advice to suppress his desires. Similar forces might have enjoined forbearance on No Water. Perhaps elders were involved in the dialogue resulting in No Water's refusal to divorce Black Buffalo Woman, which would indicate the seriousness with which Crazy Horse viewed his relationship with her and the wish to formalize the situation with formal divorce and remarriage. To go beyond these outer limits of speculation, however, would require suspending critical faculties and, like village gossips, offended husbands, and romantic novelists, creating a pleasing fiction.

By late summer, Lakota political debate continued to center on the reservation issue. Reports to the military agent at Whetstone indicated that the northern

Oglala leadership was contemplating a goodwill visit to the agency. Even Red Cloud had dropped his categorical opposition to the Missouri reservation. The spring changeover in akicita clearly was a factor, but continuing depletion of game resources in the upper Powder River country was fundamental. Through the 1870s, buffalo range would perceptibly contract north into Montana. As fall approached, Shoshones gathered in strength to reoccupy their Wind River hunting grounds, and the Oglalas were left with a choice: seek government rations or move farther north.[17]

In 1869 a new concept emerged in the Oglala political lexicon. In the familiar context of resolving threats to tribal solidarity, chiefs and elders formulated a middle way in defining future relations with the Americans. Amazingly enough, the concept is known from a rarity: a political speech by Crazy Horse. "Living with the wasicu *gradually*" (*iwastela*) became such a buzz phrase that even Crazy Horse was forced to use it. The iwastela concept recognized that the old nomadic life was not indefinitely sustainable: game was contracting, and Lakotas would eventually have to adopt the reservation solution to their predicament. What was at issue was the timeframe for the transition. Iwastela proponents envisaged a gradual adoption of farming and reservation life spread over a generation or more. Bands and individuals might move easily between reservation and hunting grounds, easing tensions and reducing the demands placed on the buffalo herds.[18]

By the end of summer, a trickle of disaffected Oglalas gravitated back from the reservation. Their reports were not encouraging. Rationing and supply problems were compounded by a proliferation of unsupervised whiskey traders, threatening Lakota communities with disruptive violence. Reminded of their pledge to provide healthful campsites, Crazy Horse and the Shirt Wearers demurred from the incipient consensus. Council agendas shifted, iwastela was put on hold, and the Oglalas shifted north to Tongue River in September.

During the cooling Moon of the Black Calf, new arrivals in the village confirmed the closure of Lakota hunting options. A straggle of families arrived from the Republican River hunting grounds of the southern Oglalas. Twenty-one-year-old Little Killer was among them, the younger brother of Club Man, husband to Crazy Horse's sister. From now on, Little Killer would travel with his brother's family, which split its time between Black Twin's tiyospaye and the Hunkpatilas. Little Killer told Crazy Horse that troops had cleared the central plains of Indians, defeating the Dog Soldier Cheyennes at Summit Springs in July and driving the fugitives in flight—south to the Indian Territory reserve below the Arkansas, or north to refuge in Lakota country. Many more southern Oglalas were trekking into the reservation to seek safety in Spotted Tail's peace party village. General Sherman's path smoothed by reckless warrior outrages, he had been able to wrest control of an unceded hunting-ground zone recognized in the treaty of 1868. Uncontested by Indians, American hide hunters moved onto the central plains. The expansion of transcontinental railroads facilitated a new market for buffalo products, just as steamboat power had driven the robe trade of the previous generation. Over the next five years, hide hunters would hunt out the remaining buffalo on the central plains, shipping millions of hides to feed the demand in eastern factories for industrial belting.[19]

Debate intensified on resuming hostilities by targeting the growing mining community in central Wyoming Territory. Man Afraid of His Horse and other moderates could point to Cheyenne outrages as triggering the last round of hostilities, legitimizing army intervention on the central plains. The Hunkpatila chief argued for moving winter quarters to the reservation, where diplomacy could buy time. Underlining the growing bitterness between the two leaders, Red Cloud moved to polarize the debate, arguing that only Lakota military capacity could secure their ends. To serve notice of his conviction, Red Cloud personally led a war party south to the Sweetwater valley, returning early in October with a valuable haul of mules. The Bad Faces had shifted away from the iwastela compromise.[20]

As fall wound on, these tensions snapped tighter. In an unforeseeable twist, John Richard, Jr., wanted for killing a corporal at Fort Fetterman, fled with his Oglala wife to sanctuary on Powder River. Volatile, vengeful, and packing six kegs of gunpowder, Richard used the ammunition to rebuild his Oglala kinship networks, arguing for reprisals against the offending garrison. After Red Cloud accepted some of the powder, widening the scope of hostilities, Man Afraid of His Horse angrily withdrew from council. Detaching twenty lodges, his own personal following, he left the village, bound for the reservation, splitting the Hunkpatila band. Many Hunkpatilas like Crazy Horse were prepared to return to a war footing. About this time, Crazy Horse left his natal band to join the Oyuhpes, where the Shirt Wearer Big Road maintained a simple line of minimal relations with the Americans. The move demonstrated once more Crazy Horse's disenchantment with the poisoned politics of Hunkpatila–Bad Face relations and his determination to remain a simple fighting man.[21]

Over the next weeks, scouts and raiders infested the upper North Platte, gathering stock and intelligence, killing straggling soldiers and civilians. Seven or eight parties of twenty-five men apiece were in the field, Crazy Horse among them. Richard maintained contact with his family and, with access to Wyoming newspapers, learned of alarming developments in the territorial capital, Cheyenne. Wyoming entrepreneurs were unhappy with the treaty of 1868, which confirmed the status of the Powder River country as unceded Indian lands, and through the winter of 1869–70, powerful forces organized a springtime invasion of Lakota territory, openly flouting the treaty. The projected Big Horn Expedition would field a massive civilian survey of northern Wyoming's agricultural and mineral resources. Furnished with a military escort and armed to the teeth against Lakota reprisals, it threatened to set back Indian relations to total warfare.[22]

Through December the war parties grew. Groups of seventy or more targeted mail patrols between forts Laramie and Fetterman, making attacks of surprising boldness. Crazy Horse took an increasingly central role in war party organization, co-coordinating tactical activities. In midwinter John Richard spread word of the Big Horn Expedition down the Powder River valley. Although Sitting Bull's Hunkpapas registered no interest in the news, many Miniconjous vowed to join the Oglalas in resisting the invasion. High Backbone's tiyospaye joined the Oglala village. A few Sans Arc warriors ignored their chiefs' counsel and joined the growing war faction. More war parties were recruited, constantly traversing the country down to the Union Pacific line to secure mules, scalps, and news. In January, three parties of one hundred men each left the Oglala village.[23]

En route to Whetstone, Man Afraid of His Horse's small following fragmented. Checked by news of the Big Horn Expedition and reports that drunken violence was rocking Whetstone after Spotted Tail's self-defense killing of Loafer chief Big Mouth, the Hunkpatila chief turned back. The crisis over the Big Horn Expedition only convinced him further that a diplomatic solution must be found to the impasse, and that Red Cloud must be brought aboard the peace process.[24]

In a startling shift, another principal emerged to play the peace card: John Richard, Jr., thinking of his future in a changing world, realized that bringing Red Cloud aboard the peace train might net him a pardon. Through the winter, Richard remained in touch with developments on the frontier and in the East. He was aware that a sea change had taken place in Indian policy. The army's massacre of 173 Blackfeet Indians on the northwestern plains outraged the eastern public, discrediting the hardline militarism of General Sherman. President Grant moved to counter criticism by removing reservation administration from the military and placing it in control of the churches—Grant's Indian "peace policy" was born. Astute playing of the new Washington mindset could reap dividends.[25]

The national controversy was echoed in the northern Oglala village. The aftermath of the treaty had at least convinced Red Cloud of the necessity of an ongoing dialogue with the government, and with coaxing from Richard and Man Afraid of His Horse, he decided that the channel of negotiation should not be closed. Prompted by Richard, the two leaders sent a joint message to Fort Laramie in the first week of March 1870. They announced that they would arrive at the fort by month's end, ready to trade or to fight. The intransigent tone appeased all shades of opinion. Immediately the village broke up and started south. The main camp advanced up Powder River, as the second, with the more suspicious Oyuhpe band at its core, moved down the west flank of the Black Hills. Augmented by dissident Hunkpatilas and Miniconjous, the Oyuhpe village numbered about 150 lodges.[26]

In the Oyuhpe camp, Crazy Horse organized a war party to reconnoiter the Sweetwater valley, now a mining center and a possible avenue for the Big Horn Expedition. The party numbered some of his closest relatives, including Young Little Hawk and his eighteen-year-old cousin Eagle Elk. High Backbone, mourning the death of his mother, may have been in the party. Entering the Wind River country late in March, they found uncomfortable allies in the northern Arapahos, still pursuing their negotiations with the Shoshones. Although the Arapaho chiefs were committed to peace with the neighboring Americans, younger warriors were browbeaten or coaxed into joining Crazy Horse's party. Scattering into the Sweetwater country, warriors targeted mining communities, picking off stragglers. Six civilians were killed on April 2, prompting the miners to mount a bloody reprisal, attacking the Arapaho camp four days later and killing the principal chief, Black Bear.[27]

With the warm moons opening, Crazy Horse knew the departure time for the Big Horn Expedition was near. To begin coordinating a screen of war parties operating across southern Wyoming, he departed for the Oyuhpe camp, two hundred miles east. Young Little Hawk remained in the west, his fifty or more warriors continuing to harry miners, troops, Shoshones, and even Utes, relaying reports to Crazy Horse.[28]

As Crazy Horse journeyed east, new developments changed the situation out of all recognition. Red Cloud and Man Afraid of His Horse, their village still advancing up Powder River, had forwarded a more placatory message to Fort Fetterman, stating they wanted peace and permission to trade. Army top brass and the Cabinet predictably rejected the proposal out of hand, but the diplomatic gamble was about to pay off handsomely for the Oglala leaders. Signaling the new independence of the Indian Office, the commissioner of Indian Affairs announced that the government was ready to locate a trading post "at such point in the Indian Territory as Red Cloud may select as his camp." This artfully phrased concession was redrawing the political map in the Oglala camps. In the main village near Pumpkin Buttes, Red Cloud and Man Afraid of His Horse were creating consensus for a dramatic break in the logjam of U.S. relations: an Oglala delegation to visit Washington and resolve the burning issues of trade, trespass, and agency location. The iwastela policy was back on track.[29]

These developments had yet to take root in the warier Oyuhpe camp on Rawhide Creek, where the council remained on a war footing. Crazy Horse started a new war party south, bound for the Union Pacific line to monitor the Big Horn Expedition's departure from Cheyenne. On the morning of April 19, the warriors forded the North Platte just north of Fort Laramie, then fanned out to reconnoiter the post. Crazy Horse, riding alone up a ravine one-half mile from the fort, confronted a civilian, George Harris, riding down the defile to hunt ducks. With no time to draw rein, Crazy Horse instinctively raised his rifle and snapped off a passing shot that shattered Harris's leg just above the ankle. Immediately, more shots echoed, and several warriors appeared on the hills around the post. A shocked garrison turned out, ready to repulse any charge through the open parade ground. Colonel Franklin F. Flint ordered a detachment of mule-mounted infantry in pursuit. Crazy Horse signaled disengagement, and the warriors withdrew across the North Platte, firing at a civilian wagon but doing no damage. Save for Harris's amputated leg, the little skirmish claimed no casualties but was notable for yielding the earliest printed notice of Crazy Horse by name.[30]

Throughout late April, warriors from the Oyuhpe village continued to scour the environs of Fort Laramie. Scouting parties were constantly seen on the hills across the river, and patrols followed a crisscross of trails between outlying ranches. Crazy Horse coordinated a party that fanned out across the country south of the fort, gathering stock and intelligence south toward the railroad and east to the Nebraska line. On the afternoon of April 28, the sleepy mail station on Chugwater Creek was jerked awake by the sudden rush of twelve warriors on the stock corral. A second party of eight warriors joined the assault, but the defenders laid down a heavy fire. Crazy Horse knew stationmaster Portugee Phillips to be a resourceful frontiersman from the Bozeman Trail War, and the Oglalas withdrew up the creek, then struck Ben Mills's herd camp, killing several cattle and cutting off two cowboys. Nearby, several warriors made a dash on a mule herd to be met by herders' lead that killed two and wounded a third. As the Moon When the Ponies Shed opened, Crazy Horse moved his men down to the Union Pacific. The Big Horn Expedition had announced a mid-May departure from Cheyenne.[31]

While Crazy Horse's war parties were busy, Red Cloud and Man Afraid of His Horse had won agreement in the main village to send a delegation to Washington. They elected to open dialogue at Fort Fetterman, weaker and more remote than Fort Laramie, where a number of trusted interpreters and officers were based. After the Indian Office concession on trade, the village council approved a placatory opening gambit: the Oglalas were ready to settle permanently on the reservation if a suitable sector could be agreed on away from the Missouri. They would demand trade, ammunition, and rationing for their people while the delegation was gone. John Richard, indicted murderer and gambling man, was the chiefs' ace in the hole. The Oglalas would present themselves as his captors—and protectors. Asserting Richard's diplomatic immunity, they would insist on taking him to Washington as interpreter. There Richard would abide the decision of the federal authorities. The Richard gambit elegantly summed up the Oglala position, matching conciliation with force.[32]

By late April, the village had reached consensus on this stance. The Bad Face peace chief Brave Bear lent his seniority to the cause, and several warrior societies, meeting for their spring renewals, approved the proposals. Then, in a development that undercut Crazy Horse's militant position, the Oyuhpe band came on board the iwastela process. Fundamental to this transformation was Red Dog, one of the strategic architects of the Bozeman Trail War victory. Now, convinced of the game crisis on the plains, he threw all his organizational and oratorical skills behind iwastela. The Oyuhpe village started west to join the Oglala Proper. Even before the villages united, Red Cloud, Man Afraid of His Horse, Brave Bear, and Red Dog were named as envoys to open dialogue. Four warrior societies served as escort, validating the chiefs' credentials. On April 25, they opened four days of talks with the Fort Fetterman commander, urging that their proposals be telegraphed east.

On the twenty-eighth, the same day Crazy Horse's raiders struck the Chugwater, the envoys departed, promising to unite all the bands and leaving Young Man

Afraid of His Horse to relay messages from the fort. Days passed in tense silence. In Washington the president was absent, and General Sherman once more opposed the Oglala initiative. Then, on May 3, a Cabinet meeting signaled the limits of Sherman's influence under the new dispensation, approving the delegation. A grim-faced Sherman followed up with authorization for limited rationing at Fort Fetterman. Departmental headquarters wired the news to Fort Fetterman, and Young Man Afraid of His Horse, with his father and Red Cloud, departed on May 7.[33]

Crazy Horse's war parties were still in the field in the first week of May. His own party shadowed the railroad on the Laramie plains, west of Cheyenne. On the Sweetwater, Young Little Hawk's party clashed with a Second Cavalry patrol on May 4, suffering casualties in a stiff pursuit. To the Oglala tribal council, these eyes and ears were suddenly loose cannons, endangering the success of the delegation. Messengers were probably sent to announce a truce and summon the war parties home immediately after the Fort Fetterman dialogue, and Crazy Horse was undoubtedly dismayed at the news. Leaving some warriors in the field, he and a bodyguard of faithful warriors rode to the Fort Fetterman area, where Crazy Horse conferred with a local Loafer about the latest developments.[34]

From there Crazy Horse's party struck north to join the united village, 350 lodges strong, at the head of Powder River. For weeks he had worked tirelessly, skillfully co-coordinating warriors and scouts across a two hundred-mile front, but no hero's welcome awaited this return. According to an anonymous Lakota report at Fort Fetterman, Crazy Horse's party had been singled out for exemplary punishment. Akicita turned out to meet him, demanding the party turn over seven horses and mules stolen along the Chugwater. When the warriors refused, the akicita whipped them and turned over the stolen stock at Fort Fetterman to confirm the return of peace.[35]

Events left Crazy Horse no time to brood. Lakota society moved quickly to rehabilitate offenders, and councils were constantly in session to finalize the delegation, even proposing Crazy Horse be a delegate. But as Thunder Tail recalled, Crazy Horse "did not have confidence" and quietly refused the invitation. He made his first remembered speech in council: "This nation will," he conceded, "gradually [iwastela] be living with the wasicu," but he went on to spell out his misgivings: "I fear the land will be taken under duress without payment." Urging the messenger to return to the North Platte, he confirmed, "Soon I shall come. If I were present," he reiterated, "I would not sell [the land] to the wasicu. So take the message: I shall go slowly [iwastela]." The speech skillfully summed up his doubts, identifying his minimal demands of the delegation while assuring the council that he remained committed to dialogue. Finally, he turned the season's buzzword around and placed his own take on iwastela, playing on its literal and figurative connotations to assert the primacy of his own agenda.[36]

A major raid on the Crows was being planned, an enterprise to unite all shades of opinion. The Crow Owners Society was staging its spring reunion, and society leaders nominated Crazy Horse as one of its lance bearers. A pair of black-painted officers, stuffed crowskins fastened to their hair and feather bustles at their hips, man-handled Crazy Horse to the society shade and seated him roughly on the floor space. Beside him sat He Dog, the pair chosen once more to illustrate tribal solidarity. Thrust into the ground before the candidates were two short lances, bound with otter skin and mounted with a crow's head. As a herald harangued, the society singers led the membership in songs memorializing previous bearers. Lance owners were chosen to die, pledged to thrust their lances through their society sashes and peg themselves to the ground in battle. As Crazy Horse and He Dog grasped the lances, they vowed to go immediately to battle—"to tempt his fate, or to test his virtue."[37]

The Fight When They Chased Them Back to Camp would go down in Lakota annals as one of the great set-piece battles against the Crows.[38] Now, in the second week of May 1870, it united the northern Oglalas around a common cause. Warriors streamed north, following Crazy Horse, He Dog, High Backbone, and a score of lesser leaders: Bad Heart Bull, Sun Eagle Feather, Iron Magpie, Little Big Man, and Pumpkin Butte. A village of Miniconjous and Sans Arcs was gathering on Rosebud Creek, its warriors scheduled to join the war party, but the Oglalas felt confident enough to open the fighting alone. The main Crow camp was located on the west side of the Bighorn River, near the modern community of St. Xavier, Montana, hundreds of tipis lining the bank. The Crow horse herd, several thousand head grazing on the east side of the river, made an irresistible target. In the morning, Lakota raiders were sent ahead to round up the herd and start driving them east. A few warriors rode boldly down to the water's edge and reined in to let their ponies drink. Crazy Horse, carrying the Crow Owners lance, joined High Backbone, distinctive in red turban and cape, in this display of cool machismo.

In the Crow village, pandemonium broke out. Mounting the war ponies tethered outside lodges, hundreds of warriors strung across the river to combat the Lakota menace. Hooves thundered as the Oglala raiders started the Crow herd to a run, and a long chase began over the flats toward the Little Bighorn, fifteen miles east. The Oglalas were hoping for the Miniconjou reinforcements to turn the tables on the pursuit, but the miles went by without a sign. Here and there, warriors turned to challenge single combatants, but as the sun climbed to noon, fresh Crow horse-flesh was wearing out jaded Oglala mounts. The Crow assault poured forward. High Backbone tried to form a defensive line atop a hill. A cluster of Oglala warriors drew rein. As the line of Crows swung to charge along the slope, twenty-two-year-old Thunder Tail would remember, the Lakotas touched up their wotawe paint designs. Pointing to the bloody trophies waved by the Crows, High Backbone taunted his men to vengeance: "When it is a day like this it is men who are brave. Get busy!"[39]

It was not enough to stem the tide, and the Oglalas fled again. At length they splashed across the Little Bighorn and urged their ponies up the slope. Here, six years later, Crazy Horse would secure his greatest victory against the Americans.

Suddenly, across the eastern hills, dust signaled the arrival of the Miniconjous. As if by a collective nerve, the fleeing Oglalas stiffened and turned to confront the pursuit. A knot of Miniconjous and Sans Arcs, all wearing trailer headdresses and waving warrior society lances, swept down on the Crows. Amidst fleeing comrades, one Crow dismounted as if pledged to die. High Backbone shot him, and Crazy Horse, shadowing his kola, struck the coup. The chase reversed itself, traversing the same country back toward the Bighorn. Out on the plain one Crow's pony foundered, and the warrior stood at bay as the Lakota line approached. Crazy Horse and High Backbone, still working as a team, closed in. The Crow bravely bluffed at Crazy Horse, but the Oglala snapped off a shot that dropped him. High Backbone rode forward to take this coup.

The pursuit continued late into the afternoon. As they entered the Bighorn valley, the Crows were strung out, riding double; a man scuttled along holding onto the tail of a comrade's mount. At length the Lakota war leaders called a halt and turned exhausted horses for home. When They Chased Them Back to Camp was over.

Days later, this period of fevered activity in Crazy Horse's life closed with the departure of the delegation to Fort Fetterman. Led by Man Afraid of His Horse and Red Cloud, the party numbered over twenty members, several taking along their wives. A retinue of five hundred people made a colorful exit from the village. Final word from the fort cleared a last-minute sticking point: President Grant had wired Cheyenne to order the Big Horn Expedition not to intrude in the unceded territory. With the wisdom of iwastela confirmed, the delegates left with a firm agenda agreed to by chiefs and warriors. Removal to the Missouri River was unacceptable. Fundamental to all Oglalas was the right to trade on the North Platte. Fort Laramie was the prime choice, but the delegates were empowered to agree to a site as far east as Scott's Bluffs. An agency so located would secure Lakota rights in the unceded territory, preventing future intrusions. Preservation of the unceded territory overrode all other concerns. Early attempts to locate permanently in the reservation interior were to be underplayed, a position possibly adopted to keep Crazy Horse aboard the peace process.[40]

Scattering by bands, the Oglalas intended to gravitate to Fort Laramie to meet the returning delegation six weeks hence. Before departure, Red Cloud presented his hair-fringed shirt to He Dog, transferring seniority to his nephew for the duration of the trip. American Horse would handle diplomacy at the forts.[41] As the camps started east from Powder River, Crazy Horse was left idle for the first time in seven months. He had suffered privations, struggled with logistical problems, and coordinated activities across a huge arena, using his visionary power and sublimating his personal desires to the tribal good. In idleness, he must have been rankled by the bitterness of his position. His own warriors had lost their lives in the action for which he had been whipped by akicita upholding the new conciliation policy. His mood threw into relief his own needs from life. All through the war years, he had been seized on as a mediating force, binding the frayed interests of Hunkpati-las and Bad Faces. His summary punishment by their police called fundamental allegiances into question.

His outlet from the suffocations of political life had always been war. Calling in comrades like Little Big Man and He Dog's younger brother Little Shield, he proposed a small-scale war party against the Crows. Still, something was missing; something could no longer wait. In the Bad Face camp, No Water was absent, probably accompanying Red Cloud's party to Fort Fetterman. It was not the best idea, but Crazy Horse paused once more to talk with Black Buffalo Woman.

Four

WAR CHIEF

13

UP AGAINST IT

About ten days after the Fight When They Chased Them Back to Camp, Crazy Horse departed for the Crow country once more. There was no colorful parade, just a small war party of a few followers only, leaving piecemeal in the early light to rendezvous a few miles from camp. The party struck north and west across the plains toward Powder River. A screen of trusted comrades led by Little Big Man flanked the little column, while scouts fanned out after game and vantage. Riding some distance ahead of the party was Crazy Horse. Beside him rode Black Buffalo Woman. She had elected to leave her husband and elope with Crazy Horse. The pair would take the consequences of their passion.[1]

All day the party continued across the treeless plain dividing the Belle Fourche drainage from the Powder. Late in May the prairie swells are vivid with new grass, and here the plains earn their clichéd sobriquet of a sea of grass. Centering on modern Gillette, Wyoming, the Thunder Basin region held strong attachments for Crazy Horse. Pasture was rich for horse herds and buffalo, and the startling weeks of spring growth may have retained a honeymoon association for him. As afternoon drew on, the party paused somewhere along the low ridges of the divide, where eastward-draining coulees interface with draws running west to the Powder. Youths were sent to fetch water and pasture the horses. Cooking fires were lit, and the war party settled down for the night.

We have no way of knowing the events of the night, but people would consider the elopement as a real if unorthodox marriage: He Dog viewed Black Buffalo Woman as his comrade's first wife, and we may assume that he ascribed a sexual dimension to this phase of the relationship at least. The months of irresolution were over, and as the preparations of camp went on, the couple had time to reflect and anticipate. In eloping with a married woman, Crazy Horse had put himself in a dangerous position. Ideally, a husband should rise above jealousy, but No Water was within his rights to demand his wife's return: in such brittle face-offs lay the germ of many a bloody feud. Putting aside reprisals, Crazy Horse must have known that he was unfitting himself to continue as a Shirt Wearer. As much as anything, the sudden resolution of the affair signaled his own disillusion with the political process that had culminated in the Washington delegation and his followers' beating by council akicita.

Black Buffalo Woman had, if anything, even more to lose. In theory, a woman could terminate her marriage by abandoning her husband, but in practice that was subject to a host of imponderables. If reclaimed, she could expect corporal punishment and even mutilation at the hands of her husband. Even if permitted to make a life with a new partner, she forfeited her property rights, and most significant, she lost all claims on her children. Early that morning, Black Buffalo Woman had left her three children with friends and relatives before joining Crazy Horse. The finality of that separation, the vulnerability of her position, must have weighed on her as darkness fell. No eavesdropping witness recorded memories of that night, so we can only infer the totality of need and desperation to be assuaged by recognizing its obverse in all that was left behind.

On the afternoon of the second day, the country began to break toward the river. Scouts sighted scattered clusters of tipis: several tiyospaye of Lakotas were camped around the crossing. The war party descended into the valley, where the wide gray belt of Powder River, braided with mudbanks, swings between white clay bluffs. Cries of recognition went up from the tipis. Miniconjous, including many of Crazy Horse's maternal relatives, were encamped here, as well as Oglalas whom Black Buffalo Woman could call kin. Friends and relatives invited the war party to spend the night with them. After two days in the saddle, the warriors were glad to accept.

That night a double tipi was raised on the campground to accommodate visitors. A social dance was staged, with lines of young men and women facing each other across the fire, chastely pairing off in a circle while singers shrilled the bittersweet joys of love. Around the perimeter of the lodge sat the guests, men grouped along one side, women on the other. At the honor place sat Crazy Horse, chatting with his host Touch the Clouds. Enjoying an evening of respectability, Black Buffalo Woman sat with the matrons, while Little Big Man sat on Crazy Horse's right. Several more of the war party, including Little Shield, clustered near.

Sharp ears might have made out the noise of new arrivals outside. As night fell, a second war party had ridden into the camps. Their leader, dismounting from his pacing mule, was No Water. Returning home to a deserted lodge, he had soon rounded up his children and pieced together the story. He recruited followers and rode night and day in pursuit. He too had relatives here, and he first searched out his kinsman Bad Heart Bull. On the pretense that he wished to go out hunting, No Water asked to borrow Bad Heart Bull's pistol—according to one account, a small .41 caliber Derringer.[2] Hunting at midnight with such a sidearm seemed an unlikely proposition, but Bad Heart Bull gave the pistol to No Water. The aggrieved husband and his followers rode into the main camp and dismounted outside the double tipi.

Inside the lodge, as tired dancers were ready to settle to the feast and women bustled around the fire, No Water stepped through the open door space. The circle fell silent as he stalked around the fire to stand four feet in front of Crazy Horse. "My friend," he rasped, leveling the pistol: "I have come!"[3] Touch the Clouds and Crazy Horse sprang up simultaneously, the latter reaching for his belt knife only to feel a restraining hand close on his arm. Trying to prevent an escalation of violence, Little Big Man had seized his comrade just as No Water squeezed the trigger. The gun barked, scarcely a foot from Crazy Horse's face. Crazy Horse reeled against Little Big Man as the bullet struck just below his left nostril, plowing a surface wound along the line of his teeth and fracturing his upper jaw before exiting his neck at the base of the skull. Released by Little Big Man, Crazy Horse took a step, then pitched forward unconscious into the cooking fire.

The floor space was suddenly electric with motion and noise. Touch the Clouds stepped between his fallen kinsman and No Water. Under the pall of powder smoke, Black Buffalo Woman scrambled to the back of the tipi, pulling up the cover and crawling out into the night air. She raced across the campground to locate a tipi of relatives, begging through sobs for protection.

As the shot died away, No Water hurried out of the lodge. His followers knotted anxiously around as he told them he had killed Crazy Horse. Warriors exited the tipi. Touch the Clouds, towering over the throng, snatched away No Water's pistol. To fading cries of alarm and defiance, the panicky party dissolved into the night, No Water not pausing even to reclaim his mule. Riders mounted to carry the horrific word that Crazy Horse was dead.

Inside the tipi, Crazy Horse's followers lifted him from the fire and carried him to the nearby camp of his Miniconjou uncle Spotted Crow. The headman and his womenfolk prepared a warm bed for their nephew while healers were called to attend. The ugly wound, blackened by powder smoke from the point-blank range, was cleaned, then a poultice of herbs was secured by a bandage covering much of Crazy Horse's lower face. The brief examination suggested that he was in no mortal danger, and more riders galloped out to correct the premature reports of Crazy Horse's death.

Out in the night, warriors scoured the valley for No Water. At length, they turned on No Water's hapless mule and shot it dead, then sullenly returned to make their base at Spotted Crow's camp. Elsewhere in the darkness, No Water's men had spirited their leader from danger. At a remote spot, they built a sweat lodge, and in a hurried ritual, purified him of what they believed to be the killing of Crazy Horse. "Then," remembered He Dog, "he disappeared." Close by stood the Badger Eaters camp of No Water's older brothers. After a few days of wandering, No Water sought protection there. Black Twin told his brother, "Come and stay with me, and if they want to fight us we will fight."[4]

Black Twin's remark reflected a dangerous escalation of tension. Even after Crazy Horse's recovery was assured, his warriors remained "very angry and thought they ought to have No Water turned over to them to be punished."[5] When messengers returned to the Spotted Crow camp to report Black Twin's defiance, some of Crazy Horse's followers argued for an open attack on the Badger Eaters. Black Twin tried to bully Horn Chips into an admission of complicity, claiming that Horn Chips had provided Crazy Horse with love charms to seduce Black Buffalo Woman. Horn Chips denied the charges but rapidly made himself scarce, permanently leaving his natal tiyospaye. "For a while it looked as if a lot of blood would flow," concluded He Dog.[6]

Spotted Crow and his two brothers Ashes and Bull Head, the senior headmen in the Miniconjou camp, hosted feasts in which they worked for reconciliation. Touch the Clouds added his weight to their advice. In visits to Crazy Horse's sickbed, he counseled the wounded man to drop his claims to Black Buffalo Woman, gradually applying the unanswerable authority of an older brother. Initially, Crazy Horse resisted, expressing his fears for Black Buffalo Woman's safety if she returned to No Water—a concern hinting at his depth of feeling for the woman.

Other forces were soon in play. Bad Heart Bull and his brother He Dog felt implicated in the feud because No Water had used Bad Heart Bull's pistol. The brothers matched Spotted Crow's efforts by approaching Black Twin and his relatives, smoothing the way to peacemaking. As the atmosphere gradually calmed, they established a toehold for diplomacy by convincing Black Twin that, whatever Crazy Horse's offense, No Water's attempt on his life had been an act of culpable folly. A corner had been turned. After consulting Crazy Horse's warriors, He Dog hammered out a deal with Black Twin to "cover" the shooting. Tethered near No Water's tipi were two of his favorite ponies—a "very fine" roan and a "fine" bay. On prompting from He Dog and his brother, No Water sent an intermediary with these ponies, and a third good horse, to Spotted Crow's camp "to atone for the injury he had done."[7]

Touch the Clouds stepped up his efforts to secure a total reconciliation. Unrecorded factors played their part. By happy chance, many of Crazy Horse's war party were Bad Faces, with relatives in Black Twin's camp. Conciliatory forces probably took root there. At length Crazy Horse gave in, and Bad Heart Bull was called to the sickbed. Insisting on the condition that No Water should not punish his wife, Crazy Horse gave his consent to Black Buffalo Woman's return. Bad Heart Bull carried the proposal to Black Twin's camp and secured No Water's assurance. At the Miniconjou camp, the council deputed Spotted Crow and warriors Sitting Eagle and Canoeing to escort Black Buffalo Woman home. Fulfilling the terms of the agreement, they left her at Bad Heart Bull's tipi. Bad Heart Bull added his personal guarantee to No Water's, and the escort departed. "If it had not been settled this way, there might have been a bad fight," He Dog summed up.[8] Although private feelings continued to rankle, as a matter of public concern, the affair was at an end. Crazy Horse and Black Buffalo Woman would not speak again.

As the Moon of Making Fat opened, the Oglala bands continued sifting southeast toward the rendezvous point of Rawhide Butte. Gradually Crazy Horse regained strength, but he would remain convalescent for several months, nursing his broken jaw in much pain and discomfort. The days confined to bed were conducive to reflection, and he pondered carefully his attitude toward both his chieftainship and his personal future.

Man Afraid of His Horse returned from Fort Fetterman to report that the delegation had departed for Washington on May 22. The official line would be that he had taken sick, but others would recall that the Hunkpatila chief "backed out" of the trip east, unhappy at the favor shown Red Cloud. As the key architect of the iwastela policy, Man Afraid of His Horse must have been rankled to see it coopted by the hitherto intransigent Red Cloud. Man Afraid of His Horse's return permitted a session of the chiefs' council to debate the issue of Crazy Horse's adultery. It came to an inevitable conclusion: Crazy Horse had made himself unworthy of his status as Shirt Wearer, and the elders formally demanded that he return his ceremonial shirt.[9]

Crazy Horse's reflections had prepared him for the decision. The tribal adoption of the iwastela policy toward the Americans imposed restrictions on him that he was no longer willing to tolerate. For over a decade, he had honed a self-image as *the* Lakota warrior, using Thunder's power to protect the people. From now on he "[d]isdained the compliment of being great—a great leader, or anything of that sort."[10] According to a late oral tradition, Crazy Horse brought the shirt to the council tipi, saying simply, "I'd rather be a plain warrior. I'm not an orator, I'm not a politician."[11]

In the private sphere, too, the enforced days of idleness had spurred reassessment of his life. His father and stepmothers redoubled their efforts to ensure a secure domestic life for Crazy Horse. The crisis underscored what they had been saying for years: their son needed a good marriage to stabilize him. Crazy Horse at last agreed. The stalled negotiations with Black Shawl's family were reopened. The menfolk had already agreed on a bride price, and after a final gift of horses was sent to Black Shawl's family, the mothers moved to finalize details. By the middle of June, barely a month after the disastrous elopement, preparations were complete.[12]

On the day of the wedding, Black Shawl rose early. After bathing, her mother, Red Elk Woman, orchestrated the preparations. She and her kinswomen carefully painted Black Shawl, outlining the part of her hair in red and sketching in the fine stripes of the hunka ceremony. Her hair was plaited in two braids to hang, in recognition of her new status, over her breast. She was dressed in the finest of clothing, moccasins and knee-length leggings topped by a graceful dress of fringed buckskin, its yoke heavily embellished with beadwork.

Other relatives had packed a number of ponies with Black Shawl's dowry. A bride was expected to take with her the minimal requirements of family life: a tipi, a pair of robes, and the basic domestic toolkit of awl and thread, kettle, axe, and knife. Mother and aunts packed the materials for a feast. Black Shawl's brothers, Iron Horse and Red Feather, led the best of Crazy Horse's gift ponies and helped their sister into the saddle. Holding the bridle, they led a procession from the Oyuhpe camp. Well-wishers watched as the line, flanked by singers, approached the Hunkpatila lodges. In Worm's tipi, Black Shawl sat on the buffalo robes that marked Crazy Horse's bed space, shyly facing away from the lodge interior. At length, her new mothers-in-law, attended by Crazy Horse's sister and other kinswomen, welcomed her, coaxing the shy maiden to turn and face her new relatives.

They too dressed Black Shawl in finely decorated clothing, presenting gifts of body paints and dress accessories, tying ribbons and ornaments to her braids. Worm could be heard outside the tipi welcoming his new in-laws. While women and children formed a circle around a group of drummers, and Black Shawl's mother and aunts joined Worm's wives in readying the feast, Worm had horses packed with goods led forward. A herald called the names of the poor, announcing that Worm was giving away in honor of his son and daughter-in-law. Singers extemporized songs of praise to Crazy Horse and Black Shawl, and the women of both families served the feast. For the first time, the two principals sat together, at the head of the circle surrounding the kettles. Confirming that Black Shawl was his favored choice for daughter-in-law, Worm may have had a white down plume fastened to her hair, signifying the ultimate honor of making her hunka. The day of celebration closed with the newlyweds being led in procession to their new tipi. To public joy, the bashful smiles of sisters, and the giggling of knowing children, they were at last left alone.

Black Shawl had little time for honeymoon bliss. Her husband remained debilitated by his wound, and his appearance at the wedding—sporting unsightly bandages or displaying a barely healed scar that drew his mouth into a fierce grimace—was at odds with Worm's conventional pieties. Black Shawl must have wondered about Crazy Horse's commitment to her. His courtship had been civil but passionless and, as gossips had always claimed, had run parallel to his affair with Black Buffalo Woman.

The first shock to the couple's new married life came within days, and from an unexpected quarter. A straggle of warriors rode into camp from the southwest, their loosened hair hacked short, leading a riderless pony. Familiar trappings hung from the saddle—to instant howls of grief from Crazy Horse's female relatives, the warriors quietly stated that Young Little Hawk had been killed. While Black Shawl laid out food for their guests, they confided the details to her husband. After hearing of Crazy Horse's shooting, the war party had shifted east down the Sweetwater valley, shadowing the course of the Union Pacific across the North Platte and over the Medicine Bow range, probably uniting with the party Crazy Horse had left on the Laramie plains six weeks earlier. Since hearing word that the Big Horn Expedition had been called off, the warriors had not troubled wasicu, but they were spoiling for a fight. They scoured the mountain trails for sign of Shoshone or Ute hunting camps. A skirmish or two followed, and in one fight, Young Little Hawk was killed.[13]

The exact identity of his killers is uncertain. Worm would recall that Shoshones were responsible, but Crazy Horse's cousin Flying Hawk identified American "settlers" as the killers. Most of the fragmentary statements bearing on the killing confirm Flying Hawk. It is not impossible that Shoshones and civilians, united against the Lakota threat, aided each other in the skirmish. As the surviving brother, Crazy Horse would have felt it incumbent on him to seek vengeance, but obstacles stood in his way. He still had not fully recovered from his wound, and even more significant, the iwastela policy remained tribal consensus. Shirt Wearers and Deciders had issued edicts forbidding war parties against the wasicu. Undoubtedly, elders and chiefs urged Crazy Horse to forego vengeance.[14]

Just as certainly, Crazy Horse pondered the Male Crow disaster and remembered the slanders that had torn apart his childhood. Unable to recruit a war party, he at least had to see that his brother's bones received a proper burial. In an idiosyncratic take on the sort of honeymoon visit that followed a wedding, Black Shawl agreed to join her husband on a solitary 150-mile trip into the mountains. With no public announcement of their destination, the couple headed southwest, Crazy Horse leading his brother's war pony.[15]

During the journey, probably acting on runners sent by Crazy Horse, the war party he had recruited over three months earlier started home. Between June 22 and 27, Union Pacific stationmasters wired reports of large war parties seen repeatedly crossing the tracks west of Fort Sanders (modern Laramie, Wyoming), with signal fires visible on the Medicine Bow Mountains. Troops were hurried west to patrol the line, and in a sharp skirmish on the 27th, a Second Cavalry detachment tangled with a reported two hundred warriors, losing one trooper and killing several of the Lakotas. An attack on a wood train near Fort Fetterman two days later may have been a reprisal by the same party, bound homeward.[16]

The timing of these demonstrations coincided with the return of the Red Cloud party. The attacks served notice that the new Oglala conciliation policy was not without its detractors, but for now, Crazy Horse satisfied himself with locating his brother's body. He collected the remains and buried them under a cairn of stones, then shot Young Little Hawk's pony so that it might carry its owner to Wanagi-yata, the Spirit Land. The couple remained in the vicinity for nine days, camping in high country timber. According to Flying Hawk, Crazy Horse scoured the district, killing several straggling wasicu.

It was an eye-opening start to married life for Black Shawl: Crazy Horse, bitter and reflective, was rarely at home. Nevertheless, a pattern was set. Through the seven years of their married life, the couple would make regular solitary trips, and if their relationship was not grounded in the passion that bound Crazy Horse to Black Buffalo Woman or that would bind him to Nellie Larrabee, it clearly grew into a stable companionship founded on mutual respect. Black Shawl was supportive of her husband's imperatives, the uncompromising opposition to American encroachments, and the vision questing that drew him repeatedly from home. On this first and eeriest journey, she grew to know her man, revealing the vulnerable mystic beneath as she replaced bandages and renewed dressings. In these first weeks of marriage, their physical relationship ignited to secure an early pregnancy. At last, Crazy Horse had had enough of cold vengeance. "He killed enough to satisfy," recalled Flying Hawk, "and then he came home." Early in July, Crazy Horse and Black Shawl rode together into the tribal village to find that the Oglala world had again moved on.[17]

Moon of Red Cherries, July 1870: The northern Oglalas gathered at Rawhide Butte for the Sun Dance, joined by bands of Miniconjous and Sans Arcs to greet the return of the Red Cloud delegation. Red Cloud's party arrived at Fort Laramie on June 26, and after final talks with General John E. Smith and post commander Colonel Franklin F. Flint, they crossed the North Platte to rejoin their people.[18]

For ten days, chiefs, headmen, and warriors debated the results of the Washington trip. The delegates were eagerly debriefed, and their anecdotes of the massive eastern cities; the ironclad warships moored in the Potomac; the factories and foundries producing firearms and artillery; the passenger ships in New York harbor landing tens of thousands of new wasicu settlers—these were weighed and assessed at feasts and society meetings. Skeptics might question the veracity of the delegates, but Red Cloud's party convinced most that the network of railroads spreading across the plains would soon shunt settlers west, filling the prairies with homesteads, ranches, mines, boomtowns, and cities, eroding further the contracting gamelands. The ever-improving arsenal of military weaponry they had seen could be used with devastating effect against those Lakotas that chose military resistance. A true turning point had been reached for Red Cloud: he persuasively urged that iwastela was the only road the Oglalas could take.

Debate now turned on the substance of Oglala meetings with government representatives. How well had the delegates fulfilled their agenda? Here, the record was definitely mixed. The agency location had not been finalized, although the Indian Office agreed to ship Oglala annuities for this year only to Fort Laramie. This concession, and the limited trade approved at the fort, won Red Cloud measured approval. He parlayed a half-promise of a goodwill issue of ammunition into a substantial diplomatic victory.

Far less clear-cut were the full implications of the treaty the Oglalas had signed two years earlier. The delegates had spent an uneasy afternoon in the Indian Office listening to a litany of clauses and subclauses. In 1868 Oglalas signed the treaty to reestablish peace. Verbal agreements with the commissioners had been fundamental to Oglala acceptance of the treaty, but these were not represented in the legal instrument acclaimed by the Senate. For every sentence promising the security of the Indian domain, another committed the Lakotas to approving future rights-of-way, railroads, and military expeditions.

The unceded hunting grounds constituted the delegation's real minefield. Warrior societies had demanded guarantees of the tract's security. The recognition of the Powder River country as unceded had been one of the diplomatic coups of 1868—"the country . . . given up to the Sioux under 'Red Cloud' and 'Man afraid of his horse,'" as reservation Lakotas understood the concession.[19] Now Red Cloud had to admit that the promise seemed far from watertight. The Oglalas had overlooked its always vague northern boundary, but the officials urged a minimalist reading coterminous with the northern line of Wyoming Territory, slicing out the Yellowstone valley from the tract. The rider "so long as the buffalo may range thereon in such numbers as to justify the chase" carried a real sting. An optimist in 1868 might have interpreted it as a metaphor for an indefinite future. Two years later, with mounting evidence of diminishing buffalo herds, it rang hollow.

In off-the-record talks, Red Cloud tentatively approved a proposal that the hunting grounds retain their unceded status for thirty-five years. For the same term, the delegates reported, annuity goods would be paid to the Lakotas. The term, matching the period left under the 1851 treaty, before its controversial amendment by the Senate, was not accidental. Red Cloud sold it heavily as his reclaiming of diplomatic ground lost by the older generation of chiefs. Indeed, in seizing so dramatically the initiative of the iwastela policy, and by stressing his critical engagement with the officials at the expense of Man Afraid of His Horse's standoffishness, Red Cloud was able to portray himself to Oglalas and Americans alike as the true guarantor of the new high plains order.[20]

Warrior societies warily came on board. Crazy Horse's comrade Little Big Man made a far-reaching commitment on the hunting grounds. Reviewing the diminishment of game, he urged the warriors to approve Red Cloud's thirty-five-year agreement, "for I thought it would be as long as I should want a country."[21] Consensus crystallized on this crisp formulation, and faced with qualified approval, Red Cloud conceded some ground to the warriors. During the Washington talks, he had tentatively approved location of an agency trading post southwest of the Black Hills, within the hunting grounds. Now, prompted by visiting northern Lakotas, the warriors demanded that not so much as a storeroom be built on Lakota land: the Americans must concede an agency located on the south side of the North Platte, on neither reservation nor unceded land. The old Ward and Guerrier trading post eight miles north of Fort Laramie was their favored site: Red Cloud would demand it when the "good men" from the East brought out the annuities.

Red Cloud had carried the day. Warriors agreed to extend indefinitely the truce that had held since spring. Red Cloud sketched a summer of shuttle diplomacy, scheduling major assemblies on the Powder late in July, and at Bear Butte in August, to secure a national consensus for peace. With Oglala support assured, Red

Cloud departed the Sun Dance village in mid-July, leading a deputation to engage Cheyenne and Arapaho cooperation.[22]

Crazy Horse arrived home in the middle of these debates—an unsettling vengeful presence in the acclaim for peace. He declined to address the council, but gossip had it that during the trip home, he had twice stalked troop details, single-handedly killing as many as four soldiers. "Those are the things," remembered his eighteen-year-old cousin Eagle Elk, "that aroused the people." That these feats remained stubbornly apocryphal is proof that Crazy Horse did not advertise them as war honors or use them directly to subvert the consolidation of iwastela. Instead, the fragmentary evidence suggests that another pattern of behavior was establishing itself. After a period of intense physical, mental, emotional, and spiritual activity, Crazy Horse was suffering burnout. The nervous energy of Thunder power, which had carried him through nine months of living on a war footing, concluding a long-standing love affair, and traveling upwards of two thousand miles on the warpath, was exhausted. As the bands scattered, Crazy Horse remained silent. Almost unnoticed, Crazy Horse departed to join his new wife's people.[23]

As summer drew on and Black Shawl announced that she was expecting a child, Crazy Horse could have been forgiven for settling into the private stabilities of family life. Newlyweds customarily joined the bride's tiyospaye for a protracted sojourn before permanently settling down, typically in the husband's band. Black Shawl's father was dead, and the family could use an extra provider. Moreover, the Big Road tiyospaye was congenial: like Crazy Horse, it remained skeptical of American entanglements. In his new home, Crazy Horse had to master complex social skills. Etiquette prescribed that a man show respect for his mother-in-law by complete avoidance. He soon established a good working relationship with Black Shawl's brothers. Iron Horse was probably close to Crazy Horse in age, and the pair maintained a respectful affinity, seasoned by the brash sarcasm of brothers-in-law. As so often happens, Crazy Horse had a special bond with Black Shawl's younger brother, seventeen-year-old Red Feather. Inducted into the Crow Owners Society that season, Red Feather plainly idolized his new brother-in-law and was overjoyed at every mark of favor. In the vacuum left by Young Little Hawk, some of Crazy Horse's nurturing protectiveness, his delight in mentoring the younger generation, was transferred onto Red Feather.[24]

By contrast, Red Cloud's summer was one of vigorous political activity. Although faced with low-key sniping by isolationists, Red Cloud met everywhere with a wary consensus for peace. Early in September, the Oglalas rendezvoused at Bear Lodge Butte, and chiefs prepared to meet the Washington officials and resolve the agency issue.

Although Red Cloud was empowered to concede that deteriorating resources necessitated a new modus vivendi with the Americans, change was to be expressly on Lakota terms, at Lakota speed. Even minor intrusions on the Lakota domain would be vigorously contested. Plans for educating Lakota children, one of the treaty's underpinnings, must be deferred: "We want that by and by."[25]

It was not lost on the most tractable chiefs that American respect for their people was rooted in Lakota valor. Oglala oral histories establish that somewhere in the north, at an unspecified date after his removal as Shirt Wearer, Crazy Horse was nominated tribal war chief: the most likely context is Bear Lodge, September 1870, at a great council attended by hundreds of chiefs, elders, and warriors. The consolidation of iwastela meant that such a title was honorific, but should the council ever declare a state of war, tribal leadership would inhere in the war chief. Like Sitting Bull among the Hunkpapas, his Oglala counterpart would be invested with decision-making power in strategy, tactics, and negotiations.

A caucus of "the older, more responsible men of the tribe" empowered three chiefs—Man Afraid of His Horse, Bad Wound, and Big Road—to make the final decision.[26] Crazy Horse remained the people's greatest warrior. Moreover, since July he had tacitly cooperated with the iwastela policy. The chiefs might have concluded that, unworldly and apolitical as he was, Crazy Horse could always be swayed by their counsels.

At the great council, Crazy Horse was led from his seat among the warriors to sit with the three chiefs at the honor place. As the chiefs held their pipe to his lips, heralds proclaimed Crazy Horse the okicize itancan, war chief of the nation. A three-foot war club, set with three knife blades, was placed in his hands. Marking again the comradeship that had often smoothed over interband tensions, He Dog sat beside Crazy Horse as the war chief's akicita. Loud acclaim greeted the appointments, and pledges were made to defend the Lakota domain. Then Crazy Horse led a parade of the Oglala warrior societies in a triumphant circuit of the campground. After the unacceptable limitations of his Shirt Wearer status, the new war chief was happy to ride as a Thunder dreamer: hair streaming loose, naked but for breechclout and moccasins, his body painted yellow, for the power of the Rock, and dotted with hailstone spots. Crazy Horse's self-image at last coincided with his outward role. From now on he was determined to remain the warrior protector of his people and their land.[27]

On the same day that the main village started for Fort Laramie, a smaller camp turned north from Bear Lodge. Numbering perhaps fifty lodges, it comprised families from each of the main three northern Oglala bands, Hunkpatila, Bad Face and Oyuhpe, people determined to maintain as long as possible the old hunting life without wasicu interference. Big Road, Black Twin, and He Dog were their peacetime leaders, but war chief Crazy Horse would always remain their principal man, the key to village consensus. Tracking buffalo herds northward, as fall opened, they moved into the valley of the middle Yellowstone in south-central Montana Territory.[28]

The shift was prophetic, for the contracting buffalo range would increasingly draw them north in the years to come, away from their agency kin and into an ever-tightening association with the northern Lakotas—Sitting Bull's people. The same forces were drawing the nonagency Hunkpapas steadily west up the Yellowstone valley. The indications are that immediately, in October 1870, Sitting Bull and Crazy Horse agreed to a policy that for the present complemented iwastela. Their people would remain on the hunting grounds but would not challenge the Red Cloud strategy of implementing a gradual transition to reservation life. Sitting Bull even declared an end to his own bands' four-year war against the military posts on the upper Missouri. Provided they were not interfered with, his and Crazy Horse's people would try to live apart from the Americans—so long as the game held out.[29]

Rosebud Creek, Moon of the Changing Seasons: Crazy Horse decided on a last war journey before winter. A select party of comrades would strike the Shoshones. Sixteen men made up the party, including High Backbone, Bald-Face Horse, Chasing Crow, and a Bad Face warrior whom Crazy Horse would increasingly rely on as a battlefield subordinate, twenty-five-year-old Good Weasel. Two relations through marriage were along, emphasizing the tight-knit affinity of the party: Little Killer and young Red Feather, recruited as the pipe owner's servant.[30]

The party camped below the Painted Cliffs, a tall bluff marked with ancient petroglyphs believed to be the work of wakan beings. Lakotas believed that the designs changed to foretell coming events. Crazy Horse and several followers solemnly smoked and made offerings to the power that etched the rock drawings. The following morning they returned to take a reading and were disturbed to make out markings that suggested they would get the worst of any encounter.

Crazy Horse suggested that the party turn back, but High Backbone curtly dismissed his kola's caution. After a pause, Crazy Horse reluctantly indicated his assent. "Yes, we're looking for death, let's go."[31] A formulaic response, yet the words resonated with significance, echoing the fatal remarks of Male Crow exactly twenty-six years earlier. The party pressed ahead down the spine of the Bighorn Mountains. By mid-October Shoshone camps would be tracking buffalo herds north from Wind River, through the very district where Male Crow had died, adding to Crazy Horse's sense of foreboding. His party struck southwest, descending from the mountains by the tortuous trails called the Sioux Pass. Persistent rain lashed the party, forming muddy pools that frosted overnight into slush. Along Bad Water Creek, an eastern tributary of the Wind, they made a miserable war camp. The temperature dropped, and darkening clouds threatened an early snow. Thoroughly discouraged, Crazy Horse again urged abandoning the expedition. As usual, the reversal in his confidence was extreme, and he was unable to secure agreement over the opposition of High Backbone. When scouts reported a large Shoshone village on Wind River, the warriors quickly acclaimed High Backbone's suggestion of a dawn attack.

Before dawn, they were in place, making their final adjustments to weapons, applying wotawe paint designs to face and body. As light grayed behind them, they rode forward under cover. Through a thin drizzle, the outline of at least 150 tipis became visible in the gathering light, the whickering of a sizeable pony herd audible on the near side of camp. The warriors clapped heels to their mounts and raced toward the lodges, whooping and firing their guns in a bid to startle the herd. Indiscriminate shots rattled through lodgeskins, felling several Shoshones. Crazy Horse had picked his men well, and the herd was soon on the move. Behind them two hundred startled Shoshone warriors mounted tethered war ponies for the pursuit.

As the chase strung out over the plain, the drizzle turned to light snow. This further echo of the Male Crow disaster was not lost on an increasingly despondent Crazy Horse. Slushy pools dotted the plain, slowing the retreat. The sixteen men were scattered and exhausted, struggling to keep the captured stock on the move: only the lead they maintained on the pursuit was saving their lives. High Backbone proposed a stand and sent riders forward after Crazy Horse, who urged a retreat into the mountains. "I wonder if we can make it back to Cone Creek," he told the messengers, "I doubt if our horses can stand a fight in this slush. They sink in over their ankles."

The riders strung back to High Backbone, who once more dismissed his friend's misgivings. "This is the second fight he has called off in this same place! This time there is going to be a fight." He urged his pony to catch up with Crazy Horse. "The last time you called off a fight here," he chided, "when we got back to camp they laughed at us. You and I have our good name to think about. If you don't care about it you can go back. But I'm going to stay here and fight."

"All right," replied Crazy Horse, "we fight, if you feel that way about it. But I think we're going to get a good licking. You have a good gun and I have a good gun, but look at our men! None of them have good guns, and most of them have only bows and arrows. It's a bad place for a fight and a bad day for it, and the enemy are twelve to our one."[32]

The two men rethought tactics. High Backbone was persuaded that a retreat into the mountains offered the best chances of survival, but Crazy Horse agreed that straight flight was ill advised. A holding maneuver should be made to deter the pursuit. Warriors turned exhausted ponies toward the enemy, but the sight of Shoshone outriders on their flank, cutting off the direct trail to the high country, signaled a deteriorating situation. Along the Bad Water, the pursuit repeatedly tangled with the Oglala rearguard—"but the Shoshones had the best of it," and a desperate fight ensued. Several warriors, including Chasing Crow and Bald-Face Horse, were wounded. Soon the Oglala warriors were scattered in precipitate flight. By late afternoon only Crazy Horse, High Backbone, and Good Weasel remained to hold back the pursuit. "It was a running fight, with more running than fighting," recalled He Dog, and "only these three were fighting at all."[33]

Crazy Horse took the left of the enemy line, drawing fire and cutting zigzag dashes across the gap between his men and the Shoshones. High Backbone and Good Weasel took the center and right. A hail of Shoshone lead ripped through the closing gap, and when Crazy Horse met his comrade at the middle of the line, High

Backbone's pony was stumbling. "We're up against it now," he told Crazy Horse; "my horse has a wound in the leg."

"I know it," replied Crazy Horse. "We were up against it from the start."[34]

The men urged weary horseflesh to another charge. In the broken terrain, Crazy Horse's comrades were soon lost to view. Zigzagging back to the center, he made out only Good Weasel riding toward him. Breathlessly, Good Weasel told what he had seen. A sudden Shoshone rush had threatened to cut off the rearguard, but he had managed to escape. High Backbone had not been so fortunate. An unlucky shot toppled the Miniconjou's wounded pony. Good Weasel saw High Backbone leap from the saddle, then face the enemy charge to fight hand to hand. A press of Shoshones surged over the massive Lakota, clubs swinging. Another horrified glance backward showed nothing of his comrade—only dismounted Shoshone warriors hacking at something on the ground. There was nothing to be done, he assured Crazy Horse: "None of us could go against such odds." Reluctantly, Crazy Horse agreed, and the pair loped after their comrades.[35]

The killing of High Backbone satisfied Shoshone vengeance. Aware they had killed a great man, the pursuit dissolved. Good Weasel pressed on, but Crazy Horse separated, as if to ride back to his kola's body. Meanwhile the scattered Oglalas climbed the Bighorn foothills, searching for a suitable place to camp. At sundown, the main party found a spring, dismounted, and tended to their wounded. As night fell, Bald-Face Horse died. The exhausted company nervously scanned the darkness. In the distance a wolf howled, then again, nearer. Good Weasel answered the call several times until Crazy Horse rode alone out of the night.

Unable to locate High Backbone, Crazy Horse had his warriors bury Bald-Face Horse. The other wounded were soon remounted or placed on makeshift travois as the war party started up the mountain trails. On the fourth day, safely across the Bighorns, Crazy Horse and Red Feather turned back to bury High Backbone's remains. Quartering the bleak battlefield, the pair at last came upon a skull and a few other bones. Coyotes had devoured everything else. Much as his sister had done only four months earlier, Red Feather warily watched Crazy Horse as the full significance of his loss sank in. He was, according to another contemporary, so "beside himself with grief and rage . . . [that from] that very hour . . . Crazy Horse sought death."[36]

14

IRON ROAD

No year in Crazy Horse's life was more momentous than 1870. It saw the death of his brother and the spectacular failure of a love affair, hastily followed by an arranged marriage and political upheavals, ending with the death of his closest comrade and first mentor in war. The loss of Young Little Hawk and High Backbone cut away two of his props. The pair had formed a constellation in Crazy Horse's life. In their reckless courage, they resembled each other more than they resembled Crazy Horse, whose bravery was always tactically calculated. With High Backbone, Crazy Horse had enjoyed a relationship of friendly, if occasionally pointed, rivalry, seasoned by the banter of warriors. Competitiveness was missing in his relationship with Young Little Hawk, to whom Crazy Horse had always shown the elder brother's balance of nurture and provocation, pushing the younger man to prove himself without consideration of Crazy Horse's exploits.

In these complementary relationships, Crazy Horse showed a maturing warrior's awareness of accepting and setting examples, of the dual imperatives of battlefield bravado and protectiveness. With the loss of Young Little Hawk and High Backbone, something of that holistic spirit hardened and contracted. In his brother-in-law Red Feather, Crazy Horse found a junior to bring on, but no one would replace High Backbone. He no longer had an example to measure himself against, or a revered partner to deflate his own propensity to brood.

As winter drew on, what optimism Crazy Horse could muster pointed to the deeper future, to the intimacies of domesticity rather than the public spheres of war and diplomacy. It lay in Black Shawl's swollen belly and in the incremental affection that was building between husband and wife. As Worm had hoped, the marriage matured into a stable companionship, sealed early in 1871 with the birth of a baby girl. Crazy Horse entered a brief period of personal happiness, security, and confidence. The baby was born along the Yellowstone as winter turned to spring.

As Black Shawl's family affectionately acknowledged, the girl resembled her father—evidence for the transmission of nagila, spiritual essence, across the generations. Kokipapi, Crazy Horse called her, They Are Afraid of Her: pointedly, the name of one of his mother's sisters. Accounts, though fragmentary and unsatisfactory, indicate that Crazy Horse found in his daughter an outlet for suppressed spontaneous affection.

Although Crazy Horse and Black Buffalo Woman never renewed their affair, the bad blood between Crazy Horse and No Water remained. The disfiguring wound on Crazy Horse's face stood for the rest of his life as a reminder of the feud. For many weeks, only soups could have passed his lips. Even after the wound healed, it left a visible scar, smudged by the powder burn, that drew Crazy Horse's mouth down, rendering his reflective features morose. Although we have no medical records, the wound must have left him with recurring problems in his teeth and plagued him painfully in cold weather.

During the winter 1870–71, the trouble with No Water flared up again. Several months after the elopement, Black Buffalo Woman had given birth to a daughter with light hair. No proof was ever adduced that the child was Crazy Horse's, but gossips' tongues were set wagging again, doubtless reflecting on the relative potency of the scandalous woman's lovers. After a buffalo surround near the mouth of the Bighorn, across the Yellowstone, Crazy Horse and his hunting partner Iron Horse, Black Shawl's brother, were starting homeward when they came upon Moccasin Top, still dressing his meat, with his buckskin racer tethered beside him. Approaching from the opposite direction, a fourth man came into view—No Water. At that distance, Crazy Horse did not recognize his rival, but as the two groups neared each other, No Water untethered Moccasin Top's pony, sprang into the saddle, and galloped south.

"Are you here?" asked the nonplussed Crazy Horse, "Then who was the man who just rode off on your buckskin horse?" "That was No Water," replied Moccasin Top.

"I wish I had known it! I would certainly have given him a bullet in return for that one which he gave me." With that, Crazy Horse uncinched his pack, leapt astride his own mount, and galloped toward the Yellowstone. Crazy Horse gained, but No Water plunged the racer over a cutbank, straight into the river, and toward the southern shore. After that, No Water permanently quit the northern Oglala camp. He traveled south to join Red Cloud's people, remaining at the agency until the last months of the war of 1876.[1]

No Water's departure highlighted the increasingly bitter issue of the agency location. After leaving Crazy Horse's camp the previous September, the main Oglala village had traveled to Fort Laramie to counsel with the "good men" from Washington. Talks deadlocked over the agency location issue and the promised guns and ammunition withheld from the annuity distribution. Skeptical warriors demanded the guns before they would approve a location, but opposition eroded, and in June 1871, accommodationist chapters of warrior societies approved the siting of the first Red Cloud Agency, on the North Platte thirty-two miles downstream from Fort Laramie.[2]

Cynical observers concurred with Sitting Bull, who declared that Red Cloud had seen "too much" in Washington. The wasicu, he contended, had "put bad Medicine over Red Cloud's eyes to make him see everything and anything that they please." Key supporters of the iwastela compromise, like the Shirt Wearer Sword Owner, were dismayed by what they claimed to be American bad faith.[3] Many shifted back to the minimalist reading of treaty obligations that Crazy Horse had helped formulate in 1868, and from which he had never wavered. As the Sun Dance circle gathered in 1871, Crazy Horse was heartened to mark the return of many who had succumbed to the appeal of government rations.

Some forty lodges of Hunkpatilas were among the arrivals. At Fort Laramie they had nominated Yellow Eagle III, Crazy Horse's old war comrade, as their chief. Yellow Eagle crystallized opposition to Man Afraid of His Horse's conciliatory leadership, rejecting the agency solution. Worm's kindred, and that of Little Hawk, backed Yellow Eagle. They were joined by tipis following the seventy-two-year-old Human Finger—Oyuhpes and Miniconjous drawn to the Hunkpatila camp during the Bozeman Trail War years.[4]

For Crazy Horse, this was a period of consolidation. Following the annus horribilis of 1870, the war chief put down roots, relieved for politics to take a back seat. He served among the blotahunka, coordinating an expedition to avenge High Backbone, but apart from the usual Crow raiding, he stayed at home, enjoying the bedrock pleasures of family life.

No amount of politically correct revisionism will make a Lakota father fit modern ideals of "hands-on" parenthood. Care of They Are Afraid of Her devolved entirely on Black Shawl and other female relatives. But Lakota fathers were traditionally indulgent of daughters, and Crazy Horse seems to have doted on the growing girl. Frank Grouard stated that "in his savage way, [Crazy Horse] idolized" the child. They Are Afraid of Her began to assert her independence of mother and cradleboard, attempting halting steps with the help of a favorite doll and a fond father's hands, rummaging curiously among the parfleche cases at the back of the tipi, racing on all fours in pursuit of some hapless puppy. Then, in precious moments that delighted both parents, she began to experiment with words, threading strings of gobbledygook with the bright lucidities of *ina* (mommy) and *ate* (daddy).[5]

Wasicu activity in the Yellowstone valley late in 1871 alerted nonagency Lakotas to a new threat to their homeland. In the two years since the Union Pacific railroad west from Omaha had met the Central Pacific line at Promontory Point, Utah, the era of the transcontinental railroad had dawned. Completion of the Union Pacific severed the two regional buffalo herds, what Lakotas called Pte Waziyata and Pte Itokagata, the Buffalo North and the Buffalo South. Already new tracks across

Kansas brought settlers by the thousands, eager to secure free land under the Homestead Act; shipped millions of buffalo hides east; and created an infrastructure of American society that marginalized Indian occupation. Crazy Horse and his compatriots were determined to avoid such a future on the unceded hunting grounds in the Powder River country.

Plans had long been maturing, however, for a northern railroad linking the Great Lakes to the Pacific Northwest. Military surveys had singled out the Yellowstone as the best route to the Rockies, and in fall 1871, surveyors probed the lower valley ahead of a large-scale reconnaissance planned for the following year. General Sherman dubbed the Northern Pacific a "national enterprise," recognizing its potential to transform the unceded territory into productive cattle range, industrious homesteads, and lucrative mines.[6]

Lakota councils earnestly assessed this prospect through the winter. The issue raised the recurring question of the unceded territory's vague northern boundary. Did it coincide with the northern line of Wyoming Territory, or extend west from the northern boundary of the reservation proper? Such niggling issues had been raised in Washington, but to the northern bands, they were academic. To them, Lakota hunting ranges extended west to the Bighorn and north to the upper Missouri valley. Northern Lakotas viewed the Yellowstone valley as the heart of their hunting grounds. Elk River teemed with winter game. As the edges of the northern buffalo herd in Alberta and Wyoming contracted year by year, the Yellowstone range became ever more fundamental to Lakota self-support. Lakotas quickly concluded that the railroad would frighten the buffalo away—"that their only source of subsistence and wealth, would be dried up, and that they would die before they would permit it."[7]

Crazy Horse's views neatly dovetailed with those of Spotted Eagle, the Sans Arc war chief, who asserted at his people's agency that no Lakota "properly authorized to speak for his people" would ever permit the Northern Pacific to build along the Yellowstone. Spotted Eagle would personally "fight the rail road people as long as he lived, would tear up the road, and kill its builders." Colonel David S. Stanley, selected to lead a military escort for the Northern Pacific surveyors, warned him that resistance would spell the ruin of his people. Spotted Eagle replied that "the driving off of the Buffalo was death to his race," and he would rather "fight knowing he would be beaten in the end" than capitulate.[8]

Spotted Eagle's visit demonstrated that even to hardline Lakotas, the agency represented a vital channel of communication to the wasicu world. Almost alone, Crazy Horse still declined even to visit and trade at the agencies. In mid-February 1872 some 430 lodges of Oglalas and Miniconjous, with a straggle of Sans Arcs and Hunkpapas, rendezvoused southwest of the Black Hills. Cold weather privations, and the urgency of dialogue with government officials, at last bore out Red Cloud's arguments to visit the agency named after him. Lone Horn, Black Twin, Elk Head— an impressive list of leaders chose to go in and sample Red Cloud's generosity.[9]

Only Crazy Horse resisted Red Cloud's blandishments. The Hunkpatila band council repeatedly met to feast and to debate the linked issues of the railroad and the reservation. Yellow Eagle, the nominal band chieftain, presided at first, but increasingly he deferred to Crazy Horse, honoring the war chief's total commitment to the hunting life. Indeed, he did more than defer; he relinquished the honor place in band councils to Crazy Horse. Flanked by elders like Worm and Human Finger, their circle filled with rising men like Iron Crow and Standing Bull IV, Crazy Horse would sit as Hunkpatila chief for the rest of his life. He was still the most diffident of public speakers, usually asking Little Hawk to speak for him, but he quietly focused debate, unraveling issues, exploring themes. When he tersely indicated that he would not visit the Oglala agency, the band headmen unanimously acclaimed the decision. Little Big Man brought a few Bad Face lodges to join his old war comrade. Late in February, Moon of the Dark Red Calf, as the main village started south, their thirty lodges pressed west toward Powder River.[10]

The split was bitter. Crazy Horse and Little Hawk recruited war parties to harry the upper North Platte valley, driving away horses and mules from outposts and waystations. Drover Levi Powell was killed on the north fork of Laramie River, and Hunkpatila raiders drove his ten horses into Red Cloud's village near Fort Laramie. Red Cloud was at a delicate juncture in talks with the post commander and civilian agent Jared W. Daniels, regarding a proposed relocation of the agency to White River, within the reservation boundary. Unwilling to endanger village solidarity by deploying akicita, Red Cloud impotently disavowed Little Hawk's raiders. The Hunkpatila example fired the mood of Bad Face warriors all too suspicious of their principal chief. The White River relocation slipped off the radar. When Little Hawk returned north, he could report that Red Cloud had settled at the agency, but that thirty or forty tipis of disillusioned Bad Faces were following Black Twin back onto the hunting grounds.[11]

As summer approached, political imperatives reasserted themselves. A great gathering had been scheduled at the Powder River forks to debate the Northern Pacific issue. Black Twin's camp, including He Dog's tiyospaye, had joined the Hunkpatilas in April. Early in June, most of the Oyuhpes arrived, disenchanted with their visit to the agency. Sitting Bull's people arrived from across the Yellowstone. The redoubtable Spotted Eagle led a disillusioned contingent of visitors from Cheyenne River. Sitting Bull and Crazy Horse were now the most famous of the Lakota leaders uncompromisingly committed to the old life. A wary rivalry still circumscribed their relationship, but the pair grew ever closer on national policy. Crazy Horse remained the junior partner. Now forty years old, Sitting Bull possessed a reassuring gravitas that grounded the nervy charisma of his Oglala counterpart. Reflecting these factors, and the larger proportion of Hunkpapas in the north, Sitting Bull occupied the honor place in the council tipi. He recognized Crazy Horse as his second-in-command, habitually seating him in the guest's place on his left.[12]

Through the following summer, the two men sought to foster an ideology of unity among the disparate bands, creating a single Northern Nation, Waziyata Oyate, that would respond decisively to new American intrusions. Although the pair could rely on the support of war leaders like Spotted Eagle, the great council was still unconvinced of any real urgency. Moderate voices like Black Moon's and Lone Horn's argued against premature war commitments.

Underlining the unity of the Northern Nation, on August 3, four tribal circles attended a Sun Dance sponsored by the Sans Arcs, at which intertribal activities were coordinated by a leader from each village: Sitting Bull, Crazy Horse, Fireboat (Miniconjou), and Turning Bear (Sans Arc). A major raid on the Crows was planned to start soon after the ceremony, but on the eighth, scouts reported troops marching down the Yellowstone: the Northern Pacific surveyors were approaching the Lakota country.[13]

The concerted response revealed the streamlining of Northern Nation leadership. "We'll go out and meet them," declared Sitting Bull, "and warn them off. They have no business in our country." While he and Fireboat organized the village's withdrawal downstream, Crazy Horse and Turning Bear coordinated the warrior response. A party almost one thousand strong started up the Yellowstone. Late on August 13 scouts sighted the troops in camp on the north side of the river opposite the mouth of Pryor Creek. Some seventy wagons and military ambulances defined the camp of Major Eugene M. Baker and his escort of over 350 troopers. Armed civilians augmented Baker's effective strength to better than four hundred. This was Crow country, and the chiefs ordered the warriors not to precipitate premature fighting. Sitting Bull wished to parley, but the fall of darkness riddled the sketchy akicita deadlines, and by midnight, eager warriors strung across the Yellowstone, driving away stock. About 3:00 A.M. desultory shots announced the opening of battle.[14]

Crazy Horse and Sitting Bull hurried the main force across the river, topped the northern bluffs, and circled downstream to front the troop position. The two chiefs remained atop a hill jutting into the valley at the left of the Lakota line. A quarter mile of bottomland separated the line from the troops, and as dawn grayed, individual warriors galloped along the flat to draw soldier fire. Almost immediately, one man, charging close, was shot dead, and several others were wounded as Baker's men deployed behind a cutbank. Sitting Bull ordered a pause, but grumbling warriors continued to try their medicine. At length, Crazy Horse, having dotted his face with white paint, laid aside his rifle and mounted. Dressed in white buckskin shirt and leggings, flourishing the Crow Owners Society lance, he charged at a dead run across Baker's line. Repeated runs attracted heavy fire, but Crazy Horse was unscathed. On the hilltop, warriors whooped their approval.

Not to be outdone, Sitting Bull walked alone down the hillside and sat on the prairie a hundred yards ahead of the Indian line. After filling his pipe, he called out for men to smoke with him. Four dumbstruck warriors, wincing at the bullets soon plowing up the dust all around them, took up the invitation. Sitting Bull smoked meditatively, then cleaned the pipe, thoroughly unfazed even when a charging warrior's horse was killed right in front of the little group. At length, he rose and strolled back uphill to renewed whoops of acclaim. "That's enough! We must stop!" Sitting Bull shouted, as he remounted his bay war pony: "That's enough!"[15]

One of the four who had smoked with Sitting Bull, his Miniconjou nephew White Bull, jostled next to Crazy Horse, who turned and remarked, "Let's make one more circle toward the soldier line. You go first."

"Go first yourself," replied White Bull. "I'll follow." Crazy Horse galloped downhill and veered his mount along the line, White Bull at his heels. Again, ineffectual soldier fire rattled out. Then, just as the pair turned their ponies at the end of the line, a volley crashed, and Crazy Horse's pony pitched forward, dead. White Bull veered left for the hilltop, leaving Crazy Horse to jump up, unhurt, from the dust. Alone, he ran uphill. Already, warriors were stringing along the bluffs downstream after Sitting Bull. A comrade lingered and Crazy Horse jumped up to ride double as the party turned to ford the Yellowstone and head home.[16]

The attack was little more than a show of force. Baker's casualties—one slain sergeant and a mortally wounded civilian—were minimal, but the survey expedition thought better of entering the Lakota domain. After scouts reported this news, the Northern Nation debated developments before the village broke up. Each division counseled separately. In the Oglala camp, the mood was uncertain. Some people were openly dismayed at the prospect of hostilities. The intertribal council closed with summary statements by the two war chiefs. Crazy Horse was brief: "My friend, if any soldiers or white men come in here and do not shoot first, we'll not bother them. But if they come shooting, we'll go after them."[17]

"Friend, you are right," agreed Sitting Bull. "I hear there is a government of white men somewhere east, and it is sending many soldiers to fight us. That is no way for them to act; it is not right. But if they come, we'll fight them and kill them. Some Indians will be killed, too, until we reach a settlement." With that, the camps separated. The two war chiefs were at pains to smooth over dissent, but their statements exposed subtle policy differences between the Oglalas and Hunkpapas. With whatever misgivings, Crazy Horse tacitly upheld the more moderate Oglala position. It speaks much for his growing maturity that, despite the rivalry both men displayed in the Baker fight, Crazy Horse instinctively supported Sitting Bull's harder line.[18]

In June 1873 the Oglala, Miniconjou, and Sans Arc villages reunited along the Little Bighorn. Although troops were known to be assembling at Fort Rice on the Missouri, intelligence indicated no departure for the west. The Lakota war leaders were happy to press their favorite concern: the controversy-free war with the Crows. The Mountain Crow village, augmented by forty lodges of Nez Perce visitors from across the Rockies, was on the Yellowstone, and in the first days of July, as chokecherries ripened, a large Lakota war party struck across country toward its target. Confident in their warriors' success, a contingent of women accompanied the party.

Crazy Horse was surely glad to be away from the seethe of politics. On the morning of July 9, he and the line of blotahunka drew up atop the bluffs overlooking the mouth of Pryor Creek. As warriors fanned along the ridge or grouped in the valley bottom, the war chiefs surveyed the Crow camp circle across the creek, opening on the Yellowstone. The defenders had been busy, for an arc of rifle pits fronted the village, and many horses grazed on an island in the river. To the accompaniment of drums, the Crow chiefs harangued for resolve. Along the Lakota lines, heralds rode also, their cries faintly audible to the massing Crows. Warriors, sporting magnificent warbonnets, galloped their fleet ponies back and forth to exhaust them and win the second wind necessary for battle. "I have never seen a more beautiful sight," recalled Crow warrior Plenty Coups, "than our enemy presented."[19]

At length a few brave men made dashes toward the creek to draw out the Crows. The defenders responded in kind, and the battle set in for a comfortable stalemate. "[T]here were too many leaders among the Sioux," recalled He Dog wryly, to shape a coherent strategy, and the Crows maintained the advantage of a strong defense. After an hour of this, dismounted warriors began to make demonstrations, standing atop low rises to taunt the enemy to the staccato bark of rifle shots.[20]

Recognizing individual mixed bloods and Americans in the Crow ranks, Lakotas shouted laconic insults, daring them to cross the creek and capture a Lakota wife: "They are better than your Crow woman."[21] Others exchanged news of mutual acquaintances, inquired about wasicu and other relations, or simply sat their ponies stock still and shook their lances to attract fire. Women called out obscene insults or shrilled in praise of their warriors. All in all, it proved a relaxing day's diversion, with minimal casualties until, late in the afternoon, the Lakota heralds noisily ordered back the women. Realizing that the foe was about to disengage, the Crows advanced toward the creek, but the Lakotas fired a Parthian shot, loosing a heavy volley into the enemy front before retreating over the bluffs.

Hundreds of vengeful Crows streamed in pursuit. In a reversal of the Fight When They Chased Them Back to Camp, the Lakota retreat turned to rout. Across fifteen miles of prairie stretching east toward Fly Creek, Lakotas fled. Several warriors were cut down and scalped by the pursuit, then mutilated by the women. Daylight was failing as the Lakotas approached the creek, adding to the demoralization in their ranks. Crazy Horse and several other leaders fanned back to hold the line at the creek. Beyond the sketchy cover of brush and cutbanks, warriors turned their ponies to open fire on the pursuit, and the fight became equal.

With night about to fall, the Crows were ready to disengage, and a flurry of action closed the day's drama. Crazy Horse almost lost his life in these last-minute maneuvers when a bullet smashed into his mount's right leg. Awkwardly, Crazy Horse managed to turn the pony, but the Crow line overtook him and turned to cut him off. As his pony lurched, the war chief sprang from its back and began to run. Several Oglalas tried to cut through the Crows at his front, only to be repulsed by the enemy rush. The situation was desperate, and a fate like High Backbone's looked inevitable until Spotted Deer laced through the enemy line. Crazy Horse leapt up behind his comrade, and the pair broke for the open. Closely pursued by the Crows, they reached the breathless Lakota line.[22]

Fired by the rescue of Crazy Horse, the Lakotas at last turned the Crow pursuit. Several warriors had been killed, and over two hundred ponies were lost to the Crows. Such a battle hardly stretched the tactical acumen of Crazy Horse, but he liked this sort of clash, which afforded room for the individual exhibitions of courage that made reputations in the Plains Indian world. Each side got a chance to field its champions, air some cathartic insults, and strike coups enough to make the combat meaningful. Considering the Second Arrow Creek Fight, or Battle of Pryor Creek, was one of the largest set-piece battles in the Lakota-Crow wars, losses remained low, and each side could claim something of a victory. Such battles gave life meaning.

During July, when a few Cheyenne warriors started down the Yellowstone to reconnoiter the expected approach of the Northern Pacific surveyors, Crazy Horse was happy to resume the congenial duties of scout. With a coterie of trusted Oglalas, he cut across country. On the morning of August 4, in the bottomland opposite the mouth of Tongue River, scouts alerted the party that troops were approaching. Augmented by Hunkpapas from Sitting Bull's nearby village, as many as three hundred warriors prepared a reception. No longer shackled by the no-first-strike policy of the previous summer, Crazy Horse was determined to attack. Once the warriors were hidden in the timber, a decoy party was hurried downstream.[23]

The approaching troops were two companies of the Seventh Cavalry, commanded by Lieutenant Colonel George Armstrong Custer. A further eight companies of the regiment completed the cavalry component of the survey escort. After the Lakota demonstrations of the previous summer, Washington was taking no chances. With nineteen more infantry companies, two Rodman cannons, a caravan of almost three hundred wagons, and a sizeable contingent of civilian and Arikara scouts, fully fifteen hundred men made up the Yellowstone Expedition of 1873. The army chartered two steamboats to ship supplies for the expedition. This formidable force reflected the premium that military chiefs placed on the Northern Pacific. Instructing General Sheridan to afford every assistance to the railroad surveyors, Sherman predicted that the Northern Pacific would "help to bring the Indian problem to a final solution."[24]

The Yellowstone Expedition had departed Fort Rice on June 20. Thirty-three years old (ten months older than Crazy Horse), Custer had earned a vivid if checkered reputation as an Indian fighter on the southern plains, matching a glorious Civil War career. Showy, individualistic, and charismatic, Custer was undeniably brave and a brilliant field commander. Nevertheless, he commanded a regiment

bitterly divided between his adherents—many of them related by blood or marriage—and his detractors.[25]

As Custer led the cavalry escort up the Yellowstone valley, he welcomed
the prospect of another, bigger Indian war in which to prove himself. Custer was
no Chivington, not the psychotic butcher or brute racist of revisionist 1960s
demonology. Cast in a romantic mold, he had sympathies for the Indian predicament that were not shared by the hoary cynics in control of army policy, but in the
final analysis, the plains were simply an arena in which Custer dreamed of winning
unimpeachable honors. His adversaries could take their chances.

Warned by expedition commander Colonel Stanley not to underestimate the
fighting abilities of the Lakotas, Custer led a trail-breaking patrol up the north side
of the Yellowstone valley. As a baking sun climbed toward noon on August 4,
Custer's ninety-strong detachment made for the shade of a grove of cottonwoods.
Suddenly, the noon stillness was shattered by whoops as six Indians charged for the
picket line. Custer was nothing if not prompt in his response. Men hurried to
deploy and lay down a heavy fire. The warriors turned and galloped upstream.[26]

In pursuit with a twenty-man detail, Custer soon outstripped the rest of his
command. To Crazy Horse and the other war leaders readying the ambush two
miles upstream, this impulsiveness seemed heaven sent. But Custer read the situation cannily. Like Crazy Horse's, his risk taking served tactical ends. When he and
his orderly spurred ahead of the halted detail, Custer gained his desired result: the
premature springing of the trap, as a rush of warriors from the timber swarmed
toward him. Custer galloped back to his men's dismounted skirmish line. Rising
suddenly from the grass, the troopers loosed three volleys at the warriors, who
melted away, regrouped under cover, then crawled forward to infiltrate Custer's
lines. Reinforced by the rest of the detachment, Custer formed a hollow circle of
men around his horses and began a slow withdrawal to the timber, under persistent
pressure. There he sketched out a defensive perimeter behind the cutbanks, deter-
ring charging warriors with accurate fire. Others tried torching the grass, but there
was no wind. The fight stalemated in desultory sniping. About 3:00 P.M. a cloud of
dust signaled the approach of more cavalry. As the warriors withdrew upstream,
Custer led another charge that effectively dispersed the enemy.

Few skirmishes in the Plains wars can have been as elegant as this. Throughout
the engagement, the troops fought effectively, with conviction and verve. Custer, a
distinctive figure in red shirt with flowing yellow hair, made a vivid impression. His
neat reversal of the decoy tactic was a ploy that must have won ironic plaudits from
the watching Crazy Horse. In response, the war chief and his lieutenants raised
their own game. Contrasting with the set-piece formalism—and the disorganized
retreat—of the Crow battle four weeks before, the warrior tactics were fluid and
responsive. Custer conceded that their charge was "in perfect line, and with as
seeming good order and alignment as the best drilled cavalry."[27]

Recalling his conclusions from the Bozeman Trail War, Crazy Horse strove to keep the battle mobile and isolate the troop units. Remembering High Backbone's victory against Fetterman, he maintained an unusual level of tactical control. After the initial repulse, lesser leaders would have withdrawn their warriors, contenting themselves with some long-range sniping. Instead he pressed forward, varying infiltration tactics with dashing charges. Always, a strong spine of warriors moved to enclose, to press and overwhelm the foe. "For three hours the fight was kept up," remarked an officer of the Seventh, "the Indians maintaining a perfect skirmish line throughout, and evincing for them a very extraordinary control and discipline."[28] True again to the instincts honed in engagements like the Wagon Box Fight, Crazy Horse only slackened the assault when Custer formed a strong defensive position. He had the warriors to overrun the timber, but the inevitable losses would have been unacceptably high. Already a handful of warriors had been lost. At sight of troop reinforcements, he ordered disengagement.

The warriors' firepower impressed itself on the men of the Seventh. In contrast to the weaponry used against Baker just one year earlier, the proportion of Henry and Winchester repeaters seemed high, making for a rapid and persistent fire that surprised the troops. Beginning in 1873, the northern Lakotas had traded intensively for improved firearms with agency traders, Métis from the Canadian plains, and unlicensed itinerants increasingly entering the Lakota country, finding a ready market for repeating carbines in exchange for that prized frontier commodity, a good mule. By 1876 repeaters composed about one-fifth of the Indian armament, and one-half of the warriors owned some kind of firearm. While hardly armed to the teeth with cutting-edge technology, as claimed by military apologists after the Little Bighorn, this represented a quantum advance on 1866, when barely one in ten warriors owned some patched-up percussion relic or fur trade fusil. Custer's troops were the first to confront this more formidable foe, well armed, well led, and filled with a supreme conviction to defend their country.

Crazy Horse's party withdrew up the Yellowstone. Near the junction with the Rosebud stood Sitting Bull's village, some four hundred lodges strong. Warned of Custer's approach, Sitting Bull ordered lodges struck. Crazy Horse's warriors hurried across the Yellowstone to warn their own villages on the Bighorn. The four circles moved downstream to join their Hunkpapa allies and by August 9 were encamped only four miles south of the junction of the two rivers. Aware that Custer's entire command was tracking Sitting Bull's retreat, Crazy Horse and the other war chiefs led their formidable warrior force down to the Yellowstone. They reached the valley to meet the Hunkpapas fording the strongly running river, six hundred yards wide. Women skillfully propelled round bullboats stacked precariously with household goods and meat stores, while men and youths rousted horses into the deep treacherous current. Custer's force was only hours behind. To ensure the safety of the women and children, the village was hurried across the benchlands to join Crazy Horse's people. Just before dark, scouts observed Custer and his 450 men arrive at the crossing and go into camp. Through the following day, warriors rode down to reconnoiter the enemy movements.[29]

A scan of the far bank revealed that their families were in no immediate danger. Custer's force was unable to emulate the Indian feat and had to give up repeated attempts to ford the river. The war leaders obviously debated a response. Undoubtedly, the issue that had divided the northern Lakotas the previous summer was again in play: Should the soldiers be attacked before they made any hostile demonstration? All Crazy Horse's instincts—and his actions throughout the war years to come—confirm that he was at one with Sitting Bull in this matter: intruding soldiers should be repelled by force. Now their counsels convinced the moderates to mount a concerted first-strike response.

During the early hours of August 11, as many as one thousand warriors approached the south bank of the Yellowstone. While some well-armed men took up positions in the timber facing Custer's bivouac, Crazy Horse and hundreds more spread out to ford the river. Behind the men, a screen of women and old folk formed around Sitting Bull to witness the action from the bluffs. Just at daylight, a single shot from across the river alerted the troops that an attack was imminent. When Custer ordered forward some of his own sharpshooters, a ragged but accurate fire opened. His Arikara scouts exchanged noisy taunts with Lakotas across the river. To add to the clamor and strike a surreal note, the regimental band played "Garry Owen," Custer's favorite march tune.

Increasingly, the Indian marksmen found the range, their shots striking along Custer's picket lines. After thirty minutes of this sniping, Custer ordered his force to move toward the foot of the bluffs. Dust upstream warned of fresh warrior movements, and as the cavalry formed in line, troopers noted still more Indians fording the river upstream and down. To combat these threats, Custer implemented a characteristic strategy, spreading his command along a broad front. Two companies were hurried west and two more east, while Custer held the center. Barely was Custer's line dressed when scouts reconnoitering the blufftops scrambled down the slope, shouting "Heap Indian come!"

Crazy Horse's attack came hard and probed everywhere along the line. Downstream, Captain Thomas H. French came under increasing pressure. Upstream, waves of warriors flung themselves against Captain Verling K. Hart's two companies. Hart ordered a platoon to secure a ridge on the extreme left of the line, but barely had the men crested the slope when one hundred warriors almost overran it. Lieutenant Charles Braden ordered a volley, but even as the Springfields roared, a second wave charged the ridge. Meanwhile, at the center of the line, warriors charged right up against Custer's position. A well-placed shot barely missed the commander, dropping his mount in the dust. Concerted volleys along the line eventually discouraged the attackers, and keen ears made out, above the renewed clamor of the band, the ominous thunder of artillery: Colonel Stanley's infantry column was approaching. Already, the war leaders observed, well-placed shells were being lobbed across the river and exploding along the bluffs. The warriors began to disengage, their line unraveling upstream.

After twenty minutes of intense action, Custer ordered the whole command to mount and charge. Having topped the northern bluffs, the companies veered and twisted to check the warriors scattering to reach the river and their families. Action spread across the bottomlands. Although the Indians were in retreat, this was no panic, and they fought in tight formations, frequently turning to check the pursuit, probing to cut off isolated men and units. At length, having discouraged too close a pursuit, they recrossed the river, guarding the retreat of their women from Stanley's cannonade. The Battle of the Yellowstone was over.

Although a tactical victory for Custer, the Northern Nation had achieved its strategic goal of dissuading further operations against their families, for minimal losses. Reunited with the main expedition, Custer's cavalry attempted no further pursuit. Instead, the survey party pressed west, out of the Lakota country, to complete the work started the previous summer. For five days, warriors monitored its progress as far as Pompey's Pillar, where the expedition turned north out of the Yellowstone valley. Contenting themselves by firing a harmless fusillade into a gang of swimming troopers, the warriors withdrew.

Distant events would soon postpone the march of the Northern Pacific. That fall the Panic of 1873 sent shock waves through the industrial economies of North America and Europe, ruining businesses and closing banks. The financiers who had underwritten the railroad's capital outlay withdrew their support, and the Northern Pacific was declared bankrupt. Track laying ended abruptly at the Missouri. There, a new frontier boomtown, Bismarck, briefly bloomed, and along the track east of the river, settlers funneled in by the thousands to checkerboard the prairie with homesteads. Army chiefs might fret the failure of Manifest Destiny, but on the high plains, the threat to the Lakota way of life was briefly lifted.[30]

That fall, a party of Oglala and Sans Arc scouts, riding along the Yellowstone in search of buffalo, came upon a line of wooden stakes driven into the earth—surveyors' markers for the route of the iron road. Leaning from their ponies, they pulled up all they could find and threw them aside. Scarcely eighteen months since Spotted Eagle issued his warning to Colonel Stanley, Crazy Horse and his allies had indeed "torn up the road."[31]

When the Oglala warriors rode home the afternoon of the Battle of the Yellowstone, Little Hawk noticed a stranger on the campground. Dressed as a Lakota but clearly of wasicu origin, twenty-two-year-old Frank Grouard, the son of a Mormon missionary and a Hawaiian mother, already had a colorful frontier past. A mail rider along the upper Missouri while still in his teens, he had been captured by the Hunkpapas about four years previously, becoming a trusted aide and intermediary for Sitting Bull. More recently, however, the pair had quarrelled, and Frank was on the lookout for a new refuge. If a single theme ran through Grouard's life, it was the ability to be all things to all men. As Frank searched the camp for his strayed mule, Little Hawk was struck by the youth's vulnerability and invited him to eat at his tipi. After hearing Grouard's tale of woe, Little Hawk advised him to stay with the Oglalas when the villages separated. He Dog, recently married and feeling expansive, invited Frank to move into his tipi. For the next eighteen months or so, Grouard would live with the northern Oglalas.[32]

Grouard had already met Crazy Horse, surrounded by a coterie of warriors on the campground. The war chief made a strong impression on Frank, who recalled his unusual features, light hair and skin, and the "few powder marks on one side of his face." Amid his boisterous comrades, Crazy Horse "didn't talk much." Grouard was the first observer to note that, at nearly thirty-three, Crazy Horse "appeared much younger than his age." Sitting in village councils, Grouard observed Crazy Horse's diffidence. Even when sitting with the Deciders, Crazy Horse was at pains to demonstrate that he "did not consider himself the chief." Indeed, remarked the perceptive new arrival, Black Twin and his brother White Twin continued to be "the most prominent among the older men in the village."[33]

Crazy Horse and Grouard became friends, hunting and associating together, and the unlikely bond was soon strengthened by tragedy. As a regular visitor to Crazy Horse's tipi, Grouard observed the depth of the father's affection for They Are Afraid of Her, now a feisty two-and-a-half-year-old. Likely within a month or so of the Battle of the Yellowstone, before the village would begin traveling east to the Little Missouri, Crazy Horse led out his usual late-season war party against the Crows. In his absence, They Are Afraid of Her was suddenly taken sick by an unidentified illness. With appalling swiftness, her condition deteriorated, and despite all that Worm and the other healers did, the girl died. Black Shawl assumed the garb of a mourner. Dressed in ragged clothing, she hacked off her fine hair, slashing open her thighs and shins with a butcher knife, perhaps slicing off the first joint of her little finger. Howling her loss as kinsmen erected a scaffold grave, she wept inconsolably when the tiny body, wrapped in robes and blankets, was lashed to the bier. Bereft and alone, she joined the procession as the village wound sadly east.[34]

Several days later Crazy Horse's war party returned home. Grouard was present, and observed that, when the unsuspecting war chief heard the news, "his grief . . . was pathetic." Like Black Shawl he hacked off his hair. Perhaps he hosted a wacekiyapi, a public mourning, enduring the insertion of pegs through his arms and legs. Certainly, he took the agony in to himself, neither accepting comfort nor giving it. Just as with Young Little Hawk's loss, he told no one of his plans. If Grouard's account is to be trusted, however, he privately asked Frank to accompany him on a pilgrimage to the grave. Seventy miles lay before them, but Crazy Horse was determined to make the trip. Without announcement, the pair rode out and, after two days' travel, approached the rocky outcrops overlooking the Little Bighorn.

The pair reined in near the scaffold, and Crazy Horse asked Frank to go and prepare a campsite while he visited the grave. Leading his friend's pony, Frank paused long enough to watch Crazy Horse clamber up onto the platform. He carried no food or drink, but lay down beside the pathetic bundle as if in a final embrace. For three days and nights beside his campfire, Grouard heard the sustained keening of the bereft man. Crow war parties were known to be crisscrossing the district, and Frank regularly checked on the safety of his friend. Each time he saw Crazy Horse atop the scaffold, loudly "mourning for the departed one."[35]

At sunrise of the fourth day, Grouard was stirred awake. Crazy Horse knelt above him and declared that he was ready to leave. For the first time since arriving, he ate sparingly and drank from the waterskin while Frank readied the horses. The vigil had gaunted him again, and as the pair rode homeward, his fierce gaze belied the stolid mask, already pulled over the intransigent knot of griefs within. He cannot but have looked back over the catalog of loss—Rattle Blanket Woman, Lone Bear, Young Little Hawk, High Backbone, and now the hardest one to bear, this child who briefly had afforded him an outlet for spontaneous affection and unconditional love. During the journey home he resumed his silence, so we have no access to his deepest thoughts, but it is safe to say that, after They Are Afraid of Her, no death, least of all his own, would ever mean so much again.

15

THIEVES' ROAD

The home Crazy Horse returned to in the fall of 1873 was, in Frank Grouard's phrase, "desolate."[1] With the tiny voice of their daughter stilled, Crazy Horse and Black Shawl were thrown on each other's comfort. Warm affinities reached across the generations and through the extensive network of relations, but their grief was still harrowingly personal. Grouard reveals that Crazy Horse once more closed down, withholding his plans, hiding his heartbreak behind the warrior's mask of stoical acceptance. Black Shawl seems to have shared something of her husband's solitary self-dependence—unusually for a Lakota widow, she would not remarry after his death.

Like any marriage, the relationship was complex. Their daughter had been born at an awkward time of year, in the privation weeks as winter turns to spring; hardship and illness might have made that birth difficult, which could explain the couple's failure to have more children. In any case, as pious Lakotas, Crazy Horse and Black Shawl would have taken seriously the injunction to refrain from sexual relations while their child was nursing. At only two and a half, They Are Afraid of Her was by Lakota standards young to yield the breast: it is therefore quite possible that mother and father were still celibate. Moreover, Black Shawl remained intermittently sickly, debilitated by the illnesses that had stalled their courtship. She was keenly aware that her recurrent condition compromised their sexual life and left her husband comfortless at times of deepest crisis.

Although never directly remarked on to outsiders, Oglala gossip knew of strains on the marriage—strains that all too clearly echo the relationship of Worm and Rattle Blanket Woman. Over sixty years later, when David H. Miller conducted research with Pine Ridge old-timers, he heard that "numerous other affairs followed" the intrigue with Black Buffalo Woman. The gossip may be just that, but one alleged affair has some support. According to modern Lakota informants, Crazy Horse had an adulterous affair with Shell Blanket Woman, wife of the Sans Arc warrior Stands Straddle. Legal testimony from the 1920s establishes that Stands Straddle divorced his wife about 1873, possibly following the affair with Crazy Horse.[2]

Divorce was simple in Lakota society. If he had been terminally unhappy in his marriage to Black Shawl, Crazy Horse could have announced a public separation by simply beating a drum and throwing the stick onto the campground at a warrior society meeting. Instead, Crazy Horse obviously valued and sought to consolidate his place among his wife's relatives. The measure of his success is in the affection and respect evinced by Black Shawl's brothers in their accounts of their brother-in-law.

What, then, are we to make of Crazy Horse's marriage to Black Shawl? It was the longest lasting of his three significant relationships with women. Black Elk's observation that Crazy Horse was "[s]ociable in the tipi" indicates a measure of contentment in the intimacies of family life.[3] Two further anecdotes are suggestive of a deep if unspoken companionship. Sometime in the first years of marriage, Crazy Horse led a horse-stealing expedition to Fort Laramie, making off with two blooded mares belonging to interpreter Baptiste Pourier. Gangly "Big Bat" had recently married an Oyuhpe woman, Fast Thunder's sister, whom Crazy Horse called cousin. Big Bat rode to Crazy Horse's camp and asked the war chief to return his horses. Always admiring of courage, Crazy Horse asked Black Shawl to bring the animals, but his wife demurred—she "did not want to give them up," remembered Pourier. Crazy Horse insisted, saying the horses rightly "belonged to Bat," and at length Black Shawl led them in. This snapshot of life in the war chief's tipi hints at the support Black Shawl afforded her husband in his war exploits, with the amusing twist that the woman of the household was the one prepared to take this particular situation to the limit. Perhaps Crazy Horse and Pourier smilingly shook their heads at female intransigence.[4]

Black Shawl supported more than just his war expeditions. One oral tradition expands on Crazy Horse's enigmatic self-reliance. "He never tried to dress well like other chiefs. He was always by himself. He made his own power. When someone wanted him, they could always get his wife, Black Shawl, to go after him."[5]

Although late and nonspecific, the statement fits with other evidence. It may be significant that the Shell Blanket Woman affair predated the death of They Are Afraid of Her. As their marriage deepened, Crazy Horse grew to trust Black Shawl, disclosing his plans, his whereabouts, and something of the spiritual imperatives that led him increasingly from home. That deepening may have begun in the bleak weeks of despair that followed their daughter's death.

Deep into the winter, Crazy Horse remained in *wasigla*, the withdrawn asceticism of mourning. He and Black Shawl would have given away all they owned. His face blackened, hair loose and hacked off at the shoulder, the war chief reflected on fundamental concepts. As the 1870s progressed, Crazy Horse turned increasingly to the holy men and healers who had shaped the visionary path of his youth. His hunka Horn Chips had left the hunting grounds after the trouble with No Water, but Worm was on hand, as was another man to whom Crazy Horse frequently turned. Long Turd, like Horn Chips, was a Rock dreamer, a practitioner of the cult practice *yuwipi*, in which the dreamer was bound hand and foot inside a darkened tipi. Long Turd was a superlative practitioner. To awestruck audiences the tipi shook, flutes sounded from the smokehole, blue sparks played around the lodge, and mysterious stones—round black pebbles and glassy crystals—struck the floor space. At the end of the performance, Long Turd, Houdini-like, stood at the door, the robe, lariat, and bowstring that had bound him neatly folded between a sturdy pair of digging sticks. Then Long Turd prophesied, predicting war exploits or locating missing objects.

"When you've suffered the loss of anything," Long Turd proclaimed, "they say then there should be a yuwipi feast." Small wonder that Crazy Horse was drawn to Long Turd's sings. Yuwipi was an intimate ritual, without the showy pageantry that the war chief distrusted. It dwelt on themes that became ever more important to him—of things lost and restored, imprisoned and liberated, hidden and revealed. Although Crazy Horse was not yet of an age to abandon the warpath and take up a calling as a holy man, Long Turd and other adepts must have seen in his mysticism the outline of his older years.[6]

To purify body and spirit, the mourner took sweat baths. Within the blistering hiss of steam, Crazy Horse was constantly adjured to be not frantic in grief but rather *iwastela cansicin*, reflectively sad. "There is but one road," the holy men repeated, urging the war chief not to spend too much time alone but to draw on the sympathy of relatives at this most difficult of times.[7]

For three or four months, Crazy Horse withdrew from the concerns of political life. As the Moon of Frost in the Tipi—January 1874—opened, however, news from Red Cloud Agency demanded his attention. Early in August, the agency had been successfully relocated to the controversial interior site on upper White River. During the fall, thousands of Lakotas had left the hunting grounds to spend the cold months testing the government's bounty. Upwards of four hundred lodges descended on Red Cloud and on Spotted Tail's agency, located forty miles downstream.[8]

The visitors placed the wasicu and the new agency on trial. Every ten days, rations were issued. Beef cattle were delivered on the hoof, and warriors staged chases that sadly echoed the buffalo run. Eked out with issues of flour, beans, bacon, coffee, and sugar, the rations often fell short, though the people vastly exaggerated their own numbers to maximize entitlements

A short ration day was a flashpoint for trouble, but even more contentious was the annuity issue. That spring the Oglalas and their northern guests had approved the relocation on the understanding that the 1873 annuities would be shared. Gifts of guns and ammunition were specifically demanded to validate the territorial concession.[9]

To the displeasure of the northern guests, the goodwill firearms were not part of the October issue. Animated by grievances large and small, real and imagined, the northern warriors rioted, shot up the agency, and made their own beef issue. Agency akicita responded impotently to the gathering crisis. In any case, agency warriors were easily swayed by their guests, agog at their stories of fighting the soldiers on the Yellowstone. Increasingly the northern akicita, marginalizing their own civil chiefs, demanded influence over agency affairs.

The census at Red Cloud proved the defining quarrel. An Indian Office directive ordered agent John J. Saville to make an accurate count, but the northern visitors declared that the census was unacceptable unless the arms and ammunition were released. Through January, tensions continued to rise, and as news of the crisis filtered north, Crazy Horse was forced to emerge from the hibernation of mourning.[10]

Typically, an end to public grief was announced by the visit of a respected chief. Near the northern Oglala winter camp, at the junction of Clear Fork and Powder River, was the one-hundred-lodge village of Miniconjous that had resisted the lure of the agencies. Lame Deer and Black Shield were the principal Deciders. Either of these men might have been involved in the rehabilitation of Crazy Horse and Black Shawl. At a warrior society feast, they were coaxed to put aside their grief. Their unkempt hair was combed, and black face paint was replaced with sacred red, the color of the life-giving sun. While well-wishers presented robes, household goods, and horses, food was served, and the chief lectured, "Though you have come up against troubles, weep over [her] only so much, have compassion for your . . . [other] relatives . . . good men and friends have you eat."[11]

Whatever their role, Lame Deer and Black Shield were instrumental in engaging Crazy Horse's return to political life. The two Deciders had fielded reports from the agencies through the winter, and after consulting their warriors, had reached a decision. When word arrived that Agent Saville had requested a reinforcement of troops, Lame Deer and Black Shield sent messengers to order Miniconjou guests at Red Cloud to decamp.

Threatening that they would return to destroy the agency in spring, the visitors urged Red Cloud's people to join them and depart for the hunting grounds. Haltingly, the agency leaders began to form a united front against their kin. Infuriated Miniconjous launched a scatter of small war parties. In the small hours of February 9, Kicking Bear, Crazy Horse's cousin wintering in Lone Horn's camp, shot down the agency clerk Frank Appleton. As Kicking Bear fled north, a mounting wave of violence seemed about to break.[12]

On Powder River, Lame Deer called an emergency council. A large coalition of Miniconjous and Hunkpapas threatened to advance on the isolated White River agencies, but the northern Oglalas were divided over the crisis. Black Twin urged moderation, arguing for a spring visit to Red Cloud, to parley and trade—in effect, the formal recognition of the agency Black Twin had so long withheld. Crazy

Horse was less conciliatory. Nevertheless, he was not quick to break openly with Black Twin. Intelligence gleaned by Red Cloud indicated that for some time, Crazy Horse was torn between conflicting loyalties. The outcome, however, was not in doubt: "Crazy Horse will probably join the War party," concluded Saville. During the second week of February, as the agency violence climaxed and army intervention became inevitable, the Oglala war chief came to a decision.[13]

"Crazy Horse has declared for war," Saville updated the situation on February 20; "Crazy Horse is on the war Path."[14] Behind the laconic telegraphese, imagine a council tipi packed with upwards of 250 Miniconjou and Oglala chiefs and warriors, with Crazy Horse and Lame Deer at the honor place. In a terse sentence or two, Crazy Horse announced his decision: war against the intruders on the Lakota domain. It would be left to Lame Deer to expand on the declaration, asserting that American bad faith left the Lakota people no choice but to withdraw from the peace made with the wasicu. War meant not simply military action, but unraveling the tentative accords established since the treaty of 1868, dismantling the policy of conciliation enshrined in the whole reservation system.

News of Crazy Horse's declaration startled the agency Oglalas. As tribal war chief, he targeted his words as much at Red Cloud's people as at his immediate audience. The agent, swinging between panic and the reassurances of the Oglala chiefs, renewed his appeal for military assistance: "Affairs among the Indians," Saville concluded, "are too complicated to trust to them for protection." Almost immediately, however, the agency Oglalas reasserted control of the situation. American Horse took the lead in building consensus to preserve order at their agency. Crazy Horse's old enemy No Water was one of the first men to be recruited as an agency "soldier."[15]

Convinced of his supporters' solidarity, Saville tried reversing his appeal for troops. It was too late. From headquarters in Chicago, Division of the Missouri chief Phil Sheridan had already authorized the transfer of troops to Fort Laramie. The anarchy created at the White River agencies afforded the opportunity that he and General Sherman had awaited. Sheridan hurried to Fort Laramie to oversee affairs personally. Over March 2–3 he watched eight companies of cavalry and eight of infantry march out of Fort Laramie, a total of 949 officers and men, backed by two new Gatling machine guns and 120 supply wagons, ordered to seize control of the White River agencies and establish permanent military posts.

News of the march panicked the Oglalas. Large numbers of agency people fled toward the Black Hills in the wake of the decamping northern visitors. Smith established Camp Robinson one mile upstream of Red Cloud Agency, and Camp Sheridan at Spotted Tail's location. Four infantry companies were left at each post, busily replacing sketchy tent camps with permanent log buildings. The army was in the Lakota interior to stay.[16]

News of the military takeover forced a reunion between Black Twin and Crazy Horse. The army invasion smoothed differences in opinion between the war chief and his principal rival. Deepening the trend of the previous twelve months, Black Twin moved closer to Crazy Horse's agenda of rejecting all treaty links with the wasicu. The two men had briefly been dangerous enemies after the No Water shooting, and since 1870 had warily competed for primacy, but for the next two years, they would evince growing cooperation, presenting a united northern Oglala front as government pressures piled up against the nontreaty Lakotas. As in his deepening affinity with Sitting Bull, Crazy Horse's fence mending with Black Twin speaks to a growing maturity in the war chief, a capacity for patient diplomacy that promised the emergence of a great chief.

Crazy Horse knew that strong leadership remained rooted in warrior solidarity. As spring drew on, he moved to consolidate his authority. Conditions at the agencies vividly demonstrated the shortcomings of the warrior societies as mouthpieces of a united nontreaty ideology. The Kit Fox Society had assumed a role policing the annuity distribution, while the Omaha Society oversaw the beef issue. In 1874 Man Afraid of His Horse united the chapters of the White Packstrap Society around a pledge to keep order at Red Cloud Agency.[17]

Even the Crow Owners, Crazy Horse's club, had relaxed its position, when his kola and fellow lance owner He Dog briefly visited the agency before removal. After 1873 the war chief evidently dropped his membership. Instead, Crazy Horse had observed Sitting Bull's own creative juggling with the problem of warrior society solidarity. Repeatedly, the Hunkpapa leader countered wavering unity by forming clubs of core supporters, creating channels of influence both to the chiefs and elders and to the key brokers of warrior opinion. To ensure a loyal body of committed followers, he recruited an informal bodyguard—"Sitting Bull's Soldiers"— of devoted supporters. Loyalty was focused not on a diffused hierarchy of officers, but on Sitting Bull himself.[18]

Crazy Horse recruited his own personal bodyguard, Hoksi Hakakta, the Last-Born Child Society, to solve the problem of warrior solidarity. With characteristic idiosyncrasy, Crazy Horse selected as members the younger sons of prominent families. Older sons, Crazy Horse was well aware, were typically favored with preferment and the family birthright, and therefore, they were most amenable to the consensual compromises of the elders. With less to lose, the Last-Born were more likely to hold stubbornly to the principles of nontreaty status. Psychologically, too, Crazy Horse showed keen insight into warrior motivation. Society member Eagle Elk observed that younger sons were fiercely competitive. "If they did great deeds or something very brave, then they would have greater honor than the first child. They were always making themselves greater."[19]

Crazy Horse selected over forty members. "They were all very brave warriors," continued Eagle Elk, "and always went out with him and fought with him." In size, the Last-Born resembled a typical warrior society, but true to the war chief's individualism, there was no hierarchy of officers or regalia. Even the ritual feast that concluded society meetings was dropped in favor of an informal meal and conferral at

Crazy Horse's tipi. Culled from across the northern Oglala tiyospaye, the member-ship roll stressed the war chief's concern to maximize his authority outside the Hunkpatila band.

Of the known members, only Little Killer habitually traveled with the Hunkpatila, and significantly, he spent as much time in Black Twin's tiyospaye. Other key Bad Face recruits were He Dog's youngest brother, Short Bull, and Good Weasel, a man Crazy Horse increasingly trusted as a battlefield aide. From the Oyuhpe band, the Last-Born recruited the redoubtable Low Dog and two of Crazy Horse's cousins: Kicking Bear, the killer of the agency clerk, and Eagle Elk. Target-ing the support of his mother's people, Crazy Horse invited Flying By, Lame Deer's son, and Looking Horse, a son of Miniconjou headman Roman Nose, to join the club. Most of these men were between five and twelve years younger than Crazy Horse, evincing his consistent concern with the coming generation. At thirty-eight years old, only Shell Boy, another Oyuhpe who may have served as society herald, is known to have been older than the war chief.[20]

Scouts reported buffalo drifting northward from the east flank of the Bighorns toward the upper valleys of Rosebud Creek and the Little Bighorn River. Crazy Horse's people, still nursing winter-poor stock, tracked slowly after the herds. Oglalas fleeing the army takeover at Red Cloud began to swell the camp. In the vil-lage reorganization, Crazy Horse and Black Twin were renamed as Deciders. Part of the Miniconjous, drifting back from the Black Hills, joined the Oglalas for com-munal hunting. Prominent among their warriors was twenty-seven-year-old Hump, a nephew of High Backbone who had earned his reputation as a youth fighting with Crazy Horse in the Bozeman Trail War. It was probably at the spring 1874 village organization that Crazy Horse named Hump as one of the four head akicita for the village. The young Miniconjou was invested with a hair-fringed war shirt by the northern Oglala council.[21]

The tightening of warrior organization soon proved well founded. Early in April, messengers from Sitting Bull appeared to warn of new intruders on the hunting grounds. About March 27 Hunkpapa scouts spotted a train of twenty-two wagons and two artillery pieces trekking east toward the lower Rosebud. The civil-ian Yellowstone Wagon Road and Prospecting Expedition had left Bozeman, Mon-tana, six weeks earlier to assess rumors of gold deposits in the Powder River country. Some 150 men, well organized and armed to the teeth with the latest breech-loading rifles, made a formidable reconnaissance force.[22]

On April 4 Sitting Bull's warriors launched an assault on the train as it ascended Rosebud Creek, only to be repulsed by the expedition's devastating firepower. Crazy Horse and Hump cooperated with Sitting Bull in planning a second attack at the head of Ash Creek, an upper fork of the Little Bighorn. When Crazy Horse found the defenders well fortified in rifle pits, he called off the charge, restricting the assault to long-range sniping, the Lakota marksmen felling twenty-one horses. The defenders were capable and ruthless. Having recouped their stock losses by capturing Indian ponies, they laced abandoned provisions with strychnine. On the Little Bighorn they buried a slain Lakota in a shallow grave, booby trapping the body with a howitzer shell overlaid with bolts, nails, and scrap iron that hurled the curious Oyuhpe warrior High Bear thirty feet through the air.

Along Lodge Grass Creek, beyond the Little Bighorn, some six hundred warriors struck the moving train simultaneously from front and rear. As in the survey clashes of the previous summer, the warriors were well armed. Although the majority still relied on smoothbore muskets, revolvers were becoming common, and Spencer and Winchester repeaters ever better represented. Several .50 caliber Sharps carbines boomed from the Lakota lines, reflecting intense winter trade at the agencies. Despite the improving firepower, neither Crazy Horse nor Sitting Bull could instill the necessary courage to overrun the defenders' concerted fire. After a determined sortie cleared a ravine of warriors, and the two cannons began shelling the timber, Crazy Horse and the other leaders ordered a withdrawal. With relief, scouts reported late in April that the Yellowstone Wagon Road and Prospecting Expedition had forded the Bighorn bound for home. Although outfought by the civilians, the Lakotas had dissuaded further intrusion from the Montana settlements.[23]

The season continued to mock the nontreaty bands' resolve. The coalescing buffalo herds of spring were smaller than ever and rapidly tracked across the Yellowstone into lands held by the Crows and Blackfeet. The Oglala circle, augmented by agency deserters to perhaps three hundred lodges, was the strongest it had been since the agency divided the people, but scarcity of game ate at tribal solidarity.[24]

Two more serious wasicu incursions were mounted during the summer, both at the personal order of General Sheridan. The first came from an unexpected quarter. During midsummer, raiders had targeted the Shoshone reservation. Crazy Horse's people, Cheyennes, and Arapahos had all participated in the cycle of raids. Sheridan, arriving at Camp Brown on an inspection tour, ordered a determined pursuit. Guided by Washakie and his eager Shoshone warriors, Captain A. E. Bates and a single company of the Second Cavalry struck the northern Arapaho village on July 4. In the battle, fought in the southern Bighorn mountains not far from where High Backbone had been killed in 1870, about twenty Indians were killed, including an old Oglala visiting from the agency. Although the defending warriors mounted a stiff counterattack, the Arapahos fled toward the sanctuary of Red Cloud.[25]

Preliminary reports at the agency indicated that Crazy Horse's village had been attacked, but, despite this error, the Bates Battle had a compound effect on northern Oglala morale. Hunger already weakened the young, the old, and the infirm, and there was much sickness in the village. The prospect of a hungry season dodging the soldiers held little appeal for the unaligned. Within days of the Bates Battle, a groundswell of opinion favored visiting the agency. Crazy Horse and Black Twin refused to sanction the visit, but by mid-July, the village broke up. Many northern Oglalas assured the agency visitors they would shortly follow them to Red Cloud.[26]

Preoccupied with disagreement and meat, Crazy Horse's people were in no state to oppose the most serious of all trespasses on the Lakota domain. Through 1873 Sheridan had urged an army reconnaissance of the Black Hills to locate a military post controlling the road between the agencies and the hunting grounds. Fort Abraham Lincoln, headquarters of Custer's Seventh Cavalry, was selected as the departure point. Over the vocal protests of Indian rights' supporters, Sheridan ordered Custer to ready a reconnaissance in force. Besides assessing locations of military potential, two civilian "practical miners" were to assay the Black Hills streams for paying quantities of gold.[27]

In loosing the miners, Sheridan was appeasing Dakota Territory boosters who had been talking up the rumors of untold wealth in the Black Hills and arguing for a reduction in the Great Sioux Reservation. He also scored a public relations coup in a year of economic downturn following the panic that bankrupted the Northern Pacific. In "golden age" America, a gold strike was seen as a national panacea. If the rumors proved true, an irresistible public mood, fed by the newspapers and adeptly surfed by politicians and army chiefs, would demand the sale, transfer, or confiscation of the Black Hills from the reservation land base.

Custer's reconnaissance departed Fort Abraham Lincoln on July 2 with a column over one thousand strong. Testifying to the intense media interest the expedition was contrived to generate, three professional journalists and a photographer accompanied Custer's staff.

As far as Indian resistance was concerned, the expedition was a profound anticlimax—most Lakotas were on the hunting grounds or settled at the agencies. On July 30 the practical miners turned up pay dirt in the gravel of French Creek. After three days of assay work, they announced gold in moderately paying quantities. While the jubilant troops pressed every utensil into panning service, guide Charley Reynolds was dispatched to carry the news to Fort Laramie. Then Custer marched home, arriving at Fort Lincoln on August 30. Already the transcontinental telegraph lines were humming with Custer's sensational dispatches, announcing to an America wallowing in slump that within the Black Hills of the Great Sioux Reservation there was "Gold from the grass-roots down!"

Through the fall of 1874, the impending Black Hills crisis underwrote a mood of foreboding in the Lakota country. Sheridan's forcing through Custer's expedition over a storm of high-level protest underlined that the highest echelons of the Grant administration were now prepared to abandon the conciliation policy that had dominated Indian Affairs for five years. Since 1857 Lakotas had defined the Black Hills as the geographical and spiritual heart of their domain, and they deeply resented the intrusion. Agency chiefs knew of the gold fever infecting the American towns across the Missouri and along the Union Pacific. They realized that Custer's reports made likely a mass invasion of the reservation by ordinary men made gold-hungry prospectors after the Panic of 1873. In December, an advance party penetrated the hills and started prospecting along Custer Gulch.[28]

Showing amazing forbearance, the Lakotas protested at the trespass but mounted no reprisals against the miners. Briefly, it seemed as if the government would act to protect Lakota land rights. Unlike military surveys, civilian parties remained illegal trespassers on the reservation, and General Sherman had to order their expulsion. On September 3 Sheridan issued a reluctant directive to his field commanders to halt civilian trains and burn their wagons—a measure forceful enough to satisfy even suspicious Lakotas. Everyone recognized that a diplomatic response to the Black Hills crisis must be formulated. The remarkable calm points to a crucial new factor threatening to unravel completely Crazy Horse's nontreaty ideology: hunger. At the close of a truly defining year on the northern plains, the realization that the old life was unsustainable was taking hold. Holy men might trust in prayer to renew the Buffalo Nation in their caves beneath the earth, but Sun Dance pleas and the cries of the hungry were not answered. The Buffalo North remained stubbornly beyond reach.

To empty bellies amid thinning herds, the only alternative was the reservation. Down the length of the northern plains, Lakota hunting bands drifted into the agencies, not as visitors but as people forced on hard times. Hunkpapas and Lone Horn's Miniconjous were shifting toward the Missouri River agencies. During August the northern Oglalas also started south. Some two hundred lodges drifted in to Red Cloud over the next two months. Frank Grouard was one of the visitors, curious to see American faces again. By September only about eighty tipis, the tiyospaye of Crazy Horse, Black Twin, Big Road, and He Dog, lingered uncertainly near the Black Hills.[29]

Reflecting the maturity of the relationship between the two leaders, Crazy Horse moved tacitly to reciprocate the concessions made to him by Black Twin. Maintaining their public unity, the two Deciders acknowledged that a visit to the agency was desirable. Early in October, they sent Little Big Man to assess the mood at Red Cloud. The positive response, coupled with the sufferings of his people, convinced Crazy Horse finally to consider the unthinkable. He sent word to Saville, which the agent released to a visiting journalist: Crazy Horse "will soon come in and draw his rations regularly hereafter," confidently predicted the Denver press on October 11. Updating the situation on the nineteenth, Saville wired the Indian Office that "All of the Ogallallas will be here this week."[30]

Messages from Red Cloud, resentful of the agent's independent channel to the nontreaty Oglalas, played on their wariness and insecurity to queer the momentous visit. Crazy Horse and Black Twin stayed out. Then, late in October, buffalo herds disturbed by Crow hunters recrossed the Yellowstone and sifted up Powder River. Jubilantly, Crazy Horse's people moved away from the agency hinterland. Nevertheless, Little Big Man assured Agent Saville they would come to the agency as soon as winter hunting closed in February, to trade robes and to parley. Saville presented Little Big Man with gifts to share with Crazy Horse and Black Twin. Little Big Man left the agency with Frank Grouard, carrying a far-reaching proposal from Saville. Although no direct response was heard from the war chief, Crazy Horse did not reject the agent's presents. To the suggestion of a new delegation to Washington, to settle the Black Hills issue with full representation of the northern bands, Crazy Horse indicated assent, provisionally agreeing to meet the man that agency Lakotas called their Great Father. After the war council of barely ten months earlier, this was a startling about-face.[31]

Besides Little Big Man's people, hundreds more lodges of Miniconjous and Sans Arcs had descended on White River. A crisis rose early and was nipped in the bud. When Saville attempted to raise the Stars and Stripes over the Red Cloud stockade on October 23, Miniconjou warriors hacked up the flagpole while Red Cloud sat calmly smoking atop a pile of lumber. The White Packstrap Society, backed by troops from Camp Robinson, was left to intervene. Disgusted at their kinsmen's accommodation of American interests, most Miniconjous drifted away, some following Lame Deer west to join Crazy Horse's people. Many hundreds more trekked in to their home agency at Cheyenne River during the first weeks of 1875. Lone Horn's people knew that the hunting grounds could no longer sustain them, and they reluctantly prepared to settle down.[32]

Despite Little Big Man's promise to Saville, the northern Oglalas did not appear at Red Cloud. Briefly, buffalo were back along Powder River. Surpluses had to be rebuilt, and the cold weather lingered, with blizzards sweeping the plains into the first week of April. Then again, Crazy Horse and Black Twin were the victims of competing agendas. Red Cloud's messages continued to confound, and runners from Sitting Bull argued against premature concessions. The Hunkpapa war chief scheduled a Sun Dance on Rosebud Creek, a ceremony to unite the Northern Nation as never before behind his uncompromising ideology.

Then, in mid-April, Oglala envoys appeared to announce a sudden acceleration of the diplomatic calendar. Fort Laramie post trader John S. Collins had made semi-official overtures to the chiefs at both Red Cloud and Spotted Tail. Advising them that the government was powerless to prevent a massive invasion of the Black Hills, Collins proposed that the Lakotas sell the entire tract of land between the forks of Cheyenne River. The chiefs requested an urgent audience with the president. Although in disagreement over the details of compensatory payment, Red Cloud and Spotted Tail Lakotas roughly agreed that a sale was acceptable. An Indian Office telegram directed the agents at Red Cloud, Spotted Tail, and Cheyenne River to ready delegations. Underlining the urgency of the Washington officials, they outlined a tight timetable. Agent Saville should be ready to entrain his Oglala delegates at Cheyenne by May 1.[33]

Knowing that northern Oglala consent was essential, Saville ordered envoys to Crazy Horse and Black Twin on April 1, but immediately a fierce blizzard closed down travel. Finally departing on the eighth, the messengers projected a fifteen-day round trip, but the crammed timetable proved unworkable. Upon arrival at the northern Oglala village, the envoys had to press for an immediate response and a virtually overnight start for the agency. Not surprisingly, talks stalled. Quizzed about affairs at Red Cloud, the envoys were forced to reveal unsettling facts—bickering among chiefs, agent, and traders about the trip, the size and composition of the delegation, and the approval of rival interpreters, as well as Red Cloud's ongoing feud with Saville. To secure a tribal consensus and a coordinated strategy, Man Afraid of His Horse had proposed that the united warrior societies nominate delegates, but dissension ensured that councils remained divided at band level. In December Crazy Horse had "purposed accompanying" the delegation, but the news left him suspicious, silent, and unhappy at the unwonted speed urged on him. Most of all, his instincts revolted at the ease with which the agency people contemplated the sale of Paha Sapa.

After protracted talks, the two chiefs announced another united position. "Crazy Horse and Black Twin refuse to come in," summarized Saville. In the guest place next to the chiefs, Lame Deer concurred, and the headmen sounded their validating hou. Expanding on his refusal, Crazy Horse declared he had "concluded to remain behind to guard the Black Hills." The disappointed messengers turned for home, followed by a straggle of goodwill visitors, including Frank Grouard, who had privately concluded that the hunting life was finished.[34]

Through the winter, several hundred miners had staked claims along French Creek. Amid January blizzards, an army eviction exercise mounted from Camp Robinson was called off. On April 7, cavalry patrol out of Fort Laramie succeeded in evicting from a rudimentary stockade one small party, but the expulsion was token, and defiant miners warned they would return.

To monitor this situation, Crazy Horse chose to remain on the hunting grounds. His words cut two ways—a warning to new intruders and an injunction to the delegates to make no premature sale. In a formalization of the war chief's role, the northern Oglala council charged Crazy Horse and his old comrade He Dog with guarding the Black Hills. According to the memories of He Dog's son, Oglala elders and holy men lectured the pair that the Black Hills were the "Heart of the Earth . . . and they were to guard this place because there were buffaloes, antelopes, and elk, and all kinds of game there in the Heart of the Earth." Crazy Horse and He Dog each nominated two "orderlies" to act as their messengers and scouts, including closely monitoring the mining parties in the hills. With spring opening the trails, that duty would be a demanding one—and dangerous: within one year, as tensions tightened and both sides became trigger-happy, miners had killed two of Crazy Horse's scouts. Yet something of the orderlies' success is reflected in the tight coordination of Oglala response to developments in the Black Hills throughout 1875.[35]

The village prepared to unite with Lakotas returning from the reservation. The White Horse Owners' council recalled Crazy Horse and Black Twin to sit in the honor places in the council tipi. This year Little Hawk and Little Big Man were summoned to share the honor, the four presiding over council deliberations, shaping agendas, and controlling village movements. A rendezvous had been announced on the west edge of the Black Hills, on the busy trail between the hunting grounds and the White River agencies. By mid-May some four hundred lodges, including Hunkpapas, Miniconjous, and Sans Arcs, had gathered within seventy miles of Red Cloud. With new grass spelling revived solidarity, the nontreaty bands grew increasingly skeptical about the negotiations opening in Washington.[36]

More new arrivals brought the bitterest news. After receiving their annuities early in May, many northern Cheyennes had left the agency, bringing with them some seventy lodges of southern Cheyenne relatives. Like the refugees after Sand Creek ten years earlier, the visitors were desperate, grieving, and bitter. Their story held unsettling parallels with the predicament of the northern plains peoples. Frustrated at encroaching reservation controls, the anger of Kiowas, Comanches, southern Arapahos and Cheyennes had boiled over at the tide of American hide hunters rolling south across the Arkansas onto the last buffalo grounds in the Texas panhandle. Through the summer and fall of 1874, commanders from three military departments had coordinated a massive pincer campaign that gradually squeezed shut every option but surrender for the southern plains tribes.

On April 7 fighting erupted at the Darlington Agency over the shackling of surrendered warriors. A core of irreconcilable Cheyennes broke away, scattering north toward refuge with the northern Cheyennes. Halfway home, as they crossed the old buffalo range of the Republican River country, now dotted with ranch and homestead buildings, one band was surprised along Sappa Creek on April 23. Half the party managed to escape, but some twenty-seven people were caught afoot and trapped in a dry gully. Under slow sniping attrition, every one—all but seven of them women and children—was killed.[37]

The venerable Medicine Arrow, most revered of Cheyenne holy men, was among the arrivals. Visiting at the Cheyenne Sacred Arrow tipi, reverently seated before the tribal ark of the Arrow Bundle, Crazy Horse knew that these grieving people mourned more than their relatives: as the army enforced total control across the southern plains, and hide hunters targeted the last scattered buffalo herds, the old nomadic Plains Indian culture was dead everywhere south of the Platte. The Powder River country was a last refuge for his way of life. Processing the intelligence of his scouts from the Black Hills he had pledged to guard, the war chief was only more determined to protect his homeland.

This spring buffalo were not thick, but the year promised better than the famine of the previous season. For a little longer, the pull of the agencies could be resisted. Crazy Horse and the other Deciders ordered the village to follow the northward shift of the spring herds. Along the Little Bighorn, they rendezvoused with Sitting Bull's people. The Hunkpapa war chief had formulated a new ideology of resistance, one that he would vocally propound through the summer. First, Sitting Bull would hold a great Sun Dance and forge a sacred unity for all the disparate peoples met here as the Northern Nation.

Crazy Horse continued to have little time for the great set-piece pageants of Lakota ceremonialism. Perhaps too he realized that opportunities for the sort of carefree horse raid he loved would be few in the months to come. He had Black Shawl prepare a feast for Last-Borns and other warriors, representing all the tribes present but centered on old comrades—Eagle Elk, Kicking Bear, and Low Dog, from the Oglalas; Lame Deer's son Flying By and Iron Plume from the Sans Arc circle. In all, thirty-seven men gathered. Outside, Sitting Bull and the holy men were readying the village for the ritual camp removal before locating the Sun Dance circle. Over their pipes, Crazy Horse's warriors agreed on a little extracurricular activity: "We do not feel like having [a] good time," his cousin Eagle Elk recalled their irreverent conversation; "We are going out like men and try to take some ponies from enemies."[38]

The party rode north at a fast clip, swimming the Yellowstone and cutting across the divide and the Musselshell valley. Scouts reported that a large war party of Crows, Nez Perces, Flatheads, and Atsinas was descending the Missouri. Crazy Horse decided on a rapid crossing to get ahead of the enemy. Approaching the river, the party intercepted a buffalo herd and paused to hunt and cut saplings for bullboats. Over a long willow framework, the warriors lashed green bullhides. After pitching the seams, they loaded their war gear into the canoes. A few men skilled with horses rousted the herd into the turbulent, June-high Missouri. Confined between steep banks, the 250-yard span of water ran deep, snaggy, and turbid. The wary animals balked, but when a lead mare was prompted into the surge, the other ponies followed. Meanwhile, most of the men stripped to cross with the canoes. Hide ropes were lashed to the boats, and while comrades steadied the gunwales, the strongest swimmers headed for the north bank, their teeth clamped on the lines. Safely across, the war party hid their bullboats in the bottomland cottonwoods.

As they cut across the Little Rockies, Crazy Horse steered his followers in a night journey through unfamiliar terrain, skillfully evading the Crow scouts. As a new day dawned, the Lakotas found themselves on a butte top, viewing the wide valley of Milk River that stretched north toward Unci Makoce, Grandmother's Land, the British possessions of Queen Victoria. Off to the west, the choppy ridges climbed to the Bearpaw Mountains, fronting the white-peaked splendor of the Rockies, but square north lay their objective. Around the log buildings of the Fort Belknap Agency clustered hundreds of Atsina, Assiniboin, and River Crow tipis. Horse herds grazed far out over the flat.

Two scouts approached from the plain. Crazy Horse assumed the pipe owner's seat at the center of the arc of blotahunka. The pipe was lighted and a stack of dried buffalo chips was raised, which the reporting scouts kicked over before kneeling, panting, before their chief. Each took a whiff from the proffered pipe, then made his report. The scouts urged an immediate attack. The large village was breaking up and scattering over the valley. Several bands were approaching the butte, they concluded, so "as long as they are just small parties coming up here we had better attack now instead of waiting until the next come."[39] After surveying the plain, Crazy Horse concurred. Keeping to the gullies, the war party looped toward the approaching camps. After the enemy paused at noon, Crazy Horse shouted the order for a charge, placing himself far in advance of the long line of Lakotas slicing toward the grazing herd. With a whoop, the warriors dashed among the enemy horses, stampeding the herd and wrenching up the picket ropes of tethered war ponies. With almost two hundred horses galloping south, the kicamnayan tactic of unexpected sudden attack had worked again.

When rearguard scouts indicated they had outpaced the pursuit, Crazy Horse ordered a halt along a timbered ridge. After the captured herd was turned out to graze and while men ate hastily from their pemmican wallets, shots suddenly rang out and an enemy dash swept away almost half the herd. The stampede drove off several of the warriors' trained war ponies. While most of the party scrambled downhill into the wooded breaks, Crazy Horse turned his pony to form a hasty rearguard.

"Cousin," he called to Eagle Elk, "be of courage and be brave. Let's fight to the finish even if we have to be killed." Two other mounted warriors joined the pair, and Crazy Horse told them to fan higher along the ridge, taking advantage of whatever cover they could find. Eagle Elk dismounted in a patch of timber and levered a rapid fire from his Winchester at the enemy atop the ridge. Crazy Horse, thumbing cartridges into his Springfield carbine, coolly combed the hillside with lead. Four more Lakotas rode up to reinforce the rearguard. "Everybody be of courage and let's fight them," came the war chief's cry. "It would not do to see the enemy kill all of us. Fight them until some [of us] do get away alive. There has to be someone left to tell the tale."[40]

The rearguard pressed uphill, but when Eagle Elk approached too closely, an enemy charge swept toward him. Circling, he galloped downhill to join the main party guarding their herd in the breaks. Four of the rearguard scrambled after him, leaving Crazy Horse and one comrade to deter the enemy advance. Slowly, with determined fire, they withdrew downhill in the twilight. With dark closing in, the enemy scattered homeward, and Crazy Horse urged his followers on a night ride through the hills. The party trekked into the Missouri bottom, dragged the bullboats out of the trees, and relaunched, as tired horses were whooped across the river.

When the warriors drove their nearly one hundred horses along the length of the moving village, however, they encountered an anticlimactic reception. Although Crazy Horse had demonstrated cool tactical acumen, bravery under fire, and the rarer capacity for protective care of his men, not a single coup had been counted nor scalp taken. The village was humming with word of the Sun Dance on Rosebud Creek, where Sitting Bull had staged a dramatic pageant of intertribal unity. Riding into the crowded dance arbor, Sitting Bull had asked one Lakota and one Cheyenne elder to present him their calumets. Then, his stripped body vivid with paint designs symbolizing his wakan helpers, he had danced toward the center pole, waving the pipe stems in mystic rapture. His painted war pony paced behind him as he approached the pole, retreated, approached again, all the time sweeping out his arms, declaiming, "I have nearly got them." A fourth time his arms swept out, and then he closed the pipestems to his chest, as if surrounding his enemies. "We have them," he proclaimed, holding up the calumets to the sky: "Wakan Tanka has given our enemies into our power . . . we are to wipe them out." Seven hundred warrior voices joined his chant of thanksgiving.[41]

Crazy Horse talked with friends and relatives about the promise of victory. No one knew the identity of the enemy, but the petroglyph scratchings on the face of the Painted Rocks, just upstream of the Sun Dance site, now showed soldiers with their heads hanging down.[42]

The identity of the defeated enemies remained unclear, but Sitting Bull used the intertribal conclave to articulate an ideology of total resistance. Envoys from the agencies were expected to update the Northern Nation on the delegations' business in Washington, and it was time to propound a rhetoric of unity. After the Sun Dance, Sitting Bull was ready to reveal his reflections on the crisis facing his people. One factor in the resounding Lakota silence following the invasion of the Black Hills was a general uncertainty about the region's significance in a time of unprecedented crisis. To all Lakotas, it was the symbolic center of their domain, in Red Cloud's phrase, "the head chief of the land." It held powerful sacred connotations as the setting of ancient myths, the scene of vision quests, and the home of awesome spiritual beings. Awe readily translated into avoidance, however, for the Lakotas had never lived year round in the region. The Northern Nation roamed the high dry plains west and north of the Black Hills, and the agency Lakotas—having to think the unthinkable in this era of momentous change—were forced to consider the benefits of a sale. Sitting Bull knew that this would be the burden of the envoys' message, and he moved to counter it.

Over half a century later, old people still remembered the persuasive sway of Sitting Bull's oratory in the summer of 1875. It is easy to picture him on his feet within the crowded council shade, a slight limp favoring an old bullet wound, the stocky figure exuding an unassuming dignity as he turned to address the arc of elders, the warriors grouped behind them, and the outer press of women and children. Crazy Horse's Miniconjou cousin Standing Bear recalled, "At this time I was about fifteen years old and I heard Sitting Bull say that the Black Hills was just like a food pack and therefore the Indians should stick to it." Expanding on his theme, Sitting Bull reiterated, "That is the food pack of the people and when the poor have nothing to eat we can all go there and have something to eat."

Like all successful political concepts, the idea of the "food pack" was both simple and suggestive. Standing Bear—and hundreds of others—went away and pondered. "At that time I just wondered about what he had said and I knew what he meant after thinking it over because I knew that the Black Hills were full of fish, animals, and lots of water, and I just felt that we Indians should stick to it. Indians would rove all around, but when they were in need of something, they could just go in there and get it."[43]

Sitting Bull's metaphor was characteristically precise. A food pack was a container for storing dried meat and vegetables. It identified the Black Hills, properly husbanded, as a guarantee against times of scarcity, an alternative to the reservation dole. The idea of selling them should be anathema to every right-thinking Lakota. As the round of councils lengthened, the confirming rumble of "hou, hou" echoed every iteration of the food pack theme.

As August, Moon of Black Cherries, opened, the expected envoys arrived from Red Cloud Agency. One hundred men strong, the party was met by a discouragingly hostile reception from the northern warriors. The leaders were Young Man Afraid of His Horse and Louis Richard, the half-Oglala brother of John Richard, Jr. Riding with them was Frank Grouard. They immediately called on Crazy Horse, and while the war chief hosted a private meal, Worm harangued the noisy Oglala circle "to listen to what we had to say."[44]

The warriors' anger reflected news from the Black Hills. Another military survey was assessing mining prospects; moreover, within the last six weeks, the number of miners had mushroomed to fifteen hundred—more men than the Oglala tribe could muster. Inside Crazy Horse's tipi, the envoys announced a council of all Lakotas to be held in September between the two White River agencies. Following the breakdown of delegation talks, commissioners had been appointed to settle the Black Hills crisis. Young Man Afraid of His Horse sold the council as a pan-Lakota summit, an opportunity to forge a truly national policy. Crazy Horse was polite, his tone judicious and moderate. As the leader of the northern Oglala warriors, he stated that he had no objection to the council—"all who wanted to go in and make this treaty could go," he acknowledged.

Grouard pressed the point of the war chief's own participation, but Crazy Horse demurred. "I don't want to go," he declared. But he repeated his commitment to consensus: "[W]hatever the headmen of the tribe concluded to do after hearing our plan, they could and would do." The war chief even agreed to facilitate dialogue with the Hunkpapa hardliners in Sitting Bull's tipi.

The following morning, a council of all adult males, over one thousand men, was convened on the campground, and the envoys delivered their formal invitation. Responding for the Miniconjous, Black Shield flatly refused to meet the commissioners: "All those that are in favor of selling their land from their children, let them go."

Sitting Bull spoke to the same effect for the Hunkpapas, mocking Richard as the commissioners' mouthpiece: "Are you the Great God that made me, or was it the Great God that made me who sent you? If he asks me to come see him, I will go, but the Big Chief of the white men must come see me. I will not go to the reservation. I have no land to sell. There is plenty of game here for us. We have enough ammunition. We don't want any white men here."[45] Sitting Bull ordered Grouard directly to tell the wasicu at Red Cloud that he would fight any Americans in his country from this time on. As long as the game remained, his people would never visit the agencies.

Sitting Bull resumed his seat. Eyes turned on the Oglala Deciders, but after an uneasy moment, Crazy Horse declined to speak. Instead, Little Hawk rose: "My friends, the other tribes have concluded not to go in, and I will have to say the same thing." Over the next few hours, some one hundred speeches reiterated northern resolve and the determination of the envoys to promote their council as a national forum. After the envoys announced they would remain in camp for another three days, the northern chiefs conceded Crazy Horse's private line—all who wished to attend might cross Tongue River and accompany the envoys to the agency.

The envoys spent an anxious night. According to Grouard, a faction of irreconcilables plotted their massacre, but Crazy Horse intervened to protect his relatives, invoking Lakota obligations of hospitality. "He said that he supposed that when anybody came in amongst them they would feed him, water him, and give him a smoke. He called the parties together who were the leaders of the proposed massacre, called them by name, and told them it would have to be stopped. He said: 'My friends, whoever attempts to murder these people will have to fight me too.'" The plot fizzled out.

For the next two days, the envoys hosted talks. Although the Hunkpapas, Miniconjous, and Sans Arcs remained adamant, with the Oglalas the envoys made significant progress. Little Hawk had toed the Sitting Bull line, but in private talks, the other Deciders proved more amenable. To close relatives, Young Man Afraid of His Horse could reveal something of the complexity of the situation at Red Cloud. Far from simply selling out their birthright, the agency chiefs were seriously considering the future. With game palpably vanishing from the hunting grounds, the Americans might reclaim the unceded territory. Young Man Afraid of His Horse was among leaders proposing a new agency on Tongue River. If the government could be held to its treaty obligations, the depleted hunting grounds might subsist future generations of Lakotas as ranch lands.

Furthermore, the agency council had sent its own fact-finding mission to the Black Hills. Brigadier General George Crook, newly commanding the Department of the Platte, had convened a meeting of miners and issued a deadline—all must leave by August 15 or face military expulsion. At Red Cloud, the White Packstrap police welcomed the deadline, which would remove the miners "before the northern Indians came down to the great council."[46] Sure enough, Young Man Afraid of His Horse's announcement de-escalated tensions. The key was Black Twin, and, after a year of conciliating Crazy Horse, he was ready to call in his political debts. Little Big Man would lead an Oglala delegation to meet the commissioners. The council was unprepared to commit the village to attending the summit, citing the lateness of the season and the necessity of hunting for tipi skins. Nevertheless, it promised the long-deferred visit for spring 1876, when they could trade winter robes and parley. Both Crazy Horse and Black Twin conceded that they might visit the agency "in a while," but regardless of that, "they will agree to any treaty that is made by the Indians at [Red Cloud] Agency." With this encouraging news, the envoys departed one day early, to arrive home on August 16.[47]

In the long history of Lakota–U.S. diplomacy, no negotiations were more tortured than those of the Black Hills councils of September 1875. What triggered the repolarization of Lakota society in the weeks following Young Man Afraid of His Horse's mission was one simple fact: the miners did not leave the Black Hills. When General Crook's ultimatum expired on August 15, no significant evacuation had taken place, and Crook's troops attempted no systematic expulsion. Talks that could have been desensitized by removal were poisoned from the start.

Crazy Horse's messengers kept the village informed of these developments, which forced a hardening of attitudes, realigning northern Oglala flexibility to the rejectionism of Sitting Bull. The village shifted east, toward favorite fall haunts around Bear Lodge Butte, where the crisis in the hills could be monitored. Little Big Man departed for the summit at Red Cloud with as many as three hundred warriors. With the stakes upped by the failure of Crook's ultimatum, Little Big Man's mission was simple: to speak out against any sale of the people's land, and to disrupt proceedings if necessary. As they traveled, the warriors extemporized a song that pithily summed up their position:

> The Black Hills is my land and I love it
> And whoever interferes
> Will hear this gun.[48]

At the agency, the commission had arrived on September 4, but more than two weeks passed before substantive discussion opened, when commission chairman William B. Allison proposed that the government lease the hills and purchase outright the section of the unceded territory lying west of a line drawn from the northwest corner of Nebraska to the intersection of the 107th degree of west longitude with the Yellowstone River. To the chagrin of the commissioners, Indian Office personnel advised their wards of the true worth of the hills, urging an asking price of at least $30 million. Even so, a strong antisale sentiment existed. Red Dog, leader of the agency faction of the Oyuhpe band, formulated a proposal that slowly achieved consensus. A limited-term leasing of the inner hills would be funded through subsistence spending and payments to the next seven generations of Lakota people. Although Spotted Tail distanced himself from the Seven Generations Plan, Red Cloud tentatively approved the scheme. Delegations from the Missouri River agencies, and representatives of the Cheyennes and Arapahos, all affirmed it. A vocal minority of younger men remained opposed to any lease or sale, arguing bitterly until Red Dog brought warily on board the Kit Fox Society, strongest of the warrior lodges.[49]

Just as consensus formed, Little Big Man's party arrived from the north. The northern leader angrily rejected the Seven Generations Plan. On September 24 he made a public threat, wrote the Omaha Weekly Bee's correspondent, "to shoot the first chief that spoke in the council in favor of making a treaty."[50] As talks opened that afternoon, Little Big Man rode onto the council ground astride a painted war pony, waving a Winchester carbine and a fist stuffed with cartridges, declaring he would have the blood of a commissioner. Young Man Afraid of His Horse had his White Packstrap police disarm the firebrand, but the demonstration succeeded in breaking up the talks. Little Big Man rode home confident that the Black Hills sale was off the agenda.

He was right. Asked by Spotted Tail to present their formal offer for the hills, the commissioners read out a final proposal on the 29th. The sums offered—four hundred thousand dollars per year to lease the hills, or $6 million for an outright sale—were plainly inadequate. The agency leaders, warned that current subsistence spending was charity, not treaty guaranteed, were determined to ensure that any sale translated into continued government support. As the commission itself conceded, annual spending on Lakota annuities and rationing was now in the order of $2.4 million. Their leasing arrangements would fund a mere two months' subsistence out of the twelve; the sale figure, spread over fifteen annual installments, little more. A second offer, of $15,000 per year for ten years to cover sale of the unceded territory, was roundly rejected when the chiefs acknowledged that those lands were too precious to the northern Lakotas to be sold. Talks wound down. Weary and disheartened, the commissioners made their way east.

In the Bear Lodge district, Crazy Horse was preparing to leave for the buffalo grounds. As the Oglalas traveled, he decided to repeat the vision quests of his youth. Near Powder River forks, he left the village alone, and climbed the rugged hills flanking the valley. Atop an isolated butte, he marked off a square of ground with wands to mark the Sacred Directions. From each wand he hung wopiye, a sacred bag filled with offerings. Then, as in the turbulent days of adolescence, he took his position within the vision pit, pleading with the wakan powers for a vision of guidance.

On the morning of the third day, Crazy Horse gathered up the wands and descended the ridges to the village. After purifying himself in the sweat lodge, he sat quietly while Black Shawl placed before him a bowl of buffalo meat. In solitary meditation, he smoked his pipe until the door flap swung open and Worm stepped in, followed by his Miniconjou kinsman Touch the Clouds. The pair sat in silence until finally, Crazy Horse acknowledged their presence with a murmured "hou." Worm asked if his vision quest had revealed anything of significance. Crazy Horse quietly stated that his dream had showed him, in vivid, concrete images, the total scattering of the buffalo herds. He had seen Lakotas reduced to poverty, forced upon reservation charity. With grim tenacity, he declared his determination to protect his homeland.[51]

Touch the Clouds had spent most of the year at the White River agencies as envoy for his father, Lone Horn, who had engaged closely in the intensive round of diplomacy, mindful that a negotiated solution was imperative. But Lone Horn had bitterly rejected the Seven Generations Plan. After the talks, he rode north to assure Sitting Bull personally of his continued solidarity, and sent Touch the Clouds and other messengers to apprise Crazy Horse and Lame Deer of the news. After the unsettling revelations of his vision, Crazy Horse probably viewed the report as more evidence for avoiding all American entanglements.[52]

Positions hardened on both sides following the failure of the Black Hills summit. Early in October, Lakota independence was underwritten by the return of buffalo from the north. Crossing the Yellowstone, sizeable herds again filtered south, up the Tongue River valley. Through the fall, agency relatives, distinguished by their bright new tipis of reservation-issue duck cloth, journeyed north to unite with Crazy Horse's people. As the new arrivals detailed the role of Red Cloud, Crazy Horse and his headmen distanced themselves. Dismissing the Seven Generations Plan as inadequate—or irrelevant—they singled out Red Cloud as "a cheap man" and froze the conciliatory dialogue that had marked the previous twelve months.[53]

With thousands more miners pouring into the Black Hills, the council approved retaliations. Uniting with disaffected agency relatives, northern Lakota war parties targeted the miners, their wagon trains, and the settlements blooming along the east edge of the hills. As the season snapped cold, the Oglala war chief had begun to reconnoiter the Black Hills personally. He saw that simple panning operations were being replaced by hydraulic systems that raised scaffolding and sluices above the creek bottoms he remembered from childhood. In valleys and parkland meadows that had been buffalo wintering grounds, log cabins and frame buildings were replacing miners' tents. The fifteen hundred prospectors in August had, before winter's end, grown to fifteen thousand: as many miners as people in the whole Lakota nation were living within the heart of the Great Sioux Reservation.[54]

In Washington, too, opinions were hardening. Within a week of the breakdown of the Black Hills summit, President Grant telegraphed General Sheridan to attend a White House emergency session. Convening on November 3, the meeting hosted, besides the president and his Division of the Missouri commander, the secretaries of War and the Interior, and the commissioner of Indian Affairs. General Crook, as Sheridan's field commander on the ground, completed the roll of top brass and high officialdom. In conditions of high secrecy, the summit meeting projected a strategy to neutralize the Lakota threat and seize the Black Hills.[55]

Sheridan and Crook readily agreed to withdraw troops from eviction duty in the hills. As the pressure of events forced agency chiefs toward a sale, Indian reprisals could be used to justify ration stoppages on the reservation and military operations on the hunting grounds. Jurisdiction of the off-reservation Indians would be transferred to the military. An ultimatum would be announced to the northern Lakotas. If they failed to enroll promptly on the reservation, troops would march them there, breaking their capacity to block another sale proposal.

The summit's decisions were implemented with speed and efficiency. Just six days after the meeting, the Indian Office produced a report recommending preemptive military action against the people of Sitting Bull and Crazy Horse, while winter kept them fixed in snowbound, hungry camps. During November, the report passed through channels from the Indian Office to the Interior Department to the secretary of War. Finally, on December 3, the secretary of the Interior instructed the commissioner of Indian Affairs to order the nontreaty bands onto the reservation. Three days later, a circular letter, the Smith directive, was prepared for all Lakota agents. Messengers should immediately be sent to summon the nontreaty people. Any bands that had not responded by January 31, 1876, would be turned over to War Department control and driven in. The stage was set for war.

With winter already slowing communications, it was December 20 before the Smith directive appeared at Red Cloud Agency. The new agent, James S. Hastings, secured reluctant messengers only on the promise of substantial payment. Early in January 1876, the villages on Tongue River had broken up. Alarmed by Crow raiders and a new minicrisis—the establishment by Montana adventurers of Fort Pease, a stockade opposite the mouth of the Bighorn—many agency visitors sifted toward the reservation. While the Miniconjous moved down the Yellowstone valley toward Powder River, Crazy Horse and Black Twin had moved back toward the Black Hills. Along the Belle Fourche, deep snows halted their progress, and they went into camp near Bear Lodge Butte. Hastings' messengers arrived the third week of January. The response to the agent's tobacco was vague but reassuring. Black Twin affirmed that the people would come to the agency in early spring. For now, he indicated, snow blocked the trails. Diplomacy must wait. The army deadline, with not three weeks to run, was underplayed by everyone.[56]

Similar responses were made by Lame Deer and Spotted Eagle, promising a spring visit to trade and consider settling permanently at Cheyenne River. Even from Sitting Bull's camp, the response was encouraging.[57]

But the army was set on war. As its deadline expired, the Interior transferred jurisdiction over the nontreaty bands to the War Department on February 1. From his Chicago office, General Sheridan readied his long-projected winter offensive against the Lakotas. He had originally conceived the sort of pincer operation that had crushed the southern plains tribes, but the extremes of a northern February indefinitely stalled deployment of the Department of Dakota's offensive. Not to be outdone by the Wyoming winter, General Crook concentrated his Department of the Platte forces at Fort Fetterman, springboard for an offensive up the old Bozeman Trail. A force of almost nine hundred officers and men, comprising five companies each of the Second and Third Cavalries, and two of the Fourth Infantry, was augmented by Crook's famous packtrain, a crack civilian unit the general had used against the Apaches in Arizona. Some eight hundred mules, and a rearguard of eighty supply wagons, would carry Crook's provisions and forage. On March 1, as a window of fine weather opened across the region, the command crossed the

North Platte and started north. Fanned far ahead of the column traveled a contingent of thirty-one civilian scouts and guides. Beside Louis Richard, Big Bat Pourier, and a cluster of iyeska recruited from around Red Cloud Agency rode Crazy Horse's old comrade Frank Grouard.[58]

Through the Moon of the Dark Red Calf, the northern Oglalas sat out the closing storms of winter. Then, in an unpredictable twist, Black Twin died. For five years the Bad Face Shirt Wearer had guided the nontreaty Oglalas. Twice in 1872 he had led his personal followers to share annuities with Red Cloud's people but had never conceded the Oglala agency the approval of a formal visit. Together with Crazy Horse, he had tightened his opposition to American intrusions in the mid-decade, but over the previous year, he had steadily moved the war chief toward accepting the inevitable—negotiating with the reservation leaders and the wasicu officials.[59]

A vital voice of moderation was stilled, and Crazy Horse was freed from constraint. The war chief ordered a camp move—not south, toward the agency, but north, down the windswept rim of the Little Powder valley. Wary of Crazy Horse's inflexibility, He Dog's tiyospaye joined the Cheyenne camp on Powder River, also preparing to travel to Red Cloud. Lame Deer and Sitting Bull's camps were barely forty miles north across the Blue Earth Hills.[60]

Through late February and early March, messengers and visitors from Red Cloud continued to appear, bearing invitations as well as warnings of Crook's imminent march. One of the last to appear was Crawler. To his brother He Dog, he presented gifts of coffee, sugar, and tobacco, with a personal message from their uncle Red Cloud: "It is spring," Crawler recited curtly; "we are waiting for you." When hunters sighted soldiers descending the Tongue River valley, He Dog conferred with his headmen and the Cheyenne chiefs. The joint council declared the camp should reunite with Crazy Horse, then work "in slowly toward the agency." The camp descended Powder River to a point forty miles upstream of the forks. There, despite repeated reports of troops traversing the snow-lashed Tongue River divide, the people squirreled into their sleeping robes the night of March 16.[61]

Atop the western hills, the pitch black sky snapped with oncoming snow. Frank Grouard examined the hunters' trail, then led down the tortuous ridges into the Powder River valley. Behind him strung out Crook's strike force, six companies, 374 officers and men, under the command of General Joseph J. Reynolds. Just before daybreak, Grouard declared the village was in the valley bottoms, one thousand feet below. As the weary, frozen men gingerly led their mounts down the precipitous slopes, broken with gullies and snarled with fallen timber, the gathering daylight revealed through the bare plum thickets and ragged cottonwoods a cluster of seventy-four tipis. Beside the frozen river, a stir of movement became audible with the whicker of ponies and then, still distant but closer with every step, the barking of dogs.

Dividing his force to deliver a frontal assault, contain the enemy flight, and secure the vital horse herd, Reynolds ordered his troops to the attack. As the thunder of ironshod hooves and the clink of cavalry harnesses alerted He Dog's people of the charge, at 9:00 A.M., March 17, 1876, the phony war of ultimatums was over. The Great Sioux War had begun.

Forty miles across country, Crazy Horse's camp was unaware of the imminent approach of war. His fifty-odd tipis represented a core of people who had longest resisted the lure of the agencies. They included "some of the strongest men from a mental stand point that the Sioux as a nation possess today," conceded one officer who would face them in battle and in council: such men like Crazy Horse "worked from conviction and held fast to their non treaty ideas."[62] Yet even Crazy Horse had to face the necessity of opening dialogue at the agencies, if any part of their old life and hunting range was to remain.

Crazy Horse was thirty-five years old. For a nineteenth-century Lakota, he was approaching a key transitional phase in life. Typically, in his later thirties, a man might be grooming a teenage son to succeed him as hunter and warrior. He would begin to drop out of war expeditions, spending more time in camp, bringing up the new generation more by word than example. Crazy Horse had no son, and he would never forget the incomparable rush of battle, yet in the past few seasons, he had haltingly evinced a growing maturity. These qualities were those of a great Lakota leader in embryo. With his mystical leanings, they suggested a future as a wise councillor and holy man. Already younger warriors sought Crazy Horse's aid in painting protective designs on shields, respecting his unparalleled favor from the wakan.[63] Visions over the next year would sketch out a possible calling as a healer like his father. They suggest something of the human possibilities of a complex, multilayered personality.

But war consumes. Because the Great Sioux War is now a distant pageant, alive with courage, dash, and the moral example of dogged endurance, tuned to the quick tempo of horseback action and the glorious verve of Lakota and Cheyenne warriors—"the finest light cavalry in the world," as one officer conceded—it is easy to forget that, like all wars, it devoured human potentialities.

Crazy Horse was not to realize those capacities for personal growth and the service of his people. Nineteen months later, he would be dead.

Five

DAYS OF THE WHIRLWIND

16

I GIVE YOU THESE BECAUSE
THEY HAVE NO EARS

Late in the Moon of the Snowblind, on the morning of March 23, 1876, the war
came to Crazy Horse's camp. Across the bleak white benchlands rimming the Little Powder, early hunters and horse herders made out a dark moving string of people. At the head rode He Dog and a knot of Cheyenne leaders. All were half-naked
in the fierce cold, some clothed in ragged shirts and dresses, and here and there a
figure huddled in a salvaged winter robe. Gaunt women opened meager packs to
feed chunks of jerky to hungry, frostbitten children.

Crazy Horse briefly conferred with He Dog, while his people rushed out to
greet the refugees. Householders stood outside their tipis, calling, "Cheyennes,
come and eat here." Eagerly, the new arrivals responded. In every tipi, matrons
roasted what fresh meat was to be had, or boiled up nutritious broths. Every family
donated spare robes to the guests and supplied lodgeskins or bark sheeting to construct dome-shaped wigwams.[1]

Six days earlier, He Dog told Crazy Horse, soldiers had attacked his camp on
Powder River. A mounted charge from upstream swept away the horse herd. Slashing open lodge covers, families fled toward the bluffs, seeking cover in the ravines
and plum thickets while their men laid down a determined covering fire. Clutching two rifles, a revolver, and his bow and quiver, He Dog first assisted his wife onto
a picketed horse and ordered Little Shield to get her safely away; then he knelt
behind a big cottonwood to fire into the bluecoats re-forming for a follow-up
assault. Reinforced by Cheyenne snipers like Black Eagle and Two Moons, He
Dog's ragged fire ultimately killed or wounded ten soldiers.

The resistance stalled Reynolds' attempt to head off the refugee flight, but as He
Dog's comrades disengaged, they were forced to watch troopers torching their lodges,
igniting tons of vital stores, household gear, family heirlooms, and craftwork master-
pieces. As the flames grew higher, the explosion of gunpowder kegs propelled stacks

of eighteen-foot lodgepoles as if they were matchsticks. Then, demoralized by the Indians' fire, Reynolds ordered a hasty withdrawal, driving away seven hundred ponies but abandoning four dead troopers on the field. With Indian casualties confined to one man, a youth herding horses, and a woman, shot in her lodge and abandoned, the defenders had won the tactical encounter, but the true losses were in lodges and winter stores. All afternoon, the freezing fugitives scavenged the charred remains of their homes for robes and unburned meat stores, then pitched camp amid the wreckage.

As Crazy Horse digested his friend's story, Short Bull took up the thread. An adept Oglala horse thief, Short Bull and a gang of comrades had tracked Reynolds' retreat and driven off 376 of the precious ponies. One of the herders, fleeing "like a scared rabbit," Short Bull observed, had looked like Frank Grouard.[2]

For another day, the fugitives had huddled amid the frozen wreckage while warriors distributed recaptured ponies and dried meat. Then, after a sudden chinook thawed the valley, the people had struck across country to find Crazy Horse, enduring rain, mud, and nighttime freezes. The evening of their arrival, Crazy Horse hosted a council. The Cheyenne headmen fielded Two Moons, an officer in the Kit Fox Society, to plead eloquently for aid in arms and ponies, before a fight to the finish with the troops.

In the pause between speeches, Crazy Horse assessed the mood, then made his laconic response. Turning to acknowledge Two Moons, the war chief declared, "I'm glad you are come." Then, to rising murmurs of "hou," he quietly concluded, "We are going to fight the white man again." The Cheyennes warmly approved the Oglala war chief's declaration of a war in defense of the hunting grounds.[3]

Scout reports established that Crook's reunited force had already withdrawn to Fort Fetterman, but everyone knew that continued resistance depended on national unity. Crazy Horse's own depleted stores were soon used up, and after five days of recuperation, heralds ordered the camp struck, and the procession angled northwest along the Powder divide to Sitting Bull's village in the Blue Earth Hills. Augmented by Lame Deer's Miniconjous, the host camp numbered 125 lodges. The refugees were welcomed at two great tipis set up on the campground. Matrons shuttled back and forth carrying steaming kettles. Sitting Bull called for his people to double up their families and donate their tipis to the guests. Women and girls presented families with robes and lodgeskins, while men brought up horses, saddles, and ammunition; some replaced pipes and sacred items.[4]

For the next week the people feasted, visited, conferred. The heroes of the Reynolds fight were honored in song:

> The soldiers charged our village, my friends cried,
> soldiers and Sioux charge, and my friends cried.

Hitherto moderate chiefs called for war. Two Moons repeated his harangue, but Sitting Bull did not need convincing. The destitution of his visitors bore out his conviction that full-scale war must follow. Skeptical Cheyennes were won over by Hunkpapa generosity. Intelligence from the agencies confirmed that fresh troop movements were being planned for spring.[5]

"This is it," declared Crazy Horse, predicting the coming fight. According to visitors from Red Cloud, he declared in open council that he had "never made war on the white man's ground, but that he would now strike a blow that would be remembered by those who invaded his country." For over a year, the war chief had resisted calls to contest the occupation of the Black Hills, but the Reynolds fight was the last straw. As the camps prepared to move after buffalo, Crazy Horse departed south, alone. Scouting a freight route in the Black Hills, he spied a small party leaving the French Creek diggings. Prospector Charles Metz, with his wife, their maid Rachel Briggs, and three other men, was returning to Cheyenne. As they passed through Red Canyon, Crazy Horse picked off the party one by one. The maid fled up the canyon, but her body was found with a single arrow through the back. In the lone warfare style of a Thunder dreamer, Crazy Horse had emphatically declared that for him, the war had begun.[6]

Late in April, a straggle of Santees, following the implacable Inkpaduta, arrived from Canadian exile, welcomed as refugees from an earlier cycle of American aggression. Crazy Horse returned about the same time. Although the war chief did not proclaim the Metz party killings as coups, Inkpaduta acclaimed Crazy Horse as a worthy heir—"a swift hawk" against his people's enemies.[7]

Turning west over the greening divide, the growing village—now exceeding four hundred lodges—camped on Tongue River through early May. As ponies fattened, hunters made successful surrounds. Messengers including Little Big Man were dispatched to the agencies. "It is war," they declared, inviting all to attend the Northern Nation Sun Dance on the Rosebud in early June.[8]

Hunts continued successfully as the Northern Nation swung west into the valley of Rosebud Creek. Food packs were filled, and clean white tipis replaced the smoke-smudged skins of winter. Warrior societies held reunion feasts, stoking the rhetoric of total resistance. On May 21, as tipis were pitched barely seven miles upstream from the mouth of the Rosebud, scouts topped the ridges overlooking the Yellowstone. Across the river were visible the white tents and unlimbered wagons of a major troop bivouac. One element of Sheridan's spring campaign had reached the hunting grounds.

The new troops were the Montana column of Colonel John Gibbon. Conceived by Sheridan as a blocking force to hold the nontreaty bands south of the Yellowstone, Gibbon's command numbered barely 450 men, comprising six companies of the Seventh Infantry and four from the Second Cavalry. Reflecting the preoccupation of the Lakotas with another attack from the south, their hunters, war parties, and scouts had all repeatedly missed Gibbon's command.[9]

On May 22 and 23, however, warriors targeted Gibbon's hunting parties. Their intelligence convinced Crazy Horse and the other leaders that the Montana column would stay put. Confidence in Lakota fighting superiority was affirmed by another visionary experience of Sitting Bull, who dreamed he saw a great dust storm approaching from the east, soldiers' arms and horse gear glinting behind the storm front. The wind smashed into a tranquil cloud formed in conical peaks like a tipi camp. Because the storm dissipated, leaving the cloud intact, Sitting Bull told Crazy Horse and the other chiefs his dream assured the people of a great victory. Scouts were posted to warn of any troop approach from the east.[10]

A new Cheyenne contingent reported that forces were assembling at Fort Laramie for Crook's second crack at the Northern Nation. Patrols were already policing the Black Hills Trail as agency-based war parties targeted the spring traffic. Processing all reports, Crazy Horse and the other chiefs ordered the villages moved slowly upstream on May 25.

During the second week of May, Little Big Man's recruiting mission had departed from Red Cloud Agency with an estimated one hundred lodges of Oglalas. A further twenty, as well as fifty lodges of Brules and a straggle of northern visitors, also departed White River. They carried substantial arms and ammunition for the war effort. Red Cloud's son Jack bore a symbolic weapon—the engraved Winchester presented his father in Washington in 1875.[11]

Traveling via Bear Lodge Butte, Little Big Man's party hurried north to find the Sun Dance village. From Cheyenne River and Standing Rock, similar parties were heading onto the hunting grounds, answering Sitting Bull's call for one big fight with the soldiers.[12]

The departures underlined the urgency of Crook's role in the Sheridan strategy. Approaching the hunting grounds from the south, Crook was to hammer the Indians against Gibbon's Yellowstone anvil. Throughout May, Crook's command reassembled at Fort Fetterman. Over one thousand officers and men made the Big Horn and Yellowstone Expedition the strongest of the summer operations. Ten companies of the Third Cavalry, five of the Second, and five infantry troops formed the core of the command, tailed by 120 wagons and a mule train expanded to one thousand animals. Urgent requests for Shoshone and Crow scouts had been wired to their tribal agencies. On the morning of May 29, Crook's command started once more up the Bozeman Trail.[13]

Still off the Lakota radar, Sitting Bull's dust storm from the east had blown out of Fort Abraham Lincoln on May 17. The last arm in Sheridan's pincer strategy, the Dakota column, was commanded by departmental chief General Alfred H. Terry. Over nine hundred men strong, it comprised the entire Seventh Cavalry and three infantry companies marching with the 150-wagon supply train. A battery of three Gatling guns accompanied the command, while forty Indian scouts—Arikaras and in-married Lakotas—broke trail. Nominally second-in-command, Lieutenant Colonel George Armstrong Custer rode at the head of the Seventh. The Terry column planned a juncture with Gibbon along the Yellowstone. Steamboats established a supply base at the junction of Glendive Creek, but the projected union slipped off schedule as Terry's command battled across prairie rendered gumbo by spring rains. Crazy Horse's intelligence reports still lacked any knowledge of the Dakota column.[14]

As the Moon When the Ponies Shed closed, the village shifted slowly upstream. The first substantial agency defections began filling out the six camp circles. The advance of Little Big Man's party, hurrying on from Bear Lodge, was one of the first. Crazy Horse dispatched scouts to escort in the new arrivals: "Everyone rejoiced to have us back there," recalled Crazy Horse's twelve-year-old cousin Black Elk. More White River defectors were approaching via the east side of the Black Hills. The first increments from the Missouri River agencies were within ten days' travel, but the main body was still gathering along the Little Missouri, 120 miles east.[15]

On June 4 the villages repitched camp for the Sun Dance. Sitting Bull had pledged to undergo the ordeal of the ceremony so that Wakan Tanka would assure his people of strength and abundance. Sitting Bull sought to secure the presence of Crazy Horse, pointedly absent from the previous year's ceremony, since the warrior named to fell the Sun Dance tree was Good Weasel, Crazy Horse's battlefield lieutenant. Holy men reverently painted the pole while warriors hung from its leafy forks sprouts of chokecherry, and rawhide cutouts of a buffalo and a male human, for power over game and enemies. Warrior societies danced to pound down the earth, to the harangue of the Ceremonial Decider, Nape of Neck, who closed the day's events with two songs—"very beautiful ones," recalled Good Weasel—encouraging the people to dance and give gifts.

Daylight of the fifth saw the line of pledgers enter the arbor and sit at the honor place. Among the pledgers, two men were to be pierced through the chest. Holy men, murmuring prayers, held up skewers to the sun before assistants pierced the pledgers' breasts and looped over the skewers the ropes hanging from the center pole. Each mentor seized his pledger around the waist and pulled back hard, four times, to a general wail from the watching women. As blood started from their wounds, pledger were each given a staff and ordered to start the slow shuffling dance step. Nape of Neck addressed the sun, asking that the pledgers' wishes be fulfilled, then held up before each dancer a glassy crystal and ordered him to look through it at the sun. Then the pledgers threw themselves backward, to tear away the skewers.[16]

Despite the interruption of a torrential downpour, dancing continued through the sixth. The dancers stopped only when a final pledger entered the arbor alone. Naked from the sweat lodge, Sitting Bull first offered a pipe to the powers and the assembled leaders. Then he sat against the center pole. His adopted brother knelt beside him, prizing fifty small pieces of flesh from each of Sitting Bull's arms. With blood streaming down his sides, Sitting Bull danced for hours before the pole, gazing at the sun. Suddenly, he stopped. His body wavered but did not fall, as if momentarily held at the still center of the world. Through a stretched silence, he peered sunward. Then he staggered, and a press of assistants and bystanders helped him lie on the earth. Water was dashed in his face to revive him. After drinking, in a low voice he confided to Black Moon what he had seen in the intense burn of vision. Then, exhausted and half-blinded by his ordeal, Sitting Bull sank into semi-consciousness.

Hushed with anticipation, the crowd listened attentively as Black Moon walked over to the center pole and called out, "Sitting Bull wishes to announce that he just heard a voice from above saying, 'I give you these because they have no ears.' He looked up and saw soldiers and some Indians on horseback coming down like grasshoppers, with their heads down and their hats falling off. They were falling right into our camp." The murmur of wonder built to exultant cries. Crazy Horse and the row of seated chiefs, convinced of Sitting Bull's prophecy, enthusiastically affirmed the vision as proof of a great victory at hand. The ceremony, with another two days to run, wound anticlimactically down after that. On June 8 the village moved up the creek, its screen of hunters and scouts urged to greater vigilance. At any moment, the upside-down soldiers might arrive.[17]

Ever since Sitting Bull's vision the previous year, people had pondered the identity of the vanquished foe. Now the debate took on new urgency. Clearly, the enemy was not Gibbon's Montana column, still fixed across the Yellowstone but moving slowly downstream, away from the Northern Nation. As the village marched, Crazy Horse remembered that the dust storm would come from the east. In fact, at dusk that same day, June 8, General Terry arrived on the Yellowstone, conferred with his forward supply base, and arranged a summit with Gibbon for the next day. Bivouaced at Powder River, still almost one hundred miles northeast of the Lakotas, Custer and his cavalry contingent impatiently awaited marching orders.

More immediate, a threat lay sixty miles south of the village. Incoming bands continued to update the war chiefs of Crook's approach. A rumor among Crook's staff and ranks held that Crazy Horse had sent a message by his iyeska scouts to Crook, warning that "he would begin to fight the latter just as soon as he touched the waters of the Tongue River."[18] One day previously, June 7, Crook's command went into camp at the junction of the Tongue with Prairie Dog Creek, straddling the Montana-Wyoming boundary. The local knowledge of his guides was wearing thin, and Crook awaited the promised arrival of Shoshone and Crow auxiliaries.

Late in the afternoon of the eighth, after a twelve-mile march up the Rosebud, the procession of villagers stopped. The Cheyenne camp was already raised when a returning war party streaked into the circle shouting the news of Crook's march. Along the length of the village, to the shouted summons of heralds, councils convened. Not waiting for the chiefs' decision, a party of young men departed south after nightfall. At 6:30 P.M. on June 9, as Crook's horse herd was driven in, the warriors poured a heavy fusillade into the lines of Sibley tents across the Tongue. The command answered in kind, quickly dispersing the warriors.[19]

For three days, spring rains lashed the Rosebud, keeping the Indians in camp. Crazy Horse and his peers debated the intelligence from Tongue River. Convinced by Sitting Bull that the real threat would come from the east, Crazy Horse was reluctant to commit his strength to combating the southern menace. They agreed that scouts would continue shadowing Crook, but no further preventive action would be taken unless he came within a day's march of the village. Even in such an eventuality, only half the warrior force would challenge Crook, lest the people be caught off guard by a double blow. Instead of numbers, Crazy Horse affirmed, astute tactics and precision planning should be used to disadvantage the enemy, and every chance seized to stampede his horses. The war chief was relieved, late on the eleventh, when the word he wanted arrived: that morning Crook's command had turned around and started south, as if withdrawing from the hunting grounds. When day rose bright and cloudless on June 12, the heralds ordered another move. Satisfied that Crook was neutralized, the villagers continued upstream twelve miles.[20]

In the days following the Sun Dance, the first arrivals from the Missouri River agencies began to trickle in. Crazy Horse asked closely about soldiers from the east, but the new arrivals could do little more than confirm reports of troop aggregation at Fort Abraham Lincoln. Still no news of the dust storm of soldiers Sitting Bull had predicted.

On June 16 the village started west, eventually descending the ridges to the forks of Sun Dance (modern Reno) Creek. Two miles separated the Cheyenne camp from the Hunkpapa circle. At the Cheyenne council tipi, a meeting of all the chiefs was heavy with the threat of impending danger.

Cheyenne intelligence once more alerted the villagers. As darkness fell and hunters returned with meat, a series of approaching wolf howls sounded, and presently a knot of dusty riders dismounted to report that through the daylight hours, they had shadowed a massive army crossing from the Tongue toward the head of the Rosebud. Its line of march clearly indicated that the troops would continue down the Rosebud tomorrow. A screen of 262 Crow and Shoshone scouts, far ahead of the column, probed dangerously near the village approaches. Uproar seized the camps. As heralds' announcements rang out, women hurried to pack everything but immediate essentials. Some even began striking their lodges. Men and youths hurried into the darkness to guard the pony herds.[21]

Crazy Horse and his peers anxiously debated the reports, augmented by fresh intelligence. Lakota hunters targeting the buffalo herd south had swapped insults with outlying Crows, and one party had spotted scouts with soldiers going into camp scarcely twenty miles south. Talks bogged down in confusion, focusing on the sudden appearance of the enemy. Fearful of a decoy strategy, elders swung consensus against premature action. Reinstating the line Crazy Horse and Sitting Bull had so long resisted, the elders had heralds cry the camps, "Young men, leave the soldiers alone unless they attack us."[22]

As Crazy Horse quickly divined, the army was Crook's, reinforced by his tardy Indian auxiliaries. That morning, Crook had departed his Goose Creek base, cutting loose from the supply train in response to Crow intelligence of the Lakota presence along Rosebud Creek. Just hours before, his column had camped at the source of the Rosebud's south fork, anticipating a second day's march downstream.

Augmented by Indian and civilian reinforcements, Crook's effective force numbered more than thirteen hundred men—significantly outnumbering the Lakota strength. But convinced of their rightful victory, warriors ran for weapons and ponies. Dabbing hurried paint, they mounted and paraded the camps. The council hurriedly agreed that Crazy Horse lead the defense. Heralds updated the situation: "The scouts have returned and they have reported that the soldiers are now camping on the Rosebud River, so young warriors, take courage and get ready to go meet them."[23]

As the drain of warriors started up the creek, Crazy Horse and Good Weasel joined them, a string of Oglalas knotting behind. A straggle of visiting Brules, convinced of Crazy Horse's medicine, attached themselves to the party. At the Hunkpapa circle, riders milled outside Sitting Bull's tipi. The Hunkpapa chief, still afflicted with sore eyes and swollen arms after his Sun Dance ordeal, restricted himself to urging courage. But younger war leaders rallied the men. Then, following Crazy Horse and the rest, some 750 warriors streamed into the darkness.[24]

A thirty-mile ride separated the two armies. Traveling through the night in isolated groups of comrades, communication failed. Everyone knew that it was too late to intercept Crook at his bivouac, that he must be caught on the march. One party struck through the Wolf Mountains. Their only plan to lay straight into Crook, they steered toward a break in the hills, meeting the Rosebud near its upper bend. Through the morning, other groups in scores or hundreds laced the hills. One group of two hundred, including Crazy Horse, sliced across country toward the Rosebud ten miles farther downstream. One or more camps of agency people were known to be just across the Rosebud on Trail Creek, and the time gained permitted a concerted ambush. Just before daybreak of June 17, as they neared the Rosebud, the Trail Creek contingent met them. Jack Red Cloud, sporting a superb trailer headdress and his father's famous Winchester, stood out among the reinforcements. The growing throng unsaddled and let their ponies graze.

Crazy Horse and the other leaders conferred quickly. Akicita were drafted to ride a deadline. None should pass upstream of Trail Creek. Just what the strategy was is unclear, but persistent reports credited the Indians with preparing a massive ambush for Crook. Strategy would have been flexible, but the course of Rosebud Creek upstream of the deadline is deeply cut for several miles, its canyon broken with gullies blocked with brush, timber, and even old Indian corrals—ideal terrain for an ambush. Recalling High Backbone's success in 1866, the leaders undoubtedly considered some variant on the decoy tactic.[25]

But events quickly rendered all planning redundant. Four scouts were selected to cut over the hills and monitor Crook's progress, while the warriors prepared for battle. For the untried, fathers and mentors prayed as they attached wotawe charms or shook out war shirts and bonnets, explained paint designs, and imparted quiet

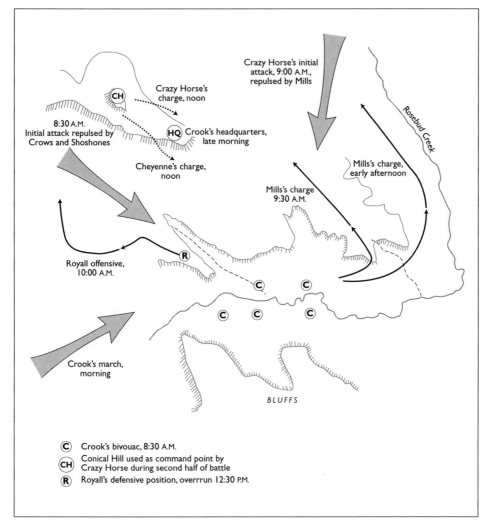

The Battle of the Rosebud, June 17, 1876

advice. Suddenly shots sounded upstream, and everyone strained to see four Crows, skylined on a distant ridge, shooting at the Lakota scouts before whipping northward, yelling "Lakota! Lakota!" Before the akicita could restrain them, a rush of men poured in pursuit and, to a mounting barrage of gunfire, the war chiefs were forced to order a general attack.

Meanwhile, Crook's command, on the march before dawn, had halted to eat breakfast beside the Rosebud ten miles upstream. Men settled to coffee and cards while the Indian scouts reconnoitered the northern bluffs. Convinced of the proximity of the enemy, the Crows were restive, but Crook was skeptical until he heard distant shots, as his outriders met Crazy Horse's scouts—a pause, then more shots sounded closer. Barely had Crook assessed the threat from his right, downstream, when more scouts galloped down the hills. "Heap Sioux!" they cried, as a line of painted warriors—the Wolf Mountains contingent—swept into the valley from upstream and raced straight at the left of Crook's halted line.

Amid wild confusion, officers hurried to rally their men, but many acknowledged that their position would have been overrun if not for the superb courage of the Crows and Shoshones. The general was able to dress skirmish lines, but for twenty minutes the battle teetered in the balance. Crook's allies gradually forced the Cheyennes and Lakotas back onto the hills. Even as the general hurried men to seize the blufftops, however, more warriors poured across the hills on his right, opening a new phase of the battle.

Crazy Horse and his warriors had streamed up the Rosebud toward the sound of the guns. A westward bend in the creek obscured the action, but with a mounting barrage sounding to their right, Crazy Horse's followers sliced up a side canyon onto the tableland to survey the battleground. From the valley bottom, units of cavalry and dismounted troopers were deploying uphill along a broad front. Atop the slopes to the west, hundreds of Crows and Shoshones were galloping in pursuit of the retreating first assault, and many Lakota ponies were bleeding or dropping from exhaustion.

Forced to abandon any ambush plan, Crazy Horse had to think on his feet. A more mobile battle was possible, such as he had envisaged in the aftermath of the Bozeman Trail campaigning. First priority was to save their comrades, and the new arrivals poured a charge downhill through a gap in the bluffs. In these minutes, two actions stamped their imprint on Indian memories of the Battle of the Rosebud. In one not redounding to Oglala honor, Jack Red Cloud's pony was shot from under him. Fleeing uphill, Jack was quirted by Crow scouts.

By contrast, a Cheyenne maiden riding to assist her brother won immortal honor when his horse was also brought down. Ignoring a closing line of enemy scouts, Buffalo Calf Road Woman galloped through the gap, hauled her brother across her pony's withers, then whipped uphill amid a hail of lead from Crook's right. From the boulders and crevices above the east slope of the gap, dismounted warriors poured heavy fire into this dangerous unit, pinning down the bluecoat line until Captain Anson Mills's determined cavalry countercharge swept uphill and secured the rocks. Crazy Horse and his comrades ordered disengagement, the Indian line unraveling to re-form atop a bluff one mile west. Many Cheyennes infiltrated a long ridge extending from the bluffs into the valley bottom, commanding Crook's left.

Sensing the advantage, Crook ordered Mills to reprise his charge and take the peak. Crazy Horse, implementing his own fallback strategy—"to lead detachments in pursuit of his people, and turning quickly cut them to pieces in detail," according to campaign diarist John G. Bourke—urged retreat, and the Indian resistance again melted away. As Crazy Horse's warriors regrouped on a conical hill three quarters of a mile northwest, staccato mirror flashes signaled the presence of a strategic leader,

one that newsman observer John F. Finerty surmised was Crazy Horse. Crazy
Horse's men opened a desultory fire on Mills's six companies. They galloped across
the ridge, slapping their buttocks in derisive provocation. Mills dismounted his men
and took up skirmish lines around the hill crest, where Crook hurried to establish
his headquarters, joined by his infantry and civilian auxiliaries.[26]

Simultaneously with Mills's action, Lieutenant Colonel William B. Royall
launched a second cavalry charge, countering the growing presence along the high
ridge on Crook's left. In a series of stirring charges, Royall's five companies pushed
the warriors back, then regrouped along the contested ridge. "In the Rosebud fight
the soldiers first got the Sioux and Cheyennes on the run," Short Bull said of the
first half of the engagement.[27] After almost two hours of action, the Battle of the
Rosebud seemed over.

"This was a pitiful long stretched-out battle," remembered one Hunkpapa
youth. With fatigue setting in, the war chiefs rallied their followers. From the conical
peak, Sitting Bull harangued, "Steady men! Remember how to hold a gun! Brace up,
now! Brace up!" Crazy Horse rode among the warriors, holding aloft his Winchester and calling for courage: "Hold on, my friends! Be strong! Remember the helpless! This is a good day to die!." He saw that Royall's charge had dangerously
extended Crook's line across a mile of broken terrain. The strategy he had formulated
over ten years, of isolating troop units and breaking them piecemeal, was beginning
to crystallize. Sensing the key to the battle, Crazy Horse called for renewed pressure
on Royall. Oglala subordinates—Bad Heart Bull, Black Deer, Kicking Bear—echoed
the war chief's resolve. Akicita Good Weasel, shadowing his war chief over the field,
added coercive persuasion to Crazy Horse's words. "When these five commenced to
rally their men," recalled Short Bull, "that was as far as the soldiers got."[28]

Like Crazy Horse, Crook perceived a defining moment. He hurried couriers to
recall Royall. With Indians developing around his left front, the general wished to
consolidate his command and advance obliquely right, where scout intelligence—
and fierce resistance—indicated that the enemy village was located. Moreover,
the wide coulee separating Royall from the headquarters position was a potential
avenue for attack. Repeated couriers ordered Royall to close the gap, but mounting pressure from the heights slowed disengagement. Crook still viewed the Indian
maneuvers as more irritant than threat. He detailed Mills to push speedily down
Rosebud Creek with eight companies and seize the (nonexistent) village. The
Indian allies would flank his movement, and the whole command would follow as
soon as Royall disengaged.

On the bluffs, Crazy Horse observed Mills's departure with grim satisfaction.
While Crook's command regrouped to fill the line, he and his war leaders ordered
a charge to stampede the horses picketed in the valley, with sharpshooters pinning
down the troops. Warriors started the herd, but fire from the southern heights
forced them to abandon it. Once more, the Crows and Shoshones responded mag-
nificently, pushing back the enemy in a flanking charge that, if supported, could

have secured the field. Instead, as the auxiliaries topped the western bluff, their pursuit came to a halt—and a precipitate reverse downhill.

While Crook continued to consolidate his hold on the center of the field, pressure mounted on Royall, still isolated across the coulee. As many as five hundred warriors were swarming over the ridge, encircling the blue skirmish lines. Every fourth trooper fell out as a horse holder while his comrades formed a segmented skirmish line stretched along the ridge. Each time Royall attempted a withdrawal, warriors poured charge after charge against his position. Zigzag lines of riders rippled across the field, striking obliquely at an unprotected flank, dissolving into the rolling terrain, levering their Winchester and Henry repeaters from the saddle. The desperate troopers threw back a blistering fire, but Crazy Horse would not give ground. In some of the hardest fighting army veterans had seen since the Civil War, Crazy Horse pressed Royall downhill, away from Crook's support. From the headquarters hill, Crook detailed two infantry companies to support Royall. Throughout the battle, Crazy Horse's men had given the infantry a wide berth, testimony to the foot soldiers' deadly accuracy. As the "walk-a-heaps" deployed, the warriors redoubled their assault on Royall's line.

Warriors tore through the position of Captain Peter D. Vroom, leaping from their ponies to fight hand to hand, killing five troopers outright. To prevent the infantry deployment from uniting Crook's divided command, Crazy Horse and the other war leaders atop the bluffs poured in a broad charge that pressed everywhere along Crook's lines. Part swept down the coulee at Royall. Another raced for Crook's headquarters position.

Chanting in unison, warriors led by Crazy Horse swept around the north side of Crook's ridgetop defenses. Guide Bat Pourier vividly remembered the war chief's presence and his miraculous survival of a hail of bullets—"they couldn't even hit his horse."[29] With the Cheyennes taking the riverward side of the ridge, the charge swept on, tangling in hand-to-hand combat with the desperate defenders, pressing to envelop the center. Only the timely deployment of Crook's reserve companies, exposing the Lakota assault to a withering crossfire, dissipated the charge. Many warriors veered downhill toward Royall. Taunting Crook, one party raced down the coulee, crossed his morning bivouac, and galloped around the Rosebud bend to reappear along the northern bluffs. Vividly assured of imminent encirclement, Crook sent a courier to recall Mills and consolidate the command.

The beleaguered Royall ordered his men to mount. Taking advantage of the moment of critical imbalance—the kicamnayan tactic of the Thunder Beings—Crazy Horse unleashed a final charge from the northwest. In a riot of dust, panicked horseflesh, gunfire, whoops, and curses, the lines collided. Some bluecoats were unhorsed by lance thrusts and swinging knife clubs. Panic gripped the soldiers. One trooper surrendered his pistol, only to be clubbed down. Another, one foot in his stirrup, was clubbed to the ground and his revolver wrested away by another warrior. As he crawled, stunned, the first rider shot him dead. Cavalry mounts spun away as their riders were forced into desperate close-quarters struggle. Warriors raced in to kill and coup. Troopers ran in panic, dropping carbines in their flight. The prospect of utter rout loomed. Only when the infantry relief opened a bull-throated volley from their Long Tom rifles did Royall manage to extricate his crippled battalion. With many troopers doubled up, he managed the sudden dash to Crook.

Crazy Horse's men melted back onto the bluffs, persistently hemming the general's north front. After the rush of action, a stalemate of sniping ensued. Then, about 2:30, dust across the tableland signaled the return of Mills at the Indians' rear, cutting the angle of the creek. For the warriors it was enough. "It was a [hot] day like this," recalled young Iron Hawk, "and they announced they should quit and go back and take care of their women."[30] Knowing that Crook had been fought to a standstill, Crazy Horse had no wish for further casualties. At least eight warriors were dead, and many more seriously wounded. He detailed scouts to shadow Crook and led a final triumphant charge down the coulee. As it melted back into the hills, the Battle of the Rosebud was over.

A stunned command was left to regroup. At least nine troopers lay dead. Twenty-three were wounded, most from Royall's mauled skirmish line, whose dire predicament would foreshadow the fate of another command barely one week later. One Indian scout was killed and seven of his comrades wounded. Crook withdrew to his Goose Creek base camp. His Indian auxiliaries decamped for home, anxious to block Lakota reprisals. Crook claimed a victory for holding the field in a battle of the Indians' own choosing, but for six weeks, his command was demoralized by the strength, verve, and conviction of the Indian force. Crook's role in Sheridan's pincer campaign had been neutralized.

Crazy Horse had fought with accustomed dash—*na hel ake Tasunke Witko lila wohitika*, summed up Black Twin's son Thunder Tail: "and there again Crazy Horse was very brave."[31] The new armament, particularly Winchesters and Henrys, had been critical to warrior confidence. If proportionate to their deployment in the Custer battle, the guns were probably in the hands of fewer than one hundred warriors, but the men used them with stunning effect. Unlike the flintlocks of old, the new sixteen-shot shock weapons transformed set-piece charges into deadly blows. Instead of loosely circling enemy positions, warriors could strike the soldiers head-on or smash into the flanks of company lines, unraveling whole units.

Once army units were isolated, the command structure that was its chief asset broke down. Unlike Indian warriors, who would fight desperately but coolly to the end, or else independently disengage to fight again, troops stripped of command cohesion panicked. This, Crazy Horse knew, was what he must build on. The battle had been a laboratory for the new tactics. Unlike the campaigning along the Bozeman Trail, the Great Sioux War saw huge armies on the offensive. Lakotas were faced not with besieged forts, tiny patrols, or trapped detachments, but with whole regiments marching openly through their hunting grounds. As the first phase of the Rosebud demonstrated, the old decoy tactic, relying on massed warriors in fixed positions, was unworkable in this mobile warfare. Instead, Crazy Horse and his comrades had perfected—literally on the hoof—a more elastic tactic, retreating to draw out units, stretching troop lines until critical pressure could snap their strained connections. The battle had not gone all their way. Crook's men fought with solid professionalism, and his Indian auxiliaries with a resolve that saved the day at least once for the embattled general. Yet, despite being significantly outnumbered, the Lakotas and Cheyennes had bested the Big Horn and Yellowstone Expedition. It was a victory of which High Backbone would have been proud.

Three days after the battle, the last of Crazy Horse's scouts returned from Goose Creek to assure him that Crook did not intend to test again the courage of the Northern Nation. Still, Crazy Horse was reluctant to be drawn into the victory celebrations. He remained convinced that this was not the victory promised in Sitting Bull's visions—the victory over the dust storm from the east, the soldiers falling upside down into the village. Until that challenge was overcome, he could not rest.

In the week following the Battle of the Rosebud, camps rode into the village daily, leaving the trail from the Rosebud scratched and overlain with hoofprints and travois tracks, until the village comprised about one thousand lodges.[32] About June 20 a party arrived from Spotted Tail Agency. They had seen Terry's Dakota column marching west along Heart River three weeks earlier. For two days, Hollow Horn Bear had followed the troops as they negotiated the Badlands. Combined with Hunkpapa reports of a new steamboat landing on the Yellowstone, stacked with supplies and forage, the news led Crazy Horse and the chiefs to conclude that while Gibbon's Montana column pegged the Yellowstone, the Dakota column would be outfitted to push against the Northern Nation from the east. At last the dusty whirl of prophecy was hardening into fact.[33]

With buffalo dispersing south, decisions had to be made about meat. Briefly, the councils favored a move toward the mountains, defying Crook at Goose Creek. Then scouts sighted concentrations of pronghorn antelope northwest, grazing the flats across the Bighorn, and the councils decided to move down the Little Bighorn two short days' travel. The move was risky, nearer any army movements based from the Yellowstone. In the atmosphere of uncertainty, holy men in both the Sans Arc and Cheyenne circles announced predictions of imminent attack, but early on June 24, the village decamped.

After crossing the Little Bighorn to the west bank, the great procession of six thousand people moved eight miles down the bottomland. Warriors flanked the clustered line of striding elders, packed travois, and grandmothers striking recalcitrant pack dogs to their duty. Mothers marshaled their families; groups of maidens astride pacing ponies struck attitudes for the brash youths shadowing warrior idols or riding in noisy gangs of cousins. As they approached the campground agreed on by the Deciders, heralds pointed out the spaces for each circle. Cheyennes pressed ahead to anchor their camp, 113 lodges, on the riverbank at a ford opposite the mouths of two coulees. Next rose the Sans Arc circle, 110 lodges, and behind them the 150 tipis of Miniconjous. Holding the rear of the village, one mile upstream of the Cheyennes, rose the largest circle, the Hunkpapa camp, at 260 lodges. Filling in the gaps, the tipis of less well-represented Lakota divisions stood irregularly next to the larger circles.

Away from the cottonwood-lined bottomland, angled one-half mile northwest of the Hunkpapa circle, the Oglala hoop rose. Augmented by Brule visitors, it counted about 240 tipis. This year's ranking Decider, Big Road, had selected the site, and the herald Iron Hawk announced band locations within the circle. By noon, the village was returning to everyday activities.[34]

Late in the afternoon of the twenty-fourth, three scouts rode in, their ponies jaded after a fifty-mile ride. Two days earlier, explained Owns Bobtail Horse in the council tipi, his party had seen a strong party of troops marching up the Rosebud, which the scouts shadowed until 6:30 that morning, when they left the soldier force at the Sun Dance site. The evidence was clear: here was the dust storm of soldiers promised them. The village must be ready, for the soldiers could follow its tracks and be in place for attack by the morning of June 26. If marched through the night, Crazy Horse probably reflected, they could arrive by noon the next day.[35]

According to one oral tradition, he seemed nervous and preoccupied as he left the council tipi. With dusk settling, he rode quickly from circle to circle, briefly visiting at the tipis of key leaders to urge total vigilance. But many seemed unconcerned. Assembling in the early evening in the Cheyenne circle, the intertribal elders' council optimistically declared that the new soldiers might wish to talk, not fight. A war chief in an uncharitable mood might well have reflected that, between warrior complacency and the senility of elders, his work was cut out for him. The elders agreed to post the Kit Fox Society as night sentries, but Crazy Horse was still frustrated when he called on his Hunkpapa counterpart. Privately, Sitting Bull advised Crazy Horse that after darkness, he intended to climb the hills to commune with the wakan powers.

As Crazy Horse hosted a feast for Elk Head and other leaders, dry lightning played over the western benchlands, and thunder rolled above the village. Pitifully sounding through the rumble, a human voice cried and sang from the ridges across the river—the voice of Sitting Bull, imploring that Wakan Tanka aid his people once more.[36]

The column located by Crazy Horse's scouts had left Terry and Gibbon's base at the junction of Rosebud Creek with the Yellowstone at noon on June 22. Comprising 597 officers and men of the Seventh Cavalry, it was commanded by Crazy Horse's old opponent, George Armstrong Custer. Sacrificing firepower for mobility, Custer declined to take along the Gatling guns hauled from Fort Abraham Lincoln. Accompanied by fifty civilian and Indian scouts, the regiment was under orders to probe west along the Rosebud, into the upper valley of the Little Bighorn. There, the latest intelligence suggested, the "hostiles" were currently located. As Custer advanced, the Terry and Gibbon commands would ascend the Yellowstone and lower Bighorn rivers, expecting to crush the Indian alliance between them. Although a coordinated campaign was projected, Custer's orders left him sufficient latitude to strike alone should the situation dictate.

Just as Crazy Horse had probably feared, Custer pressed a hard day's march, halting where the village trail swung west out of the Rosebud valley, then impatiently rousing his command at midnight. At 12:30 A.M., June 25, 1876, the grumbling, cursing men were under way again, following a screen of Crow and Arikara scouts over the difficult terrain of the Wolf Mountains. The scouts were filled with misgivings. In one of the sweat lodges at the Sun Dance site, the Arikaras had inspected a mound of sand imprinted with marks depicting two rows of hoofprints, between them scratches that signified soldiers with their heads upside down, falling toward the Lakota camp.

17

A GOOD DAY TO DIE

Sunday, June 25, 1876, found a people at play along the Little Bighorn River. Victory dances had continued through the night, many young people returning to their beds only as dawn paled the sky. In the tipi next to Crazy Horse's, the night had been punctuated by occasional cries and the bustle of female relatives: Red Feather's wife was going into labor with their first child.[1]

Although the Kit Fox warriors continued to ride the hills, even key akicita such as Low Dog continued to be openly skeptical of an attack. Anticipating another short remove in the afternoon, some of the more enterprising women began the work of packing and dismantling tipis, but most people scattered to other activities.

Along the river, women and children swam, while some youths and boys sought quieter spots to fish, sending younger brothers to scour the banks for grasshoppers to use as bait. In the shade of the cottonwoods, a few young men were still sleeping off the activities of last night, and groups of young wives had gathered to gossip and exchange news.

June, the Moon of Making Fat, was a prime month for gathering activities, and gangs of women with dutiful daughters in tow had scattered to the western benchlands to dig prairie turnips. As usual, a few older men, like Crazy Horse's brother-in-law the Miniconjou headman Red Horse, accompanied them. East of the river, a few early risers had gone to hunt and locate stray horses. A party of six Red Cloud Agency Oglalas (one spiriting away an eloping sweetheart) had left the village during the nighttime dancing, crossing the divide toward Rosebud Creek soon after sunrise. Later in the morning, four or five lodges of agency Bad Faces also started home.[2]

Crazy Horse joined the spectators on the Oglala campground, where young men were playing the hoop and pole game. At noon, men and youths, singly or in gangs of friends and cousins, strolled far out on the western flats to drive the horse herds to water, then back to the village, raising a dust visible for miles. Crazy

Horse's cousin twelve-year-old Black Elk had herded several families' stock to the river, and after eating, greased his body to join friends for a swim before bringing the ponies back to camp. It was now about 2:50 P.M.[3]

Crazy Horse remained alert to action outside the Oglala hoop. A commotion became palpable near the river. Opposite the Miniconjou circle, a Sans Arc rapidly circled his pony, crying a warning. Almost simultaneously, the Bad Face party raced into the upstream end of the village, shouting that soldiers were rapidly descending Sun Dance Creek, following the village's trail.[4]

Dawdling toward his swim, Black Elk heard the commotion. "At the Hunkpapas I heard the crier saying: 'They are charging, the chargers are coming.'" Children still naked from the river raced over the flats toward camp. On the benches, the turnip-digging gangs sighted dust upstream and the commotion in the village. Strings of women ran frantically for their families.[5]

In the Oglala circle, all was confusion as the first shots rang out beyond the Hunkpapa lodges. Elders spilled from the council tipi. Mothers screamed for children as naked youngsters raced in from the river. Crazy Horse shouted for the people to pack and move north, away from the gunfire. He called to youths to hurry in his ponies, then ran to grab weapons and bridle. The herald Iron Hawk gradually calmed the panic as he called warriors to ready their horses and prepare to defend the camp. As the first wave of Oglala warriors rode upstream to meet the attack, Iron Hawk could see a line of soldiers drawing up in skirmish formation beyond the Hunkpapa camp. By the soldiers' chronometers, it was 3:18. They began to shoot, and Iron Hawk could see their company guidons flaring above the smoke. The herald hurried toward the action, joining youths and warriors, many without horses, who gathered near the riverbank between the Hunkpapa circle and the soldiers' right flank.[6]

Red Feather, still sleeping off the victory celebrations, grumpily surfaced just as shots began to ring out. Hurrying outside, he too could see the line of dismounted soldiers about a mile upstream, "shooting at Sitting Bull's camp. The people in Sitting Bull's camp ran to the Oglala camp. The Oglalas ran, too."[7]

On the campground, all was still confusion. From his tipi Crazy Horse emerged holding his bridle and a Winchester carbine. "Our ponies aren't in yet," he observed to his brother-in-law. Red Feather snapped back, "Take any horse." Red Feather mounted and galloped toward a hill on the west side of the valley commanding the soldiers' left flank. "The hill was covered with men, warriors congregating from the Oglala and Uncpapa camps." Behind him, Red Feather recalled, "the other camps were now in commotion." Ahead of him, the Battle of the Little Bighorn had opened.[8]

At first light on Sunday, June 25, Custer's scouts had viewed the Little Bighorn valley from a vantage high on the divide, making out the smoke and pony herds that marked the Lakota and Cheyenne village as well as small parties of Indians who were plainly aware of Custer's presence. Terry and Gibbon planned to be in place along the Little Bighorn by the 26th, sketching a timetable for coordinated action, but the prospect of losing the element of surprise convinced Custer of the imperative of immediate attack. He hurried his force over the divide, and as the men briefly nooned, divided his command by battalions. Mindful of Terry's order to prevent the Indians scattering south, Custer ordered Captain Frederick W. Benteen to take three companies and probe the upstream approaches to the Little Bighorn. After leaving a single company to escort his packtrain, Custer organized a mobile strike force. He assigned a further three companies to Major Marcus A. Reno and took personal command of the remaining five: C, E, F, I, and L.[9]

Just after noon, Custer's and Reno's battalions began descending Sun Dance Creek on its twelve-mile course to the Little Bighorn. Fearful only that the Indians would escape, Custer ordered Reno to hurry forward and charge the village, promising the support of his own battalion and "the whole outfit."[10]

Reno crossed the Little Bighorn and paused to water the horses and regroup. Through the mounting dust cloud above the village two miles north, warriors could be seen riding out—not in Custer's dreaded "scatteration," but to defend their families. Just after 3:00, Reno advanced down the west side of the valley in an accelerating charge. Arikara scouts swung left to drive off the horse herds; others raced for the timber just north of the Hunkpapa camp. Across the river, Custer received Reno's advice at the same time as his own command sighted sixty or seventy-five Indians on the eastern bluffs. To prevent village dispersal, Custer ordered his battalion north along the bluffs. The change in tactics meant that Reno could expect no support from the rear, and committed Custer to a strategy of enveloping the village.[11]

As Reno's charge neared the village, warriors continued to stream out across his front. Ordering a halt about six hundred yards short of the Hunkpapa circle, Reno dismounted to form a skirmish line across the valley, its right flank anchored in the timber but its left dangerously exposed in the open valley. Volleys smashed into tipis along the southern arc of the Hunkpapa circle. The Arikara scouts in the timber cut off several small groups of women and children, killing ten noncombatants, including two of Hunkpapa war chief Gall's wives and three of his young children.[12]

These killings galvanized a warrior force already confident of its superiority. First, they forced Reno onto the defensive. Dauntless charges turned Reno's left flank. The troopers moved into the bottomland timber, sketching out a rough defensive perimeter that reduced the next few minutes' action to a stalemate of sniping. He Dog, slow to catch his pony, had joined Red Feather and the warriors massing on the hillside west of the valley. The Lakotas here were impatient, "getting ready for word to charge in a body on soldiers at timber." One warrior shouted, "Give way; let the soldiers out. We can't get at them in there." Down in the bottoms, warriors and youths infiltrating the timber were also conscious of an impasse. Heralds harangued to keep up morale. By 3:45 a mood of tense expectation had settled over the warriors, anxious for a defining moment that would break the deadlock.[13]

Twenty-five minutes earlier, as Red Feather had galloped out to meet Reno, he had left Crazy Horse waiting for his horses to be driven in. As volley firing and whoops signaled the progress of the fight a mile upstream, Crazy Horse continued to prepare himself methodically for battle. A knot of the war chief's bodyguard and his closest comrades, including the brothers Kicking Bear and Flying Hawk, awaited his preparations. Crazy Horse, naked but for moccasins and a short breechclout, painted his face and body solid yellow, over which he dabbed dots of white. He tied the stone wotawe charm under his left arm and fastened a single hawk feather in his loosened hair. Hanging the eagle wing–bone whistle around his neck, he selected his weapons, a Winchester carbine and a stone-headed war club that he pushed under the cartridge belt buckled at his waist. He smoked and talked at length with the holy man Long Turd, invoking the aid of their patron Inyan, the Rock.

Then he gathered up some earth from pocket gopher burrows, sprinkling it over himself and a few key followers, rubbing it into his hair and body. With his horses driven up, he selected a white-faced pinto pony, streaking its flanks with the protective earth and tracing light blue wavy lines down its legs. He looped the bridle over the pinto's ears and jaw, then sprang onto its bare back. These lengthy preparations had taken twenty minutes or more, but despite restive followers, Crazy Horse refused to be rushed, acting "very coolly" all the while.[14]

Extending his arms to the sun, Crazy Horse called on Wakan Tanka to help him. Then, signaling the critical significance of the day's fighting, he addressed his followers. Riding along the line, his right hand raised in admonition, the left cradling the Winchester against his hip, Crazy Horse talked "calmly to them[,] . . . telling them to restrain their ardor till the right time when he should give the word; that he wanted Reno's men to get their guns hot so they would not work so well." Red Hawk remembered Crazy Horse closing his speech with the words "Here are some of the soldiers after us again. Do your best, and let us kill them all off today, that they may not trouble us anymore. All ready! Charge! [Hokahe!]" At about 3:45, Crazy Horse turned his pony toward the battle. Followed by Kicking Bear, he led a stream of Oglala warriors at a run.[15]

As Crazy Horse's followers raced upstream, knots of women and children still fled across the valley toward the western benchlands. Other women, clustering on the hillsides, sounded the tremolo of praise, a note picked up by the shrill of war whistles as Crazy Horse approached the battlefield. Down in the timber, Black Elk heard, over the clamor, the "thunder of the ponies charging," and voices shouting, "Crazy Horse is coming!" On the hillside, the cry for a charge was heard, "Hokahe!" and hundreds more warriors streamed toward the timber.[16]

Racing ahead, the front of Crazy Horse's charge sliced into the timber. Three Oglala warriors, Kicking Bear, Hard to Hit, and Bad Heart Bull, almost collided

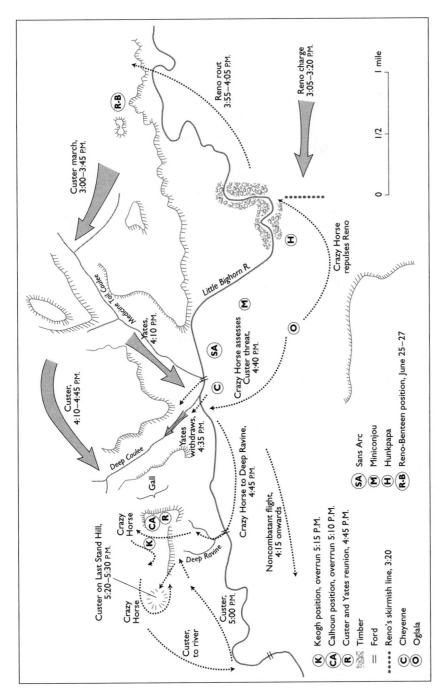

The Battle of the Little Bighorn, June 25, 1876

with Reno's right flank. The startled troopers had just mounted for a retreat. Hauling in their ponies, the three Oglalas levered a rapid fire from their repeaters into Reno's front. According to one participant, Kicking Bear's shot felled the Arikara scout Bloody Knife, spraying his brains into Major Reno's face. The panicked commander cried out an order to dismount and then immediately to remount. Simultaneously, many dismounted warriors, infiltrating from the riverbank, burst through the timber and opened a withering crossfire. The troopers charged from the timber. By luck or design, Crazy Horse had struck Reno at the moment of critical imbalance, applying the kicamnayan tactic of his Thunder vision with devastating effect.[17]

The sudden emergence of Reno's battalion from the timber actually threw some of Crazy Horse's men into confusion. Private Roman Rutten, of Company M, was cool enough to observe the recoil of a line of up to two hundred whooping warriors, slicing in from the right—"being about as badly excited as the soldiers and apparently undecided as to what movement the soldiers were about to execute." It was the first test of Crazy Horse's resolve. Acting quickly to galvanize the warriors, he shouted, "*Come on! Die with me! It's a good day to die! Cowards to the rear!*" Hefting his war club, he urged the pinto along Reno's line. If a story told Lieutenant Bourke is to be credited, Crazy Horse made the most of a movielike melodramatic moment and hurled himself at a trooper struggling with an unmanageable horse. In the shock of collision, Crazy Horse grappled the luckless foe from his saddle, brained him, and leapt astride the cavalry mount to the exultant cries of his followers. Inspired by Crazy Horse's example, the warriors streamed along Reno's right flank as the soldiers careered upstream.[18]

Within moments, whatever tactical cohesion Reno's battalion had retained was lost: "It was like chasing buffalo," more than one participant would remember. Warriors laced through the rout, selecting individual troopers as targets. Soldiers were shot out of their saddles, their horses gathered up by warriors pausing in the pursuit. One trooper riding a wounded horse made a target for Crazy Horse, who squeezed off a shot from his Winchester that hit the soldier squarely between the shoulder blades, pitching him forward out of the saddle.[19]

The war chief's cousin Eagle Elk witnessed another assault that involved Crazy Horse during the race upstream. "There were two Indians, one on a black and the other on a white horse, chasing the soldiers. Suddenly, the man on the white horse got among the soldiers. He had a sword and used it to kill one soldier. The other Indian fell off his horse," which fled toward the village. Crazy Horse caught the black pony as he galloped on and brought it to the unhorsed warrior. As Eagle Elk paused in the race, Crazy Horse continued in pursuit.[20]

Without pausing to cover the crossing, soldiers plunged their horses down the bank and into the river. "Crazy Horse was ahead of all, and he killed a lot of them with his war-club," recalled Flying Hawk; "he pulled them off their horses when they tried to get across the river where the bank was steep. Kicking Bear was right beside him and he killed many too in the water." Many warriors paused to snipe into the stream. "The Indians could kill the soldiers in the water as they tried to swim [across]," recalled Eagle Elk.[21]

Men and horses floundered over the river, scrambling up the high miry bank onto the east side of the Little Bighorn. The soldiers continued their flight up the steep hillside to the blufftop. The front of Reno's rout reached the top at 4:10, the battered rear dragging and scrambling up the slope for several minutes under heavy fire. Leaving forty dead troopers on the field, Reno's fight was a costly prelude to the main action at the Little Bighorn.[22]

The Indians too had sustained casualties. In addition to the ten women and children killed by Reno's scouts, nine Lakota and two Cheyenne men had been killed in the first hour of the battle. Although most warriors stayed across the river to gather horses and loot clothing, arms, and ammunition, a sizeable force followed the rout over the Little Bighorn. Crazy Horse, followed by a group of Oglalas, scrambled his pony up the hillside just downstream of the soldiers. As the warriors topped the bluff, they saw the soldiers forming skirmish lines. A few long-distance shots were exchanged. Beyond Reno's new position, more soldiers moved downstream: Captain Benteen's battalion, having closed its futile scout for south-fleeing Indians, was approaching to reinforce Reno. Crazy Horse began to ride along the hilltop, scanning the line of bluffs downstream to assess the overall situation. His keen eyes suddenly noticed a larger body of troops climbing a ridge, two miles northward, that commanded the lower end of the village.[23]

Short Bull rode up to the war chief, bantering, "'Too late! You've missed the fight!'"

"'Sorry to miss this fight!' [Crazy Horse] laughed. 'But there's a good fight coming over the hill.'" Pointing north, Crazy Horse said, "'That's where the big fight is going to be. We'll not miss that one.'

"He was not a bit excited; he made a joke of it."[24]

After the days of uncertainty, Crazy Horse had regained his composure in the heat of battle. Faced with the political task of maintaining Northern Nation unity, he had swung between anxious action and gloomy withdrawal: in combat, about to face his greatest test, he laughed. Wheeling his pony, Crazy Horse led his followers back across the river. They set their horses at a steady run for home, passing warriors and youths still herding away cavalry mounts or scalping and looting dead soldiers. As they neared the upstream camps, ragged fire became audible from the vicinity of the village ford; minutes later, a double volley sounded from the eastern ridge where Crazy Horse had first noticed the new soldier threat. From the Cheyenne and Sans Arc camps, a stream of women and children fled down the west side of the valley.[25]

Passing the Hunkpapa circle, Crazy Horse would have heard Sitting Bull haranguing his people. During the Reno fight, women had started dismantling tipis in the Hunkpapa and Miniconjou circles. Returning from Reno's rout, Sitting Bull rode his pony among the fearful families, calling for calm, before turning his pony west. With a coterie of trusted warriors, he hoped to establish the women and children in a strong place on the benchlands west of the Cheyenne camp.[26]

Sitting Bull was acting as a peace chief whose prime responsibility was the protection of the helpless. Crazy Horse, the Northern Nation's first war chief, hurried into the almost deserted Oglala circle about 4:30 to prepare for more fighting. On the open campground, the holy man Long Turd had built a fire of buffalo chips. As Crazy Horse's followers paused to gather fresh ponies, he briefly conferred again with Long Turd, praying and making offerings over the fire. At his tipi, he donned a white buckskin shirt and leggings before riding toward the gunfire at the village ford, followed by Flying Hawk and a cluster of comrades.[27]

One and a half hours before, Custer had led his five companies down the eastern bluffs at a fast trot. Pausing on the hilltop where Reno would later dig in, he viewed the valley and Reno's charge toward the village. A first messenger was hurried down the back trail to hurry the ammunition packtrain across country to join Custer. Should Captain Benteen's battalion also be met, "tell him to come quick— a big Indian camp."[28]

The column trotted on for a few minutes before pausing in the shallow defile of Cedar Coulee. Scouts scrambled to view Reno's action from the bluffs, scanning the back trail for sign of the packtrain and Benteen. The protracted pause in Cedar Coulee indicates tactical rethinking. Another courier was dispatched with an urgent written order for Benteen to "Come on. Big village. Be quick. Bring pacs. P.S. Bring pacs."[29]

Expecting support at any moment, Custer continued to idle in Cedar Coulee, but each minute endangered Reno's command. From the hilltops east of the valley, a score or two of Cheyenne warriors opened a long-range skirmishing action—no serious challenge, but a threat to any surprise attack from downstream. At last, Custer ordered the battalion to turn left into Medicine Tail Coulee, a long shallow draw draining northwest into the Little Bighorn at the village ford 1.25 miles away. Here a strong charge could secure the downstream end of the village and relieve the pressure on Reno. At the very least, capturing the village and the women and children would neutralize the Indian attackers, Custer's successful strategy at the Battle of the Washita. But barely had he begun his advance when his scouts reported the worst: Reno's precipitate flight from the timber. For Custer and his company commanders, several minutes of intense debate followed. Their options were clear: to press on with the attack without support, before warriors could reoccupy the village, or to withdraw and consolidate the regiment upstream.[30]

The events of the next minutes decided the fate of Custer's battalion. Over a century of speculation has failed to reconstruct Custer's strategy categorically, but his officers likely agreed to a compromise that would characterize the next hour's action: an increasingly awkward juggling of offensive and defensive priorities. The battalion was divided into two wings. Two troops, the gray-horse Company E, ubiquitous in Indian accounts of the battle, and Company F, led by Captain George

W. Yates, would trot down the coulee and secure approaches to the ford. Custer and the other three companies, under immediate command of Captain Myles W. Keogh, would climb onto the next ridge downstream and view the unfolding tactical situation as reserves. Should Benteen's support materialize, or conditions otherwise permit, the option to charge via the ford could be exercised. The two wings separated, and Yates began his descent to the ford.[31]

As he trotted down the coulee, Yates learned that the village was not as undefended as it had appeared. A light Indian fire opened from behind the riverbank. Yates returned fire. Company E, leading its distinctive grays, pressed forward to a high cutbank at the downstream end of the bottom. More dismounted warriors opened a heavier fire from across the river. Mounted warriors began crossing the low ridge south of the coulee, threatening to outflank Yates's position.[32]

Other warriors, joined by early arrivals from Reno's retreat, probed Keogh's new position atop the ridge. At both points, individual warriors made brave runs along the soldier lines, drawing fire and frightening the horses of the dismounted troops. About 4:25 Keogh's wing fired two volleys. This new decision reflected developments visible from Keogh's position. As Yates approached the ford and skirmishing began, a new flow of noncombatants drained from the lower villages, fleeing downstream along the west side of the Little Bighorn. As their flight peaked, hundreds of women, children, and old men would have been in sight from the ridge. Ever since making his battalion divisions, Custer's overriding concern had been the "scatteration" of his quarry. His plan now was to reunite the battalion and, following the ridgetops downstream, find an uncontested crossing and cut off the noncombatants' retreat.[33]

Still only lightly engaged, Custer was not yet prepared to yield his famous luck. Instead, he and Keogh had the double volley fired: dissuading their attackers; rousing Reno; and alerting Yates to disengage. Then they ordered their three companies to mount and parallel the valley downstream, intending to regroup along a ridge that extended toward the river one and one-half miles northwest. At the ford, Yates's two companies competently disengaged, Company E covering the withdrawal up a second coulee, angling northeast. As Yates withdrew uphill, many more warriors galloped across the river to pursue and flank his retreat.[34]

About 4:35 Crazy Horse rode to the village ford, between the deserted Cheyenne and Sans Arc circles. Soldiers were visible withdrawing up the coulee, pursued by a stream of warriors, "stringing up the gulch like ants rushing out of a hill." Crazy Horse and other war leaders conferred. The Cheyennes present advised Crazy Horse of Yates's approach and the skirmish across the river. In conference with the Cheyennes and Crow King, the Hunkpapa war leader, Crazy Horse reviewed these developments and assessed Custer's strategy.[35]

Several hundred yards uphill from Yates, Custer's three companies were descending from the eastern ridges. Increasing warrior numbers had paralleled Custer's rapid march, compelling his wing to fire volleys repeatedly from the saddle as they traversed the ridges. To Flying Hawk, watching beside Crazy Horse, the three companies seemed to pause to view the evolving tactical situation as they approached the coulee. Downstream, the flight of noncombatants was still visible. Sitting Bull had secured the rear of the exodus in a defensive position on the benchland west of the village, but the vanguard was hurrying north. Assessing army strategy, Crazy Horse and his companions came to a quick decision.[36]

"Custer," stated Horned Horse, in an 1877 press interview as spokesman for Crazy Horse, "seeing so numerous a body, mistook them for the main body of Indians retreating and abandoning their villages, and immediately gave pursuit. The warriors in the village, seeing this, divided their forces into two parts, one intercepting Custer between their non-combat[ant]s and him, and the other getting in his rear." Ten years later, Gall told photographer David F. Barry how the Indian force divided. While Crow King led his Hunkpapa contingent up the coulee in pursuit of Yates, Crazy Horse acted to secure the protection of the women and children. Keeping between Custer and the refugees, he would cross at a second ford north of the village and seek to envelop the command, pressing it against Crow King's warriors.[37]

The leaders turned to address the warriors gathering behind them: "Crazy Horse and Gall and Knife Chief were haranguing the Indians to get together so they could make another charge on the soldiers," recalled Red Hawk. Then Crazy Horse galloped 1.25 miles downstream, followed by Flying Hawk and a knot of Oglala comrades. A stream of Cheyenne warriors followed the war chief's party as Crazy Horse splashed through the shallows of the Little Bighorn and urged his pony up another coulee. Called Deep Ravine from its sharply cut, brush-filled lower banks, the gully drains a long rolling hillside, forking into a fan of shallow draws. To Short Bull, viewing from the village, Crazy Horse looked as self-possessed as ever. "I saw him on his pinto pony leading his men across the ford. He was the first man to cross the river [at Deep Ravine]. I saw he had the business well in hand. They rode up the draw, and then there was too much dust. I could not see any more."[38]

Flying Hawk recalled, "Crazy Horse and I . . . came to a ravine; then we followed up the gulch to a place in the rear of the soldiers." After ascending the ravine, the pair turned right up the long shallow cut of what would be known as Calhoun Coulee. From there, Custer's battalion would be visible as it topped Calhoun Ridge at the reunion point. Crazy Horse and Flying Hawk dismounted, and the war chief "gave his horse to me to hold along with my horse. He crawled up the ravine to where he could see the soldiers." After his customary scan of the enemy position, Crazy Horse sighted along his Winchester and began levering off a rapid series of shots at the ridge. According to Flying Hawk, each shot dropped a trooper from his saddle: "He shot them as fast as he could load his gun. They fell off their horses as fast as he could shoot." Hyperbole aside, as those shots rang out and Crazy Horse scrambled for cover, the final phase of the Battle of the Little Bighorn was opening.[39]

While Crazy Horse accessed the battlefield from downstream, Custer's five companies had reunited along Calhoun Ridge about 4:45. Of approximately 210 men, only one would survive the next hour. Curley, a young Crow scout, would leave the command within the next ten minutes to take news of the battle to General Terry. Curley's recollections of these crucial minutes as Custer rethought his tactics offer critical insights into the commander's evolving strategy.[40]

A party of warriors crested the ridge and galloped east, just as warriors had decoyed Royall from Crook's support eight days previously. The main body of warriors threatened from the rear, constantly reinforced by new arrivals from the Reno fight. After officer's call was sounded, Custer and his subalterns debated the position. The ridge they commanded extended east one-half mile to its terminus at Calhoun Hill. From there a long hogback ridge reached north one mile to terminate at another low hill, their angles framing the Deep Ravine drainage that Crazy Horse's warriors were beginning to infiltrate. From the hogback, Custer might launch an attack that would envelop the refugees. Considering defensive priorities, the officers could have concluded that this broken high ground offered the best position to reunite the command and to protect the horses. Custer detailed a squad of troopers to ride hurriedly in advance. The troopers turned north, riding along the riverward side of the hogback. After several hundred yards, they deployed beneath the ridge crest.[41]

The main command followed along Calhoun Ridge, leaving a second squad at the reunion point. Within a minute or so, however, new fire combed the ridge. A detachment was ordered to fall out of line, dismount, and fire into the coulee, briefly pinning down the warriors. But a second flurry of shots from the draws "quickly killed" the squad left at the end of the ridge, Curley observed—echoing Flying Hawk's observation of Crazy Horse's sniping. These developments forced another consultation as the command paused on Calhoun Hill.[42]

A plan to charge and clear the coulees "had to be given up" when substantial Indian reinforcements, advancing from the village, swept into the draws of Calhoun Coulee. Crazy Horse and his followers began to fan up the hillside, creeping from cover to cover or leading their ponies at a walk. Even more than the Rosebud, this would be in an action in which Crazy Horse unpredictably alternated infiltration tactics with sudden sweeping charges. Once again, Custer divided his battalion into two wings. He would accompany Yates's left wing of Companies E and F in a probe north along the hogback ridge, the dual objectives of securing a crossing and a defensive position in uneasy balance. To maintain communication lines south to Reno, Keogh's right wing, Companies C, I, and L, would hold the south end of the ridge against the warriors still massing from the village approaches.[43]

As Custer's wing departed, about 4:55, two volleys were fired. Then, with E Company in the lead, Custer's left wing trotted smartly along the east side of the hogback, leaving a nervous right wing to deploy. Many men seemed reluctant to dismount, and as Curley saddled for departure, he noticed a few panicked troopers actually run after Custer's wing. Almost immediately, they came under fire "from a ravine full of warriors" east of the hogback. A sudden crossfire poured in from "a large force of Indians shooting" from the riverward side of the ridgetop—Crazy Horse's warriors, switching from infiltration to frontal advance. These warriors suddenly "charged up from the direction of the river," driving the small advance squad over the ridgetop. The squad, like the panicked stragglers from the right wing, hurried to catch up with Custer as his wing approached the hill marking the northern termination of the hogback ridge.[44]

Captain Keogh deployed his three companies along the half-mile stretch of the hogback terminating at Calhoun Hill. At that point, Company L formed a dismounted skirmish line fronting the main threat: the hundreds of warriors from the south, infiltrating the gullies fanning the gentle slope up to the ridge. Opportunistic warriors soon began sniping at L's skirmish line, shooting arrows or snapping blankets at nervous horse holders to startle the four mounts each man controlled, stampeding thirsty horses—and their precious ammunition saddlebags—downhill toward the river.[45]

A sudden Indian charge rushed up from the draws, lacing through L Company's line to overrun the ridge, stampeding more horses over the ridgetop. Company commander Lieutenant James Calhoun ordered a volley fired. Many warriors melted back into the draws, immediately seeking new avenues for attack. Some turned east to seek new positions on the right wing's flank. Cheyennes veered left down the flank of Calhoun Ridge.[46]

To counter the Cheyenne threat, a squadron from Lieutenant Henry M. Harrington's Company C was deployed to resume the position at the reunion point near the riverward end of Calhoun Ridge. A trumpet sounded, and I and L Company horse holders were repositioned in the upper draws of Calhoun Coulee, covered by Harrington's company and away from the main threat from the south. For the right wing, there followed ten or more minutes of low-key action. The precarious lull overlaid mounting tension as warriors—constantly reinforced by late arrivals from the Reno action—infiltrated the draws, occupying every nook of cover, crawling in a tightening ring from coulee to sagebrush clump to draw.[47]

Meanwhile, Custer's left wing had passed beyond the hill defining the northern terminus of the hogback, swinging west toward the river. Lieutenant Algernon E. Smith's E Company paused while Custer and his headquarters staff accompanied Yates and F Company in a probe to the river. Curley, who had departed the command five or ten minutes earlier, observed some of these maneuvers from the hills. He described the battalion wings deploying, one "circularly to the left, and the remainder similarly to the right," suggesting that Custer's descent to the river synchronized with the right-wing redeployment down Calhoun Ridge. As he descended into the valley, Custer's quarry was in clear sight, barely one-half mile across the river. Custer, observed Flying Hawk, "was right above the women who had collected down the river."[48]

The refugees had gathered in the brush-lined bottom of Squaw Creek, opposite a ford offering Custer instant access to the exhausted fugitives. A scattering
of Cheyenne youths and old men had crossed the ford to protect their exhausted
families, and as Custer's company approached the bottoms, they opened ragged
fire from the willows that emptied one or two saddles, perhaps killing *New York
Herald* correspondent Mark Kellogg. Custer ordered F Company back uphill.
Events quickly accelerated. Scores of warriors—chiefly Cheyennes and Hunkpapas—crossed at Deep Ravine and veered left onto the flats below Custer's position
on the long ridge. They opened fire on the left wing. Warriors engaged in brave
runs across Custer's front—no serious threat, but compelling the troopers to take
up skirmish lines. In a V-formation, F Company fronted the river, while E—its gray
horses highly visible to warriors viewing from the right-wing siege—faced the
threat from Deep Ravine and the flats. In the following minutes, both wings of the
battalion were held in suspension, forced to assume defensive positions that would
shortly face critical pressure.[49]

Meanwhile, Crazy Horse and his followers crested the hogback ridge and
dropped into the gullies beyond, where a long coulee drains northward, framing
the hogback. Along it, warriors infiltrated the flanks of both battalion wings. As the
battle climaxed, warriors accessing the field from the Squaw Creek crossing would
feed around the nose of the battle ridge, meeting up with Crazy Horse's warriors
along the coulee to effect a complete encirclement of Custer's battalion. Right
now, a thin screen of warriors tracked Custer's progress around the ridge, opening
up a light fire from the hill at the rear of his skirmish lines, and sending a party that
rushed through the gap between the companies, stampeding a number of cavalry
horses into the valley.[50]

Crazy Horse, however, continued flanking the right wing. Indeed, he rode farther up the ravine to a position perhaps four hundred yards northeast of Calhoun's
L Company. The growing body of warriors was able to snipe at the rear of Calhoun's position atop Calhoun Hill and at Keogh's I Company, dismounted as
reserves along the east slope of the hogback. After the L Company volley at the
charge from the south, more warriors from that sector worked east to reinforce
Crazy Horse. One of these was White Bull, the Miniconjou. Impatient at Crazy
Horse's long-range sniping, he began to urge a charge, but the Oglala war chief
would not be drawn into premature action. Crazy Horse knew that the right-wing
position held the key to the battlefield. It held open Custer's line of communication to Reno and Benteen. From the encirclement strategy expounded at the village ford, Crazy Horse had been forced to trim his tactics—but, in stark contrast to
Custer's inflexible strategy, he proved himself master of a fluid tactical environment.
He hoped that warriors in the northern sector could pin Custer's left wing east of
the river and isolate the two battalion wings. With many more warriors fronting
the right wing, Crazy Horse awaited a critical moment when the wing could be
overwhelmed by a series of interlocking assaults from the coulees. The Indian force

could then envelop the weaker left wing and save the exhausted, frightened women and children waiting in the brush along Squaw Creek.[51]

That moment neared. Warriors gradually infested the riverward hillside to within forty yards of the Company I position. Two Moons recalled that sixteen right-wing horse holders were the first victims as the battle climaxed. To counter the coulee infiltrators, Company C charged from its position at the west end of Calhoun Ridge, flushing warriors like quail. After five hundred yards, the company halted, dismounted, and drew up a skirmish line. Their expected volley was never fired. Almost simultaneously, a double blow struck. In the lower coulee, the Cheyenne Lame White Man rallied the retreating warriors and led a charge that overran Company C, while Yellow Nose's Cheyennes opened a sustained fire from Greasy Grass Ridge. A "great roll of smoke seemed to go down the ravine," remembered the Two Kettle Runs the Enemy.[52] Moving Robe Woman, a Hunkpapa widow fighting to avenge the deaths of her brother and husband, saw the soldiers "running up a ravine, firing as they ran. The valley was dense with powder smoke. I never heard such whooping and shouting." Company C fell back hurriedly to its position atop Calhoun Ridge, leaving at least four men dead in the coulee.[53]

On Calhoun Hill, Company L turned its skirmish line to face riverward, firing a volley to cover their comrades' retreat. As Harrington's company won back to the ridge, it sought to reestablish a defensive position, mounted troopers holding the horses of dismounted skirmishers. Yellow Nose drove a hard charge over the ridge that sent Company C running to join Company L, leaving another dozen or so troopers dead. Under an intensifying fire from all quarters—including Crazy Horse's party in the eastern ravine—L Company's firm skirmish line broke as C Company survivors joined them at Calhoun Hill. Troopers broke ranks to form little knots of comrades firing haphazardly. At this moment of critical danger, the warriors from the south formed for another charge. Behind a shock barrage from their Winchester and Henry repeaters, the warriors, led by Gall, poured up the south slope of Calhoun Hill and overran the position. Twenty or more troopers were killed; their comrades fled along the west side of the hogback toward Company I's position.[54]

The overrunning of the L Company position marked the beginning of the end for Custer's doomed battalion. Battle veterans explaining the action to Colonel Miles two years later stated that to that point it had been an "even fight": after it, the troops began to unravel along the hogback, with the warriors "rolling [Custer's] command up in confusion and destruction." As Gall's warriors paused to loot bodies of their guns and ammunition belts, the fleeing troops won a brief reprieve.[55]

Four hundred yards to the right, White Bull had sickened of the long wait. Just as the retreat from Calhoun Hill began, he whipped up his pony, hugging its neck as he dashed between Companies I and L, drawing I Company's fire before looping back to rejoin Crazy Horse. Seeing the C and L Company survivors in full retreat, White Bull decided to repeat the run, declaring, "This time I will not turn back." Crazy Horse surely realized that the moment of critical imbalance for the right wing had arrived. With a stream of warriors stringing behind him, Crazy Horse charged after White Bull. The Calhoun Hill retreat turned suddenly to rout, men racing to join their I Company comrades.[56]

The warriors collided into the rout in a chaos of dust and powder smoke. Some mounted soldiers deserted their unhorsed comrades in the race for safety. Riderless cavalry mounts, still running in formation, sped ahead of panicked troopers racing along the hogback. A few troopers breasted the hogback and raced downhill toward the river. Gall's contingent smashed into the rear of the retreat, firing looted carbines and revolvers in a chaotic reprise of the Reno flight.[57]

Mounted men were shot from their saddles as Crazy Horse's charge smashed into their right flank and turned to track the flight, warriors and soldiers all mixed up in the melee. I Company horse holders had brought up their remaining mounts from the coulee, but as Keogh's trumpeter sounded the order to mount, the charge enveloped the I Company line. The battle was breaking right for Crazy Horse. The same moment of kicamnayan imbalance that had almost consumed Royall's men at the Rosebud opened for Keogh's right wing. The Indian charge stampeded a great number of Keogh's bays over the ridge crest. Warriors whooped the mounts down to the river, where women and old men—leaving their refuge points now that the troops were on the defensive—herded them together. White Bull had wrestled a trooper from his mount, striking the first coup before Crazy Horse rode up to count the second.[58]

Crazy Horse saw that the head of the retreat was passing the I Company position, fleeing toward the hill commanding the head of the battle ridge. If he wished to ensure the isolation of the battalion wings, he would have to act quickly. He whipped up his pinto and began to ride the length of the I Company line, strung along the east face of the ridge. Keogh's men delivered a disciplined volley at Crazy Horse's followers, who hung over the offside of their ponies' necks as they charged after the war chief. An Arapaho warrior, Waterman, was one of the observers. Given the inherent chauvinism of Plains Indian life, his testimony is an incomparable tribute to Crazy Horse's bravery. "Crazy Horse, the Sioux Chief, was the bravest man I ever saw. He rode closest to the soldiers, yelling to his warriors. All the soldiers were shooting at him, but he was never hit."[59]

Crazy Horse's brave run inspired many Lakotas and Cheyennes to follow him. Nearing the end of the I Company line, he veered sharply to the left and rode right through the soldiers. The charge cut through one of the hogback gaps to the riverward side of the ridge, "cutting the line in two," and "split[ting] up [the] soldiers into two bunches," as He Dog observed. Up ahead, the front of the retreat hurried on to the hill "where the final stand was made [recalled Runs the Enemy], but they were few in numbers by then." No more than twenty survivors of the right wing made it through to the hill. The rest were about to be engulfed around I Company's position.[60]

Most of Crazy Horse's warriors closed in to finish off Keogh. Around I Company's position, Flying Hawk remembered, "they made another stand . . . and rallied a few minutes." Simultaneously, a new warrior charge from the river crested the ridge. While more cautious warriors continued to circle Keogh's crumbling line, bolder spirits smashed through the troops, fighting at close range with war clubs.[61]

As the last defenders fell, warriors paused to loot carbines, revolvers, and ammunition, then moved up the east side of the ridge to where the last stage of the action was unfolding. By now, a thin screen of old men and boys, having advanced around the north end of the battle ridge, was calling encouragement from the safety of the gullies farther east.[62]

As Crazy Horse and a stream of followers breasted the hogback, he became instantly aware of a changed tactical situation. In the previous five chaotic minutes, Custer's left wing had finally maneuvered in support of their comrades. Remounting, Companies E and F had charged four hundred yards south to the entrenched gully of Deep Ravine, then swung left along its north branch to a new position in the shallow basin below the hogback ridge. Within one-quarter mile of Keogh's position, F Company dismounted and threw out a skirmish line along the draw. Across the hogback, the dust and uproar signaled onset of the right-wing collapse. White Bull, cresting the hogback in pursuit of Keogh's bays, saw the new soldier line. From this point, White Bull asserted, Custer "don't go any farther" toward the right wing. While the commander and his staff remained with F Company, E was detailed to secure the low hill at the head of the ridge—the best defensible position for the battalion to have a chance for survival.[63]

Company E moved four hundred yards north to a point high up the long ridge below the hill, dismounting a few feet north of the modern Custer Battlefield Visitors' Center. From there, E was forced to back up the remaining three hundred yards toward the hill, under increasing pressure from riverward threats.[64]

E Company fired a volley to pin down the infiltration from the river. Fifteen-year-old Standing Bear was in the breaks, keeping his head down under the barrage.[65] The volley bought E Company a minute's reprieve, and they pressed up the slope. This was the situation when Crazy Horse cut the retreating line and crested the battle ridge midway between Keogh's position and the refuge hill. He could see the dismounted gray-horse company, barely four hundred yards obliquely left. Observing the warriors charge over the hogback in pursuit of right-wing comrades, E Company poured in a raking volley. Crazy Horse and his followers rode over the hogback for cover.[66]

Momentarily, pressure slackened on E Company, but the continuing flow of reinforcements via the lower crossings now permitted a breakthrough charge like those that had unraveled the right wing. Twenty Lakota and Cheyenne warriors—evidently members of the Strong Hearts Society and its Cheyenne counterpart the Crazy Dogs—had pledged themselves to die in defense of their people. Heralds announced that the "Suicide Boys" would ride up from the river. In a sudden charge, followed by scores of warriors incited to bravery by the Suicide Boys' example, they cut across the long ridge from the Squaw Creek crossing, smashing into the rear of E Company.[67]

Part of the charge aimed for the company's horses, scattering a score or more of the grays down the course of modern Cemetery Ravine. Infiltration warriors in the breaks ran forward to join the breakthrough, overran E's line, and rolled on up the slope, the "fronters" breasting the battle ridge to join the final carnage in the Keogh sector. Young Standing Bear saw the stunned E Company men "sitting with their hats off." Nevertheless, officers regrouped their men and renewed their fire, desperately maintaining the defense.[68]

Other warriors grappled in hand-to-hand combat with dismounted troopers, sending some scattering to join comrades in the F Company line. The main charge veered downhill after them. Some panicked troopers galloped toward the refuge hill, but the warriors turned to drive them across the hogback. A deadly hand-to-hand melee followed, but the hundreds of warriors leaving the Keogh position were on hand to overrun the tiny stand, concluding action along the hogback. Upwards of seventy more troopers had been killed since the flight from Calhoun Hill; half of Custer's battalion was already dead. A general rush of warriors now flowed up the east side of the hogback toward the refuge hill.[69]

In the shallow draw that heads Deep Ravine, F Company also came under pressure. Over the ridgetop, the action was climaxing in the Keogh sector, and a dozen or so troopers fled downhill, probably joining F. Inevitably, warriors tracked the flight: White Bull, pursuing horses, could not resist the opportunity for coups; Yellow Nose, the Cheyenne, bearing L Company's guidon as his coup stick, also laced through the line. Barely was this repelled when part of the Suicide Boy charge took F from the rear. It is to the credit of Custer and Captain Yates that they were able to effect an orderly withdrawal up the ridge to the hill where right-wing survivors were grouping.[70]

Across the hogback, White Bull rode up to Crazy Horse and returned to his favorite argument: A swift charge could stampede E Company's remaining grays. Crazy Horse concurred, but recognizing futile bravado, he "backed out." White Bull slashed another solitary brave run across the E Company front as it approached the hill under heavy fire. Officers maintained tactical cohesion; horse holders led their plunging animals, guarded by dismounted skirmishers. Only in the last few yards, as they neared their comrades at the refuge point, did the orderly company lines collapse, and "the soldiers turned and rushed to the top of the hill."[71]

They joined the twenty or so survivors of the right wing in a grim defensive knot. E Company took up positions along the southwest slopes, F deploying around the southeast segment. Some men lay; others knelt or stood behind their horses. Foolish Elk observed that the one hundred or so soldiers on the hill were "all in confusion." Nevertheless, E Company delivered another volley that sent warriors, advancing from the river in the wake of the Suicide Boys, scrambling over the ridge to the north. As the survivors prepared for further action, barely two hundred yards away, Crazy Horse and hundreds of warriors from the Keogh sector milled in the gullies, awaiting the final assault.[72]

"All dismount" heralds cried as they paced through the throng. Elders like the Miniconjou chief Flying By harangued for courage. Infiltration tactics were employed again, warriors creeping from cover to cover to encircle the east and north flanks of the hill, sniping at men and horses. Occasionally a warrior darted out to catch a loose horse. Arrows were fired in high short arcs to fall among the troopers. If a warrior showed his head, soldiers snapped off a shot, one trooper managing to kill a Lakota warrior whose headdress made too conspicuous a target. As horses fell from Indian shooting, troopers hunkered down behind these ready-made breastworks.[73]

The customary brave runs of individual warriors punctuated this brief infiltration phase. Yellow Nose, a surreal figure with his Stars and Stripes guidon defiantly wrapped around his body, charged right over the hilltop, striking down an officer with a blow from the flat of an old saber. Sensing an end, infiltrators from the draws crept uphill. Soldiers fronting this sector fired again, briefly pinning down the assault. Standing Bear kept up his head long enough to note that there still seemed "many [soldiers] there," then dropped down as a heavier barrage of Indian shooting opened, from a position behind a low knoll southeast of the battle hill. As these ragged volleys faded, Standing Bear noted that there now seemed "very few of [the soldiers] left" standing.[74]

Suddenly, to cries of "They have gone!," the troopers drove most of their surviving mounts down the north slope of the hill, where waiting boys hurried to head them off in their thirsty career to the river. A ragged volley sounded, and a trumpet was heard. Then, in a desperate bid to reach the river, about forty-five soldiers—Company E and assorted stragglers—raced off the hill. "They are gone!" went up the cry. Across the river, young Black Elk observed the pathetic flight: "They were making their arms go as though they were running, but they were only walking." A body of Hunkpapa warriors rose to meet them, and the troopers veered left to run down the spiny ridge toward Deep Ravine. Two or three mounted troopers swung left again to race for Calhoun Coulee and a southward escape: they were cut off. The troopers, firing wildly overhead, were met above the head wall of Deep Ravine by a force of Cheyennes coming up from the river. "We could see some Indians right on top of them whirling around all over the place," Black Elk recalled. A dozen or so men fell here; twenty-eight managed to leap into the brushy ravine where their mopping-up would occupy several more minutes.[75]

On the hill, the survivors awaited the end. As sniping resumed through a thickening pall of dust and smoke, Crazy Horse decided a defining moment had again arrived. With a shrill blast on his eagle wing-bone whistle, he kicked the pinto into a gallop and "rode between the two parties." As Crazy Horse circled the hill, the surviving soldiers "all fired at once, but didn't hit him. The Indians got the idea the soldiers' guns were empty and charged immediately . . . right over the hill," overrunning the last defenses. Warriors raced up from the ravines to envelop the hill's southern approaches. Standing Bear recalled the terrific barrage as all these Indians converged on the hill: "Then I could see the soldiers and the Indians all mixed up and there were so many guns going off that I couldn't hear them. The voices seemed to be on top of the cloud."[76]

On the hill, Flying Hawk remembered that there "was so much dust we could not see much, but the Indians rode around and yelled the war-whoop and shot into the soldiers as fast as they could until they were all dead." A second bunch of about a dozen soldiers suddenly sprang up and raced downhill, where continuing shots from the gulch of Deep Ravine at least signaled continuing resistance. A mounted party of warriors poured down the hill to cut off these soldiers.[77]

On the hill, Crazy Horse was finishing off soldiers with his war club. A few troopers made a last break down the hogback only to be cut off on its western slope. As the dust cleared, one soldier was seen "running away to the east but Crazy Horse saw him and jumped on his pony and went after him. He got him about half a mile from the place where the others were lying dead."[78]

By the time Crazy Horse returned to the hill, all resistance was over. It was about 5:30, barely forty-five minutes since Custer's battalion had reunited along Calhoun Ridge. The furious action since the overrunning of Calhoun Hill had occupied perhaps twenty minutes. Warriors rode around the field, shooting into the bodies. Downslope, the last shots faded in Deep Ravine.[79]

Already women were climbing the slopes from the refuge points across the river to search for loved ones, to loot clothing and apparel, to hack and mutilate the bodies of the wasicu soldiers who had come to kill or capture them and their families.[80]

Upstream, Reno's and Benteen's battalions showed little appetite for supporting their commander. By 4:30 all the Indians had withdrawn to fight Custer, but the demoralized troopers remained behind their lines. Only when Custer's signal volleys from Calhoun Ridge alerted some officers to their commander's plight did a puny, uncoordinated force venture downstream. Topping the outcrop of Weir Ridge about 5:25, they were in time to see the closing moments of "action" on the battlefield: groups of Indian warriors riding their horses in slow circles and shooting at objects on the ground. As the warriors sighted the feeble troop advance, they started after the new foe. A sharp running skirmish followed, but by 6:10, Reno's and Benteen's men had regrouped at their refuge point. Confirming that they were now on the defensive, the men began digging breastworks topped with packs and cracker boxes to withstand a siege.[81]

It was evening, but warriors settled along the ridges to snipe while the light lasted, killing another five soldiers, wounding six more. Only darkness ended the barrage. The war leaders conferred and agreed to keep relays of warriors in the field all night: "We couldn't get at the soldiers," recalled Standing Bear, "so we decided we would starve or dry the soldiers out."[82]

At sundown, the first relay of warriors rode back to the village to find it repitched in a tighter formation downstream. Fires were lit all across the campground, but everyone was too keyed up to celebrate. They knew that their great victory had come at a price: sixteen warriors had been killed in the action against Custer, to add to the nineteen people lost in the Reno fight. And another youth, riding too close to the defenses, had been killed in the evening siege.

Before dawn, heralds ordered warriors to relieve their comrades. Beginning at daybreak, the surviving 362 officers and men of the Seventh Cavalry were subjected to a relentless fusillade. Tired warriors even mustered a charge. A final two Lakotas were killed in these clashes, totaling Indian fatalities at about thirty-eight. The Indians' galling fire killed another seven troopers, wounding thirty-nine, but clearly, the defenders would hold. About noon, Sitting Bull ordered disengagement, and the warriors slowly drifted away from the field.[83]

By early afternoon, rumors of troops approaching from the north were rife. Crazy Horse, coordinating village defense, detailed Short Bull and He Dog to scout down the Little Bighorn. Fifteen miles northward, the combined commands of Terry and Gibbon were probing gingerly up the river, aware that the smoke pall some miles ahead betokened a great Indian presence.[84]

Crazy Horse monitored incoming reports, noting with dismay the presence of Gibbon's infantry. "They saw infantry," Oglala veterans told interpreter John Colhoff, "and they don't seem to like them—they bury themselves in the ground like badgers and it's too slow fighting." Crazy Horse detached up to three hundred warriors to make a reconnaissance in force. Others torched the grass to deter pursuit. With panic already gripping the women and children, there was little to do but order a remove south. At sundown, the massive procession retraced its trail up the west side of the valley. Over two miles long, spreading half a mile across the bottomland, the Northern Nation paraded past Reno's and Benteen's beleaguered command. As they passed, a ragged cheer rose from the ranks of these survivors of the great dust storm from the east.[85]

18

WALKING THE BLACK ROAD

Deep into the night, the people ascended the river, pausing at dawn to nap and break out a hurried meal from the food packs. At daylight, the camp heralds cried "Get ready, we are going," and women hurried to reload packs and hitch travois. Having made sixteen miles from the battlefield, the two-mile procession neared the forks of the Little Bighorn midmorning on June 27. The well-watered flat made a favorable campsite, and the village was repitched for the night.[1]

At noon on the 28th, the people broke camp and started south. Satellite camps fanned up the two easterly forks, searching for better prospects in game and pasture. The main body followed along Lodge Grass Creek, camping at the foot of the Bighorn Mountains. On the sacred fourth night after the victory, people prepared to celebrate. Crazy Horse still anxiously awaited news of Terry's march, and in the evening, alarm briefly flared when the shout went up "The soldiers are coming!" A line of blue-coated men riding abreast neared, then broke into whoops of laughter at the excitement. The pranksters in looted uniforms declared, "Terry was not following us and everything was safe." After relieving the huddled survivors of the Seventh Cavalry on the 27th, Terry's and Gibbon's men had spent this day burying the dead in shallow battlefield graves.[2]

At this reassuring news, villagers lit bonfires and began victory dances. Some already knew that the slain commander was Pehin Hanska, Long Hair Custer, and singers extemporized satirical chants:

> Long Hair, guns I hadn't any.
> You brought me some.
> I thank you.
> You make me laugh![3]

Over the next few days, intelligence continued to demonstrate that the Montana-Yellowstone commands were neutralized. Short Bull's scouts arrived early on July 1, reporting that Terry and Gibbon had withdrawn down the Little Bighorn, carrying Reno's wounded on horse-drawn litters to load aboard the steamboat *Far West*, along with Terry's staff, at the junction with the Bighorn. Gibbon marched the command to Terry's new headquarters at the civilian stockade Fort Pease. There, like Crook on Goose Creek, the stunned, demoralized command took stock amid the wreckage of Sheridan's summer initiative.[4]

Freed to restock the packs, hunters sought buffalo and small teams of uncles and cousins threaded into the mountains after deer and elk. Women and girls gathered early cherries, and boys scoured streams for fish, fowl, and small game. Family groups scattered to cut lodgepoles as the village moved slowly through the high country. For several nights, victory dances continued. One name was constantly sounded in the praise songs. "After the battle," Standing Bear recalled, "I heard a lot about Crazy Horse."[5]

Over the following months, military commentators would also conclude that Crazy Horse's contribution was crucial to the victory over Custer. Penning his summary report on the course of the Great Sioux War, after debriefing surrendering warriors, Lieutenant William P. Clark concluded that the Battle of the Little Bighorn "brought Crazy Horse more prominently before all the Indians than any one else. . . . Before this he had a great reputation[;] in it he gained a greater prestige than any other Indian in the camp."[6]

The most famous Lakota victory of all time was not Crazy Horse's triumph alone. He was no Caesar or Napoleon, moving warrior brigades like chess pieces across the field. His life story has repeatedly demonstrated just how individualistic was Indian warfare. At the Little Bighorn, warriors knotted around a score of other tactical leaders. Gall helped coordinate the massed repeater volleys that broke the tactical integrity of Calhoun's position. Elsewhere, One Bull, Knife Chief, Spotted Eagle, and Iron Star all distinguished themselves as "big braves." Lame White Man, Yellow Nose, and other Cheyennes played significant roles on sections of the field.

Other Oglala blotahunka, like Low Dog and Big Road, led parties distinct from Crazy Horse's. Such groups rode into battle, ten, twenty, fifty men strong. One of the largest was the Hunkpapa Crow King's group: eighty warriors. But one unfazed trooper witness estimated two hundred men in the party that followed Crazy Horse against Reno. As the battle progressed, it attracted new followers: significantly, given the clannish loyalties of Plains Indians, many Cheyenne warriors chose to follow Crazy Horse across the Little Bighorn. Like their Lakota counterparts, they trusted the Oglala war chief's luck and medicine; his generosity in foregoing coups set up by his maneuvering; his reputation for cool bravery combined with tactical acumen; and not least, his ability to deliver results with minimal casualties. Just as at the Rosebud, Crazy Horse was the leader whose contribution at every stage of the battle evinced an overall grasp of strategy and tactics, implemented not at a single point or phase, but across the field. Even his notoriously deliberate preparations prior to repulsing Reno underwrote his exemplary authority, the compelling self-belief that this battle would run on his terms, at his speed.

A war leader "might give orders to fight," summed up one Hunkpapa, "but he does not direct how to proceed."[7] Orders might be given to a trusted lieutenant like Good Weasel, but they were implemented by example, not command. Followers, independent and used to taking the initiative, exploited the tactical configuration their leader shaped—or disengaged if circumstances deteriorated. Such a following, strong but flexible, loosely coordinated by a responsive core of subalterns like Kicking Bear, Bad Heart Bull, and Flying Hawk, could make the difference in a battle. Repeatedly, they did. In three separate phases of the Little Bighorn—the charge on Reno's retreat; the overwhelming of Keogh and the severing of the right wing retreat; and the final overrunning of Last Stand Hill—Crazy Horse sensed the defining moments of the battle. At each of these turning points, he acted swiftly to inspire and encourage, so that the rawest youth present was animated to emulate him. And each time, devoted lieutenants delivered the backup that transformed a solitary brave's run into an incremental, critical segment of the total victory.

Those moments of crucial troop imbalance, intuited through Crazy Horse's unraveling of Thunder's revelation, demonstrate that the battle was a sequence of localized actions, fought on the terms that Crazy Horse had identified after the Bozeman Trail campaigning. Troop unit isolation, leading to tactical breakdown, command erosion, and demoralized panic were the responses Crazy Horse had observed on the frozen ridge of the Fetterman battle. For ten years he had worked to deliver another such victory. Fighting Crook's brigade, Crazy Horse had achieved a dazzling tactical victory. Eight days later, on the Custer field, faced with a less wary foe, Crazy Horse was able to implement more fully the sort of mobile, strung-out strategy that had, midway through the Battle of the Rosebud, threatened to overrun Royall's battalion and unravel Crook's lines.

As Custer's lines of communication stretched between his battalion wings, Crazy Horse patiently awaited the right moment to sever them. He forcefully declined White Bull's repeated taunts to lead a premature charge—until the bloody chaos of Gall's onslaught reduced Harrington's and Calhoun's companies to a panicked shambles. Deprived of the leadership of their commissioned officers, the two troops collapsed, contrasting the brittle hierarchy of the army command structure with the flexible Indian leadership. Captain Keogh was able to rally his unit, but the surprise of Crazy Horse's kicamnayan charge overwhelmed their position, perfecting the dry run he aimed at Royall eight days earlier. Varying momentary frontal charges with protracted infiltration phases, Crazy Horse was able to soften up Custer's battalion as it belatedly consolidated a defensive position around Last Stand Hill. As the rate of fire from the hill deteriorated, Crazy Horse once more identified the crystallization of command breakdown, leading a last charge that poured over the hill to meet his circle run.

Earlier commentators have adduced several technical factors, ascribing troop collapse to the blocking of carbines after overfiring caused cartridge ejection failure. Individual guns undoubtedly blocked, and Crazy Horse exhorted his warriors to get the soldiers' "guns hot so they would not work so well." Unfortunately for the sake of literary neatness, one of the solid conclusions of the latest archaeological research is that breech mechanism failure was statistically insignificant.[8] Similarly, the troops were not inadequately supplied with ammunition. Indian testimony confirms that, despite seizing many cartridges from the saddlebags of stampeded cavalry mounts, most slain troopers were found with ammunition to spare.

Nor were the soldiers simply outgunned. The Springfield carbine was a sturdy arm, its single-shot mechanism rapidly reloaded, its range and power superior to most Indian armament. Statistical analysis of expended nonarmy shells on the Custer field suggests that about one in ten warriors—no more than about two hundred—was armed with a repeater. Building on the successful deployment of repeaters at the Rosebud, Indian leaders maximized their shock effect by concentrating groups of warriors armed with Winchesters and Henrys. Even a small group levering their carbines into a fixed troop position could have devastating effect—when Kicking Bear, Hard to Hit, and Bad Heart Bull opened fire into Reno's column, their demoralizing barrage kicked off the rout from the timber. Similarly, archaeological work at Calhoun Hill demonstrates that the troop skirmish lines there came under blistering pressure from lines of infiltrating warriors armed with repeaters. As in the Reno fight, troops exposed to concerted rapid fire were ripe for panic and could be overrun.

Custer's collapse reveals larger issues. Commentators have suggested several scapegoats in the most famous defeat of U.S. arms in history, but the fact that stands out in assessing leadership on the ground is how inflexibly Custer pursued his singleminded determination to prevent at all costs Indian "scatteration." Disregarding deficiencies in intelligence about the Indian strength, Custer repeatedly committed his regiment to pursuit of straggling parties of scouts and hunters. He was still skeptical of the presence of a sizeable village until after ordering Reno's charge down the Little Bighorn. Even after witnessing Reno's stalemate and realizing the full strength of the village, and following a lengthy pause that smacks of serious strategic reassessment, Custer elected to recommit his battalion to containing scatteration. Repeatedly dividing his immediate command into overextended wings deployed as strike force and reserve, he committed an inadequate force over a field that stretched like taffy—the ideal terrain for Crazy Horse to test his reading of army psychology.

In the broadest sense, morale differentials were crucial to the outcome of the battle. Debates of Indian firepower and the technical shortcomings of military armament obscure a central structural fact: troops were inadequately trained in the use of firearms. Limited army appropriations were reflected in the premium on live ammunition. Crazy Horse was right to conclude that, facing critical pressure, ill-trained troops would collapse into aimless, haphazard fire. Older studies suggested that the

Seventh Cavalry was an outfit dominated by raw recruits, but analysis of regimental composition suggests that the Seventh was not exceptionally green. But, excluding rest halts, the men and horses entering battle at 3:00 P.M. on June 25 had been on the march for all but five of the previous thirty-four hours. Fatigue had already worn down men's physical and mental reserves. By contrast, the warriors rushing to meet them were fresh. Already fired with the justness of their cause and Sitting Bull's assurance of total victory, the immediate threat to their families honed an edge to warrior conviction that even supremely professional troops could not blunt.

Undoubtedly, the force that overran Last Stand Hill, or reduced Reno's retreat to rout, vastly outnumbered Custer's divided battalions. Man for man, the troops were outnumbered three to one. But that fact is subject to nuanced interpretation. One strength the Indian force distinctly lacked was rapid-response deployment: some Oglalas and Cheyennes were still awaiting the arrival of their ponies fully one and a half hours after the first alarm was cried. Consequently, Reno was bluffed into halting and forming a skirmish line by a fraction of the total warrior force. Perhaps nine hundred were engaged in the climax of action against Reno; and once Reno and Benteen consolidated, they faced up to six hundred. Even after these warriors disengaged to counter the threat from Custer, the defenders sat tight. They had been outfought, and key officers were demoralized by the sheer speed and conviction of Indian deployments.

The same factors operated against Custer's command. The idea that Custer was immediately crushed by some juggernaut of red warriors does not withstand inspection. During initial phases of the Custer battle, only scores of warriors were engaged. Once his battalion reunited along Calhoun Ridge, the majority of Indians on and accessing the field were at his rear, positioned between Custer and the village. Although this presence patently threatened his communications to Reno, Custer elected to extend another strung-out offensive—one that could net him the prize of two thousand unarmed fugitives, cowering and exhausted, across the river.

Any true assessment of the Indian victory must take into account how the flight of the fugitives compromised Crazy Horse's strategic response. At the village ford, he and Crow King had divided their forces. Pursuing Yates across the river, Crow King and Gall interposed their warriors between Custer and the village. Crazy Horse elected to screen the fugitives from Custer's riverward probes. Infiltrating the drainage of Deep Ravine, Crazy Horse had to open a holding action rather than the retreat-and-regroup tactic with which he had threatened Royall at the Rosebud. Crazy Horse's responsive flexibility to the evolving tactical situation contrasts starkly with Custer's obsessive strategy of pursuit and containment. Only after Custer's left-wing threat to the fugitives was neutralized by a new influx of warriors did Crazy Horse feel secure enough to unleash the offensive against the right-wing reserve.

Fugitive safety opened the strategic configuration of the battle; minutes later, Gall's onslaught on Calhoun Hill delivered the tactical initiative for Crazy Horse to unravel the right wing completely. Indian witnesses recognized his charge on Keogh's position as pivotal.[9]

Only after Crazy Horse's charge at Keogh's troops and the consolidation of Custer's survivors on Last Stand Hill was the total warrior force brought to bear in the fearsome new odds of fifteen to one. Predictably, the battle barely lasted five more minutes, but the truth remains that the victory had been assured in a series of interlocking actions in which the odds had not been so one sided. No Indian generalissimo coordinated every battlefield maneuver as Hollywood and some earlier historians would have it. But, as Lieutenant Clark's Lakota informants asserted, no war leader contributed more to the overall victory than Crazy Horse. The praise songs of victory dancers, and the proliferation of military reports singling out Crazy Horse as the key to Northern Nation resistance, faithfully reflect his incomparable example at the Battle of the Little Bighorn.

Victory dances wound up, and as buffalo disappeared, the people were forced to butcher horses. High country pasture was soon eaten off, and the southward movement placed the village within thirty miles of Crook's becalmed base camp. This proximity was vividly illustrated on July 7, when a small scouting party including Flying Hawk tangled with twenty-five Second Cavalry troopers under Lieutenant Frederick W. Sibley.[10]

The village chiefs decided to shift downcountry, but a screen of warriors continued to harry Crook's pickets, torching the grass to deter pursuit. Their activities, compounded by the July 10 bombshell news of the Custer disaster, kept Crook confined to his base for another three and a half weeks. Free again from pursuit, on the eighth, the Northern Nation moved down the Little Bighorn toward the plains. The tempo of movement picked up, and the village swung down Rosebud Creek. Game was still scarce, and every day the people were compelled to move. With every military threat contained, meat, not warfare, became the overriding concern, and for the next two months, the war council that had coordinated Northern Nation activities yielded primacy to Deciders and hunt akicita. Outriders set fire to the plains behind them to promote grass growth and to lure the northward trending herds back across the Yellowstone in time for fall hunts.[11]

On July 14 the village, approaching the ambit of Terry's field of operations in the Yellowstone valley, swung east to camp on Tongue River. At last, the compelling logic of subsistence dictated dispersal, and several bands drifted south and east, some drifting toward the agencies. The main village swung down the Tongue, eventually catching up with the northering herds. For two weeks, removals slowed as hunters made successful surrounds and women labored to dry meat, prepare robes, and renew lodgeskins.

Crazy Horse took pride in acting as provider not only for his own tipi, but for the lodge of his father and stepmothers. Assured of food, and with intelligence that neither Crook nor Terry had stirred from their bases, warriors looked for opportunities. Some war parties targeted the Black Hills miners. Crazy Horse, after looking eagerly around for a little late summer raiding, led a large party, two hundred strong, across the Yellowstone, targeting Assiniboin bands near Wolf Point Agency on the Missouri. Gall accompanied him, keen to have some of the Crazy Horse medicine rub off, as did the Miniconjou Flying By, a member of Crazy Horse's bodyguard. Having stolen a herd of "nice horses," the party moved to rejoin the village by the start of the Moon of Black Cherries, low on the Powder River.[12]

On July 29 the war party whooped its herd homeward across the Yellowstone, stopping to camp and to inspect the remains of Terry's former supply base. Sacks of corn and oats were still stacked on the landing stage, and Crazy Horse had his men load up until the shrill whistle of the steamboat *Carroll* alerted the party to danger ascending the river. Bluecoats lined the decks, and shots were exchanged across the water with Lieutenant Colonel Elwell S. Otis's Twenty-second infantry detachment. One trooper fell, and Otis had the steamer pull to shore and land a company to chase the warriors. Disengaging, Crazy Horse led his men into the timber, hurrying homeward.[13]

Over the next couple of days, the village descended the Powder. Alerted by Crazy Horse to the prospect of plunder, a large body of people arrived at the landing stage early on August 2 and ripped open the forage sacks. Indian ponies balked at the oats, and the contents were poured out across the dock, the sacks retained for camp use. Women had loaded the travois with corn for parching when the hoot of another steamboat dispersed the gathering. The *Far West* had arrived to rescue the forage stocks and ship them upstream to Terry's new headquarters. In a day of low-key skirmishing, the boat's twelve-pounder shelled the bottomlands, gradually forcing the Lakotas to withdraw. Crazy Horse's comrade Runs Fearless was killed.[14]

On Powder River, the great village was ready to break up. New arrivals from the agencies compounded the problems of food and pasture. About sixty lodges of Cheyennes, led by Dull Knife, arrived in camp with word of increased military activity around Red Cloud Agency—the war chiefs concluded that Crook's summer hibernation was about to end.[15]

Buffalo were scattering downstream and across the Yellowstone. Already Hunkpapas opposed to Sitting Bull's leadership, like Iron Dog, were ready to track northward to hunt: a few even spoke of continuing north across the invisible medicine line of the 44th parallel to seek refuge where Inkpaduta assured Lakotas of a welcome, in Grandmother's Land. Others were ready to depart for home agencies. Neither alternative was acceptable to Crazy Horse, but subsistence demanded an immediate solution. The Deciders agreed that the core of the village would press east across the Little Missouri. Prospects for deer hunting were good in the wooded uplands like Killdeer Mountains, Slim Buttes, and Short Pine Hills; and more Hunkpapas, Sans Arcs, and Miniconjous were ready to travel to Fort Berthold to trade horses and robes at the harvest fair of the Arikaras, Mandans, and Hidatsas.[16]

Back in camp only a few days, Crazy Horse was already impatient for the warpath. With no prospective military pursuit, he was free to plan another small-scale raid. Black Fox, Dog Goes, four Cheyenne warriors, and bodyguard members Looking Horse, Short Bull, and Low Dog agreed to follow him into the Black Hills. Such a party might couple raiding activities with intelligence gathering on the intruders in the hills, even looting vital provisions. About August 3, while the main village continued east, smaller ones fanned south. As Crazy Horse's war party angled southeast onto the Little Missouri divide, they would have seen behind them the black rolling cloud of smoke that covered the Montana plain, billowing high above fires set to call homeward the elusive Buffalo North.[17]

Two days after the Northern Nation scattered, General Crook finally broke camp on Goose Creek. Reinforced by Colonel Wesley Merritt's Fifth Cavalry, units of the Second and Third Cavalries, and ten infantry companies, Crook commanded a force of over eighteen hundred effective troops. Two hundred fifty Shoshone scouts and two hundred civilian guides and packers completed the roll of the strongest command ever to penetrate the Lakota domain. Early on August 5, it started down the Tongue to unite with Terry.[18]

As the steamboat traffic observed by Crazy Horse demonstrated, Terry was also readying his command to march. Reinforcements were busily shipped up the Missouri and Yellowstone rivers to Terry's new headquarters at the mouth of the Rosebud. As he prepared to march on August 8, he could count seventeen hundred effective troops, consisting of the reorganized Seventh Cavalry, four companies of the Second Cavalry, and four battalions of infantry. Notable among the walk-a-heap reinforcements were six companies of the Fifth Infantry, under their regimental commander Colonel Nelson A. Miles. Able and supremely ambitious, more than any other officer Miles would set his stamp on the campaigning to come.

On August 10 Crook and Terry foregathered on Rosebud Creek. Following the month-old village trail across fire-blackened plains quagmired by late summer rainstorms, the two commands turned east. With intelligence focusing on Hunkpapa movements crossing the lower Yellowstone, Terry detailed Miles to patrol the crossings, while he oversaw provisioning of a new post at the mouth of Tongue River, intended to headquarter Miles's infantry in the field. With water falling daily in the Yellowstone, Terry worked to transfer steamboat shipments from Fort Buford to supply trains outfitting Tongue River Cantonment.

Crook was convinced that Crazy Horse—for the first time reckoned by military analysts as equal with Sitting Bull—and his Oglala, Brule, and Cheyenne followers would not cross north of the Yellowstone. Instead, they would veer south toward the Black Hills, threatening the security of his Department of the Platte. On August 26 Crook followed the main trail east from Powder River, making slow progress over the rain-lashed plains; on September 3, as the command straggled into the Little Missouri valley past the landmark of Sentinel Buttes, the main trail finally broke up, lost beneath three weeks' worth of Badlands gumbo. Crook's dispiriting dispatch convinced Terry to wind up his campaign on the fifth, dispersing his command to posts overseeing the agency Lakotas.

As Crook's bedraggled command crossed the Badlands, conditions worsened, and by September 5, barely two days' provisions remained. When scouts located a more recent trail pointing south, Crook ordered pursuit. Camping in mud, reduced to eating foundered mules and horses, the command soon found the crisscross trails of people dispersing after security and small game. On the seventh, Crook ordered Captain Anson Mills to take the trail to Deadwood, the nearest mining settlement, and buy supplies on army credit. In the last light of evening, with Frank Grouard in the lead, some 154 officers and men of the Third Cavalry followed Mills south. The following afternoon, near Slim Buttes, Grouard reported sighting Indian ponies, then a cluster of tipis. Three months after the Rosebud, Crook's command was again in contact with the enemy.[19]

Crook's vanguard had entered the fall hunting zone. By early September, the Indians were grouped in two large villages and ten or more satellite camps. On the north fork of Grand River, barely seven miles west of the main command, camped up to four hundred lodges of Miniconjous, Sans Arcs, and Hunkpapas. Tracked by Terry, their satellites had drifted north, away from the war zone toward sanctuary in Canada.

The second large village, some three hundred lodges, was the main Oglala-Cheyenne camp, situated on the headwaters of the south fork of Grand River. In the wooded hills all around, satellite camps were hunting deer. One camp, thirty-seven lodges, was tucked away on the east side of the Slim Buttes. Iron Plume's tiyospaye had been joined by relatives drifting south from Sitting Bull. Disheartened inside their rain-soaked tipis, some people favored surrender. Messengers opened a dialogue at Cheyenne River, indicating that the Crook-Terry pursuit had reinstated the war leadership in both main villages. Crazy Horse again presided in Oglala councils, assisted by akicita leaders Little Big Man, Kicking Bear, and He Dog.[20]

The war chief had returned from the Black Hills the third week in August. Since Crazy Horse's April hike through the hills, settlements had grown. Boomtowns like Deadwood, Crook City, and Custer City flourished. Trails were lined with supply trains, incoming miners, and a new stagecoach service. To feed an insatiable market for meat, cattle and even sheep were being herded in high country pastures. Almost overnight Paha Sapa had become one of the most densely settled sections of the trans-Mississippi West.

In the misty dawn of September 9, Captain Mills' detachment charged Iron Plume's sleeping camp, quickly rounding up most of the four hundred ponies. Behind door flaps lashed tight against the rain, people cut their way out of tipis. Two men and a woman were killed in the first minutes, but most managed to flee behind a determined fire from their warriors. Soon they were stringing over the buttes to Crazy Horse's village, twenty miles away. Others took refuge in a ravine and mounted a fierce defense as they witnessed their camp looted—three tons of dried meat, dried fruit, and a cache of flour making a welcome dietary supplement for the veterans of the "Horsemeat March." Pitiless firing into the ravine soon killed another warrior, three women, and one infant. Crook soon arrived on the scene, and by midafternoon, the entire command was bivouacked in a natural amphitheater, surrounded on three sides by the pine-topped crags and outcrops of the Slim Buttes. Led by the mortally wounded Iron Plume and his brother Charging Bear, the twenty-one survivors in the ravine were persuaded to surrender. With the first military victory of the war under its belts, the command settled to naps and cooking fires.[21]

A funeral service had begun for two soldiers and a civilian scout when, at about 4:15 P.M., the crack of distant Winchesters snapped Crook's pickets into action. Crazy Horse had arrived. Alerted in midmorning of the attack, as many as five hundred warriors had followed the Oglala war chief. The odds were severely stacked against them. Expecting to confront Mills's detachment alone, Crazy Horse had projected a Rosebudlike charge to sweep away the captured herd and release the captives. Instead, he faced the largest army ever engaged in the Plains Indian wars. Despite odds of four to one, Crazy Horse urged his warriors forward. A frontal assault was no longer feasible, but the warriors took up positions on the granite outcrops and poured a heavy fire into Crook's camp from the southwest.

Warriors spread around the hills, following the war chief's lieutenants—Kicking Bear, Wears the Deer Bonnet, He Dog, and Brave Wolf. One of their contingents darted forward to cut off some stampeding cavalry mounts, but a corporal's cool presence of mind turned the lead horse. Crook ordered his units forward. Testifying to the conviction of the Lakota attack, the general had to commit his whole force. While a unit of mounted cavalry protected the open eastern flank, infantry and dismounted cavalrymen advanced under steady fire toward the hills. Smoke hung low in the moist atmosphere, wreathing the slopes. As at the Rosebud, the range and accuracy of infantry rifles availed. The right of the Indian line first gave way, as the bluecoats secured the hilltops. Although Crazy Horse was able to preserve order, his line unfolded west, fighting a protracted duel across a five hundred-yard gap.

At the extreme left, one Lakota contingent even mounted a bold charge at the Third Cavalry position, snaking across the plain and darting for gaps in the skirmish line behind volleys from their repeaters. A distinctive figure, believed by reporter Finerty to be Crazy Horse, "mounted on a fleet white pony, galloped around the array and seemed to possess the power of ubiquity" as he urged on the attack.[22] The dazzling maneuver was worthy of the victor of the Rosebud and the Little Bighorn, but the odds were too much. Facing concerted fire, the charge dissolved to regroup beyond range. Finally, as the wet dusk turned to darkness, the warriors disengaged. It was no precipitate flight but, faced by overwhelming odds, none of their tactical objectives had been achieved. "There was no one commander," summed up Short Bull. "No leader did anything extraordinary."[23]

The following morning, as Crook's command prepared to march, renewed fire from the hills signaled that Lakota resolve was not eroded. Through the rainy morning, as troops torched the camp, lines of converging warriors charged on the cavalry rearguard, seeking to cut off units as at the Rosebud and the Little Bighorn. After a two-mile running fight, the warriors conceded the engagement. Most of the captives had been freed, and Crook was able to push his exhausted command toward the Black Hills. While his men camped near Deadwood, the general was summoned to a strategy summit with General Sheridan at Fort Laramie.

Over the next month, the Big Horn and Yellowstone Expedition trended south. They were no longer a military threat, but the screen of Lakota scouts monitoring their progress only confirmed what Crazy Horse had learned a month earlier. The massive infrastructure of communications and supply lines that already linked the booming Black Hills settlements to the Union Pacific line had achieved what no army could: the seizure of the heart of the Lakota domain. Processing these reports, and new intelligence from the agencies, Lakotas would commemorate the Battle of Slim Buttes as The Fight Where We Lost the Black Hills.

During the centennial summer of 1876, news of the Custer catastrophe convulsed a nation celebrating a landmark in its history. One hundred years after the American War of Independence, the United States stood on the world stage as a powerhouse of the new industrial age and a symbol of liberty and opportunity to millions of European emigrants fleeing oppression and poverty in the Old World. The status of world power beckoned. To visitors at the great centennial exposition in Philadelphia, confidence in American enterprise and know-how seemed justifiably unbounded. The startling word wired to press agencies early in July—that a horde of painted savages had annihilated the flower of the U.S. Army on a remote stream in Montana Territory—stunned the nation. Through the second half of 1876, the public mood in the East swung sharply against conciliating the brutal killers of Custer.

General Sheridan adeptly cruised the zeitgeist. Besides ordering units from across the Division of the Missouri to converge on the war zone for a projected winter campaign, the general tightened control of the Great Sioux Reservation. Since spring, he had argued forcefully that the reservation Lakotas gave aid and comfort to hostile bands on the hunting grounds. To halt the drain in manpower, materiel, and intelligence, Sheridan urged that the agencies be turned over to army control. On July 22, in the wake of the national scandal of the Little Bighorn, he finally received the go-ahead from Washington. That same day, wires from the Indian Office were transmitted to the agents, and over the ensuing weeks, the army assumed command of the Great Sioux Reservation.[24]

Reinforcements were rushed to Camp Robinson. Colonel Ranald S. Mackenzie assumed command of the District of the Black Hills on August 13, bringing six companies of the Fourth Cavalry. Units of the Fifth Cavalry, the Fourteenth

Infantry, and the Fourth Artillery followed, quadrupling the effective strength of Camp Robinson to some 850 officers and men.

Tensions heightened at Red Cloud Agency when a new commission arrived on September 6 and in short order browbeat the chiefs into signing an agreement surrendering title to the Black Hills and to hunting rights in the Powder River country. Over the objections of the Oglalas and Brules, the commissioners insisted on the removal of their agencies: either to the Missouri River or, more alarming, to new locations in Indian Territory—the hot arid plains of modern Oklahoma. Through the fall, the commission toured the other agencies, securing agreements from bitter chiefs who were told the alternative for their people was starvation.[25]

Disquiet at the commission's work and the tightening army control of the reservation forced a new exodus from the agencies. Moderate leaders like Touch the Clouds and Roman Nose refused to submit their bands to army counts and the surrender of arms and ponies. With about sixty-five lodges leaving Cheyenne River alone, the policy of repression and confiscation was backfiring badly.[26]

The capitulation confirmed Crazy Horse's fears about the reservation leadership. Disregarding the stark economic realities that lay behind the enforced signing, the Oglala war chief would reject every agency overture for the next five months. Feelings ran high at the news that the unceded territory was included in the cession. War chief and council declared Red Cloud Agency off-limits. Families favoring surrender would be soldiered into line, deserters whipped, their property confiscated or destroyed.

As fall approached, game dispersed and pasture thinned along the Little Missouri. If the northern Lakotas were to remain free, they had to hunt to build winter surplus. Crazy Horse and the Oglala leaders argued for a return to the Powder River country, a move the Cheyennes also favored. Sitting Bull argued for a move north across the Yellowstone, where he could reunite his Hunkpapas. Most Miniconjous and Sans Arcs warily approved Sitting Bull's line.

At the very end of September, the Northern Nation again divided. Up to 465 lodges followed Sitting Bull slowly down the Little Missouri valley. Almost as many Oglalas and Cheyennes followed Crazy Horse west. At the junction of Powder River and Clear Fork, the people divided again. Most Cheyennes trended up the creek into the Bighorn Mountains. Locating their fall hunting operation along the upper Bighorn River, the Cheyennes happily renewed their feud with the Shoshones. When the Cheyennes settled into winter quarters high up Red Fork of Powder River, during the third week of November, they signaled a clear intention of sitting out future hostilities.[27]

From Clear Fork Crazy Horse's people turned northwest. About 250 lodges—comprising Oglalas, some Brules, ten Cheyenne families, and straggling Miniconjous and Sans Arcs—followed the war chief, but along Tongue River, game still proved elusive. Pushing on to the head of the Rosebud, the village trekked over plains still blackened from the summer burning. But here the progress slowed. For about a month, the village moved along the upper Rosebud, an indication that the Buffalo North had made its hoped-for crossing of the Yellowstone.

For a few weeks, life settled into old routines, and Crazy Horse was happy to mount his traditional end-of-season raid into the Crow country. Crazy Horse was victorious in the skirmish, "and brought back a lot of scalps," recalled Black Elk. A Crow woman was killed, reportedly by Crazy Horse, and one hundred vengeful Crow warriors agreed to enlist as scouts for Colonel Miles against the Lakotas. On November 12 a Crow reprisal party made off with some Oglala ponies, but a fresh Crow scalp added to the illusion of life as normal.[28]

In truth, Crazy Horse's war council was already troubled by news of the new military presence on the hunting grounds. Scouts confirmed that Miles was settling in for the winter along the Yellowstone, establishing Tongue River Cantonment as winter quarters for his regiment and six companies of the Twenty-second. From Glendive Creek, Lieutenant Colonel Otis's command, comprising four more troops of the Twenty-second Infantry and two of the seventeenth, escorted the supply trains that channeled provisions, forage, and even a beef herd upstream to Miles. In mid-October, as Sitting Bull's village crossed the Yellowstone, he began to harry Otis's trains, varying frontal attacks with dialogue through reservation visitors.

Miles promptly marched on Sitting Bull, dispersing his village in a two-day running battle. Along the Big Dry, the bands of Sitting Bull, Gall, and Pretty Bear reunited with some of the satellite hunting bands that had peeled off the main village in August. But fifty-seven lodges of Hunkpapas, following headmen Iron Dog, Long Dog, Little Knife, and Lodge Pole, pushed farther north, camping just across the border of the British possessions. The theme of refuge and exile in Grandmother's Land had been sounded.[29]

More amenable to dialogue with Miles were the Miniconjous and Sans Arcs. On October 26 five leaders gave themselves as hostages, pledging the surrender of their people at Cheyenne River Agency within thirty-five days. During the talks, the headmen wrung off-the-record concessions out of Miles. When the chiefs raised Lone Horn's old plan of an agency near the Black Hills, Miles made some favorable noises. Once more, the prospect of an agency to secure their homeland in perpetuity animated Indian negotiators.[30]

Crazy Horse was disturbed by the reports from his Miniconjou kinsmen. Clearly, Miles—whom the messengers already called Bear Coat, after his winter apparel—intended to remain in the field through the cold months. Unlike Crook and Terry, Bear Coat was unfazed by Lakota courage and ferocity and had already formulated a total strategy, forcing a wedge between the two main blocs of non-treaty people. If Sitting Bull could be pegged north of the Yellowstone, and Crazy Horse south, the two blocs could be defeated piecemeal. Miles's dangling of a Black Hills agency, and the prospect of safe winter hunting in Canada, only further eroded Northern Nation unity. As the council progressed, Crazy Horse revealed something of the strains beginning to wear on his self-possession, indignantly protesting that he would not face the "whole force of the whites alone."[31]

Also attending the council were a number of new arrivals from Red Cloud Agency. Posing as goodwill visitors, they were in fact informers for General Crook. Guardedly, they revealed to Crazy Horse something of crucial developments south. At Fort Laramie, General Sheridan had outlined with Crook plans for a second winter campaign. As preparations matured, Crook had arrived at the Oglala agency late in October to enlist scouts. He also privately recruited a number of spies to infiltrate Crazy Horse's village. The informers' instructions were to talk up surrender, subtly undermine northern morale, and report on village movements once Crook's command was in the field. Knowledge of these Oglala fifth columnists is unsatisfactory, but their number may well have included Crazy Horse's old enemy No Water.[32]

At Fort Fetterman, Crook assembled eleven mounted companies, drawn from the Second, Third, Fourth, and Fifth cavalry regiments, as well as fifteen infantry troops and the Fourth Artillery. Augmented by the civilian packtrain and four hundred Indian auxiliaries—Pawnee, Shoshone, and Bannock volunteers serving alongside the Lakota recruits—Crook's command topped twenty-one hundred effective men. On November 14 the Powder River Expedition started up the familiar route north from Fort Fetterman.

Sixty-three Oglala warriors, fifty-five Arapahos, and ten Cheyennes served as scouts. They believed their motivation was patriotic. They realized that, although Lakota courage and leadership might yet win battles, the army's logistical backup would prevail once winter pinched bellies and blanketed pasture. Continued warfare could lead only to futile suffering, and would further compromise Lakota claims to their hunting grounds—even to the reservation. Only after surrender, the scouts reasoned, could Crazy Horse's people engage in the vital dialogue that might preserve the nation's homeland.[33]

Crazy Horse's reading of scout motivation was not so charitable. The paranoia of betrayal that would characterize his final weeks had its roots in the troubled fall of 1876. Privately, he withdrew ever deeper from the prospect of dialogue with the agency leadership. But the village mood was subtly shifting, and Crazy Horse made no public objection when six of his warriors left for Red Cloud on November 19 to investigate conditions at the agency.[34]

Whatever Crazy Horse's private inclinations, his village had no heart for an offensive against Miles. Hunting to provide meat and winter robes would engage all the energies of his fighting men for weeks. Scouts located buffalo herds farther west, high up the Little Bighorn. To move there would only compromise the stretched communications with Sitting Bull. In mid-November Crazy Horse dispatched a Sans Arc messenger to locate Sitting Bull, urging that the Northern Nation reunite on Powder River and counter the threat posed by Bear Coat.[35]

More heartening was word from the east. After its parley with Miles, the main Miniconjou–Sans Arc village had swung south to Slim Buttes. During the second week of November, a significant break took place. Only a minority of about forty lodges, close relatives of the hostages taken by Miles, decided to honor their pledge to surrender at Cheyenne River. Three hundred more lodges decided to return to the hunting grounds. The village council nominated four new Deciders—Miniconjous Lame Deer and Black Shield, and Sans Arcs Spotted Eagle and Red Bear. All determinedly wedded to the old life, the Deciders notched up akicita resistance to capitulation at Cheyenne River.[36]

Their messengers proposed a union with Crazy Horse. Eager to consolidate, Crazy Horse announced a rendezvous between the Tongue and Powder rivers. Crazy Horse was gratified to learn that Lame Deer and his fellow Deciders were united against further capitulation at the agencies, but a strong sentiment favored following up on the negotiations with Miles. Oglala leaders were also amenable to a dialogue that might be an entering wedge to secure their territorial rights to the Black Hills and the hunting grounds. Although the constituted village leaderships of Deciders and war chiefs maintained a fastidious distance, they chose not to interfere with the peace process.

Early in December, Crazy Horse's people were camped along Beaver Creek, a small east tributary of Tongue River, barely sixty miles from Miles's headquarters. Food packs were thinning, and some people were reduced to butchering weak ponies. Then, on December 6, a straggle of half-naked people staggered into camp. All that day and for several more, the drain continued. Destitute and hungry, many of the newcomers were disfigured by frozen extremities and limbs; many more nursed terrible wounds. On November 25 Crook's cavalry arm, commanded by Mackenzie, had struck the Cheyenne village in the Bighorn Mountains. Cheyenne warriors mounted a stiff defense, but by midafternoon, the troops' firepower prevailed. With forty people killed and their village torched, Cheyenne families watched seven hundred of their ponies divided among Mackenzie's blue-coated Indian scouts.

For eleven days, the frozen survivors fled over the mountains and the wind-scoured plains. Each night children died from exposure and hunger. Exhausted horses were cut open and babies held inside the steaming bellies to preserve warmth and life. At last the vanguard met hunters from Crazy Horse's village. Reprising their reception after the Reynolds battle, Oglala heralds assembled the ragged procession on the campground. Again matrons brought out kettles and readied a feast of welcome. After eating, the Oglalas presented gifts of dried meat and pemmican. Robes, blankets, and packsaddles were stacked up, and the heralds announced that every married woman would receive skins enough to construct some kind of shelter. Men drove up horses and presented friends with tobacco.[37]

The first arrivals, comprising a majority of people committed to the war, would echo the verdict of Wooden Leg: "The Oglala Sioux received us hospitably."[38] As the days passed, filling out the makeshift shelters with demoralized people who leaned toward surrender, that generosity narrowed. Stores were failing, and Crazy

Horse ordered his akicita to consolidate resources. They circuited the tiyospaye clusters, collecting clothes and tipi covers. "We helped the Cheyennes the best we could," admitted Short Bull a little defensively: "We hadn't much ourselves."[39]

To many Cheyennes, Crazy Horse seemed preoccupied, detached. As winter deepened, an uncharitable observer might have read his steely resolve as pitiless. Crazy Horse "received them with very slight manifestations of pity," surrendering Cheyennes would bitterly complain. Some late arrivals even found themselves forced to trade for the few lodgeskins and shelters left. Increasingly, Crazy Horse channeled resources into bands and warrior factions supportive of the war front. Moderate chiefs like Dull Knife and Standing Elk were marginalized. Instead, the Lakotas recognized Black Moccasin and his nephew Ice—whom Crazy Horse remembered from his bulletproofing experiment nineteen years earlier—as principal leaders: men who had followed the Oglala village throughout the fall and were against any surrender.[40]

In meetings of the war council, Crazy Horse sought to tighten village resolve. Intelligence from Red Cloud Agency reported that some incoming men from the hunting grounds not only had been forced to surrender arms and ponies but had been imprisoned at Camp Robinson. The village council declared the Oglala home agency completely off-limits, echoing Crazy Horse's personal paranoia. Every arrival from the agencies was suspected as a spy. Camp removed fifty miles southwest, to the junction of Tongue River and Hanging Woman Creek. Impatiently Crazy Horse awaited a response from Sitting Bull, eager to launch a new offensive against Miles.

Through November, Sitting Bull's village had evaded Miles's patrols. Sitting Bull agreed with Crazy Horse's determination to rid the hunting grounds of the new bluecoat war house. Ammunition stocks, so badly depleted during the summer, had to be renewed if any offensive was to be launched. Early in December, Sitting Bull and his people spent a few intensive days at the border, trading with the Métis, eagerly exchanging their robes and dried meat for powder, lead, and cartridges. When Sitting Bull readied his people to reunite with Crazy Horse, his bodyguard warriors were able to organize a mule train to rival Crook's—packing fifty boxes of fixed ammunition to equip the warriors for a winter campaign.

On December 7 Sitting Bull recrossed the Missouri, followed by 122 lodges, but the pull of sanctuary continued to draw his people across the 49th parallel. Another fifty-two lodges, the tiyospaye of Black Moon, White Guts, and Crawler, opted to join relatives in Canada. For now, Sitting Bull could invoke Northern Nation unity to keep on board restive headmen like Four Horns and No Neck. Another disaster, though, might shatter that brittle consensus.[41]

The Miniconjou–Sans Arc village had located on the Yellowstone only a few miles downstream from Tongue River Cantonment and reopened talks with Miles. On the morning of December 16, five delegates approached the post. A group of Crow scouts met them with handshakes. One Crow, the husband of the woman killed by Crazy Horse's war party, recognized his wife's horse and shot the rider, Miniconjou delegate Gets Fat with Beef, from his saddle. Other Crows wrenched his comrades from their ponies, clubbing and hacking the Lakotas to death before fleeing the scene. Vainly, Miles had iyeska scouts carry presents and placatory messages to the village, but it was too late. Within hours of the killings, Lame Deer and his fellow Deciders had their people moving to rejoin Crazy Horse.[42]

Apprised of the tragedy, Crazy Horse immediately declared that the Crow atrocity was no unforeseeable tragedy but had been carried out at Miles's orders. "Crazy Horse thought the soldiers had helped the Crows to do this," remembered Black Elk, "so [the people] were mighty sore over this." Nevertheless, village councils insisted that reprisals be limited to the Crow contingent, reflecting a growing consensus to limit the scale of hostilities.[43]

Crazy Horse left the village alone. Vengeance was out of the question since Miles, still hopeful of placating Lakota opinion, had dismissed all his Crow scouts. Crazy Horse restricted operations to reconnaissance, surveying a quadrangle of log barracks and blockhouse stores built between the west bank of the Tongue and the Yellowstone. Miles's infantry alertly manned the post. Crazy Horse recognized that the troops' accurate firepower more than compensated for their lack of mobility: behind the extended range of their rifles, the inflexible squares and skirmish lines of the walk-a-heaps were less susceptible to panic than those of their cavalry comrades. A frontal assault on the post was out of the question. Only by drawing Miles far from his base, into the broken foothill country southward, was there a chance of neutralizing his strength.

By about December 20, four villages—Oglala, Cheyenne, Miniconjou, and Sans Arc—were clustered at Hanging Woman Creek. As many as eight hundred standard tipis lodged a massive winter concentration, approaching the peak summer strength of the Northern Nation. Crazy Horse stepped up his war talk. In a characteristic surge of energy, he urged the new arrivals to join his offensive. Lame Deer and the Deciders were relatively easy to convince, but fear, hunger, and faction ran deep. After Slim Buttes and the Mackenzie fight, many people "were in a constant state of suspense and fear of a like disaster."[44]

The case for caution seemed all the stronger when Hunkpapa messengers brought shocking news. On December 18, three companies of the Fifth Infantry, led by Lieutenant Frank D. Baldwin, caught Sitting Bull's people unawares on the divide between the Missouri and the Yellowstone. Baldwin's howitzer salvo found no target but served a warning to the Hunkpapas, who fled across the bleak tableland, abandoning their tipis and winter stores. Sitting Bull's warriors were alert enough to save the ammunition mule train, but vital supplies were lost. The Hunkpapas had to scatter to restock food packs and refit lodges. Given winter privations, and the lure of Canada, Sitting Bull would have to exert every ounce of his moral strength to keep reunion with Crazy Horse on track.[45]

The Oglala war chief was unwilling to sit out events. Any day blizzards might close the country, indefinitely delaying the offensive. War leaders, warriors, and cautious elders were at last swayed by Crazy Horse's resolve. Fifty Oglala and Cheyenne warriors would draw out the troops from Tongue River Cantonment. In contrast to the highly mobile tactics deployed at the Rosebud and the Little Bighorn, this would be an even more ambitious decoy strategy than High Backbone's exactly ten years previously. Minute attention to detail would be necessary to ensure that Miles's command was lured into an ambush one hundred miles south, where the broken terrain of the upper Tongue afforded the attackers some advantage.[46]

Some reluctant headmen were intimidated by an increasingly dictatorial akicita force. Something of their misgivings, and the febrile paranoia that was taking hold of Crazy Horse, is suggested by the observation of his Miniconjou brother-in-law Red Horse. The headman was bemused by Crazy Horse's insistence on keeping the offensive secret from the women and children. In a society as open as the Lakota, such secrecy was transparently futile and speaks to the conviction that public knowledge of the offensive would terminally polarize the villages. When the warriors left, about December 23, Crazy Horse was prepared to enforce total solidarity. Hitherto always respectful of local autonomies, famously compassionate to the poor and unfortunate, now he readied himself and his bodyguard to intervene wherever dissension appeared, or the cries of the hungry, the cold, and the frightened would signal the will to conciliate, compromise, and capitulate.

19

ALL THE RIVERS LIE
ACROSS MY ROAD

Within hours of the decoy force's departure, the brittle solidarity Crazy Horse and his akicita had imposed on the Northern Nation was threatened. Two Lakotas dismounted in the Miniconjou and Sans Arc villages. Packages of tobacco wrapped in blue and red cloths made patent their purpose—envoys from the reservation had finally arrived to talk surrender. Relatives of the hostages secured by Miles pending surrender at Cheyenne River, envoys Important Man and Fool Bear stressed the predicament of the prisoners, pointed to the privations of winter, and urged immediate surrender.[1]

A series of talks was hosted throughout the villages. Although Crazy Horse made no personal attack on the envoys, the Oglala response was immediate, negative, and intemperate. The Cheyenne war leadership, centered on Crazy Horse supporters like Ice and Two Moons, backed the Oglalas: "[T]he Cheyennes and Ogallalas would not listen," reported the pair, "and abused us very much." In a council presided over by Red Bear of the Sans Arcs, the envoys laid their tobacco before the Deciders, explaining that it came from Lieutenant Colonel George P. Buell, commanding the post overseeing Cheyenne River. The Deciders probed. Uncomfortably, Important Man and Fool Bear conceded that Buell's terms were unconditional, demanding the surrender of all ponies and arms. Their account of the army takeover only compounded the unease audibly transmitted through the council tipi. Politely but firmly, the Deciders rejected the envoys' tobacco, and the council closed.

The envoys wasted no time in visiting the tipis of the hostages' relatives. Over private meals, they assessed the deep underswell of opinion. Away from the public forum, many people admitted their fears and misgivings. White Eagle, a Sans Arc headman related to one of the hostages, had repeatedly tried to leave the village with his four tipis, but each time, akicita prevented a departure. Dissatisfaction with the dictatorial war front was deep rooted, but fear of punishment ran deeper. Crazy Horse was mentioned everywhere as the ideological architect of total resistance.

As the envoys listened to the litany of increasing repression, the door flap was thrown open, and Crazy Horse stooped to enter the tipi. The Oglala war chief and a knot of bodyguards sat, and in a village not his own, without constituted authority, and riding roughshod over that of the Deciders, Crazy Horse openly threatened both envoys and their nervous hosts. "[W]e would never be allowed to take any one from that camp," the envoys reported. "If any left they would be followed and killed."

After Crazy Horse's astonishing declaration, Important Man and Fool Bear assumed a low profile, working to effect a secret departure. About December 25, thirteen lodges slipped away after nightfall, the envoys breaking trail over the frozen ridges. "We got quite a ways," they reported, "supposing we had got away, when all at once 'Crazy Horse['] appeared with a good many warriors." Backed by Little Big Man and the Oglala akicita, Crazy Horse ordered the breakaways to halt. Then the Oglalas "shot all our horses, took our arms and knives, and all our plunder, and then told us if we wanted to go to the whites to go on, but the snow was so deep we could not travel without horses, and we had to return to the hostile camp."

The unprecedented intervention hardened attitudes against Crazy Horse within the Miniconjou–Sans Arc villages. Through the next day, the envoys openly pressed a daylight departure. Upwards of 150 lodges approved the proposal. Slowly, women began the work of packing and striking tipis, but then akicita threw a cordon around the villages. Eagle Shield recalled the heralds' announcement: "[N]o Indians could leave that camp alive." A defining moment passed, and the women started to pitch their tipis again. Akicita ordered Important Man and Fool Bear to leave the village, but over succeeding nights, they returned singly to lead away four lodges, close relatives of the hostages. Some moderate headmen sent word to the Cheyenne River authorities, arguing for concessions, hoping to deepen dialogue.

The final departure of Important Man and Fool Bear marked a hiatus in the diplomatic offensive against Northern Nation solidarity. What it did not remove was a disturbing level of mistrust aimed at Crazy Horse. Moderate leaders were appalled at his marching into other villages and deploying his bodyguard to threaten and cajole. Although the constituted village leaderships supported the no-surrender line, many must have resented the high-handed intervention in their affairs. Dissatisfaction grew. Through the first half of January 1877, leadership began to shift ground.

No Water, invisible since his fall arrival from the agency, is twice mentioned in a Cheyenne account as being in the Oglala village. No Water could exploit this juncture to talk up conditions at the agency. Hitherto dismissed as propaganda for the dependency culture, his reports of the weekly beef issue, or the distribution of blankets and lodge coverings, took on a different cast in the Moon of Frost in the Tipi. With the new year, an incipient polarization was once more threatening Oglala society.[2]

As this drama had unfolded, the decoy warriors arrived near Tongue River Cantonment. Skilled horse thieves targeted Miles's stock, driving away 150 head of cattle from the beef contractor's herd. Miles took the bait. He detailed three infantry companies to follow the raiders' trail, and on December 28, the patrol clashed with four warriors guarding the herd, recapturing 108 head. The easy victory persuaded Miles to commit more men to the pursuit, and later that day another company marched out from base, hauling a twelve-pound Napoleon gun.[3]

On the 29th Miles assumed command of operations. In thirty-below-zero cold, three more Fifth Infantry companies, including a detachment mounted on captured Lakota ponies, followed their commander up the Tongue. Huddled in buffalo skin overcoats and sealskin caps and gauntlets, Miles's entire command numbered 436 officers and enlisted men. A second artillery piece, a ten-wagon supply train, and a handful of civilian and Indian scouts completed Bear Coat's strike force. Compared with Crook's brigades, it seemed puny. The men were tired after a punishing winter. Even after the troops united with the forward detachments on the thirtieth, Crazy Horse's warriors could hope for another victory such as their leader had shaped throughout the past year.

On New Year's Day, 1877, and again on January 3, gunfire was exchanged between scouts and Bear Coat's troops. Miles had projected a pursuit for sixty or seventy miles, but the carefully staged demonstrations recommitted him to the chase. About the 5th, as the command neared the village site at Hanging Woman, Crazy Horse and the war council ordered tipis struck and declared that the villages themselves would assume the decoy function, leading the soldiers up the Tongue through the foothills of the Wolf Mountains. The bold but dangerous plan speaks of Crazy Horse's supreme confidence, after the Little Bighorn, in his ability to exploit the military mindset. Alarm sounded among the moderate, and dissension probably lay behind a split in the villages. The main Oglala village pressed straight up Tongue River. With them traveled Ice and Two Moons, leading the core of Cheyennes still committed to resistance. Another group of Cheyennes and Lakotas followed up the valley of Hanging Woman Creek. Snow lay over a foot deep, and both parties traveled slowly through the subzero cold and stinging snow flurries.

Behind them, Miles's command passed the deserted village sites on January 6. On the seventh, the command bivouacked early on the east side of the Tongue, in a pocket of timber below an elevation that Indians called Belly Butte. The valley was hemmed by the foothills of the Wolf Mountains, a jumble of rugged ridges, their north-facing slopes whitened with snow. That afternoon Miles's scouts rounded up an unwary group of seven Cheyenne women and children and one shame-faced youth, traveling between the two camps. Word of the troops' approach had passed quickly upstream. Seeking the security of numbers, the contingent following Hanging Woman had quickly crossed the ridges to reunite with Crazy Horse.

On the Tongue, the people encamped near the mouth of Deer Creek, about thirty miles upstream of Belly Butte. A full council debated the crisis of the captives.

Some argued for a parley, others for an immediate assault. The Cheyenne Sacred Arrows Keeper, backing the latter option, staged a dramatic ritual. An arrow was fired straight into the air. Startled Oglalas remembered that, as it fell to earth, the arrow circled the throng of Cheyenne warriors, each man holding out his own arrow to gain some of its awesome power. At length councilors reached an uneasy compromise. The Cheyenne White Frog recalled that a strong party "went back to meet Miles and [to] fight *or* make peace." Black Elk's recollection indicates that two chiefs were named to represent the factions. The Cheyenne Dull Knife was on hand to temporize, and Crazy Horse represented the war front.[4]

The two hundred warriors attempted no negotiations. Espying a second sortie by Miles's scouts, an advance party attempted a small-scale ambush of its own. The civilians were only extricated by Miles ordering his mounted unit to cross the Tongue, secure a commanding hill, and plant one of the field pieces. As dusk settled over the valley, firing briefly flared, until darkness and several artillery rounds dispersed the attackers.

At the village, dissension rocked councils into the night, as men debated Crazy Horse's demand for a full-scale assault. Many wished to hurry the village south to safety. At length the headmen turned over the decision to the warrior societies. The war front itself showed signs of serious fracture. Some urged that the decoys continue operations, luring Miles into the broken country farther upstream. Others argued for an immediate offensive. Two miles upstream of Belly Butte, the breaks of Wall Creek afforded excellent terrain for an ambush. Crazy Horse knew that infantry demanded a different response than the frontal close-quarter fighting he had mastered against cavalry. A fixed-position ambush offering maximum cover to the attackers was the best tactic.

Backed by Little Big Man, Crazy Horse urged this option. Ice and Two Moons concurred for the Cheyennes. Despite the backing of Hump, most Miniconjous wavered. The authoritarian excesses of the war front had, disturbingly, alienated many of Crazy Horse's traditional supporters among his mother's people. Soon after midnight, a party of five to six hundred warriors—little more than half the available force—mounted and turned their ponies downstream. With anger at the half-hearted response breaking his composure, Crazy Horse ordered the assembled people "to go down and meet [Miles] . . . or else move camp."[5]

Snow flurries stung the blackness. Soon after 6:30 A.M. on January 8, overeager Cheyennes showed themselves atop a ridge upstream of Miles's bivouac. The alert commander, scanning from the dawn heights, made out massed Indian movement and hurried to make his dispositions. Crazy Horse and his war leaders, pausing only to divide the force—most Cheyennes crossing to the east bank of the frozen Tongue, Lakotas continuing down the west—poured in a charge like the one that almost carried the day at the Rosebud. Topping the heights above both banks, lines of warriors briefly drew rein and shouted a challenge to the breakfasting troops.

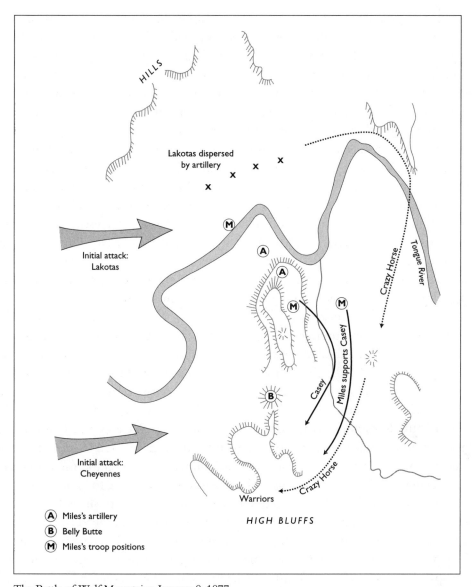

The Battle of Wolf Mountains, January 8, 1877

As Winchesters barked an opening salvo at 7:00 A.M., Crazy Horse's warriors raced along the western bluffs. Defying a single company line drawn above the west bank, the charge sought to outflank the main command across the river. The shrill of war whistles signaled orders and directions. Warriors galloped from the timber for a position directly opposite the wagons, unlimbered in two rows beneath a sheltering cutbank. Riding back and forth along the snowy slopes, they levered a persistent fire into Miles's camp. Suddenly, from emplacements above the opposite bank, the two artillery pieces opened up. Shells burst along the bluffs, exploding in midair and propelling screaming shrapnel among the warriors. From their tight infantry formations, buffalo-coated troopers poured in heavy fire. Ponies reared in fright, slipping on the ice, or fell under the hail of lead. A passing artillery shell momentarily felled horse and rider before it passed on to leave them miraculously unhurt. Crazy Horse was one of the unlucky riders. The last of nine or more war ponies to die beneath the Oglala war chief was shot from under him, leaving him to scramble up behind a comrade as the warriors withdrew out of range.

Crazy Horse made a quick reassessment of the tactical situation. The main action was now on the east side of the river, where the Cheyenne contingent had seized a line of ridges and bluffs extending south from Belly Butte. Although a troop unit controlled an isolated knoll, these heights commanded both it and the bivouac. Offering the cover of ravines, boulders, and the cedar-studded crests, a consolidated position there could neutralize the infantry strengths of unshakable lines and accurate fire. Crazy Horse and his fellow war leaders decided to concentrate the attack there. A force of warriors was left in the bottomland timber to apply continued pressure from the rear. As midmorning drew on under iron gray skies, Lakota warriors swung down to the river. Around a sheltering bend, they strung across the ice, then up the far bank. Dismounting in the ravines, they scrambled on to the heights.

Snow had resumed falling. Crazy Horse was among the warriors who seized the exposed spur of Belly Butte, taking up positions behind the boulders and loosing a sustained barrage from their repeaters and Sharps carbines. Across the flat crest, in full view of the troops, the Cheyenne Big Crow capered, sniping with his Custer battle Springfield. Miles ordered Captain James S. Casey and Company A, Fifth Infantry, to seize the butte. In double time, the unit hurried in line up a draw, exposed to heavy fire. Crazy Horse and his comrades flattened themselves behind the boulders, dodging ricocheting bullets before peeping out to shoot as Casey's men stormed uphill. The low elevation caused most warriors to shoot futilely over the troopers' heads, but the army fire raked the crest. One shot felled Big Crow, and while warriors tried to retrieve his fatally wounded body, a blistering fire enfiladed their position. Undaunted, Crazy Horse's contingent made a charge on foot as A Company topped the ridge. Amidst thickening snow, the contending forces fought briefly hand to hand, the Indians wielding their carbines as clubs. One or two Lakotas were killed in the close-quarters fighting. At length, the warriors disengaged to augment comrades along the southern heights.

Casey's sally was now exposed to flanking fire, and Miles threw forward another company to take the second line of ridges. Stumbling up the icy boulder-strewn slope, the walk-a-heaps marched relentlessly forward. Officers shouted commands, and the line halted to fire volleys up the slopes. In a gathering blizzard, the warriors mounted a stiff resistance behind rocks and fallen cedars, levering a rapid fire into the whiteout. Blinded by the snow and disconcerted by the resumption of shelling from the Rodman gun, the warriors withdrew. It was noon, but the deteriorating conditions made it seem like nightfall, and the engagement had lasted five hours.

As the war party paused at Wall Creek, a small rearguard fell out. Crazy Horse detailed ten warriors to follow the command. Then, as the main body pressed homeward, Crazy Horse and three comrades screened the retreat. For two days, Miles lingered at Belly Butte, mounting reconnaissance patrols upstream but attempting no further advance. Careful to avoid the charges laid at General Crook's door, he waited until January 10 to abandon the field and withdraw to base, arriving at Tongue River Cantonment on the eighteenth. The deteriorating weather and the exhaustion of Miles's men and stock marked the end of winter campaigning in the Great Sioux War.

Nearly equally matched, Indians and troops had acquitted themselves well in the Battle of Wolf Mountains. Both Miles and Crazy Horse had projected a campaign to end the war; both had been disappointed in a clash that ended in strategic stalemate. Contemporary military reports acknowledged that the battle was far from a walkover. "Nor was Crazy Horse, the Indian leader, that day, an adversary to be despised," conceded Captain Edmond Butler in a dispatch to the *Army and Navy Journal*. "He tried every point of our lines, but [Miles] . . . anticipated every move and foiled and punished each successive attempt."[6]

In fact, Wolf Mountains represented another tactical breakthrough for Crazy Horse and his war leaders. Fighting infantry had been the Indian blindspot throughout the war. Crazy Horse's mobile tactics could match anything the cavalry deployed, but Lakotas frankly admitted they were stalemated by infantry defenses and firepower. If the Rosebud, in its frontal charges and close-quarter combat had been an unusual Plains Indian battle, Wolf Mountains' protracted duel over the commanding heights was positively anomalous. Posterity has favored Miles at the expense of Crazy Horse. Taking the commander's own claims at face value, historians have asserted that the tactical defeat convinced the Indians of the inevitability of surrender. In truth, the factors compelling capitulation were already in place. They related more to deep-seated morale problems, reservation diplomacy, and winter game dispersal than to the short-term effects of a battle many warrior recollections treated as an inconsequential skirmish. Miles's withdrawal, like Crook's after the Rosebud, in fact freed the Indians to resume hunting. Short term, the battle, and a brief interlude of successful surrounds, actually boosted war front morale.

Late on January 10, Crazy Horse and the rearguard rode wearily into the village. Near the junction of Tongue River and Prairie Dog Creek, it had regrouped in two sprawling camps—one of Oglalas and Cheyennes, and one of Miniconjous and Sans Arcs. Scouts reported buffalo herds only miles north of the villages, and hunters replaced depleted stores. A flurry of feasts relieved the pressure on the war front.

One week after Wolf Mountains, the cycle of celebration spun into higher gear. On January 15 Sitting Bull made his long-deferred arrival. After Baldwin's attack, his people had regrouped along lower Powder River. One hundred Hunkpapa lodges and the ammunition train represented a welcome fillip to Crazy Horse. Feasts, dances, and councils went into overdrive as he and Sitting Bull propounded a united line of total resistance. Tales of arrests and internments rebuked moderates who dared to talk surrender.[7]

Sitting Bull presided over the redistribution of the Métis trade goods. Besides ammunition for the warriors, blankets and beads targeted the flagging support of the women, while tobacco conciliated wavering elders. Miniconjou Decider Black Shield publicly welcomed the revival of the war spirit. One of the architects of the victory against Fetterman ten years previously, Black Shield lent his prestige to the war front, stating, "he wants to fight—wants war." Others were able to channel Sitting Bull's ammunition to further the war front's strategy. Holy man Yellow Grass cornered the Sans Arc consignment. He hosted a series of yuwipi-like night rituals, conjuring up ten boxes of cartridges at one meeting.

Within twenty-four hours of Sitting Bull's arrival, private feasts testified to the underlying discontent. Roman Nose, a Miniconjou leader with strong ties to Spotted Tail Agency, recruited the tacit support of moderates, including Crazy Horse's kinsman Touch the Clouds, and deputed two Brules, Charging Horse and Make Them Stand Up, to slip away to Spotted Tail Agency "to get the news." They were to request that Spotted Tail "go there to them with tobacco," assuring agency chiefs and army officers that the embassy would net large-scale surrenders—at least one hundred lodges. The two messengers left secretly that day, January 16.[8]

Still others favored surrender at Cheyenne River. Crazy Horse's brother-in-law Red Horse recalled good treatment and regular rations there. Addressing the skeptical war chief, he stated that he recognized the U.S. president as his Great Father, conceding the government the kinship status that Crazy Horse so bitterly disputed.[9]

In the ten days after Sitting Bull's arrival, the mood of fractious division deepened. If the war front could have proclaimed a united strategy, it might have convinced waverers—or soldiered them into obedience. After the first days of reunion, however, it was not common ground that was on display, but the distance between the leaders. Still supremely confident in his military capabilities, Crazy Horse intended for the Northern Nation to remain on the hunting grounds, even in the certainty of renewed campaigning.

Sitting Bull, however, was pulled toward Canada. On the plains of the Northwest Territories, the Buffalo North still grazed in substantial herds. The pace of wasicu settlement was much slower than in the United States. Building on old British trade ties, coexistence seemed possible with the red-coated North-West Mounted Police. Now headmen like Four Horns argued vehemently for an early start to unite with their tribespeople already gone into Grandmother's Land. Seeking to maintain coalition solidarity, Sitting Bull declared that his people intended to cross the Missouri once more to trade, leaving ambiguous his long-term plan—a return to the hunting grounds, or refuge in Canada.[10]

Illustrating the crippling divisions within the Miniconjou–Sans Arc village, ranking Decider Spotted Eagle was shifting toward the Canadian option. Lesser leaders, like the Miniconjou chief Flying By, headman Red Thunder, and Sans Arc war leader Turning Bear, were also swayed by Hunkpapa reasoning. As if the defection of the emerging peace party was not enough, a third faction crystallized around Lame Deer, who supported Crazy Horse's position.

By late January deep snow drifted over the valley of the Tongue, keeping hunters indoors. As the game failed, the factions broke apart. Sitting Bull hosted a final feast to announce that his people would seek refuge in Canada. Soon soldiers would return, and the people were not prepared for another season of warfare. Gall underlined Hunkpapa unity on the issue. Agency defections, Gall told Crazy Horse, would leave the Northern Nation too weak to contest the hunting grounds.[11]

According to Stanley Vestal's Lakota informants, Crazy Horse responded with some of the bitterness he had expressed after learning of Sitting Bull's fall negotiations with Miles. But a new note, of fatalistic despair and sullen last-ditch intransigence, was also sounded. "My friend," he began, "the soldiers are everywhere; the Indians are getting scattered, so that the soldiers can capture or kill them all. This is the end. All the time these soldiers will keep hunting us down. Some day I shall be killed. Well, all right. I am going south to get mine!"[12]

"I do not wish to die yet," Sitting Bull quietly observed. The long maturing of the two men's relationship as figureheads of the Northern Nation meant that no open break took place. Both were at pains to smooth over their differences and assert an integrated strategy. Remaining on the hunting grounds, Crazy Horse would try to "hold our land" against the inevitable army reprisals. If defeated, or seriously weakened by desertions, he might lead his core followers after the Hunkpapas: "He is looking at me to see if it is still good here," declared Sitting Bull upon arriving in Canada.[13] Sitting Bull told Crazy Horse that his people would move first to the forks of Powder River, near where buffalo herds were reported, and a later rendezvous on Blue Earth Creek was debated before final departure for Grandmother's Land. Crazy Horse moved to conciliate, shaking hands with each of the Hunkpapa headmen before he departed. For all the assurances of solidarity, the parting was melancholy. The two men, who in the past seven years had risen above so many tribal differences to assert a national ideology, would not meet again.

On the following day, Sitting Bull led out fifty lodges of Hunkpapas. Many other people, uniting around the charismatic Spotted Eagle, agreed to rendezvous with him. The departures included significant numbers of the people most resolutely opposed to the Americans. They punctured the mood of unrealistic optimism that had followed Wolf Mountains. Key leaders in the war front—Crazy Horse's akicita chief Little Big Man, Cheyennes Ice and Two Moons—sensed a turning and began to moderate their opposition to all conciliation.

A significant break immediately appeared in the Oglala facade of total resistance. The council deputed a headman named Red Sack to go to Red Cloud Agency "to ascertain how matters were and to return and let them know as soon as possible." The reopening of dialogue indicated that the situation was slipping out of Crazy Horse's control. Faced with council consensus, the war chief chose not to press the issue and rupture what remained of village goodwill. On January 24 Red Sack departed.[14]

The nearly simultaneous exit of another party bore no council imprimatur. When fifteen lodges of Brules, Oglalas, and Miniconjous started for Spotted Tail Agency, Crazy Horse deployed the akicita. In a sinister echo of army surrender terms, the warriors seized the defectors' arms and ponies. The confiscation hardened the resolve of the deserters and secured the pity of their tribespeople. The fact that friends and relatives secretly outfitted the party with fifty-four horses and a handful of firearms, to enable a nighttime departure, testifies that the war front was dangerously alienated from its own people. Although Crazy Horse might in the short term tighten his control, Lakota society could not run against the grain of public opinion.[15]

Through the last days of January, moderates defied the war front. At a warrior feast, Red Horse raised the stakes, telling his brother-in-law, "I was going where the whites lived and [would] give myself up to them. I told him he must not send his soldiers to intercept me, better for his cause if he did not for . . . there are many of his own people who like me." Crazy Horse registered no immediate objection. Visiting his tiyospaye relatives, Red Horse arranged a piecemeal departure under cover of darkness, projecting a reunion on Powder River. Spotted Elk secured the cooperation of his kindred, and the defectors met no resistance as they slipped away. The Sans Arc White Eagle made the mistake of scheduling an open daylight removal. As White Eagle's womenfolk completed their packing, Crazy Horse led "about a hundred of his soldiers, [and] surrounded my camp. Some of them dismounted, entered our lodges and took our guns . . . I was very angry then at the soldiers, and pulled down my lodge and started right in the face of them. They shot down two of my horses, but I moved on." Some thirty-nine lodges, 229 people, left with the three headmen for Cheyenne River.[16]

Even in the Oglala village, defectors multiplied. On January 26 White Eagle Bull, with another man and a woman, left for Spotted Tail; three days later, five lodges of Brules followed. Already the akicita resistance had the feel of marking time. A final incident took place on February 1. The Cheyenne chief Little Wolf ordered struck the shabby windbreaks that his relatives occupied. Four families of ragged people rigged travois to skeletal ponies and started from the village. Crazy Horse led a line of akicita across the campground, but the redoubtable Little Wolf defied the war chief. The line closed around the defectors, and in an angry face-off, the akicita seized eleven Cheyenne ponies, shooting several to die kicking in the bloody snow. Undaunted, Little Wolf led away his people, swearing vengeance on Crazy Horse.[17]

Then, in the first days of the Moon of the Dark Red Calf, the facade crumbled. Bound for Canada, Spotted Eagle led away 150 lodges of Sans Arcs, Hunkpapas, and Miniconjous to reunite with Sitting Bull. Most remaining Miniconjous and Sans Arcs, another 150 lodges, soon drifted uncertainly in their wake. The mass departures left about 370 tipis, mostly Oglala and Cheyenne, on Tongue River. Lodges were cramped, some crowded with two families. Many Cheyennes remained housed in pathetic shelters stretched over branches. Famished people were desperate for meat and skins. Scouts reported sizeable buffalo herds grazing in the Bighorn foothills, barely forty miles to the west.[18]

Consensus quickly favored the Bighorn option. Only two leaders argued against the western move—for diametrically opposed reasons. No Water at last declared his hand, speaking openly for immediate surrender. Aware that Bear Coat would exploit the yawning distances between their villages, Crazy Horse proposed a move east to reunite with Sitting Bull at Blue Earth Creek. Most people were unconvinced by No Water's trust in the army regime at Red Cloud, and only twenty lodges of Lakotas followed him south. Their departure was uncontested, however, revealing the total collapse of the war front. But if consensus failed to firm around the defectors, it totally eluded Crazy Horse. Testimony to the alienation even of key followers, only the war chief's own tiyospaye elected to follow him east. Unthreatened by any troop movements, the main village, now comprising some 310 lodges, switched to the peacetime organization of Deciders and hunt akicita. About February 3 it headed west, over the bleak divide into the upper Little Bighorn valley.[19]

For a day or two, Crazy Horse lingered at the old campground, as if expecting a change of heart, then he too ordered his tipis struck. Only ten lodges strung behind Crazy Horse, the families most intimately bound to him by blood, marriage, and adoption. Worm and Crazy Horse's stepmothers urged their ponies through the drifts. Red Feather, always the devoted brother-in-law, and his little family were on hand to aid their sister Black Shawl. Oyuhpe warrior Tall Bull—at six feet, eleven inches and 280 pounds, "a corpulent and festive Sioux"—chose to remain with the war chief. Relatives and associates whom Crazy Horse could remember as lifelong neighbors, like the Iron Whiteman family, filled out the tiny procession as it wound into the valley of Powder River. In the bare bottomland timber at the junction with Clear Fork, where hunters might expect to flush deer and elk, they pitched camp. As family teams scattered to hunt and forage, for a few days the fact of war was suspended in the immediate imperatives of winning a living.[20]

For Crazy Horse, it was plainly a pause for reflection and reevaluation. Political disunity was one lesson—even the Hunkpatila band, united for years behind his leadership, had broken under the intolerable strains of martial law. Of the three constituent tiyospaye, Little Hawk's remained with the main village, while brothers Iron Crow and Running Horse had followed Miniconjou relatives toward Canada. Only Worm's old Kapozha had followed the war chief. But above all, it was a time of personal reckoning. The extremities of the winter had pushed Crazy Horse to one of life's threshold experiences, the abrupt turning point in the sudden silence of isolation.

Thrown back on the intimacies of tiyospaye life, he was forced to confront the consequences of resistance at all costs. Widows, and the old, always his first thought in peacetime, had suffered most. Elders like his aunt Big Woman, sharing Worm's tipi, and seventy-eight-year-old Human Finger should be living comfortably, well provided for by dutiful children. Instead, they were hungry, anxious, and cold. Women, the guardians of family life, had suffered too in the blind obsession of resistance. Black Shawl was suffering from a resumption of the coughing sickness that had blighted their courtship. Surveying this legacy of the months of dictatorial control, Crazy Horse drew back.

"To hold our land"—so Crazy Horse had pledged himself to the departing Sitting Bull. What was to be done? The war chief realized that the answer, elusive as it was, had to encompass what had been unthinkable even days before: that the remnant Northern Nation could no longer resist the blue-coated troops he had last year defeated. He knew that some leaders were prepared to cooperate with the army commanders and seek a compromise on territorial rights. As winter ended, any day might witness the reopening of the stalled diplomatic initiative from the reservation.

Discouragements multiplied. Belated messengers brought the news that Sitting Bull, although stalling on the headwaters of the Big Dry, clearly planned to regroup in Canada, with only the sketchiest plan to return to the hunting grounds. "Our land" had become uniquely Crazy Horse's burden.[21]

To any pious Lakota, the acquisition and manipulation of sicun was a process subject to wastage. In Crazy Horse's case, the revelation of Thunder power was tripped by an on-off switch that left him periodically drained, burned out. Such phases emphasized the contradictions of the man, rendering him one day masterful and the next, terminally irresolute. To receive guidance and rebuild sicun, he must acquire more power from the wakan beings. Consulting the elders, he decided to renew his vision questing. "There were things that he had to figure out," recalled young Black Elk, "and he was wanting the spirits to guide him. He would then go back to his people and tell them what he had learned."[22]

Then, about February 11, events twisted to demand Crazy Horse's public engagement. The cottonwood grove rang to shouts of visitors coming. Through the trees, thirty Lakotas rode into the cluster of shabby smoke-blackened tipis. A wary reunion yielded to joy as relatives recognized each other, and the visitors were led to the council tipi. Matrons donated meat for a feast. With no need of summons, all war-proven males assumed seats around the circle. Flanked by the elders and key warriors, Crazy Horse sat at the honor place. Then the visitors placed meat packs and packages of tobacco, wrapped in blue and red cloths, before the war chief. The peace talkers had arrived at last.[23]

With winter campaigning closed, the renewal of diplomacy marked a political offensive by the increasingly competitive field commanders—Miles on the Yellowstone, and Crook from the Department of the Platte. First to engage were Bear Coat's envoys, who departed Tongue River Cantonment on February 1. Locating the main Oglala-Cheyenne village in the Bighorn foothills, the messengers spent several days in intense debate, until key proponents of the Cheyenne war front backed dialogue. Both Two Moons and Ice, staunch Crazy Horse supporters in the winter soldiering regime, crystallized support. About February 12 a deputation of twenty-nine men, chiefly Cheyenne but including the Miniconjou Hump and three other Lakotas, left for Miles's headquarters to discuss terms.[24]

Three hundred miles south, the White River agencies hosted intense talks between Crook's subordinates and the reservation chiefs. Courted personally by Crook, Spotted Tail declined to lead an embassy until unconditional surrender terms were relaxed. At the Oglala agency, however, army proposals met with a warmer response, and thirty warriors volunteered. Representing all the agency Oglala bands, their leader was Hunts the Enemy, a nephew of Red Cloud and an akicita leader in the Bad Face band.

The party departed on January 16, making slow progress over the winter plains. At last, along the Little Powder, the envoys "met three Indians who told them that Crazy Horse was encamped some little distance above on Powder River and that Sitting Bull was just below the mouth of Little Powder." Targeting Oglala relatives, the delegation swung upstream. A day or so later, they reached Clear Fork and were ushered to feast and parley with Crazy Horse.[25]

The war chief was surprisingly gracious, in deep contrast to his reception of the December envoys. After the meager feast, Hunts the Enemy made a forceful presentation. Skimming the unconditional surrender terms, he stressed the need for Oglala tribal solidarity in a new diplomatic battle to retain their lands. Other envoys spoke. "Their speeches," they reported, "were not [immediately] responded to."[26]

Etiquette prescribed that messengers sleep at the host camp after making their proposal, leaving the council to debate the issues. Red Feather recalled his kinsman's mood. "Crazy Horse didn't want to go [to the agency]. He didn't answer them for a long time." The second day's talk, hosted by the visitors, was manifestly a stalling exercise. Nevertheless, the war chief continued to be gracious, affirming that the envoys "were relations and should be friends." The envoys reported that after smoking their pipe, Crazy Horse spoke at length: "The smoke was good. He did not commence the war. His relations were at the Agencies; he could send for all the [Northern Nation] Indians and let them decide what they should do; that if he told them to stay they would do so, even if they were to die, but he would let them say." Politely, he declined to open the tobacco. Instead, he told Hunts the Enemy to take it to the main Oglala village in the Bighorn valley. Whatever their decision, he reiterated, he would "do the same as the others did."[27]

The speech revealed the depth of Crazy Horse's change of heart. Careful to invoke his authority as war chief, for the first time he acknowledged its limits. The deputation divided. Only Hunts the Enemy and three comrades pressed on to the main Oglala village. Crazy Horse outfitted each man with a horse from his own herd, underscoring his tentative endorsement of their mission.[28]

In only two days of talks at the main village, Hunts the Enemy secured an Oglala consensus. Herald Iron Hawk announced the council decision—to travel to Red Cloud Agency and open diplomacy with the army. Hedged with provisos and warnings that travel would be slow, Iron Hawk's speech nevertheless broke the impasse in dialogue. Debate on the problematic issues of pony and arms confiscations was postponed. On this momentous issue of peace and war, a decision had been reached without consulting Crazy Horse. Everyone was at pains to stress his amenability to consensus, but the council was now acting independently of its war chief.

Soon after the big council, runners from Crazy Horse arrived to invite all bands "to meet him on little Powder river." They announced that six messengers from Spotted Tail had now arrived at Crazy Horse's camp. The Brules brought the war chief a formal announcement that Spotted Tail was mounting the biggest peace initiative yet.[29]

On February 10 messengers Charging Horse and Makes Them Stand Up had arrived at Spotted Tail Agency. To the Brule head chief they carried the invitation to open dialogue. Immediately Spotted Tail went into intensive talks with Crook. Two days earlier, the first newspaper reports of Miles's "victory" at Wolf Mountains had forced the general to drastic conclusions. Lest Miles scoop all the glory, off-the-record concessions were made to secure capitulations within the Department of the Platte. Crook agreed that all surrendered stock be turned over to enlisted Lakota scouts, who would be free to redistribute them to northern relatives. He pledged his influence in stopping the government drive to relocate the White River agencies on the Missouri. Even more significantly, the general would recommend to the Great Father that the Northern Nation be assigned a separate reservation on the hunting grounds, once all warring bands had surrendered. Armed with these concessions and a mule train of presents, Spotted Tail departed his agency on February 13, taking the trail along the east edge of the Black Hills. With him were 250 Brule headmen and warriors, including band chiefs Swift Bear, Two Strike, and Iron Shell.

Crazy Horse attempted to orchestrate a concerted response before Spotted Tail's arrival. After dispatching runners to every village and camp, during the last week of February, he led his tiyospaye over the bleak divide into the upper valley of the Little Powder, camping in deep snows. A group of the envoys remained with the camp, and as it traveled, 110 lodges from the main Oglala-Cheyenne village, responding to the call for rendezvous, caught up. Briefly, Crazy Horse could have hoped for a revival of Northern Nation solidarity.

Game was poor, and the camps scattered along the valley. Many of the new arrivals were already committed to surrender, as soon as the trails were cleared. Whoever the leaders—Little Big Man, establishing a role as the moderate northern leader, is a real possibility—they were careful not to establish a village in which the war chief could reassert martial law.[30]

Straggling buffalo herds were sighted, and as February turned into the Moon of the Snowblind, two successful surrounds were made. Farewell feasts marked Hunts the Enemy's departure for Red Cloud. The moderate leaders, confirming surrender, "requested that beef, rations &c. might be sent out to meet them at Hat Creek." Pressed to speak, Crazy Horse reluctantly agreed he would "come in and hold a council" during the spring.[31]

The full extent of the alienation from Crazy Horse was only beginning to register. Outside of the people already committed to surrender, no one responded to the war chief's runners. The main Miniconjou–Sans Arc village moved east to the Little Missouri, responding warily to Spotted Tail's request for dialogue. From Sitting Bull, no response was heard. Compounding Crazy Horse's isolation, on February 26–27, Spotted Eagle's village crossed the frozen Yellowstone, hurrying up Cedar Creek to overtake the Hunkpapas. The curt rejections of Crazy Horse's tobacco ironically underscored just how deeply his war front had rocked national morale.[32]

As if this were not enough, his own tiny following had begun to fragment. Four lodges, including Worm's, left on a hunt down the Little Powder. Most demoralizing of all, another four tipis turned south to catch up with No Water's party, surrendering at Red Cloud on March 14. The victor of the Little Bighorn was left with a following of two lodges. On March 3 Four Horns crossed into Canada with fifty-seven lodges of Hunkpapas. On the 4th, the delegation sent to talk with Miles arrived home in the main Oglala-Cheyenne village on the Little Bighorn. To people capitulating at Tongue River, and enlisting as scouts against hostile Indians, Bear Coat offered a home—effectively a reserve on the hunting grounds. Several Cheyenne leaders acclaimed the news. Most were more wary, but the council called a formal end to hostilities. Heralds "cried through the camps that the war was over, and that no more hostile expeditions would be allowed against the white man." The village was struck and moved slowly toward Tongue River.[33]

After the departure of Hunts the Enemy's party, news from the agencies focused on the Spotted Tail mission. Locating a base camp on the upper Moreau River, Spotted Tail opened dialogue with the Miniconjous and Sans Arcs. His runners arranged a grand council of the Northern Nation to be held on the Little Powder three weeks hence.

The prospect of total capitulation loomed. Spotted Tail's co-opting of Crazy Horse's own abortive rendezvous can only have rankled, but deeper misgivings animated the war chief. Spotted Tail had been the idolized uncle of his boyhood, but over the past twenty years, he had traveled further than any other Lakota chief on the wasicu road. Crazy Horse correctly concluded that the integrity of the northern hunting rounds was low on Spotted Tail's priority list. Profound distrust was only compounded by Crazy Horse's fear that Spotted Tail might invoke an uncle's compelling authority.

Since the village breakup, Crazy Horse had felt the need to seek guidance from the wakan powers in this greatest crisis of his nation's history. Wary, suspicious,

Crazy Horse was yet realistic enough to realize that to "hold our land" might now be possible only through negotiation. Visionary revelations might give him the moral strength to engage with the Spotted Tail delegation, and with the army hierarchy controlling his people's destiny. He underwent the purification of the sweat lodge, reimposing the self-denying celibacy of the vision seeker. About March 5 Black Shawl packed their tipi and belongings. Her condition made solitude impracticable, so a second family accompanied the couple. In weather still subject to savage reversals, the tiny procession angled northwest, into the snowy hills between the forks of Powder River. For three weeks they would disappear off even the Lakota radar, confounding envoys and runners as Crazy Horse sought the vision of guidance in what Lakotas called *mani'l*, the vast absent space of the wilderness.[34]

20

TO KEEP MY COUNTRY

For three weeks, Crazy Horse disappeared into the bleak hills east of Powder River, straddling the modern Wyoming-Montana boundary. Only one eyewitness account exists from those missing weeks. Soon after his departure, the Black Elk family, hurrying in to surrender, happened upon the family.

> We found Crazy Horse all alone on a creek with just his wife. He was a queer man. He had been queer all of this winter. Crazy Horse said to my father: "Uncle, you might have noticed me, how I act, but it is for the good of my people that I am out alone. Out there I am making plans—nothing but good plans—for the good of my people. I don't care where the people go. They can go where they wish. There are lots of caves and this shows that I cannot be harmed. . . . This country is ours, therefore I am doing this," said Crazy Horse.[1]

For days at a time, carrying only pipe and tobacco bag, Crazy Horse left his tipi to seek the vision of guidance. Sheltering in caves and cliff overhangs when late winter storms blasted the plains, he fasted and prayed, wept and begged for the vision that could show him how best to preserve his people's lands—a vision that eluded him. At the end of endurance, he would return home to take purifying sweat baths, but characteristically, Crazy Horse revealed little. Building on the prophetic vision of 1875, when he saw his homeland despoiled, he could offer only raw convictions. To Sitting Bull he had spoken of "holding our land." Over the troubled months to come, he would remark of his will "to keep my country." To Red Cloud, he observed, "*makoce kin tewahila,* I cherish the land."[2] This bedrock principle of preserving the hunting grounds would animate his remaining months of life. The lonely ordeal of *hanbleceya* only deepened the commitment.

As the days of solitude lengthened, however, other issues impinged on his meditations. Black Shawl's health increasingly concerned Crazy Horse, focusing the subliminal energies of the dreamer. By late winter her condition was deteriorating. Army surgeon Valentine T. McGillycuddy attended Black Shawl during the following summer, diagnosing tuberculosis. Fits of bloody coughing recalled the troubled days of courtship; under the extreme privations of the wartime winter, the fits were exacerbated, leaving Black Shawl exhausted, feverish, and bed bound. The interminable weeks before spring continued to weaken her. Concern for her condition contributed to Crazy Horse's slow realization that surrender was inevitable.[3]

In this same intense phase of vision questing, Crazy Horse was granted new spiritual power. After appealing through his old guardian spirit the red-tailed hawk, he received aid from the spotted eagle, the bird that flies closest to the powers of the Upper World. Passed down through three or four generations of practitioners on the Pine Ridge Reservation, the origin of Eagle doctoring is still attributed to Crazy Horse. That this is no facile piece of New Age hokum is confirmed by the red hawk connection—and still more significantly by the fact that the rite is used specifically to treat cases of tuberculosis. The eagle imparted key instructions to Crazy Horse. Over succeeding weeks, through consultations with the holy men, he would shape the raw data of vision into a ceremony of healing.[4]

About March 26 Crazy Horse, gaunted by three weeks of hunger and exposure, rode into the valley of Powder River twenty miles north of the forks. During his absence, messengers had kept him apprised of political developments and camp movements. During the Moon of the Snowblind, diplomacy focused on Tongue River Cantonment and the Spotted Tail mission. Little Hawk, and the Hunkpatila akicita Hard to Hit, participated in a second round of talks with Miles but rejected Bear Coat's overtures. Instead, the main Oglala village projected a rendezvous with envoys from Red Cloud at Bear Lodge Butte. Spotted Tail's mission secured surrender pledges from the majority of Miniconjous and Sans Arcs. First Touch the Clouds, with seventy crowded lodges, agreed to surrender at the Brule agency, responding to assurances that Spotted Tail had secured not only Crook's approval of a northern agency but also crucial concessions on surrendering arms and ponies. In a final round of talks near Powder River forks, Spotted Tail convinced Roman Nose and Black Shield to surrender ninety more lodges.

Worm, visiting in the village with his four tipis, was won over by his brother-in-law's arguments—exactly as Crazy Horse had feared. Concerned by the war chief's no-show, Spotted Tail pressed for information on his whereabouts. Worm was guarded, saying simply that his son "was out hunting by himself." Nevertheless, Crazy Horse had authorized his father to assure Spotted Tail that he remained committed to the wishes of his people. Worm said that his son would come to the agencies, "and shakes hands through his father the same as if he himself did it." To interpreter Jose Merrivale, Worm presented a pony "as a token that Crazy Horse himself makes peace."[5]

Spotted Tail detailed one Brule and one Oglala warrior to take tobacco and search for the war chief. Dissatisfied with the reports of the new rendezvous at Bear Lodge Butte, from which the Oglalas projected a simple courtesy visit to parley and trade at the agencies, Spotted Tail sent his last package of tobacco to Bear Lodge, warning the Oglalas "not to come in unless they brought their women and children—that they must bring their wives and children with them."[6]

Early on March 26, Spotted Tail turned homeward. Thirty miles southwest, Crazy Horse returned to the Powder River valley, the end of his vision questing coinciding suggestively with the completion of the Spotted Tail mission. The main Oglala-Cheyenne village approached from the west. For the first time in seven weeks, village and war chief were reunited.

Testifying to a tight synchronization of movements, ten agency envoys also arrived. Seven Cheyenne delegates quickly convinced a majority of their tribespeople that surrender at Red Cloud was the best remaining option. Three Oglala messengers—Bear Don't Scare, Shoulder, and Standing Rabbit—assured their relatives that they would be well treated. Contrary to scare stories, no one was being punished for his role in the war. "If [Crazy Horse] would go in to the agency," the spokesman intimated, "the agent would issue rations, blankets, and clothing, and then allow him to go back home." Most listeners divined that this statement was loaded with well-meaning optimism, but as they surveyed their people's poverty, they found little to range against it. Once more, Iron Hawk crystallized the consensus position. "You see all the people here are in rags," declared the herald, "they all need clothing, we might as well go in."[7]

Eyes turned to the war chief. "They thought that Crazy Horse would have lots to say to them because he had been out meditating in the wilderness," Black Elk recalled. Instead, Crazy Horse sat silently through the debate. He indicated his tacit approval, reiterating his weary mantra of acceptance. "Crazy Horse said whatever all the rest decided to do, he would do," recalled Red Feather. "So they all agreed to go in. They promised to go over, get the rations and the clothing, and return west of the Black Hills again." Solemnly, the pipe was lit and smoked. A morning departure for Bear Lodge was agreed, and the council broke up.[8]

As Crazy Horse returned to his tipi, the inevitability of surrender bore in. To Spotted Tail, Worm had pledged his son's capitulation; now Little Hawk had promised Miles that he "would take [Crazy Horse] and the entire camp" to surrender, either at the agencies or on Tongue River.[9] On every side, options were closing down, funneling the war chief toward the indignity of defeat. Even the weeks of vigil had left him unenlightened. Then, as he sat silently with Black Shawl, visitors arrived and told Crazy Horse that Lame Deer had remained on the Little Powder that morning. Rejecting Spotted Tail's tobacco, the Miniconjou war chief planned to leave the following day for a buffalo hunt along the Tongue.

Only fourteen lodges remained with Lame Deer, the visitors admitted, but the report galvanized Crazy Horse. His commitment "to keep my country" seemed to dovetail with Lame Deer's objectives. The hunt offered a last opportunity to reunite the Northern Nation. Perhaps he reasoned that a dramatic departure would force a break in the Oglala village, with the core nonagency contingent following their war chief. Needing the solitude to contemplate, Crazy Horse walked up the hills overlooking camp. He met He Dog, seated on the slope, and confided his plan.

He Dog was dismayed at his kola's intransigence. "You think like a child," he chided. "You smoked the pipe of peace the same as I." He pleaded for Crazy Horse to reconsider, but "Crazy Horse said nothing." After a while He Dog rose, leaving the war chief lost in reflection.[10]

The following day, March 27, as the Oglala village forded Powder River, en route to Bear Lodge Butte, the next staging point on the trail to Red Cloud, Crazy Horse turned his pony and started down the valley. If he expected a break in village unity, his hopes were quickly dashed. Black Shawl followed her husband, leading a string of gaunt pack ponies. Low Dog, irreconcilable to the last, and his family tracked the war chief, then a straggle of other lodges. No more than a dozen, most were from Hump's Miniconjou tiyospaye. Their willingness to defy their headmen's order to surrender to Miles testified to the authority Crazy Horse could still command among his mother's people. But there the drain of support ended. The main village strung east, bound for Bear Lodge and surrender. In a last bid for defiance, Crazy Horse's party urged jaded horseflesh northward.[11]

The union with Lame Deer fizzled into anticlimax. For several days, the little camp zigzagged across the plains in search of game. To preserve their horses, the people were compelled to make short removes. Their vulnerability to a new strike by Miles was plain to all. Slowly, the reality of the situation bore in on Crazy Horse. Lame Deer had no strategic aim, stating simply that he wished to make one more buffalo hunt; then he might turn in his camp at Cheyenne River.

A few more irreconcilables strung into camp. From the Cheyenne village, a small group—fourteen or fifteen men, only half of them with families—following White Hawk, raised a tipi or two and a scatter of shelters and wigwams. They reported that the delegates from Miles had prevailed on some three hundred people, composing forty-three lodges of Cheyennes and four from Hump's tiyospaye, to surrender. Already these people were drifting uncertainly toward Tongue River Cantonment. Most Cheyennes, however, were swayed by assurances of good treatment at Red Cloud Agency. After the council declared that every Cheyenne should choose a place of surrender, almost six hundred people opted to follow Standing Elk and Dull Knife to the Oglala agency—that place of sufferance that yet was the best home they knew.[12]

More arrivals only compounded Crazy Horse's deepening sense of futility and despair. Five lodges of Hunkpapas arrived from Sitting Bull. Reunion with the Hunkpapas had animated Crazy Horse's hopes for the hunt, but their news was categorical. Camped in the Missouri River bottoms forty-five miles north of Fort Peck, Sitting Bull's village had been caught by a sudden thaw on the morning of

March 17. His camp destroyed again, the Hunkpapa leader had withdrawn toward the Canadian border. Spotted Eagle's village still shadowed Sitting Bull northward. As soon as grass fattened the horses, their people would make the final push into Grandmother's Land.

For the rest, there were only promises. At Bear Butte, from the Miniconjou–Sans Arc village en route to Spotted Tail, thirty lodges would break away. A few scattered family hunting parties also trended toward Lame Deer. Peaking at sixty-three lodges, wavering between defiance and the nostalgic wish for one last hunt before surrender, the camp offered no military solution to Crazy Horse's quandary. For him, the dream of a revived Northern Nation, strong enough to defy another summer of army reprisals, was over.

A final consideration turned Crazy Horse's thoughts homeward—Black Shawl. Her condition was patently deteriorating. Her hacking bloody cough had dominated their domestic life for weeks. Intimacy was compromised by the sickness. Through succeeding months, more disturbing symptoms accumulated: a badly swollen arm testified to secondary infections inflaming the joints. Unsightly and painful, it reduced Black Shawl's capacity to run her own household. Further hurried removes between hungry camps would fatally undermine her health. To the end, Crazy Horse would remain solicitous of his wife's welfare. If during his vision quest, his wakan helpers had extended to him the strength to heal, to test that calling required taking Black Shawl home, to the security and care of relatives.[13]

Crazy Horse readied his lodge to travel. Probably at this time, to aid Black Shawl in running the tipi, relatives offered to accompany the pair. The gigantic Tall Bull, now a fixture next to the war chief, two women, and two boys joined the couple, living in the family tipi.[14] A travois nag hauled the lodgeskins. Other ponies were hitched with the lodgepoles or carried the packs, parfleches, and saddlebags that contained what was left of the family's wealth—mostly worn buffalo robes, many that had been cut down to share with the winter refugees; household implements and a few metal items like battered kettles and a coffeepot; depleted meat packs of rawhide etched in fading paint; and Crazy Horse's weapons. Tall Bull's boys rousted the loose stock, and Black Shawl was attended by her kinswomen.

About April 3 the party approached the fluted volcanic upthrust of Bear Lodge Butte. Between cutbanks of red earth and meanders studded with bare cottonwoods, the Belle Fourche wound its placid course. Along the near bank stood a circle of tipis—*cangleska wakan*, the sacred hoop of the northern Oglalas. With no announcement, the little group rode through the entrance gap and across the campground to the Hunkpatila segment of the circle. Between the tipis of Iron Whiteman and Little Hawk, the women quietly unlimbered the lodgepoles and began the work of making camp. Crazy Horse had come home.

By early April, agency Oglalas prepared to welcome their relatives from the north. Reports were still ambiguous about the intentions of Crazy Horse, but from the statements of returning envoys, General Mackenzie concluded that the war chief was unlikely to surrender, and that the winter roaming segments of the nontreaty Oglalas and Cheyennes "will almost certainly stay out."[15]

Oglala diplomacy fashioned a twin strategy to secure total surrender. After debriefing his brother, the envoy Running Hawk, Young Man Afraid of His Horse revived his plan for an agency in the north. Taking account of northern aspirations as well as the rivalry between the Department of the Platte and Miles's independent command, he meshed his scheme with Crook's plan for a northern reservation. In mid-March, after enlisting the support of fellow band chiefs American Horse and Yellow Bear, he approached Mackenzie. In return for locating their three bands, over two hundred lodges, at a new reserve on Tongue River, the chiefs promised to make peace with neighboring tribes and work as scouts against hostile Indians. Mackenzie reported favorably up the chain of command.[16]

Simultaneously, another enlistment of Indian scouts was going forward. Crook's aide Lieutenant William P. Clark, Second Cavalry, was in command of the operation at the White River agencies. Handsome and charismatic, Clark had mastered the sign language to better manage his duties. Of all Crook's proteges, Clark was the most sensitive to the nuances of Indian culture and politics. Some Oglala veterans of the Mackenzie campaign were already devoted to Waposta Ska, White Hat Clark. Although few were prepared to fight their relatives, everyone understood the necessity of ending the war. By the beginning of April, 120 Lakotas had been enlisted. Cheyennes eagerly enlisted under their chief Little Wolf, expressly "that they might go out to fight 'Crazy Horse's['] people." At both agencies, scores more warriors lined up to don army blue.[17]

A trickle of surrenders continued. On April 5 Spotted Tail arrived at his agency to announce the imminent approach of the Miniconjous and Sans Arcs. The Brule chief's report only deepened the enigma of Crazy Horse's intentions. If a spring campaign was necessary, Crook and Mackenzie must implement immediate plans. More envoys were readied to accelerate the peace process. Crook personally conferred with Red Cloud on April 10. Over three days of talks, both Crook and Lieutenant Clark played on the chief's insecurities following the general's elevation of Spotted Tail to lead both agencies. Promised appointment as first sergeant of scouts, Red Cloud agreed to lead a deputation to Crazy Horse. Behind the press-release facade of unconditional surrender, Red Cloud was assured of concessions. Besides the head chief, Oglala band chiefs Yellow Bear, Slow Bull, and the lately surrendered No Water would lead the eighty-man party. Accompanied by interpreters Antoine Ladeau, Antoine Janis, and Joseph Marrischale, trailing the obligatory packtrain of rations and presents, Red Cloud's embassy left the agency on April 13. While the Camp Robinson garrison anxiously anticipated the outcome, Red Cloud's party swung up the west flank of the Black Hills toward Bear Lodge Butte.[18]

At Bear Lodge, after the frantic activity of winter, the pace of Crazy Horse's life shifted abruptly down gear. The Oglala village took time to regroup, resting and recouping stock. Gradually, the Moon of Red Grass Appearing, ushering warm sunshine and spring downpours, yielded a carpet of nourishing green for the winter-worn pony herd. Small family hunting parties scattered to forage in the foothills. Wedges of northering geese signaled the anxious people of the reassuring cycle of the seasons.[19]

After two months of dispersal, the village reorganized into a single circle of about 155 lodges, almost one thousand people. Most were Oglalas, but approximately twenty-five lodges of Brules, ten of Miniconjous, and five of Sans Arcs were scattered among relatives. The elders nominated Little Hawk, Little Big Man, Old Hawk, and Big Road as Deciders and named He Dog as head akicita, while Iron Hawk reprised his regular function as village herald. Kicking Bear, Good Weasel, Little Shield, and Hard to Hit were among the warriors recruited as police. The appointments left ambivalent the status of Crazy Horse. With peace proclaimed, the function of the war chief was in abeyance, but everyone knew that Crazy Horse's cooperation was crucial.

During the week after his return, Crazy Horse seemed listless, despairing. "This country is ours, therefore I am doing this," he had told the Black Elk family a month before. Now, oral tradition affirms, he seemed to believe that "[a]ll is lost anyway ... the country is lost."[20] News would continue to confirm his despair. The main Miniconjou–Sans Arc village surrendered at Spotted Tail Agency on April 14. Reports from the north located Sitting Bull's village high up Milk River, within fifty miles of the Canadian line. Comprising 135 tipis of Hunkpapas, Sans Arcs, Miniconjous, and a few Oglalas, it would finally cross into Grandmother's Land during the first week of May, bringing the total of refugee Lakotas in Canada to some three hundred lodges.

During early April, the Cheyenne village straggled past Bear Lodge en route to surrender. Still lodged in wretched shelters, many Cheyennes nursed personal grievances against Crazy Horse. Matching Little Wolf's promise, they declared that upon surrender many would volunteer as scouts.

Yet as the days passed, Crazy Horse underwent a change of heart. More envoys appeared at Bear Lodge. In private talks with them and the Deciders, Crazy Horse mulled over Crook's offer of a separate reservation. As the plan matured, Crook had sectioned off the southeast corner of Montana Territory for the projected reserve. Bounded on the west by the Little Bighorn and Bighorn rivers, on the north by the Yellowstone, the tract served as a bargaining counter on which diplomacy might build.

Furthermore, the Deciders told Crazy Horse that the presidential election of 1876 had placed a new Great Father, Republican Rutherford B. Hayes, in Washington. Hitherto Crazy Horse had denied the kinship status of the president and the U.S. government, but word that Hayes was an old Civil War comrade of Crook's boosted confidence that the general really could deliver on his promises.

Gradually, Crazy Horse began to formulate a more measured response to the offer of peace. He warily accepted that only through diplomacy could his people retain their lands. He remained reluctant to undergo the humiliation of surrender, but in solitary contemplation, he decided that he would gamble on Crook's promise and go to Red Cloud Agency. Over twenty years, the most far-sighted of Lakota leaders—Man Afraid of His Horse, Lone Horn, Spotted Tail, and Red Cloud—had progressively concluded that only legally guaranteed reservations could preserve the Lakota land base. Now Crazy Horse reluctantly embraced the principle. In a startling shift toward pragmatism, he even approved two provisional agency sites— one on upper Tongue River, the second west of the headwaters of Beaver Creek, barely fifty miles south of the village at Bear Lodge Butte. The Deciders moved to lock the war chief into the peace process and announced a feast and council in Crazy Horse's honor.

About April 10 akicita rolled up the lodgeskins to permit public view of the great assembly. Haltingly, Crazy Horse made the briefest of speeches and immediately resumed his seat: "This day I have untied my horse's tail and layed [sic] my gun aside and I have sat down."

The envoys pressed him to order the camp moved. Respectful of the Deciders' jurisdiction, Crazy Horse demurred: "Not until I rest, then I will be willing to go. But before I go, give lots of ammunition to my people. I have set a place for my people that will be the reservation."[21]

Crazy Horse acknowledged the new Great Father in Washington, "who was a very good man, and would probably do more for the Indians than any who had preceded him." The simple concession of kinship status to the president was itself a radical departure for the war chief. The decision at last had been made. Six messengers, including the Strong Hearts Society headman Moccasin Top, were sent to Red Cloud with positive word. The village would leave Bear Lodge and cross the Belle Fourche on April 16, hoping to arrive at the Oglala agency as early as the 28th.[22]

Several more days of layoff afforded time for fattening stock for the journey. Even Crazy Horse began to relax, able at last to contemplate matters other than the overriding obsession with "my country." All but invisible to the military authorities that would increasingly circumscribe Lakota activities, Crazy Horse witnessed in the last four months of his life a florescence of his spiritual questing. Over the summer, one military observer learned that Crazy Horse habitually left camp as many as three times a day, to pray and meditate on his visions.

One vision that commanded immediate attention was the gift of Eagle power. With Black Shawl's health to consider, Crazy Horse needed to consult with other healers and holy men, grounding the revelation in the matrix of Lakota ceremonialism. Rooted in the yuwipi rituals of his friends Horn Chips and Long Turd, Eagle doctoring shared the spectacular nighttime displays of sparks and flashing lights, the flitting whispers of mysterious objects. Inside the blacked-out lodge, startled participants felt the whirring brush of wings and the prick of eagle claws. Yet Eagle power would evince a unique combination of elements. Crazy Horse dispensed with the theme of binding and escape. He did not use sacred stones in the divinatory rites. Given the rationing culture to which he would be shortly exposed, it is significant that later practitioners have insisted that only native foods like dog and pemmican be served at Eagle meetings.

To relatives and elders who still loved him, the move into the sphere of healing must have been a heartening development. They would have remembered that Worm, at the same stage of his life, underwent the crisis of Male Crow's death. Rising above personal and tribal tragedy, Worm was able to shape a worthy life as a holy man. Like many difficult sons, Crazy Horse was assuming the characteristics of his father. One final time he was able to demonstrate his belief and love in the coming generation of Lakotas. Two Oyuhpe youths, Living Bear and Little Warrior, in later life transmitted knowledge of Eagle power into the twentieth-century Lakota world. The development speaks of the hard-won maturing of Crazy Horse, spiritual growth born during the sternest weeks of his life. The dim outline of a future beyond the war chieftainship shows the ghost of an aborted human possibility.

Since the 1930s, and the publication of John G. Neihardt's hugely influential *Black Elk Speaks*, much has been written on Crazy Horse as a "mystic warrior of the plains." As we enter the twenty-first century and New Age gurus weave grab-bag religions from Buddhism, astrology, Jungian psychology, and Native American shamanism, it is important not to lose sight of the intimate human truths that underlie their ecumenical generalisms. Just as Jesus Christ might have difficulty in endorsing many of the churches founded in his name, so Crazy Horse would not have recognized himself as the spiritual ecowarrior proclaimed in scores of books, CD-ROMs, and self-help manuals for the terminally bewildered.

Ultimately, these readings are based on Neihardt's own dualistic Christian ideology. Expanding on Black Elk's terse account of his cousin, Neihardt claimed that when Crazy Horse secured his youth vision, he "went into the world where there is nothing but the spirits of all things. That is the real world that is behind this one, and everything we see here is something like a shadow from that world." In battle, Crazy Horse "had only to think of that world to be in it again, so that he could go through anything and not be hurt."[23] Built on by Mari Sandoz in her portrait of a Lakota Christ, this account is unrecognizable in Lakota terms but readily translates into Neihardt's Christianized Neo-Platonism. It foreshadows postmodern deconstructions of the past and its inhabitants—where wish fulfillment and narcissistic self-projection create not men and women, but demons and impossible saints.

Crazy Horse's real—only vaguely understood, cut tragically short, but real—mystic career demands our sympathetic critical engagement with the scanty sources. As in his youth, begging for power to conquer his people's enemies, Crazy Horse sought the sicun that would enable him to shape events in *this* world, whether they be the great tribal issues of land and peace or the intimate concerns of his family's health and well-being. Such strength and visions were given by the wakan powers in return for self-denying observances and taboos. They came at the price of perpetual vigilance, alert reinterpretation, and profound reflection. Out of such meditation, many holy men grew into *woksape*, wisdom. More elusive than the other cardinal virtues that Crazy Horse had so gloriously embodied, wisdom resonated with mystical insight and the ability to consider the greater good of the people. Like us in this, at least, the war chief moved haltingly along the Red Road that represents spiritual growth. During these final months of life, wisdom would sit beside suspicion, paranoia, and the reflex to violence as a political solution, in the protean enigma that remains Crazy Horse.

True to the schedule announced by their messengers to Red Cloud Agency, the Deciders ordered camp struck on Monday, April 16. Craftswomen had put the two-and-a-half-week layoff to good use, and the people turned out in their best clothing for the march. About April 20, within sight of Pumpkin Buttes, scouts reported the approach of Red Cloud's deputation. Red Cloud's heralds had a simple message: "All is well; have no fear; come on in."[24]

Nervousness was inevitable as the agency leaders and northern Oglalas met, but Red Cloud handled the amenities well. He reassured Crazy Horse and the Deciders that no arrests would follow surrender. Carefully he explained the procedure of surrendering stock. All would be given up to the agency scouts and later redistributed among the northern village. The herd, though still in poor shape, was exceptionally large, about twenty-two hundred head. Every person in the village owned more than two ponies on average. Keen to affirm their kinship status with the deputation, the northern Oglalas pledged five hundred head as presents. On the subject of firearms, Red Cloud could offer no good news. All guns would have to be turned in, he explained, perhaps sniping at Spotted Tail, who allegedly claimed that the army would demand only captured weapons. Here was the first flashpoint for trouble, but Crazy Horse merely remarked, "All right, let them have them."[25]

If any leader needed careful handling, it was Crazy Horse. A startling concession was immediately matched by resistance over minutiae. The firearms issue provoked no response, but to simple inquiries about his intentions, Crazy Horse lashed back defensively. "Hehe, Yes, yes," he snapped, declaring that he "would not be ready to endure just anything" to make peace—the unconditional surrender originally demanded. Warning the deputation not to apply pressure, he affirmed that although "you Lakotas make me feel unsure of myself, I am going." Signaling something of his deep-seated misgivings, and the premonitory dreams that would trouble the weeks ahead, he concluded darkly, "I am aware that I will not live."[26]

The following morning, the village started. "We all went in to the agency in good spirits," recalled Short Bull; there "was no bad feeling among the chiefs or anybody." That night, a council was called to debate another momentous issue. Red Cloud explained that a delegation of Oglala leaders would be invited to Washington to counsel with the president about Crook's reservation proposals. Another switch had tripped in the war chief's mental defenses. Asked outright if he would go, Crazy

Horse answered with unexpected conviction: "Hou. *Mni kte lo*, Alright, I will go." Welcoming the opportunity to lay the Northern Nation's case before the new Great Father, Crazy Horse questioned Red Cloud closely about delegation protocol.[27]

Despite thaws and hard rains that reduced trails to mud, about April 25, in a happy state of reunion, the village forded the South Fork of Cheyenne River opposite the mouth of Beaver Creek. In the symbolic geography of the region, the crossing represented a significant transition. Hitherto the village had traveled through country the Northern Nation claimed as its own. Now they approached the zone controlled by the agency Lakotas. Another council was staged to reflect the shift. Rising from his seat at the honor place, Crazy Horse personally spread a buffalo robe for Red Cloud to sit on. Then, in a startlingly conciliatory gesture, he removed his war shirt and placed it over Red Cloud's shoulders, transferring symbolic primacy in the village to the agency chief.[28]

Assured of his mission's success, Red Cloud hurried six messengers homeward to report that the village should arrive about May 4. Fatigue and anxiety were setting in, however, and the village made one more short move. At a point on the Fort Laramie–Black Hills road three miles north of the Hat Creek stage station, progress stopped about April 27. Lodges were pitched along the quagmire of Sage Creek, within fifty miles of the agency. Six more northern messengers were selected. Rations were now essential, and Red Cloud sent word that the village was "out of supplies, stuck in the mud."[29]

The messengers found Red Cloud Agency buzzing with activity in preparation for the expected surrender. General Crook had been on hand to receive the capitulations at Spotted Tail Agency, but divisional headquarters called him to a conference in Chicago. By a potent irony, General Sheridan was about to apply the brakes on the northern reservation scheme just as surrenders climaxed.

To expedite surrender, Lieutenant J. Wesley Rosenquest was ordered to take out ten wagons of rations and one hundred beef cattle. Accompanied by a small detachment, agency interpreter Billy Garnett, and fifty Oglala scouts led by American Horse, Rosenquest left Camp Robinson on the morning of April 30. On the 31st, five miles short of the village, Rosenquest ordered a halt. The scouts washed and painted by the creek, then each donned a crisp white cotton shirt (courtesy of the agency trader's store), mounted, and galloped wildly around the circle of tipis.

The northern Oglalas rode out to meet their kinsmen. American Horse had the scouts sit in a row across the trail. As the northern people halted, there were scenes of great joy at the symbolic reunion. Each scout was presented with a pony. To Rosenquest's surprise, his hand, too, was clamped on the rein of a gift horse, a token of the village's desire for peace. And, in a pregnant moment, Crazy Horse came forward silently to shake hands with the officer.[30]

After weeks of hardship, the people feasted all too well on beef, hardtack, tea, and pilot bread, overeating so that "nearly all the children sickened, and the march could not be resumed next day."[31] Over Rosenquest's protests, the village lay over a further two days, but under the facade of conviviality, old anxieties reemerged. After shaking hands with the lieutenant, Crazy Horse refused to talk further. He Dog tried to coax his friend to accept the situation gracefully, but even he was troubled at developments. Only as they neared the agency, He Dog recalled, "I found we were coming to surrender," and would not be allowed to return immediately to the north. Little Killer, catching up with one of the last hunting parties, remembered that Crazy Horse remarked he had been "'captured,'" believing himself a defeated enemy rather than an equal making peace.[32]

There were causes enough for disquiet. Although they repeatedly tried to clarify the matter with Red Cloud, people were uncertain just what they would have to surrender. During the layover, Iron Shield, a Lakota messenger from Bear Coat Miles, appeared. Besides reporting the April 22 surrender of three hundred Cheyennes and Miniconjous at Tongue River Cantonment, he claimed that Miles sent private word to Crazy Horse. Bear Coat allegedly warned the war chief that if he surrendered at the agencies, the authorities would "arrest the young men, and put them in the Guard-House."[33]

Iron Shield's insinuations were not without foundation. Although Crook prevented arrests in his department, Sheridan and Mackenzie favored punitive measures once surrenders were complete. According to Thunder Tail, images of pursuit and arrest were deliberately deployed to provoke Crazy Horse. Asked if his people would resist if scouts and soldiers came to arrest him, the war chief tried to defuse the dangerous turn in the conversation: "Hiya, No," he insisted. Frankly, he acknowledged his priorities: "I live with the Northern Nation, and I cherish the land."[34]

These were not the only misgivings broached. On the march, Crazy Horse would have been able to confer about Young Man Afraid of His Horse's plan for an agency on Tongue River. Now American Horse could tell the northern leaders that the proposal had been quashed by the army high command, driving home just how problematic was Crook's northern reservation. The agency chiefs renewed their appeal for the northern Oglalas to join with them in a concerted bid to win a just peace in Washington.[35]

Most disturbing of all, however, was news that Crook and Mackenzie had already exerted pressure on the Cheyennes to accept relocation to the southern Cheyenne and Arapaho reservation in Indian Territory. Briefly, the council considered boycotting the Oglala agency and surrendering at Spotted Tail. In the village at large, however, the mood remained buoyant. People were happy at the prospect of regular rations, a distribution of annuity goods, and reunion with Oglala relatives. Still, Crazy Horse remained deeply disturbed. He quizzed Iron Shield closely about Lame Deer's movements.[36]

When the march resumed on May 3, the war chief and He Dog remained on the deserted campground. The friends shared a pipe. At last the war chief's patience snapped. "I am going back to Lame Deer," he exclaimed. He Dog soothed the war chief, invoking their pledge of peace, but the comical fact that their ponies had

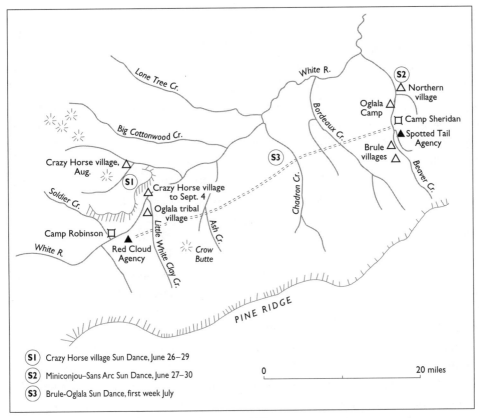

Red Cloud and Spotted Tail agencies and environs, 1877

strayed deflated the situation. The friends were forced to walk all the way to the next campsite, and by the time they reached home, Crazy Horse's anger had burned itself out.[37]

As the village neared the agency, nerves wore thin. It made only eight miles on May 4; scarcely four or five on the fifth. As the villagers approached the high white-clay bluffs of Pine Ridge, a sudden fusillade of shots ahead of the column panicked the whole village. Women and children galloped for the bluffs, and quiet was restored only after it was understood that some warriors had happened upon a herd of antelope. After another downpour, the evening of the fifth found the village camped high up a creek feeding out of the bluffs, within eight miles of the agency.[38]

The sun dawned on a momentous day, Sunday, May 6, and in the gray light, Lieutenant Rosenquest got his wagons moving, escorted by American Horse's scouts. Soon after daylight, the Deciders ordered the march, and the column threaded up onto the pine-capped bluffs. Crazy Horse mounted a white pony and rode to the head of the column. By midmorning the trail topped the Pine Ridge, then intersected with the south-flowing Soldier Creek. Scouts sighted the quadrangle of buildings grouped around the Camp Robinson parade ground; and beyond, along

White River, the tipi camps clustered around the Red Cloud Agency stockade. Winding up the creek rode a company of twenty blue-coated Oglala scouts, led by a single officer wearing a jaunty white hat.[39]

At 10:00 A.M., five miles out from the agency, Lieutenant Clark's party drew rein. Down the defile approached a row of ten chiefs and headmen. Several yards in the lead rode Crazy Horse. All was silent as he drew up and ordered a stop. One hundred yards behind the leaders, six companies of warriors halted, each "formed regularly in single rank" behind a headman.[40] Along the low bluffs above the creek, hundreds of women, children, and elders watched Crazy Horse dismount and sit deliberately on the ground. Red Cloud rode forward, asking Clark to approach alone. The lieutenant sat facing the war chief, a few yards apart. Five minutes of silence passed. Then Clark rose and offered his hand. Through Red Cloud, Crazy Horse made it known that he wished to shake hands while seated, "because that was the sign that the peace made was to last through life and forever."[41]

Clark sat again, and Crazy Horse held out his left hand. "Kola," he began, "I shake with this hand because my heart is on this side; I want this peace to last forever."[42] Gingerly, the two men shook. Then Rosenquest, several of Clark's scout escort, and a *Chicago Times* correspondent each offered his hand to the war chief. Clark and the others walked to greet the warriors—a few offered nervous fingers, but most "gave a good hearty grip, and seemed to mean it," intoning the "hou, kola" of informal greeting.[43] Clark's party turned back and reseated themselves before Crazy Horse. Little Hawk and He Dog had joined the war chief. At a signal from Crazy Horse, the other Deciders came forward. Each shook hands warmly with Clark, then joined the circle of seated men.

Crazy Horse observed that now was the "best time for smoking the pipe of peace." He spoke in an undertone to Red Cloud, who remarked that Crazy Horse would not speak again, but would now smoke and "invoke the Great Spirit to make [the peace] eternal." After the pipe was lighted and passed around the circle, He Dog arose. "I have come to make peace," he declared, "to those that I like and have confidence in. I give these." Just as Crazy Horse had conceded primacy to Red Cloud, now He Dog indicated his submission to General Crook's representative. After gesturing Clark to stand, he pulled off his magnificent war shirt and drew it over Clark's shoulders. Then he removed his headdress and placed it on Clark's head. Holding up the pipe to the sun, He Dog placed it and a finely beaded pipe bag in the lieutenant's hands, endowing him with honorary Decider status. Finally, the akicita leader presented Clark with his own war pony. From the saddle, He Dog removed a fine buffalo robe and spread it at the honor place on Crazy Horse's left.[44]

Clark sat, then made the keynote speech. "We have come to make a lasting peace, never to be broken," he began. "We had a rain last night that has washed out all bad feelings. . . . The sun is now shining brightly. All shows the Great Spirit is pleased with our actions." He stated that all arms and ponies must be given up, after camp was made on the site chosen by General Mackenzie. The people would have to be counted, "so as to provide them with rations." Their names would be sent to the Great Father in Washington. There, Clark assured them, General Crook was "looking out for your interests."

The Deciders sat in awkward silence. Crazy Horse observed, "I have given all I have to Red Cloud." After consultation, Red Cloud advised Clark to go easy. "Crazy Horse is a sensible man. He knows it is useless to fight longer against the whites, and is now willing to give himself up." But, continued Red Cloud, Crazy Horse did not consider himself defeated, deeming "it best as a matter of policy to surrender." The northern leaders asked that they be allowed to give up their arms voluntarily, without the indignity of force. Each man would advance, lay down his gun, and give his name. Clark approved the proposal, and the talk wound up on a positive note: "[A]ll bad feeling of the past," Clark asserted, "must be buried."[45]

Clark and his entourage remounted at noon on a brilliant spring day. The lieutenant still wore He Dog's headdress. To many of the Indians, remembered Shave Elk, "he looked so comical that . . . we . . . laughed."[46] The relaxation of tension was palpable as Crazy Horse signaled the village to resume its march. Early in the afternoon, the procession hove in sight of Camp Robinson. At the head rode Clark and Rosenquest, with Red Cloud and the scouts and envoys forming a stolid column behind. After a quarter-mile gap rode a row of six men—Crazy Horse, the Deciders, and He Dog—ahead of the warriors. The men spread across the widening valley of Soldier Creek, but as the post buildings appeared, warrior societies grouped in five regular companies, each of forty men.

On cue, a voice struck up a song, soon taken up along the two-mile length of the column. Curious officers at the post, come to witness a surrender, observed instead a march of victory as the northern Oglalas descended, to the stately measure of their great "Song of Peace," into the White River valley. Behind the warriors strode the elders, leading the throng of women, children, and pack animals. Boys raced their ponies back and forth. Toddlers squalled from seats on the travois. Youths flanked the loose stock, brood mares trailing nervy colts in the cloud of dust. A screen of pickets brought up the rear.

At 2:00 P.M. the head of the procession approached the agency, one mile beyond the post. Immediately north of the agency compound, the ground fell away steeply to a narrow arc of bottomland in a curve of White River. Riding across the stream, Crazy Horse and the Deciders drew up on the flat. The order to halt was called, and immediately the singers fell silent. Lieutenant Clark turned to Crazy Horse and told him, "You want to take up all the guns and ponies."[47] Women immediately set to work pitching camp, and in short order the circle of tipis stood on the campground.

While the women worked, the ponies were surrendered. The weeks of careful husbanding had paid off, and the herd seemed in "very good order," many animals being captured U.S. mules and cavalry mounts. Thomas Moore, Crook's chief packer, kept a tally until he reached seventeen hundred, then let through the rest, at least five hundred head more. Behind him, Oglala scouts waited to drive the herd away. Red Cloud harangued to forestall trouble, assuring Crazy Horse's people that their horses would be returned to them. He was pledged a personal gift of seven hundred head in recognition of his efforts for peace. Subverting Sheridan's rationale, the Oglalas would be free to dispose of the ponies as they pleased. Beginning the following morning, in scenes of orchestrated largesse, most would be redistributed among the northern villagers.[48]

The pony surrender went ahead smoothly. Clark turned to the twin issues of counting and disarming people. Asked that all scouts and wasicu spectators withdraw, the lieutenant humored the Lakotas. Only Clark, Lieutenant Rosenquest, Lieutenant Charles A. Johnson, and interpreters Garnett and Leon Palladay remained. At 4:00 P.M. the warriors gathered on the campground, and Crazy Horse led off the disarming, laying down a rifle on the grass. Throughout the surrender, observed Crook's aide Lieutenant John G. Bourke, Crazy Horse "behaved with stolidity, like a man who saw he had to give in to fate, but would do so as doggedly as possible." The Deciders and He Dog followed suit, then some fifty warriors. With just seventy-six guns turned in, Clark waited, then addressed Crazy Horse firmly: "[T]hat wouldn't do." From American Horse, the lieutenant had precise reports of the northern arms. Clark repeated that every piece must be "turned in at once, and that now was their time to show a genuine desire for peace."[49]

Crazy Horse sat in stoical silence, but other headmen offered flimsy excuses. Clark told the warriors they could take their arms to their lodges, but he would search every tipi until all were surrendered. As the campground emptied, Clark sent for a wagon and several scouts. Frank Grouard was on hand to assist and interpret. Agency commissary clerk Charles P. Jordan was charged with counting the Indians. Each attended by an interpreter, Clark and Jordan started around the camp circle. At each tipi, Jordan took down the names of all adult males, then counted the occupants. His enumeration tallied 145 lodges, housing 217 men, 312 women, 186 boys, and 184 girls, for a total of 899 people.[50]

Everyone remained surprisingly cool, won over by Clark's "firmness and fine judgment."[51] Occupants sat calmly while Clark gathered up every gun and had them placed in the wagon. Holdouts were approached by scouts and instructed to give up specified weapons. From Crazy Horse's lodge, they removed three Winchesters; next door, Little Hawk surrendered two. The process took upwards of three hours, and it was 8:00 before the lieutenant was satisfied to return to post. Some 114 weapons were surrendered, comprising forty-six breechloaders, thirty-five muzzleloaders, and thirty-three revolvers.

With Clark's departure, the village relaxed into everyday routines. At dusk women served up the evening meal. A few visitors from the agency bands paid social calls and were offered food and coffee. Some brought gifts of meat and clothing. Here and there, reunions were made in the heightened pitch of tears. Crazy Horse had invited Frank Grouard to supper, and Crook's favorite guide walked to the tipi with Lieutenant Bourke. As they approached, Bourke observed Crazy Horse, a man lithe and sinewy, seeming scarcely thirty years old for all his care-worn appearance. During the day, the war chief had seemed "sullen and gloomy" in the unwelcome glare of center stage. In repose, his face remained "quiet, rather morose, dogged, tenacious, and resolute. His expression is rather melancholic." Yet, when Frank called his name, Tasunke Witko, Crazy Horse's features "lit up with genuine pleasure." Frank explained that Bourke was akicita to Three Stars Crook, and Crazy Horse, still seated, favored the lieutenant with a friendly glance, then gave him "a hearty grasp of the hand."[52]

Night fell on one of the defining days of Crazy Horse's life. He had acquitted himself well. If officers like Mackenzie balked at the war chief's "proud and almost contemptuous behavior," that pride was rooted in a national esprit.[53] Unlike earlier surrenders, people dragging into the agencies in demoralized poverty or in charges of sham bravado, the Oglala capitulation was a well-judged dignified performance. The people reclaimed their place within the Oglala tribe, believing that the strengthened hoop could win from the wasicu a just peace. To this optimism Crazy Horse clung. His misgivings were obvious, but his bright welcome for Grouard hinted at the human warmth behind the facade of sullen pride. "I came here for peace," he would repeatedly state through the coming summer. And now it was time to seize the prizes of peace.

This iconic image depicts Crazy Horse as the Thunder dreamer, his body paint vivid with lightning and hail—the destructive powers of the storm—in the greatest victory of his life, the Battle of the Little Bighorn. Drawing by Amos Bad Heart Bull, reprinted, with permission, from *A Pictographic History of the Oglala Sioux*, by Amos Bad Heart Bull, text by Helen H. Blish (Lincoln: University of Nebraska Press, 1967; copyright renewed 1995).

Red Cloud, 1872. During the warfare of the 1860s, Crazy Horse acted as a tactical war leader, implementing the strategic vision of Red Cloud. The relationship soured after Red Cloud decided to shape a new accommodation with the United States and became terminally embittered after Crazy Horse's 1877 surrender at Red Cloud Agency. The older chief sought to protect his primacy by plotting against Crazy Horse. Courtesy National Anthropological Archives, Smithsonian Institution (NAA INV 01 601 305).

Spotted Tail, 1870. Young Crazy Horse revered his warrior uncle until Spotted Tail's conversion to an accommodation strategy alienated his nephew. The men remained suspicious of each other through the tragic sequence resulting in Crazy Horse's death. Courtesy Denver Public Library (X-32002).

Young Man Afraid of His Horse, 1877. As peers and comrades, Young Man Afraid of His Horse and Crazy Horse retained a mutual respect after the former's move to the reservation. Young Man Afraid remained committed to integrating Crazy Horse's followers into the smooth running of agency life and stayed apart from the intrigues that resulted in the war chief's death. From John Gregory Bourke Diaries, courtesy U.S. Military Academy, West Point.

He Dog, 1877. Crazy Horse's friendship with his lifelong kola (pledged comrade) He Dog was frequently invoked to smooth tensions between the Hunkpatila and Bad Face bands. As Red Cloud's nephew, He Dog left the Crazy Horse village in the tense weeks before the latter's death, but he remained loyal to the war chief in friendship and memory. Courtesy Nebraska State Historical Society (NSHS–B7747).

Little Big Man, 1877. Former comrade turned political rival in the months after surrender, Little Big Man posed the greatest challenge to Crazy Horse's leadership at Red Cloud Agency. His role in the war chief's death alienated many followers, terminating his political ambitions. Courtesy National Anthropological Archives, Smithsonian Institution (NAA INV 06530900).

Hunts the Enemy (George Sword), 1877. Nephew of Red Cloud and later captain of the Pine Ridge Reservation police, Hunts the Enemy's diplomacy was crucial in effecting the surrender of Crazy Horse's followers. Courtesy Nebraska State Historical Society (NSHS-1392: 39-4).

Little Hawk and Lieutenant W. P. Clark, 1877. Half-brother of Crazy Horse's father, Little Hawk was a forceful supporter of Crazy Horse within the council of chiefs and elders. Lt. Clark commanded the scout troops in which Crazy Horse enlisted after surrender. His disillusion in the war chief was sudden, total, and critical in the events leading to Crazy Horse's arrest and death. National Anthropological Archives, Smithsonian Institution (SPC BAE 4605 01600909).

General George Crook. As commander of the Department of the Platte, Crook faced Crazy Horse in war and in diplomacy. Bested at the Rosebud, Crook repulsed Crazy Horse at Slim Buttes—but it was his offer of an agency in the hunting grounds that netted the war chief's surrender and the end of the Great Sioux War. Courtesy Library of Congress (LC-BH826-2600).

Lieutenant Colonel George Armstrong Custer. Civil War hero Custer first clashed with Crazy Horse in 1873. At the Little Bighorn three years later, Custer obsessively sought to contain the "scatteration" of his foe, his regiment paying the ultimate price against a supremely flexible warrior force led by an inspirational Crazy Horse. Courtesy Library of Congress (LC-USZ62-63838).

Colonel Nelson A. Miles. The army's supreme self-publicist, Miles clashed with Crazy Horse at Wolf Mountains in January 1877. After a tactical standoff, Miles returned to base. Winter privations and agency diplomacy orchestrated by Miles's rival Crook secured mass surrenders the following spring. Courtesy Library of Congress (LC-B813-2044).

Kinsman and friend to Crazy Horse, the Miniconjou leader Touch the Clouds (seated far left) sought a diplomatic solution to the crisis in U.S.-Lakota relations. He remained loyal to the war chief, accompanying him on the final ride to Camp Robinson to ensure fair play. Seated next to Touch the Clouds in this 1877 photograph are (left to right) Sharp Nose, Black Coal, and Friday (Northern Arapahos). The standing Lakota is Young Spotted Tail. Courtesy Library of Congress (LC-BH832-523).

Oglala delegation to Washington, 1877. This classic Matthew Brady image includes key agency leaders Red Cloud and Little Wound (seated, first and second from left), plus northern headmen Iron Crow, He Dog (seated, second from right and extreme right), Little Big Man, and Big Road (second row, first and second from left). Courtesy Library of Congress (LC-BH832-850).

Low Dog, 1881. Redoubtable warrior, and irreconcilably hostile to the Americans, Low Dog was one of Crazy Horse's key supporters in the Oyuhpe band of Oglalas. Courtesy Denver Public Library (B-430).

Spotted Eagle, 1881. War chief of the Sans Arcs, Spotted Eagle organized the opposition to the Northern Pacific Railroad in 1872. Among the leaders to choose exile in Canada over surrender, after Crazy Horse's death, Spotted Eagle emerged as his most widely influential successor. Courtesy Denver Public Library (X-31563).

Black Shawl. This image from the collections of the Standing Bear family is believed to be of Crazy Horse's wife. The seven-year marriage was the most stable of his personal relationships, and despite illness and the death of their daughter, Black Shawl remained loyal to the war chief, riding with him in the flight to Spotted Tail Agency on the eve of his death. Courtesy Donovin Arleigh Sprague, Crazy Horse Memorial.

Crazy Horse's funeral cortege. This newspaper image depicts the procession of Crazy Horse's family en route to Spotted Tail Agency, September 6, 1877. From *Frank Leslie's Illustrated Newspaper*.

Crazy Horse's scaffold burial at Camp Sheridan. Spotted Tail agent Jesse Lee ordered the plank fencing built to protect the scaffold on which Crazy Horse's body was buried. Lee's sympathy persuaded Crazy Horse's father not to join the flights to Canada in the chaotic aftermath of the war chief's death. From John Gregory Bourke Diaries, courtesy U.S. Military Academy, West Point.

Six

I CHERISH THE LAND

21

I CAME HERE FOR PEACE

Early on the morning of May 7, the people of the northern Oglala village gathered to meet the military agent, Lieutenant Charles A. Johnson. For the first time, Crazy Horse viewed the Red Cloud Agency compound, and he and He Dog visited Frank Yates's trading store. The trader presented his prominent new clients with gifts of blankets. Outside, a talk was held with the officers. Short Bull recalled that Crazy Horse plainly stated his priorities. Prepared to concede the Tongue River location, he insisted on his second-choice site: "There is a creek over there they call Beaver Creek; there is a great big flat west of the headwaters of Beaver Creek; I want my agency put right in the middle of that flat." Citing the good grass at the site, he concluded that "after the agency was placed there he would go to Washington and talk to the Great Father." Then, from the issue bastion at the southeast corner of the agency stockade, clerks disbursed a portion of annuity goods. The agent, recalled Red Feather, "gave them rations, clothing and blankets. Everyone was very jolly."[1]

Women hurried back to the village to start making clothes from the rolls of bright-colored flannel, calico, and stroud. Others gathered on the campground to be taught the use of some of the new comestibles. Supplied with skillets and flour, they observed Crook's ubiquitous packer Tom Moore demonstrate the preparation of fry bread—already a major item in the agency Lakota diet. Army contract surgeon Valentine T. McGillycuddy visited the village and attended Crazy Horse's tipi at the war chief's request to examine Black Shawl. The northern menfolk meanwhile had been invited to attend a giveaway staged by Red Cloud. Agency scouts redistributed to northern relatives the ponies just surrendered. Only U.S.-branded stock was retained by the army.[2]

As morning progressed, all the northern people gravitated over the prairie to a cluster of corrals marking the agency beef-issue station. Under the eye of butcher Ben Tibbetts, Oglala herders rousted some thirty head of stringy longhorns.

Declining meat that had been prebutchered "on the block," the Deciders requested that their issue "be turned over to them alive, so that they could enjoy a sensation next to that furnished by a buffalo hunt."[3]

Hunters rode forward as Tibbetts's herders whooped the cattle into a run. "All the thrilling whoops of battle, the terrific feats of horsemanship and the skill of the savage with his rudest weapon were exhibited in a twinkling," observed a Denver journalist. The longhorns raced toward White River, flanked by the hunters. "Every moment a poor brute would receive its death wound from the unerring shaft, and occasionally one made fairly mad would turn and delight his pursuers by a plucky resistance." Within twenty minutes, all the cattle were slain. Drying racks outside the tipis were soon hung with sheets of wafer-sliced beef and looped with coils of guts, the image of a camp living fat—if only on reservation rations.[4]

The beef issue ushered in a week of binge eating. Agency leaders hosted feasts and dances, and the Camp Robinson officers' mess was happy to welcome Lakota veterans of the Great Sioux War. A few days after surrender, Billy Garnett invited Crazy Horse and the Deciders to eat at his cabin. As Billy's Oglala wife served the meal, Crazy Horse gingerly sat on a chair and pulled up to the table. Away from the public eye, he dropped his mask of reserve and silence, telling Billy that he wished to be shown how to handle a knife and fork: "He said he had got it to do."

Crazy Horse continued to quiz Billy about the journey east. How would the delegation travel, he asked; how were bodily functions performed on the weeklong railroad journey to Washington? Billy patiently explained to Crazy Horse's satisfaction. When his guests departed that evening, the interpreter was confident that the war chief was entirely committed to the road of peace.[5]

The eating continued unabated. Overfed on unfamiliar foods, many people fell ill. At the officers' mess, strawberries and cream were on the menu, until the unaccustomed richness of diet left the visitors violently sick. Soon after dinner with the Garnetts, Crazy Horse took to his bed, so ill that for several days—according to a hyped-up newspaper account—he was "not expected to live." Although his symptoms persisted through midmonth, by May 13, just a week after surrender, Crazy Horse began to recover from the worst effects.[6]

Ill or not, the war chief had a busy week. On May 8 Colonel Mackenzie convened a general council at which he stated that he knew all firearms had not been surrendered. Already sick, Crazy Horse had begged off attending, but when he learned Mackenzie's ultimatum, he personally "went from tepee to tepee, consuming nearly the entire night, coaxing and commanding by turns, that if any guns could be found they must be turned in before daylight." A few rifles were turned in at the agency early on the ninth—proof of Crazy Horse's commitment to the peace process.[7]

At the annuity distribution, Agent Johnson had remarked to Crazy Horse that he should enlist as an army scout—keeping order at the agency and handling diplomacy with the holdouts up north. The northern council decided a mass enlistment would be advantageous to their cause. At a private feast, Crazy Horse said that he "didn't wish to go," but Red Feather "coaxed" his brother-in-law to accept the invitation and articulate the council consensus.[8]

Crazy Horse made a short but conciliatory speech to Mackenzie. He "wanted to 'get along straight and well' at the Agency," and "'he would like a hundred of his best men enlisted'" as scouts. Careful to keep the northern agency atop everyone's agenda, Crazy Horse closed his remarks by urging that the agency "be removed north, where the land is better and where the children would be properly brought up." In private conversation with Lieutenant Clark, Crazy Horse agreed to enlist.[9]

Preparations were hurried forward. Clark agreed to sign up Crazy Horse and fifteen of his leading men. Of the Deciders, Little Hawk, Little Big Man, and Big Road were enrolled. The herald Iron Hawk and akicita leaders He Dog and Four Crows were also approved, all members of the Sore Backs kindred. That tiyospaye's solidarity was underlined by the enlistment of Bad Heart Bull and Crazy Horse's comrade Good Weasel. The war chief's brother-in-law Club Man and relative Whirlwind Bear represented the Hunkpatilas, while Thunder Tail represented Black Twin's old tiyospaye. Of the Siksicela band, Crazy Bear enlisted. The Oyuh-pes following their Decider Big Road included Charging Hawk and White Bear. In what amounted to a concession to Crazy Horse, another ten northern men from Spotted Tail Agency were taken on the army payroll. Led by the Hunkpatila elder Iron Crow, the men would bring their families—perhaps eight or nine lodges—from Spotted Tail to join Crazy Horse's village.[10]

On Saturday, May 12, the enlistment took place at Camp Robinson. "A remarkable scene occurred," reported the *Cheyenne Daily Leader*'s correspondent, "when these red soldiers were sworn into Uncle Sam's service. They swore with up lifted hands to be true and faithful to the white man's government." Of Crazy Horse and his comrades, the journalist contended, "the sullen, discontented look worn by the hostiles when they first came in, is fast disappearing now." The issue of Sharps carbines and Remington revolvers, with ammunition, went far to create the atmosphere of goodwill. The new intake, salted with a few agency trusties, was organized into a regular unit as Company E. As top sergeant, Crazy Horse headed seven subordinate noncoms: sergeants Little Big Man, Little Hawk, He Dog, and No Water; and corporals Iron Hawk, Four Crows, and Pawnee Killer. The enlistment closed with a significant statement by Lieutenant Clark. The chain of command now ran down from Clark and Spotted Tail Agency chief of scouts Captain George M. Randall, through three top sergeants: Spotted Tail, Red Cloud, and Crazy Horse.[11]

By mid-May Crazy Horse had time to take stock of the situation at the White River agencies. The new enlistment asserted a Lakota hierarchy at the Oglala agency headed by Red Cloud and Crazy Horse. Reflecting his status, the war chief paid his infrequent visits to the agency, commissary clerk Charles P. Jordan remembered, "accompanied by a body guard of 6 or 8 men." Further emphasizing his distinction, Crazy Horse always sat on a chair to face the agent or Lieutenant Clark, while the bodyguard sat "on the floor—3 or 4 on each side of him." His position in the chair asserted two facts that sat in uneasy alignment: his attempt to master the forms of wasicu protocol, and his unswerving belief in his own figurehead status as principal Lakota.[12]

Crazy Horse had also had time to assess the attitudes of the agency Lakotas. Some 530 lodges of agency Oglalas were organized into five bands, scattered over the prairie two or three miles south and east of the agency itself.[13] In the years following the split in the Oglala tribe, Crazy Horse soon saw that changes had continued apace. On ration days, many agency families drew up in wagons. Lakotas dressed in manufactured clothing. Underlining the cultural sea change Crazy Horse had so long resisted, Red Cloud appeared for formal events in civilian dress clothing; had his iyeska relatives look after a growing herd of cattle he owned; and permitted his wife to keep a noisy batch of chickens. If such developments disturbed the war chief, a substantial amount of goodwill prevailed between the Oglalas and their northern guests. Most northern families were happy to be warm, secure, and well fed, and for most people, the reunion of the tribe was an occasion for simple joy. Oglala women began to prepare scores of little gardens in sheltered spots near the camps. Some of the newcomers showed unexpected interest in planting their own tiny plots of corn and beans. Underscoring unity of aspiration, the Payabya, Loafer, and Spleen bands had already requested an agency on the hunting grounds, and as the month progressed, Red Cloud's camp council moved gradually toward adopting a similar position.

Many of these issues found expression in a "grand peace council" hosted on May 11. Chief Little Wound sent out invitations to the whole Oglala tribe "to talk over a lasting peace and agency reforms" with Lieutenant Clark. Little Wound welcomed his guests in a huge double tipi, while akicita strangled a dozen dogs for the cooking pots.[14]

Crazy Horse sat close to Little Wound and the other chief guest, White Hat Clark. A holy man rose to invoke the favor of Wakan Tanka on the gathering, before each of the chiefs rose to speak. For two hours the speakers forcibly presented the case for peace: only Crazy Horse remained silent—"stolid and relentless," concluded a Denver newsman.

As the meal was consumed, the hundreds of women and children crowding outside the lodge parted to allow through an old man, leaning on a cane and supported by a young warrior. In a staged exhibition of the generosity Lakotas—and their American allies—owed each other, Little Wound stood and "pulled off his fine new blanket and presented it to the sufferer." Other chiefs shed their own blankets and other garments and—to the accompaniment of tremolos of praise—presented the old man with their gifts. Crazy Horse was never outdone in generosity. As singers took up his name in an extemporized chant of honor, the war chief stood and stripped off his clothing. Stepping forward, he presented the old man with his blanket and other garments. From outside, Crazy Horse's pony was led onto the floor space. Its reins were put into the indigent's hands, and a herald rode the circuit of the campground, proclaiming the greatness of Crazy Horse's name. After a closing prayer, "the assembly adjourned in excellent spirits."[15]

The grand peace council highlighted the ideology of Oglala tribal unity that had emerged in the days since surrender. Clark was able to report to his hosts that General Crook was now returning from the East and would hold a major council at Red Cloud Agency. With the general, the summer's diplomatic schedule could be finalized. Meanwhile the Oglalas began to determine the ceremonial calendar. In keeping with the new mood, the northern village proposed that it host the tribal Sun Dance at the end of June. The Oglalas believed that Crook's imminent arrival meant an early departure for the delegation and return from the capital by the time of the ceremony. If all went as planned, the Oglalas might depart White River for the new northern agency site immediately after the end of the Sun Dance.

As the Moon When the Ponies Shed entered its second half, Crazy Horse moved to consolidate his position. He wished to unite his village with the Miniconjous and Sans Arcs who had surrendered at Spotted Tail. The Scout enlistment had provided a handy excuse for permitting several transfers: Crook's impending visit to Red Cloud and the Sun Dance supplied two justifications for adding more visitors to Crazy Horse's circle.

As news of Crook's itinerary firmed up, the Oglala bands sent invitations to Spotted Tail Agency for Brules and northern Lakotas to camp with them. Since surrender, Spotted Tail had succeeded in keeping the northern village at his agency well in line: the Miniconjous and Sans Arcs were not allowed to forget that they were guests, and that generous Brule hospitality could easily turn into stern sufferance. Many people grew restive, favoring transfer to Crazy Horse's village. According to one reminiscent account, the Miniconjous and part of the Sans Arcs even acknowledged Crazy Horse as their head chief—dangerously alienating Spotted Tail from his nephew's interests.[16]

No clearer evidence of Oglala unity could be demonstrated than the formation of the tribal village that greeted Crook late in May. Two miles southeast of the agency, the bands raised a single hoop. Tribal consensus formed around the northern reservation. Chiefs and elders deputed two leaders to make keynote speeches to the general: Young Man Afraid of His Horse and Crazy Horse, as the principal Lakota proponents of the scheme, would articulate the tribal position. Red Cloud, faced with the restoration of a united Hunkpatila band, could only follow in the wake of the tribal consensus.

At noon, May 23, General Crook arrived at Camp Robinson. Two days were spent finalizing details for the departure of Colonel Mackenzie's Fourth Cavalry to its old stations on the southern plains. Crook and Mackenzie also counciled with Cheyenne leaders about joining their southern Cheyenne relatives in Indian Territory. Demoralized by the war and uncomfortable with their Lakota hosts, many Cheyenne chiefs were still dubious about such a move. Pressured by the military, however, a brittle consensus formed around agency leaders keen for preferment: the Cheyennes agreed to an early departure for the south.[17]

Crook had returned to White River with little that Crazy Horse could endorse. In the East, Crook had run into a wall of opposition from his superiors Sheridan and Sherman. The military chiefs had agreed on a strategy of ensuring total surrenders followed by agency relocations to the Missouri River. The official correspondence is muted, but Sheridan berated Crook about the leniency of his surrender terms. Sheridan favored the arrest and imprisonment of key war leaders and disavowed Crook's northern reservation scheme. Crook conceded to Sheridan that he thought the Lakotas could be persuaded to move to the Missouri, but he requested permission to travel to the capital to confer with the Indian commissioner.[18]

During the same weekend of Crazy Horse's surrender, Crook held a lengthy meeting at the Indian Office and persuaded the commissioner to postpone any removal until October.[19] The respite bought everyone time: Crook could continue to use his influence in the Hayes administration to secure a northern reservation; the Washington officials, preoccupied with a summer of unprecedented labor unrest, could place the Lakota delegation question on hold; and the military high command could reassure itself, with numbing cynicism, that "a Later removal is not Objectionable Especially if the approach of Winter makes [the Lakotas] more manageable."[20]

Thus Crook had little of substance to offer the Lakotas. Even the delegation, confidently expected to follow his return to Red Cloud, was indefinitely shelved. Some concession would have to be made to keep Crazy Horse on board the peace process. The idea of an army-monitored buffalo hunt in the north, first floated by Crook to the Miniconjous and Sans Arcs in April, seemed the best solution, although even this would have to be approved up the chain of command.

Nevertheless, the mood was upbeat as the Oglalas and their guests from Spotted Tail prepared to meet the general. So affable was Crazy Horse that he granted his first and only press interview. At Camp Robinson on the afternoon of the twenty-fourth, a *Chicago Times* correspondent approached Lieutenant Clark to secure an audience with the war chief. Accompanied by interpreter Billy Garnett, Red Dog, and the northern headman Horned Horse, Crazy Horse answered questions, concentrating on the Custer battle. Although he left most of the talking to Horned Horse, Crazy Horse gave his approval to an account of the battle that revealed a surprising amount of the war chief's strategy. All seemed to bode well for the next day's diplomatic round.[21]

Shortly after noon on Friday, May 25, General Crook and his staff assembled outside the main gate at Red Cloud. East of the agency buildings, Lieutenant Clark had drawn up some six hundred mounted warriors. Atop a long rise, hundreds more mounted Indians milled to view the scene. At 12:30 Clark gave an order, and the warriors wheeled their horses. Forming into eighteen platoons, they executed a precise drill to pass in review before Crook "in fine style," according to a watching correspondent. Throughout the maneuver, Crazy Horse rode at Clark's side on the right of the line. As they passed Crook, the chiefs wheeled out of line. Crook advanced alone, dressed characteristically in shabby civilian coat and slouch hat. The chiefs dismounted and walked forward to shake hands. In contrast with the general, many chiefs wore sergeant's jackets and army-issue hats: but no one could match Little Big Man for visual impact when the northern Decider, "conspicuous for his almost complete nudity," sprang from his pony.[22]

Even Little Big Man's exhibitionism was upstaged by Crazy Horse, however. The first chief to dismount, he dropped to one knee in front of Crook before rising and holding out his hand to shake. "Three Stars," he addressed the general, "I have seen the white man. He is very strong. My heart is good."[23] Crazy Horse stepped back, but his gesture, the accustomed stance of a scout reporting to his chief, was followed by most of the other leaders. It was a startling token of conciliation from the war chief.

After a pause for lunch, the council was convened inside the agency stockade. At 3:00 P.M. Crazy Horse arose to open the proceedings. After shaking hands with Crook and Mackenzie, Crazy Horse sat on the open ground in front of the general. He spoke in anticipation of a rapid solution to the issue of the northern reservation:

> You sent tobacco to my camp and invited me to come in. When the tobacco reached me I started out and kept moving till I reached here. I have been waiting ever since arriving for Gen. Crook, and now my heart has been made happy. In coming this way, I picked out a place where I wish to live here after. I put a stake in the ground to mark the spot. There is plenty of game in that country. All of my relatives here approve of my choice. I want them to go back with me and always live there together.[24]

Young Man Afraid of His Horse endorsed the northern reservation, stressing the potential of the region for raising stock.[25] Red Cloud too expressed "a desire to be moved north," requesting also the long-promised schools to educate the coming generation of Lakotas. Other speakers, including No Water, echoed the new consensus, while Iron Hawk sounded the note of conciliation: "The time has come by," announced the northern village herald, "when the Indians will laugh at the words of the Great Father. Hereafter they will take his word as law."[26]

Speaking for the northern contingent at Spotted Tail, Sans Arc Decider High Bear reprised the demand for a northern agency: "I want a place somewhere in my own country north where we can get some game, where we can run around and see my people hunt buffalo. We want a large agency so we can be free." Spotted Tail wound up proceedings with a crowd-pleasing dig, which united Indians and the military against invidious civilian treaty commissions.[27]

Posing as the man of deeds and few words, Crook stated that he "would do all he had agreed to—no more, no less." Assuring the Lakotas that he would forward their request for "a reservation in the upper country," and that he hoped soon to accompany the delegation east, he dismissed the council but accepted an invitation to the Oglala tribal village later in the afternoon. The chiefs left the agency happy with the proceedings.[28]

When Crook was welcomed to the great council shade in the village, Young Man Afraid of His Horse opened the talk by first echoing Spotted Tail's criticism of the Black Hills commissioners, angrily rejecting the Indian Territory relocation, then arguing forcefully that the surrenders had been negotiated on the understanding of "an agency in our own country."[29]

A northern spokesman, perhaps Little Hawk, contended that for his people, the Great Sioux War had been one of self-defense, and stated that they had "come in" in response to requests from the agency bands to help prevent relocation to Indian Territory. "These scouts told us," he concluded, "if we came in you would help us to get an Agency in this country."

Discontented rumblings were quieted by council moderator Red Dog, who called on Crook to speak. The general was affable, stating that his soldiers had only fought the Indians when fired upon. Addressing the time table, he reminded the Oglalas that "a few stragglers [were] out yet" on the hunting grounds. Crook insisted that all must surrender, although he conceded that Sitting Bull's Canadian exiles were beyond call. Once the surrenders were complete, Crook said, "[we] will go to Washington and there I will help you. I have to ask for help from the President . . . [but] he has a great many things to attend to; so we will go when he has more time."

Although manifestly a stalling exercise, the speech went down well enough. The general's arrival had again spelled disaster for the village's dogs, and women now carried in steaming kettles to honor their guests, as Iron Hawk delivered a ten-minute oration blessing the food. Crook won Oglala affection by wolfing down his canine portion, while to much amusement, the fastidious Clark passed his bowl and a dollar piece to the Lakota seated behind him.·

Before the council broke up, some Lakotas pressed the points they felt had been passed over. Crazy Horse and other northern leaders were concerned by the slippage in the diplomatic schedule. The chiefs pressed for assurances and concessions. Crook reviewed the subject of a hunting expedition to the north. He promised that once all stragglers had surrendered and "no hostiles remained on this (South) side of the Yellowstone, he would not object to their having an escort of a Battalion of Cavalry, while they engaged in a Buffalo hunt in the Big Horn Mtns to the West of [Cantonment Reno]."[30]

This undertaking fell far short of the guaranteed northern reservation Crazy Horse had seized on in April. What it did do was to preserve the schedule projected for the second half of the summer: the ceremonial season would climax with the Sun Dance, and provided all stragglers had surrendered, the northern Lakotas could leave for a lengthy hunt prior to the delegation's departure. For Little Big Man, identifying a new consensus for pragmatism, this was enough. If Crazy Horse was suspicious, the public mood favored no premature break with the wasicu, and the winter soldiering regime had left mental scars on the war chief: however deep the crisis he perceived as threatening his people, Crazy Horse would not lightly seek to reimpose martial law on them. For now, he would continue to bide his time, perfecting strategies that kept the northern reservation a live issue.

The uniting of the two northern villages was his favored tactic, and Crazy Horse sought to secure transfers and defections from the Brule agency. Iron Crow, an early transfer, was promoted to Decider status by the northern council.[31] Northern Oglala leaders used the talks with Crook to raise the topic of the Miniconjou and Sans Arc hostages taken by Colonel Miles the previous fall, arguing for their release at Red Cloud and hoping to secure the hostages' relatives to their circle.[32]

Although the evidence is unsatisfactory, about fifteen lodges of Oglalas, Brules, Sans Arcs, and Miniconjous seem to have joined Crazy Horse at the end of May without permission. Worm, with four lodges of his Kapozha kindred, successfully appealed to the new Camp Robinson commander for an official transfer from Spotted Tail.[33]

Three weeks after surrender, despite illness and doubts expressed in continued mood swings, Crazy Horse remained committed to the peace process. "Crazy Horse had come to the Agency with nothing but honorable intentions," was the considered evaluation of Billy Garnett. For much of May "his frame of mind was tranquil and pacific."[34] The talk with Crook found the war chief at his most conciliatory, most united with the agency hierarchy. But the talk taught him that a successful conclusion to the summer's diplomatic activity demanded a strong and united Lakota people. Crazy Horse needed to redouble his efforts to unite the two northern villages. He could hope that the impending Sun Dance would instill deeper unity in his people, rechartering the Northern Nation and creating a united hoop that would shape events this summer on White River.

22

MOON OF MAKING FAT

On Saturday, May 26, the day after the council with Crook, Lieutenant Colonel Luther P. Bradley, Ninth Infantry, assumed command of the post and the District of the Black Hills from the departing Colonel Mackenzie. Bradley was an able and humane officer with long experience of the plains. Like Crook, Bradley opposed top-brass attempts to force the Lakotas to relocate. All things considered, Bradley was a sensitive choice to take control of the district and its Indian affairs.[1]

"All the principal men among the Indians are here today," Bradley wrote his wife that evening. Lieutenant Clark was on hand to make introductions to the chiefs. "There are a great many fine looking fellows among the wild Indians who lately came in." In particular, Bradley continued, "I had an introduction to Crazy Horse, and a handshake." Like many observers, Bradley was struck by the war chief's unassuming manner, but he was alert to the potential for command: "He is a young[,] slender and mild mannered fellow but he is evidently the leader of his band."[2]

Two days later, 972 Cheyennes left Red Cloud Agency for their new home at the Southern Cheyenne and Arapaho Agency in Indian Territory. The Cheyenne removal, and the departure of Mackenzie's five hundred officers and men, created a subtle change in Crazy Horse's attitude.[3]

Some hours after his tribe's departure, a lone Cheyenne warrior rode out of the northern bluffs. Lieutenant Clark was on hand to debrief him. Crazy Horse sat in, gleaning the first substantive news from the hunting grounds. The Cheyenne declared he came from Lame Deer's camp. Three weeks earlier, the day after Crazy Horse's surrender, Miles's command had surprised the village on a tributary of Rosebud Creek. Lame Deer was killed, and sixty-three tipis, thirty tons of dried meat, and 450 horses were captured. Led by Lame Deer's son Fast Bull, the people were regrouping near the forks of Powder River, before "all Coming into this agency."[4]

The surrender would complete the diplomatic initiative demanded by Crook. Immediately, the war chief detailed three warriors to carry tobacco to Fast Bull. These envoys, Clark advised Crook, will "start at once to ascertain the facts and will exercise the utmost dispatch."[5]

The cooperation with Clark marked a deepening of the relationship between the two men. Although too wary to be friends, each recognized a mutual dependence. To the lieutenant, Crazy Horse was a key facilitator of peace. Crazy Horse understood that Clark's continued support was vital to the northern reservation scheme. As June opened, each cultivated the other. In particular, they discussed in detail the hunting expedition tentatively agreed to by Crook. Crazy Horse seized on the hunt as an essential stage in his diplomatic strategy. Escorted by troops to Cantonment Reno, Crazy Horse could secure approval for his agency location on Beaver Creek, locking in military support before traveling to Washington.

After a month at the agency, Crazy Horse believed he had the measure of the situation. Deepening cooperation with the army, enhancing his status as peace facilitator, was to be matched by forceful reminders of his latent military potential. Crook's aide Lieutenant Bourke observed that after the Cheyenne departure, "'Crazy Horse' daily grew more insolent and intractable, thinking perhaps that he could manage matters better to suit himself."[6] The departure of Mackenzie's battalion of cavalry reduced Camp Robinson to four hundred men, less than half its springtime strength. Lieutenant Clark would come to believe that Crazy Horse ascribed all kindness to weakness. In reality, the war chief was remaining true to his own concept of loyalty to the northern Lakotas, ensuring that Crook's promises did not slip from the schedule.

Having offered Clark assistance in inducing Lame Deer's camp to surrender, Crazy Horse needed to assert his autonomy. After the talk with Crook, the northern village moved to a new location on Little White Clay Creek, six miles northeast of the agency. Moreover, the plans for the Sun Dance were well advanced. In a move calculated to raise the political temperature, the village council decided to hold the ceremony, scheduled for the last week of June, north of White River. Participating bands would depart for the hunt after the ceremony.

In Lakota political geography, the course of White River demarked the independent domains of northern and agency bands. In effect, Crazy Horse was reclaiming the village primacy he had yielded to Red Cloud during the march to surrender. While agency leaders pondered a response, Crazy Horse's willingness to force the issue of northern autonomy was leading to tension within his village. A significant section favored a more accommodating manner. By late May, the moderate faction had found a forceful spokesman in Little Big Man. Though initially less influential than his fellow Decider Little Hawk, Little Big Man had begun to carve out an independent constituency. He would repeatedly polarize the village throughout the summer, challenging Crazy Horse as its key decision maker. At a date probably late in May, the two men quarrelled violently, recalled an infantry noncom at Camp Robinson. "I don't know what it was about, but at all events the two were deadly enemies from that time forward."[7]

Horn Chips did know "what it was about," and he revealed, "Crazy Horse in camp one time had forbidden L[ittle] B[ig] M[an] to sleep with one of the squaws. They got into a fight over it and were never friends after that."[8] After a campground altercation, Little Big Man "gathered his followers together and separating from Crazy Horse, established his camp at a point two miles up" Little White Clay Creek, nearer the agency.[9]

No further demonstrations followed until the next ration day. About to issue cattle to Crazy Horse, military agent Johnson was interrupted by the interpreter telling him that Little Big Man "had asked that his cattle be issued separately." Johnson asked the interpreter for advice, acutely aware that he must offend someone. Assured that he should accede to Little Big Man, the agent compounded his offense by serving the Decider ahead of Crazy Horse. The war chief "flew into a fury, refusing to accept his share, and [rode] back to camp, followed by his people."[10]

As the Moon When Ponies Shed closed, Crazy Horse was in no mood to smooth matters with either Little Big Man or the agent. He was strengthening his village, not just in raw numbers but in spiritual power. On May 29 the Spotted Tail agent authorized the transfer of Worm and four lodges to Red Cloud. Their number included the revered elder Human Finger and a Sans Arc Sun Dance priest, Foolish Heart, invited by Crazy Horse to coordinate the coming ceremony. During the first week of June, the northern village crossed White River to a new campsite three miles north of the agency. The responses to the Sun Dance–hunt invitations reveal much about Oglala politics a month after surrender. Of the five agency camps, two sent positive responses. Young Man Afraid of His Horse, of the Payabyas, and Yellow Bear, for the Spleen band, sent presents to the northern village, indicating that their bands wished to accompany the hunt.[11]

Young Man Afraid of His Horse represented a strand of the agency leadership that wished to reintegrate Crazy Horse's people into tribal life. By contrast, Red Cloud sought to marginalize the war chief and reduce his influence with the wasicu. Red Cloud seized on Crazy Horse's camp move as the justification he needed. Also disenchanted with the war chief was American Horse. Evidence from censuses suggests that Red Cloud and American Horse instructed their akicita to forbid all movements to Crazy Horse's village.[12]

On this note of unresolved tension began the second week of June. Beef issue was scheduled for June 9. While Crazy Horse continued to cooperate closely with Lieutenant Clark, he remained unprepared to conciliate the agency hierarchy. Butcher Ben Tibbetts had received a particularly good batch of beef cattle, weighing well above average. Tibbetts selected twenty-nine head for distribution to the northern village. Herders drove the cattle out of the corral, and northern akicita circled the herd to drive them homeward. Just then, Crazy Horse rode up, and in conversation with the warriors, objected that the village was used to receiving thirty-one head. Turning to Johnson and Tibbetts, Crazy Horse "refused to take the cattle, and ordered his braves to drive them back into the corrall [*sic*], which they accordingly did. In the meantime, a steer had escaped from another corrall. Crazy [Horse] saw it, and ordered it captured. He then ordered the twenty-nine turned out, and with the thirty head, he started homeward." Although Johnson "said he would take the extra steer out on the next beef day," he had been comprehensively outmaneuvered by the war chief.[13]

Lieutenant Clark was on hand but chose not to press the point directly with Crazy Horse. Clark was aware of the threat. "Some of the young bucks here are a little restless," he acknowledged to departmental headquarters, "and I also think the moral influence which was exercised by the great number of troops which were here is lacking to suppress the growth of any insubordinate feeling." Crazy Horse's cultivation of Clark evinced a rare degree of psychological acumen: indeed, Clark's low opinion of Johnson suggests that the war chief was astutely playing off the two officers.[14]

To civilian visitors, Crazy Horse continued to be welcoming. Later in the day of the beef issue, Richard and Clay Dear, brothers of the agency trader, took a party to the northern village. The visitors were welcomed by Crazy Horse, "seated on the ground . . . surrounded by his principal chiefs, who were in council." The war chief presented the party with a pair of moccasins. Richard Dear reciprocated with a "slight present," and the visitors returned to the agency pleased.[15]

On the following day, Sunday, June 10, Clark called a council to discuss the issue of Fast Bull's camp of fugitives. Crazy Horse, the northern leaders, and all the agency chiefs were present. Clark reminded the Lakota chiefs "that it is detrimental to their interests" to let the fugitives stay out, "particularly so if they dont come in before they [the agency delegations] go on to Washington." The leaders conferred and agreed that once the three northern scouts returned with positive news, the council would decide on a course of action. Clark continued to press the issue of proactive Lakota diplomacy and won a wary consensus around coercing the fugitives to surrender. If necessary, a united Oglala akicita would act to "bring them in[,] forcibly if they find it necessary."[16]

On June 13 the scouts returned from the north. At the invitation of the northern council, Clark had ridden out to Crazy Horse's village to discuss the latest developments on the hunt. The scouts reported that they had located Fast Bull's deserted campsite near the forks of Powder River and followed its trail for three days to the Blue Earth Hills. There they gave up the chase but confirmed the belief that Fast Bull was bound ultimately for surrender at either Spotted Tail or Cheyenne River. The scouts emphatically stated that no other Lakotas or Cheyennes remained on the hunting grounds.[17]

"The application to go out hunting was renewed," Clark reported; "they will want to start in about twenty five days." As for participating bands, most of the northern village, the Payabya and Spleen bands, and a few Kiyuksas would want to go from Red Cloud Agency—more than three hundred lodges. The mooted departure date of July 8, just after the close of the scheduled Brule Sun Dance, demonstrated that Crazy Horse expected substantial increments from Spotted Tail Agency. To help effect that, Clark continued to be a useful ally. Several days earlier, the lieutenant had asked Crazy Horse to accompany him to Spotted Tail. Compensation money for ponies confiscated from the Wazhazha band the previous October had come through to Camp Robinson, and Clark proposed to present it personally. "I . . . will take over one or two of Crazy Horses [sic] Band—perhaps that chief himself if he wants to go over," Clark had opined. At the council with Crazy Horse, the lieutenant announced his intention to ride to Spotted Tail the following morning. Although Clark's sketchy reports give us no follow-up detail, Crazy Horse likely made the trip.[18]

Clark's three-day visit to the Brule agency is the best context for two eyewitness statements that place Crazy Horse at Spotted Tail during the summer. The first recalls a visit paid by the war chief to the agency store of George Jewett. Twenty-year-old Susan Tackett, daughter of trader James Bordeaux, had driven to the store. Susan's Lakota mother-in-law

> pointed [Crazy Horse] out to me. He was a very handsome young man of about thirty-six years or so. He was not so dark. He had hazel eyes, nice long light brown hair; his scalp lock was ornamented with beads and hung clear to his waist; his braids were wrapped in fur. He was partly wrapped in a broadcloth blanket. His leggings were also navy blue broadcloth; his moccasins were beaded. He was above medium height and was slender.[19]

The vivid word picture describes a relaxed and confident Crazy Horse, enjoying the sort of intimate socializing that appealed even to his reserved nature. The second eyewitness pictures a very different Crazy Horse, working secretly to bolster northern Lakota solidarity. The war chief's principal purpose in visiting the Brule agency was to step up pressure on the Miniconjous and Sans Arcs to attend his Sun Dance and join the hunting expedition—over Spotted Tail's objections. Crazy Horse soon found the leadership divided. Now he went underground, privately urging known supporters to attend his Sun Dance. It was a high-risk strategy, and poor manners: detection risked ill feeling and a strain on northern solidarity.

Sure enough, a break came. One night, Touch the Clouds' family was disturbed by the chief's sister, wife of the Oyuhpe war leader Black Fox: "Crazy Horse had come to their tent and was trying to induce Black Fox to go North and . . . she objected and came to tell" her brother. Touch the Clouds was hosting a feast for some of the scouts. He led them to Black Fox's tipi nearby and rebuked the Oglala war chief for interfering with the smooth running of his village. Crazy Horse was forced to return home with his mission a failure.[20]

When Clark and Crazy Horse returned home on June 17, the village was undergoing the final preliminaries to the ceremony. Augmented by new arrivals from the agency bands, about 185 lodges formed the Sun Dance camp when it formally raised its hoop on June 22. Located on Spring Creek, the village was surrounded by clusters of satellite tiyospaye preparing to join the northern hoop.[21]

As a public pageant, the Sun Dance did not appeal to the war chief's heyoka introversion, but this year's ceremony was essential to his plans, and he surely sat with Foolish Heart and the ceremonial Deciders as the four holy days began on Tuesday, June 26. Early that morning, the village made a short move, pitching the formal ceremonial circle amid whirling dust storms and ninety-degree heat. Foolish Heart ordered a scouting party to locate the tree that would become the Sun Dance pole, the axis linking earth and sky. In the evening, the scouts returned to report a suitable tree had been found, and on the following morning, the whole village turned out to see the tree felled and brought home as a captive enemy. Accompanied by White Hat Clark, the people rode out in all their finery. It was a holiday atmosphere, and people paused to cut boughs and foliage with which to enclose the dance arbor, weaving garlands of clematis for themselves and their ponies, or leaf shields of green shrubbery—the vegetation that declared earth's renewal. Two miles out, the procession approached the cottonwood marked by the scouts. A cluster of old women gathered at the tree, dancing and singing as Foolish Heart ordered four of the bravest warriors and two virgins, resplendent in dresses bright with beading and elk-teeth ornamentation, to fell the tree.

As the first warrior advanced, he picked up an axe and recounted a coup, one of the great deeds of the Sioux War. He struck the tree a light blow and presented two sticks to the old women, vouchers for a pony apiece promised to the poor. His comrades did likewise, before the virgins stepped forward and struck the final blows to fell the cottonwood, as a great cheer went up from the hundreds of spectators lining the ravine. After the virgins had trimmed the fallen tree, a team of headmen, including the four Deciders and the head akicita, carried the pole on sticks to the first rest point. After the holy men had offered the pipe to the sun, the headmen tied the pole to a wagon. This innovation, doubtless proposed by one of the Little Big Man faction, attracted some grumbling.

Meanwhile, the effigy of an enemy man had been erected at the center of the campground. After the final rest a half mile out, all the warriors in the procession remounted and drew up in a line. At a signal, they raced wildly for the village, each man determined to be the first to strike the effigy, winning luck to strike the first coup of the following season. Clark climbed a hill to watch the pageant and the sham battle that was to follow. This year the battle had been planned to commemorate the Custer fight, with the northern village warriors reenacting their own roles. In a distinctly ill-considered move, the agency visitors were cast as Custer's force. As Clark watched the giddy race and the wild charges across the campground, he saw that the sham battle was threatening to become a real one.[22]

Down in the noisy, dusty circle, Billy Garnett was riding with the agency visitors. "When the fight was on," Billy recalled, "instead of striking the Custer party lightly as was usual[,] some of the others struck their opponents with clubs[,]and war clubs [give] hard blows."The agency men became "enraged [and] they opened fire with their revolvers on the other side and drove them out of the dancing camp."At that moment, Clark galloped up. Shouting orders, he "stopped the firing and prevented what might have been a serious affair."[23]

Although no overt act would disturb the rest of the ceremony, the sham battle revealed the growing bad blood between agency and northern Lakotas.As the ceremony climaxed on June 29, Lieutenant Colonel Bradley was a privileged guest. He took his seat with two thousand Lakotas to see the final stages of the ritual. At 2:00 P.M. all the dancers underwent the ordeal of "being cut on the upper arm in half a dozen places so that it would bleed freely, and afterwards [were] painted all over in the most fantastic style."The dancers were then "decorated with chaplets of leaves with feathers on the sides." Only three men had actually pledged to undergo the full self-torture, but late in the proceedings, four more volunteered.These men were "adorned with the most elegant war-bonnets."[24]

The seven pledgers, already weak from fasting, were visibly daunted by their ordeal. Foolish Heart and other holy men encouraged them with whispered exhortations as they applied paint or rubbed their hands with sacred sage. By this time, the arbor was filled with spectators, and the dance area itself was busy with processions of women bearing kettles of steaming food or piles of blankets and cloth to give away in the name of honored children. A line of female relatives, filled out by selfless sweethearts, formed to allow the holy men to cut their arms as a gesture of solidarity with their loved ones. At length, the leading dancer was led forward and laid on his back, where he waited as Foolish Heart knelt and pierced his breast with a knife, running skewers through each cut and, as the dancer stood, securing them by thongs to one of the ropes hanging from the pole. Drummers beat out a faster tempo as the other six dancers followed, blowing shrill notes from their whistles and holding looking glasses to the sun as they began the steps of the dance.[25]

With all their strength, the dancers "commence[d] their effort to tear themselves loose, dancing and surging back on the ropes with the whole might of their bodies." One dancer freed himself within fifteen minutes; for the rest, the ordeal lasted another hour. Clark "saw one Indian throw himself back with all his force and might, but he could not tear himself loose; he had to wait for a slight decay of the muscles. One or two were very weak-kneed, heart-sick with fear and fasting; and if I ever saw regret, it was on their painted faces."[26] Another dancer "fainted dead away at the pole, and the rope was torn out by his friends to save his reputation."[27] As each man broke free, he was led to a seat at the back of the arbor. The exhausted were carried on blankets to the sacred tipi, where the holy men "kindly and carefully cared for" them.[28]

The drama of captivity, transcendence, and liberation was ended. As the sun sank on June 29, Crazy Horse may well have reflected on the spiritual metaphors he had seen enacted. After the unpropitious opening, the ceremony had united northern and agency Lakotas. But the unity looked dangerously thin. The climactic day saw two thousand people gather in the dance arbor—an impressive gathering, but less than half the total Lakota population at Red Cloud. With a projected departure for the hunting grounds only nine days away, Crazy Horse could not afford to let up in his drive to unite the Lakota people behind the northern reservation scheme. Early the following morning, he departed for Spotted Tail Agency, to lend his presence to the two Sun Dances being organized there.

The new agencies had already been located by bureaucrats unconcerned with Lakota wishes. The imperatives of Sheridan and Sherman and of Indian Office cost-cutting on transportation neatly dovetailed with Dakota Territory boosters determined to win lucrative reservation contracts. Members of the Board of Indian Commissioners had ascended the Missouri River to scout locations early in June. They advised that a site for Spotted Tail's people had been fixed at the mouth of Whetstone Creek—the hugely unpopular location abandoned only six years earlier. Meanwhile, the "agency for Red Cloud's band of Indians has been selected at the mouth of Yellow Medicine River on the banks of the Missouri River." A collision course had been set.[29]

23

BUYS A BAD WOMAN

Midsummer was the peak of the Lakota ceremonial year, and three other Sun Dances were scheduled on White River. Despite the best efforts of agency leaders, each dance highlighted the supreme charisma of Crazy Horse. At Spotted Tail Agency, the Miniconjou and Sans Arc leadership had conceded Spotted Tail's rejection of the Crazy Horse Sun Dance, but when they organized their own ceremony, the central drama was co-opted by kinsmen of the Oglala war chief. The brothers Kicking Bear, Black Fox, and Flying Hawk, all wartime comrades of Crazy Horse, underwent the self-torture to offer prayers for him. Another cousin, Fast Thunder, was selected to make the piercings. As the dance climaxed on June 30, Crazy Horse appeared to mingle with the crowd and to sit with the holy men as his cousins fulfilled their pledges.[1]

Crazy Horse's departure from Red Cloud spelled collapse for a third ceremony, sponsored by the agency Oglala bands. Few people appeared at the dance ground, and the ceremony had to be abandoned. After the spectacular pageant at Crazy Horse's village, this was a serious embarrassment to the agency chiefs.[2]

The Brule leadership had scheduled their own Sun Dance to open about July 1, inviting bands to attend from both agencies. Brule invitations to cohost their ceremony offered a face-saving alternative to the Oglala leadership, and a great gathering assembled at the crossing of Chadron Creek. Crazy Horse and his retinue were again in evidence. Renewing his efforts of two weeks earlier, Crazy Horse prevailed on key headmen to accompany him to the Oglala agency in time for the projected hunt departure on July 8. None of the northern Deciders would agree to leave the Brule agency, but Black Shield, fretting at his loss of influence on the reservation, agreed to join Crazy Horse. Two other Miniconjou headmen, Wounded Hand and High Lodge, agreed to the move. Black Fox, still recovering from the scars of his own Sun Dance vow, also accepted the war chief's tobacco. Most significant of all, in this hoop that proclaimed the strength and unity of the

Lakota people, Crazy Horse won over Elk Head. The Sans Arc holy man was the Keeper of the Sacred Calf Pipe, most revered of Lakota sacred bundles, and a living embodiment of Lakota sacral values. Although only twenty-three lodges of Miniconjous, Oglalas, and Sans Arcs followed him, in moving the Calf Pipe to the northern Oglalas, Elk Head transferred supreme religious sanction to the Oglala war chief and the hunting expedition in the north.[3]

At Red Cloud Agency a new civilian agent had assumed control on July 1. Dr. James S. Irwin would oversee Oglala affairs for the next eighteen troubled months. Irwin was unimpressed at his first meeting with the war chief. Crazy Horse assumed his gauche manner, and Irwin concluded, "[H]e is but a bashful girlish looking boy." Faced with the defections from Spotted Tail, Irwin saw no threat. He approved the transfer on July 7, over the initial objections of the Spotted Tail agent.[4] The transfer raised Crazy Horse's strength again, to about 250 lodges. Of these, some 140 were Oglala; their guests approximated 45 lodges of Miniconjous, 40 of Brules, and 25 of Sans Arcs. Crazy Horse's village was now the strongest band at Red Cloud Agency.[5]

Reorganization of the Indian scouts also secured Crazy Horse's status. All scout enlistments expired on June 30, but Lieutenant Clark had prepared to strengthen and streamline the system. Beginning July 1, Clark oversaw new enlistments. The scouts were reorganized into five companies, three serving at Camp Robinson, two at Camp Sheridan. Each company was commanded by nine noncommissioned officers—one first sergeant, four sergeants, and four corporals—drawn from the recognized chiefs and headmen. Company A, chiefly comprising Arapahos, was commanded by Sharp Nose and the ranking Arapaho chiefs and men's society leaders. Agency Oglalas formed the majority of Company B, to whose leadership Clark promoted Little Wound as first sergeant. Major chiefs Red Cloud, Young Man Afraid of His Horse, Yellow Bear, and American Horse served as his sergeants.

At Spotted Tail, Brule chief Swift Bear assumed command of Company D, while Company E was formed around the leadership of the northern village at Spotted Tail. Touch the Clouds was named as first sergeant, with the two Sans Arc Deciders, Red Bear and High Bear, as sergeants. However, the process of integrating agency and northern Lakotas was reinforced in the command hierarchy at Spotted Tail. Brule leaders Two Strike and Whirlwind Soldier completed the complement of sergeants in Company E.[6]

The Spotted Tail Agency enlistments underlined the relatively smooth integration that characterized political life there. Spotted Tail had made no secret of his opposition to Crazy Horse throughout the summer, as the Oglala war chief poached disaffected Miniconjous and Sans Arcs from the Brule agency. After the Sun Dance, officers recognized that a "little rivalry" existed between Crazy Horse and Spotted Tail, about "who shall have the largest following of the northern Indians."[7]

The organization of the third scout company at Red Cloud gave the greatest concern to agency Lakotas unhappy with the preferment of Crazy Horse. The thirty-seven privates of Company C were fairly evenly divided between northern and agency warriors, including such Clark trusties as the brothers Charging Bear, Bear's Foot, Woman Dress, and No Neck—all sons of old chief Smoke and identified with the Red Cloud interest. The command structure of the company, however, was organized around the leadership of the northern village. On July 4, upon his return from Spotted Tail's Sun Dance, Crazy Horse was reenlisted as first sergeant, while the village Deciders Little Hawk, Little Big Man, Big Road, and Iron Crow were all enlisted as sergeants. Herald Iron Hawk and akicita leaders He Dog, Four Crows, and No Water served as corporals.[8]

Moreover, the integration of agency and northern contingents reinforced Crazy Horse's influence. Clark's effective demotion of Red Cloud threatened a power vacuum that a determined man might exploit. Red Cloud's suspicions of the war chief's intentions were deepened by the corrosive corruption of jealousy. Rumor even had it that General Crook would use the Washington trip to have Crazy Horse recognized by the president as head chief of the Oglalas. Although Camp Robinson commander Bradley assured General Crook that "Clark [has] done extremely well in this business and I think he is entitled to much credit for his good sense and patience," the jealousies created by the scout reorganization only deepened the potential for critical factionalism on White River. Some of the intermarried community believed that too much leeway was being given Crazy Horse.[9]

At a scout meeting held in Clark's quarters at Red Cloud one week later, the layout of the room vividly illustrated these issues. Seated "on the rim of an office chair, with his feet on the seat, high enough to see and be seen," Clark addressed his audience in fluent sign language. Seated in an arc on the office floor, thirty sergeants and corporals passed the pipe. Red Cloud was notable by his absence but, in a second chair close to Clark's desk, Crazy Horse occupied a position unmistakably elevated above his fellow officers.[10]

With both Red Cloud and his own Company C sergeants absent, Crazy Horse was as aware as Clark was of the theater of space and hierarchy. His occupancy of the chair asserted a strong self-belief in his supremacy among the Lakotas, and was a clear statement of his parity of status with Clark. For the moment, supremely assured in his own leadership, and confident in the implementation of Crook's springtime promises, Crazy Horse continued to place that highly symbolic chair beside the lieutenant. But as the second week of July opened and departure day neared, that confidence would be shaken and his self-assurance would begin to be undermined. Crazy Horse would not again relax in easy trust of his own willpower and wasicu promises.

Affairs in the distant East ensured that the long-deferred diplomatic schedule would stall and founder. The year 1877 was critical one of labor agitation, and in July the season climaxed with a railroad strike and rioting in Chicago. Preoccupied with civil unrest, the Hayes administration stalled the Lakota delegation trip. General Crook was summoned to join army chiefs of staff for emergency talks on the national crisis. Crook would not return to the West until the final days of August. His departure put on hold the White River delegation for critical weeks.

The projected hunting expedition had been conceived as immediately preceding the trip to Washington. As the delegation timescale slipped, so did army support for the hunt. The schedule was further delayed when Lieutenant Clark was called to Fort Laramie on detached service, leaving Camp Robinson for eleven days beginning July 16. The departure date of July 8 had already slipped from the schedule. Just before Clark left, he and Bradley met with Crazy Horse and the Lakota chiefs at Camp Robinson. After explaining the circumstances, insisting that only a modest delay was involved, the two officers succeeded in reassuring the chiefs. They then proposed a new twist to the long-delayed schedule: "We have advised them," Bradley wrote Crook, "to defer [the hunt] until the return of the delegation from Washington," reversing the original sequence.[11]

The northern Deciders chose not to contest the decision. Since hunting operations were the specific preserve of the Deciders, Crazy Horse registered no open complaint. But as the days stretched into the second half of the month, the war chief began to feel some misgivings about his easy acquiescence. Short Bull recalled that the issue of the trip east began to sour at this point: "This was the only cause of misunderstanding at the time. Crazy Horse wanted to have the agency established first, and then he would go to Washington. The officers wanted him to go to Washington first. The difference of whether Crazy Horse should go to Washington before or after the site of the agency was settled upon brought on all the trouble little by little."

Short Bull's brother He Dog recalled pressing Crazy Horse to accept the new schedule. With a hint of impatience, the war chief replied, "First, I want them to place my agency on Beaver Creek west of the Black Hills. Then I will go to Washington—for your benefit, for my benefit, and for the benefit of all of us. And that is the only reason why I will go there."[12]

Crazy Horse had begun pondering the case of the Cheyenne exile to Indian Territory. Reflecting on the Washington trip, he feared that if he traveled east "before the site of his agency was settled upon, the authorities might try to intimidate him into signing a transfer of his people to Indian Territory."[13] It is impossible to gauge how much this apprehension arose from Crazy Horse alone and how much was insinuated by Lakota rivals. Certainly, the latter were now exploiting the relocation issue to marginalize and discredit the war chief. By July key agency leaders were jealous of the attention afforded Crazy Horse. Civilian visitors continued to seek Custer's conqueror. Clark's preferment of the war chief only honed the unrest. Little Killer suggested that agency chiefs like Red Cloud fed Crazy Horse's doubts. "When Crazy Horse first came to Fort Robinson, he wanted to go to Washington. But other Indians were jealous of him and afraid that if he went to Washington they would make him chief of all the Indians on the reservation. These Indians came to him and told him a lot of stories."

Rumors of arrest and punishment resurfaced. As if that were not enough, the tribal consensus for a northern agency evaporated in July. While still opposed to the Missouri River relocation, Red Cloud and other leaders favored a compromise site near the forks of White River, within the existing reservation. Undermining Crazy Horse's position, they assured the new civilian agent that the site was acceptable to most Oglalas.[14]

The new mood of suspicion, and the communication vacuum following Clark's departure, began to overshadow village solidarity. After advising Crook on the sixteenth that "We are as quiet here as a Yankee village on a Sunday," Bradley conceded that undercurrents were evident: "Crazy Horse and his people say nothing about going on the hunt, at present, *though they may take a notion to start at any time*" (my emphasis).[15]

For the moment, the war chief chose not to press the issue. Crazy Horse repeatedly told comrades, "I came here for peace. No matter if my own relatives pointed a gun at my head and ordered me to change that word I would not change it." His close working relationship with Clark clearly gave him confidence in the fulfillment of Crook's promises. The takeover by the new civilian agent also seemed to bode well for affairs at Red Cloud. Bradley reported that the Indians "appear to like [Dr. Irwin] and he seems disposed to make them satisfied and contented," concluding, "I think he will succeed here."[16]

After his return to Camp Robinson, Clark also paid tribute to the new agent. "Dr. Irwin makes a superior agent, conservative and yet sufficiently firm."[17] Irwin completed a new census before the end of July, on which rationing could be more fairly based. Although Irwin recognized that "'Crazy Horse' and his northern band of Indians were not so well disposed," the public mood was upbeat. Crazy Horse would find little support for a premature break with the authorities.[18] But another unexpected factor underlay the war chief's sitting out of events. In the most startling development since surrender, Crazy Horse had fallen in love.

Between the agency compound and Camp Robinson stood a cluster of cabins and fifteen Cheyenne lodges. Flanked by two or three ragged lodges housing widowed relatives and their dependents stood the cabin of Joe Larrabee. Fifty-year-old "Long Joe" had spent much of his life with the Cheyennes, moving to the reservation from Colorado after the treaty of 1868. By his two wives, Joe would father nine children. The teenage sons, Philip and Alex, were already old enough to be noted by name in the agency census. Joe's four daughters went unnamed, classified anonymously as "adult females" or "children females," but Helen, the second daughter, was a handsome girl of eighteen.

To the family she was Nellie, to Lakota acquaintances, Brown Eyes, but as she entered marriageable age, she remained a girl of daunting self-will—flighty, flirty, and widely admired, with a string of suitors haunting the Larrabee dooryard. Gossip even placed White Hat Clark among the callers. Another of the besmitten was Little Bear, a Loafer band Oglala whose nickname Sioux Bob reveals he inhabited the same multiethnic bilingual community as the Larrabees. Long Joe looked with some favor on Sioux Bob's suit and had accepted gifts preliminary to a bride price for Nellie. Whatever Nellie's feelings in the matter, Sioux Bob considered himself betrothed.[19]

Just when the paths of Crazy Horse and Nellie Larrabee crossed is unknown. That unsatisfactory fact actually demonstrates an important truth: the courtship was conducted with some discretion. Speaking to Judge Eli S. Ricker thirty years later, Billy Garnett touched on the couple's first meeting, but Ricker's syntax immediately grows opaque with Victorian propriety. The meeting may have been at some public gathering: beef-issue day was an opportunity for beauties to promenade and young men to show off their riding skills. Whatever the circumstance, Nellie fixed on Crazy Horse her "captivating gaze." To a man used to the shy glances of proper Lakota girls, that forthright stare was unsettling—and thrilling. True to Crazy Horse's reserve, however, the relationship would not be carried on in the public eye. Instead, by early July, Crazy Horse was making discreet evening visits to the Larrabee household. Crazy Horse even had kinsmen drive several ponies across the river and up to the Larrabee door. When Joe had his boys drive them in with the family herd, it was clear that Sioux Bob had a serious rival in the matrimony stakes.[20]

A Lakota marriage was not contracted in isolation. Conservative Lakotas could be prim, and many of the war chief's followers disapproved of the affair. Crazy Horse took a pipe and consulted his most trusted advisers—who confirmed the negative assessment. But Crazy Horse was already in too deep. Before Lieutenant Clark left Camp Robinson, Crazy Horse met him for an informal chat. When the subject of Nellie arose, Clark teased his first sergeant, encouraging the relationship. Realizing that a period of courtship and domestic bliss could mellow Crazy Horse, Clark sought to counter the arguments against the marriage. According to Baptiste Pourier, Clark positively persuaded Crazy Horse to go ahead and marry Nellie.[21]

For Crazy Horse the courtship neutralized but did not remove the political issues at stake. During the third week of July, these issues snapped into focus. "[N]early all of [Crazy Horse's] leading men with their friends partially separated from his band," stated Agent Irwin in his monthly report.[22] Revealingly, the initiative did not lie with the preoccupied war chief. As he continued to raise his objections to traveling to Washington, more moderate voices began to argue against him. The principal articulator of the moderate line was the man emerging as his archrival: Little Big Man argued persuasively for accepting the new schedule. He also began to echo the suspicions voiced by agency leaders opposed to Crazy Horse, insinuating that if he went east, Crazy Horse might be arrested and killed for his notoriety as leader in the Custer battle. Such rumors awoke the paranoia Crazy Horse had felt before surrender.[23]

When Crazy Horse continued to express doubts about the new schedule, Little Big Man again led a significant section of the village nearer to the agency. The separation remained, in Irwin's phrase, only "partial." No open break had occurred to rupture solidarity irretrievably. Such movements could always be rationalized as for better pasture, or fresh water: reunion was anticipated, and everyone took care not to force a premature crisis.

Events late in the month showed the wisdom of moderation. The return of Lieutenant Clark suggested a firm timetable might soon be forthcoming. And new developments in the tortured negotiations with Fast Bull's camp of fugitives indicated an imminent surrender. Over July 22–23 nine lodges, mostly Sans Arcs, surrendered at Spotted Tail. They had left Fast Bull's camp on the upper Moreau River, waiting "to hear how they were received." If satisfied, Fast Bull "will come in immediately[;] if not he will cross the Missouri River and join 'Sitting Bull.'" On July 25 Agent Lee dispatched three Miniconjou messengers northward, predicting Fast Bull's imminent surrender.[24]

Crazy Horse could conclude that the diplomatic process should now accelerate and approval of the Beaver Creek site follow speedily. With significant differences between him and Little Big Man removed, the two camps reunited in a single village during the last week of the month. War chief and Decider agreed once more to submerge their personal differences and, in a symbolic gesture, donated their family tipis to build a new council lodge for the village.

On the morning of Friday, July 27, Crazy Horse's confidence seemed well founded. Lieutenant Clark returned from Fort Laramie and immediately invited the chiefs and headmen to hear a message from General Crook. Some seventy headmen took their seats in the agency council room. Crazy Horse and Little Big Man sat beside Red Cloud and the agency leaders, a row of warriors at their backs. Dr. Irwin was invited to attend, accompanied by Indian Office Inspector Benjamin R. Shopp. Shopp's report summarizes a crucial council and its aftermath. First, Clark read out the message from Crook. The general

> had promised that the Indians should go on a Buffalo Hunt. He was about to redeem that promise, and all who wished to might start as soon as they could make the necessary arrangements and be absent about 40 nights, then to return to the Agency. He would exact from them, however, certain terms. They were to go on the Buffalo hunt, conduct themselves peaceably and all return at the time agreed upon. Permission had also been obtained from the Hon. Secretary of the Interior for 18 Indians to visit Washington, D.C. with a view of presenting their grievances as to the contemplated change of the Indian Agency to the vicinity of the Missouri River. They should select their best and strongest men for this mission and not go for their own gratification merely but for the protection of their interests, and seek an interchange of views as to what would ultimately result to their good. They were expected to be in readiness to leave there by the 15th of September next. An opportunity was then given for an expression of their views either approving or disapproving the order, but no feelings of disapprobation were mani-

fested. During the reading of the message or the delivery of the "talk" or explanation of the Lieutenant, they were apparently pleased.

A feast had also been promised to them as was customary on the assembly of councils. Young-man-afraid-of-his horses suggested that the feast be had at the lodge of Crazy horse, and his partner Little-big-man. No oral objections to this proposition were made, although Red Cloud and one or two others left the room. Dr. Irwin promised to issue an order giving them three cattle together with some coffee and sugar, as soon as they should determine to whom it was to be issued. The council then adjourned.[25]

When the headmen left the compound and mounted their ponies, Crazy Horse had every reason to be pleased. His belief in Crook's promises at last seemed vindicated. The hunting expedition had been restored to the top of the schedule. Crook had authorized an early departure date: the hunting expedition could leave for the north no later than August 5, only nine days hence. Final details needed to be hammered out, but for Crazy Horse, the peace process was back on track as he crossed White River and headed homeward.

More disturbing was the early departure of Red Cloud and his band headmen. Young Man Afraid of His Horse's proposal that the northern village host the tribal feast continued his efforts to integrate Crazy Horse and the northern leadership into the smooth running of agency life. Red Cloud had served notice that he and the Bad Face band had withdrawn support for that policy, and later that evening, Red Cloud sent two messengers to call on Dr. Irwin and explain his rationale. First explaining that they "represented Red Cloud and several other bands," the visitors launched into a sustained attack on Crazy Horse before asserting

> that there was considerable dissatisfaction among them as to the proposition to hold the feast with Crazy Horse. He having but lately joined the agency it was but right and a matter of courtesy for him to come to them, and they were not disposed to go to him, as such action indicated a disposition to conciliate him. He had always been regarded by them as an unreconstructed Indian, he had constantly evinced feelings of unfriendliness towards the others, he was sullen, morose and discontented at times, he seemed to be chafing under restraint, and in their opinion was only waiting for a favorable opportunity to leave the agency and never return. The time had now come. Once away on the hunt, he with his band of at least 240 braves, well armed and equipped, would go on the war path and cause the Government infinite trouble and disaster. The other Indians these men represented, had no confidence in him. He was tricky and unfaithful to others and very selfish as to the personal interests of his own tribe. The ammunition that would be furnished to them would be used for the destruction of the whites, against whom they seemed to entertain the utmost animosity.[26]

It was a bitterly partisan account. With just enough grounding in reality for plausibility, it reflected the alarming deterioration in relations between Crazy Horse and Red Cloud. When Red Cloud's messengers left Irwin's quarters, they had begun a systematic campaign to discredit Crazy Horse with the agent. They left an indelible impression on Irwin, coloring all his subsequent dealings with Crazy Horse and the northern village. Shopp's subsequent conversation with the agent showed that, while he doubted the ostensibly "friendly attitude" of the northern village, Irwin had as yet no significant personal dealings with Crazy Horse sufficient to confirm or refute the Bad Face spin. Red Cloud's bid to marginalize his perceived rival was now operating on a dual front. Playing on the war chief's insecurity, he was trying to force Crazy Horse's withdrawal from the Washington trip, neutralizing him as a diplomatic player. Red Cloud opened a second front by eroding Crazy Horse's credibility with the civilian authorities. Although Red Cloud's aims were confined to maintaining his own edge as principal Oglala chief, no one could say where the intrigue would end.

Unaware of Red Cloud's escalation of the intrigue, Crazy Horse had every reason to be satisfied with developments as the council with Clark closed. With the hunt restored to the top of the agenda, the following day brought more encouraging news. At the regular ration issue, Black Shawl and other claimants were issued new tickets. Having completed his revised census, Dr. Irwin had authorized ration increases of 15 percent—increases that went some way toward alleviating the northern village's repeated demand for an increase in the beef ration.[27]

Lieutenant Clark also received instructions from General Crook on the 28th, lifting restrictions on sales of ammunition. Indians preparing for the departure of the hunting expedition could stock up on powder, lead, and fixed ammunition. The stores of J. W. Dear and Frank Yates prepared to order new supplies. Influenced by Red Cloud's assessment of the hunt question, Irwin was reluctant to cooperate with the new military directive and advised his superiors of his concern.[28]

24

MANY BAD TALKS

August, the Moon of Black Cherries, opened auspiciously at Red Cloud Agency. The northern village was in better temper than at any time since the surrender. Even Crazy Horse's suspicions were allayed by the announcement about the hunt: Billy Garnett recalled that the war chief seemed "well satisfied" by the latest developments.[1]

Busying itself with the preparations for the hunt, the village was in a happy hum of activity by August 1. Farewell feasts were announced to assure agency hosts of the northern village's intentions to return in time for the delegation's mid-September departure for Washington. On the 1st of the month, Lieutenant Clark reported to Crook that he had received invitations for no fewer than three such feasts.[2]

From Washington, authorization for the trip east finally arrived. The Indian Office wired Crook on August 2, asking the general to "select a delegation of 15 or 20 Indians from Red Cloud and Spotted Tail Agencies [to be sent] to Washington under charge of Agent Irwin, or some suitable army Officer."[3] Instructions were promptly wired to Camp Robinson. The news coincided with the lifting of the ban on ammunition sales, and the two trading stores opened for a day or two of boom business. In the agency council room, Clark hosted another talk and read Crook's telegram aloud. It met with measured approval, although the Oglala leaders were emphatic that a larger group should be authorized.[4]

Aware of the need to field a representative body of leaders, Clark advised that the recognized band chiefs form the core of the delegation. Addressing the issue of northern village representation, Clark proposed Crazy Horse and Little Big Man as the obvious candidates. This too was accepted quietly. As the meeting broke up, Clark held an informal talk with the northern leaders. At their request, he went over the telegram's main points again, explaining it "kindly and fully."[5] Crazy Horse's party then rode home to make their final plans for the journey north.

Several hours earlier, in the northern village, Crazy Horse's Miniconjou kinswoman Iron Cedar Woman noticed a strange woman walking across the campground. Crazy Horse's tipi skins were rolled up, and Black Shawl was inside, sewing. The stranger entered and spoke quietly to Black Shawl. To the intense interest of village gossips, Nellie Larrabee had arrived and entered a long conversation with her lover's wife.[6]

In the month or more of courtship, the one unknown quantity had been Black Shawl's attitude to her husband acquiring a second wife. Nellie forthrightly told Black Shawl of the depth of feeling between her and Crazy Horse. However divided might be her feelings, Black Shawl decided not to stand in the way. Despite medical care from the Camp Robinson surgeon, her respiratory sickness lingered and she nursed a painfully swollen arm. She generously told Nellie that a new wife might "enliven [Crazy Horse's] spirit." Black Shawl would offer no objection if Crazy Horse wished to bring home a second wife.[7]

Black Shawl's generosity of spirit was matched by Nellie's courage and determination. Aware of the opposition to her marrying the war chief, Nellie may have feared that the first thrilling weeks of courtship were stalling into impasse. Later in the afternoon, the northern leaders returned from the agency. As Crazy Horse tethered his pony, Nellie stepped out of the door place, and to the war chief's surprise, she told him she had won Black Shawl's consent to their match. A little abashed, Crazy Horse accepted the unorthodox proposal and awkwardly told Nellie to move in her gear. As the gossips watched agog, Nellie reentered the tipi. For the next thirty days, she would be Crazy Horse's second wife.[8]

On the following morning, Nellie's father and mother appeared in the northern village. After some words with their daughter in her new home, they returned to announce the news to her worried brothers and sisters. For the moment, Long Joe decided to accept his daughter's headstrong fait accompli, but he was disgruntled with the development and made no secret about the agency of his displeasure.[9]

Within a day or two, Crazy Horse's goodwill was placed under sudden and serious strain. On August 5 a message from Lieutenant Clark arrived at Spotted Tail Agency instructing military agent Lieutenant Jesse M. Lee that all Indians who desired could join the hunting expedition with Crazy Horse's village. Immediately, the Brule leadership moved to quash the plan. Upon leaving the agencies, Spotted Tail contended, the northern Indians might resume hostilities, or even make a break to join Sitting Bull in Canada.[10]

Spotted Tail and Swift Bear pressed Touch the Clouds and the northern Deciders at Spotted Tail Agency to postpone the hunt. Since the delegation was due to leave in six weeks, this amounted to cancellation. At Red Cloud, the agency leadership also favored deferring the hunt, asserting the overriding importance of formulating a united tribal position to present in Washington. Even Young Man Afraid of His Horse, key agency supporter of the hunt, agreed on the preeminence of diplomacy.

At Crazy Horse's village, though, plans for departure were already complete. One newspaper report indicates that Yellow Bear and part of the agency Spleen band, also committed to the hunt project, were readied for departure. Fulfilling Crook's schedule, on August 5 the Deciders led a short move to Little Cottonwood Creek.[11] Seven miles north of the agency, the campsite was squarely on the trail to the hunting grounds, skirting the edge of Hat Creek Bluffs before angling northwest toward Warbonnet Creek and the crossings of the South Cheyenne.

But now word was received from Touch the Clouds that his village would not join the northern Oglalas on the hunt. At the same time, Clark began renewing his invitations for talks on the Washington trip. He made at least one personal visit to the village. Crazy Horse told him that "he wanted to do right, but wanted plenty of time to consider" the delegation matter. Clark decided not to press Crazy Horse for an immediate decision, "hoping that the influence of his head men might be sufficient."[12]

Further messages followed up Clark's visit, inviting the northern leaders to private talks at his quarters at Camp Robinson. Little Big Man and the other Deciders, in formal control of the hunt operation, rode to the post, but Crazy Horse, recalled Billy Garnett, "did not like this arrangement." Yet another delay was added when the army paymaster visited Camp Robinson and all scouts were invited to draw their back pay on August 7. Again Crazy Horse refused to attend. Concluding that protracted talks were indefinitely deferring departure, Crazy Horse told the village council that "he wanted to go on with the hunt" immediately.[13] He repeatedly declined Clark's invitations, still refusing to state categorically whether or not he would go to Washington. In a bitter play on words, the war chief told Clark's messengers that he "was not looking for any Great Father [the President]. *His* father was with him and there was no Great Father between him and the Great Spirit."[14]

The message harked back to wartime rhetoric. Dissatisfied with delay, Crazy Horse began to listen to voices that reawakened all the old suspicions of wasicu intentions. Images of arrest and even death, first kindled in the days preceding surrender, returned to haunt him.

Clark asked Frank Grouard to pay a call on Crazy Horse and "do what he could" to talk him around. Grouard found his old friend grimly resigned, as in the days after the death of They Are Afraid of Her. Crazy Horse told Grouard he had woken from a dream in which he stood on a mountain peak and watched an eagle soar far above him. Suddenly, the eagle folded its wings and fell dead at Crazy Horse's feet, its body pierced by an arrow. In the vivid super-logic of dream, Crazy Horse knew the eagle was himself, and told Grouard "he was looking for death and believed it would soon come to him."[15]

The dream shook him, its memory disturbing his sleep patterns. Nellie Larrabee became a key influence during these critical days. She confirmed Crazy Horse's deepening paranoia, telling him the delegation was a trick, that once in the government's power, he would be imprisoned and never allowed to return.

Although later historians have been quick to discredit Nellie, imputing a bewildering mix of malign motivations, she was only repeating the gossip of the intermarried community at Red Cloud, gossip that had its roots in newspaper stories, off-the-record talks around Camp Robinson, and the spin placed on events by a Byzantine array of political factions. Rumor it may have been, but we shall see that much of Nellie's suspicion had a strong grounding in reality.[16]

Nellie's intervention marked the beginning of a new phase in Crazy Horse's alienation. Hitherto, the voices discouraging him from going to Washington had been those of political rivals. Now his closest associates and relatives also urged withdrawal. His Miniconjou uncle Spotted Crow advised Crazy Horse that "going to Washington is only a decoy. They want to get you away from us and then they will have you in their power." Another uncle, Black Elk, concurred with Nellie's analysis and even brought over his son-in-law, half-breed John Provost, to supply supposed inside information. An enlisted scout demoted from sergeant in the July reorganization, Provost confirmed Black Elk's claims, stating that Crazy Horse would be imprisoned if he went east, perhaps on an island in the sea.[17] Aware of the fates of southern plains war leaders, incarcerated in a Florida prison since the Red River War in 1875, Crazy Horse grew ever more suspicious.

But Clark, as well as Agent Irwin and Lieutenant Colonel Bradley, only pressed the issue harder. Clark primed the more tractable Deciders and akicita leaders to bring around the war chief. Irwin did the same with agency leaders, which only deepened Crazy Horse's distrust of Red Cloud and the other chiefs.[18]

Crazy Horse had always resented this sort of pressure, retreating into silence. He Dog, one of Clark's go-betweens, remembered, "after a while Crazy Horse became so he did not want to go anywhere or talk to anyone."[19] After a visit to Red Cloud, Major George M. Randall observed that Crazy Horse was being "talked to too much, but if they would let him alone and not 'buzz' him so much he would come out all right."[20]

But the "buzzing" only got worse. Crazy Horse was also aware that not all Clark's runners were messengers. About midmonth, the lieutenant asked a few of his most trusted Oglalas to watch the war chief. Woman Dress, a cousin of Red Cloud's serving in Crazy Horse's scout company, had a plausible pretext for loitering in the northern village. Woman Dress, the brothers Lone Bear and Little Wolf, and Frank Grouard operated as Clark's key informers. Little Wolf began to visit regularly the tipi next to Crazy Horse's, paying court to the daughter of the lodge and, holding her in the chaste embrace of the Lakota suitor, listening with one ear to the conversations next door.[21]

From now on, Crazy Horse's nerves would suffer from exhaustion both mental and physical. The war chief's behavior echoed the profound mood swings of the previous winter, but the cycle of resignation and furious activity began to spin faster, its troughs deeper and its peaks more frenzied and desperate. Tensions deepened in midmonth. A military rethink on the hunt issue resulted in a War Department directive rescinding Crook's permission for the agency traders to sell ammunition to the Indians.[22]

Realizing that the hunt was becoming a dead letter, Crazy Horse prepared to notch up his opposition to the delegation. Many followers began to feel disquiet at their war chief's intransigence. A slow drip of defections began during the second week of August, as the moderate began to consider seriously the option of attaching themselves to the bands of agency relatives. Red Cloud in particular stepped up appeals to kin to leave the northern village ahead of a final reckoning.

The first defector of significance was Crazy Horse's old comrade He Dog. Already nursing serious misgivings about the war chief's alienation, He Dog was asked by Clark to extend a personal invitation for Crazy Horse to come with him to the post. He Dog was hurt when Crazy Horse was pointedly absent from home, and "felt bad" when, upon finally contacting the war chief, Crazy Horse flatly turned down the invitation. Nevertheless, Crazy Horse was not simply evasive or negative. For Clark's information, he reformulated to He Dog his position on relocation: "If they would have the agency moved over to Beaver Creek, then he would go to Washington as they asked him." But He Dog felt snubbed and ordered the lodges of his Sore Backs tiyospaye struck. As Red Cloud's nephew, He Dog had the strongest ties with the agency hierarchy. Moving across the White River valley, the Sore Backs pitched camp near his uncle.[23]

After ten days of withdrawal and reflection, Crazy Horse was ready to launch one of his intense bursts of activity, seeking to formulate a strategy that could shape events rather than merely react to them. When a new invitation from Bradley asked Crazy Horse and Little Big Man to attend talks at post headquarters, the war chief accepted the tobacco—perhaps another gibe at Clark's expense. On August 15 Crazy Horse and Little Big Man rode to Camp Robinson. Bradley reiterated, "the Great Father at Washington had sent word to them that he wanted them to come and see him. 'Little Big Man' immediately gave his consent to go, but 'Crazy Horse' would give no satisfactory reply as to what he would do."[24]

Bradley was left still in doubt about Crazy Horse's intentions. He telegraphed departmental headquarters that Crazy Horse "refuses now" to go to Washington, leaving open the possibility that after further deliberation he might agree to go east.[25] This only restated the position taken ten days before. But Crazy Horse's actions show that he was now pursuing a dual strategy. In meeting Bradley, he was appeasing the moderate wing of the northern village, and buying time with the military authorities.

Yet immediately upon return to camp, Crazy Horse began implementing his second line of strategy. As evening drew on, he invited twenty trusted followers to a private talk where the war chief outlined his plan. Under cover of darkness, the party, headed by Two Lance, was to make the forty-mile journey to the northern village at Spotted Tail Agency and invite Touch the Clouds and the other leaders to move their camp to unite with Crazy Horse on Little Cottonwood Creek. As dusk deepened, the envoys left the village "secretly" and slipped quietly east.[26]

As private messengers of the war chief, Two Lance's party represented the first clear-cut break in the village organization. Crazy Horse was now willing to risk the delicate accord between him and the Deciders. Crazy Horse was willing to act unilaterally in a high-risk strategy that he calculated would force matters to a head. As always, that strategy was rooted in uniting the two northern villages. Such a union would create a joint village of about four hundred lodges, fielding a warrior force of over five hundred fighting men—a force that could shape events on White River. Then, Crazy Horse might finally force a resolution of the impasse stalling the fundamental question: relocation to the hunting grounds.

Crazy Horse would already have been aware of what threatened to become a crucial factor in the situation. The Oglala agency bands were preparing to form a united tribal village to facilitate debate over the Washington trip and to formulate a single tribal policy on the new agency location.[27] All too aware that union might lead to compromise, or even the acceptance of an agency site on the hated Missouri River, Crazy Horse felt the need for allies who would staunchly uphold the northern reservation scheme. He must have awaited anxiously the return of Two Lance's party.

During the day, August 16, the messengers returned quietly from Spotted Tail Agency, piecemeal like a defeated war party. At a hurried night council, distinctly not the done Lakota thing, Touch the Clouds and the other Deciders had given the messengers "a very cool reception."[28] Crazy Horse's tobacco packages were returned unopened. Just what reasons the Miniconjous and Sans Arcs gave Two Lance is unreported. But at the Brule agency, the hunt was already a dead issue. On agency location, the Brules had agreed to retain the existing site, naming Wounded Knee Creek, farther down the White River valley, as a fallback position. A northern site was emphatically not on the Brule agenda. Spotted Tail was determined to present a united Brule front in Washington and was already pressuring northern leaders to toe his line.[29]

As further inducement, a special annuity distribution for the Miniconjous and Sans Arcs had been scheduled for August 20, only five days away.[30] If Touch the Clouds moved his village to join Crazy Horse, he would jeopardize his people's receiving the blankets, clothing, and domestic implements they still badly needed after the winter's privations. Village consensus favored no intemperate action in accepting the Oglala war chief's tobacco. Crazy Horse could expect no support from the Miniconjous and Sans Arcs.

On August 17 all Oglala and Arapaho leaders were called to Red Cloud Agency and addressed by both Agent Irwin and Lieutenant Clark. Clark read aloud the latest telegram from Crook, stressing that Crazy Horse was requested "particularly to go" on the Washington delegation. Reporting to Crook the following day, Clark stated:

> I explained to [Crazy Horse] that in addition to the other interests involved, you wished him to come on with the others and work with you in regard to

their Agency and, if possible, prevent any undesirable change. That the President wanted him to come and you were anxious to have him go; that it was important and necessary for us all to work earnestly and honestly together in the matter &c &c.[31]

Crazy Horse remained silent through all this. The discouragements of the previous day had eroded whatever remained of his patience with the niceties of diplomacy. Red Cloud's leaders, their cooperation taken for granted, were restive as Clark and Irwin continued to press for Crazy Horse's agreement. At the close of business, Irwin gave the war chief a voucher to collect two extra beef cattle. Drawing on the Camp Robinson stores, Clark presented the northern leaders with more provisions with which to hold a feast and "talk over the matter and decide" on their representatives. As the council closed and the agency chiefs filed out of the building, the lieutenant once again spoke briefly with Crazy Horse and the northern leaders, inviting them to attend his quarters at Camp Robinson the following day and give their decision.

No record exists of the talks held later that day in the northern village, but a deconstruction of Clark's account of the next day's proceedings reveal that Crazy Horse clearly dominated the debate. Invoking his status as Oglala tribal war chief, he claimed the right to a final say on the composition of the delegation. Little Big Man and the other Deciders chose not to press the matter. Neither did they seriously challenge Crazy Horse as he proceeded to make a still more startling claim: that he could veto the delegates of the agency bands, not only here at Red Cloud but at Spotted Tail Agency too, and personally nominate their representatives. Reflecting the military context of the next day's talk, with only Clark representing the wasicu, Crazy Horse was nominated sole speaker for the party.

The following morning, a large group of northern leaders and warriors rode into Camp Robinson and was welcomed to Lieutenant Clark's quarters. Crazy Horse alone spoke. Contrasting with the temporizing and silence of the previous two weeks, the war chief spoke forcefully and at length. For the first time he declared flatly that he would not accompany the delegation east, saying that "he had no business with the Great Father and he would stay with his people and take care of them," according to one account.[32]

"I am not going there. I wanted to go, but you have changed my mind. . . . Still deep in my heart I hold that place on Beaver Creek where I want my agency. You have my horses and guns. I have only my tent and my will. You got me to come here and you can keep me here by force if you choose, but you cannot make me go anywhere that I refuse to go."[33] Instead, he continued, he had "brought up the men he had selected to go." Moreover, he wished certain of the key agency chiefs—singling out Red Cloud, Spotted Tail, and Little Wound—to be "thrown away": only the men Crazy Horse had named, mostly northern leaders, should be accredited as delegates. On relocation, Crazy Horse told Clark that he "had already said where he wanted his Agency, and if [the officials in Washington] wanted to know anything more, these men would tell them &c."

Clark was taken aback, but he replied "kindly but firmly," explaining that the broad composition of the delegation was already agreed on, and would consist of the recognized chiefs. This, continued Clark, "was a matter that [Crazy Horse] could only decide for himself" and his own village. The northern Oglala village "was only a small part of the total" at the White River agencies, Clark continued. Red Cloud, Spotted Tail, and the Arapaho Sharp Nose were Crazy Horse's equals and would attend the Washington summit. Then, reviewing the previous day's talk, the lieutenant told the war chief that "he had been asked if he would work with the President and [General Crook] in this matter[,] and I wanted to know if he would do so."

The tension must have been palpable as Crazy Horse replied, "I have already stated I am not going." The talk stalled. Crazy Horse left before Clark held his customary private talk with Little Big Man and the other Deciders. Sounding out their opinion, Clark found the Deciders guarded about criticizing the war chief, but he was convinced they "are all right, and dead against him in this matter."

Clark was still surprised by Crazy Horse's intransigence several hours later, when he sat down to report in detail to Crook the events of the past few days. After two weeks of gathering impetus, a profound shift had crystallized in Clark's thinking. From viewing Crazy Horse as a key facilitator of peace with the Lakotas, he now perceived the war chief as the main obstacle to stable relations. The mood of uncertainty in the northern village, and the emergence of rivals to leadership such as Little Big Man, made this an auspicious time to attempt a political coup. Crazy Horse's "power could be easily broken at the present time," he asserted, fatefully concluding, "and I believe it necessary." Only force, he concluded, "will work out a good condition in this man's mind; kindness he only attributes to weakness." Reluctantly abandoning his cherished belief that "any Indian could be 'worked' by other means," Clark reiterated that "absolute force is the only thing" for Crazy Horse. Clark's ego bruised by what he saw as Crazy Horse's deception, he was henceforth firmly opposed to any conciliation of the war chief.[34]

After the council of August 18, Clark saw the way forward for the northern village as the removal—in effect the arrest and imprisonment—of Crazy Horse and the recognition of a moderate leader as his successor. In the subtext of his report's conclusion lay the assumption that delay in Crazy Horse's removal would necessitate even more drastic measures if hostilities were to be averted.

The aborted talk between Crazy Horse and Clark was a turning point for Lakotas too. After August 18, friction worsened between Crazy Horse and the Deciders. Crazy Horse's misjudgement on the delegation vetting issue was all too plainly the sign of a mind, unbalanced by sleep loss, losing its purchase on Lakota realities—or else obsessively determined to force a crisis at all costs. The majority of the northern village took the pragmatic view that no departure from the agency should take place, at least until the return of the delegation from the East. In the week following the final talk with Clark, some of the Deciders and akicita leaders began paying regular visits to Agent Irwin's office. They complained that Crazy Horse's "dictatorial manners, and disregard for the comfort of his people" were causing great dissatisfaction in the northern village. Moreover, they were disturbed by Crazy Horse's "want of truthfulness" in the last round of talks with the officers at Camp Robinson.[35]

Irwin's sympathetic reception of the Deciders encouraged the moderate wing of the village to distance itself from the war chief. During the same week, another break took place in the village. On August 25 Irwin drafted his annual report and advised the Indian Office that "the leading men of [Crazy Horse's] band . . . have drawn off from him . . . [stating that] they are determined to carry out their promise to General Crook, and their original intention to obey orders and keep the peace."[36]

These events demonstrated the changing fortunes of the Deciders. At surrender Little Hawk had been recognized as the most influential of the Deciders, but the widest sway was now enjoyed by Little Big Man.[37] The war chief's rival had become the most politically visible player in northern affairs after Crazy Horse himself. From mid-August, relations between the two men would terminally deteriorate.

Little Big Man attempted to build a united front with the other Deciders. Easiest to persuade was Big Road. This Oyuhpe band Shirt Wearer had until surrender paid no recorded visit to the agencies. Nevertheless, his record as sergeant of scouts had impressed the officers at Camp Robinson with his prudence and moderation, and he was a kola to Little Big Man. The two friends "had agreed to walk the white mans [sic] road together."[38]

Of the other two Deciders, Iron Crow was warily amenable to the moderate line. Leader of a tiyospaye of intermarried Hunkpatila and Oyuhpe Oglalas, with strong marriage links to the Miniconjous, Iron Crow was reckoned as the Decider with the widest influence after Little Big Man.[39] As the fourth Decider, Little Hawk was in a difficult situation. His instincts were less suspicious and hostile than those of his brother's son, and he would have been under intense pressure to adhere to a united front with his three peers. But to the Lakotas, kin solidarity was all, and Little Hawk surely remained loyal to Crazy Horse when the other Deciders ordered tipis struck. A significant section of the northern village followed Little Big Man three miles southeast, camping on the north side of White River opposite the mouth of Little White Clay Creek. Both sides took care to mask the cracks in village unity. Moderates stressed to Irwin that the separation was "partial," and by implication temporary. Both sides clearly hoped soon to reabsorb the other peacefully.

Two related events, about August 20, supplied the immediate causes of the village break. Lieutenant Clark finally issued a directive cancelling the hunting expedition. The Oglala agency bands formed their united tribal circle.[40] Clark's order forced Crazy Horse to raise the stakes once more. By now an unmistakable battle of wills was under way between the two men. The memoir by Spotted Tail agent

Jesse Lee, though partial and self-serving, is nevertheless insightful in its reading of the Clark–Crazy Horse relationship. Although Clark was "successful in almost every move" in his determination to control affairs at Red Cloud, Lee observed that he was "overreached by the wily Crazy Horse, whose unfettered will would consciously brook no mastery."[41]

The ban on the hunt demanded an equivalent response if Crazy Horse was to reassert his "mastery" of the situation. Crazy Horse had hitherto accepted the reality of the delegation to Washington, however much he might seek to dictate its agendas. After the hunt announcement, Crazy Horse withdrew all support for the delegation, and pursued a policy of total noncooperation with the military and the civilian agent. Crazy Horse issued orders to the northern villages at both agencies, forbidding participation in the delegation. The Deciders referred to this new twist in the war chief's attitude as his "dictatorial manner," and Crazy Horse's withdrawal of even minimal courtesies from the agent and his personnel—refusing to "touch the pen" to receipts for rations, for instance—were cited as instances of his "small regard" for his people's comfort, provoking the moderates to break away soon after August 20.[42]

The formation of the agency Oglala camp circle posed an even more serious challenge to Crazy Horse's mastery of events. Counting approximately 575 lodges, its strength was over twice that of the northern village. For the first time that summer, Crazy Horse could be dominated by a united Oglala tribe.[43]

In the great council shade, the huge gathering of chiefs and warriors debated for more than a week the key issue: agency relocation. The Oglala chiefs wanted a united tribal line on which to negotiate with the officials in Washington. Unity, however, was no foregone conclusion. Of the five major bands of agency Oglalas, four had originally favored the northern agency scheme. During the Sun Dance season, American Horse, ever the political realist, and Red Cloud, jealous of the attention accorded Crazy Horse, had withdrawn support of the Loafer and Bad Face bands. Young Man Afraid of His Horse's Payabya and Yellow Bear's Spleen bands continued to support the hunt. In early August, therefore, a significant section within the Oglala tribe remained conciliatory to Crazy Horse and the interests of the northern village.

Two significant new factors were now in the equation. The journey to Washington was less than one month away, and pressure was intense to iron out band differences and formulate a tribal policy on relocation. Second, Crazy Horse had just made his extraordinary claim to nominate delegates for all bands at both agencies, "throwing away" as chiefs Red Cloud and Little Wound, his key political opponents at the agency, into the bargain. One cannot underestimate the effect of this insult in uniting the agency bands against Crazy Horse. As reports of the war chief's defiance multiplied, and he ignored repeated invitations to attend the tribal council, a consensus emerged for either retaining the existing agency or locating farther down the White River valley, within the boundaries of the Great Sioux Reservation. Reluctantly, Young Man Afraid of His Horse withdrew support for Crazy Horse's unilateral stance; a nervous Yellow Bear, too, removed his Spleen band contingent into the tribal circle. In deference to the President's status as "Grandfather" to the Lakota people, the Oglalas would allow him and his great council the final say on the exact location of their agency. The Oglala delegation to Washington would not support a northern homeland.[44]

Crazy Horse would attend no talks with such an agenda. What is more surprising is that, even after the village break, Little Big Man and other moderates did not attend the tribal council. Little Big Man had not given up the goal of a northern agency. The moderate faction began to formulate a compromise solution, arguing not for a simple return to the nomadic life on the hunting grounds, but for the separate reservation promised them by General Crook, where they could be issued cattle, seed, agricultural tools and equipment, and be trained toward self-sufficiency for the changing times ahead.[45]

The political initiative had slipped away from Crazy Horse. After the fevered activity of midmonth, the war chief was reduced to another of his deadlocks. The vagueness of the Deciders' statements to Irwin indicates that Crazy Horse had no concrete plans, beyond his absolute opposition to the delegation. With continued pressure from the agent, the military, and the agency Oglalas, Crazy Horse's following might have completely unravelled during the last week of August and Lieutenant Clark's goal been peacefully achieved—effective deposition of the war chief and complete village control transferred to the moderate wing.

On Saturday, August 26, however, intelligence reached White River that passed back the initiative to the war chief. The sequence of events had begun ten days earlier and three hundred miles northward, when startling news reached Colonel Miles's headquarters at Tongue River Cantonment: "Sitting Bull has had a disagreement with British authorities, recrossed the line, and reached the Milk River. If he crosses the Missouri River, I will endeavor to use my force against him."[46]

This intelligence, gleaned from sources Miles regarded as trustworthy, had no relation to any facts. For over two weeks, however, it would keep military telegraphers busy. By the time Sheridan finally laid it to rest in a September 9 wire to the adjutant general in Washington, the rumor had reaped a whirlwind at the White River agencies.[47]

Thirty-one Lakota scouts, serving on upper Tongue River with a battalion of the Fifth Cavalry, were ordered home on August 20. With tension building on White River, General Crook wished to concentrate loyal scouts in case of an outbreak. But the scouts' return on the twenty-sixth only heightened tensions. They brought with them the "news" of Sitting Bull's return from Canada, and the update that the Hunkpapa war chief was definitely "coming south to his old home" in the Powder River country.[48]

The two factions of the northern village were reunited by the report. Startled by the development and anxious at renewed rumors of preemptive pony confiscations, Crazy Horse's camp struck its lodges and joined Little Big Man's moderates on White River. Although the hardline faction had made the move, some people saw trouble ahead and wanted no part of it: two lodges slipped down to the agency and won Irwin's permission to transfer immediately to Spotted Tail; some more quietly attached themselves to the Oglala tribal village.[49]

Defections were minimal, though, as Crazy Horse hurried to reimpose total control. Although our sources are uniformly biased against the war chief, it is plain that Crazy Horse seized on the news of the Hunkpapa return to the hunting grounds, arguing that a prompt departure from both agencies could reunite the Northern Nation in time to make fall hunts.

In the words of intelligence reports reaching Lieutenant Colonel Bradley's Camp Robinson headquarters, Crazy Horse had "become hostile" during the days immediately following August 26.[50] Such terms are loaded. The inherent bias of the sources requires them to be critically assessed. There is no real evidence that Crazy Horse advocated actual hostilities: as the August 31 showdown with Lieutenant Clark would show (see chapter 25), he still justified his actions in terms of the pledges made to him by Crook and the agency leaders in the weeks leading up to surrender. The "hostile" charges were loaded with all the spin that Crazy Horse's detractors could apply. But to assert that the accusations were simply trumped up, blackening the name of an impossible innocent, is to read the sequence of events with the false naivety of the apologist. Crazy Horse would state in open council on the thirty-first that he intended an immediate departure for the hunting grounds.[51]

Crazy Horse's return to domination of village affairs in the week leading up to September 2 demonstrates that formal primacy in the village had been transferred back to the war chief.[52] This might be a merely symbolic action in normal times, but the highly charged atmosphere on White River clearly implies that this transfer followed an intense power struggle with Little Big Man. As tensions escalated with the military, elders normally wary of intemperate action were concerned to place the village under strong protection. All these factors were in play as the northern village council declared martial law, with the war chief in supreme authority.

Crazy Horse invited a carefully chosen group of war leaders to form the blotahunka, supplanting the peacetime council for the duration of the military threat. He nominated Black Fox, another Oyuhpe Shirt Wearer, as his chief lieutenant, empowered to act as village chief in case of Crazy Horse's absence. The elevation of Black Fox, a July transfer from Spotted Tail Agency, was a clear indication of Crazy Horse's determination to marginalize Little Big Man and the moderate wing. His bypassing of the constituted akicita is indicated by the key roles played in the next few days by members of his Last-Born Child Society bodyguard.[53]

Crazy Horse pressed ahead with plans for an imminent departure. On Wednesday, August 30, "information was received" at Camp Robinson that Crazy Horse and his warriors were now ready to "decamp and join Sitting Bull."[54] Lieutenant Colonel Bradley and his staff debated earnestly the measures to be taken to prevent a new Sioux War. By grim synchronicity, yet another wild card had been dealt that day. After news that the outbreak of Nez Perce Indians from their home in the Pacific Northwest had spilled onto the Montana plains, Lieutenant Clark had ordered the commander of scout Company C, first sergeant Crazy Horse, to prepare for action in the north.

25

PUTTING BLOOD ON OUR FACES

The Nez Perce war posed a new and unexpected crisis for Military Division of the Missouri chief Phil Sheridan. Eight hundred Nez Perce Indians, resisting relocation to an Idaho reservation, had led Department of Columbia troops in a fighting retreat through the Rockies. Early in August they crossed the Continental Divide and entered Sheridan's military jurisdiction. Sheridan moved to mobilize troops from the departments of Dakota and the Platte. General Crook, in the East for most of the summer quelling labor riots, was ordered back to his Omaha headquarters.[1]

Sheridan wired the Department of the Platte to ready the Fifth Cavalry for action. Regimental commander Colonel Wesley Merritt was ordered to Camp Brown, overseeing the Shoshone reservation in central Wyoming. Five companies of the regiment were ordered ready to entrain west. Another five companies were on detached service, patrolling the upper Tongue River in the aftermath of the Lame Deer campaign. Sheridan advised Omaha to order battalion commander Major Verling K. Hart to move his patrol west to the Bighorn River.[2]

Sheridan was also keen to learn the dispositions of the Lakota and Arapaho scouts enlisted at the White River agencies. He was disappointed when Omaha wired that Crook had ordered home Hart's complement of scouts just one week earlier. On August 28 Sheridan advised Crook, then still in Maryland, to order one hundred scouts to rejoin Hart immediately. Early on the 29th, Omaha wired Camp Robinson to ready the scouts, following up with a request for yet more Indian auxiliaries. For First Sergeant Crazy Horse and the northern Lakotas, a fateful series of events was now in motion.[3]

In a series of rapidly arranged consultations, Clark and Bradley sounded the agency Oglalas and the Arapahos throughout August 29 and 30. Sharp Nose, first sergeant of scout Company A, assured the officers of total Arapaho cooperation.[4]

PUTTING BLOOD ON OUR FACES

An encouraging reaction was also received from the agency Oglala chiefs. The chiefs expressed concern that active service might postpone the delegation's departure for the east. Clark wired Omaha to request authorization to defer the Washington trip. Sheridan responded that the delegation could not be delayed. Despite the confusion, Clark was confident enough in the Oglalas to leave final negotiations to agency personnel. By afternoon of the thirtieth, the Oglalas stated that, besides enlisted scouts, one hundred volunteers were willing to join the campaign. Clark ordered the Oglalas and Arapahos to be ready to move immediately, and an evening departure from Red Cloud Agency of 150 scouts was predicted.[5]

Not all was going according to plan. Spotted Tail, although no longer enrolled as a scout, had to be consulted over Brule participation. At Red Cloud on the thirtieth, he stalled talks with Clark over details of pay and conditions. Before the issue could be resolved, Spotted Tail departed for home, leaving Clark and his superiors in doubt over Brule participation.[6]

Spotted Tail's conspicuous loyalty meant that Clark could not openly criticize the Brule chief. Not so with the northern leadership, however. Like Spotted Tail, northern Deciders had been summoned to counsel with Clark. Touch the Clouds and High Bear rode to the Oglala agency on the twenty-ninth. Over the next twenty-four hours, it became clear that Clark wished sixty scouts from Spotted Tail to go fight the Nez Perces. This announcement caused "hubbub and excitement among the Indians," recalled Agent Lee. In particular, the "northern Indian scouts did not take to this measure with much zest."[7]

The northern Lakotas perceived their scout duties as performing traditional akicita functions: keeping order in the village and acting as peace envoys in the ongoing dialogue with the Lame Deer holdouts. Touch the Clouds told Clark's messengers, "The Great Father has washed the blood from our faces, if we put it on again we will never take it off."[8] Nevertheless, Touch the Clouds agreed to meet Clark and discuss the situation the following day. First, he rode into Crazy Horse's village to try to patch up relations and to forge a united bargaining position.

Touch the Clouds found Crazy Horse's village in intense debate. Early that morning, the council had declared its readiness to depart immediately to join Sitting Bull on the hunting grounds. The arrival of Clark's messengers asking that Crazy Horse and twenty Company C scouts join the Nez Perce campaign resulted in a protracted debate that would last all day. Asked to accompany the scouts and troops, Crazy Horse's initial reaction echoed that of Touch the Clouds: "You have asked us to become peaceful, how can you ask us now to go to war again?"[9]

Yet as afternoon wore on, the mood of the northern council began perceptibly to turn. Little Big Man focused debate, but Crazy Horse also shifted from a purely obstructionist position, as he grasped that his desire for an immediate departure could be dovetailed with Clark's proposal. If northern warriors agreed to serve as scouts, the war chief concluded, that could serve as "an excuse which [Crazy Horse] thought would enable him to get away and go north"—not as a pursued fugitive, but as a valued ally of the United States.[10]

Crazy Horse immediately sought to reopen diplomatic relations with the agency bands. In a characteristic burst of energy, Crazy Horse did "all in his power to induce other Indians, (especially the enlisted scouts,) to accompany" the departing northern village.[11] Messengers linked the issues of the hunt and the campaign, urging that all scouts depart for the war zone with the northern village. Crazy Horse contended that American troops were unable to fight against Indian enemies, and that the scouts should be free to employ their own tactics. Crazy Horse's envoys deployed enough finesse to keep the talks going into the following day.

A united line was forged between Crazy Horse and Touch the Clouds late on the thirtieth. Crazy Horse would demand an unprecedented salary raise for combatant scouts: "thirty-five dollars a day for himself and each of his men," as Red Feather remembered, illustrating how debate had shifted to fine detail. Although he remained uncomfortable with the concept of combat duty for his scouts, Touch the Clouds tentatively approved the Crazy Horse plan. A message was dispatched ordering Company E scouts to come to Red Cloud, ready for orders.[12]

They also agreed on the broad substance of the next day's speeches. Clark would be told that both northern villages were ready to depart immediately on the hunt. Once on the hunting grounds, scouts and additional volunteers would assist the troops in rounding up the Nez Perces. With this bottom line agreed on, chiefs and warriors returned to their family tipis. Touch the Clouds could congratulate himself in mending fences with Crazy Horse, and on helping bring a note of realism into the northern Oglala council after five days of brinkmanship.

In a life characterized by enigma and misunderstanding, few events have been so misrepresented as Crazy Horse's meeting with Clark on August 31. Misunderstanding began with the context of the talk itself. There is no evidence to indicate that Clark had specifically scheduled a meeting with Crazy Horse at all. Although Crazy Horse's personal intentions regarding the scouting project remained unclear to the lieutenant, and the planned departure of scouts on the previous evening had not taken place, by the morning of the thirty-first, Clark was reasonably confident of the cooperation of most Red Cloud Agency scouts. He had invited Touch the Clouds and High Bear to approve scout Company E's participation in the Nez Perce campaign. Crazy Horse's presence was simply as a guest of his kinsman Touch the Clouds. The Oglala war chief was empowered to speak in support of the solidarity of the two northern villages, but his role in the talk was conceived as secondary.

A twenty-man party of northern Lakotas left the northern village early on the morning of the thirty-first. The fact that most were Crazy Horse's own young men—including bodyguard members from the Last-Born Child Society—indicates that, whatever the formal status of the party, the Oglala war chief was asserting his own presence. At 9:00 A.M. they were ushered into Clark's quarters, taking seats on the floor of his office. Touch the Clouds, flanked by Crazy Horse and High Bear, sat in front of the arc of warriors, facing Clark's desk: the chair so often occupied by Crazy Horse stood empty as Clark, accompanied by Frank Grouard, as interpreter, and Three Bears, representing the agency Oglala village, entered to open the proceedings.[13]

Through Grouard, Clark proposed that the scouts go north to help fight the Nez Perces. Touch the Clouds rose to make the keynote response, reviewing events since surrender in an "earnest and forcible speech."[14]

"We washed the blood from our faces," he began, carefully echoing his first response to Clark's messengers, "and came in and surrendered and wanted peace." He went over the assurances of the Great Father and General Crook that had promised "absolute peace" to the northern Lakotas. Now he and his people were asked "to go on the war-path, a thing which he violently condemned as a breach of faith." Asserting his own record of loyalty since surrender, he reminded Clark that he had been ordered first to

> give up his gun and he did it; then it was to enlist as a scout to keep peace and order at the agency, and he did that; then he was asked to throw away the buffalo hunt and he did that; then like a horse with a bit in its mouth, his head was turned toward Washington, and he looked that way; now the Great father, the "Gray Fox" (General Crook) and "White Hat" [Clark] *put blood on their faces and turned them to war.*

Touch the Clouds stressed his unhappiness at this course of events: "You ask us to put blood on our faces again, but I do not want to do this," he continued, turning to acknowledge his guest as he added, "Neither does Crazy Horse. You," he reproached Clark, "enlisted us for peace." Both he "and Crazy Horse had been *deceived* and *lied to*," and this "latest plan of yours is hard medicine." Nevertheless, underlining the northern Lakotas' consistent record of loyalty, both he and Crazy Horse would reluctantly "*do as 'White Hat' said*, and war it would be! They would *all* go north and fight," he contended, demanding that the scouts fight under their own leaders. "We will surround the Nez Perces," Touch the Clouds concluded, "and whip them and then there will be peace all around."

The Miniconjou sat down to a "hou" of approval from Crazy Horse, and the Oglala war chief arose to make a briefer speech.[15] In accordance with his guest status, Crazy Horse at first confined himself to reaffirming Touch the Clouds's statements:

> The big chief, Gen. Crook, sent out word to us that if we would come to the Agency we would be well treated, and should live in peace and quiet. We believed him, and we came in with our hearts good to every one; and now we are asked to put blood upon our faces and go on the warpath, almost in the same breath with the request to go on a mission of peace to Washington.[16]

Crazy Horse stressed that when he surrendered to Clark in May, "it was with the understanding that he would never have to make war against any nation," and that he had not intended to go "back on that agreement."[17] Now, however, Clark and the wasicu insisted that he fight *for* them.[18]

With substantive speeches made, Clark now hoped to begin dialogue, but the hunt issue immediately raised its head. Clark repeated his direct question: would Crazy Horse assist the military in the north against the Nez Perces? Crazy Horse responded, "I was going out there to hunt."[19] This statement, followed by an increasingly heated exchange between the war chief and the lieutenant, soon reduced the talks to a shambles of argument. What was really said, and—even more important—what was understood by the two speakers, their interpreter, and the other Lakotas in the office?

Fundamental is that Crazy Horse made an unambiguous statement that the northern Oglala village would leave on its hunt imminently, "that he didn't intend to stay any more and would leave at once."[20] According to Clark, "[Crazy Horse] told me that he did not like the country about here, that he never promised to stay here, and that he was going North with his band, that he had made up his mind and was certainly going."[21]

Clark asked how the Indians could make a successful buffalo hunt with ammunition sales closed. Crazy Horse allegedly replied that "he was going out, and that if ammunition was not issued or sold him he would break the doors open [of the agency trading posts] and take it himself." Although this statement may reflect the distortion of Grouard's mistranslation, by this juncture in the conversation, Crazy Horse's manner (less easy to misrepresent) was already "very overbearing and insulting" to Clark.[22]

Although not yet present at the talk, Billy Garnett's summary of this stage of the council seems fair: Crazy Horse "talked very badly" to Clark, Garnett stated less than a year later. "He said he would not go out with the troops, but that he would move out slowly with his entire village and when overtaken would help to fight the Nez Perces."[23] Although the tenor of debate was rapidly deteriorating, Crazy Horse continued to offer the quid pro quo: permit the hunt and he would cooperate in the scout scheme.

Clark told Crazy Horse "he must remain where he was."[24] He insisted "he didn't want the lodges and women; that he just wanted the men."[25] At this point the council reached a crisis. With Clark flatly refusing to permit the northern villages to leave on the hunt, Crazy Horse taunted Clark, "[I]f the White man could not conquer his enemies, he could do it for him. *But if any went North they would all go*" (my emphasis).[26]

As temperatures rose, Grouard began to mistranslate statements by Crazy Horse and Touch the Clouds. Grouard was flustered, less than competent as interpreter, and by his own account frightened at the course the interview was taking. The personal motivation behind his mistranslations remains unclear, but the actions of

Three Bears suggest that Oglala factions determined to discredit Crazy Horse wished to ensure that dialogue between the war chief and the army totally broke down. Perhaps Grouard had been reluctantly persuaded to assist in disrupting proceedings.[27] Grouard was now twisting key statements. Already, according to one account, he had mis-represented Touch the Clouds by stating that the Miniconjou said that "if it was insisted that the Indian scouts take part in the Nez Perce war they would join the Nez Perces and fight the soldiers."[28] Another remark by Crazy Horse was misrepresented: "Crazy Horse could see that the Government wanted to fight and that he would go back to his village and the Government could send troops and kill them all."[29]

These statements do not seem to have unduly disturbed Clark. Perhaps he had added a judicious pinch of salt of his own to Grouard's words. But as the talks degenerated into a duel of wills between the lieutenant and the war chief, Grouard's distortions became more serious. Camp Robinson surgeon McGillycuddy, not an eyewitness, stated that Crazy Horse concluded his remarks to Clark by stating, "We are tired of war; we came in for peace, but now that the Great Father asks our help, we will go north and fight until there is not a Nez Perce left."[30]

If this was indeed the climax of the council, it is significant that this late in the proceedings Crazy Horse—whatever his manner—was willing to concede to Clark the principal point of the whole talk: the military cooperation of the northern Lakotas. But Grouard misinterpreted again, according to McGillycuddy's information, telling Clark that Crazy Horse said, "We will go north and fight *until not a white man is left!*"[31]

The room was in chaos. Crazy Horse and Clark were furious with each other, and Grouard was badly frightened. Into this tinderbox, Three Bears now chose to throw his own fuse. Picking up the theme of killing, Three Bears asserted that Crazy Horse and his party were planning to murder Clark. As scout Company B corporal, and first war leader of the Oglala Kiyuksa band, Three Bears was one of Clark's most loyal and distinguished trusties. He sprang up from the floor and roared at Crazy Horse that "if he wanted to kill anybody, to kill him, as he would not be permitted to kill his (Three Bear's [sic]) friend, that not one of the conspirators would get out of the building alive if they raised any trouble, that the place was full of armed soldiers, ready to do their share of the killing."[32]

"Considerable confusion followed the speech of Three Bear[s], and Crazy Horse did not seem to know what to do."[33] Grouard concluded that the situation was now "too hot" for him. He slipped out of Clark's quarters and, meeting Billy Garnett, told him to take over the interpreting.[34]

Clark told Garnett to ask Crazy Horse once more if he would not go out with the scouts and serve against the Nez Perces. Garnett crossed the room to engage in a brief private conversation with the war chief. He could see that Crazy Horse was "not right." In the minutes following Three Bears's outburst, Crazy Horse had come to a new decision. When Garnett asked him if he would serve with the scouts, Crazy Horse answered unequivocally, "Hansni, No." As Garnett remained at his side, Crazy Horse explained to the interpreter, "I told him [Clark] what I want him to do. We are going to move; we are going out there to hunt." Turning to address the lieutenant through Garnett, he taunted Clark, "You are too soft; you can't fight."

Clark sought to explain that the new war on the hunting grounds foreclosed any possibility of hunting, but Crazy Horse cut him short: "If you want to fight the Nez Perces, go out and fight them; we don't want to fight; we are going out to hunt."

His patience worn away, Clark snapped, "You cannot go out there[,] I tell you." Even as Garnett framed the interpretation, Crazy Horse turned to his warriors and remarked, "These people can't fight, what do they want to go out there for? Let's go home; this is enough of this." Crazy Horse rose, and Touch the Clouds, High Bear, and the rest followed him from the office.

Clark wasted little time in alerting Lieutenant Colonel Bradley of the depth of the crisis, as he perceived it. "Crazy Horse and Touch-the-Clouds with High Bear came up and told me that they were going north *on the war-path*" (my emphasis).[35] This summary statement represents the situation as Clark understood it. Although it reflects Grouard's distortion of the two chiefs' repeated statements about leaving on the hunt, it is worth pointing out that most of the more lurid embroideries ascribed to Grouard are not mentioned. Perhaps Clark was able to reach a more measured understanding of the situation from Garnett. Nevertheless, the situation could not be plainer. Although willing to assist in the Nez Perce campaign at the start of the interview, by its close, Crazy Horse had withdrawn all offers of cooperation. Both he and, more qualifiedly, Touch the Clouds intended an immediate departure of their villages for the hunting grounds. Bradley set the post telegrapher's wires busy with reports to Omaha and Chicago.

Bradley also wired Fort Laramie to request cavalry reinforcements. He intended to surround both Crazy Horse's and Touch the Clouds's villages and prevent any departure, but his stripped-down garrisons were unequal to the task. Bradley was able to secure the reconcentration of elements of the Third Cavalry. Early on September 1, Major Julius W. Mason started a forced march from Fort Laramie, commanding Companies E and G. Messages were hurried through to Company F at Hat Creek Station, and to Company's D and L, scouting the Black Hills Trail, ordering them to march immediately to headquarters.[36]

Meanwhile Crazy Horse too was making his dispositions. At the northern village, a council was hurriedly arranged. Crazy Horse and Touch the Clouds reviewed the morning's events. Explaining their refusal to aid the military, they asserted that Major Hart's battalion on Tongue River was not really bound against the Nez Perces: instead, Hart was marching to intercept Sitting Bull and prevent his return to the Powder River country. All cooperation must be withdrawn from the army, both chiefs argued.[37]

Throughout the morning, Crazy Horse's envoys had continued their dialogue with the agency bands, but the abortive talk with Clark changed the whole tenor of the situation. After hearing Three Bears' account of the furious duel of words in Clark's office, those scouts who had given support to Crazy Horse rapidly rethought their plans. In the Oglala tribal village a final council, of all 864 adult males, was being held "to take the sense of our people" on the critical issues facing their nation. At the close of talks heralds announced that the Oglala people "want no more fighting and from this out we will live in peace."

As well as agreement on agency relocation within the White River valley, there were pledges to control the Crazy Horse village by force. Oglala chiefs had sought to conciliate Crazy Horse and bring him "into a better state of feeling—but we can do nothing with him." Now, if necessary, Oglala akicita would be deployed against Crazy Horse if he attempted to leave or made any warlike demonstration within a twenty-two mile radius. Beyond that line, the council conceded, the army could take over in pursuit of fugitives.[38]

That evening Oglala chiefs reported their decision to Irwin, spokesman American Horse assuring the agent "that they would see that 'Crazy Horse' did nothing about the Agency that would hurt my feelings."[39]

As evening deepened, tensions grew. Clark had continued working with the scouts, hoping once more to ensure a daytime departure. Although some seemed disgruntled, and others who had performed active service during the summer complained of the poor condition of their stock, by dusk a contingent of 150 scouts awaited Clark's final orders. In addition to the Company A and B scouts already agreed to go, the promised fifty scouts, drawn from both Spotted Tail Agency companies, had arrived. One hundred volunteer warriors were ready to leave, after Sheridan wired approval to loan them army-issue firearms. Even some of Crazy Horse's own Company C scouts, still anticipating the departure their war chief had approved before the final row with Clark, were among the contingent that by evening was forming near the agency.[40]

Night was drawing on when akicita appeared from Crazy Horse. Proclaiming the war chief's assertion that the Nez Perce campaign was a front for action against Sitting Bull, they announced that Crazy Horse and Touch the Clouds forbade any cooperation with the army: all scouts must go home. In a clear echo of the Oglala tribal edict placing deadlines around the agency, Crazy Horse ordered that any scout departure would be opposed by the full force of the Northern Nation. Reflecting his long duel with Clark, Crazy Horse's order asserted his unmediated control over all scouts. Contested that control might have been, but the scouts decamped. From the perspective of the White River agencies, the Nez Perce campaign was in a shambles.[41]

Through the night, the exchange of military telegrams grew more heated. General Crook, on board the Union Pacific to Camp Brown, picked up Bradley's warning that the scouts were reluctant to depart and advised Bradley and Clark not to force the issue. Crook was confident that he could enlist Shoshone scouts, more familiar with the country west of the Bighorns. An angry Sheridan wired Crook to countermand this advice, then telegraphed Bradley of the imperative need for the scouts to march immediately.[42]

Bradley fired back a lengthy wire that revealed the new complexities of the situation, concluding ominously, "There is a good chance for trouble here and there is plenty of bad blood. I think the departure of the scouts will bring on a collision here." Bradley followed up with a request that Crook come to Camp Robinson.[43]

Sensing the limits of the situation, Crook wired Sheridan from Grand Island to request that all orders to mobilize the scouts be countermanded. At 1:00 A.M. on September 1, Sheridan, aware that the Nez Perce campaign was a minor operation compared to the threat of a new Sioux war, requested Crook to leave the railroad at Sidney and proceed immediately to Camp Robinson. He conceded that all scout mobilization would be held pending Crook's arrival. Crook detrained at Sidney, acknowledged Sheridan's dispatch, and waited for the morning stage.[44]

As morning of September 1 rose on the upper White River valley, Bradley and Clark prepared messages for the chiefs and their scout companies: "[N]otice was . . . given," reported Billy Garnett, "that the scouts would not be required" for the Nez Perce campaign.[45] If Crazy Horse persisted in leading the northern villages onto the hunting grounds, it would now most certainly be construed as an act of war. The stage had been set for an endgame on White River.

26

MOVING ACROSS THE CREEK

September 1 was a day of anticlimax in Crazy Horse's village. Clark's latest message, suspending all scout movements, deflated the mood of tense expectation. Supporters of Crazy Horse and of Little Big Man were aware that the new order undercut the war chief's position: he could no longer legitimize departure for the north by scout participation in the Nez Perce campaign. This, and related developments, quickly began to pick at the stitching of village consensus. Other critical factors weighed in the balance of northern Lakota opinion. Already rumors were circulating about troop movements, impending arrests, and confiscation of arms and ponies.

Also crucial in northern village debate was the growing impatience with Crazy Horse evinced by the agency Oglalas. Leaders like Red Cloud and American Horse had for almost three months argued against conciliating the war chief. In the past two weeks, Crazy Horse's intransigence had alienated his last allies in the agency hierarchy, Young Man Afraid of His Horse and Yellow Bear. Over the next thirty-six hours, rhetoric would intensify, with the tribal council ultimately issuing an order that any northern departure would result in the breakdown of all friendly relations: a state of war would exist between agency and northern villages.[1]

A third issue weighed in the balance. Clark's trusties reported that Crazy Horse had received messengers from Sitting Bull in the last few days. If so—and an envoy from the Hunkpapa chief probably did visit the northern village early in September—their message could only dampen enthusiasm for a breakout: Sitting Bull was not preparing to leave his sanctuary in Grandmother's Land. Flight would commit the breakaways to a month-long retreat into the British possessions, or else to a new war on the hunting grounds. Only the truly intractable would face a third winter campaign. Inevitably, more people sided with Little Big Man.[2]

Crazy Horse was also in communication with the Fast Bull holdouts. Their fifty lodges were moving indecisively along the western edge of the Badlands, within fifty miles of Red Cloud Agency. During late August a nervous consensus had emerged favoring surrender at Spotted Tail Agency. On August 27, twenty-two people surrendered and were dispersed among the Brule bands. However, the Hunkpapa contingent in Fast Bull's camp continued to argue for flight to Sitting Bull. Certainly, the surrender process stalled for several days corresponding to the formation of the war council in Crazy Horse's village. Dialogue with the Oglala war chief seems likely, perhaps through key aides Kicking Bear and Shell Boy. Yet by the first days of September, a second party of fifteen lodges, including Crazy Horse's comrade Low Dog, was preparing to surrender; it was confidently expected that the rest would follow within a few days.[3]

All these factors contributed to the new mood of insecurity in Crazy Horse's village. Against increasingly vocal objections, Crazy Horse continued to press for an imminent start throughout the first. Aware that an order to strike the tipis in daylight would precipitate a crisis, he argued for a nighttime departure.

Supported tentatively by Big Road and Iron Crow, Little Big Man began rebuilding the moderate consensus. The war council could field no speaker as persuasive as Little Big Man. Thrown back on the support of young war leaders with little debating power, Crazy Horse heard support ebb away. By the afternoon of September 2, more than one hundred lodges were prepared to break with Crazy Horse.[4]

First to rethink matters had been Touch the Clouds. The Miniconjou chief had been tugged in Crazy Horse's wake through the meeting with Clark, but the latest developments convinced him of the need to be on hand for his own people. Moreover, when he left for Spotted Tail Agency, eight lodges of Miniconjous living in Crazy Horse's village accompanied him. Led by Low Bear, they first traveled to the Red Cloud stockade, where Agent Irwin tallied the sixty-two people, issued them rations, and authorized their transfer, doubtless relieved at even the smallest defection from Crazy Horse.[5]

No open break attended the striking of Low Bear's tipis—Crazy Horse could not risk a quarrel with Touch the Clouds—but their departure augured poorly for the uniting of the two northern villages. The defectors included the family of Crazy Horse's war comrade Red Hawk. Moreover, the Miniconjou contingent in Crazy Horse's hoop, about forty-five lodges until September 1, had been conspicuously loyal to his leadership. The loss of Low Bear's tiyospaye must have dismayed the war chief.[6]

Touch the Clouds's return to Spotted Tail led to alarm and reassessment of the evidence by the military hierarchy at Camp Sheridan. He was preceded by two dispatches from Clark, the first claiming that the Miniconjou chief was behind yesterday's conflict with Crazy Horse; the second, carried by Frank Grouard, advising of the imminent surround of Crazy Horse's village, to be synchronized with that of the northern village at Spotted Tail. That evening Touch the Clouds convinced the officers that he did not intend to depart for the north, and in a heated exchange with Frank Grouard, accused him of lying and mistranslation, accusations backed up by the agency interpreter, Louis Bordeaux.[7]

Agent Lee and Camp Sheridan commander Captain Daniel W. Burke were satisfied with the loyalty of the Miniconjous and Sans Arcs. Moreover, with negotiations well advanced for the surrender of Fast Bull's camp, any round-up operation might trigger a panicked flight. Determined to plead the cause of his northern contingent, Lee started for Camp Robinson early on the morning of September 2. Lucy W. Lee, who taught a small class of Lakota children at the agency school, accompanied her husband.[8]

Meanwhile, Camp Robinson continued to hum with activity. Following a forced march from Fort Laramie, Major Mason's two companies arrived at the post on the second. After a wearing eighty-mile journey from the railroad at Sidney, General Crook and his aide, Lieutenant John G. Bourke, arrived at headquarters early that morning. After assessing reports, Crook asked Clark for the opinion of the agency Indians. Clark assured him that their chiefs all agreed that "the safety of all demanded the deposition of 'Crazy Horse' and the dismemberment of his band."[9]

Confident that all reinforcements would be in place before night, Crook ordered Bradley to supervise the simultaneous surrounds of the northern villages early the following morning. Bradley was to command operations at Crazy Horse's village. Expanding for the first time on his intentions, Crook added that the warriors were to be totally disarmed. Reflecting the wishes of Red Cloud and the agency chiefs, Crook advised that the villages be broken up, enrolling individual families with relatives in the agency bands.[10]

Keenly aware of Indian sensitivities, Crook issued an order for all loyal Oglalas to raise a united village at a point on White Clay Creek two miles southeast of the agency. Crook arranged to meet the Oglalas in full council there the following afternoon, September 3. Nothing was publicly said of the intended surround of the northern villages, but Crook envisaged keeping the operation secret until night, when Red Cloud and the other chiefs could be involved in last-minute consultations. A private message was sent to Spotted Tail, inviting the Brule head chief to confidential talks with Clark at Red Cloud Agency.[11]

The Oglala council agreed to a statement that would meet with approval from Crook: "[T]he Indians had been a powerful people, but were now reduced to their present small numbers by fighting the whites, upon whom they were now dependent"; therefore, they unanimously "resolved they were now in favor of peace." Any departure for the north would be treated as grounds for war. Tightening the peace zone they had defined two days previously, they asserted that all Lakotas remaining north of White River would be treated as enemies by the Oglala Nation. Ratcheting up the pressure, No Water, at a meeting of scouts, declared he would kill Crazy Horse.[12]

Matching ultimatum with conciliation, however, the council decided to send Crazy Horse a final deputation. He Dog was chosen to make the keynote speech.

Attired in their finest war clothing, mixing Lakota gear with the blue uniforms of the scouts, the envoys made a colorful parade around the Oglala village before turning their horses toward White River.[13]

At Camp Robinson, the situation continued to change by the hour. Agent Lee arrived from Spotted Tail early in the afternoon. Lee made his views known to Bradley, insisting that he "was certain [Touch the Clouds] had no intention of going north for war." He assured Crook of the complete loyalty of all Indians at Spotted Tail. Crook and Bradley were given pause. They told Lee he should talk to Clark about the business, and the lieutenant was called in.

Priding himself as the man of action, intuitively in tune with his Indian allies, Clark reacted angrily when Lee called into question his reading of Indian affairs. Crook weighed his subordinates' accounts and slowly began to shift his ground. Gravely, Crook told Lee he was glad he had come. "Mr. Lee," he continued, "I don't want to make any mistake, for it would, to the Indians, be the basest treachery to make a mistake in this matter." Turning to Bradley and Clark, he told them that the surround of Touch the Clouds' village should be suspended. The next day's operations would be confined to Crazy Horse's village.[14]

While Lee and Clark sparred, the northern village council prepared to welcome Red Cloud's embassy. The war chief would not be present to receive the envoys. After the heated debate of the first, Crazy Horse had withdrawn into himself again. Sensing the swing in consensus toward accommodation, still finding no rest in sleep, he had talked into the night with Nellie. She continued to advise her husband of the talk around the agency, now focused on rumors that the army was planning his imminent arrest. Concerned for his safety, Nellie began to advise that he seek refuge at Spotted Tail Agency.[15]

Early in the afternoon, two unknown wasicu had appeared in the village. Dressed in civilian clothing, without an interpreter, they made it known that they wished to speak to Crazy Horse. Shown to his tipi, they managed to tell Crazy Horse that they were army officers and were inviting the war chief to attend the big council with Crook to be held the following day on White Clay Creek. The two men shook hands with Crazy Horse. Then, fumbling for a goodwill present, they pooled two cigars and a penknife, its blade unclasped and bare. With awkward farewells, the two men left Crazy Horse's tipi and presumably rode back toward Camp Robinson.[16]

The visit, only known through Crazy Horse's conversation with He Dog later that afternoon, remains as mysterious and unsettling as it seemed to the war chief. The identities of the two men are uncertain. One, according to He Dog, was "the soldier chief from Fort Laramie." Perhaps he meant Major Mason, commanding the newly arrived reinforcements. The badly orchestrated social call, minus interpreter, demonstrates that Lieutenant Clark was not involved. Nevertheless, both Crazy Horse and He Dog believed the men to be officers. It may be that Crook, more disturbed by Lee's protestations than he showed, asked Mason or his lieutenants to pay an off-the-record visit to Crazy Horse and, in a spirit of fairness, give him an opportunity to return quietly to the fold. That would be consistent with Crook's actions later in the evening. Or perhaps Mason, an old Camp Robinson hand, simply fancied his abilities as mediator and paid an off-duty courtesy call on the war chief.[17]

Either way, the visit backfired. Continuing to sit by his sleeping place at the back of the tipi, Crazy Horse stared gloomily at the penknife, trying to divine the intention behind the gift. Uneasy at the meeting, his judgment impaired from sleep loss, that naked blade seemed to mean "trouble was coming," the announcement of weapons being unsheathed for war. At length, troubled and in need of solitude, he stuffed the knife and the two cigars under the blankets of his bed and left the tipi. Although his whereabouts for the next hour or two are unknown, he likely sought a quiet place outside the village where he could try through prayer, direct communication with Wakan Tanka, to resolve the tensions besetting him.[18]

About midafternoon the deputation from the Oglala council rode into the northern village. Once seated in the council tipi, the envoys faced the arc of elders, headmen, and warriors who had hurried to attend. With unease He Dog's party registered that Crazy Horse was absent, Little Big Man and the other Deciders occupying the honor place. The envoys concentrated on a single theme: Crazy Horse's intransigence could lead only to disaster. Even now, Three Stars Crook was at Camp Robinson coordinating a major military operation. At the very least, Crook envisaged arrests and confiscations of both arms and stock. Such an operation might easily lead to bloodshed. Moreover, the Oglala tribe took seriously its promises of peace to the Great Father's people and had committed itself to aiding the troops in controlling hostile relatives.

A way out of this crisis did exist, the speakers continued. General Crook had ordered the peaceful Lakotas to move their village to White Clay Creek. The agency bands had already raised their hoop at that point, ready to counsel with Crook tomorrow, in a talk intended to restore peace to the Oglala agency. The northern village should set aside Crazy Horse's leadership and move across White River out of the war zone declared by the Oglala tribe.

The envoys, including such compelling speakers as the herald Iron Hawk, spoke persuasively. It was left to He Dog to close the envoys' address. He Dog scanned his audience and the throng of spectators outside, proclaiming, "All who love their wife and children, let them come across the creek with me. All who want their wife and children to be killed by the soldiers, let them stay where they are."[19]

The council adjourned, and as He Dog and Iron Hawk walked across the village circle, a message was brought to them: Crazy Horse was now at home and wished them "to come to his tipi." Crazy Horse again sat before his bed. As his guests entered, he turned and, reaching under the blankets, brought out the cigars and knife left by his earlier visitors. With no preamble about the council, Crazy Horse recounted the story of the two wasicu visitors.

> He said this was a present [recalled He Dog] brought him by two visiting white men who had come to see him that afternoon. He did not like the way they shook hands with him, and he did not like their talk, and he did not like their gift. He thought the gift of the knife meant trouble was coming. He thought they shook hands with him as if they did not mean him any good. He was afraid there would be trouble at that council [with Crook].[20]

Focused disturbingly on private obsessions, only Crazy Horse's last sentence showed any concern with the wider predicament facing his people. Dismayed by his old comrade's state of mind, He Dog tried to laugh off the penknife, then turned to the real issue.

"Does this mean that you will be my enemy if I move across the creek?" he asked.

Crazy Horse laughed. "I am no white man!" he replied. "They are the only people that make rules for other people, that say, 'If you stay on one side of this line it is peace, but if you go on the other side I will kill you all.' I don't hold with deadlines. There is plenty of room; camp where you please."[21]

Dusk was falling before the Deciders reached a consensus. Little Big Man articulated their decision. The northern village would move to the south side of White River. Moreover, while Little Big Man carried the support of fellow Deciders Big Road and Iron Crow, Little Hawk's loyalty to Crazy Horse precluded unanimity. A characteristic face-saving device, when coercion would be fruitlessly divisive, was a declaration permitting tribespeople to make their own decisions. Such an announcement was made, and the village bustled with preparation. About 115 lodges followed Little Big Man and a straggle of elders a short distance across the twilit valley, where the lodges were pitched once more in the security of the peace zone.[22]

The departure left scores of spaces in the vacated camp circle. Some one hundred tipis remained standing, however, about six hundred people remaining loyal to their war chief. The clearest identifying characteristic was age: a preponderance of younger men predictably chose to follow Crazy Horse and his war council.[23] Yet other distinctions were clear, too. Little Big Man's declaration had probably swayed a clear majority of the 115 lodges of northern Oglalas in the village. Most of the Bad Faces in the village had followed Little Big Man, while significant numbers of Oyuhpes and a few Hunkpatilas followed Big Road and Iron Crow.

Of the Hunkpatila band, Little Hawk's tiyospaye and the few lodges of Crazy Horse's own immediate relatives were left. A cluster of Oyuhpes, centered on the old Wakan tiyospaye that had been loyal to Crazy Horse for twenty years, completed the Oglala contingent in the rump village. Many of these remaining Oglala warriors were lodge members of Crazy Horse's bodyguard.

The majority of the thirty-seven remaining lodges of Miniconjous, twenty-five lodges of Sans Arcs, and some of the thirty-eight lodges of Brules that had also composed the united village, remained with Crazy Horse. Their elders and headmen, the Miniconjous Black Shield, Wounded Hand, and High Lodge, and holy men like the Sans Arc Elk Head, Keeper of the Calf Pipe, expected no favors from the agency hierarchy and chose to stay with the war chief.[24]

At Camp Robinson, news from Camp Sheridan advised that runners from Fast Bull's camp had just visited Touch the Clouds. The camp was now ready to surrender at Spotted Tail: its vanguard, led by Shedding Bear, might even "be there in a very few hours." Bradley hurriedly discussed the development with General Crook. It confirmed the general's caution in ordering the suspension of operations against Touch the Clouds, but it also threw into question the whole issue of surrounding Crazy Horse's village. Mindful of Agent Lee's warnings, Crook and Bradley weighed the factors. "There was much reason to fear," as Crook's aide Lieutenant Bourke would write some months later, "that if 'Crazy Horse's' village should not be completely surrounded and his warriors not all captured, those that escaped might get mixed-up among those of [Fast Bull's] band and some of the latter might be killed or wounded." Crook was at pains not to repeat the errors of judgment he had ascribed to Colonel Miles, when in May Fast Bull's father, Lame Deer, was killed during the aborted parley on Muddy Creek.[25]

At last Crook came to a new decision. He suspended the surround of Crazy Horse's village and announced that messengers were to be sent to Crazy Horse's village early in the morning, inviting the war chief to the council on White Clay and giving him "one last chance for self-vindication."[26]

Clark sent for He Dog, who had returned with the envoys from the northern village, and asked him "to get Crazy Horse to talk to them some more." He Dog hurried home while Clark sent a large amount of provisions. He Dog told his wife to prepare a big feast and then sent invitations to the officers at Camp Robinson. Another messenger was hurried across the river to invite Crazy Horse: an informal meal, hosted by an old friend, was envisaged, at which public face might be retained while defusing tensions unresolvable in open council.

The day was too far advanced, however. Weary and suspicious, Crazy Horse yet managed to be gracious for the sake of He Dog. "Tell my friend," he observed to the messenger, "that I thank him and I am grateful, but some people over there have said too much. I don't want to talk to them any more. No good would come of it."[27]

A momentous day was over. Crazy Horse had seen his following halved, isolating him and his core following. As Oglala chiefs were apprised of Crook's decision to suspend immediate operations against Crazy Horse, and to invite him to attend tomorrow's meeting between the general and the tribal council, their deliberations must have focused on furthering their diplomatic gains. If Crook's initiative succeeded and Crazy Horse was brought back into the fold, the prospect of Crazy Horse's restoration to army favor was not appealing to sections of council opinion.

Crazy Horse was dangerously isolated by nightfall on September 2, an isolation as much mental as political. The war chief's meeting with the officers betrays a mind fixated on minutiae. Outside the thrill of battle, Crazy Horse's mind had always leaned to the otherworldly. Since surrender, with no outlet for physical action, his meditative instincts had deepened. He left the village three times a day, according to Spotted Tail Agent Lee, to engage in private prayer. According to Lee's wife, in these same days, Crazy Horse's fitful sleep was disturbed by another equivocal dream, "that he was not to die between sun and sun, nor by a bullet." On such brittle shards of vision, he expended mental energies frayed by fatigue.[28]

This otherworldliness was in danger of becoming pathological. His mind tortured by the political demands placed on this most apolitical of men, his own personal imperative to "keep my country" at all costs, the relentless tide of talk, gossip, and rumor, and the consequent weeks of sleeplessness, had all robbed him of essential perspectives. An unclasped penknife fixated his mind, but faced with a defection that would halve his following, Crazy Horse showed no interest whatsoever.

The war chief's tragedy was that his commitment to "keep my country," was inconsistent with the increasing privacy and quietism of his spiritual life—the calling as a healer that had first sounded six months previously. To try to keep the country was an intensely political act. Deserted by comrades willing to negotiate a compromise solution, leadership now devolved solely on Crazy Horse, leaving him open to the distorting perspectives of messianism. Torn apart by these pressures that pulled him toward passivity and defiance, Crazy Horse brooded another night. Still suffering from her swollen arm, Black Shawl slept alone, while Crazy Horse and Nellie sat talking late. It is to be hoped that the couple took from each other what comfort they could, for it would be their last night together on earth.

27

THEY REFUSED TO FOLLOW

Daylight of Monday, September 3, rose over the upper White River valley. Shortly before midnight, the last of Bradley's reinforcements had gone into hasty bivouac on the prairie north of the Camp Robinson quadrangle. Eight companies of the Third Cavalry and three infantry companies were now concentrated at Camp Robinson. Even at chronically low levels of manning, over six hundred regulars were at Bradley's disposal. The agency Oglalas could field over seven hundred warriors to aid their wasicu allies. The Arapahos, also loyal to Crook, could mount more than one hundred active warriors.

Such a force outnumbered Crazy Horse's depleted following by almost ten to one. Apprised of the latest troop arrivals, the northern villagers began once more to change in mood. The air of sullen defiance became increasingly anxious as the morning progressed. Crazy Horse registered the change in mood. As the day began, the war chief made one of his drastic shifts of mind and decided to reopen dialogue with the military. Perhaps this reflected his latest conversations with Nellie, who was seriously worried by her husband's position. Certainly, he was influenced by the anxiety among even die-hard supporters. Although the warriors continued to support Crazy Horse's argument for a secret nighttime departure, "fear of punishment" by troops and Oglala relatives was breeding serious misgivings.[1]

The arrival of messengers from Crook seemed to offer a way out. They extended a personal invitation from the general for Crazy Horse to attend the council at the Oglala tribal village that afternoon, where Crook could "hear what [Crazy Horse] had to say for himself."[2] Only the previous evening, the war chief had refused He Dog's invitation to a preliminary feast. Now, warily, he responded to Crook's olive branch. "Crazy Horse called [Clark] to the council," recalled Red Feather. "He wanted to tell White Hat that he and his people were ready to go back where they came from."[3]

This only repeated what everyone had known for over a week. But the air of moderation, of a calm exchange of information, was new. Crazy Horse's singling out of Clark was also significant, and the return to an open departure, negotiated with the military, addressed the obvious anxiety of the war council. In a day of about-faces, this was one of the most surprising. Briefly, it seemed that an exit strategy was shaping from the impasse of intransigence and mistrust.

Late in the morning, a decisive twist in events prevented such an outcome. Crook and Clark boarded an ambulance at Camp Robinson bound for the council. They had arranged to pick up as interpreters Billy Garnett and Baptiste Pourier at Frank Yates's trading store, just outside the agency compound. As the ambulance lumbered up, its passengers saw Garnett and Pourier deep in conversation with an Indian.[4]

Billy introduced the Lakota as Woman Dress, one of Clark's trusties, and told the general that Woman Dress had just warned them that Crazy Horse was coming to the council. Sixty warriors would accompany the war chief. Once talks opened, Crazy Horse planned to pick a verbal quarrel with Crook and then, approaching the general as if to shake hands, stab him to death. His followers would rise up and fall on Clark and any other officers with him. In the confused aftermath of this bloody scene, the northern village could make a break for the hunting grounds.

The astonished general quizzed Garnett and Woman Dress. Warily, Garnett and Pourier vouched for the veracity of the Oglala, who insisted that the whole council should be called off. Crook pressed for verification, asking Woman Dress if he personally had overheard Crazy Horse's plan. The Indian replied that Little Wolf, another of Clark's trusties, had eavesdropped outside the war chief's tipi the previous evening and reported to his brother Lone Bear. In turn, Lone Bear had informed Woman Dress.[5]

Still incredulous, Crook chewed over this information but was convinced by Clark to return to the post. Clark then instructed Garnett to attend the tribal council and summon the loyal agency chiefs to Camp Robinson for confidential talks. Stressing that the northern leaders must not be informed of this development, Clark turned back with the general.[6]

Billy arrived about noon to find the Oglala tribal council in session. He noted that neither Crazy Horse nor any northern leaders were present, which sat uneasily with Woman Dress's story. American Horse stepped out of the council lodge to talk to the interpreter. American Horse announced to the council that Crook's plan had changed: that the general had received a letter on the way to the village and had to return to the post. After repeating that Crook "won't be here today," American Horse slipped quietly around the circle, whispering to the chiefs the summons to headquarters. Garnett, assured that American Horse would bring the chiefs presently, hurried back to Camp Robinson.[7]

By early afternoon, as the officers awaited the arrival of the Oglala chiefs, the general was convinced of Crazy Horse's treachery. A final invitation was sent to

Crazy Horse to attend the talk at post headquarters, but Crazy Horse, claimed Bourke, "paid no attention" to the summons.[8]

About 2:30 P.M. the agency chiefs were shown into Colonel Bradley's quarters. Awaiting them were Crook, Clark, and three interpreters: Garnett, Pourier, and the reinstated Frank Grouard. Colonel Bradley was at the adjutant's office across the parade ground. Fourteen Oglala leaders sat around the room. American Horse had been liberal with Clark's invitations. All the major band chiefs were present: scout sergeants Red Cloud, Little Wound, Young Man Afraid of His Horse, American Horse, and Yellow Bear were accompanied by Red Dog, High Wolf, Slow Bull, Black Bear, Daylight, and Blue Horse. Representing the warriors were akicita leaders Three Bears, No Flesh, and Crazy Horse's old enemy No Water.[9]

Crook expanded on a favorite theme: the loyalty the Lakota people owed to a government that fed and clothed them. After retelling Woman Dress's story of Crazy Horse's planned treachery, at which the chiefs expressed surprise, Crook told them the Oglalas were being led astray by the war chief's folly. To assure the Great Father of Oglala loyalty, they must assist in the arrest of Crazy Horse. The chiefs talked briefly among themselves, then stated that Crazy Horse "was such a desperate man, it would be necessary to kill him." The interpreters concurred.[10]

Crook demurred but asked what would be the best way to capture Crazy Horse and disarm his band. A strategy was quickly formulated. Each chief present would select two of his best warriors to coordinate the operation. They would select a strong war party, which would surround Crazy Horse's village that night, and then call to the war chief and all enlisted scouts to come out and give up their arms. If this summons drew no response, then the Oglalas would use force against Crazy Horse and his warriors. Approving this scheme, Crook ordered Clark to issue the necessary ammunition and told the chiefs to then return to their village and prepare for the night's work. Impressing the Oglala chiefs with the need to keep the plan secret from the northern village, Crook left to prepare for his own departure for Cheyenne.[11]

In conversation with Clark, the chiefs returned to the theme of killing Crazy Horse. Reluctantly, Clark conceded a reward of three hundred dollars and his own famous sorrel racer. Then he led the chiefs to the commissary and issued them ammunition. When they departed for their village, it was already late in the afternoon.[12]

Crazy Horse's fragile trust in renewing dialogue with the military was already exhausted. First Crazy Horse learned that the talk with Crook had been cancelled; then Crook's messenger brought a summons for Crazy Horse to come to Camp Robinson. Although unaware of the lies Woman Dress had told about his intentions, Crazy Horse must have viewed these about-faces with suspicion. Signaling a termination to all dialogue, he gave no reply to the general's message.

Instead, Crazy Horse returned to stepping up the pressure for an immediate departure. Another mood shift took place—and as quickly reversed itself. Abandoning his acquiescence of the previous day, the war chief decided to force the reunion of his divided village. A body of akicita was sent across the river to order Little Big Man's camp of defectors home, only to be plainly rejected by He Dog.[13] Faced with these mounting disappointments, Crazy Horse once more left the village to seek out a quiet place to pray.

As the Woman Dress incident demonstrated, elements in the Oglala tribal village were also prepared to step up the pressure. There had been no truth in the alleged plot to murder General Crook. Little Wolf, the Clark trusty whom Woman Dress claimed had overheard the plot, was a familiar figure in Crazy Horse's village. With their blankets hooded over their heads, he, his brother Lone Bear, and their comrades Long Chin and Woman Dress had often been seen idling around the war chief's tipi. Perhaps Little Wolf had observed Crazy Horse's meeting with He Dog the previous evening, and, overhearing talk of officers and knives, had exaggerated the story out of all recognition. Or perhaps Woman Dress applied the murderous spin to an inconsequential tale. Either way, it had no truth. "This was not true," Red Feather simply dismissed the tale. Ten years later, Little Wolf claimed to have never told such a story.[14]

The origin of the Crook murder story remains a tantalizing clue in the intrigue against Crazy Horse. The fact that the Oglala tribal council had received no report of a murderous plot allegedly overheard on September 2 until Crook told the chiefs of Woman Dress's story, at midafternoon on the 3rd, is another indication of its fabrication. Any such news would have been instantly relayed to the tribal village. In all likelihood, Woman Dress and persons unknown agreed on the story early on the morning of the third. The story is unlikely to represent any plot by the Oglala tribal council as a whole. Instead, a few leaders most opposed to the northern war chief met privately to discuss how best to ensure that Crazy Horse could not be restored to military favor.

Who those leaders were can never be precisely known. According to Lieutenant Bourke's late published account, Woman Dress told Crook that he had been sent by "'Spotted Tail' and the other Indians."[15] On the face of it, this seems improbable: Woman Dress was an Oglala and would be unlikely to carry messages for the Brule head chief. However, Spotted Tail was at Red Cloud Agency by the afternoon of the third, and it would be natural for him to have visited in the Oglala village en route between the agencies. Of the Oglala band chiefs, Red Cloud and American Horse seem the most likely candidates. Woman Dress belonged to Red Cloud's Bad Face band, was the chief's first cousin, and "always stayed with" Red Cloud, according to Red Feather. The rivalry between Red Cloud and Crazy Horse needs no further elaboration. American Horse was even more robustly opposed to the war chief. According to his own account, he would have shot Crazy Horse dead on September 5 if others had not gotten in the way.[16]

American Horse took the lead in orchestrating another demonstration against the war chief. The chronology seems to fit late afternoon of the 3rd, after the Oglala chiefs returned from their talk with Crook. A plan was made within the Loafer band to force a crisis with Crazy Horse by abducting Nellie Larrabee. Such an act carried the risk of Crazy Horse's violent opposition—a variation on the shoot-him-down plan proposed to Crook. At a Loafer band council, head akicita Red Shirt was present, as well as key warriors High Bear, Apples, and Eagle Horn. A more reluctant guest was Little Bear (Sioux Bob), the hapless betrothed of Nellie Larrabee before Crazy Horse appeared on the scene.

To Little Bear's alarm, a scenario was storyboarded in which he marched up to Crazy Horse's tipi and demanded the return of his woman. Leaving Little Bear no time to back down, Red Shirt led his party straight into Crazy Horse's village. Dismounting before the war chief's tipi, they marched in line toward his door. Only Little Bear, marching rather stiffly at the head of the column, struck a discordant note amid this display of Lakota machismo. When Little Bear's voice unaccountably failed him, Red Shirt and the others spoke up, demanding that Nellie return with them. The moment of truth seemed at hand, but Worm emerged from the lodge to explain that his son was not at home. Into the tense silence, Nellie herself appeared, stooping to leave the tipi. As she was compelled to mount Little Bear's pony, Red Shirt's party shot dead the war chief's best horse, standing tethered beside the lodge. No resistance was offered to this act of calculated defiance.[17]

For the northern village, this was a defining moment. In a classic case of Lakota bluff, the Loafers had successfully cowed the victors of the Little Bighorn. For many of the young warriors, their war chief's recurring absences, as he sought through prayer the guidance of his wakan helpers, must have seemed ever more disturbing. Now a crisis had come, and Crazy Horse was not even present to save his warriors' face. Before the end of the day, many of the demoralized openly favored crossing White River and joining Little Big Man's camp of defectors.

No account records Crazy Horse's reaction to the loss of his second wife. For the war chief, their passionate union had evolved into a relationship of unusual trust and communication: he can only have felt the loss intensely. What the open abduction demonstrated in political terms was the determination of elements of the agency Oglalas to force a crisis with the northern village. Crazy Horse would have realized that Red Shirt's party had been prepared to shoot him down. After Crazy Horse returned, these matters were anxiously debated in the council tipi. Careful not to escalate the potential blood feud, Crazy Horse declined to respond to the Loafers' challenge. "Crazy Horse never did any thing," recalled his cousin Eagle Elk, "[he] only stayed away from [the Loafers] altogether."[18]

By the end of the afternoon, the war council's morale was at its lowest ebb. The mercurial Crazy Horse had proved unable to give his followers a clear lead in the day since the village breakup. Now, when he restated that "he desired to move away" immediately, ahead of further interventions, they demurred. Black Fox, Crazy Horse's principal lieutenant in the blotahunka, and other key warriors "refused to follow" their war chief. As the evening drew on, the mood of unease deepened.[19]

At the agency and at Camp Robinson, developments had continued. As plans for the nighttime operation were revealed, key players registered their dissatisfaction with the course of events. Agent Irwin called on Lieutenant Colonel Bradley with He Dog in tow, each man of the three disturbed by rumors of an impending arrest operation. Crook, preoccupied with Nez Perce developments, and Clark, jealously guarding his intelligence, had left the post commander and civilian agent out of their loop of communication—and here was a northern defector breaking the news to them. Bradley quizzed interpreter Garnett about the afternoon council.[20]

Bradley quickly decided to change the plan. Uncomfortable with the prospect of a covert operation, and in any case aware that the essential element of surprise was lost, he immediately summoned Clark. Bradley told him that he wished to reschedule the whole operation; the arrest should take place the next morning. Both Clark and Crook had envisaged an essentially Indian policing operation. Bradley insisted that the army should be fully involved in the arrest and disarming. Although General Crook played no direct role in events after leaving Bradley's quarters earlier in the afternoon, he evidently indicated his approval of Bradley's reevaluation.[21]

Lieutenant Lee was one of the first to be apprised of the news. Upon hearing that a morning arrest was planned, the Spotted Tail agent asked if word had been sent to Camp Sheridan. Advised of the secrecy of the operation, he insisted that word be sent to prevent any "stampede" from Touch the Clouds's village. The revelation that Spotted Tail was then at Red Cloud Agency, involved in hush-hush talks with Clark, was the last straw. Lee and Clark engaged in another heated debate. Both Clark and Bradley wished Spotted Tail's participation in the arrest tomorrow, but Lee was adamant that the Brule chief's presence would be necessary to prevent trouble at his own agency. Once again, Lee wrung a concession. Bradley reluctantly permitted Lee and Spotted Tail to leave for the Brule agency after midnight.[22]

Returning along the parade ground to his quarters, Clark summoned Billy Garnett from his stool at the sutler's bar. "These Indians can hold nothing," grumbled Clark before outlining the change of plan. He ordered Billy to hurry to the tribal village and inform the chiefs that Bradley had decided against a night operation. Instead, all loyal Oglala chiefs were to report with their warriors to Camp Robinson before sunrise. There they would be issued arms and ammunition for the daytime arrest of the war chief and the disarming of his village.[23]

Evening was deepening when Billy rode again into the Oglala circle. Dismounting, he noticed "a bunch of Indians back of [American Horse's] lodge plotting up something." To the Loafer headmen, Billy briefly reviewed Clark's instructions. "I told them not to bother themselves; not to kill Crazy Horse that night; that this was the message that Lieutenant Clark gave me, but to report to [Camp Robinson] before sun-up and draw ammunition and guns."[24]

At Crazy Horse's village, the approach of night brought only fresh misgivings and fears. One visitor to Red Feather told of the parley with Clark and the promised reward to the killer of Crazy Horse. Red Feather hurried to his brother-in-law's tipi with the news. He found Crazy Horse subdued and fatalistic. The war chief unfastened his scout Sharps rifle from the lodgepoles above his bed. He presented the rifle in its scabbard to Red Feather in a symbolic act of abdication, then indicated the knife at his waist. "He was waiting like that for the soldiers," recalled his brother-in-law. Crazy Horse was now prepared to fight and die as a simple warrior in defense of the village.[25]

An anxious Red Feather rode to Camp Robinson to confirm the army's plans. Crazy Horse had given up any hope of leading his followers north. Instead, a growing number of people spoke of joining Little Big Man; yet others favored flight to Spotted Tail Agency. Although Black Fox, on whom leadership was devolving, continued to urge solidarity, before daylight fully half the village would exercise one of these options.

With the village in meltdown, and Crazy Horse in a mood of fatalistic despair, the day drew toward midnight. For the war chief it had been a day of dizzying mood swings and political shifts. Grimly, he relinquished his position as war chief, relieved at the lifting of an intolerable burden. Expecting the momentary attack of troops and agency relatives, Crazy Horse was prepared to die fighting, alone like a Thunder dreamer, in defense of what remained of the Northern Nation.

28

BAD WINDS BLOWING

Few were sleeping when Red Feather left the northern village to ride up to Camp Robinson. At the post, all was bustle. Having assessed the activity, Red Feather sought out Billy Garnett. The interpreter told him that "the scouts and soldiers were going after Crazy Horse." After meeting another Lakota scouting the post, Red Feather and he pooled their intelligence and rode back to the village. Together they entered Crazy Horse's tipi "and told him the soldiers were coming." The war chief offered no remark. He continued to sit, the knife at his belt his only visible weapon, "waiting like that for the soldiers."[1]

Not all were so fatalistic. Inside every tipi, the evolving situation was assessed. Many people were fearful that retribution was at hand. No organization or leadership sought to coordinate action. The Sans Arc Pistol Maker, for example, led his family and fled to relatives at Spotted Tail. A larger number elected to join Little Big Man's camp. Piecemeal, twenty-five or thirty families slipped into the darkness to cross the river to safety. No akicita turned out to prevent the movement: Crazy Horse had withdrawn into silence, and Black Fox was unwilling to rupture what remained of village solidarity.

Of one hundred tipis standing before dusk, seventy-three remained when intelligence began to filter to Camp Robinson. As the sun rose and news of the troop movement crystallized, another twenty or more lodges were struck. By midmorning the village had been halved again: some fifty tipis remained standing on a campground littered with abandoned lodgepoles and baggage; three hundred people remained to face a day of whirlwind.[2]

At the Oglala tribal village, Billy Garnett had brought Clark's revised summons for all to report to Camp Robinson before daylight. Runners were dispatched to Little Big Man's camp, and as night deepened, the northern Deciders and defecting akicita rode up to sit in the tribal circle.[3]

The Oglala chiefs succinctly informed He Dog and the other northern defectors that troops were to be sent to arrest Crazy Horse. Trouble was expected from the war chief's warriors, and Lieutenant Clark had told the Oglalas "to prepare [their] guns and ammunition" for a morning operation.[4]

The Oglala tribal council was not content to serve as mercenaries for the army: the tribe's prime concern was to rehabilitate its northern relatives. The Oglala tribe would take into its protection those northern Lakotas who rejected Crazy Horse's leadership. Little Big Man agreed to move his camp into the tribal circle. Those in Crazy Horse's village who agreed to the council's terms would also be made welcome. To accelerate this process, before dawn Little Big Man rode back to the northern village.[5]

Those northern people who "had no ears" could expect summary punishment. Crazy Horse was singled out as a target. Although individuals like Young Man Afraid of His Horse might nurse misgivings, the council's mood now favored the permanent removal of Crazy Horse from the equation of Lakota politics. The Oglala band chiefs "all say Crazy-Horse would not listen to them," observed the *New York Tribune*'s reporter three days later; "that he was obstinate, dictatorial, stubborn, and objected to every measure which was taken for their and his good . . . and opposed every effort . . . to pacify him." As the Oglala warriors prepared for the day's action, several anonymous leaders remarked "that they would like to kill [Crazy Horse] like a dog if he resisted." The plan to kill the war chief was no longer a whispered plot but the Oglala council's public decision.[6]

Some four hundred Oglala men mustered at Camp Robinson soon after 7 A.M. From their camp north of the post, one hundred Arapaho men had also gathered; a few Cheyennes were on hand from the small camp still clustered around Joe Larrabee's cabin. Extra ammunition was issued by Lieutenant Clark, and firearms supplied to those who needed them.[7]

General Crook had departed in the small hours for the railroad, and Lieutenant Colonel Bradley oversaw the operation. He assigned immediate command of the cavalry contingent to Major Julius W. Mason, who formed his eight companies of the Third Cavalry into two battalions. Companies D, G, F, and E, under command of Captain Guy V. Henry, were to march down the north side of White River to Crazy Horse's village. Captain Frederick Van Vliet took charge of Companies C, B, H, and L, which would march along the south side of the river. Lieutenant John Murphy, Fourteenth Infantry, accompanied Van Vliet's battalion in charge of a single twelve-pounder cannon. Joined by Lieutenant James F. Simpson as adjutant and V. T. McGillycuddy as surgeon, Major Mason took his place at the head of Van Vliet's right-wing battalion.[8]

In consultation with Lieutenant Clark, the Oglala chiefs made their dispositions, using Mason's division by battalions to further their own aims. The vanguard of Henry's left-wing battalion were the Indians perceived as most loyal: Sharp Nose and Black Coal, with their one hundred Arapahos and Cheyennes, and the Oglala contingent from the Kiyuksa band. Three Bears, the Kiyuksa war leader, was placed in tactical command of the Indian left wing, reporting directly to Clark.

In front of Mason's right wing rode the main Oglala contingent, their vanguard fronted by chiefs acting as mediators. Red Cloud, Little Wound, Young Man Afraid of His Horse, American Horse, and Yellow Bear rode at the head of the wing, each chief carrying a calumet pipe in the crook of his left arm. About 9 A.M. the two battalions began their march east, "to surround, attack, dismount, and disarm Crazy Horse and his braves."[9]

Billy Garnett joined the column leading a contingent of reinforcements from the tribal village, who attached themselves to the right wing. Defectors from the northern village formed the core of the reinforcements, following Big Road, Iron Crow, and He Dog. In the event of action, Clark was concerned that northern auxiliaries might defect to Crazy Horse, and the lieutenant ordered Garnett to direct the right wing to form two divisions. Those considered most trustworthy were formed into a division riding on the extreme right, under command of Young Man Afraid of His Horse. Between them and the river rode the northern contingent, with a group of agency warriors, led by American Horse, with He Dog acting as akicita.[10]

As the march resumed, the column of four hundred cavalry, in skirmishing formation, and at least five hundred Indian allies could not be kept secret. A rattle of gunfire, when the Arapaho contingent flushed a coyote, signaled the approach, and Indians appeared along the rolling hills flanking the march. Crazy Bear brought the first news of the march back to the northern village. Once more, no coordinated response was in evidence: the rump village seemed in a paralysis of morale.[11]

Depleted by nighttime desertions, the fifty lodges remaining had faced daylight with misgivings. Many women struck tipis and loaded travois in preparation for flight. In the urgency of fear, many belongings were left where they lay. Women and children hurried northwest, where the lee of the Hat Creek bluffs offered refuge and the first toehold on the trail north. As morning progressed, more of the non-combatants raced for the bluffs. What leadership remained in the village, grouped around Black Fox, managed to keep most of the men on the campground: that was the limit of its success. Crazy Horse remained incommunicado within his tipi.[12]

Crazy Horse's inaction accelerated the freefall of village morale. Little Big Man was in the camp, doing what he could to pacify people, securing the surrender of several straggling families. Meanwhile, news of the march at last galvanized the rump war council. In a hasty meeting, a quick trawl of opinion favored negotiation. Crazy Horse's brother-in-law Red Feather galloped toward the column with word that the men in the northern village "promised to give up [their] guns and move near" Red Cloud Agency.

Red Feather met the column three or four miles from the village. In a hurried talk with Clark, he passed on the war council's message. Then, "[t]he soldiers told me to tell Crazy Horse they were coming, and he was to do as they said."[13] Red

Feather galloped homeward. During his absence, something had happened to break the deepest of Crazy Horse's deadlocks. When Red Feather left the village, about 9:20 A.M., the war chief had been in a state of paralyzed resignation. Within half an hour, he was moving swiftly to implement a new course, just as if he had received a new surge of the Thunder power of his vision. Although a radical, possibly spiritual, boost in personal morale had taken place, Crazy Horse had probably been galvanized to action by earthly visitors.

His key aides Kicking Bear and Shell Boy entered the tipi soon after Red Feather's departure. A rapid review of options was probably passed over. As the march cut off flight to the bluffs, an immediate break for the north was impossible. In the face of collapsing morale, armed resistance was futile, surrender, unthinkable. Until now Crazy Horse had been opposed to fleeing to Spotted Tail Agency, where the Brule chief effectively controlled the northern Lakotas. Suddenly flight to Spotted Tail seemed to open up a range of options, just as they were being slammed shut at Red Cloud. Most important for Crazy Horse's sense of humanity, atrophying in paranoia, was Black Shawl's health. She remained sickly from winter privations, and her arm was still grotesquely swollen. A healer in the small Oglala camp near the Brule agency was trusted by Crazy Horse and Black Shawl. Moreover, her uncle and her widowed mother both lived there. His wife could be left with her closest relatives in the event of any further crisis, not at the mercy of vindictive reprisals by Red Cloud Agency Oglalas.[14]

Furthermore, the Brule agency offered a new haven for the northern Lakotas. As a minimal option, Crazy Horse might find safety from agency Oglalas bent on his arrest or death. Spotted Tail represented a sanctuary where the Northern Nation might be reunited: Crazy Horse's goal throughout the summer. As a final, and possibly critical, factor, fourteen lodges from Fast Bull's camp had crossed White River early that morning. Led by Shedding Bear and Low Dog, they had now entered Touch the Clouds's village ahead of surrender at the agency. Their arrival created the sort of tension and uncertainty that determined leadership might unbalance— the kicamnayan moment that Crazy Horse had mastered in battle—to provoke a mass breakout. About 9:50 A.M. Crazy Horse stepped out of his door flap, carrying bridle and saddle.[15]

Black Shawl packed a few essential items. Crazy Horse hurried to drive in the couple's horses. Little Big Man hurried upriver with word for the Oglala chiefs that "Crazy Horse is either going to fight or he is going to run away: he is catching his horse."[16]

As the troops neared the village, lone northern warriors made brave runs. Looking Horse, a Miniconjou scout from Crazy Horse's village, charged across the front of both wings, "scolding" Clark and the agency chiefs.[17]

The Oglala tribe would not tolerate this defiance. Woman Dress shot Looking Horse's pony. As the animal sank to the earth, Looking Horse sprang clear, but another scout pistol-whipped him to the ground. White Cow Killer, an Oglala brother of the hapless warrior, dragged his senseless body into the shade of a cottonwood, then hurried to rejoin the moving column.[18]

Clark ordered the scouts forward, instructing them not to fire first.[19] The scouts prepared for battle, dismounting to remove saddles and strip off shirts and army jackets. Little Big Man galloped up to report that Crazy Horse was fleeing the village, then turned his pony and raced back toward the village, as the column started on his trail.[20]

Half a mile east, all was chaos. Escorted by Kicking Bear and Shell Boy, Crazy Horse and Black Shawl had mounted and started riding downstream at about 10:00 A.M. Before leaving, Crazy Horse informed the war council that he was going to Spotted Tail Agency. Black Fox declined to follow the war chief, ordering his seventy men to follow him across White River. The warriors formed a row along a knoll some six hundred yards south of the river. In full panoply of Lakota war gear, they made an imposing sight as the right-wing battalion of Oglalas and troops approached the mouth of Little White Clay. At the same time, the left wing was approaching the deserted campground. Fanned out to the north and west, Clark's contingent could see a few families straggling out for the bluffs. Some of the people in the rear, disheartened and fearful, drifted back to surrender, but all eyes were now on the south side of the river. There Little Big Man drew up his pony again before the chiefs and officers, warning them that the northern warriors were "going to show a fight." As he spoke, Black Fox's warriors began to advance down the hillside toward the right wing. Darting ahead of them on a swift pony, a Sans Arc youth waved a revolver. Sixteen years old, Crayfish was a veteran of the Custer battle and utterly fearless. The right wing was ordered to halt as Crayfish charged the column, threading between some of the lead riders before whipping back up the hill toward his comrades.[21]

The scene was now set for the height of the drama. From the center of the northern line, Black Fox nudged his pinto forward. He carried a Springfield carbine, with a revolver belted at his waist. In magnificent war gear topped by a superb trailer headdress, he appeared the epitome of Lakota valor. Kicking his pony into a gallop, Black Fox harangued the Oglalas and troops, "I have looked all my life to die," he chanted; "I see only the clouds and the ground; I am all scarred up." He drew his knife and clamped it between his teeth, riding headlong for the line of chiefs and officers. From that line, American Horse and He Dog stepped forward. American Horse held aloft his pipe, saying, "Brother-in-law, hold on, let up, save the women and children. Come straight for the pipe; the pipe is yours. Hold on," American Horse repeated, as Black Fox reined in, "we have not come down for anything like that; we came down to save you. Don't you make any trouble."[22]

At length, Black Fox drew up and assented "hou." Tentatively, American Horse and Black Fox shook hands and sat on the ground some fifteen feet in front of the line of agency leaders. The pair smoked together while behind them thirty northern warriors executed a precise series of mounted maneuvers. Black Fox declared that Crazy Horse had run away with his wife to Spotted Tail Agency. "He listens to too many bad talks. I told him we came in for peace, but he would listen to them. Now he is gone and the people belong to me. I come to die, but you saved me."[23]

American Horse told him that they had come to arrest Crazy Horse and disarm the village, but with the war chief having fled, his following would probably only have to come to Red Cloud Agency and join the tribal hoop. "If this is all" replied Black Fox, "I am glad to hear it." He rose to address his followers. "All over," he shouted. "Hey, stop this running and get back there." Without a word, still riding in perfect order and ready to fly or fight at a word from Black Fox, the warriors turned their ponies to cross the river onto the campground. Mightily impressed by Black Fox's command, Billy Garnett remembered, "That very man had the control of that village."[24]

As the tense standoff dissolved, Mason ordered officers' call. Just then Crazy Horse was seen, topping a distant rise to the east. Officers and chiefs huddled to identify the little party. Riding at the front was Black Shawl, with her husband and his two comrades, Kicking Bear and Shell Boy, in a protective arc behind her. Even as they appeared, the four riders vanished over the rise. Clark detailed No Flesh to take ten of his Kiyuksa warriors and capture Crazy Horse. As he lashed up his pony, No Flesh announced he intended to kill the war chief.[25]

The group of officers and chiefs paused a while. Reviewing "further particulars," Clark ordered No Water and a second detail of ten scouts from the right wing to "arrest [Crazy Horse] and bring him to my house" at Camp Robinson. "I promised No Water $200 if he accomplished his mission." As No Water's party loped east, the officers crossed the river to the campground. American Horse led a scout detachment to bring the rest of the women and children back from the bluffs. By 11 A.M. Mason and Clark had started the procession back to the agency. Before noon some forty-three lodges had surrendered, relieved at the leniency of their reception. Soon after midday, they pitched tipis in the tribal circle rising outside the Red Cloud Agency compound. As the work began, Clark scribbled a hurried note to apprise Lee at Spotted Tail of the morning's events and of the flight of the Oglala war chief toward his agency.[26]

Forty-five miles east of Red Cloud Agency, Beaver Creek takes its rise in the uplands of the Pine Ridge, flowing north through a valley confined by low pine-topped bluffs and ridges. In 1877 the valley was the home of more than one thousand lodges of Brule Sioux and their northern Lakota relatives. Spotted Tail Agency, located twelve miles south of the mouth of the creek, and its military post, Camp Sheridan, three-quarters of a mile to the north, were the points of reference in the political geography of the valley. Upstream of the agency in three vast tipi camps were the host Brules. Three miles north of Camp Sheridan, at the forks of Beaver Creek, was Touch the Clouds's village. Lining the creek between the northern village and Camp Sheridan were a few Oglala tipis. Worm was living there, as were kin like Standing Bear and Fast Thunder, several of Black Shawl's relatives, and Crazy Horse's hunka brother Horn Chips.[27]

Agent Lee and Spotted Tail had left Camp Robinson at 4:00 A.M. and approached their agency late in the morning. They found Captain Burke receiving the surrender of Shedding Bear's fourteen lodges. As Burke tallied people, stock, and firearms, Lee explained the situation at Red Cloud. Before departure, Clark had assured Lee he need not fear: Clark could lay his hands on Crazy Horse at any time he wished, and no disruption would spread to the Brule agency. Neither Lee nor Burke was so sanguine. Camp Sheridan was manned by one company of cavalry and one of infantry, and the officers agreed that preparations for the worst must be made.[28]

The Shedding Bear camp had been accompanied to the agency by three of the northern Deciders. After the situation was outlined to them, Touch the Clouds and Red Bear agreed to return to their village, "to try to hold their people steady." Roman Nose would remain at the agency to dampen excitement there. Spotted Tail had already departed to prepare the Brule villages.[29]

The hours passed in mounting tension until 2 P.M., when an Indian courier raced into the agency, declaring, "the soldiers were fighting Indians over at Red Cloud." Roman Nose quelled the clamor, and White Thunder, a Brule chief and scout sergeant, was hurried down to keep Touch the Clouds in line. White Thunder took with him Black Crow, son-in-law of Spotted Tail. Lean, sharp-faced Black Crow was as ready to shoot down Crazy Horse as any of Clark's Oglala partisans.[30] As the afternoon progressed, more loyal Brules joined them and by "dint of hard effort . . . were succeeding fairly well" in controlling the northern village. About 4:00 P.M., however, news arrived that a true crisis had come.[31]

Black Crow rode into Lee's compound, shouting, "*Crazy Horse is in the northern camp!*" The Brule warrior was sent back to the village with orders for the northern Deciders to bring Crazy Horse to the post. Simultaneously, Clark's courier appeared. Lee tore open Clark's note:

> Dear Lee—There has been no fight. Crazy Horse's band is just going into camp and will give up their guns without trouble in all probability. Crazy Horse has skipped out for your place. Have sent after him. Should he reach your agency, have "Spot" arrest him, and I will give any Indian who does this $200.00.[32]

Soon after this thunderbolt, fifteen or twenty Oglala scouts rode into Camp Sheridan, No Flesh's party sent in pursuit of Crazy Horse. The party seemed anxious to hide themselves and their exhausted ponies. No Flesh requested Burke's assistance in arresting Crazy Horse.[33]

To assess the latest news, Lee and agency interpreter Louis Bordeaux rode to Camp Sheridan, where Touch the Clouds appeared "in great excitement and said that he understood that Crazy Horse had taken refuge in his camp." With difficulty, Lee and Burke managed to pacify the Miniconjou chief, who was anxious that the roundup operation was intended for his village also. At length Touch the Clouds agreed to return to his village and "retain Crazy Horse there at all hazards."[34]

Shortly afterward, Spotted Tail arrived to report that the northern village was striking its tipis. Burke and Lee agreed that they must leave immediately for the village. Spotted Tail would assemble the Brule warriors and follow. Taking along Bordeaux and post surgeon Egon A. Koerper, Burke and Lee boarded the post ambulance and started down Beaver Creek. Within a mile, they met Jose Merrivale and Charley Tackett, who announced that Crazy Horse, Touch the Clouds, and a large party of northern Lakotas were on their way to the post. After another half mile, at about 5:30 P.M., the anxious officers saw three hundred warriors drawn up in a line of battle. Many wore warbonnets. Lances and other weapons were brandished as the ambulance drew up and its passengers climbed down to meet the Oglala war chief and his escort.[35]

Seven and a half hours before the confrontation on Beaver Creek, Crazy Horse and Black Shawl had ridden out of the northern Oglala village. Although soon aware that two groups of Oglala scouts were in pursuit, Crazy Horse acted coolly. The doubts and premonitions of the last few days were put aside. In the heady rush of action, the war chief once more made quick, lucid decisions. This would be a sustained chase, and he told Black Shawl to pace the ponies. On level ground and downhill, they put their mounts to a run, but at the foot of hills and ridges, the little party slowed to climb the slope at a walk, conserving the strength of their animals. At the hilltop, the horses were fresh again and responded easily to the downhill run. At first their gain on the scouts seemed imperceptible: for hours, the pursuing dust raised twin clouds at a steady distance behind them. But both groups of scouts were using their horseflesh to exhaustion, racing uphill and down at a gallop. By the time they crossed Chadron Creek, the gap was lengthening. No Water's first pony foundered; the corporal mounted a second horse and quirted it mercilessly onward before it too collapsed and died. His party walked their mounts the rest of the way. No Flesh's party closed the distance enough for a shouted exchange with Crazy Horse, but as they crossed the Bordeaux Creek flats, their horses too played out. By 2:00 P.M. Crazy Horse and Black Shawl were free of pursuit and able to slow their sweating mounts as they approached Beaver Creek.[36]

The couple swung downstream and rode into the small cluster of Oglala tipis. As Black Shawl dismounted, relatives hurried to help her to her mother's tipi, but Crazy Horse had little time for farewells. Pausing briefly at the lodge of Horn Chips, who could warn him of the scout deployments along the valley, the war chief remounted and rode downstream.[37]

When Crazy Horse, eluding White Thunder's Brule scouts, galloped into the northern village about 3:30 P.M., "there was a wild scene," Lee learned, "beggaring description." Miniconjou and Sans Arc warriors whooped their support of the man who had led them to victory against Custer.[38]

After dispatching Black Crow to the agency, White Thunder rode boldly into the village to make his arrest. Brule scouts followed their sergeant, but facing the overwhelming force of northern warriors, they were compelled to withdraw. Supporters knotted around Crazy Horse to lead him to the council lodge. As the village briefly quieted, White Thunder deployed his followers to form a cordon around the village.[39]

Inside the council tipi, the Sans Arc Deciders presided over a council of warriors. Crazy Horse argued forcefully for an immediate flight north. After a half-hour debate, Red Bear told heralds to order tipis struck. The women hurried to comply, and the two hundred northern lodges "came down with magic swiftness." White Thunder ordered his party to ride the outer circle of tipis, haranguing the village. Asserting Brule authority, they ordered their northern relatives to stop: at length, as women paused in their work, the Brule speeches "restored some degree of quiet" to the village.[40]

An anxious hush descended. As White Thunder pondered his next move, Black Crow returned from the agency, then rode alone into the village. With no concessions to council propriety, Black Crow told the war chief "that He understood that he Crazy Horse never listened, But now he had got to listen and had got to come with him to the Commanding Officer" at Camp Sheridan. Over the murmur of objections, he stated flatly, "You must listen to me. You must come with me."[41]

Black Crow's manner left the northern leaders in no doubt of Brule resolve. To Crazy Horse's dismay, the Sans Arc Deciders issued new orders. While High Bear remained in camp to oversee the repitching of tipis, Red Bear would lead the warriors to Camp Sheridan. They would escort Crazy Horse and see that no harm was done to him. As the warriors hurried to don war clothes and untether their best ponies, Black Crow rode outside the camp circle to confer with White Thunder. Quickly the two men agreed that Crazy Horse was to be shot if he attempted escape. They ordered the rest of the "reliables" to mingle with the northern warriors. About 5:10 P.M. the three hundred-strong escort started upstream. Three riders formed the front: Red Bear and White Thunder, flanking Crazy Horse. Immediately behind Crazy Horse rode Black Crow, well positioned to shoot the war chief dead.[42]

Shortly after starting, Touch the Clouds appeared, riding hard from the post. He joined the line of leaders, riding between Crazy Horse and Red Bear as the party observed Burke and Lee's ambulance approaching them. The leaders reined in, the warriors fanning out into a long line, resplendent with warbonnets, shields, banner lances, and war shirts, across the valley. As the ambulance drew up and its passengers climbed out, the line pressed forward—"very much excited," concluded Agent Lee. First out of the ambulance was Dr. Koerper. The surgeon had recently treated Touch the Clouds's family, and he walked coolly toward the Miniconjou chief, proffering his right hand in friendship. Touch the Clouds stared straight ahead. The moment stretched; then Koerper walked the last few steps to stand on Touch the

Clouds's left. Still holding out his right hand, Koerper placed his left on the neck of the Miniconjou's pony. At last Touch the Clouds relented, and took the doctor's hand in friendship.[43]

Burke and Lee now approached the leaders. Crazy Horse leaned forward tentatively to shake the officers' hands. Through Louis Bordeaux, Burke and Lee asked that Crazy Horse accompany them to Camp Sheridan, "as they wished to talk with him."

"I have been talked to," responded the war chief, "night and day[,] until my brain has turned."[44]

Asked why he had come to Spotted Tail, Crazy Horse replied that "he had come away from Red Cloud with his sick wife, and to get away from trouble there." He at last signaled his agreement to go to the post. As the party readied itself to start, Lee observed the war chief. Lean and melancholy, "Crazy Horse was sitting on his pony with [a] very much distressed look in his countenance."[45]

With the ambulance leading the way, the procession started for the post. After a while White Thunder rode to catch up with Bordeaux, riding behind the ambulance. White Thunder advised the interpreter "to tell the officers to hurry back and get home[;] that there was danger." Bordeaux rode forward and urged Lee to speed up. The driver urged the mules to a lope, and the ambulance lurched ahead. By now nervous, Bordeaux hurried his horse ahead of the ambulance as the post appeared in sight.[46]

On the far side of the open parade ground and post buildings, another mounted force could be seen approaching from the south: Spotted Tail was bringing his promised warriors to prevent any crisis. Beyond, on the hills and benches west of the creek, Brule camps were also moving downstream, to pitch tipis around the agency. Suddenly, a new movement was detected. No Water's party of scouts, walking their punished ponies, approached the post. Seeing the uniforms of the Oglala scouts, the northern warriors burst forward from their line. White Thunder's scouts interposed themselves between the two parties, forcing the warriors back into line. At last Crazy Horse quietly told the northern warriors to fall back. Wasting little time, No Water's party mounted their beaten ponies and hurried upstream to the agency.[47]

The ambulance lumbered onto the Camp Sheridan parade ground with its escort of warriors, shouting and singing. Simultaneously, Spotted Tail's three hundred Brule warriors rode in from the south. The two parties edged forward, their flanks pressing ahead so that the lines threatened to converge and only a space at the center, about six feet by eight, was left empty. Into this arena, the officers debarked from the ambulance. Through Bordeaux and Merrivale, they asked Crazy Horse to enter the office with them, but the war chief would not speak. Impatiently, Burke told Crazy Horse that he could not stay here; he would have to return to Red Cloud Agency. Burke promised him that he would not be hurt, but Crazy Horse remained silent. Now Burke turned to address the northern warriors, asking them through Merrivale to dismount, but they did not respond.[48]

Spotted Tail nudged his pony into the gap and said, "I am Spotted Tail, the Chief of the Sioux and I want you[,] Crazy Horse[,] to go to [Camp Robinson] to talk with the White Chief." On both sides warriors continued to press forward, contracting the space in the center to "about the size of a prize ring."[49]

The officers proposed that the chiefs "go into a house for a talk; but the [northern Indians] insisted that they all had a right to hear what was said." Crazy Horse appeared ever more fearful of treachery: one woman watching from the post buildings observed that the war chief "looked like a hunted animal." The mill of warriors was growing ever louder; whoops and yells sounded as rifles and pistols were flourished openly, and Burke and the interpreters could no longer make themselves heard. Spotted Tail again seized the initiative and, speaking in "a clear, ringing voice" to Crazy Horse, facing him only six feet away, declared,

> We never have trouble here. . . . [T]he sky is clear, the air is still and free from dust! You have come here and you must listen to me and my people! I am chief here. We keep the peace. We, the Brules, do this! *They obey me!* and every Indian who comes here must listen to me! You say you want to come to this agency and live peaceably. If you stay here you must listen to me. That is all![50]

Spotted Tail's dramatic pauses were punctuated by the click of Winchester hammers, and as he closed, "400 vociferous 'hows'" acclaimed the Brule chief. Spotted Tail asked Crazy Horse if he would now talk with the officers in the adjutant's office. Crazy Horse finally offered his first words since reaching the post. "I will," he quietly agreed.[51]

Just as the situation seemed to be resolving itself, a frenzied warrior urged his pony into the gap. Buffalo Chips, a Sans Arc, turned his pony to face Crazy Horse. "You are afraid to die, but I will die for you," he shouted. Turning to Spotted Tail, he shouted again, "You are a coward!" and leapt from the saddle. Crazy Horse sat stolidly, but Spotted Tail laughed. Buffalo Chips seized Captain Burke by the shoulders, clutching at his uniform coat. He begged Burke to hang him instead of Crazy Horse.[52]

Burke laughed nervously and observed that he did not want to hang anyone. As Buffalo Chips ran out of breath, a Loafer warrior thrust his carbine into the Sans Arc's face, and a second Brule rode up. He dragged Buffalo Chips across his pony and urged it through the crowd. After the extravagant performance, the crowd quieted and began dispersing. Only a few leading Lakotas remained on the ground, and as daylight failed, they dismounted and followed the officers and Crazy Horse into Burke's private quarters.[53]

The little group sat in chairs or on the floor. Burke and Lee, with the post adjutant scribbling notes and Louis Bordeaux interpreting, faced Crazy Horse and Touch the Clouds. Spotted Tail and Swift Bear represented the Brule chiefs. Crazy Horse, recalled Lee, "seemed like a frightened, trembling, wild animal, brought to bay, hoping for confidence one moment and fearing treachery the next. He had been under a severe nervous strain all day and it plainly showed."[54]

Nevertheless, when the war chief was invited to speak, the officers were impressed. Asked to state why he had left Red Cloud to come to Spotted Tail, Crazy Horse first observed that "he should like to keep his country"; then repeated "that there had been so much trouble over at the other camp and he had been talked to so much that his head was in a whirl, and he wanted to get away."[55]

Moreover, he expanded, at Red Cloud "there were bad winds blowing. He did not understand why it was so but that there was feeling against him there and he was being misrepresented. He was desirous of having peace, for which purpose he had surrendered and he would be glad to do anything to keep out of trouble, but he did not think this would be possible over at Red Cloud."[56]

He added that he had fled the Oglala agency only when he saw a big body of scouts coming to his camp; he had gone to his kinsman Touch the Clouds to avoid disturbance. Moreover, his wife was ill, and he had brought her here to be treated. Therefore, he would like "to be transferred to Spotted Tail Agency where things were quiet and no winds blowing. He would be out of the turmoil and he would assure [the officers] that if this request would be granted they would find him a peaceable Indian."[57]

Burke and Lee asked how the "reported threats and conspiracies had become current and . . . if he had said such things in council as Grouard had reported him to have said." Crazy Horse denied them strenuously and agitated that he had been misrepresented since the talk with Clark four days previously.[58]

In a speech of unprecedented length, the war chief tried to set the record straight. He recalled his surrender, when he told Lieutenant Clark on the pipe that he would go no more to war. That promise was the reason why he had not wanted to scout against the Nez Perces. "When I was asked to take my young men to go and fight the Nez Perces I did not refuse. I said that I had come here because I was told that there should be peace and not war between the white man and the red man. Now there was war again. I am asked to take a few of my young men to go and fight. I will not do that. If the white man cannot conquer his enemies, I will take all my people and go north *and do it for him*." Pausing for a moment, he addressed his Lakota hosts, "At Red Cloud I am in constant trouble. I understand you have a good Agent here and I wish to join this Agency and stay here."[59]

After Touch the Clouds confirmed that these had been Crazy Horse's words in the talk with Clark, the door was opened to admit a courier. He handed to Burke a letter from Bradley stating that the war chief must be captured and returned to Camp Robinson. Quickly scanning the note, Burke turned to his adjutant and whispered to him "to write . . . in reply explaining the dangers and difficulties of the situation and saying that Crazy Horse would be persuaded to return." A note was quickly scribbled and hurried off to Bradley. Burke conferred briefly with Lee, explaining the new development. The officers returned to the talk just after sunset, about 8:00 P.M.[60]

Burke and Lee explained to Crazy Horse that they had received orders to send him to Camp Robinson. The "only thing for him to do was to go over there and make his statement of his case there. [Crazy Horse] was under some misgivings and did not know . . . what was best to do. If Lee and Burke would promise to intercede for him with Gen. Bradley and have him transferred to Spotted Tail, he would go."[61]

Lee took up the conversation, pledging "his word . . . that no harm should happen to [Crazy Horse]," and that he would have the opportunity to state his case fully to Bradley the next day. Moreover, both Lee and Burke would use their influence to have Crazy Horse's village transferred to the Brule agency.[62]

Lee would personally accompany the war chief the following morning and "get him a hearing."[63] Swift Bear and Touch the Clouds would use their influence to expedite the transfer. Spotted Tail was more guarded. He insisted that the "Oglala people are yours. Something good should happen to you with them." Crazy Horse had to return to Camp Robinson. As the minimum of good manners, Spotted Tail promised him a fine horse but left little doubt that he had no wish for his nephew's presence.[64]

Crazy Horse "seemed to realize his helplessness." Lee stressed he would report his words to Bradley. At last, with great reluctance, Crazy Horse granted that he would go with Lee in the morning. He asked for something to eat, food that would cement kinship relations with the Brule agency hierarchy.[65]

As a quick meal was prepared, plans were made for the night. Swift Bear suggested that Crazy Horse be permitted to sleep at Touch the Clouds's village. The Miniconjou chief pledged that he would see Crazy Horse returned to Camp Sheridan at 9:00 in the morning. Crazy Horse was given into the care of Touch the Clouds, and the two men rode back down Beaver Creek. Immediately after they left, Burke and Lee conferred privately with Spotted Tail and Swift Bear. To ensure the war chief was secured, four or five Brule scouts were detailed to watch the northern village.[66]

Night had fallen, and as Crazy Horse and his comrades wound down the valley, the scatter of Oglala tipis bloomed like lanterns. Pausing in the ride downstream, Crazy Horse dismounted and was asked into the tipi of Standing Bear, who was married to two of his cousins. Over a quiet meal, Crazy Horse asked Standing Bear to accompany him to Camp Robinson in the morning. He was anxious to recruit as many relatives as possible to ride with him, mindful of Spotted Tail's guarded warning that "something bad" might happen to him here.[67]

At his village, Touch the Clouds placed a small tipi at Crazy Horse's disposal. After a final meal in the Miniconjou chief's lodge, Crazy Horse rode out a short way, tethering his pony atop a wooded hill. Alone in the darkness "he prayed for guidance for himself." As he meditated, he must have reflected on the day's events. Of the objectives he had identified that morning, only Black Shawl's safety had been secured. "I should like to keep my country," he had told the officers, but the words already rang elegiacally, as when we prepare at last to give up an ideal long cherished. Could the future lie here, at Spotted Tail, relinquishing his role as war chief and taking up the life of a healer, marked out for him in the visions of the previous winter? Political marginalization he knew was the price of life at his uncle's agency. But even this minimal option seemed elusive: Spotted Tail's distaste for the prospect showed through the thin veneer of respect and kin obligation.

A day of real action had temporarily relieved the vicious cycle of mood swings for the war chief. Now, in tranquility, he found no peace. "He believed something was going to happen." Misgivings filled him, and when he left the hill to talk late with Touch the Clouds, he dwelled on death. He had thought long on the significance of his visions, and they now offered him what reassurance he could muster for the future. Reflecting on his lifelong affinity with the powers of Rock, he told his cousin that after death, "his bones would turn to rock and his joints to flint." Now he sought sleep, but Touch the Clouds pondered his cousin's words. To him, it seemed that Crazy Horse was "looking to die."[68]

29

THIS DAY IS MINE

Late that night a private meeting gathered in the Camp Sheridan sutler's store. Captain Burke and his adjutant welcomed Agent Lee, interpreters Bordeaux and Tackett, and Spotted Tail with fellow Brules Swift Bear, White Thunder, and Coarse Voice. Touch the Clouds had also been summoned. In a lengthy debate, the men juggled the awkward priorities of the case. Bradley had ordered an arrest, but military realities and the officers' consciences sat uneasily with any betrayal of their promises to Crazy Horse. It was finally agreed that Spotted Tail would organize the Brule scouts to escort Lee and Crazy Horse to Camp Robinson soon after 9:00 A.M.[1]

Burke was already busy at his desk when a courier rode up just before dawn with a new dispatch from Bradley:

> Camp Robinson
> Midnight.
>
> Dear Major:
>
> Your dispatch received. If you have got my dispatch written about 4 o'clock, it tells you too much. I wrote it after getting the report of Col. Mason, and Clark. We did not get the whole village, but got the greater part of it and shall get some more lodges to-night. Crazy Horse must be held as a *prisoner* and must come here as such, keep him securely and I will send a body of Indians to bring him here. All the Indians here are with us and behave well, including Little Big Man and the other Northern Chiefs.
>
> Yours Truly,
> [sign.] L. P. Bradley.[2]

Burke viewed the letter with moral and practical misgivings. It implied active disarming and physical restraint of the war chief. Early in the morning, he sent a messenger to Bradley stating simply that he would have Crazy Horse sent over in an ambulance, accompanied by scout sergeants Swift Bear, Touch the Clouds, and High Bear.[3]

Burke was not alone in having misgivings as daylight gathered on Wednesday, September 5. At the northern village, Crazy Horse had risen from his troubled sleep full of foreboding. Touch the Clouds and High Bear prepared to ride back to Camp Sheridan. Worm appeared and advised his son to unwrap his sacred bundle and invoke the aid of his guardian the red-tailed hawk. Crazy Horse declined but, as his party passed the Oglala camp halfway to the post, he prevailed on his cousin Fast Thunder to join the group. Fast Thunder, now a trusted scout, and his wife hitched up their wagon and followed the war chief.[4]

At Camp Sheridan, the scene seemed eerily calm. Crazy Horse and Touch the Clouds waited outside post headquarters, talking to Charley Tackett. Swift Bear and Black Crow rode over from the Brule camps, and Bordeaux appeared from the agency. Burke and Lee were delayed. The war chief's apprehension was palpable as they awaited the arrival of the officers. At length Crazy Horse said that "he must go back to Touch the Cloud's camp and get a saddle, he having come from his camp at Red Cloud on his horse bareback." Tackett brought permission from Major Burke, with word that the officers and scouts would follow him to the northern village.[5]

Crazy Horse leapt astride his pony and wheeled out of the parade at a run. It was a disturbing sign. Captain Burke appeared, and after a hurried consultation, Swift Bear and Touch the Clouds detailed two scout officers, Good Voice and Horned Antelope, to follow the war chief. Instructed to shoot Crazy Horse's pony should he attempt to escape, the scouts were also ordered to kill him if he resisted. Accompanied by Tackett, Touch the Clouds, and High Bear, Burke followed at a run down Beaver Creek.[6]

Minutes later Lee arrived and boarded the post ambulance with Bordeaux. Swift Bear and Black Crow also climbed aboard. The driver whipped up the four-mule team, followed by a string of scouts. At the village, Bordeaux directed the driver to Touch the Clouds's tipi, where Burke and Tackett were pacing anxiously. Lee conferred hurriedly with Burke. The war chief had changed his mind, Burke warned, and refused to return: "If I go to Red Cloud there will be trouble," Crazy Horse had confided; he "'was afraid that something [bad] would happen'" there.[7]

Touch the Clouds had placed a small tipi at Crazy Horse's disposal, and the officers repaired there. Speaking through Tackett, the war chief "asked us to go down [to Camp Robinson] without him, and fix up the matter for him and his people," recalled Lee. "We assured him we had no thought of harming him in any way; that he owed it to his people at Red Cloud to return, and we insisted on his returning peaceably and quietly." After some thought, Crazy Horse outlined some preconditions for his return: agreeing that neither he nor Lee should take arms, he requested that the agent first tell Lieutenant Clark all that had occurred since Crazy Horse's arrival at Spotted Tail. Then he wished to make a full statement of his own of "how 'he had been misunderstood and misinterpreted; that he wanted peace and quiet, and did not want any trouble whatever.'" Crazy Horse also wanted Lee to tell Clark "that Major Burke, Spotted Tail and [Lee] were willing to receive him by transfer from Red Cloud." Lee gave his personal pledge of safety but reminded Crazy Horse that such a decision rested in Bradley's hands. Clearly unhappy, Crazy Horse suddenly left the tipi to consult friends in the council lodge.[8]

Telling Lee to continue talks, "get Crazy Horse if he could and go right on," Burke decided to ride back to Camp Sheridan, gather the Brule scouts, and return to make an arrest should negotiations break down.[9] After Burke's departure with Tackett, Bordeaux rejoined the agent in the small tipi. The two men sat nervously and "waited for Crazy Horse to get ready."[10]

In the council tipi, consensus favored the war chief's return to Camp Robinson: all present "urged him to go."[11] A party of Brule scouts and akicita, led by Sergeant Whirlwind Soldier, a Decider in Spotted Tail's village, had followed from Camp Sheridan. Three Bears and Spider, Oglala messengers just arrived from Camp Robinson, accompanied the Brules. The Oglalas insisted that Crazy Horse return with them to Red Cloud Agency, but their hosts ensured that the debate remained relaxed. Whirlwind Soldier, Swift Bear, and Black Crow all spoke to the same effect, "coaxing" Crazy Horse toward compliance.[12]

Crazy Horse looked again for reassurance. His gaze rested briefly on the lean profile of Turning Bear, a Brule scout and an old comrade in the north. Crazy Horse asked Turning Bear his advice. The Brule "advised him to go and said he would accompany him" to Camp Robinson. The assurance of solidarity, the same promise of support Crazy Horse had sought from Standing Bear and Fast Thunder, was enough to tip the balance. Outside a herald could be heard, calling the war chief to eat at the tipi of Touch the Clouds. Indicating his tacit consent to departure, Crazy Horse left the council lodge.[13]

Meanwhile Lee's patience had expired. He instructed Louis Bordeaux "to go in and get Crazy Horse" just as the herald called the war chief to eat. Outside, Bordeaux met Crazy Horse, whose mood had transformed again. Crazy Horse asked the interpreter "to come and breakfast with him" as he ducked through the doorway into Touch the Clouds's tipi. After advising Lee, the interpreter joined Crazy Horse.[14]

After breakfast, Crazy Horse stepped outside, where Lee walked through the crowd, his hand outstretched. The two men shook hands. Lee agreed to Crazy Horse's conditions about the agenda of talks with Bradley and Clark, telling the war chief, "he was no coward and could face the music over there. This remark," Lee recalled, "seemed to appeal to him and he said he would go."[15]

"Hou. *Anpetu ki le mitawa*," said Crazy Horse, pausing for Bordeaux to interpret ("This day is mine") before adding that he would accompany Lee presently. The agent indicated the ambulance, but Crazy Horse asked to ride, for the vehicle would make him sick. Lee agreed, and Swift Bear stepped forward, leading two ponies, gifts from his famous herd to seal goodwill. Crazy Horse requested that seven northern Lakotas ride with him, "to see fair play." Swift Bear and Touch the Clouds ordered Good Voice and Horned Antelope to join the party riding with Crazy Horse, "to take care of him and prevent his escape." Then they clambered aboard the ambulance with Black Crow and High Bear.[17]

Crazy Horse continued to talk with friends. As Lee watched anxiously, Bordeaux "asked him if he was now ready to go. Crazy Horse replied that he was," adding that Lee should start the ambulance and he would follow. Reluctantly, Lee agreed, remarking to Bordeaux, "Let us go and cross Beaver Creek, and if he does not come we will go back here again and wait till Major Burke comes with the scouts."[18] Lee and Bordeaux climbed aboard, and the driver started the team out of the village. A string of Miniconjous rode or walked beside the vehicle, and Touch the Clouds leaned outside to order key followers to ride with Crazy Horse. Seven northern warriors, including the Miniconjou head akicita Charging Eagle, Touch the Clouds' younger brother Standing Elk, and his son Charging First, fell in line. Turning Bear and Hollow Horn Bear, Brule scouts, also joined the procession.[19]

The ambulance crossed Beaver Creek and stopped. Bordeaux looked back and saw Crazy Horse riding out of the village. Good Voice and Horned Antelope rode nearby, and then "nine or ten of Touch the Cloud's men" strung out behind. Satisfied, Lee ordered the driver to start again. Crazy Horse splashed through the creek, his party overtaking the ambulance as it lumbered forward.[20]

Meanwhile Burke and Spotted Tail had agreed on a strategy to ensure a successful outcome. Beginning about 11:00 A.M., sixty scouts would follow in three stages to reinforce the escort. Finally, about 1:30 P.M., No Flesh's and No Water's Oglalas would depart in time to strengthen the escort as it approached Camp Robinson. Fifteen miles out, as Crazy Horse's party crossed Little Bordeaux Creek, the first group of five or ten scouts overtook the ambulance. Soon another little party caught up, riding easily as if for company. At Chadron Creek, as stock was watered and grazed, a larger party appeared. Over forty scouts now constituted the escort. After the whole party lunched on scout rations, Crazy Horse arose to relieve himself. He thought himself alone, but at a footfall turned to find a scout following him. Realizing the reality of his captivity, he turned back.[21]

He asked Lee, "Am I a prisoner?" The agent assured his charge that no harm was intended, then ordered the party to mount and start on the second half of the journey.[22] Beyond Chadron Creek, the party sighted small groups of Lakotas that had left Red Cloud Agency to go on to Spotted Tail. Lee, exhausted after the strain of the past twenty-four hours, let his full stomach lull him into a fitful doze. Bordeaux also fell asleep. Suddenly, both men jerked awake. Scanning the trail ahead, they could see nothing of Crazy Horse. The war chief had "gone on ahead," explained Swift Bear, and ridden swiftly over the crest of the next rise barely one hundred yards away.[23]

Lee ordered scouts to bring back Crazy Horse. Galloping over the rise, they found him watering his pony at the next creek, talking to another Lakota party.

Their number included his old Miniconjou comrade Big Crow, Black Shield's son, and in the snatched exchange, the war chief was able to buckle on a holstered revolver beneath the red blanket belted at his waist. The scouts ordered Crazy Horse to return to the ambulance. White Thunder and Good Voice "directed [Crazy Horse] to ride immediately in the rear of my ambulance, and he saw at once he was closely guarded." Crazy Horse again "seemed nervous and bewildered, and his serious expression seemed to show that he was doubtful of the outcome. I tried to reassure his friends by telling them that I would do exactly as had been promised in presenting his case."[24]

The last increment of Brule scouts caught up with the party, reinforcing the escort to some sixty warriors. The straggling column tightened up as the ambulance paused near Ash Creek, fifteen miles from Red Cloud. Lee penned a quick note to Clark, asking whether to take Crazy Horse to the agency or to the post. He also requested that the agency authorities be asked to "keep its Indians off the road, so that we could go in quietly."[25] Lee stressed that "tact and discretion" had been used to secure Crazy Horse, implying that the war chief had not been arrested. Moreover, both he and Burke "*had promised* [Crazy Horse] *that he might state his case*, and wished when we reached Red Cloud that arrangements be made accordingly." Horned Antelope was detailed to deliver the note express to Clark. It was now about 3:45 P.M.[26]

At Camp Robinson, fevered preparations were under way. That morning, Bradley had wired the telegraph office in Cheyenne to update General Crook on the situation. After dispatches from Burke and Lee, he could report with some relief that "Crazy Horse was captured last night at Spotted Tail."[27] Lieutenant Clark sent a fuller report after the latest news from Burke: the Camp Sheridan commander would bring Crazy Horse to Camp Robinson today. Ignorant of the promises made to Crazy Horse, Clark assured his superior that the war chief "will be put in guard-house on arrival." Aware of Crook's switch to the Sheridan solution—incarceration of Crazy Horse in the east—Clark further advised that their prisoner "be started for Fort Laramie to-night," then hurried to the railroad and "kept going as far as [departmental headquarters in] Omaha, 2 or 3 Sioux going with him so that they can assure people on return that he has not been killed." Evincing the tortured ambivalences of the chain of command, Clark closed by requesting that Crook wire Bradley with instructions to this effect.[28]

At noon Crook arrived at the Union Pacific station in Cheyenne. After reading Clark's message, Crook dictated the required instructions to Bradley. Congratulating Bradley on "the successful termination of your enterprise," the general diplomatically asked that the instructions be conveyed to Clark "and others concerned. Send 'Crazy Horse' with a couple of his own people with him, under a strong escort, via Laramie to Omaha. Make sure that he does not escape."[29]

Crook then wired Sheridan about developments, indulging his superior's prejudices: "I wish you would send him off where he would be out of harm's way. . . .

The successful breaking up of 'Crazy Horse's' band has removed a heavy weight off my mind and I leave here feeling perfectly easy."[30] Crook hurried to board the westbound train. Soon after it started, Sheridan ordered Crook to have Crazy Horse sent on from Omaha to his Chicago headquarters. These instructions too were wired to Camp Robinson.[31]

After issuing a general order that upon arrival Crazy Horse be detained in the guardhouse, and posting a double guard around the post, Bradley called into the adjutant's office Captain Henry W. Wessells. He instructed Wessells to ready his unit, Company H, Third Cavalry, to leave the post at midnight as escort to an ambulance transporting Crazy Horse to Fort Laramie. The prisoner would then be taken by the Deadwood stage to Cheyenne, thence by railroad via Omaha and Chicago to imprisonment in Fort Marion, Florida.[32]

Bradley left the fine details of Crazy Horse's reception to Lieutenant Clark, who rode to the agency to assure Oglala assistance in the final stage of the operation. Little Big Man, on hand to represent the rump northern village, agreed to accompany Crazy Horse as far as Omaha. No Neck (half-brother to Woman Dress) and Plenty Wolves would also join the escort. Bat Pourier would guide.[33]

About 4:45 Horned Antelope arrived with Lee's message for Clark and news that the Crazy Horse party was within an hour's ride of the agency. Immediately, the chiefs dispatched akicita "to their villages to have it harangued for none of them to approach the party as they were passing the Agency, as it was feared that some young men might become excited, and probably make an attempt to rescue Crazy Horse."[34] Little Wound, Young Man Afraid of His Horse, and Yellow Bear would stay to keep order in the village. To ensure the securing of Crazy Horse in the guardhouse, Red Cloud and American Horse departed to lead the Bad Face and Loafer warriors immediately to Camp Robinson. Key northern scouts, including sergeants Little Big Man and Big Road, and corporal Iron Hawk, also rode to the post. Clark scribbled a note instructing Lee to take Crazy Horse straight to Bradley, handed it to Horned Antelope, and departed for Camp Robinson.[35]

The Red Cloud Agency buildings came in sight of Crazy Horse's escort, with over seven hundred Oglala tipis standing just south of the trail. Twenty Oglala scouts fell in line with the escort—the No Flesh and No Water party that had left Spotted Tail early in the afternoon. A messenger from Agent Irwin rode up to ask that the escort stop at the agency, so that Irwin could speak to Crazy Horse and "have him left there." The Brule scouts refused to stop.[36] Instead, the sergeants ordered all firearms loaded. Despite the orders of their chiefs, "great excitement" was visible in the Oglala camps. Some Oglala scouts held cocked rifles ready to shoot Crazy Horse, still riding behind the ambulance. Touch the Clouds leaned out of the ambulance to instruct his men to form a cordon on either side of the vehicle. Remember "the man," he ordered, "who first drew a gun among the Oglalas."[37]

The commotion brought Agent Irwin to view the procession. Satisfied that his Oglalas were "all Quiet," he returned to his office and penned a telegram reporting that Crazy Horse was "taken."[38]

Many Oglalas hurried after the escort. He Dog sent a messenger with orders to the escort "to bring Crazy Horse into my tipi. I meant to give him a good talking-to." This time the scouts did not even bother concocting a response. He Dog stripped his leggings and shirt, fastened his wotawe charm to his scalp lock, and clapped on his warbonnet. Stowing a shotgun under his red blanket, he did not pause to saddle his pony but rode bareback up the trail to Camp Robinson.[39]

Just at sunset, the party clattered over the bridge spanning White River. Among the escort flanking the ambulance, Charging First looked ahead up the slope and made out the post buildings and lines of soldiers drawn up for the evening parade. Turning in his saddle, he saw large numbers of mounted Oglalas catching up with the escort just as it approached the post. As they overtook the procession, spilling to the left and right around the buildings, Brule scouts harangued them, "telling the Oglalas they didn't want Crazy Horse and his people on their reservation [sic]."[40]

The post commander ordered officer of the day Captain James Kennington to the adjutant's office where Crazy Horse was to be turned over. Lieutenant Henry R. Lemly was to post his Company E, Third Cavalry, around the guardhouse, where the prisoner was to be held. Bradley then retired into his private quarters. At the far end of the parade ground, Lieutenant Clark did likewise. In an amazing abdication of personal responsibility, the two key officers on the ground chose to absent themselves at Camp Robinson's most troubled hour. Just then the ambulance appeared between Bradley's quarters and the infantry barracks, flanked by the escort and scores more Oglalas. Turning left, it cut across the parade ground and halted outside the adjutant's office. Crazy Horse reined in his pony and scanned with misgiving the thronging parade ground. It was 6:00 P.M.[41]

Already the parade was filling with excited Oglalas. Red Cloud stood with a line of Bad Face warriors extending from the adjutant's office across the parade ground, preventing Indians from infiltrating past the building toward the guard-house some sixty-six feet beyond. At the rear of the adjutant's office, American Horse had formed his Loafer warriors into a matching line to prevent infiltration from behind the buildings. Some soldiers were already falling out of barracks to assume positions around the guardhouse. As Crazy Horse observed this, He Dog rode up on his left. Defying Brule scouts who ordered him to keep back, He Dog leaned forward and shook hands with his old friend. "I saw that he did not look right," He Dog recalled.[42]

He Dog reproved Crazy Horse, "You should have listened to me and we could have gone to Washington . . . instead you listened to your people lie." At a loss for advice, He Dog concluded, "Look out—watch your step—you are going into a dangerous place."[43]

From the ambulance, the passengers alighted. As Crazy Horse dismounted at Bordeaux's instruction, a short figure in a red shirt bustled through the crowd. Little Big Man assumed "a rather superior manner . . . as though he was running the business," observed Bordeaux. Seizing Crazy Horse by the sleeve, he snapped, "Come on you coward!" Crazy Horse seemed astonished but said nothing as Little Big Man pulled on his sleeve.[44]

The two men walked to the office doorway, where Lee was talking to the adjutant, Lieutenant Fred Calhoun. The commanding officer, Calhoun explained, had left orders that Crazy Horse be turned over to the officer of the day. "Not yet," replied Lee, and asked if Crazy Horse might not speak with the commander. Calhoun stiffly referred Lee to Bradley at his private quarters. Turning, Lee asked Bordeaux to tell Crazy Horse to go into the office and sit down. "[T]his is not General Bradley's quarters," Crazy Horse observed, but with Little Big Man at his side, he entered the building, followed by Swift Bear, Touch the Clouds, High Bear, Black Crow, and Good Voice. Lee detailed a scout to wait at the door with orders to admit no one until his return.[45] Other Brules formed a line of guards outside the building, haranguing that none of Crazy Horse's followers should "go around there."[46]

Lee hurried across the parade ground to Bradley's quarters. The commander congratulated Lee on securing Crazy Horse but flatly refused to meet with the war chief, reiterating his order that the prisoner be turned over to the officer of the day. Lee pointed out the exceptional circumstances, but Bradley would not budge. Outlining his own orders from Sheridan, he insisted they permitted no latitude. Bradley grew angry as Lee importuned for clemency, snapping that it was too late to hold a talk. He ordered Crazy Horse turned over to the officer of the day. Lee could assure him that "*not a hair of his head should be harmed!*" Lee retraced his steps across the parade ground.[47]

Lee entered the adjutant's office and told Bordeaux that any hopes of a transfer for Crazy Horse had fallen through. Coaching Bordeaux to talk with the war chief, Lee insisted, "Do not tell him about this." Fearing trouble if Crazy Horse was put in the guardhouse, Lee advised, "Let us keep out of the squabble. We have brought him over here and done our duty to the government and done all we could for him." Lee concluded, "so let[']s not say anything that will stir up trouble."[48]

Lee explained to Crazy Horse that night was drawing on and that Bradley thought it too late for talks. "[I am] only a little chief and [I] cannot get you a hearing now, but the commanding officer says that if you will go with this man," pointing to Captain Kennington, "not a hair of your head will be injured." Crazy Horse and the other chiefs said "hou." Still wary, Crazy Horse scanned his friends' faces for reassurance. His own features brightened, and he shook Kennington's hand warmly.[49]

Outside, Red Feather and his friend White Calf had slipped the cordon of Brule scouts and sneaked around the back of the building. Peeking through the window, they eavesdropped as Kennington sought to explain that Crazy Horse "should go in the next house and stay there all day and after they got through supper they would take him to Washington." Little Big Man stood beside Crazy Horse, advising him that these orders came from Lieutenant Clark: "We'll do whatever White Hat says," he assured the war chief and the officer of the day.[50]

The transfer of authority complete, Lee called Swift Bear out of the office. "I have done all I can for Crazy Horse," he insisted. Swift Bear affirmed he had heard. Before departing, Lee told Bordeaux to summon Touch the Clouds and High Bear. The two northern chiefs, together with Big Road and Crazy Horse's kinsman Standing Bear, joined the little party. Lee repeated what he had told Swift Bear, adding that Crazy Horse would have an opportunity to talk with the officers at Camp Robinson in the morning. The chiefs indicated their approval. Bordeaux announced that Crazy Horse would not be harmed but would now be put in the guardhouse, in the charge of the soldiers.[51]

The group dispersed onto the parade ground. Bordeaux briefly stepped back into the office. He observed Captain Kennington take Crazy Horse by the right hand, saying, "Come with me," as he motioned his prisoner up with his free hand. Briefly, Crazy Horse held back, but as the officer pulled, he stood and stepped toward the door. Little Big Man followed and took hold of Crazy Horse's left arm, repeating, "Come on you coward." Walking between the two men, Crazy Horse stepped out of the office and onto the parade ground. His captors turned sharply left, still holding Crazy Horse's arms. As they walked, Little Big Man constantly told Crazy Horse he would stay by his side wherever they went. At sight of the officer of the day, two guards on the parade snapped smartly to attention and fell in behind the three men, bayoneted rifles held at their shoulders.[52]

As Crazy Horse was led toward the guardhouse, the crowd grew restive. "Rescue him!" someone shouted. A group of northern Lakotas began edging closer to the guardhouse, cocking their rifles and revolvers, when a body of mounted scouts rode up, hands raised in admonition. The warriors fell back.[53]

The movement toward the guardhouse was general. At least two hundred Indians were swarming around the building as Crazy Horse approached. In the half hour or so since Crazy Horse had arrived, the situation on the parade ground had changed significantly. Supporters of Crazy Horse were pressing forward on foot and horseback. Behind the two buildings, Oglala spectators were spilling up from the agency trail on foot, on horseback, and even in wagons. To meet the new tactical situation, American Horse had moved his Loafer warriors from behind the adjutant's office. With Red Cloud's Bad Faces, they formed a new line, extending out from the guardhouse front deep across the grounds. As Crazy Horse neared, the line was assailed by the press of his supporters. Men shouted at one another across the closing gap, waving cocked revolvers.[54]

Some supporters surged toward their war chief. A line of guards formed across the space between the two buildings as the little procession approached the guardhouse. In the lead was the Brule scout Turning Bear. Between Crazy Horse with his two captors and the crowd was Wooden Knife, a Miniconjou. Leaper walked behind Crazy Horse, while a few other scouts, including Big Road, Iron Hawk, and Long Bear, brought up the rear. Pausing briefly at the door, the group conferred. Manning guard post number one, a red-bearded infantryman walked back and forth in front of the building, his bayoneted rifle held at slope. At the approach of the party, he stood to attention and lowered his rifle. Turning Bear walked past him into the guardhouse. A few other scouts entered the building. Then, by sudden volition, Crazy Horse walked through the doorway. First Captain Kennington, attended by four soldiers of the guard, then Little Big Man and a few of Crazy Horse's friends, Horn Chips among them, followed the war chief into the building. At Kennington's order, the rest of the guard remained outside, facing the open door. The sentry resumed his position. The crowd quieted.[55]

Several Brules, including Swift Bear, Black Crow, Crow Dog, and Standing Bear, stayed outside the guardhouse, but Lee and many of the Brule scouts began to walk away, toward the line of officers' quarters. Bordeaux and fellow interpreter Billy Garnett continued to watch the open door of the guardhouse. Touch the Clouds, attended by his son, joined Swift Bear's group, as did Fast Thunder, just then drawing up and alighting from his wagon. The group tried to quiet the vocal protestors, but suddenly, some thirty seconds after the last of the party had entered the building, "something happened in there. I could hear the noise inside," remembered Garnett. The noise rose to an uproar, and suddenly Turning Bear ran outside, shouting, "This is a guard house."[56]

Inside the door, Crazy Horse had found himself in the main guardroom. Immediately to his right, a log wall divided the guardroom from the prison room proper. A single inner door, placed within two feet of the outer doorway, connected the two rooms. The guardroom quickly filled with twenty or more Lakota scouts and soldiers of the guard. Crazy Horse still expected only to be kept securely overnight—not to be imprisoned: Frank Grouard, watching him enter the building, saw that "he did not know that he was to be placed in confinement."[57]

Just as in the morning council, he had seized on Turning Bear's example and followed him into the guardhouse. Now for the last time, Crazy Horse's childlike capacity to trust fell through its characteristic vertigo into alarm, suspicion, and mistrust. Scanning the room, he saw the small grated window on the inner door and asked Turning Bear, "What kind of a place is this?"[58]

But the impetus in the crowded room was thrusting him toward the inner door. It swung open. Pressing behind Crazy Horse, Horn Chips heard Turning Bear offer to "be locked up and stay with him."[59] On either hand, Little Big Man and Captain Kennington continued to draw Crazy Horse forward. Suddenly, Turning Bear stopped in the open doorway, saying that "it was a hard place they were going into."[60]

Momentarily, Crazy Horse stopped. "Let us go back," concluded Turning Bear and started for the outer door. Amid a confusion of shouted orders, the forward impetus thrust Crazy Horse toward the prison room. Behind him, he could hear

Turning Bear run onto the parade ground, yelling, "It's the jail! It's the jail!" The crowd clamored. Through the inner doorway, Crazy Horse could see walls hung with shackles, and seven wasicu prisoners sitting or standing around the cell, several bound in manacles or leg irons. "I won't go in there," Crazy Horse said flatly. Behind him, the hammers of rifles clicked.[61]

Suddenly, he wrenched his arms free and flung them up, snatching at Little Big Man's face. His hand closed on a braid and pulled away his enemy's hair ornaments. "I wouldn't do that!" hissed Little Big Man. Crazy Horse thrust his arms forward. Bracing his outstretched hands on either side of the prison room door, he swung his body back against the guards. The men fell back. In the crush, the red blanket knotted at Crazy Horse's waist came undone, revealing a white-handled revolver holstered at his hip. He reached for his belt. Just then, scout Plenty Wolves snatched the revolver from its holster. "Go ahead!" shouted the scout, "Do whatever you want with him! I have got the weapon—the gun!"[62]

Crazy Horse drew his only other weapon, a butcher knife with its blade ground down for cutting tobacco. With his left hand, he snatched Little Big Man's knife from its scabbard. Crazy Horse turned and darted for the outer door. Guards presented bayonets but too late to confine the agile war chief. Captain Kennington, backing down the room, had drawn his sword and blocked Crazy Horse's exit. Brandishing both knives, Crazy Horse sprang at Kennington. The captain skillfully parried the thrusts and would have stabbed Crazy Horse had not another Lakota leapt between them. Crazy Horse darted for the gap. "Nephew, don't do that," yelled Little Big Man. "Don't! Don't do that!"[63]

As Crazy Horse bounded into the open doorway, Little Big Man sprang forward and seized him from behind, forcing the two blades against Crazy Horse's body. For a moment, Crazy Horse's impetus dragged Little Big Man on, but in the open doorway, their joint momentum braked. "Let me go! Let me go!" cried Crazy Horse. In plain sight of the baying crowd, the pair struggled briefly for mastery; then, with a surge of strength, Crazy Horse freed his right hand. With an adroit snap of his raised wrist and arm, he slashed his knife across Little Big Man's left hand, cutting the flesh between the bases of the thumb and forefinger. A second time the blade flashed down, opening an ugly gash in Little Big Man's forearm. The scout cried out and loosened his grip. Not pausing to consider the guards, Crazy Horse bounded onto the parade ground. He grunted "h'gun," the warrior's cry for courage. The crowd surged toward him.[64]

The guards facing the doorway sprang toward Crazy Horse, bayonets thrusting. Beyond them Oglala and Brule scouts were hurrying through the crowd, ordering bystanders back as they shouldered carbines or cocked revolvers. Red Cloud and American Horse roared at their followers, "Shoot to kill!" American Horse aimed his gun, but other Lakotas got in the way, and he lowered his weapon. Beyond the scouts, Crazy Horse could see his followers, many mounted, yelling defiance. He started to run, his blade bluffing a gap through the guards. He lunged at one of the scouts, as if to cut his way through. To Crazy Horse's right, Swift Bear, Black Crow, and Fast Thunder rushed up, seeking to stop the furor.[65]

Soldiers and scouts were streaming out of the guardhouse. Brandishing his sword, Kennington ran between the fugitive and the crowd, crying, "Kill the son of a bitch! Kill the son of a bitch!" Kennington momentarily blocked Crazy Horse's retreat, but the rush of Lakotas reduced him to impotently circling the throng, still crying, "Kill him! Kill him!" The swarming Lakotas forced Crazy Horse to check his run. Little Big Man, bounding outside in renewed pursuit, caught hold again of Crazy Horse's wrist. Swift Bear, Black Crow, and Fast Thunder raced up to grapple the war chief, one man managing to tackle him around the waist. With another violent effort, Crazy Horse tore himself free, but the impetus of the struggle threw him backward.[66]

Against the wall, the guardhouse sentry stood, moving his bayonet forward and back in prescribed drill. To the scout Yellow Horse, exiting the guardhouse, the butt of the rifle seemed almost to touch the wall. The sentry moved up just as Crazy Horse surged back toward him. He prodded forward with the bayonet. The blade tore through the back of Crazy Horse's shirt, on the left side above the hip. Without Crazy Horse's own reverse momentum, it might have done no more damage: Yellow Horse saw no more than a prod, "just enough to make him feel the bayonet." But Crazy Horse's own weight drove the bayonet deep between his kidneys, piercing the bowels and angling down toward the groin. The sentry tugged his rifle backward, the butt banging against the wall. Without pause, he delivered a second thrust smartly to the righthand side of the war chief's lower back. Piercing the lower ribs, the blade ranged upwards as Crazy Horse's body sagged, puncturing the right lung. The sentry withdrew the blade as Crazy Horse straightened. In the first rush of agony, his weight involuntarily bore down on his left heel, causing him to pivot right.[67]

Circling the wounded man, the sentry thrust at Crazy Horse from the front, but this time the bayonet lodged only in the guardhouse door. Little Big Man caught hold once more of Crazy Horse's arm. "Let me go; you've got me hurt now!" breathed the war chief. Just then, an uncle of Crazy Horse—perhaps the Miniconjou Spotted Crow—pushed through the crowd. He drove the butt of his rifle into Little Big Man's stomach, upbraiding the scout: "You have done this once before." Little Big Man reeled backward to sit in the dust, his hands braced to support himself. "You are always in the way!" roared Spotted Crow. A trumpeter sounded the urgent peal to arms.[68]

As Crazy Horse staggered backward, Swift Bear and his two comrades caught him, scolding, "We told you to behave yourself."[69] Groaning, Crazy Horse fell to his knees. For a moment he crouched, then the upper part of his body sagged, and he lay in the dust. The crowd, momentarily hushed, watched the wounded man begin to writhe on the ground. "I stood there, ready to drop," recalled He Dog.[70] Then people surged forward again. Frank Grouard heard cartridges being chambered and gun hammers clicking, expecting at any moment a shot that would start a battle. Infantry soldiers were hurrying from barracks. Mounted cavalry appeared from the barracks and stables behind the lower end of the parade ground.[71]

A knot of Lakotas quickly formed around Crazy Horse's body. Touch the Clouds knelt and tried to raise Crazy Horse's head. Caught in the crowd, his son Charging First shouted a warning and pushed aside the gun as an angry Lakota aimed at the Miniconjou chief. He Dog warned away another warrior who drew aim on Crazy Horse. He Dog was about to spread his own blanket over him when Crazy Horse gasped, "See where I am hurt. I can feel the blood flowing." He Dog bent to pull aside Crazy Horse's shirt. He viewed the two wounds. A lump was rising on the war chief's chest above where the second bayonet thrust had ended. Blood frothed at his mouth and nostrils. His breath came in gasps punctuated by grunts—"more from anger than pain," thought He Dog.[72]

When Closed Cloud, a Brule, came out of the guardhouse carrying Crazy Horse's blanket and knelt to lay it over him, a spasm of fury seized the war chief. He snatched at the Brule's braids and jerked his head weakly from side to side: "You all coaxed me over here," he scolded, "and then you ran away and left me!"[73] He Dog took the blanket from Closed Cloud and rolled it into a pillow for Crazy Horse. Then he covered his friend with his own blanket, reassuring him that he would "take him home." He Dog hurried across the parade ground toward Lieutenant Clark's quarters.[74]

Surgeon Valentine T. McGillycuddy wedged his way through the cordon of guards to kneel beside the war chief. A bloody spittle filmed Crazy Horse's lips, and he ground his teeth in agony as McGillycuddy turned over his body. Blood was trickling from the wound at his hip, and his pulse was faint and irregular. These were mortal wounds. McGillycuddy advised Kennington of the situation. Kennington ordered four guards to carry Crazy Horse back into the guardhouse. Barely had the men positioned themselves around the body when a powerful northern Lakota laid a hand on McGillycuddy's shoulder. Another older man leapt from his pony, clutching a bow and arrows in one hand and aiming his revolver at Kennington with the other. scouts threw him to the ground, wresting away his weapons.[75]

A row of thirty mounted men, supporters of Crazy Horse, kneed their horses through the crowd. Several Brules urged the party to stop: Crow Dog clubbed his carbine and forced the line to rein in. Bat Pourier had just appeared on the scene from Clark's office, and he pleaded with Kennington, "For God's sake, captain, stop!" As the mounted warriors paused, Pourier began talking in Lakota. Crazy Horse was badly hurt, he said, and must be examined by a doctor. He suggested that the wounded man be carried into the adjutant's office.[76]

Deep in the crowd, Pourier's words found a response. Lakotas of both factions began shouting at Kennington and McGillycuddy. Puzzled by the sea change in the crowd, unable to tell friend from foe, and without an interpreter, the two men were momentarily confused. Pourier translated the shouts: "Don't take him in the Guard House, he is a Chief." Kennington stood silent, so McGillycuddy asked, "What shall

I do with him?" Pourier translated, and the crowd shouted, "Take him there," pointing down the parade ground at the adjutant's office.[77]

Kennington demurred, but McGillycuddy volunteered to speak to Bradley. As he hurried across the parade ground, elders consolidated the mood of calm. The two factions agreed to withdraw from the scene, and the northern Lakotas moved down the parade ground toward Bradley's quarters. The scouts and agency Oglalas shifted up the grounds to Clark's quarters at the upper end of the officers' row. Crazy Horse was left on the ground, still surrounded by the nervous cordon of the guard, his body writhing in occasional convulsions.[78]

Outside Clark's quarters, the lieutenant stood talking to Billy Garnett, but he was still unwilling to take charge of the situation. He Dog angrily reproached the lieutenant, then stalked away.[79] Clark authorized Garnett to have Crazy Horse taken into the adjutant's office, adding, "You can go with him." Then, as Garnett turned to talk with the chiefs, the lieutenant returned to his quarters.[80]

At the lower end of the officers' row, McGillycuddy was having no more luck in trying to win Bradley's involvement in the crisis. Since Lee's visit a half-hour before, the commanding officer's resolve to simply follow orders had only deepened. The surgeon was dismissed and made his way back to the parade ground.[81]

The situation had changed again in the brief minutes since McGillycuddy had left the scene. The two Lakota factions remained suspicious of one another. In the absence of an officer competent to take charge of the situation, American Horse ordered his scouts to have some blankets ready on which to carry the wounded man into the adjutant's office. The scouts managed to surround the guardhouse, forming a cordon around the wounded man and Kennington's guard. In the line, Woman Dress could hear Crazy Horse moaning repeatedly, "Father, I want to see you." Other scouts threw a second cordon, several ranks deep, across the gap to the adjutant's office. As the northern Lakotas ran up, American Horse kneed his pony forward into the space between the factions.[82]

McGillycuddy hurried through the crowd and outlined Bradley's orders to Kennington, who once more ordered his detail to carry Crazy Horse into the guardhouse. Immediately, the crowd began to shout again, this time united in their disapproval of the military action. Through Johnny Provost, McGillycuddy explained to American Horse that Crazy Horse was badly hurt, and that Bradley's orders were for him to be carried into the guardhouse. There, the surgeon insisted, he would take personal care of the wounded man. Still on his pony, American Horse declared loudly for all to hear, "Crazy Horse is a Chief and can not be put in the guard house." All Lakotas approved this neat encapsulation of their mood. McGillycuddy hurried back to Bradley's quarters.[83]

Still unprepared to take personal charge of the crisis, Bradley at last "*reluctantly consented*" to McGillycuddy's proposal of the adjutant's office solution.[84] The surgeon wasted no time. He told American Horse of Bradley's approval, and the Loafer chief announced, "Maybe the man is badly hurt, and maybe he is not; we will take him into the same place where they had the talk, and see how much he is hurt, and probably the Indian doctors can save him. It will not do to let him lie here." American Horse sprang from his pony and spread his own blanket beside Crazy Horse, ready to take personal command.[85]

He Dog interposed, "No! I wouldn't have anything to do with him." Just then Little Big Man bustled up, his left arm bandaged. He shouted some orders. Standing Bull, the Hunkpatila akicita, and another warrior came up and spread their own blankets on the ground. In the pause, American Horse motioned up his own akicita, Red Shirt and Two Dogs. He helped them lift Crazy Horse onto the blankets and supervised their carrying him into the adjutant's office. The Loafer warriors bore Crazy Horse to a cot in the corner, but Crazy Horse indicated that he would not lie there. The pile of blankets was formed into a rude pallet on the floor and Crazy Horse laid upon it. American Horse stepped coolly back onto the porch.[86]

"We have been wrangling over this Crazy Horse," he shouted to the northern Lakotas, "we have got him in the house now and you can't touch him."[87] No challenge followed American Horse's taunt. Already many of Crazy Horse's supporters were slipping away down the trail to the agency. It was about 7:00 P.M., and darkness was gathering. Lights had begun to come on around the post. Troops by now lined the parade ground. Outside Bradley's quarters, the demoralized northerners passed the file of Spotted Tail Agency scouts. Blaming them for his nephew's arrest, Crazy Horse's uncle rode up to their line and pointed his revolver at Louis Bordeaux, but two Oglalas caught his bridle and led Spotted Crow aside.[88]

Disconsolate, Red Feather demanded of Turning Bear why the Brules "left Crazy Horse and ran out [of the guardhouse]. I told them," recalled the war chief's brother-in-law, "they made it worse when they said, 'Look out, this is the jail!' and ran out." Anger, grief, and frustration boiled over as Red Feather received no reply from the Brules: "I started to cry. I had my gun with me, and they thought I was starting to fight. The Rosebud men held me."[89] As the last of the northerners scattered back down the parade ground, Red Cloud stepped forward to deliver his parting harangue: "There is nothing to do. You fellows . . . [wanted it] this way, and now it happened."[90]

In the dimming adjutant's office, a lantern was lit. Touch the Clouds and Bat Pourier had followed inside, quickly joined by Spider and White Bird, key Oglala akicita. No more Lakotas were permitted in the building. Lieutenant Clark sent over Louis Bordeaux to be on hand in the office vigil.[91]

Inside, McGillycuddy and post surgeon Charles E. Munn were attending the wounded man. After McGillycuddy administered a first injection of morphine to sedate Crazy Horse, the surgeons were able to examine the wounds more closely. From the blood lacing his lips and nostrils, they knew that the right lung had been pierced. The lower wound, traversing the bowel mass, had now raised a dark purplish bruise over the right side of Crazy Horse's groin. Although little blood was visible on the body, both wounds were bleeding internally. The surgeons knew that their patient could not survive past midnight. Beyond alleviating his pain, there was little to be done. Discussion in the room centered on whether Crazy Horse had been wounded by a bayonet or his own knife. Before he slipped into unconsciousness, the war chief said that he had felt the sentry's bayonet enter his side. Anxious to save a still critical situation, McGillycuddy tried to convince the Lakotas present that Crazy Horse had inadvertently stabbed himself. He took a sheet of paper and pierced it with both the war chief's knife and a guard's bayonet. Pointing as he examined the wounds, he sought to show that their configuration matched that of the knife. His audience unconvinced, he at length laid down the paper on the office table.[92]

A little later, a commotion outside heralded a new arrival. Worm and one of his wives had arrived. Guards demanded their business, but at a word from Touch the Clouds, the guards stood aside. In the narrow orbit of the kerosene light, Worm knelt by the rude bed and said, "Son, I am here."

At his father's voice, Crazy Horse turned and forced himself through the morphine haze to respond. "Father," he gasped, "it is no use to depend on me; I am going to die." He sank back. His stepmother sobbed; then Worm and Touch the Clouds began to weep.[93] At last the little group stood back, and Touch the Clouds sent a message to call Agent Lee. While the group awaited Lee, McGillycuddy poured a glass of brandy and held it to Crazy Horse's lips. Worm objected, signing with his hands that his son's brain whirled, and the doctor withdrew. At 10:00 P.M. Lee entered the office and crouched beside the dying man. According to Lee's account, Crazy Horse took his proffered hand. Disjointedly, the war chief began to speak, first in personal justification, then in bitterness at Little Big Man, and finally in qualified exculpation of Lee. At length he sank back.[94]

His audience strained to hear more, but Crazy Horse did not speak again. Pain visibly worked his features, and McGillycuddy administered another hypodermic of morphine. Weary with the strain of vigil, Worm and Touch the Clouds sat together on the floor at the opposite end of the office. The old man was suspicious of the surgeon's medicine, and through Bordeaux, McGillycuddy told him that it was no use to let his son suffer; soon he must die. Reluctantly, Worm made the "hou" of approval. As Crazy Horse drifted into fitful slumber, the end had begun.[95]

For the little group, normal sounds took on unsettling clarity. The steady beat of the sentry outside, faint exchanges from the parade ground, the irregular exits and entrances—all punctuated the strained breathing of the dying man. Suddenly, from outside the melancholy trumpet call of Taps pealed end of day. To McGillycuddy the sound seemed briefly to rouse Crazy Horse, who murmured as if, the surgeon fancied, he woke on the afternoon of his greatest victory. Then his head sank once more.[96]

About 11:30 Pourier was admitted to relieve Bordeaux. Before he left, the interpreter felt Crazy Horse and knew he was growing cold. Despite the morphine, he turned restlessly, in great pain. Worm, knowing the end was near, rose to begin a harangue about his son's life and greatness. Newspaper accounts depict his review of the family's history, Crazy Horse's deeds in war against the Crows and Shoshones, and the causes of the late conflict in the north.[97] Every messenger from the agencies had said, "'Come in! Come in! Or the Gray Fox [General Crook] will drive you after Sitting Bull" into Canada. At last Crazy Horse had come to the reservation, and Red Cloud and Spotted Tail "had to stand aside and give him the principal place in council, and on this account they and their young men became jealous. They were the cause of his poor boy lying there. He was killed by too much talk."[98]

After a pause, Worm praised his son's dutifulness. "[H]is son had been his only protection," a journalist rendered Worm's words. "While they were north, his son had taken good care of him, and they always had plenty of game to eat."[99] He trailed off into exhausted silence. Briefly everyone drifted into reverie; then Pourier sensed that the rattling breath of the dying man had ceased. Quietly, he remarked to McGillycuddy that Crazy Horse was dead. The surgeon crossed the room and saw it was true: at about 11:40 Crazy Horse had quietly died. McGillycuddy and Pourier were unsure how to break the news to Worm, fearing that in his grief he might seek revenge. A bottle of whiskey was on hand, and Pourier suggested they give Worm a glass to steady his nerves. Nervously, McGillycuddy poured the liquor: Pourier took a good pull before passing the drink to Worm. The old man swallowed and thanked Pourier, calling him "son": "It was good, that will open my heart."

"Don't take it hard," counseled Pourier; "your son is dead." Worm wrenched and grunted a cry of grief. "My son is dead," he lamented, "without revenging himself."[100] As Worm sank into silence once more, eyes turned on Touch the Clouds. The Miniconjou surveyed the faces lit and shadowed by the lantern bloom. Slowly, he drew himself to his full height and offered his hand to each of the men in the room: to McGillycuddy and Pourier, to Captain Kennington and Lieutenant Lemly. As the wasicu anxiously awaited his reaction that, transmitted to the waiting camps, could spell peace or war, Touch the Clouds searched for the words that would complete the circle between doing honor to his kinsman's memory and preventing further agony and bloodshed. Then he stooped over his kinsman's body and drew the blanket over his face, laying his hand on Crazy Horse's breast.

"It is good," he said at last; "he has looked for death, and it has come."[101]

30

OWNING A GHOST

At daylight, September 6, an unearthly wail rose above the Camp Robinson quadrangle. Driven by two agency Oglalas, a mule-drawn ambulance started down the agency trail, bearing the body of the Oglala war chief to his tribal village. Ahead of the vehicle walked Worm and one of Crazy Horse's stepmothers, while a detail of scouts brought up the rear of the procession. Through a sepulchral hush they moved, past watching soldiers, officers' wives, and a straggle of journalists.[1]

At the Oglala village, the excitement of the night notched up once more. Hundreds of women and children stood outside their tipis, voices raised in a general wail at first sight of the procession. Part of the Crazy Horse village—about twenty lodges of Oyuhpes and Miniconjous, led by Black Fox—had stampeded during the night to join relatives at Spotted Tail, and the approach of the war chief's remains threatened to provoke more demonstrations. Red Cloud, Young Man Afraid of His Horse, Little Wound, and Little Big Man all called for calm. Crazy Horse, they cried, was "'[t]he man without ears, who would not listen to counsel.'" His death was regrettable, but he brought it on.[2]

Up the trail, the ambulance came to a halt as Crazy Horse's Miniconjou uncle leveled his gun at the driver, who fell across his comrade's lap. The latter, a cooler hand, calmed the situation, and at the nervous snap of reins, the vehicle lurched forward again. The ambulance drove onto the campground and drew up outside Worm's tipi. Worm added his voice to the calls for calm. "[T]he whites had killed his son," he harangued the crowd; but his son, he painfully conceded, "was a fool and would not listen; it was," he echoed Touch the Clouds's conciliation, "a good thing."[3]

Then he entered the tipi. Red Feather, still numb from the loss of his brother-in-law, was called to help carry the body inside. Amid incense of sage and sweetgrass, he and other kinsmen unwrapped the blanket, unbuttoned the store-bought shirt Crazy Horse had put on the previous morning, then loosened leggings and breechclout. In turning the body, Red Feather briefly observed the wound between the war chief's kidneys. Having stripped the corpse, he helped dress it in clean new buckskin. Weeping kinsfolk paused to survey their work. "Crazy Horse was a nice-looking man," Red Feather recalled over half a century later.[4]

Amid the solidarity of relatives, Worm stated his wish to perform the Ghost Owning ceremony in honor of his son. The most prestigious of Lakota ceremonies, Owning a Ghost committed mourning relatives to months of self-denying observances. No violent act could be undertaken or even witnessed by the Ghost Owner; instead, he must inculcate powers of contemplative meditation. Above all, his household, living in the Ghost Lodge, must be a byword for generosity.

A holy man first purified a knife in the smoke of burning sweetgrass. Then, as the women loosened Crazy Horse's hair, combing it out to reach his waist, the holy man cut a lock from near the forehead and wrapped it in red cloth. The hair lock, like the fringes on a ceremonial shirt, or the scalp wrenched from an enemy's head, was believed to contain a person's nagila, or spiritual essence. In preserving the lock, Worm's family was retaining part of Crazy Horse's being to remain with the people for the duration of the Ghost Owning.[5]

As the morning progressed, the village quieted into the blank silence of loss. Worm claimed that Crazy Horse had made a deathbed request to be buried at Spotted Tail. Although finessed by Worm's declaration that "Red Cloud Agency is not on hallowed ground," the move was a slap in the face to the Oglala tribal leadership. Fearful of the funeral rites sparking a landslide breakout, Oglala akicita proclaimed that anyone decamping for the north would be forcibly stopped.[6]

Then, a little before noon, the door flap of Worm's tipi was thrown open, and Crazy Horse's body was carried outside and laid upon the waiting travois. Securely bundled within rolled blankets and a haired buffalo robe, the body was lashed by rawhide thongs to the travois poles. Taking up the reins, Worm and his wife walked toward the camp entrance. Behind the travois walked Black Shawl, eyes downcast on the bundle. Behind the chief mourners, a knot of relatives followed onto the rolling prairie. Beneath the fading wails of mourners, a wary relief settled on the village and the anxious watchers behind the agency palisade.[7]

On the following morning, Worm's procession wound through Camp Sheridan. Atop the bluff opposite the post buildings, Worm and his kinsmen built a scaffold, scarcely three feet high, on which they bound the body, now wrapped in a vivid red blanket. Day and night, the eerie wail of mourners echoed through the tipi camps lining the valley.[8]

Gradually, an uncertain peace descended over Spotted Tail Agency. At Red Cloud the Oglala tribe asserted control over its northern contingent. Chiefs and officers had planned a breakup of the northern village, with families scattered among the agency bands. In the volatile atmosphere of recrimination, this plan was put on hold. Modifying rather than scrapping the village organization, the army hierarchy recognized Big Road as the ranking chief, once it became clear that Little Big Man's role in Crazy Horse's death was simply too controversial to permit his succession. Organized around a newly conciliatory leadership, willing to concede primacy to the Oglala hierarchy, the northern village lost its appeal for the Miniconjou and Sans Arc people who had flocked to Crazy Horse's chieftainship. In the wake of Worm's departure, many more people stampeded to join relatives at Spotted Tail. Inclusive of the people formally transferred to the Brule Agency during the crisis, some 173 lodges deserted Crazy Horse's village for Spotted Tail.[9]

Agent Lee sought to dissolve the new arrivals among his reliable bands, but most consolidated with Touch the Clouds's village. Now topping four hundred lodges, the agency's fragile balance was dangerously skewed by the accession of panicky, resentful Crazy Horse followers. It was further threatened by the simultaneous surrender of Fast Bull's camp. These diehards were wary and skittish. Hardly had they arrived when Fast Bull and Low Dog, Crazy Horse's old Oyuhpe comrade, began plotting the sort of breakout that had eluded the war chief. As the chiefs prepared to depart for Washington, the threat of violent outbreak seemed to be settling down, but it was a nervous and superficial calm, and the body of Crazy Horse—as much as his living presence—would prove a rallying point for competing constituencies.[10]

On September 11 Agent Lee requested that his wife prepare the wailing mourners hot food and coffee. Through Louis Bordeaux, Lee spoke briefly to Worm. The holy man stated his concern that in the night cattle might disturb his son's remains. He asked that a fence be erected. Seizing an opportunity to ease the crisis, Lee and his carpenter, Jack Atkinson, loaded a spring wagon with tools and lumber and drove back to the grave. Near each corner, and midway along each long axis of the scaffold, they planted a sturdy post. To each side of the framework they nailed four roughhewn planks, "and in a hour made a fence to protect Crazy Horse's body."[11]

In gratitude, Worm and his wife each stroked Lee's face "in devoted affection—an Indian way to demonstrate their love to a friend."[12] The kindness of the agent and his wife helped convince Worm that his place was at Spotted Tail Agency. Matching Lee's generosity, Captain Burke had the Camp Sheridan commissary supply "the best coffin the Quartermaster's department could turn out."[13] The grave validated the Lakota presence there, underpinning Brule attempts to retain the existing agency. As a Ghost Owner, Worm could not engage in the political debate, but he was in a position to make compelling symbolic use of his status—and Crazy Horse's memory. In burying his son so conspicuously, Worm asserted the necessity of a new accommodation with the wasicu world.

Eight days after his death, on Thursday, September 13, a funeral marked Crazy Horse's passing. The inner wall of planking that surrounded the scaffold was hung with red blankets. While hundreds of mourners watched, the coffin was lashed to the scaffold, and Crazy Horse's body placed inside. Beside the body were laid a pipe and tobacco, a bow and quiver of arrows, a carbine and pistol with ample ammunition, and supplies from the agency warehouse of coffee, sugar, and hard bread. A few beads and trinkets—"to captivate the nut-brown maids of paradise," opined one of the few correspondents left on White River—completed the grave goods, and the coffin lid was put in place.[14]

Crazy Horse's favorite war pony was led up and slaughtered, to fall beside the grave. The heightened emotion of the event was sufficient to dissuade even Agent Lee from attending, but at length the crowds broke up and drifted homeward. Eight chief mourners remained at the graveside, and as night drew on, the howls of grief were echoed from the villages below. About this time, recalled Red Feather, people observed that each night, a war eagle alighted and walked around on the coffin. Crazy Horse's wakan power had not deserted him in death.[15]

The funeral left only a matter of days until the delegation's departure, and at both agencies, councils hurried forward. From Spotted Tail the Brule delegation was led by the head chief and Swift Bear, with Touch the Clouds and Red Bear to represent the northern village. All would quietly endorse Spotted Tail's bid for an agency sited on Wounded Knee Creek, within the existing reservation. In one of the bitterest ironies of the Crazy Horse tragedy, Oglala tribal unity unraveled over the agency location. After so bitterly contesting Crazy Horse's northern reservation scheme, Red Cloud's Bad Face band about-faced on the issue and requested the location on Tongue River that had been Crazy Horse's first choice. Young Man Afraid of His Horse also reinstated his support for Tongue River. Accorded generous representation by the Oglala tribal council, the northern Oglalas fielded Big Road, Little Big Man, Iron Crow, and He Dog to represent them in Washington.

The delegations departed Camp Robinson for the railroad on September 17. In extensive talks in Washington, Big Road and other northern Oglala spokesmen argued cogently for a Tongue River reserve where their people could learn to raise cattle now that the buffalo were finished. President Hayes proved conciliatory. Providing that the Lakotas removed to the Missouri valley this winter, where rations and annuities were already stockpiled, they could select their permanent agency sites in consultation with a new government commission the following spring. While the existing reservation boundaries remained, and locations within the White River valley were favored, Hayes did not categorically rule out the Tongue River location.

The delegations returned home prepared to sell to their people this latest compromise. It was no easy task. During the delegation's absence, sixty lodges of northern Indians had slipped away. Brule diplomacy brought some home, but Fast Bull rejected all conciliation and led forty lodges in a dash for Canada. Through the second half of October, with winter dangerously near, thousands of disgruntled Lakotas prepared for a move no one wanted. At Red Cloud on October 25, the movement got slowly underway behind two companies of the Third Cavalry.[16]

At last, on the morning of October 29, the Spotted Tail column also started east. The Brule Deciders had decided on an upcountry trail along Pine Ridge. Freight wagons transported material and supplies, cowboys rousted a beef herd to subsist the march, and hundreds of travois straggled over the hills. At the northern village, some two hundred lodges of Miniconjous, Sans Arcs, Oglalas, Brules, and Wazhazhas remained on the campground. They had prevailed on Agent Lee to permit them to travel with the Red Cloud column down White River, assuring him that they would rejoin the Brules on the Missouri. Touch the Clouds and the other northern Deciders were among their leaders, but their assurances hid a deep discontent. Low Dog, one of the war leaders in the lately surrendered Fast Bull camp, increasingly dominated councils with his call for a breakout for Canada. The Sans Arc Decider Red Bear broke the village's fragile consensus when he endorsed Low Dog's scheme.

Worm's family was among the people who stayed behind. Preparing for departure, the family opened the coffin and removed Crazy Horse's body, lashing the bundle again to the travois for travel. Worm wished to follow the Spotted Tail column, but public opinion compelled him to remain with the northern village. Low Dog and his adherents seized on Crazy Horse's body as political capital, using the corpse to inflame warrior opinion and inspire a mass breakout. This sat uneasily with Worm's commitment as Ghost Owner, and he grew increasingly disenchanted with Low Dog's intransigence.

As the Red Cloud column made slow progress down White River, the northern village struck tipis to intercept it. On November 1 Lieutenant Clark and the Oglala chiefs held a lengthy parley with the northern leaders, failing to persuade them to rejoin Spotted Tail. Fearful that undue pressure would lead to a breakout, Clark and Agent Irwin permitted the northerners to join the Oglala march, but inadequate rations threatened a logistical nightmare. Impeded by rainy weather that reduced trails to gumbo, the march slowed to a crawl. The northern contingent traveled behind the Oglalas, dawdling to preserve its stock, firing the prairie, and making demonstrations against the small cavalry escort. Each night a few individuals slipped away north. Some people favored assimilation into agency bands, but all attempts at conciliation foundered on the resolve of Low Dog, Red Bear, and the growing body of headmen and warriors who favored flight. We "belong to the North," they taunted, exhibiting Crazy Horse's body to back-sliding kinsfolk, exhorting a breakout to carry off his remains to the sanctuary of Grandmother's Land. "[E]ven as a dead chief," Clark grimly observed, Crazy Horse "exercises an influence for evil."[17] Underlining the dangerous mood, fifty more lodges had broken away from the Brule column, laid over at the head of Wounded Knee Creek, intending to join the mass breakaway.

Worm was deeply dissatisfied at the turn of events. Each day his family traveled at the rear of the eight-mile column, a buckskin horse hauling his son's body. After his son's death, Worm wanted no more bloodshed, and flight to Canada could only defer the inevitable—accepting the reservation. On November 7, as the villages laid over near the old robe trade landmark of Butte Cache, a beef issue was organized. Amid the bustle, Worm's family quietly prepared for departure. Unreported at the time, they left under cover of darkness, evading Low Dog's akicita and angling south up the valley of Big White Clay Creek. Besides Worm and his wife and sister, Black Shawl remained with her husband's family. Crazy Horse's hunka brother Horn Chips accompanied the little group. Having left Wounded Knee on November 5, the Brules were already stringing down the south fork of White River. Seeking a permanent place with his wife's relatives, Worm was determined to catch up.[18]

First, there were other duties. Crazy Horse's body must find a final resting place. Although the exact location of this second burial is obscured by enigma and misdirection, Horn Chips indicated that it was in Pine Ridge north of the head of Wounded Knee Creek. While the women made a stopover camp, Worm and Horn Chips dug a hole and buried Crazy Horse in a rude coffin they had fashioned. Wood was scarce, and Crazy Horse's legs had to be unjointed at the knees. This was to be no scaffold grave boldly commemorating the dead, but siting it to overlook the Wounded Knee valley silently underwrote Spotted Tail's claim to a permanent home here.[19]

There was no time to pause. Turning east, the family hurried to catch up with the Brule column. Putting aside the agonies of his son's adjustment to the new life, Worm knew that the only long-term future for the Lakota people lay on the reservation. So the family urged on their ponies, soon lost to sight in the rolling folds of prairie from the lonely spot where its pride lay buried.

September 1878, Moon of the Black Calf: Lining the south fork of White River and its tributary Rosebud Creek stood hundreds of Lakota lodges. Scores of wagons, idling beside tipis or driven by Lakota teamsters, marked a people in transition toward the agrarian dream of the social improvers. Buildings under construction, heavy freight wagons, and tarpaulined stores, marked the location of the new Rosebud Agency, permanent home to Spotted Tail's Brules and their remaining northern guests. A neat row of Sibley tents signaled the presence of troops. Captain Henry W. Wessells and a unit of the Third Cavalry had established the temporary outpost of Camp Rains in the preceding weeks, once Spotted Tail received the go-ahead to depart the hated Missouri River and locate his people at the new site.[20]

Forty miles downstream, at the forks of White River, Red Cloud's people were fretfully awaiting permission to remove to their chosen location farther up the White River valley in the lea of Pine Ridge. In the months since Crazy Horse's burial, the interminable contention over agency relocation had finally narrowed to these sites within the boundaries of the Great Sioux Reservation. Although the Oglalas and Brules would continue to see their remaining land base eroded by agreements, sales, leases, and allotments, in 1878 they came home for good. Soon log cabins would replace tipis along these same creeks, as bands and tiyospaye crystallized into permanent communities around frame schoolhouses and the spires of churches. The old nomadic life was at an end.

The northern village straggled along the Rosebud, its irregular clusters marking the factional divides that had riven it during the previous twelve months. As
ever, a sentiment existed to break away for sanctuary with Sitting Bull's people in
Canada. Just as Worm had foreseen, the lure of the last buffalo herds, and the collapse of hopes for a northern reserve, had caused mass breakouts during the previous winter. His brother Little Hawk had joined the flights, along with old war
comrades of his son like He Dog and Big Road, Low Dog and Iron Crow. In mid-
September 1878, with winter impending, a few more diehards were preparing a
break. Fifteen lodges led by Red Eagle and Bad Mustang were laying down a
smokescreen of talk about joining Red Cloud, but only the troops were fooled.[21]

After them, as the reality of life in exile impinged, the drain of reservation disaffected would dry up. Exposed to renewed campaigning from Bear Coat Miles and
diplomatic pressure from Ottawa, and starved by the relentless attrition forced on
the remaining Buffalo North, the people, over the next three years, began a reverse
movement. Hungry stragglers drifted back to the reservation, or surrendered to
Miles and sat in vast transit camps at Fort Keogh, Wolf Point, and Fort Buford, until
sent by steamboat down the Missouri to the agencies that were the only home left
them. Last to surrender would be Sitting Bull, enduring the indignity of two years'
off-reservation detention before settling to the inevitability of the new life.[22]

Besides the breakaways, a larger faction of the northern village was preparing
to resettle with Oglala kinsfolk. Oglala chiefs had extended gifts and invitations to
secure the defection. Some fifty lodges, resisting continued pressure from Spotted
Tail and the Brule leadership to assimilate with their hosts, prepared to depart as
soon as word was received that the Oglala remove had begun. Black Shawl, who
had joined the household of her mother Red Elk Woman, was one of the women
preparing for the move to Pine Ridge.[23]

Yet a core of people remained for whom the Brule agency had become home.
Apolitical, prepared to accept Spotted Tail's deciding vote on any issue, they revered
Worm as their ranking elder. Now, twelve months after his son's death, Worm was
preparing for a major ceremonial to commemorate Crazy Horse and validate this
homecoming to Rosebud. Outside the Ghost Lodge stood a sturdy tripod bearing
a large bundle—the pack that contained the lock cut from Crazy Horse's hair. The
year-long Ghost Owning would culminate in a magnificent giveaway in Crazy
Horse's name, and the release of his nagila to the Land of the Spirits.[24]

A day was announced to release the soul. Worm prepared invitation wands to
summon kinsfolk from as far afield as Cheyenne River Agency, pledging gifts of
women's craftwork, food, awls, knives, tobacco, horses, blankets, and yard goods.
Outside the Ghost Lodge, a rack was set up on which to hang finery. Kettles were
laid on to boil food for the closing feast. While a ring of curious onlookers gathered, those honored to attend the ceremony entered the tipi and assumed seats
flanking the Ghost Bundle and an effigy post representing Crazy Horse, dressed in

clothing he had worn in life. Lances and shields were propped against the post and tripod. A stack of parfleches bulged with presents. Women hugged the post in a final farewell, presenting dried meat and cherry juice that the holy man mentoring the ceremony ordered poured into the earth before the effigy.

After the pipe, low chants gave way to reverential hush as the holy man gently addressed the bundle, telling it that it was about to leave on a great journey. The bundle was first presented for Worm to embrace against each shoulder, then reverently unwrapped.[25]

At sight of the hair lock at the center, the mourners wailed. Songs of gratitude were sung, recalling to all the obligations of sharing and generosity, verities that must bind the Lakota future as they had shaped the past. Now these key gifts—imprinted so powerfully with the war chief's spirit—were presented to relatives and allies. Preserved, treasured, circulated in the eternal cycle of giving, they must carry into the Lakotas' new world the strength of their greatest warrior. More goods were carried outside and laid beside the rack as a herald summoned the poor to take one last time from Crazy Horse's unequaled largesse. As soon as the rite was completed, women would rush forward to cut up the Ghost Lodge, the covers shared among guests and visitors.

Chants of praise died away as the procession exited the Ghost Lodge. The holy man led the way, bearing before him the hairlock at the heart of the Ghost Bundle. In the high singsong tone of the Lakota priest, he cried out, admonishing Crazy Horse's soul to behold his people below. Behind him stepped Worm and his wife and the chief mourners. Three times the holy man gestured forward with the hair lock, as if freeing a reluctant thing. On the sacred fourth gesture, the movement seemed cleaner, final, as if this soul might at last break its bonds to earth. Perhaps Worm, holding aloft the pipe in a final salutation, felt through the stabs of grief and memory a compensatory joy, now that his son had no more need of a country.

NOTES

Short titles are generally used in note citations. Frequently cited archival material and collections, government publications, and organizations are identified in citations by the following abbreviations:

AGO	Adjutant General's Office, War Department
ARCoIA	Commissioner of Indian Affairs, *Annual Reports*, 1851–1878
BIA	Records of the Bureau of Indian Affairs
Canadian Papers	*Papers Relating to the Sioux Indians of the United States Who Have Taken Refuge in Canadian Territory*
Carrington Papers	*Papers Relative to Indian Operations on the Plains* (*Senate Executive Documents*, 50th Cong., 1st sess., 1888, S. Doc. 33.)
CoIA	Commissioner of Indian Affairs
CRA	Cheyenne River Agency
DPR	Department of the Platte, Records from the U.S. Army Continental Commands
DWR	Department of the West, Records from the U.S. Army Continental Commands
DS	Dakota Superintendency, Field Office Records of the Office of Indian Affairs
Fetterman Investigation	Records Relating to the Investigation of the Fort Philip Kearny (or Fetterman) Massacre, Miscellaneous Unbound Records, BIA, RG 75, NARS
ID	Records of the Indian Division, Secretary of the Interior

Indian Hostilities	*Information Touching the Origin and Progress of Indian Hostilities on the Frontier* (*Senate Executive Documents*, 40th Cong., 1st sess., 1867, S. Doc. 13)
LR	Letters Received
LS	Letters Sent
NA	National Archives and Records Service
NACPR	National Archives—Central Plains Region
OIA	Records of the Office of Indian Affairs
NSOIA	Records of the Northern Superintendency, Office of Indian Affairs
PRA	Pine Ridge Agency
RCA	Red Cloud Agency
Red Cloud Investigation	*Report of the Special Commission Appointed to Investigate the Affairs of the Red Cloud Indian Agency, July 1875, Together with the Testimony and Accompanying Documents.*
RIPC	Records of the Indian Peace Commission
Sioux War Papers	Papers Relating to Military Operations in the Departments of the Platte and Dakota against Sioux Indians, 1876–96, file 4163, Letters Received (Main Series), AGO
SW File	Sioux War, File 6207, Special Files of the Military Division of the Missouri.
STA	Spotted Tail Agency
UMA	Upper Missouri Agency
UPA	Upper Platte Agency
WA	Whetstone Agency

CHAPTER 1

1. The clearest statement dating the birth of Crazy Horse (Curly Hair in childhood) is that of his father (also Crazy Horse): His son was born "in the fall of 1840." *New York Sun*, Sept. 14, 1877. The date is confirmed by Horn Chips, Crazy Horse's close friend and spiritual mentor; see Horn Chips, interview by Eli S. Ricker, Feb. 14, 1907, tablet 18, Ricker Papers. Horn Chips dates it to the fall of the year the Oglala stole one hundred horses, corresponding to the winter of 1840–41 in American Horse's winter count. Cf. Hardorff, "'Stole-One-Hundred-Horses Winter.'"

Most other oral statements are vague. He Dog links his year of birth with Crazy Horse's, but the uncertainty over his own date (ca. 1835–41) is unhelpful. A kinswoman of Crazy Horse's stated that he was born in spring of the year Left-Handed Big Nose was killed by the Shoshones—according to American Horse's winter count, 1839–40. See Bordeaux, *Custer's*

Conqueror, 22. Although this informant, Julia Iron Cedar Woman, a.k.a. Mrs. Amos Clown, was related through Crazy Horse's stepmothers, she lived most of her life with the Miniconjous and Sans Arcs.

As to location, Crazy Horse's father remarked that it was on the south fork of Cheyenne River, but Horn Chips twice stated that it was at or near Bear Butte: see also Horn Chips, interview by Walter M. Camp, ca. July 11, 1910, Camp Papers, Brigham Young University (BYU). Josephine F. Waggoner located the birth near modern Rapid City, "on Rapid River (Creek) near the [Black] Hills, at or below where Quaking Asp empties into the Rapid." Quoted in DeLand, *Sioux Wars*, 354. All these locations are along the east flank of the Black Hills.

2. Hassrick, *The Sioux*, 310–14, details a typical birth. See also Powers, *Oglala Women*, 53–57.

3. Hassrick, *The Sioux*, 310.

4. Dorsey, *Study of Siouan Cults*, 483. On the boyhood names of Crazy Horse, see Horn Chips interview, tablet 18, Ricker Papers, and statements of He Dog and his son Joseph Eagle Hawk: R. A. Clark, *Killing of Chief Crazy Horse*, 68. The latter source gives Crushes Man and Buys A Bad Woman as names used before Crazy Horse reached maturity.

5. This discussion of Lakota history follows closely K. M. Bray, "Teton Sioux Population History." Standard references on early Lakota history are Hyde, *Red Cloud's Folk* and *Spotted Tail's Folk*; also White, "Winning of the West."

6. K. M. Bray, "Oglala Lakota and the Establishment of Fort Laramie."

7. White, *Roots of Dependency*, chap. 6 (Pawnees); Hoxie, *Parading Through History*.

8. The most valuable printed sources on Lakota social life are found in Walker, *Lakota Society*. Capsule ethnographies are contained in two chapters by DeMallie: "Sioux Until 1850" and "Teton."

9. DeMallie, *Sixth Grandfather*, 102, 323. On Kapozha, see Red Feather statement, Buechel, *Dictionary of Teton Sioux*, 288; W. K. Powers, *Winter Count of the Oglala*, 34. Makes the Song seems to have been a member of the Horse Dreamer cult. His widow, [Old] "Crazy Horses Mother," aged ninety, is listed in the STA 1887 census, Northern Camp, BIA, RG 75, NACPR.

10. On the background of Hunkpatila, see Bray and Bray, *Joseph N. Nicollet*, 261; Left-Hand Heron statement, "Field Notes/Summer of 1931/White Clay District/Pine Ridge Reservation, South Dakota" (hereafter "Field Notes"), 50, Mekeel Papers.

11. Left-Hand Heron, "Field Notes," 50, Mekeel Papers. "Old" Man Afraid of His Horse (1808–89) was the third in direct line to bear this famous name (Tasunke-Kokipapi, correctly They Fear His Horse). The earliest references to him are found in C. E. Hanson, Jr., *David Adams Journals*, 19, 71, 81, 83, 86.

12. Bray and Bray, *Joseph N. Nicollet*, 261. To trace Lakota bands through the historical record, consult Culbertson, "Journal of an Expedition to the Mauvaises Terres"; Hayden, *Contributions to the Ethnography and Philology*; and Dorsey, "Siouan Sociology."

13. The four prime Lakota virtues are discussed in Hassrick, *The Sioux*, 32 ff. Central to an understanding of the Lakota ethos of generosity is the work of Yankton ethnolinguist Ella C. Deloria. For an assessment of her unique contribution to Lakota ethnology, see Raymond J. DeMallie's afterword in Deloria, *Waterlily*. An overview based on her work is Mirsky, "The Dakota."

14. On family background, see Hardorff, *Oglala Lakota Crazy Horse*; and cf. Black Elk, in DeMallie, *Sixth Grandfather*, 351, which states that Male Crow was one of six brothers, four being slain with him. The identity of Curly Hair's father as the sixth is confirmed by the Cloud Shield winter count entries for 1844–45 and 1852–53 (for discussion, see chapter 3). Short Man winter count, 1838, Walker, *Lakota Society*, 139, and pls. after 144; Ruby, *Oglala Sioux*, 96.

15. DeMallie, *Sixth Grandfather*, 350–52; Powers, *Winter Count of the Oglala*, 31.

16. Quotation in DeMallie, *Sixth Grandfather*, 351. Denig, *Five Indian Tribes of the Upper Missouri*, 21.

17. C. E. Hanson, Jr., *David Adams Journals*, 71–72.

18. Ibid., 71.

19. Cloud Shield winter count, 1844–45, Mallery, *Dakota and Corbusier Winter Counts*, 141 and pl. 45; C. E. Hanson, Jr., *David Adams Journals*, entries for Jan.–Feb. 1845.

20. C. E. Hanson, Jr., *David Adams Journals*, 85–87; Powers, *Winter Count of the Oglala*, 31.

21. Lakota informants, interviews by Kingsley M. Bray and Jack Meister, 1993–2005, Cheyenne River and Pine Ridge. Several informants requested anonymity, especially in the sensitive matters of Crazy Horse's family life. Many contributed vital information on the death of Rattle Blanket Woman. At Rosebud, Victor Douville, Lakota Studies Department, Sinte Gleska University, supplied background information: conversations with the author, Sept. 26, 2001, and May 7, 2002. This interpretation of a controversial sequence of events, however, is mine. The alleged affair between Rattle Blanket Woman and Male Crow was first hinted at by family relative Victoria Conroy, writing to Josephine F. Waggoner, Dec. 18, 1934, and quoted in full in Hardorff, *Oglala Lakota Crazy Horse*, 29–31. Hardorff skillfully unravels the confusions of this document and is the first to identify the suicide of Curly Hair's mother. Additional genealogical data was published in *Lakota Times*, Nov. 12, 1986.

22. DeBarthe, *Frank Grouard*, 181; Lt. Col. L. P. Bradley to Adj. Gen. (AG), Dept. of the Platte, Sept. 7, 1877, SW File.

23. Ruby, *Oglala Sioux*, 97; Flying Hawk, in McCreight, *Firewater and Forked Tongues*, 138–39, the invaluable memoir of Moses Flying Hawk, Crazy Horse's cousin and comrade-in-arms. For a Lakota child's developmental progress, see especially Hassrick, *The Sioux*, 315ff; also Mirsky, "The Dakota."

24. Important details of the remarriages of Crazy Horse (Curly Hair's father) are preserved in family testimony given at Rosebud Reservation in 1934, printed in Gonzalez and Cook-Lynn, *Politics of Hallowed Ground*, 402–404. Leo Combing testimony, Aug. 13, 1920, Clown family heirship files, Cheyenne River Tribal Office (copy supplied by friends at Cheyenne River). Again, I respect requests for anonymity in these controversial matters. Victor Douville provided invaluable background information (conversations with the author, Sept. 26, 2001, and May 7, 2002). See also genealogical data in *Lakota Times*, Nov. 12, 1986. Information collected by Donovin Sprague, historian at the Crazy Horse Memorial Museum, states that Curly Hair's stepmothers were named Gathers the Grapes and Corn, and affirms that they were considered sisters of Spotted Tail (conversation with the author, Jan. 13, 2004).

25. Eastman, *Indian Heroes and Great Chieftains*, 85–86. Eastman's work is cloyed by a sentimental boy-scout reading of Lakota culture, but he was a full-blood Dakota, and he obtained stories from old Oglalas during his term as Pine Ridge physician.

26. Miller, *Custer's Fall*, 94.

27. Douville, in conversations with the author, Sept. 26, 2001, May 7, 2002, discussed Crazy Horse as holy man. On the transition to holy man as a stage in adult development, see W. K. Powers, *Oglala Religion*, 59–63.

28. Little Hawk's mother was Good Haired Otter. Born ca. 1812, she still lived in her son's household in 1891.

29. DeBarthe, *Frank Grouard*, 180–81.

30. Ibid.; Eastman, *Indian Heroes and Great Chieftains*, 90. Eastman implies a significant "difference in age" between Curly Hair and High Backbone, with the latter the senior. To a direct question, He Dog replied that High Backbone was "[j]ust about the same age as Crazy Horse and I" (He Dog, in Riley, "Oglala Sources," 15). This problem is not as intractable as it seems. A difference of five or even ten years in adulthood means little; in childhood, it is crucial.

31. In 1877 Frank Grouard stated that, as a child, Curly Hair and his family were regular visitors to "one of the Missouri River Agencies," definitely Fort Pierre: Bourke diary, Dec. 4, 1876, vol. 15, 1454, Bourke Diaries. Since Oglalas did not regularly visit the Missouri River posts after 1835, this is best understood as part of a regular Miniconjou visit.

32. Sources on Miniconjou connections: Lakota informant interviews, 1993–2005, by K.M. Bray and Meister, at Cheyenne River and Pine Ridge; Douville conversations; Conroy to Waggoner, Dec. 18, 1934, quoted in Hardorff, *Oglala Lakota Crazy Horse*, 29–31; *Lakota Times*, Nov. 12, 1986; Gonzalez and Cook-Lynn, *Politics of Hallowed Ground*, 402–404. Combing testimony, Aug. 13, 1920, Clown family heirship files; Waggoner to Dr. Raymond A. Burnside, July 6, 1934, quoted in DeLand, *Sioux Wars*, 355; Sprague conversation, Jan. 13, 2004.

33. Chittenden and Richardson, *Life, Letters, and Travels of Father Pierre-Jean De Smet*, 2:631; also K. M. Bray, "Lone Horn's Peace," 30; Lucy W. Lee, dispatch of Sept. 18, 1877, to Greencastle (Indiana) *Star*, in Brininstool, *Crazy Horse*, 69–70. This source claims that, "Through Father De Smet and other missionaries who had visited the Missouri River country, [Crazy Horse] had gained a very clear knowledge of Christ and His life upon this earth, and he had taken Him as an example and pattern for him to imitate. In his troubles with the whites, he likened them to Christ's persecutors." Although uncredited to any primary source, and to be assessed critically given Mrs. Lee's role as Spotted Tail Agency schoolteacher, the statement squares nicely with the evidence for regular visits to Fort Pierre. De Smet's 1848 trip is the only one that fits the chronology. During the days after Crazy Horse's death, Lucy's husband, Lt. Jesse M. Lee, extended much kindness to the mourning family—so this may be evidence of the highest caliber.

34. McCreight, *Firewater and Forked Tongues*, 138–39.

35. The literature on Lakota religion is truly vast, but for orientation see DeMallie, "Lakota Belief and Ritual," 25–43; and W. K. Powers, *Oglala Religion*. Fundamental texts are in Walker, "Sun Dance" and *Lakota Belief and Ritual*.

36. Mathew H. King, in Kadlecek and Kadlecek, *To Kill an Eagle*, 126.

37. Eastman, *Indian Heroes and Great Chieftains*, 88.

38. Lakota buffalo hunting practices are vividly rendered in Densmore, *Teton Sioux Music and Culture*, 436ff.

39. Name changes conventionally followed a significant accomplishment or threshold experience. He Dog stated that Curly Hair was given the name His Horse on Sight at "about 10 years old." He Dog, in Riley, "Oglala Sources," 9–10. In a follow-up interview with Mari Sandoz, June 30, 1931, He Dog rendered the name Horse Stands in Sight. Sandoz Papers, part II, box 31. He Dog's son Eagle Hawk renders it Horse-Partly-Showing: R. A. Clark, *Killing of Chief Crazy Horse*, 68.

CHAPTER 2

1. Fitzpatrick to CoIA, Sept. 22, Nov. 24, 1851, ARCoIA, 1851, 332–37. Man Afraid of His Horse's role is indicated in an autobiographical statement by Sam Deon, Dec. 26, 1902, MS 2039, box 59, Sheldon Papers. Deon, a longtime trader with the Oglalas, states: "Old Man Afraid—great Sioux chief—took Indians of near Ft Pierre" to the Horse Creek Treaty in 1851.

2. No detailed exposition exists of the prewar Lakota–U.S. relationship. This discussion leans on K. M. Bray, "Teton Sioux Population History." For 1831 spending figures, see undated "Remarks" by upper Missouri sub-agent Jonathan L. Bean, UMA, LR, OIA. Bean's entire spending budget was $1,420.

3. A vivid contemporary insight into changing Lakota attitudes is Denig, *Five Indian Tribes of the Upper Missouri*, 19 (includes quotation). For oral tradition and the epidemics, see Bettelyoun and Waggoner, *With My Own Eyes*, 44–47; Left-Hand Heron (Makula) winter counts,

Waggoner Papers. For the ca. 1850 deaths of Crazy Horse's stepsisters, see Brave Bird and Afraid of Eagle testimony, July 7, 1934, in Gonzalez and Cook-Lynn, *Politics of Hallowed Ground*, 403–404; Combing testimony, Aug. 13, 1920, Clown family heirship files (copies courtesy of family descendants).

4. Wissler, "Societies and Ceremonial Associations"; Walker, *Lakota Society*, 21–39.

5. The fullest account of the 1851 treaty is in the pages of the *Missouri Republican*, Oct. 6, 17, 22, 23, 24, and 26, Nov. 2, 9, 30, 1851. My narrative follows this source. See also Fitzpatrick's official reports (Fitzpatrick to CoIA, Sept. 22, Nov. 24, 1851), and those of Mitchell to CoIA, Oct. 25, Nov. 11, 1851, ARCoIA 1851, 288–90, 324–26. Valuable details are provided by De Smet in Chittenden and Richardson, *Life, Letters, and Travels of Father Pierre-Jean De Smet*, 2:653ff; and Lowe, *Five Years a Dragoon*, 76–83. Lakota perspectives on the treaty-making process are ably reconstructed in DeMallie, "Touching the Pen," 38–53. In the following account, I restrict notes to quotations and points of interpretation.

6. *Missouri Republican*, Nov. 2, 1851 (includes quotation from Clear Blue Earth speech). At this session, September 10, the more amenable Cheyennes and Arapahos presented their candidates for head chieftainship, respectively Medicine Arrow and Little Owl. On Man Afraid of His Horse's refusal to stand as head chief, see Left-Hand Heron statement, Sept. 18, 1931, in Mekeel, "Field Notes," 51.

7. Cheyenne warrior societies also validated the treaty and approved the nominations of delegates to Washington. Denig, trading among the Lakotas in the mid-1830s, viewed the warrior societies as "of no importance in their government and with the Sioux . . . are only recognized as separate bodies during their dances and other ceremonies." Denig, "Indian Tribes of the Upper Missouri," 434. Clearly, this situation was changing by mid-century.

8. *Missouri Republican*, Nov. 23, 1851.

9. Text and signatories of the 1851 treaty are printed in Kappler, *Indian Affairs: Laws and Treaties*, 2:594–96. Signing after Scattering Bear were Clear Blue Earth, Big Partisan, Yellow Ears (Brules); Smutty Bear (Yankton); and Long Mandan (Two Kettle).

CHAPTER 3

1. Chittenden and Richardson, *Life, Letters, and Travels of Father Pierre-Jean De Smet*, 2:683–88. See also Nadeau, *Fort Laramie and the Sioux*, 81–82.

2. Bernard Moves Camp, in Steinmetz, *Pipe, Bible, and Peyote*, 19–20. This statement, by a great-grandson of Horn Chips, is fundamental to understanding the hunka relationship between Curly Hair and Horn Chips. Although brief and confused in detail about Curly Hair's family predicament (stating that his mother had remarried, her new husband and Curly Hair being unable to get on), it accurately reflects the boy's unhappiness and his feeling of solidarity with his uncles (i.e., his mother's Miniconjou brother). For Young Little Hawk's status as child beloved, consider Eagle Elk statements to John G. Neihardt, November 1944, Neihardt Papers.

3. Bernard Moves Camp, in Steinmetz, *Pipe, Bible, and Peyote*, 19–20. Details on the 1851 movement of the Badger-Eaters from Bad Wound's band are drawn from Mekeel, "Field Notes," 40, 62, 64, Mekeel Papers: see statements of Charles Turning Hawk, Joseph No Water, and Grant Short Bull. The fact that No Water I, the ranking Badger-Eaters elder, is not mentioned in these statements suggests that he fell victim to the epidemics that killed Horn Chips's parents. Leadership devolved on his twin sons. Black Twin seems to have been one of the akicita leaders at the 1851 treaty (note that he was a cousin of Scattering Bear). Black Twin was probably in his mid-twenties in 1851; his brother No Water II, significant in Crazy Horse's adult life, was a youth of seventeen. Grant Short Bull statement to Mekeel, "Field Notes," 64, Mekeel Papers.

4. Ruby, *Oglala Sioux*, 52.

5. Fundamental to any understanding of the hunka is the work of James R. Walker. See his invaluable interviews with Oglalas, documents 71–82, and his fullest synthesis, "*Hunka* Ceremony," document 83, Walker, *Lakota Belief and Ritual*. The most comprehensive regional assessment is Blakeslee, "Plains Interband Trade System." See also Hall, *Archaeology of the Soul*, ch. 10; and for a profound reading of the Pawnee ceremony, Fletcher, *Hako*.

6. The following generalized account of a hunka ceremony leans heavily on Walker, *Lakota Belief and Ritual*, documents 71–83. Comparative materials and incidental details have been drawn from Black Elk, J. E. Brown, *Sacred Pipe*, ch. 6; Standing Bear, *Land of the Spotted Eagle*, 27–32; Densmore, *Teton Sioux Music and Culture*; Ella Deloria, in Mirsky, "The Dakota," 414–15. Deloria is particularly good on the social implications of the ceremony.

As to the identity of Curly Hair's hunka father: Horn Chips' 1907 statement, "Bull Head at Cheyenne River Agency has the feather that Crazy Horse wore to his honor," may refer to the eagle down plume worn by hunka candidates (Horn Chips interview, tablet 18, Ricker Papers.) Perhaps Bull Head (1831–1923) was returned the plume after Crazy Horse's death. He Dog names Bull Head, along with Ashes and Spotted Crow, as an uncle of Crazy Horse. Complicating these issues, Sans Arc Leo Combing (born 1851) identified another Bull Head, who died before Combing's birth, as a brother to Crazy Horse's stepmothers. My feeling is that all these men (including both Bull Heads) were "sons," possibly by several wives, of the Miniconjou chief Corn.

7. Standing Bear, *Land of the Spotted Eagle*, 28.

8. Walker, *Lakota Belief and Ritual*, 237.

9. Horn Chips interview, tablet 18, Ricker Papers. The Badger-Eaters were considered a Bad Faces sub-band after 1851.

10. For Oglala-Miniconjou 1852 activities, see K. M. Bray, "Lone Horn's Peace," 32–33; H. H. Anderson, "From Milwaukee to the California Gold Fields," 58–59; "Cloud Shield Winter Count," Mallery, *Dakota and Corbusier Winter Counts*, 142 and pl. 46. An excellent source on John Richard and his family is Jones, "Those Wild Reshaw Boys."

11. Flying Hawk, in McCreight, *Firewater and Forked Tongues*, 139.

12. On the roles of fathers, brothers, and uncles in a Lakota boy's education, see Mirsky, "The Dakota," 422–23.

13. Eastman, *Indian Heroes and Great Chieftains*, 87

14. Horn Chips interview, tablet 18, Ricker Papers.

CHAPTER 4

1. Lt. R. B. Garnett to Asst. Adj. Gen. (AAG), Jefferson Barracks, June 30, 1853, Old Files, AGO, RG 94, NA.

2. On Hunkpapa isolationism, see Bray and Bray, *Joseph N. Nicollet*, 261; Denig, *Five Indian Tribes of the Upper Missouri*, 25–27; K. M. Bray, "Teton Sioux Population History," 184, and "Before Sitting Bull."

3. The fullest accounts of the Miniconjou incident are Lt. Garnett's official report (Garnett to AAG, Jefferson Barracks, June 30, 1853), and Lt. H. B. Fleming to Lt. R. B. Garnett, June 16, 1853, Old Files, AGO. Good secondary accounts are Nadeau, *Fort Laramie and the Sioux*, 86–89; Hafen and Young, *Fort Laramie and the Pageant of the West*, 209–10. Hyde, *Red Cloud's Folk*, chap. 5, remains an insightful introduction to the period 1853–56. A major synthesis is Paul, *Blue Water Creek and the First Sioux War*. Consistently useful for a military overview of Plains Indian relations with the United States, with unusual sensitivity to Indian politics, is Utley, *Frontiersmen in Blue*, and its sequel, *Frontier Regulars*.

4. Fitzpatrick to CoIA, Nov. 19, 1853, AR CoIA 1853, 127–29. The text of the treaty amendment and the list of Lakota signatories is printed in H. H. Anderson, "Controversial Sioux

Amendment," 203–205. Red Cloud's resistance is suggested by John B. Sanborn to Vincent Colyer, 1870, ARCoIA 1870. Description of Red Hawk's opposition is based on Robert Holy Dance in Lewis, *Medicine Men*, 165. The only "treaty" that fits Holy Dance's story is the 1853 amendment. For antiannuity Oglala factions, see also Wissler, "Societies and Ceremonial Associations," 9, 28.

5. Miniconjou winter counts all speak of trading Spanish/Navaho blankets from a trader White Bull calls "Jar" (Richard): Howard, *Warrior Who Killed Custer*, 18.

6. Captain E. Johnson to Bvt. Lt. Col. William Hoffman, Oct. 11, 1854, Main Series, LR, AGO. Other primary sources on the Grattan "Massacre" used in the subsequent discussion are collected in ARCoIA 1854 and U.S. House, *Information Relating to an Engagement*. See also Man Afraid of His Horse statement, LR, DPW. Several good secondary accounts exist, but see especially McCann, "Grattan Massacre"; Hyde, *Spotted Tail's Folk*, 56–62; Hafen and Young, *Fort Laramie and the Pageant of the West*, 222–32; Nadeau, *Fort Laramie and the Sioux*, 89–110.

7. Johnson to Hoffmann, Oct. 11, 1854.

8. Ibid.; Man Afraid of His Horse statement.

9. James Bordeaux, in U.S. House, *Information Relating to an Engagement*.

10. Ibid. Bordeaux does not name the speaker, but the context suggests Man Afraid of His Horse.

11. Man Afraid of His Horse statement; Hoffman to AGO, Nov. 29, 1854, Main Series, LR, AGO.

12. Hoffman to AGO, Nov. 29, 1854.

13. Ibid., 4–5.

14. Ibid., 5. On Spotted Tail's role, see Hyde, *Spotted Tail's Folk*, 67–68.

15. Hoffman to AGO, Nov. 29, 1854, 5. Upper Missouri Agent Vaughan's reports trace the escalation of hostilities in the Missouri River zone: see Vaughan to CoIA, Oct. 19, 1854, ARCoIA 1854; Nov. 21, 1854; Feb. 17, May 19, 1855, UMA, LR, OIA.

16. Thomas S. Twiss to CoIA, Sept. 3, 1855, ARCoIA 1855, 79.

17. Twiss to CoIA, Oct. 1, 1855, ARCoIA 1855, 80. On Harney's preparations, see Utley, *Frontiersmen in Blue*, 115f.

18. Twiss to CoIA, Aug. 20, Sept. 3, Oct. 1, Oct. 10, 1855, ARCoIA, 1855, 78–85.

19. Twiss to CoIA, Oct. 1, 1855, ARCoIA, 1855, 80–81.

20. Mattison, "Harney Expedition," 110ff. On the Battle of Blue Water Creek, the best secondary accounts are Paul, *Blue Water Creek and the First Sioux War*, ch. 6; Utley, *Frontiersmen in Blue*, 116–17; and Clow, "Mad Bear." Primary sources used in the following account are Harney's official report, Secretary of War, ARCoIA 1855, 49–51; Lt. Col. Philip St. George Cooke statement, *Senate Executive Documents*, 34th Cong., 3rd sess., 1857, S. Doc. 58; Drum, "Reminiscences of the Indian Fight"; Lt. G. K. Warren, journal, Sept. 2–3, 1855, J. A. Hanson, *Little Chief's Gatherings*, 103–106. In contrast to the rich documentary record, Lakota accounts of the battle are scanty, but see Bettelyoun and Waggoner, *With My Own Eyes*, chap. 8. Note that Mari Sandoz's influential contention that Curly Hair was present as a visitor in the Blue Water camps is nowhere stated in the oral and traditional record. See *Crazy Horse*, chap. 4. It is best interpreted as dramatic license. Sandoz keys the visit to He Dog's statement that Curly Hair spent one year among the Brules, when he was about seventeen or eighteen. The Brule sojourn and its chronology are dealt with in chapter 5.

21. Bvt. Brig. Gen. William S. Harney to AAG, HQ of the Army, Sept. 25, 1855; Harney to Secretary of War, Nov. 10, 1855 (includes quotation), both LR, AGO. Twiss to CoIA, Oct. 1, 10, 1855, ARCoIA 1855, 81–85; Warren journal, J. A. Hanson, *Little Chief's Gatherings*, 108–110.

22. Warren journal, Sept. 22, 1855, J. A. Hanson, *Little Chief's Gatherings*, 110.

23. Twiss to CoIA, Oct. 18, 1855, UPA, LR, OIA, RG 75, NA; Harney to Secretary of War, Nov. 10, 1855. Ruby, *Oglala Sioux*, 97.

CHAPTER 5

1. The traditional sources dating Curly Hair's first vision quest are late. Most detail is provided in interviews collected by Edward and Mabell Kadlecek in the 1960s and published in *To Kill an Eagle*. One of the best-informed interviewees was Frank Kicking Bear, son of Crazy Horse's comrade, who stated on May 5, 1969: "When [Curly Hair] was 14 years old he received the Holy Message on the top of a hill now called Scottsbluff" (116). Scott's Bluffs are a prominent landmark on the south side of the North Platte, fifty miles downstream from the Laramie River, a location confirmed by my own Lakota informants. A dating prior to fall 1855 is indicated, after the Hunkpatila band crossed south of the North Platte (late August) into the peace zone. The September bracket fits the aftermath of the Blue Water Creek battle and suggests that Curly Hair's wish for "power to serve his tribe" is in the context of that defeat and the captivity of Lakota relatives. Joseph Black Elk, in Kadlecek and Kadlecek, *To Kill an Eagle*, 80–81.

None of the oral sources confirm Sandoz's placing of the vision quest immediately after the Grattan incident (*Crazy Horse*, 40–44, 103–106), which must be viewed as obeying the dramatic unities of fiction, not historical evidence.

Literature on the vision quest is vast. Always fundamental is Walker, *Lakota Belief and Ritual*, but consult first DeMallie, "Lakota Belief and Ritual in the Nineteenth Century." In the following reconstruction, I have mapped Curly Hair's individual circumstances onto a generic account grounded in J. E. Brown, *Sacred Pipe*, chap. 4.

2. According to Oglala holy man Mathew H. King: "As a young man [Curly Hair] had a dream that he would receive his powers from the Thunder Gods" (Kadlecek and Kadlecek, *To Kill an Eagle*, 126).

3. Joseph Black Elk, in Kadlecek and Kadlecek, *To Kill an Eagle*, 80–81.

4. Henry Crow Dog and Carl Iron Shell statement, in Kadlecek and Kadlecek, *To Kill an Eagle*, 96, 116, expressly identify the Thunder as giving Curly Hair power. Luther Standing Bear, whose stepmother was Curly Hair's cousin, writes in *Land of the Spotted Eagle*, 209: "The Lakotas believe that the hawk was his protecting power," confirming the statement of Frank White Buffalo Man, in Kadlecek and Kadlecek, *To Kill an Eagle*, 149, that Curly Hair "dreamed of red hawks and received power." Hawks were believed to be messengers of Thunder. Good on Thunder visions is Densmore, *Teton Sioux Music and Culture*, 157ff, with primary accounts and invaluable song texts.

5. Frank Kicking Bear, in Kadlecek and Kadlecek, *To Kill an Eagle*, 116.

6. Hyde, *Spotted Tail's Folk*, 73–75; Carl Iron Shell, in Kadlecek and Kadlecek, *To Kill an Eagle*, 115, details Iron Shell's offer.

7. Twiss to CoIA, Oct. 18, 21, 28, 1855; Twiss to Supt. A. Cumming, Nov. 14, 1855. ; Bettelyoun and Waggoner, *With My Own Eyes*, 58, 60–61.

8. Bettelyoun and Waggoner, *With My Own Eyes*, 60.

9. Council minutes, *Senate Executive Documents*, 34th Cong., 1st sess., 1856, S. Doc. 94. Covering the Oglala negotiations, Harney to Secretary of War, Apr. 22, 1856, Main Series, LR, AGO.

10. *Senate Executive Documents*, 34th Cong., 1st sess., S. Doc. 94, 24 ff.; Vaughan to CoIA, Sept. 10, Oct. 27, 1856, ARCoIA 1856.

11. Vaughan to CoIA, Sept. 10, 1856, ARCoIA 1856; McDonnell, "Fort Benton Journal," 120, 122, 178, 186–87; K. M. Bray, "Lone Horn's Peace," 37–38.

12. On the heyoka, see Walker, *Lakota Belief and Ritual*, 155–57; Hassrick, *The Sioux*, 272ff; Wissler, "Societies and Ceremonial Associations," 82–85; DeMallie, "Lakota Belief and Ritual," 36ff. Very useful for modern comparison is Lewis, *Medicine Men*, chap. 7.

13. Wissler, "Societies and Ceremonial Associations," 85.

14. Walker, *Lakota Belief and Ritual*, 155–57; Hassrick, *The Sioux*, 272ff; Wissler, "Societies and Ceremonial Associations," 82–85; DeMallie, "Lakota Belief and Ritual," 36ff; Lewis, *Medicine Men*, chap. 7. For the activities of the mail coach raiders, see Hyde, *Spotted Tail's Folk*, 81–82.

15. He Dog, in Riley, "Oglala Sources," 9. He Dog's remarks are crucial to understanding Curly Hair's youth and to correcting earlier interpretations. He says simply: "When we were 17 or 18 years old we separated. Crazy Horse went to the Rosebud [Brule] band of Indians and stayed with them for about a year. Then he came home." With no other dating pointers, Mari Sandoz placed the Brule sojourn in the twelve-month frame ending fall 1855 (*Crazy Horse*, 69–85), fortuitously locating Curly Hair in the Blue Water Creek battle. Curly Hair would then have been fourteen, but since Sandoz's preferred year for Curly Hair's birth is 1842, she would make him only twelve or thirteen years old, decidedly not He Dog's "17 or 18." Unravelling the dating is complicated by He Dog's assertion that he and Curly Hair were exactly the same age. Estimates of He Dog's birthdate cluster in the frame 1835–41, with Pine Ridge censuses (RG 75, NA) consistently suggesting 1838–39—indicating that he was really a year or two older than his friend. He Dog probably was "17 or 18" from summer 1856 to summer 1857; Curly Hair was fifteen or sixteen. Placing the Brule sojourn later does not fit what we know of the young Crazy Horse's warrior career, which after 1857 focuses in the north against Crows and Shoshones, not in the Brule zone against the Pawnees. Moreover, the return of his uncle Spotted Tail from captivity makes a plausible context for an extended family visit in 1856, climaxing with Curly Hair's first war party against the Pawnees the following spring, and ending with his independently attested visit to the Cheyennes before an August 1857 return home.

16. Hyde, *Spotted Tail's Folk*, 77ff, ably assesses the impact of captivity on Spotted Tail and his companions.

17. Twiss to CoIA, Sept. 1, 1859, ARCoIA 1859, 134. The Oglala and Brule Kit Fox Society would act as akicita, supervising the distribution of treaty annuities, a function noted by Standing Bear, *Land of the Spotted Eagle*, 146.

18. Twiss to CoIA, Sept. 12, 25, Oct. 13, 1856, ARCoIA 1856, 87–88, 99–103, and Twiss to CoIA, Nov. 7, 1856, UPA, LROIA. For general background on the Cheyenne troubles, see Grinnell, *Fighting Cheyennes*, 111–17.

19. For Cheyenne attempts to engage the Brules in their war against the Americans, see Hafen and Hafen, *Relations with the Indians of the Plains*, 18–19n.

20. Curly Hair's first warpath is referred to in John Colhoff to Joseph Balmer, Dec. 3, 1951 (transcript in author's collection); Eagle Elk, Nov. 27, 1944, 12, Neihardt Papers; White Bull, in Hardorff, *Surrender and Death of Crazy Horse*, 268–69. The context clearly fits Curly Hair's Brule sojourn, and Colhoff's mention of "field cultivators" suggests a May 1857 dating. At this time, the Pawnees were grouped in two villages on the lower Platte, with American settlements right across the river. This confirms White Bull's location of the battle "down near Omaha."

21. Eagle Elk, 12, Neihardt Papers.

22. Ibid.

23. Wissler, "Societies and Ceremonial Associations," 84.

24. He Dog, July 7, 1930, 9.

25. Ibid.; see also Hinman's editorial note, 50. Although Hinman is surely mistaken in assuming a war honor, her point is well made that the Brules may have already adopted American attitudes toward the killing of noncombatants. Given the establishment of Twiss's police force, an attempt to impose such rules is exactly what we might expect. Sandoz, although pres-

ent at the interview with He Dog, and following up with more questioning of the old man a year afterward, gleaned no more details. Her presentation of the killing as an accidental coup in the 1855 Omaha battle (*Crazy Horse*, 69–72) is therefore a fictionalized attempt to gloss over what looked disturbingly like a blot on her hero's reputation.

He Dog may have known more than he was prepared to tell to strangers. The evidence is simply too fragmentary to admit of narrative reconstruction, but it may be significant that another of Crazy Horse's boyhood names was Buys a Bad Woman: see R. A. Clark, *Killing of Chief Crazy Horse*, 68. As a skim over the outer margins of plausible reconstruction, we might posit that Curly Hair, having proved himself in battle, felt ready to take a wife. In some unknowable combination of private circumstance and heyoka compulsion, the affair turned to tragedy.

CHAPTER 6

1. Curly Hair's hunting trip to the Cheyennes is attested by Bettelyoun and Waggoner, *With My Own Eyes*, 78. Background on the Sumner campaign against the Cheyennes is supplied in Chalfant, *Cheyennes and Horse Soldiers*.

2. Chalfant, *Cheyennes and Horse Soldiers*, chap. 4–7, is the most comprehensive account of this phase of Sumner's campaign. See also Utley, *Frontiersmen in Blue*, 120 ff.

3. For Cheyenne movements in July see Chalfant, *Cheyennes and Horse Soldiers*, 56–58, 174–76; also Powell, *People of the Sacred Mountain*, 1:211–12.

4. For the Sumner fight, see Grinnell, *Fighting Cheyennes*, chap. 10.

5. On the flight north see Chalfant, *Cheyennes and Horse Soldiers*, 218–19, 233–37; J. Hudson Snowden journal, entry for Aug. 11, 1857, J. A. Hanson, *Little Chief's Gatherings*, 178.

6. Bettelyoun and Waggoner, *With My Own Eyes*, 78. For troop movements to Utah, a handy source is Hafen and Young, *Fort Laramie and the Pageant of the West*, 284–302.

7. He Dog, in, Riley, "Oglala Sources," 9–10. He Dog states that Curly Hair returned to the Oglalas about one year after his departure to join the Brules, indicating a return in late summer 1857. On Iron Whiteman's feat, see Bad Heart Bull and Blish, *Pictographic History of the Oglala Sioux*, 503.

8. Much discussion of the 1857 council has been generated: see especially Hyde, *Red Cloud's Folk*, 82, and *Spotted Tail's Folk*, 90; Sandoz, *Crazy Horse*, 98–101; K. M. Bray, "Lone Horn's Peace," 42–43. These secondary sources follow Hyde in locating the council at Bear Butte. From Bear Butte's spiritual resonance and geographic centrality, Hyde's conjecture may be correct, but Warren, the only significant primary source, simply locates it on the Belle Fourche. My presentation of the council, expanding on the account in "Lone Horn's Peace," is based on Warren's journal for September 1857, printed in J. A. Hanson, *Little Chief's Gatherings*, 158–67; and Warren, *Preliminary Report*, 18–21, 51–53. Warren's accounts embody and quote key statements from Lakota participants, including Bear Ribs and Elk Bellows Walking. Upper Missouri Agent A. H. Redfield also learned something of the council's resolutions at Fort Clark in September (ARCoIA 1857, 424). Significant background is also supplied in Bettelyoun and Waggoner, *With My Own Eyes*, 68–69, 77–78. In the following discussion, I have limited footnoting to quotations and critical or neglected points.

9. Bettelyoun and Waggoner, *With My Own Eyes*, 69.

10. See Bear Ribs, in J. A. Hanson, *Little Chief's Gatherings*, 166; and Warren, *Preliminary Report*, 20 (includes quotation).

11. On territorial claims and the Black Hills as Lakota heartland, see especially Warren, *Preliminary Report*, 19 (includes quotations). The 1857 Belle Fourche council may be interpreted as the key event in the crystallization of Lakota proprietary concepts regarding the Black Hills,

which dominate reservation politics to this day. The most comprehensive coverage of the latter-day Black Hills issue is Lazarus, *Black Hills, White Justice.*

12. For deserters, see *Message of the President of the United States Communicating a Report of the Proceedings of a Council Held at Fort Pierre by General Harney with a Delegation from Nine Tribes of the Sioux Indians*, Senate Executive Documents, 34th Cong., 1st sess., 1856, S. Doc. 94, 27. On expulsions of white intruders, see Hyde, *Red Cloud's Folk*, 82, and *Spotted Tail's Folk*, 90; Sandoz, *Crazy Horse*, 98–101; K. M. Bray, "Lone Horn's Peace," 42–43; J. A. Hanson, *Little Chief's Gatherings*, 158–67; Warren, *Preliminary Report*, 18–21, 51–53; Bettelyoun and Waggoner, *With My Own Eyes*, 68–69, 77–78; and cf., e.g., Lower Brule speeches to Snowden party, Snowden journal, Oct. 11, 1857, J. A. Hanson, *Little Chief's Gatherings*, 185; Lone Horn speech to Indian Peace Commission, Fort Laramie, May 28, 1868, "Transcript of the Minutes and Proceedings of the Indian Peace Commission Appointed By An Act of Congress Approved July 20, 1867," vol. 2, 107–10, ID.

13. See Bear Ribs, in J. A. Hanson, *Little Chief's Gatherings*, 158–67.

14. On Sitting Bull's public career in the mid-1850s, see Utley, *Lance and the Shield*, chap. 2; K. M. Bray, "Before Sitting Bull"; Vestal, *Sitting Bull*, 30–32; G. C. Anderson, *Sitting Bull and the Paradox of Lakota Nationhood*, chap. 2. These sources, rooted in Vestal's interviews with Lakota associates of Sitting Bull, reflect the significant role that the Strong Heart Society played in articulating an ideology of resistance to American expansionism.

15. "We fight the Crows because they will not take half and give us peace with the other half": Black Horse (Cheyenne chief) speech to Col. H. B. Carrington, July 1866, Hebard and Brininstool, *Bozeman Trail*, 1:264; Bear Ribs, in J. A. Hanson, *Little Chief's Gatherings*, 165.

16. Eastman, *Indian Heroes and Great Chieftains*, 88–89, is the source for Curly Hair's following High Backbone to war against the "Gros Ventres." The term could apply to the Gros Ventres of the Missouri, the horticultural Hidatsa tribe of northern North Dakota, but consideration of Eastman's other uses of the name indicates that he means the Atsinas, sometimes known as Gros Ventres of the Prairie, of north-central Montana. The Atsinas speak an Algonquian language closely related to Arapaho.

17. For the preparations and procedures of a war party, see Wissler, "Societies and Ceremonial Associations," 54ff; George Sword, in DeMallie, "Teton Dakota Kinship and Social Organization," 150–53; Walker, *Lakota Society*, 95. High Backbone's personal organization of a later war party is recorded in Vestal, *Warpath*, 39–40.

18. A war party parade is graphically illustrated in Bad Heart Bull and Blish, *Pictographic History of the Oglala Sioux*, 202–11, 291–97, with valuable notes on the heyoka at 204.

19. Wissler, "Societies and Ceremonial Associations," 55–59.

20. He Dog, in Riley, "Oglala Sources," 10. I believe that He Dog's recollection of the fight with the Arapahos refers to the same battle reported by Eastman. Both accounts indicate that this battle was the one in which Curly Hair's adult reputation was founded, and it is unlikely that there were two such battles involving the Arapahos (or Atsinas). Some difference in age is indicated: Eastman believed that Curly Hair (born according to his reckoning ca. 1845) was sixteen years old; He Dog (after asserting that both he and Curly Hair were born in 1837–38) states that Curly Hair was "about 18" at the time of the fight. Since he believed that he and Curly Hair were seventeen or eighteen during the latter's yearlong sojourn with the Brules (and Cheyennes), the dating of the Arapaho (Atsina) battle fell within one year of and more likely very soon after Curly Hair's return. A fall 1857 dating therefore looks most likely for the fight, just as Curly Hair approached his seventeenth birthday.

The internal chronology in Sandoz, *Crazy Horse*, 115–18, dates the fight to 1860, when according to her reckoning, Curly Hair was seventeen. Having already discarded He Dog's dating of Curly Hair's birth and his Brule sojourn, she further scrambles her principal informant's chronology by placing the Atsina fight five years later. She also ignores He Dog's identification of the enemy and equates the fight with yet another tradition that the battle was fought with Shoshones or a people related to them, "speaking a changed tongue." In doing this she used details from a letter by Walter S. Campbell (Stanley Vestal) to Eleanor Hinman, Oct. 13, 1932, setting out an account of Curly Hair/Crazy Horse's war deeds obtained (through Joseph White Bull) from Owns Horn, one of Crazy Horse's Miniconjou cousins (see Hardorff, *Surrender and Death of Crazy Horse*, appendix B). In this account, two coups are credited in a fight (or fights) with "the Grass House People (who lived where the Shoshoni do now)." These enemies were probably northern Shoshones and Bannocks. This fight probably took place in 1858. Details of the fight, and the identity of the enemy, are fully discussed in chapter 7.

Sandoz took the Campbell data and synthesized it with material from Horn Chips' 1907 statement to Judge Ricker. Horn Chips also gave details of the fight in which Curly Hair received his adult name but identified the enemies vaguely as "the Crows and Rees [Arikaras] and others whose language they could not understand." (Horn Chips interview, tablet 18, Ricker Papers). The unlikely combination, underlined by Horn Chips' indeterminate catchall (converted by Sandoz into an ethnonym, "the people of the unknown tongue") and his further identification of Shoshones among the enemy, probably demonstrates simply that Horn Chips knew little of the details: there were blank spots in his knowledge of his hunka brother's life, as chapter 7 explores further.

At face value Horn Chips' dating also seems inconsistent: Ricker set down that the fight took place when Curly Hair "was just twenty-one years old," i.e., in 1861–62. However, at the end of his account of the fight, Horn Chips was at pains to state that he was four years older than Curly Hair (i.e., born in 1836). Horn Chips may have meant that *he* was "just twenty-one" at the time of the fight, placing it (per this independent reconstruction) in 1857, just as Curly Hair passed his seventeenth birthday, thus squaring neatly with Eastman's and He Dog's placing of Curly Hair in the age frame sixteen to eighteen.

Selecting her material at will, Sandoz did take up He Dog's observation that Curly Hair took two enemy scalps in the fight and was wounded. He Dog does not specify where Curly Hair was hit. The Owns Horn material, however, states that in the fight with the Grass House People, Curly Hair was wounded in the left calf. Believing, from the Hinman interviews with Red Feather, that Curly Hair was wounded only twice, the second time by No Water in 1870, Sandoz then synthesized He Dog and Owns Horn. However, Eagle Elk's 1944 statement to John G. Neihardt establishes that there was a third wound, in the arm—most likely sustained in the fight to which He Dog refers. Unlike He Dog, Sandoz makes a causal relation between the wound and the scalp taking, indicating that Curly Hair was violating the taboos of his youth vision. No such taboo is mentioned in the Ricker and Hinman interviews, Sandoz's major sources.

21. For High Backbone's war costume, see Bad Heart Bull and Blish, *Pictographic History of the Oglala Sioux*, 134, 342, 350, 375.

22. He Dog, in Riley, "Oglala Sources," 10.

23. Horn Chips interview, tablet 18, Ricker Papers.

24. R. A. Clark, *Killing of Chief Crazy Horse*, 68.

25. On the bond between kola, see Hassrick, *The Sioux*, 111; Walker, *Lakota Society*, 40–41; DeMallie, "Teton Sioux Kinship and Social Organization," 145.

26. K. M. Bray, "Lone Horn's Peace," 44. These camps were probably located along the Belle Fourche above Bear Lodge Butte (modern Devil's Tower, Wyoming).

27. He Dog, in Riley, "Oglala Sources," 10. For comparable details on a change in names, see Afraid of Bear, in Wissler, "Societies and Ceremonial Associations," 61; DeMallie, "Teton Sioux Kinship and Social Organization," 156. See also Workers, *Legends of the Mighty Sioux*, 111–12.

Customs of a victorious war party and the victory dance are synthesized from Hassrick, *The Sioux*, 88–90; Densmore, *Teton Sioux Music and Culture*, 359–363; Wissler, "Societies and Ceremonial Associations," 59–61; DeMallie, "Teton Sioux Kinship and Social Organization," 155–56; Bad Heart Bull and Blish, *Pictographic History of the Oglala Sioux*, 38, 168–69; Standing Bear, *My People the Sioux*, 57; Black Elk, in DeMallie, *Sixth Grandfather*, 369–70. Neihardt was able to write his own vivid synthesis in *When the Tree Flowered*, 100–103.

CHAPTER 7

1. Joseph Black Elk, in Kadlecek and Kadlecek, *To Kill an Eagle*, 80.

2. Eastman, *Indian Heroes and Great Chieftains*, 89; Walker, *Lakota Belief and Ritual*, 122; Standing Bear, *Land of the Spotted Eagle*, 209.

3. Walker's informants added, "Only those who have much power to do mysterious things are entitled to wear hawk's feathers." Walker, *Lakota Belief and Ritual*, 222.

4. He Dog, in Riley, "Oglala Sources," 16. On evidence for the red-tailed hawk's aid in securing healing power for Crazy Horse, see chapter 20.

5. Fast Thunder and Struck by Crow, in Curtis, *Teton Sioux*, 184, 189–90.

6. Owns Horn, in Hardorff, *Surrender and Death of Crazy Horse*, 268–69. The statement indicates that the fight took place on the modern Wind River Reservation. For an illustration of a grass tipi, see D'Azevedo, *Great Basin*, 294.

7. Owns Horn, in Hardorff, *Surrender and Death of Crazy Horse*, 268–69.

8. For information on Crazy Horse's Miniconjou visit, I am indebted to modern Cheyenne River elders who have requested anonymity. One woman vividly recalled her own grandparents' recollections of the visit.

9. On scouting, see Standing Bear, *Land of the Spotted Eagle*, 75–78; King, in Kadlecek and Kadlecek, *To Kill an Eagle*, 126.

10. The deaths of Black Shield's sons and his prompt revenge are widely attested to in the winter counts: see, e.g., Cloud Shield and White Cow Killer counts, 143, and Lone Dog Group counts, 143, Mallery, *Dakota and Corbusier Winter Counts*, 143. See also Report of Sec. War, communicating report of Bvt. Brig. Gen. W. F. Raynolds, *Senate Executive Document*, 40th Cong., 2nd sess., 1868, S. Doc. 77, for background details on 1859 events. Mekeel, "Field Notes," 53, Mekeel Papers.

11. Raynolds report (*Senate Executive Document*, 40th Cong., 2nd sess., 1868, S. Doc. 77, 52), says eleven Crows were killed. This is probably the same event as attested in the Bad Heart Bull endpapers: Bad Heart Bull and Blish, *Pictographic History of the Oglala Sioux*, 503, item 8: "Along the Greasy Grass River [the Little Bighorn], ten Crow Indians were killed." It is possibly the same attack remembered by the Crows, where eleven young men and one woman were killed: Lowie, *Crow Indians*, 324. The postscript of Upper Platte Vaccinating Agent J. C. R. Clark to Supt. IA, June 27, 1859, UPA, LR, OIA, supplies the date of the Lakota attack. See also K. M. Bray, "Lone Horn's Peace," 44.

12. Victor Douville, conversation with the author, Sept. 26, 2001.

13. Eastman, *Indian Heroes and Great Chieftains*, 91–92.

14. Black Elk, in J. E. Brown, *Sacred Pipe*, 45. For basic concepts of Lakota religion, consult especially Walker, "Sun Dance" and *Lakota Belief and Ritual*, passim.

15. For kicamnayan applied to the flight of swallows, see Lone Man's Thunder vision song "Before the Gathering of the Clouds," Densmore, *Teton Sioux Music and Culture*, 162.

16. *Chicago Tribune*, May 3, 1877.

17. Black Elk, in DeMallie, *Sixth Grandfather*, 203.

18. Flying Hawk, in McCreight, *Firewater and Forked Tongues*, 138–39. Garnett interview, tablet 1, Ricker Papers. Few events in Crazy Horse's life have been so willfully misunderstood

as the vision of the man from the lake. By far the most influential reading of the vision is that of Mari Sandoz, *Crazy Horse*, 41–43, 103–106. For dramatic impact, Sandoz treated this as Crazy Horse's only significant vision, and for added effect ascribed a dating immediately after the Grattan fight in 1854, locating it in the Nebraska Sandhills. This date and location, followed by key secondary accounts (e.g., Ambrose, *Crazy Horse and Custer*, 67–69; Josephy, *Patriot Chiefs*, 271–73) is incorrect. Garnett himself heard Crazy Horse locate the vision near a lake in the Rosebud Creek district of southern Montana. In the heart of the Powder River country, Rosebud Creek lay emphatically in the Crow domain until after 1859: the vision therefore took place soon after 1860.

19. Garnett interview, tablet 2, Ricker Papers. Although embroidered by historians as Crazy Horse's most famous vision, it was dismissed out of hand by Horn Chips: "There is no truth in the story of the horseman coming out of the pond and telling Crazy Horse what to do" (Horn Chips interview, tablet 18, Ricker Papers). Horn Chips is almost certainly overstating, perhaps because he was not called upon to interpret this vision, which fell outside the constellation of Thunder dreams that had so far dominated Crazy Horse's life.

20. Flying Hawk, in McCreight, *Firewater and Forked Tongues*, 139; Garnett interview, tablet 2, Ricker Papers; Iron Horse, in Standing Bear, *Land of the Spotted Eagle*, 180; Walker, *Lakota Belief and Ritual*, 94, 108, 118 (quotation), 122–23, 169–70; Dorsey, *Study of Siouan Cults*, 496.

21. Horn Chips interview, tablet 18, Ricker Papers.

22. The stone charm Horn Chips gave Crazy Horse is well attested. Besides Horn Chips' own statements (interview, tablet 18, Ricker Papers; interview, ca. July 11, 1910, Camp Papers, BYU), see He Dog, in Riley, "Oglala Sources," 13; Red Feather, in ibid., 31; Eagle Elk, November 1944, Neihardt Papers. Mari Sandoz conducted a second interview with He Dog to clear up a few points (June 30, 1931, part 2, folder 16, box 31, Sandoz Papers). This interview is the source for the quotation about the stone's size. He Dog claimed that the stone was black, but Red Feather, whose son Stanley owned the stone in 1930, said it was white. A number of traditional statements about the stone are collected in Kadlecek and Kadlecek, *To Kill an Eagle*. They state that Crazy Horse rubbed his body with the stone before going into battle. The best ethnographical account of the religious significance of Rock, with Lakota accounts and song texts, is provided by Densmore, *Teton Sioux Music and Culture*, 204–38.

23. Horn Chips interview, tablet 18, Ricker Papers.

24. Horn Chips interview, ca. July 11, 1910, Camp Papers, BYU.

25. The account of the Battle Defending the Tents is derived from Bad Heart Bull and Blish, *Pictographic History of the Oglala Sioux*, 126–33. Besides vivid depictions of action, Bad Heart Bull's topographic plan yields significant details of strategy and tactics. Throughout, I have also referred to Crow traditions of the battle, vividly rendered in Medicine Crow, *From the Heart of the Crow Country*, 64–78. For Crazy Horse's part in the battle, I have depended on Thunder Tail's statement on Crazy Horse, to Ivan Stars, 1915, printed in Lakota and in translation, in Buechel and Manhart, *Lakota Tales and Texts*, 2:623–33. I have occasionally amended Manhart's translation.

26. He Dog, in Riley, "Oglala Sources," 14.

27. Ibid., 16.

28. Eagle Elk, November 1944, Neihardt Papers.

29. Thunder Tail, in Buechel and Manhart, *Lakota Tales and Texts*, 2:623–33.

30. Bourke, *On the Border with Crook*, 415.

31. Friends and acquaintances described Crazy Horse in fairly consistent terms: besides statements already cited by He Dog, Red Feather, Horn Chips, and Eagle Elk, see especially Short Bull, in Riley, "Oglala Sources," 40–41; and Joseph White Bull to Stanley Vestal, Vestal to Hinman, Oct. 13, 1932.

32. Short Bull, in Riley, "Oglala Sources," 40–41; Bettelyoun and Waggoner, *With My Own Eyes*, 108–109; Irwin to CoIA, Sept. 6, 1877, RCA Letterbook, NACPR.

33. On "court[ing] the girls together," see He Dog, in Riley, "Oglala Sources," 9.

34. Quotations in this order: Black Elk, DeMallie, *Sixth Grandfather*, 203; He Dog, Riley, "Oglala Sources," 14; John Colhoff to Joseph Balmer, Nov. 17, 1951 (transcript in author's collection).

35. Garnett interview, tablet 2, Ricker Papers. On Crazy Horse and High Backbone's excellence in all fields, see King, in Kadlecek and Kadlecek, *To Kill an Eagle*, 126.

36. Billy Garnett quoted in R. A. Clark, *Killing of Chief Crazy Horse*, 100.

CHAPTER 8

1. For the parley with Bozeman, see M. H. Brown, *Plainsmen of the Yellowstone*, 136–38 (quotations on 137); Gray, "Blazing the Bridger and Bozeman Trails."

2. For the attack on Fort Union, see B.S. Schoonover to Supt. A. M. Robinson, Aug. 23, 1860, UMA, UMA, LR, OIA; and Sunder, *Fur Trade on the Upper Missouri*, 215. For northern Lakota raiding along the North Platte, see Thomas S. Twiss to Robinson, Oct. 10, 11, Nov. 1, 1860, UPA, LR, OIA; and Schmutterer, *Tomahawk and Cross*, chap. 6. These sources strongly suggest that missionary Moritz Braeuninger, while establishing a mission station on upper Powder River, was killed by Hunkpapa and/or Oglala warriors about July 23, 1860. Hunkpapas were probably recruiting Oglala support for the impending attack on Fort Union.

3. For background on the Colorado gold rush and the Plains Indians, see Coel, *Chief Left Hand*. Twiss to CoIA, Feb. 2, Oct. 2, 1859, and John Pisall [*sic*] to CoIA, Apr. 12, 1860, UPA, LR, OIA, reveal something of the Arapaho predicament.

4. Wissler, "Societies and Ceremonial Associations," 28.

5. For background on the central plains crisis, see Berthrong, *Southern Cheyennes*, chap. 7; Grinnell, *Fighting Cheyennes*, chap. 11; Hyde, *Life of George Bent*, chap. 5.

6. A. Cody to CoIA, Dec. 18, 1861, UPA, LR, OIA.

7. Wissler, "Societies and Ceremonial Associations," 9.

8. For background on the Santee war in Minnesota, see Utley, *Frontiersmen in Blue*, chap. 13, and Carley, *Sioux Uprising of 1862*. A groundbreaking analysis is G. C. Anderson, *Kinsmen of Another Kind*, chap. 12. An impeccably edited collection of firsthand Dakota accounts is G. C. Anderson and Woolworth, *Through Dakota Eyes*.

9. Twiss to CoIA, Jan. 23, 1865, UPA, LR, OIA, stresses the role of Santees in the events of 1864. A report from Fort Benton confirmed the presence of a small contingent of Little Crow's band of Mdewakanton Santees in the northern Lakota winter assemblage at the mouth of Powder River.

10. "Sword's Acts Related," 86f.

11. Garnett interview, tablet 2, Ricker Papers. Little Big Man was reportedly a "cousin" to Crazy Horse. His father is said to have been Yellow Thunder, an akicita leader in 1841 and a chief (Shirt Wearer?) by 1846; his mother (a Cheyenne) was named Her Holy Breath.

12. Collins to Loree, July 3, 1864; Loree to Supt. William M. Albin, July 13, 1864; Albin to CoIA, Oct. 12, 1864 (with enclosures); and Twiss to CoIA, Jan. 23, 1865, all UPA, LR, OIA.

13. Unrau, *Tending the Talking Wire*, 136.

14. Marquis, *Memoirs of a White Crow Indian*, 8–9; Gray, "Blazing the Bridger and Bozeman Trails," 48ff.

15. Collins, circular to "all Mountainneers [*sic*], and other Citizens and settlers," July 14, 1864; Loree to Wood, Aug. 18, 1864, both in UPA, LR, OIA; Ware, *Indian War of 1864*, chaps. 20–21; Collins to CoIA, May 12, 1865, in Spring, *Caspar Collins*, 164–68.

16. The deteriorating situation on the central plains is traced in see Berthrong, *Southern Cheyennes*, chap. 7; Grinnell, *Fighting Cheyennes*, chap. 11; Hyde, *Life of George Bent*, chap. 5. See also Hoig, *Sand Creek Massacre*, and, for a synthesis of Cheyenne oral accounts, Powell, *People of the Sacred Mountain*, 1:278–310.

17. On the northward flight, see Berthrong, *Southern Cheyennes*, chap. 7; Grinnell, *Fighting Cheyennes*, chap. 11; Hyde, *Life of George Bent*, chaps. 5 and 8; and Powell, *People of the Sacred Mountain*, 1:311ff. Collins's report to the CoIA, May 12, 1865 is an invaluable breakdown of Indian numbers and attitudes.

18. Oglala chiefs: see anonymous statement (June 12, 1867?), Fetterman Investigation. The recollections of George Bent are fundamental to all reconstructions of events in the Powder River country in 1865. See Hyde, *Life of George Bent*, chap. 8; and Powell, *People of the Sacred Mountain*, 1:311ff.

19. Bvt. Maj. Gen. Alfred H. Sully to AAG, Dept. of the Northwest, June 6, 1865, printed in "Official Correspondence Pertaining to the War of the Outbreak," 506.

20. Unrau, *Tending the Talking Wire*, 251–52; Hyde, *Life of George Bent*, 207–208; Bettelyoun and Waggoner, *With My Own Eyes*, chap. 10.

21. Bettelyoun and Waggoner, *With My Own Eyes*, 66.

22. A number of newspaper accounts of the 1877 surrenders mention the 1865 murder of Crazy Horse's brother at Fort Laramie and maintain that this was his last peacetime visit to a post or agency: See, e.g., *New York Tribune*, May 7, 1877: "[Crazy Horse] has been at war for 12 years, having left Fort Laramie in 1865 upon the occasion of the murder of his brother." Though vague, the report accurately reflects the conditions of 1865.

CHAPTER 9

1. Holy Blacktail Deer, in DeMallie, *Sixth Grandfather*, 106.

2. Utley, *Lance and the Shield*, 87.

3. Garnett interview, tablet 2, Ricker Papers.

4. The Horse Creek breakout remains a neglected action. Reports are collected in *War of Rebellion*, series 1, vol. 48, pt. 1, 322–28, 1303. For vivid oral reminiscence, see Bettelyoun and Waggoner, *With My Own Eyes*, chap. 10. Three accounts by George E. Hyde demonstrate his mastery of synthesizing official reports and Indian recollection: *Life of George Bent*, 210–12; *Red Cloud's Folk*, 120–22; *Spotted Tail's Folk*, 118–122.

5. The Battle of Platte Bridge, one of the great set-piece clashes of the Plains Indian wars, was vividly recalled by George Bent and other Cheyenne participants. Their accounts form the basis of my reconstruction: Hyde, *Life of George Bent*, 212–22; Grinnell, *Fighting Cheyennes*, chap. 17; Powell, *People of the Sacred Mountain*, 1:327ff. A book-length study is Vaughn, *Battle of Platte Bridge*. See also Spring, *Caspar Collins*, chap. 12; Berthrong, *Southern Cheyennes*, 247–49; Hyde, *Red Cloud's Folk*, 122–26; Utley, *Frontiersmen in Blue*, 319–22; Unrau, *Tending the Talking Wire*, 271–75; Nadeau, *Fort Laramie and the Sioux*, chap. 11.

6. For a strategic overview of the 1865 campaigns, start as always with Utley, *Frontiersmen in Blue*, 322ff. Official reports, journals, and diaries of the 1865 campaigns are collected in Hafen and Hafen, *Powder River Campaigns*.

7. Hyde, *Life of George Bent*, 223–33; Powell, *People of the Sacred Mountain*, 1:375–78; Grinnell, *Fighting Cheyennes*, 204–209; Bent, "Forty Years with the Cheyennes."

8. On the activities of Young Little Hawk, see two White Bull statements, in Howard, *Warrior Who Killed Custer*, 34–35; and Vestal, *Warpath*, 44–45 (which names Crazy Horse's younger brother as Cloud Man). For Red Hawk, see his own recollection, Curtis, *Teton Sioux*, 188.

9. The appalling march of Cole and Walker is documented in Hafen and Hafen, *Powder River Campaigns*. For background on the first Lakota clashes with Cole and Walker, see Utley, *Frontiersmen in Blue*, 328–29, and *Lance and the Shield*, 68–69. George Bent's accounts establish the Sun Dance dating, as presented in Powell, *People of the Sacred Mountain*, 1:383, 656, and the appearance of northern Lakota messengers. High Backbone was with the Miniconjous through midsummer 1865 but living in the Oglala village through the fall; suggesting he may have been one of the messengers.

10. Eagle Elk, Nov. 27, 1944, 12–13, Neihardt Papers. Eagle Elk's context is unsatisfactory, leading straight into an account of No Water's shooting of Crazy Horse in 1870; however, the only action that fits his attack on "some soldiers located near Powder River" is the 1865 assaults on Cole and Walker. Interpretation is probably at fault. Like most Oglalas, and Pine Ridge interpreters, Eagle Elk refers to High Backbone as Hump. Some Miniconjou informants today believe that the younger Hump was probably a nephew (sister's son?) of High Backbone.

11. Eagle Elk, Nov. 27, 1944, 12–13, Neihardt Papers. Background on the battle is from Hyde, *Life of George Bent*, 236–40; Powell, *People of the Sacred Mountain*, 1:383ff; Hafen and Hafen, *Powder River Campaigns*; Utley, *Frontiersmen in Blue*, 329.

12. Utley, *Frontiersmen in Blue*, 329–30, documents the windup of the Connor offensive.

13. Singing Bear, "Red Cloud," Sept. 1915, in Buechel and Manhart, *Lakota Tales and Texts*, 2:604–14 (quotation at 610). The Buechel and Manhart texts represent one of the greatest of future resources for Lakota studies, but they pose significant difficulties. Buechel's purpose in assembling texts was linguistic, not historic, and his interviewers showed little interest in obtaining dates and historic contexts. Singing Bear's account of the life of Red Cloud is typical in this regard. Nevertheless, its first section seems to be a detailed if partial account of the events of 1865 through spring 1866, yielding valuable clues to Red Cloud's rise to primacy in the Oglala tribe.

The account has significance for the career of Crazy Horse also. It places him as a ranking councilor in the fall of 1865, debating the issue of a proposed Crow truce. In all likelihood, this reflects the Lakota practice of nominating a blotahunka war council *after* a successful defense of the village (see Wissler, "Societies and Ceremonial Associations," 61). Red Cloud, recognized as pipe owner or leader, was probably seated at the honor place, flanked by Crazy Horse and the other blotahunka named by Singing Bear. Since such leaders were entitled to wear shirts fringed with human hair, this may explain the confusion about the date Crazy Horse was made Shirt Wearer, which is definitively dated to summer 1868, after the end of the Bozeman Trail War (see chapter 11). Mari Sandoz, probably unhappy with the implications for Crazy Horse's "hostile" credentials, chose to redate it to September 1865, at the very start of the war (*Crazy Horse*, 174–78). The only rationale for such a redating was He Dog's and Little Shield's uncertainty over the term Crazy Horse served as Shirt Wearer: [He Dog:] "It was about five years that [Crazy Horse] was a chief, maybe longer"; [Little Shield:] "It was about the fourth year that the trouble started" (Riley, "Oglala Sources," 19). Since Sandoz knew Crazy Horse was divested of his Shirt Wearer status in 1870, she used this vague statement to ignore three others that unequivocally dated the investiture. In light of Singing Bear's account, it now seems possible to hypothesize that He Dog and Little Shield were confusing the Shirt Wearer ceremony of 1868 with the blotahunka investiture of three years earlier, both involving the presentation of hair-fringed shirts. Coincidentally, the date reconstructible from Singing Bear fits with Sandoz's misdating.

14. For the Fort Sully treaties of 1865, see *Proceedings of a Board of Commissioners*; Bvt. Maj. Gen. Alfred H. Sully to Maj. Gen. J. Pope, Oct. 1, 1865, UMA, UMA, LR, OIA; also Newton Edmunds to CoIA, Oct. 14, 1865, and *Report of the Commission to Treat with the Sioux of the Upper Missouri,* both in ARCoIA 1865.

15. For Big Ribs's mission and Red Cloud's position, see Col. Henry E. Maynadier to CoIA, Jan. 25, 1866, UPA, LR, OIA. Recruited by Gen. H. M. Dodge at the *iyeska* (mixed-blood) communities north of Denver, the embassy left Fort Laramie on Oct. 15, 1865, returning on Jan. 13, 1866. See also Coutant, *History of Wyoming*, 2:541; and, for details of the Oglala councils with the treaty commission at Fort Sully, *Proceedings of a Board of Commissioners*, 93–110.

16. Man Afraid of His Horse's diplomatic engagement is attested to in Vital Jarrot to CoIA, Feb. 11, 1866, UPA, LR, OIA.

17. Jarrot to CoIA, Feb. 11, 1866; Jarrot to E. B. Taylor, Feb. 5, 1866, UPA, LR, OIA. Maj. Gen. John Pope to Secretary of the Interior, Feb. 12, 1866; and E. B. Taylor to CoIA, Oct. 1, 1866, ARCoIA 1866, 206, 210–11; also 1866 Treaty Articles, and CoIA to Secretary of the Interior, Jan. 20, 1867, both in *Papers Relating to Talks and Councils*, 19–20, 31–34.

18. On Red Cloud's role, see Singing Bear, in Buechel and Manhart, *Lakota Tales and Texts*, 2:604–14; Charles P. Jordan to Doane Robinson, June 26, 1902, Robinson Papers.

19. Maynadier to CoIA, Mar. 24, 1866; E. B. Taylor to Maj. Gen. Frank Wheaton, Mar. 12, 1866; Taylor to CoIA, Mar. 12, 1866, all UPA, LR, OIA.

20. Maynadier to Wheaton and Taylor, Apr. 5, 1866, UPA, LR, OIA.

21. A full listing of all headmen at the June 5 treaty council is printed in *Rocky Mountain News*, June 18, 1866.

22. Minuted proceedings for the Fort Laramie talks have not yet surfaced. The following account depends on Taylor to CoIA, June 9, 1866, UPA, LR, OIA; also *Rocky Mountain News*, June 18 (includes quotation), 25, 27, 1866; Taylor and Maynadier, undated report, and Taylor to CoIA, Oct. 1, 1866, ARCoIA 1866, 208–209, 210–12. For Man Afraid of His Horse's perception of these talks, see his statement to Cheyenne chiefs, Carrington Papers, 10.

23. *Rocky Mountain News*, June 18, 1866; Taylor to CoIA, June 9, 1866 (includes quotation).

24. Taylor to CoIA, June 9, 1866; Unrau, *Tending the Talking Wire*, 345; *Rocky Mountain News*, June 27, 1866 (includes quotation).

25. The evidence suggests that Bad Faces considered the land north of Crazy Woman Creek their own. As revealed by the pattern of subsequent hostilities, the land south of there, including the upper Powder River valley, was considered Hunkpatila country. The pattern reflects post-1858 expansion into Crow country. See M. I. Carrington, *Absaraka*, 94.

26. Carrington Papers, 5. In the absence of minuted proceedings, the roles of Red Cloud and Man Afraid of His Horse have been misunderstood. Contrary to the assumption of Nadeau, *Fort Laramie and the Sioux*, 209, 306–307, it is clear that they returned to Fort Laramie for the second round of treaty talks scheduled to start June 13. The *Rocky Mountain News* coverage of the proceedings establishes that as late as June 19, formal talks had not actually resumed. This is entirely consistent with the situation outlined by Coutant's informants: Red Cloud and Man Afraid of His Horse were both present at Fort Laramie, "but . . . not taking any part in the peace talks, yet doing a great amount of hard work among the tribes on the outside. Nothing was allowed to escape the attention of those chieftains." Coutant, *History of Wyoming*, 2:543.

27. F. C. Carrington, *My Army Life*, 292: Red Cloud's speech was clearly recalled by William Murphy, in 1866 a private of Company A, Eighteenth Infantry, at the 4th of July, 1908, celebrations in Sheridan, Wyoming. Murphy explicitly states that it was a "harangue to the Indians," *not* a speech to the commission as many secondary writers have assumed. The chronological context seems to fit June 14, since talks "continued for some time" after the speech, i.e., before the northern Oglala departure on the fifteenth. Margaret Carrington also implies a hiatus, suggesting that after Red Cloud, "with all his fighting men," withdrew from council, Man Afraid of His Horse remained engaged in debate "with the treaty-makers," i.e., those chiefs favoring agreement. M. I. Carrington, *Absaraka*, 79.

28. M. I. Carrington, *Absaraka*, 79–80 (includes all quotations); Coutant, *History of Wyoming*, 2:543–48. F. C. Carrington, *My Army Life*, 124–25, M. I. Carrington dates this confrontation to June 15. Frances Carrington, in an otherwise overdrawn account, notes the detail of the chiefs ordering tipis struck.

29. Carrington Papers, 10, 19. The Cheyennes told Carrington that five hundred warriors were in the Oglala Sun Dance village, suggesting an approximate count of four hundred lodges. The treaty was signed by the Brules and Oglalas remaining at Fort Laramie on June 27, and by representatives of one small Cheyenne band on June 28.

30. Ibid. For evidence of the War Deciders: Carrington Papers, 29, 32 (Buffalo Tongue); Fort Laramie, post scout reports, Nov. 1866 (Black Twin); Fire Thunder, in DeMallie, *Sixth Grandfather*, 103 (Big Road). Fire Thunder's observation, "Red Cloud was, of course, over all of us" neatly sums up the same tacit primacy implied by Singing Bear: it also echoes the literal meaning of *ataya zuya itancan*, war chief over all—see DeMallie, "Teton Dakota Kinship and Social Organization," 152.

31. Hebard and Brininstool, *Bozeman Trail*, 1:278.

32. Carrington Papers, 10 (includes quotation), 29, 32; M. I. Carrington, *Absaraka*, 119–21. The split within Hunkpatila, which finally crystallized in May 1871 (see chapter 14), undoubtedly had its origin in the first weeks of hostilities against the Bozeman Trail garrisons. Young Man Afraid of His Horse was one of the leaders in the July 23 attack at Crazy Woman Creek: John Colhoff to Joseph Balmer, Oct. 17, 1948 (transcript in author's collection). Little Hawk's presence can be inferred from his key role around Fort Reno in 1867 (see chapter 10). Buffalo Tongue (born 1819) was herald of the White Packstrap, a warrior society founded by Man Afraid of His Horse himself.

In 1866 Hunkpatila numbered approximately forty-five lodges, 280 people. Four tiyospaye are detectable: Kapozha, led by Man Afraid of His Horse and Worm; the former Standing Bull kindred, now led by Worm's brother Little Hawk (the elder); Yellow Eagle II's tiyospaye; and Payabya, perhaps associated with Man Afraid of His Horse's brother-in-law Blue Handle. Most of these family groups, with the possible exception of Little Hawk's, were divided over the war issue. Through the war years, the band underwent a complex process of splitting and regrouping, reflecting residual veneration for Man Afraid of His Horse. Politics were particularly volatile in the period July 1866–March 1867.

33. Baptiste Pourier, interview by Eli S. Ricker, tablet 13, Ricker Papers, locates Red Cloud in the attack on the Bighorn ferry, dated July 17 in the meticulous reconstruction of Gray, *Custer's Last Campaign*, 31–32.

34. M. I. Carrington, *Absaraka*, 122–24. For background on the first months of the Bozeman Trail posts, see Carrington Papers, passim; Utley, *Frontier Regulars*, 100ff; Hebard and Brininstool, *Bozeman Trail*, 1:263–96; D. Brown, *Fort Phil Kearny*, passim.

35. Carrington Papers, 20–21, 30; M. I. Carrington, *Absaraka*, 126.

36. Carrington Papers, 20–21, 30; Singing Bear, in Buechel and Manhart, *Lakota Tales and Texts*, 2:605, 611; R. A. Clark, *Killing of Chief Crazy Horse*, 100.

37. On Miniconjous, see John B. Sanborn to Secretary of the Interior, July 8, 1867 (High Backbone), in *Indian Hostilities*, 66. There were "not quite a hundred lodges" in the Miniconjou village on Tongue River by November: Fort Laramie, post scout reports, Nov. 1866.

38. By late October, few Lakotas remained on Powder River: Crazy Horse and the Buffalo Tongue camp of Hunkpatilas had therefore consolidated on the Tongue. See statement of "Bordeau Bro in Law," "Notes Taken of a Conversation with Two Indians," Fort Laramie, post scout reports, Nov. 1866. On Crazy Horse as Red Cloud's "principal lieutenant," see Whitewash, in Robinson, *History of the Dakota or Sioux Indians*, 361.

39. Whitewash and White Bear, in Robinson, *History of the Dakota or Sioux Indians*, 359–61; M. I. Carrington, *Absaraka*, 189, 191–92. An interesting note on Red Cloud as "the chief soldier, the one who *managed the war* for the Sioux in all the wars with the whites" (my emphasis) is in Red Fly statement, Aug. 5, 1903, "1902–06/Red Cloud and Sioux Indians," Box 59, MS 2039, Sheldon Collection. On Red Cloud, the standard references are Hyde, *Red Cloud's Folk*, and Olson, *Red Cloud and the Sioux Problem*. They are now supplemented by Larson, *Red Cloud*, and Paul, *Autobiography of Red Cloud*.

40. For the December 6 attack, see Carrington Papers, 36–39; M. I. Carrington, *Absaraka*, 194–97; "Indian Hostilities," 59. A full secondary account is Vaughn, *Indian Fights*, 32–43; see also D. Brown, *Fort Phil Kearny*, 174–81; and Utley, *Frontier Regulars*, 103–104. On Yellow Eagle's role, see Whitewash, Robinson, *History of the Dakota or Sioux Indians*, 359. This is Yellow Eagle III, son of the *tiyospaye* headman. He was a close associate of Crazy Horse's through the 1870s (see chapter 14).

41. Literature on the "Fetterman Massacre" is vast. Besides the sources listed in the following notes, my narrative depends on Carrington Papers, 39–50; "Indian Hostilities," 15, 28ff, 62–66; M. I. Carrington, *Absaraka*, 200–17; F. C. Carrington, *My Army Life*, 142–48; Grinnell, *Fighting Cheyennes*, chap. 18; Hyde, *Life of George Bent*, 343–46; Hebard and Brininstool, *Bozeman Trail*, 1:297–346; Vestal, *Warpath*, chap. 6; Powell, *People of the Sacred Mountain*, 1:451–51; Utley, *Frontier Regulars*, 104–106; D. Brown, *Fort Phil Kearny*, 186ff; Nadeau, *Fort Laramie and the Sioux*, 221–33; Hyde, *Red Cloud's Folk*, 145–49; H. H. Anderson, "Centennial of Fetterman Fight"; Appleman, "Fetterman Fight"; Vaughn, *Indian Fights*, chap. 2.

42. White Bull, in Vestal, *Warpath*, 53–54.

43. The winkte prophecy was recalled by Grinnell's Cheyenne informants: see *Fighting Cheyennes*, 237–38.

44. For decoys, see especially the Eli S. Ricker interviews with George Sword (Apr. 29, 1907, tablet 16) and American Horse (Aug. 18, 1906, tablet 16), Ricker Papers; also the Grinnell interview material presented in Powell, *People of the Sacred Mountain*, 1:456.

45. Red Cloud's presence along the west side of the ambush ridge is directly attested to by the statements of White Face and Big White Horse, July 30, 1903, "1902–06/Red Cloud and Sioux Indians." Disproving hearsay statements that the Bad Face leader was absent from the battle, they state: "Red Cloud was there. I saw him."

46. Bordeaux, *Custer's Conqueror*, 23.

47. American Horse's contention that he killed Fetterman as stated is strongly confirmed by the testimony regarding Fetterman's wounds of Assistant Surgeon Samuel M. Horton, July 25, 1867, Fetterman Investigation. See Hebard and Brininstool, *Bozeman Trail*, 1:312n, and the introduction, by John D. McDermott.

48. DeBarthe, *Frank Grouard*, 181; W. K. Powers, [John Colhoff's] *Winter Count of the Oglala*, 32.

49. Rocky Bear statement, n.d. [ca. 1902], Box 59, MS 2039, Sheldon Papers.

CHAPTER 10

1. Kinney to HQ Dept. of the Platte, Feb. 7, 1867, Fetterman Investigation; Bvt. Brig. Gen. H. Wessells to Gen. C. C. Augur, Feb. 14, 1867, UPA, LR, OIA; Captain J. Mix to AAG, Feb. 11, 12, 1867, DPR. Crucial to understanding Little Hawk and Crazy Horse's campaign against Fort Reno, Feb.-Aug. 1867, is Robinson, *History of the Dakota or Sioux Indians*, 371ff. Robinson's sources are probably his interviews with White Bear and Whitewash, conducted at Butte Creek issue station, Rosebud Reservation, June 11, 1904. For the makeup of the Little Hawk camp in spring 1867, I follow Vestal's account of the investiture of Sitting Bull: *Sitting Bull*, 91–92.

2. Dates of skirmishes are confirmed in Webb, *Chronological List of Engagements*, 28. For background on the Bozeman Trail garrisons, see Utley, *Frontier Regulars*, 123–25; D. Brown, *Fort Phil Kearny*, chaps. 10–11; Murray, *Military Posts in the Powder River Country*.

3. The activities of the investigative commission generated a printed report, *Indian Hostilities*, and a mass of unprinted correspondence, memoranda, testimony, and minutes of proceedings, collected in Fetterman Investigation.

4. Statement by Iron Shell's envoys, Apr. 1867, *Indian Hostilities*, 93–94.

5. Significant numbers of Bad Faces chose to follow Man Afraid of His Horse. The band chief Brave Bear, Sword Owner's father, remained with the main village, as did He Dog's tiyospaye. Black Twin, a war Decider in 1866, began a lifelong career of doing the opposite to Red Cloud. Most of the True Oglalas, following American Horse and Sitting Bear, also remained with the main village.

6. May 9, Minutes of Special Commission, Fetterman Investigation. For background on Hancock's march and the resumption of warfare on the central plains, see Utley, *Frontier Regulars*, chap. 8.

7. Webb, *Chronological List of Engagements*, 29; Robinson, *History of the Dakota or Sioux Indians*, 371.

8. On the Sitting Bull investiture, Vestal, *Sitting Bull*, chap. 14; Utley, *Lance and the Shield*, 84–89, 350–51; G. C. Anderson, *Sitting Bull and the Paradox of Lakota Nationhood*, 63–65; K. M. Bray, "Before Sitting Bull." All these are based on Vestal's interviews with pro–Sitting Bull Lakotas. Anderson and Utley have critically weighed the partisan Vestal accounts and produced more balanced interpretations of Sitting Bull's new rank and role. It seems important to contextualize the political situation. Coming after the seating of Red Cloud (1865) and High Backbone (1866) as tribal war chiefs, Sitting Bull's elevation should be seen as an attempt to streamline northern Lakota response to the American intrusion on the hunting grounds.

A word on chronology: Vestal's informants were vague on the date of the investiture, placed anywhere in the 1867–69 bracket. Anderson opts for spring 1868; Utley, for 1869. A neglected clue strongly suggests 1867. Presiding at the ceremony were the four Hunkpapa Shirt Wearers seated in 1851, including Loud-Voiced Hawk (Cetan Hotanka). The commander of Fort Stevenson noted the recent accidental death of this chief ("Ishetan-Otanka," or Hawk-bustard in his rendition) on Apr. 3, 1868: de Trobriand, *Military Life in Dakota*, 260. An obvious 1867 context exists. Writing from Fort C. F. Smith on May 4, experienced guide Jim Bridger stated: "At the present time the entire tribe of the Northern Sioux are collecting on Powder River below the mouth of Little Powder River, and their vowed intention is to make a vigorous and determined attack on each of the three posts" on the Bozeman Trail (*Army and Navy Journal*, June 29, 1867). For this reason, and because Crazy Horse's movements are traceable later in the summer, spring 1867 seems to be the correct frame for the Sitting Bull investiture.

9. Kinney to CoIA, June 4, 1867, "Indian Hostilities," 126.

10. Webb, *Chronological List of Engagements*, 29.

11. Fort Laramie council, June 12–13, Minutes of Special Commission, Fetterman Investigation; off-the-record talks are summarized in Sanborn to CoIA, June 16, 1867, "Indian Hostilities," 115–16. See also ARCoIA 1867, 268–70; M. T. Patrick to Supt. H. B. Denman, July 1, 1867, ibid., 289–90. Secondary accounts (e.g., Hyde, *Red Cloud's Folk*, 151–52) that state that Red Cloud was present are mistaken.

12. Minutes of Special Commission. See also Nadeau, *Fort Laramie and the Sioux*, 237, 309. Rafael Gallegos mentioned Man Afraid of His Horse's trade for ammunition in testimony, Aug. 4, 1867, Fetterman Investigation.

13. Horn Chips interview, tablet 18, Ricker Papers. See also H. B. Denman to CoIA, July 16, 1867, UPA, LR, OIA.

14. Webb, *Chronological List of Engagements*, 30; Kinney to CoIA, June 17, 1867, UPA, LR, OIA; White Bear, Robinson, *History of the Dakota or Sioux Indians*, 372.

15. G. P. Beauvais to Secretary of the Interior, Dec. 14, 1867, UPA, LR, OIA.

16. Black Eagle statement, accompanying Col. David S. Stanley to John B. Sanborn, Oct. 6, 1867, RIPC, ID.

17. Dog Hawk statement, in M. T. Patrick to Supt H. B. Denman, July 28, 1867, UPA, LR, OIA; Gallegos testimony, Aug. 4, 1867, Fetterman Investigation. Crow intelligence allows us to follow closely the movement of the Lakota Sun Dance village: see Mattes, *Indians, Infants, and Infantry*, 134–38, and Gray, *Custer's Last Campaign*, 66–68. See also Utley, *Frontier Regulars*, 123–25.

18. Appleman, "Hayfield Fight," 138–39, and "Wagon Box Fight," 152.

19. Literature on the Wagon Box Fight is vast. Fundamental to an overall grasp of the action and its chronology is Captain Powell's own understated report to Fort Phil Kearny post adjutant, Aug. 4 1867, reprinted in a pamphlet, Hackett, *Odds and Ends*. Indian accounts key to my reconstruction are Sword interview, tablet 16, Ricker Papers; Fire Thunder, in DeMallie, *Sixth Grandfather*, 107–108; Eagle Elk, Nov. 27, 1944, 11, Neihardt Papers; White Bull, in Vestal, *Warpath*, chap. 7; and the Cheyenne statements in Powell, *People of the Sacred Mountain*, 2:749–54. Reminiscent accounts are collected in Hebard and Brininstool, *Bozeman Trail*, 2:39–88. Valuable secondary accounts, besides Appleman, "Wagon Box Fight," are Hyde, *Red Cloud's Folk*, 159–61; and Utley, *Frontier Regulars*, 123–25, which includes an informed analysis of Indian casualties. Military historians have been loath to accept Indian recollections of as few as six fatalities, but clearly estimates of hundreds of slain warriors are laughably overblown. Even Powell's guess of sixty killed may more accurately reflect the number of downed ponies. Two weeks after the battle, Lt. George Henry Palmer observed, "the Indians lost thirty or forty killed." See Greene, "'We do not know.'"

20. The following analysis depends on contemporary records of the peace commission, RIPC, ID. An interim report summarized progress through December 1867, printed in ARCoIA 1868, 26–50. An invaluable summary of commission activities is Utley, *Frontier Regulars*, chap. 9. For an account of the Commission's dealings with the Lakotas south of the Platte, see K. M. Bray, "Spotted Tail and the Treaty of 1868."

21. G. P. Beauvais to Secretary of the Interior, Dec. 14, 1867, UPA, LR, OIA. Beauvais to John B. Sanborn, Sept. 12, 1867 (telegram); Maj. J. W. Howland to Gen. W. T. Sherman, Sept. 12, 1867, both RIPC, ID.

22. Howland to Sherman, Sept. 12, 1867; Col. John E. Smith to AAG, Oct. 1, 1867, DPR; Webb, *Chronological List of Engagements*, 32. In the action on August 16, Crazy Horse's warriors struck one of the civilian trains laid over at Fort Reno, killing two men and driving away as many as three hundred head of cattle. Five warriors were allegedly lost in the clash. One month later, a peace commission runner noted, "They have a great many oxen in their camp, and use them in moving." Black Eagle report, accompanying Stanley to Sanborn, Oct. 6, 1867, RIPC, ID.

23. Black Eagle report; Beauvais to Secretary of the Interior, Dec. 14, 1867; Howland to Sherman, Sept. 12, 1867.

24. Beauvais to Secretary of the Interior, Dec. 14, 1867; Simonin, *Rocky Mountain West in 1867*, 94 (includes quotation).

25. Webb, *Chronological List of Engagements*, 34–35; Robinson, *History of the Dakota or Sioux Indians*, 381. Col. John E. Smith to Maj. Gen. C. C. Augur, Nov. 26, 1867, DPR, expressly identifies the attackers in the fall 1867 campaign as the two bands of Man Afraid of His Horse and Red Cloud. A contemporary, if evasive, Lakota mention of the November 4 action was by Blue Handle, Man Afraid of His Horse's envoy, one month later: see A. T. Chamblin to Supt H. M. Denman, Dec. 8, 1867, NSOIA. See also Fire Thunder, in DeMallie, *Sixth Grandfather*, 108; and, for details of Crazy Horse's involvement, Bordeaux, *Custer's Conqueror*, 24.

26. A. T. Chamblin to Supt H. M. Denman, Nov. 29, Dec. 8, 1867, NSOIA.

27. Ibid.; Bordeaux, *Custer's Conqueror*, 24 (includes quotation).

28. Chamblin to Denman, Dec. 8, 1867.

29. Ibid.; Chamblin to CoIA, Dec. 8, 1867; H. M. Denman to Acting CoIA, Dec. 16, 1867, all UPA, LROIA. On the organization of the White Packstrap Society and its founding by Man Afraid of His Horse, see Wissler, "Societies and Ceremonial Associations," 34–36. Buffalo Tongue's involvement is deduced from testimony taken by the peace Commission in April 1868: see testimony by The Cook (Brule), *Papers Relating to Talks and Councils*, 74–5; for Yellow Eagle, cf. Charles E. Gueru testimony, ibid., 78.

30. Chamblin to Denman, Dec. 8, 1867. For diplomacy at Fort Phil Kearny, see H. M. Mathews to CoIA, Jan. 13, 1868 (telegram), Jan. 29, 1868, both UPA, LR, OIA; Mathews to CoIA, Feb. 18, 1868, RIPC, ID.

31. Chamblin to Denman, Dec. 8, 1867; Chamblin to CoIA, Dec. 8, 1867; H. M. Denman to Acting CoIA, Dec. 16, 1867; The Cook testimony; Gueru testimony; Bissonnette to CoIA, Jan. 29, 1868; also J. H. Strader to Acting Quartermaster/Fort Laramie, Dec. 22, 1867, RIPC, ID; Chamblin to Denman, Dec. 22, 1867, Jan. 4, 1868, NSOIA; Chamblin to CoIA, Jan. 4, 1868, UPA, LR, OIA.

32. Mathews to CoIA, Jan. 13, 1868 (telegram) and Jan. 29, 1868; Mathews to CoIA, Feb. 18, 1868; Greene, "'We do not know,'" 27–30.

33. Chamblin to Sanborn, Apr. 4, 1868 (telegram), RIPC, ID; American Horse speech, Apr. 29, 1868, and Battiste Good speech, Apr. 13, 1868, *Papers Relating to Talks and Councils*, 11, 13–15; K. M. Bray, "Spotted Tail and the Treaty of 1868," 26–27.

34. The text of the treaty of 1868 is printed in Kappler, *Indian Laws and Treaties*, 2:998–1007.

35. Ashton S. H. White to Secretary of the Interior, Apr. 11, 14, 1868, UPA, LR, OIA. This report also locates the Oyuhpes, seventy-five lodges, and the main Bad Face camp, one hundred lodges, on the Belle Fourche, and American Horse's camp, fifty lodges, at head of Bear Lodge Creek.

36. Treaty of 1868 (quotations from Articles 11 and 16).

37. Sanborn to CoIA, Apr. 24, 1868, UPA, LR, OIA; American Horse speech, Apr. 29, 1868. Northern Oglala messengers sequentially deferred the scheduled start of talks at Fort Laramie from April 1 (date deferred at commission's request) through late April, to May 12, and finally to May 21 (American Horse speech). It is significant that Man Afraid of His Horse honored this final date. For Hunkpapa intervention against the treaty, see Col. De Trobriand's journal, *Military Life in Dakota*, 259, 264–65.

38. Bordeaux, *Custer's Conqueror*, 24.

39. *Omaha Weekly Herald*, June 10, 1868.

40. On Red Cloud's son, see Olson, *Red Cloud and the Sioux Problem*, 76. On Hunkpatila movements: Ashton S. H. White to CoIA, June 15, 1868 (telegram), UPA, LR, OIA; Lt. Col. A. J. Slemmer to John B. Sanborn, Oct. 1, 1868, RIPC, ID; Charles Gueru to CoIA, July 1, 1868, ARCoIA 1868, 252–54. Rather overdrawing the point, White observes, "Red Cloud sent Yellow Eagle to the Fort to say that he was on his way down to make peace."

41. Gueru to CoIA, July 1, 1868; A. T. Chamblin to John B. Sanborn, Aug. 17, 1868, RIPC, ID. Minutes of the peace commission's councils with the Oglalas, May 24–25, 1868, are printed in *Papers Relating to Talks and Councils*, 85–88.

What exactly did Oglala signatories understand of the implications of the treaty? The official record gives little away, but in a private letter, Sanborn confided that he and Gen. Harney approved the Lakota request to be allowed to trade with their "old traders" in the Platte zone, although he insisted they understood Fort Laramie itself to be off limits (John B. Sanborn to Vincent Colyer, undated, ARCoIA 1870). The nearest thing we have to an impartial observer is

William G. Bullock, manager for the post sutler. Bullock observed that the Indians were told *"plainly* and *repeatedly* . . . that they need not go on the reservation for anything unless they wanted to go" (emphasis by Bullock). Annuity goods would only be issued them on the reservation, but "they could come and hunt and trade anywhere they wanted to on the North side of the North Platte and trade at Fort Laramie" (Spring, "Old Letter Book," 287).

42. Gueru to CoIA, July 1, 1868; H. G. Litchfield to Gen. C. C. Augur, June 16, 1868 (telegram), DPR. Messengers from Red Cloud told Bullock on July 10 that they had had no communication with Man Afraid of His Horse since the treaty (Spring, "Old Letter Book," 278).

CHAPTER 11

1. Location of the village at the time of the Sun Dance is from Garnett interview, tablet 1, Ricker Papers.

2. Wissler, "Societies and Ceremonial Associations," 39–40; Hassrick, *The Sioux,* 26.

3. A note on dating: All previous secondary accounts have followed Sandoz, *Crazy Horse,* 174–78, in placing the Oglala Shirt Wearer ceremony in 1865. Nevertheless, solid dating in eyewitness and other primary sources, with most of which Sandoz was familiar, clearly establishes that it took place in 1868. Short Bull stated the investiture of Crazy Horse and his peers was in that year: Short Bull, interview by Helen Blish, July 23, 1929, précis, no. 23, box 27, Sandoz Papers. The Garnett interview, tablet 1, Ricker Papers, precisely dates it to a month or two after the May 25 signing of the treaty of 1868. Garnett was present in the village and observed the ceremony, and his careful memory of events in the period 1867–69 closely contextualizes it. Moreover, the midsummer 1868 dating is confirmed by a contemporary notice. Maj. W. Dye to AAG, Feb. 3, 1869, DPR, observes, "The Ogallallas [*sic*] have two new chiefs, one the son of [']Man-afraid-of-his-horses,' bearing the same name: the other the son of 'Brave-bear' and called the 'Man who carries the sword' *both made within six months*: they replace their fathers" (my emphasis). Taken with Garnett, Dye's chronology establishes that the ceremony capped the negotiated settlement of the treaty.

4. The Garnett interview, Ricker Papers, is a vivid eyewitness account that I have followed closely in the following discussion.

5. On No Water, I am relying on a traditional statement made by Eddie Herman to Joseph Balmer (Balmer to author, Nov. 9, 1981).

6. Wissler, "Societies and Ceremonial Associations," 40.

7. Black Elk, in DeMallie, *Sixth Grandfather,* 322.

8. John Colhoff to Joseph Balmer, Nov. 27, 1950 (transcript in author's collection).

9. Ibid.

10. Wissler, "Societies and Ceremonial Associations," 40.

11. Military Division of the Missouri, Gen. Order No. 4, Aug. 10, 1868, ARCoIA 1868, 85–86; J. P. Cooper to Supt H. M. Denman, Aug. 27, 1868, ibid., 250–52.

12. Cooper to Denman, Aug. 27, 1868.

13. On the movement to the reservation, see M. T. Patrick to Supt H. A. Denman, Aug. 6, Sept. 16, 1868, UPA, LR, OIA; Gen. C. C. Augur to John B. Sanborn, Oct. 4, 1868, *Papers Relating to Talks and Councils,* 119–20; Lt. Col. A. J. Slemmer to AG, Dept. of the Platte, Sept. 23, 1868, ibid., 120–21. Lt. Col. A. J. Slemmer to John B. Sanborn, Oct. 1, 1868, RIPC, ID, reported that "'Man afraid of his horse,' Red Leaf and other Chief men are very much dissatisfied at their people leaving Laramie and if possible will prevent their going."

14. For conditions on the central plains, see Berthrong, *Southern Cheyennes,* 305–307, and the trenchant overview of Utley, *Frontier Regulars,* 137–39. The northern Oglala raids are treated in Slemmer to AG, Dept. of the Platte, Sept. 23, 1868.

15. He Dog, in Riley, "Oglala Sources," 10.

16. Supt H. B. Denman to CoIA, Nov. 6, 1868, ARCoIA 1868, 230; Maj. W. Dye to AG, Dept. of the Platte, Nov. 20, 1868.

17. Dye to AG, Dept. of the Platte, Nov. 20, 1868; Gen. C. C. Augur to Dye, Nov. 4, 1868 (telegram), also UPA, LR, OIA. The actions of Sherman and the Peace Commission are minuted in *Papers Relating to Talks and Councils*, 122–31.

18. Dye to AG, Dept. of the Platte, Nov. 20, 1868, details the talks with Red Cloud. A valuable eyewitness account of the informal, off-the-record meetings is Adams, "Journal of Ada A. Vogdes," 3–4; Bullock to Messrs. Robert Campbell and Co., Nov. 19, 1868, Spring, "Old Letter Book," 287.

CHAPTER 12

1. He Dog, in Riley, "Oglala Sources," 10–12. Background information on Oglala and Brule winter camp strengths and locations in 1868–69 is supplied in Maj. W. Dye to AAG, Feb. 3, 1869, DPR. The projected Crow campaign is mentioned in Dye to AAG, November 20, 1868, UPA, LR, OIA; it is likely the same campaign as mentioned in McGillycuddy, *Blood on the Moon*, 8, when—according to Man Afraid of His Horse partisans—Red Cloud was granted the temporary chieftainship of the Oglala tribe.

2. Data on Crazy Horse's courtship of Black Shawl are inadequate. The account of Bordeaux, *Custer's Conqueror*, 41, is based on anonymous oral sources, but Bordeaux had good connections. Having jettisoned much of his literary baggage, I have retained his chronological framework of approximately eighteen months separating the marriage agreement with Black Shawl's family and Crazy Horse's elopement with Black Buffalo Woman (see chapter 13). Since the latter is securely dated to May 1870, I have anchored the courtship of Black Shawl in fall 1868.

3. On the family of Black Shawl, see Red Feather, in Riley, "Oglala Sources," 30 (includes quotation). The Pine Ridge census, 1890, places Red Elk Woman, age seventy, and her daughter "Tasina sapa win, Her Black Blanket," age forty-six, in the Spleen, or Melt, band camp (site of modern Holy Rosary Mission), living next to the family of Black Shawl's brother Red Feather. As two widows, the women would have lived in their natal tiyospaye, which the Spleen likely represents. At the time of Black Shawl's marriage to Crazy Horse, however, Red Feather and his family belonged to Big Road's tiyospaye of Oyuhpes: see He Dog statement, June 30, 1931, folder 16, part 2, box 31, Sandoz Papers. Two facts point to a Miniconjou connection. John Colhoff (to Joseph Balmer, Oct. 5, 1951: transcript in author's collection) stated that John Red Feather was a nephew of High Backbone's; Miniconjou headman Red Horse, upon surrendering in 1877, stated that Crazy Horse was his "relative. He married my own sister." Red Horse statement, Col. W. W. Wood to AAG, Dept. of Dakota, Feb. 27, 1877, Sioux War, file 6207, Military Division of the Missouri, Special Files.

4. The account that follows is of a generic Lakota courtship, but given the conservatism of the Crazy Horse family, it is probably not too far from the concrete situation. For pertinent sources, see Walker, *Lakota Society*, 50ff; M. N. Powers, *Oglala Women*, 74–78; Hassrick, *The Sioux*, 124–26.

5. He Dog, in Riley, "Oglala Sources," 9; Bordeaux, *Custer's Conqueror*, 41.

6. Walker, *Lakota Society*, 53.

7. Bordeaux, *Custer's Conqueror*, 41.

8. Bullock to Campbell and Co., Nov. 19, 1868; Augur to Dye, Nov. 4, 1868; and Dye's circular, Nov. 20, 1868, UPA, LR, OIA; Dye to AAG, Feb. 3, 1869 (includes quotation).

9. Dye to AAG, Feb. 3, 1869.

10. Ibid.

11. Ibid.

12. Alex du Bois and Henry Brant to Gen. W. T. Sherman, Mar. 6, 1869; Dye to AAG, Mar. 25, 1869, both DPR; American Horse, Cloud Shield, and White Cow Killer winter counts, Mallery, *Dakota and Corbusier Winter Counts*, 144–45.

13. Oglala hostilities in the Shoshone country began on the lower Sweetwater April 20, 1869, and continued through September. See J. A. Campbell to CoIA, Sept. 23, 1869, ARCoIA 1869.

14. He Dog, in Riley, "Oglala Sources," 16.

15. Short Bull, in Riley, "Oglala Sources," 33; cf. Flying Hawk, in McCreight, *Firewater and Forked Tongues*, 139.

16. He Dog, in Riley, "Oglala Sources," 16. Sandoz's detailed account of the young love between Crazy Horse and Black Buffalo Woman is presented in *Crazy Horse*, 131–35. She states that by a cunning ploy, Red Cloud had his niece marry No Water during Crazy Horse's absence on the warpath, ca. 1862, spoiling the plans of the lovers. No primary source that I have seen bears out this tale, which smacks of a fiction to mitigate the circumstances of Crazy Horse's adultery. Despite its influence on later secondary accounts, it is time to discard the tale.

17. On movements to the reservation, see Captain Dewitt C. Poole to Governor J. A. Burbank, Aug. 14, 1869, UPA, LR, OIA; Poole to CoIA, Aug. 20, 1869, ARCoIA 1869.

18. Crazy Horse speech recollected by Thunder Tail, Buechel and Manhart, *Lakota Tales and Texts*, 2:624, 629.

19. George W. Colhoff, interview by Eli S. Ricker, ca. 1906, tablet 25, Ricker Papers, states that by fall 1869, dissatisfied Lakotas were drifting west from Whetstone Agency onto the hunting grounds. For background on conditions at the Brule-Oglala agency, see Hyde, *Spotted Tail's Folk*, chap. 6; Clow, "Whetstone Indian Agency"; and the reprint of a neglected classic—Poole, *Among the Sioux of Dakota*, with DeMallie's valuable introduction. For events on the Republican, I use Little Killer statement, Feb. 1915, Buechel and Manhart, *Lakota Tales and Texts*, 2:435–46; but for background, consult Utley, *Frontier Regulars*, 156–57; and K. M. Bray, "Spotted Tail and the Treaty of 1868," 31–2.

20. White Clay (Cheyenne) report, Captain Eugene Wells to AAG, Oct. 19, 1869, DPR; *Omaha Weekly Herald*, Jan. 26, 1870.

21. White Clay report. For background on John Richard, Jr.'s activities, see Jones, "John Richard, Jr., and the Killing at Fetterman"; also Olson, *Red Cloud and the Sioux Problem*, 87–88, 93. Garnett interview, tablet 1, Ricker Papers, provides valuable details on Richard. An untapped newspaper source is *Omaha Weekly Herald*, Dec. 8, 1869.

22. On war parties: *Plattsmouth Herald*, Nov. 25, 1869; *Omaha Weekly Herald*, Dec. 15, 1869. Olson, *Red Cloud and the Sioux Problem*, 89–92, outlines the Big Horn Expedition.

23. White Clay report; *Plattsmouth Herald*, Dec. 30, 1869; *Omaha Weekly Herald*, Jan. 26, 1870; White Swan (Miniconjou) report, Bvt. Maj. Gen. D. S. Stanley to AAG, Dept. of Dakota, Feb. 12, 1870, UPA, LR, OIA; Roman Nose (Miniconjou) report, Captain D. C. Poole to Governor J. Burbank, May 4, 1870, DS Field Office Records. Crazy Horse was definitely involved in the late phase of this campaign: given the new split in Hunkpatila, it seems more than likely that he was engaged from the start.

24. Man Afraid of His Horse left Powder River bound for Whetstone Agency with twenty lodges—"all he could persuade to go" (White Clay report). In garbled intelligence from Whetstone, the *Omaha Weekly Herald*, Dec. 8, 1869, reported his following reduced to seven lodges, still en route. They never arrived, and Man Afraid of His Horse is next heard of back on Powder River in March. For Spotted Tail's request, see Captain D. C. Poole to Governor Burbank, Nov. 24, 1869, UPA, LR, OIA.

25. Utley, *Indian Frontier*, chap. 5, cogently contextualizes the peace policy and sensitively reads the Lakota engagement with it. His paragraph on Red Cloud, 150, is a necessary departure for any understanding of the Oglala leader's postwar career.

26. Maj. Alexander Chambers to AAG, Mar. 11, 1870 (telegram), DPR. The routes are inferred from the April locations of the two villages.

27. Maj. Alexander Chambers to AAG, Dept. of the Platte, May 6, 1870 (telegram), UPA, LR, OIA, ascribes prime responsibility for killing of miners to "a band of 'Ohyacopee' Sioux and Minneconjous [*sic*] . . . Crazy-horse-Leading [the party]." Arapaho chiefs also blamed these Lakotas, although the blurred evidence indicates that some Arapaho warriors may have joined Crazy Horse's party. Eagle Elk, Nov. 27, 1944, 13, Neihardt Papers, places Crazy Horse in the war party "over the Rockies" immediately before the No Water affair, i.e., April 1870. High Backbone was with Crazy Horse and the Oglalas May–October 1870: therefore, he probably left the Miniconjous to join the Wyoming raids. For the winter 1869–70 death of High Backbone's mother, see e.g. W. K. Powers, *Winter Count of the Oglala*, 32. For background on March–April hostilities in Wyoming: Trenholm, *Arapahoes, Our People*, 231–34.

28. Eagle Elk, Nov. 27, 1944, 13, Neihardt Papers

29. Maj. Alexander Chambers to AAG, Mar. 18, 1870 (telegram), DPR; Gen. W. T. Sherman to Gen. P. H. Sheridan, Mar. 23, 1870 (telegram), UPA, LR, OIA; AAG, Division of the Missouri, to Gen. C. C. Augur, Mar. 29, 1870 (telegram; includes quotation), DPR.

30. *Plattsmouth Herald*, May 5, 1870. The relevant dispatch, one of a series penned by Fort Laramie chaplain Alpha Wright, is reprinted in Paul, "An Early Reference to Crazy Horse."

31. *Plattsmouth Herald*, May 5, 1870. Chambers to AAG, Dept. of the Platte, May 6, 1870, states that Crazy Horse's party, having engaged in hostilities in the Sweetwater region in early April, had shifted operations to attack "the Railroad, and ranches below Laramie."

32. Maj. Alexander Chambers to AAG, Apr. 28, 1870 (telegram), DPR; Gen. C. C. Augur to Gen. P. H. Sheridan, Apr. 28, 1870 (telegram); Sheridan to Gen. W. T. Sherman, Apr. 28, 1870 (telegram); Sherman to Sheridan, Apr. 29, 1870 (telegram); Governor J. A. Campbell to CoIA, Apr. 29, 1870 (telegram), all UPA, LR, OIA; Sherman to Sheridan, May 4, 1870 (telegram), DPR.

33. Chambers to AAG, Apr. 28, 1870 (telegram); Augur to Sheridan, Apr. 28, 1870 (telegram); Sheridan to Sherman, Apr. 28, 1870 (telegram); Sherman to Sheridan, Apr. 29, 1870 (telegram); Campbell to CoIA, Apr. 29, 1870 (telegram); Sherman to Sheridan, May 4, 1870 (telegram); Chambers to AAG, Dept. of the Platte, May 6, 1870 (telegram), UPA, LR, OIA. Details of the Fort Fetterman negotiations, including the warrior society escort, are in Adams, "Journal of Ada A. Vogdes," 11–12.

34. Captain D. S. Gordon to AAG, Dept. of the Platte, May 6, 1870; Chambers to AAG, Dept. of the Platte, May 6, 1870 (telegram), both UPA, LROIA. Chambers states that, within the previous day or two, Crazy Horse had "been seen and talked with by a Sioux who lives here [at Fort Fetterman]."

35. Governor J. A. Campbell to CoIA, May 12, 1870 (telegram), UPA, LR, OIA. Campbell transmits Maj. Chambers' May 11 dispatch from Fort Fetterman, which remarks: "messenger just in from man afraid-of his horses and Red Cloud returning seven horses and mules taken from Chug Water by Oyakopee Sioux and *his party whipped*" (my emphasis). In light of Chambers' earlier telegram (May 6), this means the party of "Crazy-horse Leading," implying that Crazy Horse himself was beaten.

36. Thunder Tail statement about Crazy Horse, Buechel and Manhart, *Lakota Tales and Texts*, 2: speech at 624 (Lakota), and 629 (English). Although the chronology is scrambled, the context best fits the Oglala delegation to Washington of 1870. Since both Crazy Horse's and Sitting Bull's speeches dwell on the term *iwastela*, it is plain that this was the idiom of the day following the treaty of 1868.

37. Wissler, "Societies and Ceremonial Associations," 23–25 (quotation on 24); He Dog, in Riley, "Oglala Sources," 13; Bad Heart Bull and Blish, *Pictographic History of the Oglala Sioux*, 112.

38. Bad Heart Bull and Blish, *Pictographic History of the Oglala Sioux*, 314–80, vividly illustrates the battle; additional details, including Crazy Horse's activities, are taken from the Thunder Tail account, in Buechel and Manhart, *Lakota Tales and Texts*, 2:624–25, 630–31. On dating: Crazy Horse was engaged in the war parties against the Americans from late March through the first week of May 1870. The tight sequence of events, covered in chapter 13, was completed by late June, according to He Dog's chronology. Since the Fight When They Chased Them Back to Camp is presented as the starting point of the sequence, it best fits mid-May, precisely contemporaneous with preparations for the Red Cloud delegation—and a likely context for its delayed start.

39. Thunder Tail account, in Buechel and Manhart, *Lakota Tales and Texts*, 2:624–25, 630–31 (with amended translation).

40. The most detailed secondary account of the delegation is Olson, *Red Cloud and the Sioux Problem*, chap. 7. Nevertheless, minor errors occur in Olson's chronology. Contemporary documentation shows the Oglala party arriving at Fort Fetterman probably late on May 16. After five more days of talks, Man Afraid of His Horse pleaded sickness, and the delegation departed without him on May 22, arriving at Fort Laramie on the 24th. Accompanied by Col. John E. Smith, the party departed that post on May 26 and boarded the Union Pacific at Pine Bluffs on the following afternoon.

41. He Dog statement, in H. Scudder Mekeel to George E. Hyde, Aug. 26, 1931 (précis in author's collection): "R[ed] C[loud] gave [He Dog] his shirt to wear during his trip to Wash[ington]." On American Horse's diplomacy, see Gen. F. F. Flint to AAG, June 19, 1870 (telegram), DPR.

CHAPTER 13

1. The fundamental sources for details on the elopement of Crazy Horse and Black Buffalo Woman are the Hinman interviews with He Dog, July 7 and 13, 1930, and He Dog's undated statement to John Colhoff, all in Riley, "Oglala Sources," 13–14, 15–19. These form the core of my account. Additional details are from Eagle Elk, Nov. 27, 1944, 13, Neihardt Papers; Horn Chips interview, tablet 18, Ricker Papers. Spurious dates and details spoil the traditional account presented in Bordeaux, *Custer's Conqueror*, 41–43, but I have used details of the role played by Touch the Clouds. I restrict footnoting to quotations and controversial points.

2. "Lone Eagle Gives Museum Biography of Crazy Horse," transcript in Hyde Papers, author's collection. This undated [ca. 1950] piece summarizes a talk given by Lone Eagle to the Colorado Springs Pioneer Museum. Most of its information is derived from the then unpublished Hinman interviews, but it includes a few independent details, including the assertion that Bad Heart Bull's pistol was a Derringer. There is no verification of this in the primary sources, but Lone Eagle's account is notable for its restraint, and the detail merits remark. Lone Eagle states: "An attractive young Oglala woman, Black Buffalo Woman, wife of No Water, left her man and went to live with Crazy Horse in the old Ft. Laramie (Wyo.) area about 1870."

A note on dating: if No Water had been part of the delegation escort to Fort Fetterman, he would have been able to leave the post for home on May 22, when Red Cloud's party departed for the railroad. This would place the elopement and shooting of Crazy Horse within the frame May 21–25—unverifiable in detail, but consistent with the internal logic of He Dog's chronology.

3. He Dog, July 13, 1930, Riley, "Oglala Sources," 17.

4. Ibid.

5. Ibid.

6. Ibid.

7. Ibid. The Miniconjou headmen Bull Head, Ashes, and Spotted Crow were brothers of Crazy Horse's stepmothers.

8. Ibid., 17–18.

9. Ibid., 19. Man Afraid of His Horse almost certainly presided over the divesting of Crazy Horse. Col. Franklin F. Flint, noting the delegation's arrival at Fort Laramie, observed that "man afraid of his horses [was] left sick at Fort Fetterman." Flint to AAG, May 24, 1870 (telegram), DPR. Pourier interview, tablet 15, Ricker Papers, states that Man Afraid of His Horse "backed out" of the delegation, strongly suggesting that his was a diplomatic illness.

10. Garnett interview, tablet 1, Ricker Papers.

11. King, in Kadlecek and Kadlecek, *To Kill an Eagle*, 126.

12. In the following account of a generic Lakota wedding, I have depended on Hassrick, *The Sioux*, 129–30; Walker, *Lakota Society*, 51ff; M. N. Powers, *Oglala Women*, 81–82; Standing Bear, *Land of the Spotted Eagle*, 108–12.

13. Two direct statements date Crazy Horse's marriage to Black Shawl: Red Feather (in Riley, "Oglala Sources," 30) states, "Crazy Horse married my sister six years before he was killed," i.e., ca. 1871. An 1870 dating is suggested by He Dog (in Riley, "Oglala Sources," 14): "*Shortly after* [the Black Buffalo Woman elopement, Crazy Horse] married Red Feather's sister" (my emphasis). Moreover, a statement by Moses Flying Hawk—an Oyuhpe relative and close associate of Crazy Horse's—asserts that Crazy Horse "took his wife with him" when he went to bury the remains of Young Little Hawk (McCreight, *Chief Flying Hawk's Tales*, 21). From He Dog's chronology, we know that this trip was in late June 1870. The marriage to Black Shawl therefore is to be fitted into the mid-June frame, after Crazy Horse's recovery from the No Water shooting. The tight sequence clearly implies family intervention to stabilize the crisis in Crazy Horse's personal life.

On the death of Young Little Hawk: Eagle Elk, Nov. 27, 1944, Neihardt Papers; Flying Hawk, McCreight, *Chief Flying Hawk's Tales*, 21; He Dog, Riley, "Oglala Sources," 15; also He Dog to Sandoz, June 30, 1931, folder 16, part 2, box 31, Sandoz Papers. He Dog is once again our best guide to chronology. He states that Young Little Hawk was killed while Crazy Horse was recovering from the No Water shooting—broadly, early June 1870.

14. Eagle Elk, Nov. 27, 1944, Neihardt Papers; Flying Hawk, McCreight, *Chief Flying Hawk's Tales*, 21; He Dog, Riley, "Oglala Sources," 15; He Dog to Sandoz, June 30, 1931; Worm statement, *New York Sun*, Sept. 14, 1877. Although Worm states that Shoshones killed his youngest son, Eagle Elk gives the enemy as Utes. He Dog and Flying Hawk agree that Young Little Hawk was killed by Americans, the latter stating they were civilian "settlers." All sources indicate a location in south-central Wyoming except He Dog (to Sandoz), who places the killing "near Chimney Rock." Given He Dog's veracity and the unanimity of other sources, perhaps interpreter John Colhoff confused Chimney Rock with Independence Rock, another Oregon Trail landmark in the right district. An anonymous tradition set down in Eastman, *Indian Heroes and Great Chieftains*, 91, states that soldiers killed Young Little Hawk, after a dash to stampede a post herd. Official records detail a number of skirmishes in the Sweetwater–Laramie plains country, spring 1870, but further research is needed to establish a definite context.

15. Flying Hawk, McCreight, *Chief Flying Hawk's Tales*, 21. He Dog, Riley, "Oglala Sources," 15, states that Crazy Horse "went south and found his brother's body and buried it" before the Red Cloud delegation returned from Washington. This indicates late June for the burial trip, since the delegates returned to Fort Laramie on June 26.

16. Webb, *Chronological List of Engagements*, 55; Gen. P. H. Sheridan to Gen. W. T. Sherman, June 29, 1870 (telegram); Sherman to Sheridan, June 30, 1870 (telegram); Sheridan to Sherman, July 1, 1870 (telegram), all UPA, LR, OIA. Sherman assumed the raiders to be Lakotas and northern Arapahos, consistent with the makeup of Young Little Hawk's party.

17. Flying Hawk, McCreight, *Chief Flying Hawk's Tales*, 21; Eagle Elk, Nov. 27, 1944, Neihardt Papers.

18. Col. John E. Smith to CoIA, July 15, 1870, ARCoIA 1870, 324–26. In the following summary of the Oglala delegation to Washington, I have used Smith's extensive report and the minuted proceedings of talks in Washington, UPA, LR, OIA. A full secondary account is Olson, *Red Cloud and the Sioux Problem*, chap. 7; but see Utley's insightful summary in *Indian Frontier*, 148–51. Still useful for insight and flavor is Hyde, *Red Cloud's Folk*, 174–81.

19. Poole to Burbank, Mar. 4, 1870, DS Field Office Records.

20. The agreement on thirty-five years is unnoted in the minutes of talks in Washington but was clearly fundamental to Lakotas. Red Cloud's role in winning the concession is attested by Little Big Man's 1873 statement to the Oglala agent: J. W. Daniels to CoIA, Apr. 15, 1873, RCA, LR, OIA. Brule delegates also took credit for the agreement, e.g., Swift Bear speech, Apr. 10, 1872, Daniels to CoIA, Apr. 14, 1872, RCA, LR, OIA.

21. Little Big Man, in Daniels to CoIA, Apr. 15, 1873.

22. Red Cloud's post-delegation diplomacy is detailed in the following documents in UPA, LR, OIA: Col. F. F. Flint to AAG, Dept. of the Platte, July 15, Aug. 1, 1870; Maj. Alexander Chambers to AAG, Dept. of the Platte, July 27, Aug. 2, 1870 (telegrams); Chambers to CoIA, July 8, 14, 1870 (telegrams); Flint to CoIA, Aug. 6, 29, 1870 (telegrams). See also Adams, "Journal of Ada A. Vogdes," 12–13.

23. Eagle Elk, Nov. 27, 1944, Neihardt Papers.

24. He Dog to Sandoz, June 30, 1931; Iron Horse, in Standing Bear, *Land of the Spotted Eagle*, 180–81; Red Feather, in Riley, "Oglala Sources," 30, 33. On Red Feather's membership in the Crow Owners, ca. 1870, see Wissler, "Societies and Ceremonial Associations," 66.

25. For fall 1870 Oglala attitudes, see minuted speeches in William Fayet, clerk, "Journal of the United States Special Indian Commission, headed by F. R. Brunot and R. Campbell, to the Oglala Sioux, Aug.–Oct. 1870," UPA, LR, OIA.

26. He Dog, in Riley, "Oglala Sources," 13; Thunder Tail, in Buechel and Manhart, *Lakota Tales and Texts*, 2:624, 629. For once, He Dog is unhelpful with the chronology, simply dating the investiture of Crazy Horse as tribal war chief as "early, a long, long time before the Custer fight." Necessarily postdating the divesting of Crazy Horse's Shirt Wearer status (early summer 1870), it took place at a gathering of the whole Oglala tribe; Thunder Tail adds that it was "in the north." No such gathering postdated 1870, so the early September gathering at Bear Lodge Butte, detailed in "Journal of the United States Special Indian Commission," looks to be the correct context.

27. He Dog, in Riley, "Oglala Sources," 13; Thunder Tail in Buechel and Manhart, *Lakota Tales and Texts*, 2:624, 629; "Journal of the United States Special Indian Commission." John Colhoff to Joseph Balmer, May 3, 1950 (transcript in author's collection), indicates He Dog's participation and adds that two Cheyennes and two Arapahos were similarly honored. Colhoff states that the ceremony took place just before Red Cloud's Oglalas "left for Fort Laramie" to establish Red Cloud Agency on the North Platte River, i.e., the agency negotiations of fall 1870–June 1871. In 1877 Standing Bear (married to a cousin of Crazy Horse, the daughter of Worm's sister Big Woman) depicted Crazy Horse in formal regalia, brandishing a knife club: pictograph reproduced in Ewers, "Military Art of the Plains Indians," 24–37, fig. 17.

28. Joseph Eagle Hawk, He Dog's son, states that the Oglala tribe divided on the same day as the investiture (confused with the 1868 Shirt Wearer ceremonies), part going south, Crazy Horse and He Dog "go[ing] north with their bands" (Eagle Hawk MS, "History of Chief Crazy Horse," Eddie Herman, Transcribed Letters, Spring Collection).

By late 1870, the Oglala population totalled about 635 lodges (excluding Wazhazhas). Of these, 450 attended the October talks at Fort Laramie. Perhaps 140 Southern Oglala and Loafer lodges remained at Whetstone Agency, so a maximum of fifty lodges remained in the north with Crazy Horse.

29. Sitting Bull speech, in Thunder Tail's account, in Buechel and Manhart, *Lakota Tales and Texts*, 2:624, 629–30. For background on Sitting Bull's changing relations with the United States in 1870, see Utley, *Lance and the Shield*, 90–92.

30. Chasing Crow was the son of Red Cloud's sister and trader David Adams. Good Weasel was one of the Strong Heart Society lance owners.

31. John Colhoff, in W. K. Powers, *Winter Count of the Oglala*, 32.

32. He Dog, in Riley, "Oglala Sources," 14–15.

33. Ibid.

34. Ibid.

35. Little Killer, in John Colhoff to Joseph Balmer, n.d. [ca. spring 1949] (transcript in author's collection). Little Killer laughingly dismissed Frank Grouard's claim that Crazy Horse rescued High Backbone's body, then charged the Shoshones alone armed only with his whip. "What they don't know, won't hurt them," he told John Colhoff.

Details on High Backbone's last warpath are from Colhoff statement, 32; Little Killer, in Colhoff to Balmer; He Dog, in Riley, "Oglala Sources," 14–15; Red Feather, ibid., 31. Details derived from Crazy Horse may be assumed in DeBarthe, *Frank Grouard*, 181. The death of High Backbone is noted, interestingly, in several Oglala and Brule, but no Miniconjou, winter counts.

36. Red Feather, in Riley, "Oglala Sources," 31; DeBarthe, *Frank Grouard*, 181 (includes quotation).

CHAPTER 14

1. He Dog, Riley, "Oglala Sources," 18. Moccasin Top was a Bad Face, comrade to Good Weasel as a Strong Heart Society lance owner.

2. Fayet, "Journal of the United States Special Indian Commission," UPA, LR, OIA. Olson, *Red Cloud and the Sioux Problem*, 130ff, deals in detail with negotiations leading to the establishment of Red Cloud Agency. For additional details, see John Wham to CoIA, Mar. 24, 1871, and Col. John E. Smith to AAG, Dept. of the Platte, Mar. 22, 1871, RCA, LR, OIA.

3. Olson, *Red Cloud and the Sioux Problem*, 131. On Sword Owner's reversal of policy, cf. his role in 1870 with reports from 1872—e.g., J. W. Daniels to CoIA, Sept. 22 (telegram), Oct. 25, 1872; Daniels to Col. John E. Smith, Sept. 22, 1872, RCA, LROIA.

4. For comparisons of Man Afraid of His Horse's band strength in March (seventy lodges) and December (thirty lodges, including Young Man Afraid of His Horse's tiyospaye, hunting on the Republican), see Smith to AAG, Dept. of the Platte, Mar. 22, 1871, and Smith to CoIA, Dec. 14, 1871, RCA, LROIA. I have assumed that the balance, approximately forty lodges, went north with the departures in May and June. On Yellow Eagle III's status in Hunkpatila: Colhoff to Balmer, Apr. 25, 1951, transcript in author's collection.

5. DeBarthe, *Frank Grouard*, 181.

6. Utley, *Lance and the Shield*, 111. To understand the vital connection between the railroads and army control of the plains, see Hutton, *Phil Sheridan and His Army*; Athearn, *William Tecumseh Sherman* and "Firewagon Road." For a brief overview of Lakota resistance to the Northern Pacific, see Utley, *Frontier Regulars*, 242–43.

7. T. M. Koues to CoIA, Mar. 30, 1872, CRA, LROIA. The northern boundary of the unceded territory was not defined until the Black Hills Commission of 1875, offering to buy part of the region, tacitly equated it with the Yellowstone River east of the Crow reservation.

8. Col. D. S. Stanley to CoIA, Apr. 7, 1872, CRA, LROIA. See also Utley, *Lance and the Shield*, 106–107.

9. J. W. Daniels to CoIA, Feb. 29, Mar. 21, 25, Apr. 20 (includes tabulation of bands present at RCA on Apr. 1), 1872; Col. John E. Smith to U.S. AG, Mar. 21, 1872, all RCA, LROIA.

10. John Colhoff stated that Yellow Eagle III "was the chief of the Hunkpatilas, before Crazy Horse took over the band" (to Balmer, Apr. 25, 1951). The men were allies, not rivals, indicated by Yellow Eagle's remaining with Crazy Horse through the turbulent summer of 1877 and suggesting that Yellow Eagle voluntarily relinquished chieftainship. The 1872 climate of polarization seems a clear context for choosing a hardline leader like Crazy Horse.

On numbers: Red Cloud stated that as few as "ten or fifteen lodges of that band" had refused to come to the agency (Red Cloud speech, May 27, 1872, "Report of Councils held with 'Red Cloud's' band of Ogallalla Sioux by the President of the United States and Secretary of the Interior. May 27th, 28th and 29th 1872," entry 663, item 34, Special Files, ID). Agent Daniels concluded that the right figure was about thirty lodges (J. W. Daniels to CoIA, Sept. 15, 1872, ARCoIA 1872, 267), and this fits well with what we know of Hunkpatila population. In his annual report for 1873, Daniels noted the presence of Little Big Man in the camp and an increase to forty lodges: Daniels to CoIA, Aug. 18, 1873, ARCoIA 1873.

11. Smith to AG, United States, Mar. 21, 1872, notes the crucial fact of Little Hawk's involvement in the raids near Fort Fetterman. See also Brig. Gen. E. O. C. Ord to AAG, HQ Military Division of the Missouri, Apr. 14, 1872, RCA, LR, OIA.

12. J. W. Daniels to CoIA, July 6, 1872, RCA, LR, OIA. The relative status of Sitting Bull and Crazy Horse, asserted in Hunkpapa recollections, is graphically confirmed by Oglala artist Amos Bad Heart Bull. Cf. Vestal, *Sitting Bull*, 94, and Bad Heart Bull and Blish, *Pictographic History of the Oglala Sioux*, 216.

13. Vestal, *New Sources of Plains Indian History*, 169; Daniels to CoIA, Sept. 4, 1872, RCA, LROIA.

14. For accounts of the Baker fight, see Vestal, *Sitting Bull*, chap. 18 (quotation at 126), *New Sources of Plains Indian History*, 169, and *Warpath*, 137–44; Utley, *Lance and the Shield*, 107–109; M. H. Brown, *Plainsmen of the Yellowstone*, 200–201. In the account that follows, I have restricted footnoting to quotations.

15. Vestal, *Sitting Bull*, 129.

16. Vestal, *Warpath*, 143.

17. Vestal, *Sitting Bull*, 130–31.

18. Ibid., 131; Daniels to CoIA, Sept. 4, 1872. For Sitting Bull's actions against a second survey party, see Utley, *Lance and the Shield*, 110–11.

19. Quotation from Linderman, *Plenty-Coups*, 257. The major Lakota source for the Battle of Pryor Creek is pictorial, but besides graphic depictions of action, it includes the recollections of eyewitnesses such as He Dog and Left-Hand Heron: Bad Heart Bull and Blish, *Pictographic History of the Oglala Sioux*, 34, 383–90. For Crow recollections, see Marquis, *Memoirs of a White Crow Indian*, 84–96; Linderman, *Plenty-Coups*, chap. 16. Blackfoot (Sits in the Middle of the Land), the principal Crow chief, gave a valuable contemporary report, ARCoIA 1873, 123–25. With painstaking detail, Gray synthesizes contemporary reports and newspapers to contextualize and precisely date the battle: *Custer's Last Campaign*, 97–99.

20. He Dog, in Bad Heart Bull and Blish, *Pictographic History of the Oglala Sioux*, 34.

21. Marquis, *Memoirs of a White Crow Indian*, 93.

22. For details of the rescue of Crazy Horse, see Bad Heart Bull and Blish, *Pictographic History of the Oglala Sioux*, 389, and especially Short Bull, in Riley, "Oglala Sources," 33–34.

23. Participation of Crazy Horse in the first action against Custer is noted by Cheyenne informants of Marquis: see Powell, *People of the Sacred Mountain*, 2:825–26, 1346–47.

24. The writings of Utley are indispensable to following the railroad surveys of 1873: see *Frontier Regulars*, 242–43; *Lance and the Shield*, 111–15; *Cavalier in Buckskin*, 111–27. Sherman quotation in Utley, "War Houses in the Sioux Country," 260.

25. No figure in frontier military history has attracted more controversy, sycophantic praise, and hysterical criticism than George Armstrong Custer. The unbiased reader now has a sympathetic but critical guide in Utley's *Cavalier in Buckskin*.

26. Besides Utley's secondary accounts, the August 4 action was memorialized by Custer himself, "Battling with the Sioux on the Yellowstone," and by Second Lt. Charles W. Larned, Howe, "Expedition to the Yellowstone River." For Walter M. Camp's interview with an enlisted veteran, see Liddic and Harbaugh, *Custer and Company*, 37ff. See also the Cheyenne account to Marquis, in Powell, *People of the Sacred Mountain*, 2:825–26, 1346–47; M. H. Brown, *Plainsmen of the Yellowstone*, 203–206; Frost, *Custer's 7th Cav and the Campaign of 1873*; Taunton, "Yellowstone Interlude."

27. Custer, "Battling with the Sioux on the Yellowstone," 209.

28. Lt. Larned, in Howe, "Expedition to the Yellowstone River," 195.

29. For the Battle of the Yellowstone, consult Custer, "Battling with the Sioux on the Yellowstone"; Howe, "Expedition to the Yellowstone River"; Liddic and Harbaugh, *Custer and Company*, 37ff; Powell, *People of the Sacred Mountain*, 2:825–26, 1346–47; M. H. Brown, *Plainsmen of the Yellowstone*, 203–206; Frost, *Custer's 7th Cav and the Campaign of 1873*; Taunton, "Yellowstone Interlude"; DeBarthe, *Frank Grouard*, 52–53.

30. For the failure of the Northern Pacific amid the financial Panic of 1873, see Utley, *Cavalier in Buckskin*, 124–25, and the national context outlined in Ambrose, *Crazy Horse and Custer*, 371–74.

31. Neihardt, *When the Tree Flowered*, 137.

32. DeBarthe, *Frank Grouard*, 53–54; Gray, "Frank Grouard," offers a sympathetic portrait with indefatigable detective work on Grouard's background, for which see also Utley, *Lance and the Shield*, 352. The DeBarthe biography must be read with an eye to journalistic embroidery, the more galling because Grouard's observations on Lakota life and culture are generally sound and instructive. The John Colhoff correspondence with Joseph Balmer also throws light on Grouard's eighteen months with the northern Oglalas, including He Dog's assertion that Grouard lived in his tipi: Colhoff to Balmer, Oct. 5, 1951, transcript in author's collection.

33. DeBarthe, *Frank Grouard*, 54.

34. Ibid., 181–82; Red Feather, in Riley, "Oglala Sources," 30; and He Dog, in ibid., 14. He Dog and Red Feather say, respectively, that the little girl was "about 2 years old," and "about three years old," when she died. The proposed birthdate of spring 1871 gives an age of approximately two-and-a-half at death—midway between the estimates, and a comfortable nine months after the wedding of Crazy Horse and Black Shawl. Grouard dates the death to 1873, plainly in the fall months after he joined the Oglalas. The dating is consistent with reconstructible northern Oglala village movements. The village was in the district between the Rosebud and the Little Bighorn again in spring 1874 but was farther south and east throughout the period June 1874–spring 1875, when Grouard permanently left Crazy Horse's people. Fall 1873 therefore looks definite for the death of Crazy Horse's and Black Shawl's daughter.

35. DeBarthe, *Frank Grouard*, 181–82.

CHAPTER 15

1. DeBarthe, *Frank Grouard*, 182.

2. Miller, *Custer's Fall*, 231; Leo Combing testimony, Aug. 13, 1920, Clown family heirship files; conversations between the author, Jack Meister, and Cheyenne River Reservation inform-

ants, 2001–03. Shell Blanket Woman married Stands Straddle ca. 1871, was divorced, then died in 1874. Stands Straddle was still alive in 1920.

3. Black Elk, in DeMallie, *Sixth Grandfather*, 203.

4. Pourier interview, tablet 13, Ricker Papers.

5. Frank White Buffalo Man, in Kadlecek and Kadlecek, *To Kill an Eagle*, 150.

6. On Long Turd, see the vivid recollection of Bone, 1915, in Buechel and Manhart, *Lakota Tales and Texts*, 2:452–63. Long Turd performed protective rites before Crazy Horse rode into the Battle of the Little Bighorn (see chapter 17). The literature on yuwipi and its variants, still widespread among traditional Lakota communities, is truly vast. For orientation and bibliography, see W. K. Powers, *Yuwipi*; Feraca, *Wakinyan*.

7. "Taking a Sweatbath," Brave Dog, in Buechel and Manhart, *Lakota Tales and Texts*, 2:464–67.

8. Lt. Col. J. W. Forsyth to AG, HQ Division of the Missouri, Mar. 27, 1874, LR, AGO, contains rationing lists for both Red Cloud and Spotted Tail agencies.

9. A good summary of the agency economy is provided by Buecker and Paul, *Crazy Horse Surrender Ledger*, introduction.

10. Agent Saville's monthly reports and supporting documents, printed in *Red Cloud Investigation*, 434–53, supplemented by unprinted reports in RCA, LROIA, are the best way to trace the crisis at Red Cloud Agency during the winter of 1873–74.

11. "Mourning," Brave Dog, in Buechel and Manhart, *Lakota Tales and Texts*, 2:572–73. No Flesh, tracking stolen agency stock, reported on the location and leadership of the northern Miniconjou village in Joseph Bissonnette to D. R. Risley, Dec. 26, 1873, WA, LR, OIA. Top Hair and Foolish Bear (Sans Arc?) were the two junior Deciders in the village.

12. Besides Saville's monthly reports in *Red Cloud Investigation*, 434–53, and the supplemental unprinted reports in RCA, LR, OIA, several significant secondary accounts trace the gathering crisis: Hyde, *Red Cloud's Folk*, 207ff; idem, *Spotted Tail's Folk*, 209–12; Olson, *Red Cloud and the Sioux Problem*, 159ff; Buecker, *Fort Robinson*, 4ff. Kicking Bear's role in the Appleton killing is flatly asserted by several Lakota and *iyeska* statements.

13. The situation in the northern villages on Powder River is reconstructible in bare outline from the following primary sources: J. W. Dear to Col. J. E. Smith, Feb. 19, 1874, LR, AGO; J. J. Saville to CoIA, Feb. 16, 17, 20, 1874 (telegrams); Feb. 16 (includes quotation), Feb. 23 (two reports), 1874, RCA, LROIA.

14. Saville to CoIA, Feb. 20, 1874 (telegram); Saville to Col. J. E. Smith, Feb. 20, 1874, RCA, LROIA.

15. Dear to Smith, Feb. 19, 1874; Saville to Smith, Feb. 20, 1874 (includes quotation). For bills and vouchers tracing the emergence of Oglala men's society consensus to protect their agency, see Saville to CoIA, Mar. 31, 1874, RCA, LR, OIA.

16. Forsyth to AG, HQ Division of the Missouri, Mar. 27, 1874; Buecker, *Fort Robinson*, 12ff; Grange, "Fort Robinson," 196–200.

17. Omaha Society as beef ration akicita: J. J. Saville to CoIA, Jan. 31, 1874, in *Red Cloud Investigation*, 448–49. For background on the society, see Wissler, "Societies and Ceremonial Associations," 48–52; Kit Fox Society as annuity akicita: Standing Bear, *Land of the Spotted Eagle*, 146. White Packstrap Society background: Wissler, "Societies and Ceremonial Associations," 34–36; Bad Heart Bull and Blish, *Pictographic History of the Oglala Sioux*, 105. Role as Red Cloud Agency police under Agent Saville, Amos Appleton to Mrs. A. R. Appleton, Oct. 26, 1874, Appleton Family Papers; J. J. Saville to CoIA, Dec. 29, 1873, *Red Cloud Investigation*, 435–36; same to same, May 4, Aug. 7, Sept. 28, Nov. 13, 1874, RCA, LR, OIA.

18. Vestal, *Sitting Bull*, 96, 209. He Dog stated, "I was on reservation before [war of] 1876 on the Platte": He Dog, interview by Walter M. Camp, July 13, 1910, in Hammer, *Custer in '76*, 205.

19. Eagle Elk, Nov. 27, 1944, 9, Neihardt Papers. A mid-1870s dating suits the status of Eagle Elk (born 1852) as a charter member of the society, and the 1874 drive to reunite the northern Oglalas around a nontreaty ideology seems the best immediate context.

20. Ibid. Hardorff, *Oglala Lakota Crazy Horse*, 34, reconstructs likely membership from war party associations with Crazy Horse and bodyguard status. From a critical examination of the sources, I have extended Hardorff's list of likely candidates.

21. Crazy Horse and Black Twin as 1874 Deciders: see J. J. Saville to CoIA, July 20, 1874, RCA, LR, OIA. For Hump's and Crazy Horse's bands hunting together, spring 1874, see Utley, *Lance and the Shield*, 118. One Miniconjou informant stated that Hump was made a chief or head warrior by Crazy Horse himself (Chris Ravenshead, conversation with the author, Oct. 20, 1994), bearing out Nelson Miles's contention that Hump was an Oglala head warrior, *Personal Recollections and Observations of General Nelson A. Miles*, 1:243.

22. Utley, *Lance and the Shield*, 118–19; Quivey, "Yellowstone Expedition of 1874"; Hutchins, "Poison in the Pemmican"; M. H. Brown, *Plainsmen of the Yellowstone*, 216–19.

23. Utley, *Lance and the Shield*, 118–19; Quivey, "Yellowstone Expedition of 1874"; Hutchins, "Poison in the Pemmican"; M. H. Brown, *Plainsmen of the Yellowstone*, 216–19. Utley's account utilizes valuable Lakota interview material that enables us to understand band movements and interactions.

24. White Bull, in Vestal, *New Sources of Plains Indian History*, 162.

25. The Bates Battle is covered in Fowler, *Arapahoe Politics*, 50–52; Trenholm, *Arapahoes, Our People*, 249–52.

26. J. J. Saville to CoIA, July 20, 1874. Saville summarized the game shortage: "The past year there have been very few buffalo south of the Yellow Stone. Consequently all the northern bands started for the Agencies." Saville to C. C. Cox, Dec. 16, 1874, RCA, LR, OIA.

27. The 1874 Black Hills Expedition is treated briefly in Utley, *Frontier Regulars*, 243–44, and at greater length in idem, *Cavalier in Buckskin*, 128–41; and in Jackson, *Custer's Gold*. Contemporary reports and newspaper coverage are collected in Krause and Olson, *Prelude to Glory*. Lakota sources relevant to my account are Slow Bull and Long Bear (both eyewitness) statements of Custer's seizure of Stabber, in J. J. Saville to CoIA, Aug. 3, 1874, RCA, LR, OIA; Black Elk, May 1931, in DeMallie, *Sixth Grandfather*, 158–60.

28. Parker, *Gold in the Black Hills*, contains a valuable account of the gathering crisis over the Black Hills.

29. John Burke to CoIA, Sept. 1, 1875, ARCoIA 1875; Saville to C. C. Cox, Dec. 16, 1874; DeBarthe, *Frank Grouard*, 84. Grouard's movements are also indicated in statements by He Dog and Alex Salway, in Colhoff to Balmer, Oct. 5, 1951 (transcript in author's collection). Agent Saville's incremental census, though massively inflated, traces the northern influx to Red Cloud through September: Saville to CoIA, Aug. 3, 31, Oct. 5, 1874, RCA, LR, OIA.

30. Denver *Rocky Mountain News*, Oct. 11, 1874 (first quotation), further characterized Crazy Horse as "a disagreeable and 'rambunctious' Ogallalla"; Saville to CoIA, Oct. 19, 1874 (telegram), RCA, LR, OIA (second quotation).

31. Saville to Cox, Dec. 16, 1874; Captain W. H. Jordan to AAG, Dept. of the Platte, Oct. 23, 1874; Saville to CoIA, Jan. 8, 1875 [misdated 1874 in original], RCA, LR, OIA. The *New York Times*, May 21, 1875, covering the Lakota delegation to Washington, reported, "Crazy Horse, one of the bravest and most skillful soldiers of the Ogallalas, [originally] purposed accompanying the present visitors," which is not confirmed in other sources, but is consistent

with the trend of events through fall 1874. For Grouard, Burke to CoIA, Sept. 1, 1875, ARCoIA 1875; Saville to Cox, Dec. 16, 1874; DeBarthe, *Frank Grouard*, 84. He Dog and Alex Salway, in Colhoff to Balmer, Oct. 5, 1951 (transcript in author's collection).

32. The flagpole incident is covered in Buecker, *Fort Robinson*, 36–38; Amos Appleton to Mrs. Appleton, Oct. 26, 1874, identifies the role of the White Packstrap Society. Saville to CoIA, Nov. 30, 1874, *Red Cloud Investigation*, 451–53.

33. John S. Collins to President U. S. Grant, Apr. 4, STA, LR, OIA; J. J. Saville to CoIA, Mar. 29, Apr. 8, 1875, RCA, LR, OIA. For background on the looming Black Hills crisis, see Olson, *Red Cloud and the Sioux Problem*, chap. 10.

34. Saville to CoIA, Apr. 8, 24 (telegram; includes first quotation), 1875, RCA, LR, OIA; *New York Times*, May 21, 1875 (second quotation); for Grouard, Burke to CoIA, Sept. 1, 1875, ARCoIA 1875; Saville to Cox, Dec. 16, 1874; DeBarthe, *Frank Grouard*, 84. He Dog and Alex Salway, in Colhoff to Balmer, Oct. 5, 1951 (transcript in author's collection). A dispatch to the *Omaha Weekly Bee*, May 5, 1875, indicates that, besides Black Twin and Crazy Horse, Lame Deer was on Agent Saville's invite list.

35. Joseph Eagle Hawk narrative, "History of Crazy Horse," in Hardorff, *Surrender and Death of Crazy Horse*, 133–34.

36. Martin Gibbons (Acting Red Cloud Agent) to CoIA, May 24, 1875, RCA, LR, OIA; Henry A. Bingham to CoIA, July 1, 1875, CRA, LR, OIA. Decider appointments: see the otherwise unexplained entry for June 6, 1875: "Black Twin/Little Big Man/Crazy Horse/Little Hawk," in Kime, *Black Hills Journals of Colonel Richard Irving Dodge*, 65. My reading is consistent with the key role each of these men played in the councils preparatory to the Black Hills summit. For background on the Cheyenne River Agency delegation to Washington, see H. H. Anderson, "A History of the Cheyenne River Indian Agency," 444–47.

37. The Red River War of 1874–75 is summarized in Utley, *Frontier Regulars*, chap. 13. One of the most controversial actions of the Plains wars, the clash on Sappa Creek has recently received two objective studies: Chalfant, *Cheyennes at Dark Water Creek*; and Monnett, *Massacre at Cheyenne Hole*. Martin Gibbons to CoIA, May 19, 24, 1875, RCA, LR, OIA, notes the arrival of Cheyenne refugees in the Lakota territory.

38. Eagle Elk, Nov. 27, 1944, 1–8 (quotation on 1), Neihardt Papers.

39. Ibid., 3.

40. Ibid., 4.

41. For White Bull's (Cheyenne) vivid recollection to George Bird Grinnell of Sitting Bull's role in the 1875 Sun Dance, see Powell, *People of the Sacred Mountain*, 2:928–29 (includes quotations). For cogent assessment of Sitting Bull's role, see G. C. Anderson, *Sitting Bull and the Paradox of Lakota Nationhood*, 88; Utley, *Lance and the Shield*, 122–23.

42. Saville to CoIA, Aug. 16, 1875, RCA, LR, OIA; DeBarthe, *Frank Grouard*, 85. On Painted Rocks, see Black Elk, in DeMallie, *Sixth Grandfather*, 198.

43. DeMallie, *Sixth Grandfather*, 163–64 (Standing Bear), 171–72 (Iron Hawk).

44. DeBarthe, *Frank Grouard*, 85–86 (quotation on 85). This and subsequent quotations on the Tongue River council are, unless otherwise noted, from Grouard. For additional details, see Saville to CoIA, Aug. 16, 1875; Short Bull, in Riley, "Oglala Sources," 35.

45. Bourke, *On the Border with Crook*, 245.

46. Sitting Bull of the South speech, Aug. 11, 1875, in *Red Cloud Investigation*, 303.

47. Saville to CoIA, Aug. 16, 1875. For the agency fact-finding deputations in the Black Hills, see Kime, *Black Hills Journals of Colonel Richard Irving Dodge*, 145–46, 165–66; *Red Cloud Investigation*, 300.

48. Gilbert, *"Big Bat" Pourier*, 43.

49. The official report of the Black Hills Commission is printed in *Report of the Secretary of the Interior, 1875*, 1:686–703. Significant details in my account are derived from Garnett interview, tablet 2, Ricker Papers; Charles Turning Hawk, interview by Eli S. Ricker, Feb. 19, 1907, tablet 18, Ricker Papers; Black Elk and Standing Bear, in DeMallie, *Sixth Grandfather*, 162–63, 168–70, 172. In addition to a large body of as yet untapped newspaper coverage of the councils, valuable secondary accounts are provided by Olson, *Red Cloud and the Sioux Problem*, chap. 11; Hyde, *Red Cloud's Folk*, 241ff; Larson, *Red Cloud*, 187–95.

50. *Omaha Weekly Bee*, Oct. 13, 1875.

51. Bordeaux, *Custer's Conqueror*, 48–49. Bordeaux's chronology is scrambled, with the vision quest placed anywhere in the frame August 1875–April 1876. Nevertheless, the presence of Touch the Clouds is significant because sections of Bordeaux's uneven book that feature the Miniconjou leader seem more reliable than other sections. I have therefore accepted the story and placed it in what seems the best chronological context.

52. For Lone Horn's role in the Black Hills negotiations, see especially Black Elk, Standing Bear, and Iron Hawk, in DeMallie, *Sixth Grandfather*, 169, 171–72; also Singing Bear, in Buechel and Manhart, *Lakota Tales and Texts*, 2:605–607, 611–13. Awkwardly caught between the Cheyenne River Agency consensus to sell the hills and the Northern Nation determination to keep its land, Lone Horn was torn by the pressure of competing claims. During the winter of 1875–76, the great Miniconjou chief, who had so skillfully steered the middle course between Lakota factions, died after twelve months of intense diplomatic activity.

53. Saville to CoIA, Oct. 11, 1875, RCA, LR, OIA; Black Elk, in DeMallie, *Sixth Grandfather*, 164–66, 169–70 (quotation on 170).

54. For the growth of Black Hills settlement, see Parker, *Gold in the Black Hills*.

55. The closest reading of the White House summit and the Watkins report (printed in *Senate Executive Documents*, 44th Cong., 1st sess., S. Doc. 52, 3ff), sardonically critical of government chicanery but adducing extensive off-the-record newspaper coverage, is Gray, *Centennial Campaign*, chap. 3. More sympathetic interpretations are provided by Hedren, *Fort Laramie in 1876*, 17–18; Utley, *Frontier Regulars*, 246–48.

56. Hastings to CoIA, Jan. 28, 1876, RCA, LR, OIA, outlines the response from Crazy Horse and Black Twin. Village movements are analyzed in Gray, *Centennial Campaign*, 321–22.

57. John Burke to CoIA, Sept. 1, 1875, ARCoIA 1875; Manypenny, *Our Indian Wards*, 305–308.

58. Preparations for the spring campaign are concisely presented in Utley, *Frontier Regulars*, 248–49. See also Gray, *Centennial Campaign*, 47ff.

59. The date of Black Twin's death is most clearly indicated by He Dog interview, July 13, 1910, in Hammer, *Custer in '76*, 208: "Black Twins not in [Custer] fight. Died in 1875." He Dog probably expressed this date as the winter before the Custer battle. Agent Hastings' contemporary report establishes that Black Twin was still alive in January 1876, but his complete absence from the voluminous Lakota accounts of the war of 1876 suggests a death in February. Hyde's contention (*Red Cloud's Folk*, 306) that "Black Twin died in the Crazy Horse camp, after its surrender in 1877," is not borne out by the record.

60. He Dog to Helen Blish, 1930, in (a) John Colhoff to Joseph Balmer, Apr. 7, 1952 (transcript in author's collection); (b) Bad Heart Bull and Blish, *Pictographic History of the Oglala Sioux*, 391–92; Short Bull, in Riley, "Oglala Sources," 35. General background on band movements is brilliantly presented by Gray, *Centennial Campaign*, 321–25.

61. Short Bull, in Riley, "Oglala Sources," 35. Cheyenne sources are synthesized in Powell, *People of the Sacred Mountain*, 2:937ff, 1361.

62. Lt. W. P. Clark to AG, Dept. of the Platte, Sept. 14, 1877, SW File. This crucial synthesis of accounts given Clark by Lakota scouts and surrendering warriors has been published with valuable contextual material in Buecker, "Lt. William Philo Clark's Sioux War Report," 16.

63. Victor Douville, Lakota Studies Department, Sinte Gleska University, conversation with the author, Sept. 26, 2001.

CHAPTER 16

1. On the Reynolds fight and its aftermath, see Marquis, *Wooden Leg*, 159–74 (quotation at 170). This classic Cheyenne account is amplified by those presented in Powell, *People of the Sacred Mountain*, 2:937–46. See also Vaughn, *Reynolds Campaign on Powder River*; Utley, *Frontier Regulars*, 249–51; Bourke, *On the Border with Crook*, chaps. 15–16; Greene, *Battles and Skirmishes*, chap. 1; Gray, *Centennial Campaign*, 54–58. I have used Gray's groundbreaking analysis of Indian numbers and movements in the spring of 1876 (chap. 27) as a basis for my own account throughout this chapter.

2. Lakota accounts of the Reynolds battle: He Dog to Helen Blish, 1930, in (a) John Colhoff to Joseph Balmer, Apr. 7, 1952 (transcript in author's collection); (b) Bad Heart Bull and Blish, *Pictographic History of the Oglala Sioux*, 391–92; Short Bull statements, in (a) Colhoff to Balmer, Feb. 9, 1949 (transcript in author's collection); (b) Riley, "Oglala Sources," 35; Iron Hawk, interview by Eli S. Ricker, May 12, 1907, tablet 25, Ricker Papers. According to Colhoff, He Dog stated, "We were very much peeved at Frank Grouard."

3. Two Moons, in Hardorff, *Lakota Recollections*, 132–33; Crazy Horse quotation in Two Moons, interview by Hamlin Garland, 1898, in Hardorff, *Cheyenne Memories*, 100.

4. Marquis, *Wooden Leg*, 170–72; Vestal, *Sitting Bull*, 140–41, and *Warpath*, 182–83. For assessment of Sitting Bull's role, Utley, *Lance and the Shield*, 132ff.

5. He Dog, in Colhoff to Balmer, Apr. 7, 1952.

6. Vestal, *Warpath*, 182 (first quotation). My reconstruction of the Metz party killings is based on a letter datelined "Spotted Tail Agency, May 8, 1876" and published under the headline "Crazy Horse's Revenge" in *Omaha Daily Bee*, May 15, 1876 (second quotation). This letter was based on intelligence received from agency Oglalas returning from the north. The killings, well known in Black Hills folklore, have also been ascribed to outlaws, but this earliest of accounts merits respect. It meshes with He Dog's guarded statement to Mari Sandoz, June 30, 1931: "White men say C[razy] H[orse] killed negro and his wife [*sic*] in Black Hills . . . Maybe CH killed him [*sic*]. Don't know." Folder 16, part 2, box 31, Sandoz Papers. Black Hills historian Robert H. Lee states (letter to the author, Feb. 29, 2000) that the only black fatality in the early settlement of the region, known to him, was Rachel Briggs, the Metz family maid.

7. Gray, *Centennial Campaign*, 325–28; "The Surrender," Waggoner Papers (includes quotation).

8. Vestal, *Sitting Bull*, 141.

9. For Gibbon's activities, see Gray, *Centennial Campaign*, chap. 7; Utley, *Frontier Regulars*, 252; Stewart, *March of the Montana Column*. The role of the Crow scouts is brilliantly analyzed in Gray, *Custer's Last Campaign*, chaps. 12–14.

10. Gray, *Centennial Campaign*, 82–83, 329–30; on Sitting Bull's vision, Utley, *Lance and the Shield*, 136.

11. Bourke, *On the Border with Crook*, 283–89; Gray, *Centennial Campaign*, 92–94, 336. Little Big Man's role in Red Cloud Agency defections—consistent with his shuttling between agency and hunting grounds, 1873–75—is indicated by Black Elk, in DeMallie, *Sixth Grandfather*, 170.

12. Black Elk, in DeMallie, *Sixth Grandfather*, 170–71.

13. For Crook's preparations, see Bourke, *On the Border with Crook*, 289–91; Gray, *Centennial Campaign*, 110ff; Utley, *Frontier Regulars*, 253; Vaughn, *With Crook at the Rosebud*, chap. 1.

14. Terry and Custer's preparations are outlined in Utley, *Frontier Regulars*, 252–53; Gray, *Centennial Campaign*, 86–90, 97ff.

15. Black Elk, in DeMallie, *Sixth Grandfather*, 171; Powell, *People of the Sacred Mountain*, 2:954; Gray, *Centennial Campaign*, 329–30, 336.

16. Good Weasel, in Buechel and Manhart, *Lakota Tales and Texts*, 2:374–83.

17. Vestal, *Sitting Bull*, chap. 21 (quotation at 150–51); Utley, *Lance and the Shield*, 137–39.

18. Bourke, *On the Border with Crook*, 296.

19. For Crook's march from Fort Fetterman, see ibid., 291ff; Finerty, *War-Path and Bivouac*, chaps. 5–8; Vaughn, *With Crook at the Rosebud*, chaps. 2–3; Utley, *Frontier Regulars*, 253; Gray, *Centennial Campaign*, 111ff. The action of June 9 is also covered in Greene, *Battles and Skirmishes*, chap. 2; idem, *Lakota and Cheyenne*, 21–23, contains Cheyenne recollections. Anonymous Lakota accounts are presented in Eastman, "Story of the Little Big Horn."

20. Eastman, "Story of the Little Big Horn"; Gray, *Centennial Campaign*, 115–16, 327, 331.

21. Cheyenne accounts are richest for the preamble to the Battle of the Rosebud. All are synthesized in Powell, *People of the Sacred Mountain*, 2:954–56; several are presented in original interview format in Greene, *Lakota and Cheyenne*, 21ff.

22. Marquis, *Wooden Leg*, 198.

23. Standing Bear, in DeMallie, *Sixth Grandfather*, 174. Besides the memoirs of Bourke and Finerty, Crook's movements are best followed in Gray, *Centennial Campaign*, 120–21; Vaughn, *With Crook at the Rosebud*, chap. 4.

24. Eastman, "Story of the Little Big Horn"; Short Bull, in Riley, "Oglala Sources," 37 (for Good Weasel's presence with Crazy Horse). Sitting Bull's debilitation, as observed by G. C. Anderson, *Sitting Bull and the Paradox of Lakota Nationhood*, 90, kept him out of the battle, but Vestal's interviews with White Bull and One Bull indicate that he accompanied the war party and exhorted the warriors to bravery. In assessing the warrior strength, I have accepted the low figure adduced by Gray, *Centennial Campaign*, 120.

25. For syntheses on the Battle of the Rosebud, see Vaughn, *With Crook at the Rosebud*; Mangum, *Battle of the Rosebud*; Utley, *Frontier Regulars*, 255–56; Gray, *Centennial Campaign*, 123–24. A talk by Neil Gilbert, "Did Crook Fail Custer?" delivered at Hastings Museum, Dec. 4, 1999, has also shaped my analysis. I am indebted to Neil for further advice on my treatment of the battle. These sources establish the essential framework of chronology and spatial correlations on a widely flung battlefield. Cheyenne recollections of the battle are richest (Powell, *People of the Sacred Mountain*, 2:954–56; Greene, *Lakota and Cheyenne*, 21ff), but Lakota perspectives are provided by Vestal, *Warpath*, chap. 19; and the interviews with Black Elk, Standing Bear, and Iron Hawk, in DeMallie, *Sixth Grandfather*, 174–77. Speculation that Crazy Horse planned an ambush of Crook was rife as soon as the dust settled on the battle. Later historians have tended to dismiss the idea, but the fact—noted by Grinnell's Cheyenne informant Young Two Moons (see Greene, *Lakota and Cheyenne*, 26)—that akicita "formed a line and would let [the warriors] go no farther," is consistent with a projected decoy-ambush plan.

26. Bourke, *On the Border with Crook*, 311; Finerty, *War-Path and Bivouac*, 86.

27. Short Bull, July 13, 1930, Riley, "Oglala Sources," 37.

28. Vestal, *Sitting Bull*, 153 (first quotation); Miller, *Ghost Dance*, 289 (second quotation); Short Bull, July 13, 1930, Riley, "Oglala Sources," 37 (third quotation).

29. Pourier quotation from Eddie Herman, "Noted Oglala Medicine Man Kept Crazy Horse's Secret," *Rapid City Daily Journal*, Feb. 11, 1951. Henry W. Daly (civilian packer), quoted in Vaughn, *With Crook at the Rosebud*, 109, confirms Crazy Horse's presence in this attack.

30. Iron Hawk, in DeMallie, *Sixth Grandfather*, 176.

31. Bordeaux, *Custer's Conqueror*, 52; Thunder Tail account of Crazy Horse, Sept. 1915, in Buechel and Paul, *Lakota Tales and Texts*, 2:625, 631.

32. Gray, *Centennial Campaign*, 333–34.

33. Hollow Horn Bear, in Hardorff, *Lakota Recollections*, 177–79.

34. Gray, *Centennial Campaign*, 327, 333, 356. I have accepted the relative accuracy of Gray's reconstructed lodge totals for the village as of June 24–25, 1876. Further research should yield still finer tuning, but there can be little doubt that Gray's figures are substantially correct. On Oglala leadership, I have followed Vestal, *Sitting Bull*, 143, naming Crazy Horse, Low Dog, Big Road, and "Sweat" (a nickname for Iron Hawk) as Oglala leaders. By his own account, Iron Hawk was the Oglala herald (Iron Hawk interview, tablet 25, Ricker Papers), an honor typically accorded the senior akicita officer. He Dog's status as akicita is confirmed by Gen. Hugh L. Scott's identifying him as "Crazy Horse's head soldier" in 1876 (Graham, *Custer Myth*, 98). Big Road, the Oyuhpe Shirt Wearer, was a Decider in 1877 and likely held the honor in 1876 too.

35. White Bull, in Hardorff, *Lakota Recollections*, 109n. For background on Custer's march up the Rosebud, and subsequent night march, June 24–25, see especially Gray, *Custer's Last Campaign*, chaps. 16–17.

36. Powell, *People of the Sacred Mountain*, 2:1006–1007; Utley, *Lance and the Shield*, 143–44. For Crazy Horse's anxiety, see Bordeaux, *Custer's Conqueror*, 53–55.

CHAPTER 17

1. George Close, in John Colhoff to Joseph Balmer, Dec. 3, 1951 (transcript in author's collection). George Close (Kanye, died 1949) was Red Feather's eldest son, born at dawn June 25, 1876.

2. For village activities, see especially Grinnell, *Fighting Cheyennes*, 348; Marquis, "She Watched Custer's Last Battle," 366; Red Horse, in Graham, *Custer Myth*, 57, 61; Black Bear, interview by Walter M. Camp, July 18, 1911, in Hammer, *Custer in '76*, 203–204; Miller, *Custer's Fall*, 63, 75–76.

3. Black Elk, in DeMallie, *Sixth Grandfather*, 180–81; Eastman, *Indian Heroes and Great Chieftains*, 98–99. On Custer battle chronology, the analysis of Custer's march in Gray, *Custer's Last Campaign,* provides a painstaking reconstruction figured to the half minute. Although skeptics have questioned the precision of Gray's clocktime system, its strength lies in its all but incontrovertible reconstruction of relative time elapsed. Consequently, certain anchor points seem beyond reasonable question: e.g., significant action began at Reno's skirmish line about 3:15–3:20 P.M and transferred to the Custer sector of the field one hour later, where serious resistance concluded by about 5:30. This framework forms the basis of my chronology of the battle. While Gray himself, the most fastidiously analytical of historians, would balk at back-projecting his timescale onto village events, where participants paid no heed to clock times, his achievement frees historians to impose time constraints on Indian eyewitness testimony notoriously impervious to chronology.

4. Feather Earring, in Graham, *Custer Myth*, 97; He Dog interview by Camp, July 13, 1910, Hammer, *Custer in '76*, 206.

5. DeMallie, *Sixth Grandfather*, 181; Red Horse, Graham, *Custer Myth*, 57, 61.

6. Emily Standing Bear, in Fox, "West River History," 150. Horned Horse, in Bourke, *On the Border with Crook*, 416; Eastman, *Indian Heroes and Great Chieftains*, 98–99; Iron Hawk interview, tablet 25, Ricker Papers. Historians have incorrectly assumed that Ricker's informant is the same Iron Hawk as Neihardt's 1931 interviewee. The latter was a Hunkpapa, like Black Elk, a youth in 1876; Ricker's informant, in his mid-forties at the Little Bighorn, was by that time the regular herald in the northern Oglala village.

7. Red Feather, in Hardorff, *Lakota Recollections*, 81ff.

8. Ibid.

9. The literature on the Battle of the Little Bighorn continues to grow exponentially. Vital to any study is the 1879 testimony of officers, enlisted men, and civilian scouts, Graham, *Reno Court of Inquiry*. Many older reconstructions of the action retain historiographical interest but have been superseded in the last generation by advances in archaeology and belated serious analysis of the voluminous Indian testimony. Of older overviews, Stewart, *Custer's Luck*, remains of value, but the benchmark syntheses of the last twenty-five years are Greene, *Evidence and the Custer Enigma*; Hardorff, *Markers, Artifacts and Indian Testimony*; Gray, *Custer's Last Campaign*; Fox, *Archaeology, History, and Custer's Last Battle*. Archaeological work since 1984 has been presented in Scott and Fox, *Archaeological Insights into the Custer Battle*, and Scott and Bleed, *Good Walk Around the Boundary*. A truly landmark publication of the Walter Camp interviews is Hammer, *Custer in '76*. Particularly valuable compilations of Indian accounts include Hardorff, *Lakota Recollections* and *Cheyenne Memories*; Greene, *Lakota and Cheyenne*. Michno, *Lakota Noon*, is a synthesis of Indian testimony.

10. For Custer's dispositions and chronology, I continue to rely on Gray, *Custer's Last Campaign*, chap. 19.

11. The sighting of the warrior force downstream from Custer is attested by Sergeant Daniel A. Kanipe, in (a) interview by Walter M. Camp, June 16–17, 1908, in Hammer, *Custer in '76*, 92–93, 97; (b) Graham, *Custer Myth*, 249.

12. Hardorff, *Hokahey!*, chap. 2.

13. Ibid., 42; Miller, *Custer's Fall*, 95ff; He Dog, in Hammer, *Custer in '76*, 206 (first quotation); Red Feather, in Hardorff, *Lakota Recollections*, 81 (second quotation); Black Elk, in DeMallie, *Sixth Grandfather*, 181–82; Iron Hawk interview, tablet 25, Ricker Papers.

14. Crazy Horse's preparations are outlined by Standing Bear, interviewed by Camp, July 12, 1910, Hammer, *Custer in '76*, 215 (includes quotation); Horn Chips interview, ca. July 11, 1910, Camp Papers, BYU; Masters, *Shadows Fall Across the Little Horn*, 41. His appearance in the Reno phase of the battle is probably accurately represented in Bad Heart Bull and Blish, *Pictographic History of the Oglala Sioux*, 214, 216, 232.

15. Garnett interview, tablet 2, Ricker Papers (first quotation); Red Hawk, in Nicholas Ruleau, interview by Eli S. Ricker, Nov. 20, 1906, tablet 29, Ricker Papers (second quotation); Flying Hawk, in McCreight, *Chief Flying Hawk's Tales*, 27ff.

16. DeMallie, *Sixth Grandfather*, 182.

17. Bad Heart Bull and Blish, *Pictographic History of the Oglala Sioux*, 217; Iron Hawk interview, tablet 25, Ricker Papers. Red Feather noted the concurrence of Reno's flight and Crazy Horse's charge: "Just then Crazy Horse came"—adding with Old Testament brio, "He came amongst the soldiers" (Hardorff, *Lakota Recollections*, 83–84). For Kicking Bear's killing of Bloody Knife, see Dewey Beard, in Eddie Herman to Joseph Balmer, Jan. 2, Apr. 5, 1955 (transcripts in author's collection).

18. Roman Rutten, interview by Walter M. Camp, Hammer, *Custer in '76*, 118–19 (first quotation); J. M. Lee, "Capture and Death," 325 (second quotation); Bourke, *On the Border with Crook*, 415.

19. Red Feather, in Hardorff, *Lakota Recollections*, 84; Bad Heart Bull and Blish, *Pictographic History of the Oglala Sioux*, 232. The Bad Heart Bull drawings graphically depict the "buffalo chase" of Reno's command.

20. Eagle Elk statement on the Custer Fight, Nov. 14, 1944, Neihardt Papers.

21. Flying Hawk, in McCreight, *Chief Flying Hawk's Tales*, 27 (; Eagle Elk statement on the Custer Fight, Nov. 14, 1944, Neihardt Papers.

22. Gray, *Custer's Last Campaign*, 290, establishes the chronology; idem, *Centennial Campaign*, 175–76, and chapter 24, analyzes casualties.

23. Short Bull, in Riley, "Oglala Sources," 37. Michno, *Lakota Noon*, 108ff, first correlated Short Bull's and other Indian sightings of Custer's battalion, just as Reno's men took up defenses atop what would later be named Reno Hill.

24. Short Bull, in Riley, "Oglala Sources," 37.

25. Flying Hawk, in McCreight, *Chief Flying Hawk's Tales*, 27ff; also Flying Hawk, interview by Eli S. Ricker, Mar. 8, 1907, tablet 13, Ricker Papers.

26. Runs the Enemy, in Dixon, *Vanishing Race*, 174–75.

27. Standing Bear interview, July 12, 1910, Hammer, *Custer in '76*, 215; Horn Chips interview, ca. July 11, 1910, Camp Papers, BYU; Masters, *Shadows Fall Across the Little Horn*, 41; Bad Heart Bull and Blish, *Pictographic History of the Oglala Sioux*, 214, 216, 232; Flying Hawk, McCreight, *Chief Flying Hawk's Tales*, 27ff; Flying Hawk interview, tablet 13, Ricker Papers. For Joseph White Bull's recollection of Crazy Horse's appearance in the second phase of the battle, see Walter S. Campbell (Stanley Vestal) to the Editor/University of Oklahoma Press, July 16, 1948, in Hardorff, *Surrender and Death of Crazy Horse*, 269.

28. John Martini testimony, in Graham, *Reno Court of Inquiry*, 129; Daniel A. Kanipe interview, Hammer, *Custer in '76*, 93.

29. Martini's testimony and recollections are confused and irreconcilable for this crucial interlude, but Gray, *Custer's Last Campaign*, 340ff, establishes the sequence of events during the lengthy hiatus between Custer's first sighting the village and the advance into Medicine Tail Coulee.

30. Ibid. Gray's careful elucidation of the hitherto derided recollections of Crow scout Curley, mapped onto his Reno fight chronology, once more outlines a causative sequence. The activities of Cheyenne skirmishers are indicated by John Stands in Timber, northern Cheyenne tribal historian, in Stands in Timber and Liberty, *Cheyenne Memories*, 193, 197–98; Powell, *People of the Sacred Mountain*, 2:1007, 1018.

31. The pivotal division of Custer's battalion at Medicine Tail Coulee has evoked much speculation. Debate on wing composition itself has been heated, but I have accepted the reasoning of Fox, *Archaeology, History, and Custer's Last Battle*, 141–42. What seems plain is that Custer had intended to support Reno with the whole battalion by advancing to the ford, but on learning of Reno's collapse, Custer reassessed. Gray's contention (*Custer's Last Campaign*, 360–61) is that the Yates advance to the ford was a feint, to relieve the pressure on Reno and thus reunite the regiment. It seems to me that, given the intense debate witnessed, but not understood, by Curley (he saw Custer and guide Mitch Bouyer doing "a whole lot of talking" after word of the Reno debacle), the most flexible reading of tactics is warranted. I find Fox's reading of the evidence (*Archaeology, History, and Custer's Last Battle*, 312–18) to be the most persuasive.

32. Michno, *Lakota Noon*, 121–24, 138–42, analyzes Indian testimony for action at the ford and Yates's routes to and from it. Gray, *Custer's Last Campaign*, 363–69, presents his analysis of Curley's several recollections.

33. Crazy Horse was the first eyewitness to ascribe Custer's strategy to pursuit of noncombatants. See Crazy Horse-Horned Horse interview, May 24, 1877, *Yankton Union and Press and Dakotaian*, June 7, 1877. So large was the stream of fugitives, reasoned Crazy Horse, that Custer believed it to be "the main body of Indians retreating and abandoning their villages." Fox, *Archaeology, History, and Custer's Last Battle*, 315, plausibly interprets other Indian evidence.

34. The Gray chronology posits the Reno-Benteen reunion—and entrenchment—to 4:20, five minutes before significant firing began from the Custer sector.

35. Grinnell, *Fighting Cheyennes*, 350; Gall, in Burdick, *David F. Barry's Indian Notes*, 9–15. Eastman, "Story of the Little Big Horn," though uneven, presents vital Lakota recollections of the battle. He suggests that Crazy Horse arrived at the village ford during the skirmishing with Yates, i.e., approximately 4:20–4:30. Given Short Bull's meeting with Crazy Horse near Reno Hill about 4:15, this is impossible: Crazy Horse had to ride about three miles from the latter point, via the village, to the ford. Factoring in a short stopover at the Oglala circle, he must have arrived at the latter point as Yates withdrew up the coulee (4:33–4:46 according to the Gray chronology). This is consistent with the recollection of Flying Hawk, who fought at Crazy Horse's side throughout the first phase of the battle. Stating that he "was with the leaders and could see [everything]," Flying Hawk observed Custer's wing atop the eastern ridges (Gray: 4:32–4:38 P.M.), but his view of Yates's retreat was obscured by warriors who had already "crossed the river" and advanced up the coulee. Flying Hawk interview, tablet 13, Ricker Papers.

36. Because Flying Hawk rode next to Crazy Horse, his perceptions are especially significant. He reasoned that Custer's wing, seeing the coulee full of warriors pursuing Yates, determined against a descent to the village. Instead, they "came down off the second [eastern] ridge [Gray: 4:38 P.M.] and went up onto Calhoun Hill" [to reunite with Yates at 4:46]. Flying Hawk interview, tablet 13, Ricker Papers.

37. Crazy Horse–Horned Horse interview, May 24, 1877; Gall, in Burdick, *David F. Barry's Indian Notes*, 9–15. Gall must have arrived late at the ford—but not as late as in Michno's reconstruction (*Lakota Noon*, 167–68), since Red Hawk witnessed harangues by both Gall and Crazy Horse.

38. Red Hawk, in Ruleau interview, tablet 29, Ricker Papers; Short Bull, in Riley, "Oglala Sources," 37; Flying Hawk, in McCreight, *Chief Flying Hawk's Tales*, 28; Gall in Burdick, *David F. Barry's Indian Notes*, 9–15; Mrs. Spotted Horn Bull, in McLaughlin, *My Friend the Indian*, 45–46. Crazy Horse's route onto the Custer battlefield has been the subject of much controversy. Older secondary accounts, crediting an enormous village stretching for miles along the river, had him ride to a point below its downstream end, then cross the Little Bighorn to envelop from the north what would be called Last Stand Hill, just as Gall's force closed from the south. This view has been invalidated by the closer reading of Indian testimony and the realization that the village extended only a short distance north from the village ford. See Michno, "Crazy Horse, Custer, and the Sweep"; also Fox, *Archaeology, History, and Custer's Last Battle*, 298ff. Michno argues that Crazy Horse crossed at the village ford with the main body and followed up Deep Coulee. Mrs. Spotted Horn Bull's recollection could be adduced to support this route, but Gall (consistently derogated by Michno) insists that Crow King followed one deeply cut gully, just upstream of the lower end of the village (i.e., Deep Coulee), while Crazy Horse followed "another very deep ravine" farther downstream (Deep Ravine proper). Crazy Horse was then "very close to the soldiers [united along Calhoun Ridge] on their north side. Crow King was on the South side." Note that north and south correlate respectively with downstream and upstream. Although I disagree with the contention that Crazy Horse arrived late—a point directly contradicted by Flying Hawk and Short Bull, both eyewitnesses—I concur that Crazy Horse accessed the battlefield via Deep Ravine. Interestingly, Private George Glenn referred to a gully that must be Deep Ravine as "Crazy Horse gully": Glenn, interview by Walter M. Camp, Jan. 22, 1914, in Hammer, *Custer in '76*, 136.

39. Flying Hawk, in McCreight, *Chief Flying Hawk's Tales*, 28–29.

40. For battalion reunion and Curley's accounts, see Gray, *Custer's Last Campaign*, 369ff.

41. Curley, in Hammer, *Custer in '76*, 158–59, 162–63, 167–68. On Custer's defensive priorities, see Taunton, "Yellowstone Interlude," 87–88.

42. Curley, in Hammer, *Custer in '76*, 158–59, 162–63, 167–68.

43. Ibid. For Custer's dispositions, see Fox, *Archaeology, History, and Custer's Last Battle*, 318.

44. Curley, in Hammer, *Custer in '76*, 159.

45. Gall was closely involved in this action: for his 1886 statement set down by Gen. Godfrey, see Graham, *Custer Myth*, 94–95.

46. For accounts of the first charge on the Calhoun position, see Runs the Enemy, Dixon, *Vanishing Race*, 175; Hump, Graham, *Custer Myth*, 78; White Bull (Miniconjou), Vestal, "Man Who Killed Custer"; Red Feather, Hardorff, *Lakota Recollections*, 85, 87; Two Moons, Hardorff, *Cheyenne Memories*, 102; Little Hawk, Young Two Moons, ibid., 62, 66.

47. Two Moons, Hardorff, *Cheyenne Memories*, 102; White Shield (ibid., 53) recalled these maneuvers: "Of the other companies, some left the river, *and some went toward it*" (my italics).

48. Curley, in Graham, *Custer Myth*, 11; Flying Hawk interview, tablet 13, Ricker Papers. For an assessment of the left wing's approach to the river, see Fox, *Archaeology, History, and Custer's Last Battle*, 173ff; Scott and Bleed, *Good Walk Around the Boundary*, 41–44.

49. Stands in Timber and Liberty, *Cheyenne Memories*, 199.

50. Runs the Enemy (Dixon, *Vanishing Race*, 175–76) was among the warriors who attacked the left wing from the ridge. Crazy Horse was in the draws of Calhoun Coulee in the frame 4:45–4:55, but soon after 5:00, White Bull (Vestal, "Man Who Killed Custer," 7) noted him across the hogback in the minutes prior to the Calhoun position collapse.

51. For White Bull, see Vestal, "Man Who Killed Custer," 7, and *Warpath*, 195. Vestal's original 1930 and 1932 interview notes with White Bull have been published in Hardorff, *Lakota Recollections*, 107–26.

52. Runs the Enemy, Dixon, *Vanishing Race*, 176; He Dog, in Hardorff, *Lakota Recollections*, 75; Two Moons, Hardorff, *Cheyenne Memories*, 109; Marquis, *Wooden Leg*, 231; Kate Big Head, Marquis, "She Watched Custer's Last Battle," 369. For analysis of the unit deployment down Calhoun Coulee, see Fox, *Archaeology, History, and Custer's Last Battle*, 148ff.

53. Moving Robe Woman (Mary Crawler), in Hardorff, *Lakota Recollections*, 95. At least four authentic grave markers were placed in this sector to honor fallen soldiers. The literature on the evidence of grave markers for troop dispositions is itself extensive and contentious. A cogent reading of the evidence is Taunton, *Custer's Field*. For approximations of troop fatalities per battle sector, I have drawn chiefly on Fox, *Archaeology, History, and Custer's Last Battle*, and Gray, *Custer's Last Campaign*, Fig. 7, 388.

54. Hollow Horn Bear, in Hardorff, *Lakota Recollections*, 182; Little Hawk and Young Two Moons, in idem, *Cheyenne Memories*, 62, 66; Runs the Enemy, Dixon, *Vanishing Race*, 176; Gall, Graham, *Custer Myth*, 95; Fox, *Archaeology, History, and Custer's Last Battle*, 157–61.

55. *Personal Recollections and Observations of General Nelson A. Miles*, 1:287–88. The statements of Miles's informants, like the Horned Horse-Crazy Horse interview, belie assertions that Indian witnesses could not assess strategic patterns. Camp's interview with Foolish Elk (Sept. 22, 1908, Hammer, *Custer in '76*, 199); the Ricker interviews with Nicholas Ruleau (tablet 29), Flying Hawk (tablet 13), and Iron Hawk (tablet 25); and those with Respects Nothing (Nov. 9, 1906, tablet 29) and Standing Bear (Mar. 12, 1907, tablet 13) also evince a strong grasp of the battle's overall shape. They confirm that the trend of the battle's final phase was a rapid unraveling along the hogback ridge to Last Stand Hill, where right-wing survivors consolidated with the two left-wing companies. I favor a short climactic phase—perhaps twenty minutes from the overrunning of Calhoun Hill to mopping up on Last Stand Hill and Deep Ravine.

56. White Bull, Vestal, "Man Who Killed Custer," 7.

57. Ibid.; Red Feather, Hardorff, *Lakota Recollections*, 86; Gall, Graham, *Custer Myth*, 91. Bad Heart Bull and Blish, *Pictographic History of the Oglala Sioux*, 264–68, vividly depicts right-wing collapse.

58. White Bull, in Vestal, "Man Who Killed Custer," 7, and *Warpath*, 196–97; White Bull, in Hardorff, *Lakota Recollections*, 113; He Dog, in Hammer, *Custer in '76*, 207.

59. Waterman, in Graham, *Custer Myth*, 110; He Dog, in Hammer, *Custer in '76*, 207; He Dog, in Hardorff, *Lakota Recollections*, 75; Lone Bear, in ibid., 158. White Bull's testimony on Crazy Horse's charge is badly garbled by his pride, the vagaries of translation, and Vestal's hurried writing-up of his notes. In his 1932 interview, White Bull affirmed that, after counting second coup on the trooper White Bull had jerked from his mount, "Crazy Horse ran through infantry," i.e., Keogh's dismounted I Company. In his 1930 interview, White Bull asserts that Crazy Horse "backed out" of following White Bull in a brave run. See Hardorff, *Lakota Recollections*, 113n, 115 and n. Close reading of the interviews suggests that two separate incidents are involved, the latter involving E Company's approach to Last Stand Hill.

60. For He Dog quotations, see, respectively, He Dog, in Hardorff, *Lakota Recollections*, 75; He Dog, Hammer, in *Custer in '76*, 207; Runs the Enemy quotation, Dixon, *The Vanishing Race*, 176. Dispensing with erroneous preconceptions about Crazy Horse's route to the battlefield, and the mythical onslaught from the north, enables assessment of his true tactical significance in the Battle of the Little Bighorn. Crazy Horse's charge on the Keogh position, and the breaking of the right-wing retreat, emerge as his critical contribution to Custer's defeat. For my assessment of Crazy Horse's overall role in the victory, see chapter 18.

61. Flying Hawk, in McCreight, *Chief Flying Hawk's Tales*, 29; Rain in the Face, in Eastman, *Indian Heroes and Great Chieftains*, 146–48.

62. Gall, Graham, *Custer Myth*, 91. Fox, *Archaeology, History, and Custer's Last Battle*, 162–72, presents archaeological evidence for action in the Keogh sector. His reading of total tactical collapse seems an accurate assessment of the right-wing disaster, but the evidence of bodies, markers, and Indian testimony all point to a doomed but determined rally by Keogh's I Company.

63. White Bull, Hardorff, *Lakota Recollections*, 113. Perhaps the single greatest gap in our knowledge of the Custer battle is the synchronization of wing movements. White Bull's testimony is vital in this regard. He establishes that, as action was climaxing in the Keogh sector, the two left-wing companies were deployed in (a) the north branch draw of Deep Ravine; and (b) a point nearer Last Stand Hill. Custer had therefore moved his units in response to the accelerating action along Calhoun Ridge and Calhoun Hill. This movement may be the "charge" reported by Red Horse (Graham, *Custer Myth*, 62). White Bull evidently believed that the left wing intended to consolidate with the right wing along the hogback, hence his remark that the former "don't go any farther" than the draw. Cheyenne tradition, derived from eyewitnesses like Wolf Tooth, states that from "the basin" (= White Bull's "draw"), E Company led its horses back toward Last Stand Hill. (Powell, *Sweet Medicine*, 1:116.)

64. Graham, *Custer Myth*, 62; Powell, *Sweet Medicine*, 1:116; White Bull, Hardorff, *Lakota Recollections*, 113, 115. For evidence of a skirmish line next to the modern visitors' center, consistent with the E Company deployment reconstructed here, see Fox, *Archaeology, History, and Custer's Last Battle*, 182–83, 353n44. White Bull witnessed E Company's movement: soldiers "start[ed] to run toward the hill. Most of them don't get to the top, and they lay down and start shooting."

65. Standing Bear, in DeMallie, *Sixth Grandfather*, 185–86.

66. Young Two Moons and White Shield, in Hardorff, *Cheyenne Memories*, 55, 66. This heavy fire killed Lame White Man, unhorsing the Cheyenne war leader as he raced along the west side of the ridge in pursuit of the soldiers.

67. For the role of the Suicide Boys, see Stands in Timber and Liberty, *Cheyenne Memories*, 200–201; Powell, *Sweet Medicine*, 1:116–117, and *People of the Sacred Mountain*, 2:1027–28; and Fox, *Archaeology, History, and Custer's Last Battle*, 189–92.

68. Standing Bear, DeMallie, *Sixth Grandfather*, 186.

69. Stands in Timber and Liberty, *Cheyenne Memories*, 200–201; Powell, *Sweet Medicine*, 1:116–117, and *People of the Sacred Mountain*, 2:1027–28; Fox, *Archaeology, History, and Custer's*

Last Battle, 189–92. A discrete cluster of soldier markers is grouped east of the hogback, midway between the Company I position and Last Stand Hill. These may represent the troopers cut off by the Suicide Boys and driven over the ridge.

70. White Bull, Hardorff, *Lakota Recollections*, 113–15; Vestal, *Warpath*, 197; Powell, *Sweet Medicine*, 1:117.

71. White Bull, Hardorff, *Lakota Recollections*, 115; Soldier Wolf and Tall Bull, in Hardorff, *Cheyenne Memories*, 43, 47.

72. Foolish Elk, interview by Walter M. Camp, Sept. 22, 1908, Hammer, *Custer in '76*, 199; Young Two Moons, in Hardorff, *Cheyenne Memories*, 66–67.

73. Young Two Moons, in Hardorff, *Cheyenne Memories*, 67; Big Beaver, in ibid., 149; Red Feather, in Hardorff, *Lakota Recollections*, 87.

74. Yellow Nose, in "Yellow Nose Tells"; Standing Bear, DeMallie, *Sixth Grandfather*, 186.

75. Standing Bear, DeMallie, *Sixth Grandfather*, 186; Black Elk, ibid., 193; Iron Hawk, ibid., 191. For analysis of action in Deep Ravine, see Fox, *Archaeology, History, and Custer's Last Battle*, 203–21.

76. Red Feather, in Hardorff, *Lakota Recollections*, 87–88; Standing Bear, DeMallie, *Sixth Grandfather*, 186. Hardorff conflates the overrunning of Last Stand Hill with Crazy Horse's charge at the Keogh position, but Red Feather's account clearly refers to the topography of the former locale ("The soldiers were on *one side of the hill* and the Indians on the other. . . . The Indians . . . charged right *over the hill*": my emphasis). Although annihilation was now a certainty for Custer's men, Red Feather establishes that Crazy Horse once more shaped a defining moment in the battle.

77. Flying Hawk, in McCreight, *Chief Flying Hawk's Tales*, 29; Big Beaver, Hardorff, *Cheyenne Memories*, 150.

78. Flying Hawk, in McCreight, *Chief Flying Hawk's Tales*, 29. Amos Bad Heart Bull drew a symbolic depiction of Crazy Horse clubbing Custer at the end of the battle (Bad Heart Bull and Blish, *Pictographic History of the Oglala Sioux*, 269). The picture may reflect knowledge of the incident Flying Hawk reports.

79. Flying Hawk, in McCreight, *Chief Flying Hawk's Tales*, 29.

80. Standing Bear, DeMallie, *Sixth Grandfather*, 187. The mutilations are graphically detailed in Taunton, *Custer's Field*.

81. For timing of the "Weir advance" from Reno Hill, see Gray, *Custer's Last Campaign*, 319–26. Late phases of the Battle of the Little Bighorn have been understandably neglected after the climax of action on the Custer field. A good overview is Stewart, *Custer's Luck*, chap. 17.

82. Standing Bear, DeMallie, *Sixth Grandfather*, 187.

83. Standing Bear, DeMallie, *Sixth Grandfather*, 189; Stewart, *Custer's Luck*, 420–27; Gray, *Centennial Campaign*, 181–82; Vestal, *Sitting Bull*, 176.

84. Short Bull, in Riley, "Oglala Sources," 37–38; He Dog, in Hardorff, *Lakota Recollections*, 76; Gray, *Centennial Campaign*, 188–90.

85. John Colhoff to Helen Blish, Apr. 7, 1929, in Bad Heart Bull and Blish, *Pictographic History of the Oglala Sioux*, 36; He Dog, in Hardorff, *Lakota Recollections*, 76; Stewart, *Custer's Luck*, 427–29.

CHAPTER 18

1. Black Elk, in DeMallie, *Sixth Grandfather*, 196. Gray, *Centennial Campaign*, 338–45, is a meticulous reconstruction of village movements from June 26 through late August.

2. Black Elk, DeMallie, *Sixth Grandfather*, 196. For Terry's relief of the Seventh Cavalry and subsequent burials and movements, see Gray, *Centennial Campaign*, 191–97; Stewart, *Custer's Luck*, 464–84.

3. Black Elk, DeMallie, *Sixth Grandfather*, 197.

4. Short Bull, in Riley, "Oglala Sources," 38.

5. Standing Bear, in DeMallie, *Sixth Grandfather*, 188.

6. Lt. W. P. Clark to AG, Dept. of the Platte, Sept. 14, 1877, in Buecker, "Lt. William Philo Clark's Sioux War Report," 18. Clark's report was based on the statements of Lakotas surrendering at Red Cloud Agency in 1877.

7. Robert Higheagle, in Utley, *Lance and the Shield*, 162.

8. See summary in Fox, *Archaeology, History, and Custer's Last Battle*, 238–41.

9. He Dog, in (a) Hammer, *Custer in '76*, 207; (b) Hardorff, *Lakota Recollections*, 75.

10. Flying Hawk interview, tablet 13, Ricker Papers; Gray, *Centennial Campaign*, 199–200.

11. Gray, *Centennial Campaign*, 341–42, synthesizes Indian accounts.

12. Black Elk, DeMallie, *Sixth Grandfather*, 361–62.

13. Ibid.; Gray, *Centennial Campaign*, 210; Greene, *Yellowstone Command*, 32. The July 29 skirmish is the only engagement that fits Black Elk's description.

14. Black Elk, DeMallie, *Sixth Grandfather*, 199; Gray, *Centennial Campaign*, 210–11, 343; Greene, *Yellowstone Command*, 34–35. Black Elk refers to Runs Fearless by his nickname, Yellow Shirt.

15. For the Cheyenne flight from Red Cloud and for the Warbonnet Creek skirmish, see especially Hedren, *First Scalp for Custer*.

16. Fall schedules are indicated in Gen. George Crook to Gen. P. H. Sheridan, Sept. 10, 1876, in Greene, *Slim Buttes, 1876*, 130–31; and recollected in Tall Bull (Cheyenne), interview by Camp, July 22, 1910, Hammer, *Custer in '76*, 213.

17. Vestal, *Warpath*, 206–207. White Bull recollected meeting Crazy Horse's party on its return from the Black Hills, in mid-August. Since Crazy Horse did not return from his raid across the Yellowstone until the very end of July, a departure in the first days of August is indicated. Note that Black Elk states the village dispersed one day after the skirmish with the *Far West*—i.e., August 3.

18. The movements of Terry and Crook are ably presented in Gray, *Centennial Campaign*, chap. 18; Greene, *Slim Buttes, 1876*, chaps. 1–3; and outlined in Utley, *Frontier Regulars*, 267–70.

19. Besides providing a masterly synthesis, official reports bearing on the Slim Buttes Battle are gathered in Greene, *Slim Buttes, 1876*. A shorter account is H. H. Anderson, "Battle of Slim Buttes."

20. For village composition and satellite camps, see Lt. Col. G. P. Buell to AAG, Gen. Terry's Column in the Field, Sept. 9, 1876, SW File; Crook to Sheridan, Sept. 10, 1876; He Dog, in Hammer, *Custer in '76*, 208; Samuel Charger, in Greene, *Lakota and Cheyenne*, 87–88.

21. Greene, *Slim Buttes, 1876*, chap. 4. Significant Lakota accounts of the battle are Many Shields, in Lt. Col. G. P. Buell to AAG, Dept. of Dakota, Sept. 19, 1876; Red Horse, in Col. W. W. Wood to AAG, Dept. of Dakota, Feb. 27, 1877, Sioux War Papers; Blue Hair to Walter M. Camp, Camp Papers, BYU.

22. Finerty, *War-Path and Bivouac*, 196.

23. Short Bull, Riley, "Oglala Sources," 38.

24. Events surrounding the transfer to military authority of the White River agencies are fully traced in Buecker, *Fort Robinson*, 84ff.

25. U.S. Senate, *Report of the Sioux Commission*; Garnett interview, tablet 2, Ricker Papers.

26. "Register of Whites, Indians, and Indian Bands at Cheyenne River Agency, 1876–1877," vol. 54, Fort Bennett, Post at Cheyenne River Agency; H. H. Anderson, "A History of the Cheyenne River Indian Agency," 471–72.

27. K. M. Bray, "Crazy Horse and the End of the Great Sioux War," 95–96. Particularly useful for fall Oglala movements is Respects Nothing interview, tablet 29, Ricker Papers.

28. Black Elk, DeMallie, *Sixth Grandfather*, 199; Bad Heart Bull and Blish, *Pictographic History of the Oglala Sioux*, 400; Maj. J. M. Mason to AAG, Division of the Missouri, Dec. 5, 1876, SW File; *Omaha Daily Bee*, Feb. 23, 1877. Through early November, the Crazy Horse village was encamped on Rosebud Creek; in mid-month, it moved to Tongue River below Otter Creek.

29. For Miles's fall campaigning, see Greene, *Yellowstone Command*, chaps. 4–5. Once across the international boundary, Iron Dog's camp parleyed with the north west mounted police on November 27. The Hunkpapas stated that they wished to remain in Canada, having left Powder River early in October, crossing the Missouri between Fort Peck and Wolf Point. Lt. R. H Day to Post Adjutant, Fort Buford, June 7, 1877, Sioux War Papers.

30. Spotted Elk, in Col. W. W. Wood to AAG, Dept. of Dakota, Mar. 1, 1877, SW File.

31. Kime, *Powder River Expedition Journals*, 82.

32. For Crook's activities at Red Cloud Agency, see Buecker, *Fort Robinson*, 88–89. Billy Garnett recalled details of the "spies" sent out by Crook to Crazy Horse's village. Garnett interview, tablet 1, Ricker Papers. Although No Water is not mentioned, he definitely joined the northern Oglalas in late summer or fall 1876. For his presence by midwinter, see Marquis, *Wooden Leg*, 289, 292.

33. Scout enlistments are set forth in Bourke diary, [Nov. 1876], vol. 14, 1360–63.

34. Mason to AAG, Division of the Missouri, Dec. 5, 1876.

35. Lt. R. H. Day to Col. W. B. Hazen, Nov. 25, 1876, SW File.

36. For the November 30 surrender at Cheyenne River, see Gen. Alfred H. Terry to AG, Division of the Missouri, Dec. 1, 1876 (telegram); Lt. Col. G. P. Buell to AG, Dept. of Dakota, Dec. 2, 1876, both SW File; H. H. Anderson, "A History of Cheyenne River Agency," 472. Village leadership is reconstructed from statements of surrendering Lakotas at Cheyenne River, in Col. W. W. Wood to AAG, Dept. of Dakota, Dec. 28, 1876, Jan. 24, Feb. 16, 1877, SW File

37. The Mackenzie battle is most fully covered in Greene, *Morning Star Dawn*. Cheyenne perspectives are synthesized in Powell, *People of the Sacred Mountain*, 2:1056–71.

38. Marquis, *Wooden Leg*, 287–88.

39. Short Bull, Riley, "Oglala Sources," 39.

40. Bourke diary, Aug. 1, 1878, vol. 24, 12–14. See also my discussion and additional sources in K. M. Bray, "Crazy Horse and the End of the Great Sioux War," 96.

41. For December defections to Canada, see Lt. R. H. Day to Post Adjutant, Fort Buford, Feb. 10, 1877, SW File; Canadian Papers, 9ff. For background on Sitting Bull's activities, consult Utley, *Lance and the Shield*, 177–78; Greene, *Yellowstone Command*, chap. 6.

42. Statements of Swelled Face and Spotted Elk, in Col. W. W. Wood to AAG, Dept. of Dakota, Feb. 21, Mar. 1, 1877, SW File; *Omaha Daily Bee*, Feb. 23, 1877; Black Elk, DeMallie, *Sixth Grandfather*, 199–200; Short Bull, Riley, "Oglala Sources," 39. The fullest secondary account is Greene, *Yellowstone Command*, 150–52.

43. Black Elk, DeMallie, *Sixth Grandfather*, 200.

44. K. M. Bray, "Crazy Horse and the End of the Great Sioux War," 97; Clark to AG, Dept. of the Platte, Sept. 14, 1877, Buecker, "Lt. William Philo Clark's Sioux War Report," 19 (includes quotation).

45. Greene, *Yellowstone Command*, 140–43; Utley, *Lance and the Shield*, 178–79.

46. Red Horse, in Wood to AAG, Dept. of Dakota, Feb. 27, 1877.

CHAPTER 19

1. Fool Bear and Important Man, in Col. W. W. Wood to AAG, Dept. of Dakota, Jan. 24, 1877; Eagle Shield, in same to same, Feb. 16, 1877, both in SW File. Quotations in this section are derived from these documents. Throughout chapters 19 and 20, I draw on my earlier study of these events: K. M. Bray, "Crazy Horse and the End of the Great Sioux War."

2. Marquis, *Wooden Leg*, 289, 292.

3. From a military point of view, preliminaries to the Battle of Wolf Mountains are treated most fully in Greene, *Yellowstone Command*, 155–63; but see also H. H. Anderson, "Nelson A. Miles and the Sioux War"; *Personal Recollections and Observations of General Nelson A. Miles*, 1:234–36; Utley, *Frontier Regulars*, 276–77; Powell, *People of the Sacred Mountain*, 2:1074.

4. Marquis, *Wooden Leg*, 289–90; Powell, *People of the Sacred Mountain*, 2:1074–75 (quotation at 1380n18); Little Killer, in Buechel and Manhart, *Lakota Tales and Texts*, 2:448–49; Black Elk, DeMallie, *Sixth Grandfather*, 201–202.

5. Swelled Face, in Col. W. W. Wood to AAG, Dept. of Dakota, Feb. 21, 1877, SW File. The following account of the Battle of Wolf Mountains is based on Col. Nelson A. Miles to AAG, Dept. of Dakota, Jan. 23, 1877, SW File; Greene, *Yellowstone Command*, 163–76, and *Battles and Skirmishes*, chap. 14; Powell, *People of the Sacred Mountain*, 2:1075–78; Marquis, *Wooden Leg*, 290–93; Black Elk, DeMallie, *Sixth Grandfather*, 201–202; Short Bull, in Riley, "Oglala Sources," 38–39; Eagle Shield, in Wood to AAG, Dept. of Dakota, Feb. 19, 1877, SW File.

6. *Army and Navy Journal*, Mar. 31, 1877, reprinted in Greene, *Battles and Skirmishes*, 202.

7. Eagle Shield, in Wood to AAG, Dept. of Dakota, Feb. 16, 1877, SW File. For background see K. M. Bray, "Crazy Horse and the End of the Great Sioux War," 99; Utley, *Lance and the Shield*, 179–80.

8. Charging Horse and Make Them Stand Up, in Lt. Horace Neide to Lt. Bourke, Feb. 10, 1877, SW File (includes quotations); K. M. Bray, "Crazy Horse and the End of the Great Sioux War," 100.

9. Red Horse, in Wood to AAG, Dept. of Dakota, Feb. 27, 1877, SW File; Eagle Shield, in same to same, Feb. 16, 1877.

10. Swelled Face, Wood to AAG, Dept. of Dakota, Feb. 21, 1877.

11. Bordeaux, *Custer's Conqueror*, 60–61; Vestal, *Sitting Bull*, 182.

12. Vestal, *Sitting Bull*, 182.

13. Sitting Bull speech, June 2, 1877, quoted in Manzione, *"I Am Looking to the North for My Life,"* 49.

14. Red Sack, in Lt. W. P. Clark to Lt. Bourke, Feb. 24, 1877, SW File.

15. Eagle Pipe, in Lt. Jesse M. Lee to Lt. Bourke, Mar. 6, 1877; also Lee to AAG, District of the Black Hills, Mar. 19, 1877, both SW File. This party surrendered at Spotted Tail Agency, Mar. 4–5, 1877.

16. Red Horse and White Eagle, Wood to AAG, Feb. 27, 1877. This party surrendered at Cheyenne River Agency, Feb. 25, 1877.

17. White Eagle Bull, in Lt. Horace Neide to Lt. Bourke, Feb. 16, 1877; Lt. Jesse M. Lee to AAG, District of the Black Hills, Mar. 19, 1877; Little Wolf, in Clark to Bourke, Feb. 24, 1877, all SW File.

18. Lt. W. P. Clark to AG, Dept. of the Platte, Sept. 14, 1877, reprinted in Buecker, "Lt. William Philo Clark's Sioux War Report," 19–20; K. M. Bray, "Crazy Horse and the End of the Great Sioux War," 102.

19. K. M. Bray, "Crazy Horse and the End of the Great Sioux War," 102, 114n41. The first surrenders at Red Cloud Agency (Little Wolf's Cheyenne party) were registered Feb. 24–28. Other small groups, accompanied by agency delegates, trickled in through early March. No Water's party surrendered March 14, and the Cheyennes of American Horse, Red Owl, Big Head (Tangle Hair), and Plenty Camps, on the previous day.

20. Red Feather, Riley, "Oglala Sources," 25–26; Short Bull, ibid., 39; Oglala delegates' statement, in Lt. W. P. Clark to Lt. Bourke, Mar. 3, 1877, SW Files (hereafter Oglala delegates' statement). Returning delegates were probably the source for the *Omaha Daily Bee*, Mar. 13, 1877, statement on Tall Bull (includes quotation). At surrender, Tall Bull and his family were actually living in Crazy Horse's tipi, while Iron Whiteman's lodge stood next to Crazy Horse's. Given the lifelong association of the latter family with the Hunkpatila band, it seems likely that the two traveled together through the previous weeks.

21. For Sitting Bull's movements, see Canadian Papers, 12–13; Lt. R. H. Day to Post Adjutant, Fort Buford, Feb. 19, 1877, SW File; Oglala delegates' statement includes quotation.

22. Black Elk, DeMallie, *Sixth Grandfather*, 202.

23. Oglala delegates' statement.

24. For Miles's first round of negotiations, see Miles, *Personal Recollections and Observations*, 1:239–40; Powell, *People of the Sacred Mountain*, 2:1087–90, 1123–24, 1380–81; Greene, *Yellowstone Command*, 192–94. When Hunts the Enemy's Oglala delegates arrived at the main village, about February 17, they learned that the deputation to Miles had departed five nights earlier.

25. Oglala delegates' statement. The recruitment and departure of the Oglala delegates is detailed in Gen. George Crook to [HQ, Division of the Missouri], Jan. 8, 1877 (telegram), SW File; *Army and Navy Journal*, Feb. 3, 1877; Garnett interview, tablet 2, Ricker Papers. Hunts the Enemy, who took the name George Sword later in 1877, gave his recollection to Pine Ridge physician James R. Walker. I have used the translation by Ella Deloria, "Sword's Acts Related," in typescript at Colorado State Historical Society, Denver. Thirty years old in 1877, Hunts the Enemy was the younger brother of the Shirt Wearer Sword Owner, who had died at Red Cloud Agency in 1876.

26. Oglala delegates' statement.

27. Quotations in sequence: Red Feather, Riley, "Oglala Sources," 26; Tall Man, in Lt. W. P. Clark to Lt. Bourke, Mar. 8, 1877, SW File; Oglala delegates' statement; Red Feather, Riley, "Oglala Sources," 26.

28. "Sword's Acts Related"; K. M. Bray, "Crazy Horse and the End of the Great Sioux War," 104–105. Hunts the Enemy's comrades were Running Hawk (younger brother of Young Man Afraid of His Horse); Long Whirlwind; and the Oglala-Cheyenne Fire Crow.

29. Tall Man, in Clark to Bourke, Mar. 8, 1877; *Omaha Daily Bee*, Mar. 14, 1877. For details and documentation on Spotted Tail's departure for the north, see Neide to Bourke, Feb. 10, 1877; Lt. Jesse M. Lee to CoIA, Mar. 20, 1877, STA, LR, OIA; Lee to Bourke, Mar. 6, 1877; Bourke diary, Feb. 13, Apr. 20, 1877, vol. 19, 1835, 1901, 1904–05.

30. Oglala delegates' statement; Tall Man, in Clark to Bourke, Mar. 8, 1877.

31. Oglala delegates' statement (first quotation); *Omaha Daily Bee*, Apr. 17, 1877 (second quotation).

32. For Spotted Eagle's crossing the Yellowstone, see Col. Nelson A. Miles to AAG, Dept. of Dakota, Mar. 24, 1877, reproduced in undated *Chicago Times* clipping in Bourke diary, vol. 19, 1902–03; K. M. Bray, "Crazy Horse and the End of the Great Sioux War," 105, 114n58.

33. Tall Man, in Clark to Bourke, Mar. 8, 1877; Canadian Papers, 12–13; Miles to AAG, Dept. of Dakota, Mar. 24, 1877 (includes quotation).

34. F. C. Boucher, Spotted Tail's son-in-law, stated that Crazy Horse "went out by himself" about three weeks before Spotted Tail reached the Little Powder River (Mar. 20). See Lt. Jesse

M. Lee to AAG, District of the Black Hills, Apr. 8, 1877, STA, LS, 1877, vol. 1, 667–70, BIA, RG 75, NACPR. Tall Man, however, indicated that Crazy Horse was still in camp as of March 4, when the former departed for the agency. I therefore assume that Crazy Horse departed soon after Tall Man. Boucher also states that Crazy Horse had only his own lodge with him, but Lakotas arriving at Spotted Tail Agency stated that the war chief "was out hunting . . . with two lodges." See Lt. W. P. Clark to Lt. Bourke, Apr. 2, 1877, SW File. Spotted Tail's mission is detailed at length in K. M. Bray, "Crazy Horse and the End of the Great Sioux War," 106–107.

CHAPTER 20

1. Black Elk, in DeMallie, *Sixth Grandfather*, 202.

2. Thunder Tail account, in Buechel and Manhart, *Lakota Tales and Texts* 2:626, 631–32.

3. On Black Shawl's ill health, see V. T. McGillycuddy, in Brininstool, "Chief Crazy Horse" 36; McGillycuddy, *Blood on the Moon*, 75.

4. There are several accounts of the eagle power cult on the modern Pine Ridge Reservation, but see especially Lewis, *Medicine Men*, 93–105. The late practitioner Pete Catches observed that the rite "comes from Crazy Horse by way of Good Lance" (ibid., 103), and noted the intercessionary role of the red hawk in obtaining eagle power. For an outline of twentieth-century practice, see Fugle, *Nature and Function of the Lakota Night Cults*, 8–9; Steinmetz, *Pipe, Bible, and Peyote*, 22, 26, 44; Feraca, *Wakinyan*, 53–55.

5. Spotted Tail, in Lt. Jesse M. Lee to AAG, District of the Black Hills, Apr. 5, 1877, SW File. Spotted Tail's diplomacy is treated at length in K. M. Bray, "Crazy Horse and the End of the Great Sioux War," 107–108. I have drawn extensively on my earlier article for the negotiations leading to surrender.

6. Spotted Tail, in Lee to AAG, Apr. 5, 1877; also F. C. Boucher to "Major Neide," Mar. 25, 1877, copy enclosed with Lee to AAG, District of the Black Hills, Apr. 2, 1877.

7. Red Feather, in Riley, "Oglala Sources," 26. Internal evidence in the extensive documentation on the Spotted Tail mission establishes that the Brule chief started homeward from Little Powder on March 26. Tight chronological coordination with the movements of Lame Deer, and the return of the delegates to Miles, suggests that the main Oglala-Cheyenne village encamped on Powder River later the same day. See K. M. Bray, "Crazy Horse and the End of the Great Sioux War," 108 (where March 26 is misprinted "March 2"), 115n80. For delegates, see also Marquis, *Wooden Leg*, 297f; "Departures" entries in Buecker and Paul, *Crazy Horse Surrender Ledger*, 98, 100.

8. Black Elk, DeMallie, *Sixth Grandfather*, 203; Red Feather, Riley, "Oglala Sources," 26.

9. Miles, *Personal Recollections and Observations*, 1:243.

10. R. A. Clark, *Killing of Chief Crazy Horse*, 53–54.

11. Wooden Leg noted that a "little band [of Oglalas] went down Powder River": Marquis, *Wooden Leg*, 297. Upon surrender to Miles, Hump complained that twenty-four lodges had defied his authority and stayed out. Since Hump's tiyospaye was traveling with the Oglalas in February and March, I suggest that he means that ten lodges of his own following had joined Lame Deer. Crazy Horse's departure is the best context. Low Dog, an Oyuhpe war leader, surrendered with the Lame Deer camp at Spotted Tail Agency, September 4, 1877, then played a leading role in the November 17 breakout for Canada.

12. For Lame Deer's objectives, see K. M. Bray, "Crazy Horse and the End of the Great Sioux War," 110. For the Cheyenne division, see Marquis, *Wooden Leg*, 197–300; Powell, *People of the Sacred Mountain*, 2:1124–28; Lt. W. P. Clark to HQ, Dept. of the Platte, May 4, 1877 (telegram), transmitted in R. Williams to AAG, Division of the Missouri, May 5, 1877 (telegram), SW File; Col. Nelson A. Miles to AAG, Dept. of Dakota, Apr. 22, 1877, Sioux War

Papers.

13. Black Shawl's brother stated that, by summer 1877, she was suffering with a "swollen arm": Red Feather, in Riley, "Oglala Sources," 28. Joint swellings of this nature are one manifestation of tuberculosis. (Black Shawl's other brother Iron Horse denied that his sister suffered the disease. See Standing Bear, *Land of the Spotted Eagle*, 180.)

14. For composition of Crazy Horse's household at surrender, see Buecker and Paul, *Crazy Horse Surrender Ledger*, 162. On Tall Bull, cf. *Omaha Daily Bee*, Mar. 13, 1877.

15. Mackenzie to Bourke, Apr. 1, 1877. The first word that Crazy Horse was en route to surrender came from army detachments patrolling the northern Black Hills. On April 5 Spotted Tail's interpreter, Jose Merrivale, told Captain Vroom, in camp near Crook City, that Crazy Horse had arrived in the northern Oglala village at Bear Lodge Butte. Vroom to Gen. George Crook, Apr. 5, 1877 (telegram), transmitted in Crook to Gen. P. H. Sheridan, Apr. 5, 1877 (telegram), SW File.

16. Col. Mackenzie to CoIA via HQ Dept. of the Platte, Mar. 19, 1877, Sioux War Papers.

17. Bourke diary, Apr. 4, 1877, vol. 19, 1852–55. Scout enlistments as of April 4, 1877 are enumerated in ibid., 1856–57, and updated in Clark to AG, Dept. of the Platte, Apr. 20, 1877 (copy supplied by Fort Robinson Museum). By May 2, two hundred scouts were enlisted, including newly surrendered Cheyennes, Miniconjous, and Sans Arcs.

18. Bourke diary, vol. 19, 1885–86; Garnett interview, tablet 2, Ricker Papers; Buecker and Paul, *Crazy Horse Surrender Ledger*, 99; "Red Cloud's Mission to Crazy Horse."

19. For the northern Oglala layover at Bear Lodge Butte, approximately Apr. 1–16, 1877, see K. M. Bray, "Crazy Horse and the End of the Great Sioux War," 110–12. Village leadership is reconstructed from *Army and Navy Journal*, May 12, 1877; Bourke diary, May 6, 1877, vol. 20, 1984–85; Bourke, *On the Border with Crook*, 412; "Eagle Hawk Narrative/Told to Eagle Hawk [by He Dog]," in Hardorff, *Surrender and Death of Crazy Horse*, 135.

20. King, in Kadlecek and Kadlecek, *To Kill an Eagle*, 125.

21. Black Elk, DeMallie, *Sixth Grandfather*, 203.

22. *New York Tribune*, Apr. 28, 1877; Bourke diary, Apr. 16, 1877, vol. 19, 1884; Buecker and Paul, *Crazy Horse Surrender Ledger*, 104.

23. Neihardt, *Black Elk Speaks*, 85.

24. *New York Herald*, May 11, 1877; *New York Tribune*, Apr. 28, 1877 (incorporating Red Cloud to Lt. William P. Clark, Apr. 16, 1877); Thunder Tail, in Buechel and Manhart, *Lakota Tales and Texts*, 2:625, 631. Quotation in Short Bull, Riley, "Oglala Sources," 39.

25. *Chicago Tribune*, May 8, 1877; Little Killer, in Riley, "Oglala Sources," 44 (includes quotation).

26. Thunder Tail, in Buechel and Manhart, *Lakota Tales and Texts*, 2:626, 631.

27. Short Bull, Riley, "Oglala Sources," 39; Thunder Tail, in Buechel and Manhart, *Lakota Tales and Texts*, 2:626, 631.

28. Bourke diary, Apr. 27 and 29, 1877, vol. 19, 1918, 1934; *Chicago Tribune*, May 8, 1877.

29. Bourke diary, May 1 and 3, vol. 20, 1949ff, 1974; Short Bull, Riley, "Oglala Sources," 39. Buecker and Paul, *Crazy Horse Surrender Ledger*, 114, names the northern messengers: Lodge Wing, Singing Prick, Goes for Nation Bad, Owns Sharp, Slow White Cow, Eagle Round Wood.

30. On the Rosenquest mission, see Garnett interview, tablet 2, Ricker Papers; Lt. C. A. Johnson to CoIA, Apr. 30, 1877, RCA Letterbook, BIA, NACPR; *Denver Daily Tribune*, May 18, 1877. For Camp Robinson background, see Buecker, *Fort Robinson*, 92ff. American Horse's scouts may have been a chapter of the Omaha Society.

31. Charging Bear, in Bourke diary, May 3, 1877, vol. 20, 1974; *New York Sun*, May 23, 1877.

32. He Dog, in Hardorff, *Lakota Recollections*, 79, and Riley, "Oglala Sources," 20 (first quotation); Little Killer, ibid., 44 (second quotation).

33. Iron Shield, in Mackenzie to AAG, Dept. of the Platte, May 16, 1877, SW File; Clark to HQ Dept. of the Platte, May 4, 1877 (telegram), Sioux War Papers; Bourke diary, May 4, 1877, vol. 20, 1983–84.

34. Thunder Tail, in Buechel and Manhart, *Lakota Tales and Texts*, 2:626, 631–32.

35. Gen. P. H. Sheridan, Mar. 29, 1877, Endorsement: "disapproved," to Mackenzie to CoIA, Mar. 19, 1877; CoIA to Secretary of War, Apr. 9, 1877, Sioux War Papers.

36. The Cheyenne removal is treated at length in Powell, *People of the Sacred Mountain*, 2:1149–51, 1385. For the Spotted Tail Agency option, see Louis Bordeaux, interview by Walter M. Camp, July 6–7, 1910, Liddic and Harbaugh, *Custer and Company*, 137–39.

37. "Eagle Hawk Narrative," Hardorff, *Surrender and Death of Crazy Horse*, 137. In view of Iron Shield's intelligence from Miles and Lame Deer, Crazy Horse might have meant to join the latter in surrendering at Tongue River Cantonment.

38. Charging Bear, in Bourke diary, May 3, 1877, vol. 20, 1974; *New York Sun*, May 23, 1877.

39. Primary sources on the surrender of Crazy Horse are voluminous and detailed. In the following account I have consulted these newspaper reports: *Chicago Tribune*, May 8, 1877; *Chicago Times*, May 7, 1877; *Army and Navy Journal*, May 12, 1877; *Frank Leslie's Illustrated Newspaper*, June 8, 1877; *New York Herald*, May 7 and 28, 1877; *New York Tribune*, May 7, 1877; *New York Sun*, May 23, 1877. Other detailed eyewitness reports include Bourke diary, May 6, 1877, vol. 20, 1984–94; Bourke, *On the Border with Crook*, 412–15; W. P. Clark, *Indian Sign Language*, 295–96; Garnett interview, tablet 2, Ricker Papers. In this account, I footnote only quotations and controversial points.

40. *Chicago Tribune*, May 8, 1877.

41. *New York Herald*, May 28, 1877.

42. Bourke, *On the Border with Crook*, 412.

43. *Chicago Times*, May 7, 1877.

44. All quotations except He Dog from *New York Tribune*, May 7, 1877; He Dog quotation: *Chicago Times*, May 7, 1877. For more on He Dog's role, see R. A. Clark, *Killing of Chief Crazy Horse*, 57, and caption to pictograph 9, 54.

45. Quotations from *Chicago Times*, May 7, 1877; *New York Sun*, May 23, 1877; *Frank Leslie's Illustrated Newspaper*, June 8, 1877.

46. Shave Elk (Thomas Disputed), interview by Walter M. Camp, Liddic and Harbaugh, *Custer and Company*, 126.

47. R. A. Clark, *Killing of Chief Crazy Horse*, 75.

48. *New York Herald*, May 7, 1877 (includes quotation); R. A. Clark, *Killing of Chief Crazy Horse*, 59. The seven hundred head pledged Red Cloud matched the ponies confiscated from him by Mackenzie the previous October.

49. Bourke diary, May 6, 1877, vol. 20, 1987–91.

50. Charles P. Jordan to Doane Robinson, June 26, 1902, Robinson Papers. Buecker and Paul, *Crazy Horse Surrender Ledger*, 157–64, prints the complete roll of the "Crazy Horse Sioux."

51. *Chicago Tribune*, May 8, 1877.

52. Bourke diary, vol. 20, 1991; Bourke, *On the Border with Crook*, 414–15.

53. *New York Sun*, May 23, 1877.

CHAPTER 21

1. "Eagle Hawk Narrative," in Hardorff, *Surrender and Death of Crazy Horse*, 138–40; Short Bull and Red Feather, in Riley, "Oglala Sources," 26, 40. Short Bull indicates that Crazy Horse's statement about the Beaver Creek location was made on the day of surrender, but none of the

contemporary newspaper accounts mentions such a statement. The next major talk, between the northern leadership and Col. Mackenzie, was on Tuesday, May 8, but Crazy Horse was absent due to illness. On balance, the context seems to fit the busy schedule of May 7, when distribution of rations and annuity goods necessitated dialogue between Crazy Horse and Lieutenants Johnson and Clark.

2. Red Feather, Riley, "Oglala Sources," 26; McGillycuddy, *Blood on the Moon*, 75–76. Denver *Rocky Mountain News*, May 20, 1877, establishes that northern warriors were already remounted "upon ponies obtained from Red Cloud's peace band" the day after surrender.

3. Denver *Rocky Mountain News*, May 20, 1877.

4. Ibid. For details on the agency beef issue and its economic significance to the Oglalas, see Buecker and Paul, *Crazy Horse Surrender Ledger*, 12–14.

5. Garnett interview, tablet 2, Ricker Papers.

6. *Cheyenne Daily Leader*, May 16, 1877. As late as May 18, when Frank Grouard and agency trader J. W. Dear led a party of civilian visitors to visit Crazy Horse at home, the war chief was "still suffering from the effects of a change of diet and over-feeding." *Cheyenne Daily Leader*, May 23, 1877.

7. *Denver Daily Tribune*, May 18, 1877.

8. Red Feather, Riley, "Oglala Sources," 26.

9. *Cheyenne Daily Leader*, May 16, 1877.

10. Registers of Enlistment in the U.S. Army: Indian Scouts, 1866–77, AGO. The ten men enrolled from Spotted Tail Agency seem to be Jumping Shield (Iron Crow), Looking Horse, Eats with Wolf, Flying Water Bear, High Hawk, Keeps the Horn, Little Dog, Long Bear, Medicine Bull, Pretty Elk, and Sore Tail.

11. *Cheyenne Daily Leader*, May 16, 1877. Pawnee Killer was a headman in the agency Oglala Spleen band.

12. Jordan to Robinson, June 26, 1902, Robinson Papers.

13. This breakdown of Oglala bands is based on 1877 census details in Buecker and Paul, *Crazy Horse Surrender Ledger*. Red Cloud's Bad Face band, augmented by the agency faction of Oyuhpes led by Red Dog, High Wolf, and Slow Bull, aggregated about ninety lodges. The Payabya band, led by Young Man Afraid of His Horse, counted another eighty-five tipis. American Horse's Loafers numbered some eighty lodges; the Spleen band, led by Yellow Bear, about sixty-five lodges. Largest of the bands, and the only one exceeding the northern village's strength, was Little Wound's Kiyuksa camp. The 170 Kiyuksa lodges were augmented by the remnant of the Wazhazha band (most of which had transferred to Spotted Tail late in April) to create a village of about 210 lodges.

14. Denver *Rocky Mountain News*, May 20, 1877, is the fullest account of the Kiyuksa-hosted council (includes quotation). See also *Denver Daily Tribune*, May 18, 1877.

15. Denver *Rocky Mountain News*, May 20, 1877.

16. Col. Thomas Anderson, "Army Episodes and Anecdotes," 34, Coe Papers (typescript at Fort Robinson Museum, Crawford, Nebraska).

17. *Yankton Union and Press and Dakotaian*, June 7, 1877. On Cheyenne relocation, see also *Chicago Times*, May 26, 1877, and for detailed background, Powell, *People of the Sacred Mountain*, 2:1149–51, 1385.

18. Gen. P. H. Sheridan to Gen. W. T. Sherman, Apr. 10, 1877 (telegram); Sherman to Sheridan, Apr. 11, 1877 (telegram); Sheridan to Sherman, May 2, 1877 (telegram); Sherman to Sheridan, May 2, 1877 (telegram): all in Sioux War Papers.

19. Sheridan to Sherman, May 2, 1877 (telegram); Sherman to CoIA, May 4, 1877 (telegram); Sherman to Sheridan, May 7, 1877 (telegram), Sioux War Papers.

20. Sheridan to Sherman, Apr. 23, 1877 (telegram), Sioux War Papers.

21. *Chicago Times*, May 26, 1877.

22. The fullest account of the May 25 council appeared in the *Chicago Times*, May 26, 1877. Briefer reports are found in *Cheyenne Daily Leader*, May 26, 1877 (includes quotations); and *Black Hills Daily Times*, May 28, 1877. A brief summary was submitted in Lt. Charles A. Johnson to CoIA, June 4, 1877, RCA, LR, OIA.

23. Jordan to Robinson, June 26, 1902, Robinson Papers.

24. Crazy Horse speech, *Cheyenne Daily Leader*, May 26, 1877. A slightly different version appears in the *Chicago Times* account.

25. Young Man Afraid of His Horse's speech appears in full in *Chicago Times*, May 26, 1877.

26. *Cheyenne Daily Leader*, May 26, 1877.

27. *Chicago Times*, May 26, 1877. Spotted Tail quotation from *Cheyenne Daily Leader*, May 26, 1877.

28. Crook quotations from *Cheyenne Daily Leader* and *Chicago Times*, both May 26, 1877.

29. Young Man Afraid of His Horse speech from Garnett interview, tablet 2, Ricker Papers. This is the only source on the second council and forms the basis for my account. Young Man Afraid of His Horse had led an Oglala delegation to inspect the proposed Indian Territory homeland.

30. Bourke diary, vol. 24, 34. Cantonment Reno (renamed Fort McKinney on Aug. 30, 1877) was located near the head of Powder River, on the site of the 1865–68 Bozeman Trail garrison Fort Reno. Crook had raised the possibility of an Army-policed buffalo hunt with the surrendering Miniconjous and Sans Arcs at Spotted Tail on April 15: see, e.g., Bourke diary, vol. 19, 1871.

31. When Clark reorganized the scouts in early July, Iron Crow joined Little Hawk, Little Big Man, and Big Road in being appointed sergeant of Company C, based around the leadership in Crazy Horse's village. Old Hawk, the fourth Decider at surrender, may have retired, been removed, taken sick, or even died. He does not appear in subsequent censuses.

32. Crook to Sheridan, May 26, 1877, LR, AGO. In truth, the five hostages, interned at Cheyenne River, did not want to be transferred to Red Cloud. After release in July, Black Eagle (Sans Arc) left Cheyenne River Agency without permission to join his relatives at Spotted Tail, participating in the subsequent flight to Canada. Red Skirt (Miniconjou) traveled to Spotted Tail also, but to bring his family, thirteen persons, home to Cheyenne River. Rising Sun and Crazy Thunder (Sans Arcs) left Cheyenne River with their families about February 4, 1878, ostensibly for the relocated Red Cloud Agency: their real purpose may have been to join the northern Lakotas then fleeing to Canada. White Hollow Horns, the fifth hostage, did not leave Cheyenne River, settling in the Miniconjou camp now led by his son Little Bear.

33. Valuable, if tantalizing, clues to population movements between Spotted Tail and Red Cloud are revealed in a partial census of the latter agency. See Census of Indians, May 21, 1877, PRA. Listed in the document are sixty-four families, numbered 61 through 122 (sic), then belonging to Crazy Horse's village. Judging from the document's overall emphasis on transfers and visitors from Spotted Tail, these families represent people perceived as belonging properly to that agency: i.e., mainly Brules, Miniconjous, and Sans Arcs. Some twenty-five names are recognizable from the tally of the Crazy Horse village at surrender, May 6. Others are likely to represent subsequent unofficial transfers from Spotted Tail—e.g., Jumping Shield (Iron Crow), no. 121—or brief visitors, such as High Lodge, no. 111, who is deleted and is known to have returned to Spotted Tail until official transfer in July. On Worm's experience, see chapter 22.

34. Garnett interview, tablet 2, Ricker Papers.

CHAPTER 22

1. Bradley to his wife, May 26, and Oct. 7, 1877, Bradley correspondence, folder f, box 2, Bradley Papers; also Bradley private journal, box 1, Bradley Papers.

2. Bradley to wife, May 26, 1877.

3. Clark to Crook, May 28, 1877, transmitted in Crook to Sheridan, May 29, 1877 (telegram), SW File. For full background on the Cheyenne departure, consult Powell, *People of the Sacred Mountain*, 2:1149–51, 1385. On the Mackenzie departure, see Buecker, "A History of Camp Robinson," 52.

4. Clark to Crook, May 28, 1877. For background on the Lame Deer fight, see especially Greene, *Yellowstone Command*, chap. 9.

5. Clark to Crook, May 28, 1877.

6. Bourke diary, vol. 24, 35.

7. Sgt. William F. Kelley, in *Crawford Tribune*, Special Edition, June 26, 1903.

8. Horn Chips interview, ca. July 11, 1910, Camp Papers, BYU.

9. Sgt. Kelley, in *Crawford Tribune*, June 26, 1903.

10. Ibid.

11. On Worm's transfer, see Lt. Jesse M. Lee to Lt. C. A. Johnson, May 29, 1877, STA, LS, 1876–77, vol. 2, 370–71, BIA, NACPR; and "May 30 Transferred from Sp Tail," Census of Indians, May 21, 1877, RCA, PRAP. The lodges accompanying Worm's were those of Yankton; Tall Woman (including Human Finger Necklace); and Foolish Heart.

12. The tally of people stampeding from Crazy Horse's village to Spotted Tail Agency in the wake of the war chief's death includes several men who may be confidently identified as transfers to Crazy Horse from the agency bands—e.g., Throw Him Away (from Payabya); Horse Thief, Bear Brain (Spleen); Good Horse (Kiyuksa), Back, Fox, and Quiver (Wazhazha). No Bad Faces or Loafers are identifiable. "List of Indians transferred from other Agencys [*sic*]," STA 1877 census, 63ff., BIA, NACPR.

13. *Omaha Daily Republican*, July 13, 1877.

14. Clark to Lt. W. S. Schuyler, June 10, 1877, SW File.

15. *Omaha Daily Republican*, July 13, 1877.

16. Clark to Schuyler, June 11, 1877, SW File.

17. Clark to Schuyler, June 13, 1877, SW File.

18. Ibid.; Clark to Schuyler, June 10, 1877.

19. Bettelyoun and Waggoner, *With My Own Eyes*, 108–109.

20. Affidavit of [Amos] Charging First regarding capture and killing of Chief Crazy Horse, Crazy Horse Biography File. Charging First telescopes events, believing that this event led directly to Crazy Horse's return to Camp Robinson under guard and his death. The presence of Black Fox in the northern village at Spotted Tail indicates that it took place prior to the first week of July (see chapter 23).

21. Garnett interview, tablet 2, Ricker Papers; James S. Irwin to CoIA, Aug. 25, 1877, in ARCoIA 1877. The latter source gives 1,100 as the population of the Crazy Horse village as of June 27, equivalent to 185 standard lodges. Garnett indicates the presence of satellite camps. The size of these camps is indicated by a consideration of the subsequent growth in the village. It peaked in late July–early August at about 250 lodges, including twenty-three lodges officially transferred from Spotted Tail early in July. Some forty lodges therefore remain unaccounted for. While details are lacking, most of these must be increments from the Oglala agency bands at or immediately after the Sun Dance. Some, possibly most, of these families should represent northern Oglalas who surrendered piecemeal before Crazy Horse.

22. Garnett interview, tablet 2, Ricker Papers; W. P. Clark, "Sun-Dance," *Indian Sign Language*; Bradley private journal, June 26 and 29, 1877, box 1, Bradley Papers. Dana Long Wolf recalled that "the dance was actually in charge of Chief Fool Heart and three other assistants whose names he does not now recall": W. O. Roberts, Supt. Pine Ridge Indian Agency, to Prof. E. P. Wilson, Chadron State College, June 13, 1940, copy provided by James A. Hanson, Museum of the Fur Trade, Chadron, Nebraska.

23. Garnett interview, tablet 2, Ricker Papers.

24. Ibid.; W. P. Clark, "Sun-Dance," *Indian Sign Language*; Bradley private journal, June 26 and 29, 1877, box 1, Bradley Papers (June 29 entry includes quotation); Roberts to Wilson, June 13, 1940.

25. Garnett interview, tablet 2, Ricker Papers; W. P. Clark, "Sun-Dance," *Indian Sign Language*; Bradley private journal, June 26 and 29, 1877, box 1, Bradley Papers; Roberts to Wilson, June 13, 1940.

26. Garnett interview, tablet 2, Ricker Papers; W. P. Clark, "Sun-Dance," *Indian Sign Language* (second quotation on 363); Bradley private journal, June 26 and 29, 1877, box 1, Bradley Papers (quotations from June 29); Roberts to Wilson, June 13, 1940.

27. Bradley journal, June 29, 1877.

28. W. P. Clark, *Indian Sign Language*, 363.

29. Lt. Col. P. Lugenbeel to AAG, Dept. of Dakota, June 13, 1877, Military Division of the Missouri, LR, AGO; Report of special commission to select homes for Red Cloud and Spotted Tail Indians, in Board of Indian Commissioners, 9th Annual Report, ARCoIA 1877.

CHAPTER 23

1. On the timing of the Miniconjou–Sans Arc Sun Dance, Spotted Tail Agent Lee noted that it was "in full operation" as he penned his report, Jesse M. Lee to CoIA, June 30, 1877, STA, LR, OIA. For oral tradition regarding the dance, see James M. Chase in Morning and Alfred Ribman, in Kadlecek and Kadlecek, *To Kill an Eagle*, 91–93, 143–44, also ibid., chapter 4. It is noteworthy that Kicking Bear and his brothers had evidently surrendered at Spotted Tail. Members of the Wakan tiyospaye of the Oyuhpe band, they were closely related to the Miniconjous. Kicking Bear's first marriage was to a Sans Arc woman.

2. Garnett interview, tablet 2, Ricker Papers.

3. Jesse M. Lee to CoIA, Aug. 2, 1877, STA, LR, OIA (includes enumeration of Elk Head camp, for a total of twenty-two (sic) lodges: thirteen Miniconjou, five Sans Arc, three Oglala, one Hunkpapa). The Red Cloud agent told Lee on July 7 that the party had arrived "since the Sun Dance": James S. Irwin to Jesse M. Lee, July 7, 1877, STA, LS, BIA, NACPR.

4. Irwin to CoIA, Sept. 6, 1877, RCA Letterbook, NACPR; Irwin to Lee, July 7, 1877.

5. These figures set a new baseline for the Crazy Horse village population. The numbers of Miniconjous, Brules, and Sans Arcs are rounded approximations derived from the Crazy Horse village lodges noted as transferred or fleeing from Red Cloud to Spotted Tail in the crisis period August 26–Sept. 16: see "List of Indians transferred from other Agencys [*sic*]," STA 1877 census, 63–71, BIA, NACPR. In addition to these people, sixty-six lodges of Oglalas (mainly Oyuhpes) joined in the flight. The flight left a rump northern village at Red Cloud Agency, all Oglalas, totaling approximately seventy-five lodges.

6. Registers of Enlistment in the U.S. Army: Indian Scouts, 1866–1877, AGO. I am indebted to friends Ephriam D. Dickson III and Bob Lee in compiling these data.

7. Bradley to Crook, July 16, 1877, LR, AGO.

8. Registers of Enlistment.

9. Bradley to Crook, July 16, 1877. Clark's preferment of Crazy Horse and his de facto demotion of Red Cloud seem the best context in which to understand persistent oral traditions that Crazy Horse was to be recognized by the government as the Oglala head chief. See, e.g., Little Killer, in Riley, "Oglala Sources," 44; White Rabbit, in Standing Bear, *Land of the Spotted Eagle*, 181; and Standing Bear's own remarks in ibid., 179.

10. *New York Tribune*, Sept. 7, 1877.

11. Bradley to Crook, July 16, 1877. On Clark's absence, see Camp Robinson post returns, July 1877, Fort Robinson Museum, Crawford, Nebraska. While absent, Clark remained on active duty at forts Laramie and Sanders.

12. Short Bull and He Dog, in Riley, "Oglala Sources," 25, 40.

13. Riley, "Oglala Sources," 51, editorial note 42. This statement probably reflects Hinman's conversations with interpreter John Colhoff. Hinman remarks that: "The Indians interviewed seem to have been reluctant to state these suspicions in so many words to the white interviewer."

14. Little Killer, in Riley, "Oglala Sources," 44.

15. Bradley to Crook, July 16, 1877.

16. Crazy Horse quotation from He Dog, in Riley, "Oglala Sources," 24; Bradley to Crook, July 16, 1877.

17. Clark to Crook, Aug. 1, 1877, LR, AGO.

18. Irwin to CoIA, Sept. 7, 1877, in Misc. LS by Pine Ridge Agency, 1876–1914, BIA, NACPR. This is Irwin's delayed monthly report for July, actually penned after the death of Crazy Horse.

19. On the Larrabee family, see Red Cloud Agency 1876 and 1877 registers, in Buecker and Paul, *Crazy Horse Surrender Ledger*, 41, 58. Additional details from Rosebud Agency 1887 census, BIA, NARS. For a 1944 statement by Nellie's younger brother Tom Larrabee, see Bordeaux, *Custer's Conqueror*, 97–98. Lemly, "Passing of Crazy Horse," contains some interesting if garbled details. Lemly, stationed at Camp Robinson, mistakenly believed that Nellie was the daughter of Louis Richard. See also Garnett interview, tablet 2, Ricker Papers.

20. Garnett interview, tablet 2, Ricker Papers; Lemly, "Passing of Crazy Horse," 318.

21. Garnett interview, tablet 2, and Pourier interview, tablet 13, Ricker Papers.

22. Irwin to CoIA, Sept. 7, 1877.

23. Mrs. Carrie Slow Bear (a.k.a. Many White Horses, Red Cloud's daughter), in Riley, "Oglala Sources," 42.

24. Maj. Daniel W. Burke to AAG, Dept. of the Platte, July 23, 1877; Bradley to AAG, Dept. of the Platte, July 23, 1877 (telegram), SW File; Jesse M. Lee to CoIA, Aug. 2, 1877, STA, LR, OIA.

25. Benjamin R. Shopp to CoIA, Aug. 15, 1877, RCA, LR, OIA.

26. Ibid.

27. Irwin to CoIA, Aug. 5 (telegram) and Aug. 11, 1877, RCA, LR, OIA; Irwin to CoIA, Sept. 7, 1877 ; Clark to Crook, Aug. 1, 1877. These sources strongly suggest that the military census conducted February through May was essentially complete. After transfers and late surrenders, the July 1 population at Red Cloud approximated 5,700 people. Irwin's new count raised this figure to 6,536. Subsequent counts continued the trend. At the end of his tenure, he transferred to V. T. McGillycuddy a ration book that tabulated 7,038 Indians at Pine Ridge Agency in March 1879—an overcounting of approximately 65 percent.

28. Shopp to CoIA, Aug. 15, 1877.

CHAPTER 24

1. "Billy Hunter's Account," Bourke diary, vol. 24, 78.

2. Clark to Crook, Aug. 1, 1877, LRAGO.

3. Bourke diary, vol. 24, 54.

4. Clark to Crook, Aug. 18, 1877, in Bourke diary, vol. 24, 72–76. At both Red Cloud and Spotted Tail agencies, the chiefs insisted that a larger delegation be approved. Ultimately, twenty-one Lakota and three Arapaho delegates made the trip.

5. Ibid., quotation at 73. For additional details, see "Billy Hunter's Account."

6. Julia Iron Cedar Woman (Mrs. Amos Clown), in Bordeaux, *Custer's Conqueror*, 70.

7. Ibid. On dating: the most precise statement about the date of Crazy Horse and Nellie's marriage is that of Victoria Conroy (Standing Bear), a granddaughter of Worm's sister. She stated in 1934 that Crazy Horse and Nellie had been married for "a month or so when he was killed." See Hardorff, *Oglala Lakota Crazy Horse*, 30. The marriage therefore took place in late July or early August. Iron Cedar's reminiscence discloses that Nellie rode to Crazy Horse's village on a day when the war chief was absent at a council with Lt. Clark. The only known councils in the correct frame are those of July 27 and August 3–4. Although either date might be possible, Garnett's indication that Crazy Horse's alienation immediately followed his association with Nellie Larrabee suggests that the later dating is correct.

8. Julia Iron Cedar Woman, in Bordeaux, *Custer's Conqueror*, 70

9. Tom Larrabee, in ibid., 98.

10. J. M. Lee, "Capture and Death," 323.

11. Such a move is directly affirmed by Garnett, whose 1878 account states that "the Indians had started on the hunt": "Billy Hunter's Account," Bourke diary, vol. 24, 78. He Dog's reminiscence shows that the village had moved to Little Cottonwood Creek before his own defection to join Red Cloud, during the second week of August. He Dog, in Riley, "Oglala Sources," 20.

12. Crazy Horse, undated [Aug. 1877], in J. M. Lee, "Capture and Death," 327. Lee's rendering is derived from a mid-August letter from Clark to Lee. Its context fits either the council of August 3–4, or, more likely, Clark's subsequent visit to Crazy Horse's village.

13. "Billy Hunter's Account," 78. The Camp Robinson post returns for Aug. 1877, Fort Robinson Museum, detail the paymaster's Aug. 7 visit.

14. Crazy Horse, in J. M. Lee, "Capture and Death," 327.

15. Clark to Crook, Aug. 18, 1877, in Bourke diary, vol. 24, 73; DeBarthe, *Frank Grouard*, 182. Grouard returned to Red Cloud Agency early in August after scouting duties in the Powder River country.

16. Garnett interview, tablet 2, Ricker Papers. On Crazy Horse's lack of sleep from about the second week of August, see Spotted Tail, in Lucy W. Lee's newspaper account of the death of Crazy Horse, reprinted in Brininstool, *Crazy Horse*, 62–71.

17. He Dog, in Riley, "Oglala Sources," 25; Garnett interview, tablet 2, Ricker Papers.

18. Clark to Crook, Aug. 18, 1877.

19. He Dog, in Riley, "Oglala Sources," 20.

20. J. M. Lee, "Capture and Death," 327.

21. For this week, see "Billy Hunter's Account," 78–79. On spies, see especially W. P. Clark, "Court," *Indian Sign Language*, 130. Little Wolf belonged to the Oyuhpe band and had come in from the hunting grounds to Red Cloud Agency in spring 1875, in the company of Frank Grouard.

22. Shopp to CoIA, Aug. 15, 1877, RCA, LR, OIA.

23. He Dog, in Riley, "Oglala Sources," 20. See also Short Bull, in ibid., 40. Details are also taken from R. A. Clark, *Killing of Chief Crazy Horse*, 49–68, especially 60. He Dog's defection preceded August 18, when Clark remarked that He Dog had "joined Red Cloud" (Clark to Crook, Aug. 18, 1877).

24. "Billy Hunter's Account," 79.

25. Bradley to AG, Dept. of the Platte, Aug. 15, 1877 (telegram), in Bourke diary, vol. 24, 54.

26. Details on Crazy Horse's embassy to the northern village at Spotted Tail Agency are from Clark to Crook, Aug. 18, 1877; Maj. Daniel W. Burke to Bradley, Aug. 16, 1877, folder A, Bradley Papers (transcripts at Fort Robinson Museum, Crawford, Nebraska).

27. American Horse, in Irwin to CoIA, Sept. 1, 1877, RCA, LR, OIA.

28. Burke to Bradley, Aug. 16, 1877.

29. Minutes of Lakota speeches made in Washington in September reveal how united was the Spotted Tail Agency line on agency location. See 1877 delegation proceedings, DS, LR, OIA.

30. Capt. E. A. Koerper, Surgeon, to AG, Dist. of Black Hills, Aug. 20, 1877, STA, LR, OIA.

31. Clark to Crook, Aug. 18, 1877. Unless otherwise noted, subsequent quotations on the August 17–18 councils are from this source.

32. Lucy W. Lee account, in Brininstool, *Crazy Horse*, 68.

33. He Dog, Riley, "Oglala Sources," 25.

34. Clark to Crook, Aug. 18, 1877.

35. Irwin to CoIA, Aug. 25, 1877, in ARCoIA, 1877.

36. Ibid.

37. Clark to Crook, Aug. 18, 1877, indicates the comparative status of the Deciders at this time, showing changes from the situation in the spring as outlined by Bourke. See Bourke diary, vol. 20, 1984–85, 1992; also *Army and Navy Journal*, May 12, 1877.

38. On the friendship of Little Big Man and Big Road, see Little Big Man to the "President of U.S.," Aug. 1, 1878, enclosed with James R. O'Beirne to CoIA, Aug. 27, 1878, RCA, LR, OIA.

39. Clark to Crook, Aug. 18, 1877.

40. For Clark's ban on the hunt, see Bourke diary, vol. 24, 54–55. American Horse (in Irwin to CoIA, Sept. 1, 1877, RCA, LR, OIA) dates the formation of the Oglala tribal camp to ten or twelve days prior to August 31.

41. J. M. Lee, "Capture and Death," 326.

42. James Irwin to CoIA, Aug. 31, 1877, RCA, LR, OIA. Irwin also asserts that Crazy Horse was "lordly and dictatorial with his own people and other bands of Sioux at this *and Spotted Tail Agency*" (my emphasis). The unstated context is presumably related to the linked hunt and delegation issues.

43. American Horse, Irwin to CoIA, Sept. 1, 1877.

44. Ibid.

45. See, e.g., speeches of Big Road and Little Big Man to the president, Sept. 25, 1877, DS, LR, OIA.

46. Miles to AAG, Dept. of Dakota, Aug. 16, 1877 (telegram), Main Series, LR, AGO.

47. The flurry of telegrams generated by the "Sitting Bull Returns!" rumor can be examined in the correspondence files of the Office of the Adjutant General. On September 9 Sheridan finally wired Washington that "General Gibbon has positive information that Sitting Bull is still north of the line and apparently has no intention of coming south."

48. Bradley to Mrs. Bradley, Sept. 6, 1877, folder F, box 2, Bradley Papers; AAG, Dept. of the Platte to Sheridan, Aug. 27, 1877 (telegram), LRAGO.

49. One lodge of Oglalas, head of the family Plenty Horses, was transferred to Spotted Tail Agency on August 25. On August 26, as the crisis deepened, one lodge of Brule (Guts, Brule Loafer band) and one more of Oglalas (Kills the Punch) were also transferred. See "List of Indians transferred from other Agencys [sic]," STA 1877 census, 63, BIA, NACPR. I surmise that by August 31, approximately twenty lodges had followed He Dog from Crazy Horse's village and assimilated to the Oglala tribal village.

50. Bradley to Mrs. Bradley, Sept. 6, 1877. See also Bradley private journal, August 31, 1877.

51. Sandoz, Crazy Horse, 387–91, established the paradigm apologia for Crazy Horse, followed by, e.g., Ambrose, Crazy Horse and Custer, 465–67. By contrast, purely military historians tend to reproduce uncritically the undoctored rumors of the day.

52. See Walker, Lakota Society, 86.

53. For details of Black Fox's role, and those of Kicking Bear and Shell Boy (Last-Born members) on September 4, see chapter 28.

54. New York Tribune, Sept. 7, 1877.

CHAPTER 25

1. The Nez Perce war is most comprehensively treated in Greene, Nez Perce Summer, 1877. An excellent overview is Utley, Frontier Regulars, chap. 16.

2. Sheridan to Williams, AAG, Dept. of the Platte, Aug. 28, 1877 (two telegrams); Williams to Sheridan, Aug. 27, 1877 (telegram); same to same Aug. 28, 1877 (telegram); Sheridan to Crook, Aug. 28, 1877 (telegram); all in Sioux War Papers.

3. Sheridan to Crook, Aug. 28, 1877 (telegram); Williams, Dept. of the Platte to Sheridan, Aug. 29, 1877 (telegram); Sheridan to Williams, Aug. 29, 1877 (telegram), Sioux War Papers.

4. Bradley to AG, Dept. of the Platte, Aug. 31, 1877 (telegram; copy in Fort Robinson Museum).

5. Ibid.; Clark to AG, Dept. of the Platte, incorporated in Williams, Dept. of the Platte to Crook, Aug. 30, 1877 (telegram); Sheridan to Williams, Aug. 30, 1877 (two telegrams); Williams to Sheridan, Aug. 30, 1877 (telegram), all in Sioux War Papers. Billy Garnett, Red Cloud Agency interpreter, seems to have handled some of the arrangements with the agency Oglala chiefs for Clark.

6. Garnett interview, tablet 2, Ricker Papers.

7. Lt. Jesse M. Lee to CoIA, Sept. 30, 1877, STA, LS, BIA NACPR; J. M. Lee, "Capture and Death," 328.

8. Col. Thomas M. Anderson, "Army Episodes and Anecdotes," 34, Coe Papers (typescript at Fort Robinson Museum).

9. Ibid.; "Billy Hunter's Account," Bourke diary, v ol. 24, 79–80; Garnett interview, tablet 2, Ricker Papers.

10. "Billy Hunter's Account," 80.

11. Ibid.

12. Red Feather, in Riley, "Oglala Sources," 30.

13. Garnett interview, tablet 2, Ricker Papers; DeBarthe, Frank Grouard, 175–76. Grouard's account, self-serving and melodramatized by DeBarthe, is silent on his own complicity or incompetence. Nevertheless, key factual details square with Garnett's lengthy retrospective account.

14. Gen. Jesse M. Lee, interview by Walter M. Camp, Oct. 27, 1912, folder 116, Camp Field Notes, Camp Papers, BYU.

15. Ibid.

16. Crazy Horse, in Brininstool, Crazy Horse, 68–69.

17. Louis Bordeaux, affidavit statement before Mellette Co. Judge, South Dakota, Oct. 9, 1912, in "Story of the Death of Crazy Horse, A Noted Chief of the Northern Oglala Sioux, at Fort Robinson, Sept. 6th [*sic*] 1877," South Dakota State Historical Society, Pierre. This affidavit was made to support Jesse Lee's bid for the Congressional Medal of Honor in recognition of his conduct during the Crazy Horse crisis.

18. Louis Bordeaux, interview by Eli. S. Ricker, Aug. 30, 1907, tablet 11, Ricker Papers.

19. Garnett interview, tablet 2, Ricker Papers.

20. Bourke diary, vol. 24, 38.

21. Clark to CoIA, Sept. 10, 1877, STA, LR, OIA.

22. *Army and Navy Journal*, Sept. 15, 1877.

23. "Billy Hunter's Account," 80.

24. Bourke diary, vol. 24, 37.

25. R. A. Clark, *Killing of Chief Crazy Horse*, 75–100 (quotation at 76).

26. Col. Thomas M. Anderson, "Army Episodes and Anecdotes," 34–35.

27. See chapters 26–27 for full analysis of alleged plots and conspiracies against Crazy Horse.

28. Lee interview, Oct. 27, 1912.

29. Bordeaux affidavit statement, Oct. 9, 1912.

30. V. T. McGillycuddy, in Brininstool, "How 'Crazy Horse' Died," 34. This statement derives from information given McGillycuddy by an anonymous interpreter (elsewhere identified as Louis Bordeaux) on the evening of Sept. 2, 1877.

31. Ibid.

32. DeBarthe, *Frank Grouard*, 176.

33. Ibid.

34. Garnett interview, tablet 2, Ricker Papers. All subsequent details and quotations from the meeting with Clark are derived from this source.

35. Clark to Burke, Aug. 31, 1877, in J. M. Lee, "Capture and Death," 328.

36. Bradley to Sheridan, Aug. 31, 1877 (telegram), Sioux War Papers; *Army and Navy Journal*, Sept. 15, 1877. For a concise overview of these events, see Hedren, *Fort Laramie in 1876*, 231, with documentation on troop movements.

37. Bradley to Sheridan, Aug. 31, 1877 (telegram), Sioux War Papers; Sheridan to Sec. War, Sept. 1, 1877 (telegram), Sioux War Papers.

38. American Horse, in James Irwin to CoIA, Sept. 1, 1877.

39. Irwin to CoIA, Sept. 1, 1877.

40. Details are fragmentary, but see Bradley to Sheridan, Aug. 31, 1877 (telegram), Sioux War Papers; Sheridan to Sec. War, Sept. 1, 1877 (telegram), Sioux War Papers; also Sheridan to AAG, Dept. of the Platte, Aug. 31, 1877 (telegram); Sheridan to Crook, Aug. 31, 1877 (telegram); Sheridan to Bradley, Aug. 31, 1877 (telegram), Sioux War Papers.

41. Bradley to Sheridan, Aug. 31, 1877, and Sheridan to Sec. War, Sept. 1, 1877, suggest the reconstruction that Crazy Horse issued an order during the evening or night of August 31, "and prevented the scouts from going to join Hart's command" (Sheridan to Sec. War).

42. Crook to Sheridan, Aug. 31, 1877 (two telegrams); Sheridan to Crook, Aug. 31, 1877 (two telegrams); Sheridan to Bradley, Aug. 31, 1877 (telegram), Sioux War Papers.

43. Bradley to Sheridan, Aug. 31, 1877 (telegram), Sioux War Papers.

44. Crook to Bradley, Sept. 1, 1877 (telegram), Bourke diary, vol. 24, 57–58; Crook to Sheridan, Aug. 31, 1877 (telegram); Sheridan to Crook, Sept. 1, 1877 (telegram); Sheridan to Bradley, Sept. 1, 1877 (telegram); Crook to Sheridan, Sept. 1, 1877 (telegram), Sioux War Papers.

45. "Billy Hunter's Account," 80.

CHAPTER 26

1. Such an order is implied in Clark to CoIA, Sept. 10, 1877, STA, LR, OIA. Clark states that by September 4, any unauthorized departure for the "North . . . means war with them."

2. Bourke diary, vol. 24, 37–38.

3. For a tally of the Fast Bull camp enrolled at Spotted Tail Agency, August 27–September 11, 1877, see "List of Indians transferred from other Agencys [sic]," Spotted Tail Agency 1877 census, 63–65, 71, BIA, NACPR. The August 27 surrenders included Lame Deer's son No Butcher and his Sans Arc son-in-law Leader Eagle.

4. Fundamental to an understanding of the events of September 1–2 and the northern village split is an interview given by Gen. Crook aboard the Union Pacific westbound from Cheyenne on September 5. It appeared in the *Cheyenne Daily Leader* of September 6. I consulted a syndicated version of the story, *Omaha Daily Bee*, Sept. 8, 1877.

5. "List of Indians transferred from other Agencys [sic]," Spotted Tail Agency 1877 census, 64; also Irwin to J. M. Lee, Sept. 1, 1877, Miscellaneous LS, PRA, BIA, NACPR.

6. For July-August composition of Crazy Horse's village, see chapter 23.

7. J. M. Lee to CoIA, Sept. 30, 1877, LS, STA, NACPR; J. M. Lee, "Capture and Death," 328; Lee interview, Oct. 27, 1912, Camp Papers, BYU (includes quotation). Clark's claim reversed his position of the thirty-first, when he had advised Burke that Crazy Horse had been the bad influence on Touch the Clouds.

8. Lee to CoIA, Sept. 30, 1877; J. M. Lee, "Capture and Death," 328; Lee interview, Oct. 27, 1912, Camp Papers, BYU.

9. Bourke diary, vol. 24, 40.

10. Bradley to AG, Dept. of the Platte, Sept. 7, 1877, SW File;; Clark to Crook, Sept. 5, 1877 (telegram), in Bourke diary, vol. 24, 66. Some ambiguity remained on the issue of village dispersal, for on September 5 Clark wired Crook with details of Crazy Horse's arrest, letting slip that, far from being permanently broken up, the northern Oglala village was to be reorganized under more pliable leadership. This hints at private arrangements made between Clark and Little Big Man that Crook did not rule out of court.

11. He Dog, in Riley, "Oglala Sources," 20, 22, most clearly presents an Oglala perspective on Crook's arrival at Camp Robinson on September 2. He Dog states that "orders came for everybody to go over and camp beside the White [Crawford] Butte," located "a couple of miles east of Fort Robinson." The Garnett interview, tablet 2, Ricker Papers, locates the new village site as some two miles southeast of Red Cloud Agency. Spotted Tail was at Red Cloud Agency by the afternoon of September 3, holding confidential talks with Clark.

12. Ibid.; *Omaha Daily Bee*, Sept. 13, 1877 (includes quotations); Clark to CoIA, Sept. 10, 1877. On No Water's vow, see Red Feather, in Riley, "Oglala Sources," 26.

13. Direct knowledge of the embassy to the Crazy Horse village is confined to He Dog, in Riley, "Oglala Sources," 22–24. Crook's Sept. 5 interview, *Omaha Daily Bee*, Sept. 8, 1877, indicates the council's outcome in the breakup of the village.

14. J. M. Lee, "Capture and Death," 330; Lee interview, Oct. 27, 1912, Camp Papers, BYU (includes quotation).

15. Crazy Horse's absence from the council is evident from He Dog's recollection. For Nellie Larrabee's continued advice to her husband, see Bordeaux, *Custer's Conqueror*, 70–71, 74–75.

16. He Dog, in Riley, "Oglala Sources," 22–24. I have also used details from the account of He Dog set down by his son, Rev. Eagle Hawk, in R. A. Clark, *Killing of Chief Crazy Horse*, 60–61.

17. He Dog, interpreter John Colhoff, and Eleanor Hinman struggled over the identities of the two officers. Hinman equated He Dog's "soldier chief from Fort Laramie" with Bradley.

Although Bradley had been stationed at Fort Laramie earlier in the year, he had been commanding at Camp Robinson since late May, and both Crazy Horse and He Dog would have had no trouble recognizing him. The second officer He Dog identified by his Lakota name, and Colhoff tentatively identified him as "D. H. Russell"—otherwise unknown.

18. Crazy Horse's absence from the village, a common enough occurrence, is implied by his nonappearance at the council with the Oglala envoys.

19. He Dog, in Riley, "Oglala Sources," 22.

20. Ibid., 22–24.

21. Ibid.; also, details from R. A. Clark, *Killing of Chief Crazy Horse*, 60–61.

22. This outcome of the council is indicated in Crook's interview (*Cheyenne Daily Leader*, Sept. 6, 1877; syndicated in *Omaha Daily Bee*, Sept. 8, 1877). Big Road and Iron Crow (a.k.a. Jumping Shield) were named among the Lakota leaders who assisted in attempting Crazy Horse's arrest on September 4 (see Clark to CoIA, Sept. 10, 1877; also Bradley to AG, Dept. of the Platte, Sept. 7, 1877). Little Hawk was not so named, and thus probably remained with Crazy Horse, September 2–4.

23. Crook interview, *Omaha Daily Bee*, Sept. 8, 1877.

24. As rounded approximations, 115 northern Oglala lodges, and 100 lodges of Miniconjous, Brules, and Sans Arcs composed Crazy Horse's village from late August through September 2. Very roughly, the Oglalas broke down as fifteen Hunkpatila lodges; thirty Bad Face lodges; sixty Oyuhpe lodges; and ten lodges of agency bands. Most of the Hunkpatila and perhaps twenty more lodges, chiefly Oyuhpe, remained loyal to the war chief. The line dividing Oyuhpe from Miniconjou is very blurred. Kicking Bear and his brother Black Fox, key aides to Crazy Horse, belonged to a leading family of the Wakan tiyospaye, an Oyuhpe subband with sister lineages among the Miniconjou, Sans Arc, and Hunkpapa tribal divisions.

25. Bourke diary, vol. 24, 40–41. See also Bradley to AG, Dept. of the Platte, Sept. 7, 1877; Crook interview, *Omaha Daily Bee*, Sept. 8, 1877; Bradley private journal, Sept. 2, 1877.

26. Bourke diary, vol. 24, 43.

27. He Dog, in Riley, "Oglala Sources," 24.

28. Lee interview, Oct. 27, 1912, Camp Papers, BYU; Lucy W. Lee, dispatch to the Greencastle, Indiana, *Star*, Sept. 18, 1877, reprinted in Brininstool, *Crazy Horse*, 70 (includes quotation).

CHAPTER 27

1. On the mood in the northern village, see Gen. Crook interview, *Omaha Daily Bee*, Sept. 8, 1877.

2. Bourke diary, vol. 24, 43.

3. Red Feather, in Riley, "Oglala Sources," 26.

4. The most important eyewitness statements on Woman Dress's intervention with Crook are by Billy Garnett. This account synthesizes details from the Garnett interview, tablet 2, Ricker Papers; R. A. Clark, *Killing of Chief Crazy Horse*, 77–78; and "Billy Hunter's Account," Bourke diary, vol. 24, 80–81. See also Bourke diary, vol. 24, 43–44, and Bourke, *On the Border with Crook*, 420.

5. In later years, both Little Wolf and Lone Bear would deny circulating such reports. Garnett and Pourier, who retained an interest in events not redounding to their credit, placed the blame squarely on the shoulders of Woman Dress (see Garnett interview, tablet 2, Ricker Papers). This is probably simplistic scapegoating: as Clark's spies, Little Wolf, Lone Bear, Long Chin, Woman Dress, and Frank Grouard were all involved in reporting on Crazy Horse.

6. R. A. Clark, *Killing of Chief Crazy Horse*, 77–78; Garnett interview, tablet 2, Ricker Papers.

7. R. A. Clark, *Killing of Chief Crazy Horse*, 77–78.

8. "Billy Hunter's Account"; Bourke diary, vol. 24, 81; Bourke, *On the Border with Crook*, 420.

9. Our fullest accounts of Crook's talk with the Oglala chiefs are by Billy Garnett (Garnett interview, tablet 2, Ricker Papers; R. A. Clark, *Killing of Chief Crazy Horse*, 77–78). Details are also derived from Bourke's diary and published account (Bourke diary, vol. 24, 43–44, and Bourke, *On the Border with Crook*, 420).

10. Bourke, *On the Border with Crook*, 420. In his diary Bourke records that the chiefs' proposal to kill Crazy Horse was "agreed to by the others" present but was overruled by Crook. (vol. 24, 81).

11. Apart from approving Bradley's change of plan later that evening, Crook seems to have played no further direct role in the plan to arrest Crazy Horse. He may have been preoccupied with incoming intelligence on the Nez Perce campaign prior to his departure, before daylight of September 4, for the Union Pacific at Cheyenne.

12. Garnett, an eyewitness, recalled the figure of three hundred dollars: R. A. Clark, *Killing of Chief Crazy Horse*, 79–80. Red Feather, not present, gave a figure of one hundred dollars: Red Feather, in Riley, "Oglala Sources," 27–28.

13. R. A. Clark, *Killing of Chief Crazy Horse*, 61.

14. Red Feather, in Riley, "Oglala Sources," 32; He Dog, ibid., 24. For details on Garnett's later questioning of Little Wolf and Woman Dress, see Garnett interview, tablet 2, Ricker Papers; and R. A. Clark, *Killing of Chief Crazy Horse*, 96–99.

15. Bourke, *On the Border with Crook*, 420.

16. Red Feather, in Riley, "Oglala Sources," 32.

17. Eagle Elk, in John Colhoff to Joseph Balmer, May 3, 1950 (transcript in author's collection). Eagle Elk's account of the abduction of Nellie Larrabee has no dating, but the fragmentary accounts of Crazy Horse's second marriage indicate that she was with him up to the eve of his flight to Spotted Tail Agency. The chronology seems to fit September 3 when, as the Oglala chiefs candidly revealed to Gen. Crook, elements of the agency bands were ready to force a crisis in the depleted northern village and to assassinate Crazy Horse.

18. Ibid.

19. Quotations from Gen. Crook interview, *Omaha Daily Bee*, Sept. 8, 1877.

20. Billy Garnett's accounts are once again the fullest source. See Garnett interview, tablet 2, Ricker Papers; R. A. Clark, *Killing of Chief Crazy Horse*, 80–81. Billy inflates his own role, indicating that Bradley had no inkling of the afternoon's talk between Crook and the Oglalas. Bradley was possibly trying to assess Clark's off-the-record discussions.

21. In his official report on the attempted arrest and killing of Crazy Horse, Bradley states that his final dispositions were made on Crook's orders. See Bradley to AG, Dept. of the Platte, Sept. 7, 1877, SW File.

22. J. M. Lee, "Capture and Death," 331; Lee interview, Oct. 27, 1912.

23. R. A. Clark, *Killing of Chief Crazy Horse*, 80–81.

24. Ibid. See also Garnett interview, tablet 2, Ricker Papers.

25. Red Feather, in Riley, "Oglala Sources," 28. To fight armed with only a knife was a heyoka practice.

CHAPTER 28

1. Red Feather, in Riley, "Oglala Sources," 24.

2. It is difficult to quantify precisely the breakup of Crazy Horse's village during the night and morning of September 3–4. The critical facts are that on September 3, it counted one hundred lodges, but by noon of the 4th, after the arrest operation, Lt. Col. Bradley stated that "about half of the village (40) odd lodges" were present: Bradley to Crook, Sept. 4, 1877 (telegram; transcript at Fort Robinson Museum). Thus, at least fifty lodges had left. Clark stated that "Quite a number of lodges of Crazy Horse's band left here last night" (i.e., left Red Cloud for Spotted Tail), and the "rest commenced moving early this morning before we started" (at 9:00), a process continuing until Crazy Horse's own departure about 10:00 A.M., "some going to camps here and quite a number to Spotted Tail": Clark to Crook, Sept. 4, 1877 (telegram), Bourke diary, vol. 24, 59–60. Bourke's diary account (vol. 24, 47), assembled a year later, asserts that seventy-three lodges were still in the village on the morning of the 4th, and that over fifty were captured by noon, the remainder escaping to Spotted Tail. I suggest that about thirty lodges joined the agency Oglalas, and at least twenty headed toward Spotted Tail. Of the latter, several were brought in by Oglala scouts and volunteers during the night of September 4–5: AAG, Dept. of the Platte, to AAG, Div. of the Missouri, Sept. 5, 1877 (telegram; copy in Fort Robinson Museum). Newspaper accounts also assign "about 50 lodges" to the village by September 5, (*New York Times*, Sept. 19, 1877).

3. R. A. Clark, *Killing of Chief Crazy Horse*, 61–62.

4. Ibid.

5. Garnett interview, tablet 2, Ricker Papers, states that on September 4, agency and northern Oglalas formed a single village just south of the agency compound. These moves were clearly planned during the night council. Little Big Man's mission is indicated by the fact he is not named among the chiefs and headmen directly participating in the arresting party (see *Army and Navy Journal*, Sept. 15, 1877; AAG, Dept. of the Platte to AAG, Div. of the Missouri, Sept. 5, 1877, [telegram]; Bradley to AG, Dept. of the Platte, Sept. 7, 1877, SW File; Clark to CoIA, Sept. 10, 1877, STA, LR, OIA.)); instead, Garnett shows him riding between the northern village and the column, apprising the latter of developments.

6. On "Bad Miniconjous," see Twitchell, "Camp Robinson Letters," 94. For quotations, see *New York Tribune*, Sept. 11, 1877.

7. The most precise account of the formation of the arresting party is in *Army and Navy Journal*, Sept. 15, 1877. Bradley estimated "about 350 friendly Indians" (Lakotas only?) participated: AAG, Dept. of the Platte, to AAG, Div. of the Missouri, Sept. 5, 1877 (telegram). Garnett stated to Ricker that all the Oglala leaders who had spoken to Crook on the third participated: reports indicate the involvement of Red Cloud, Little Wound, Young Man Afraid of His Horse, American Horse, and Yellow Bear (Oglala chiefs); Three Bears, No Flesh, and No Water (Oglala war leaders); Big Road and Iron Crow (northern village chiefs); Sharp Nose and Black Coal (Arapahos). See Bradley to AG, Dept. of the Platte, Sept. 7, 1877; also Clark to CoIA, Sept. 10, 1877.

8. *Army and Navy Journal*, Sept. 15, 1877.

9. Quotation from ibid. Garnett interview, tablet 2, Ricker Papers, is the most important source for Oglala dispositions on the march from Camp Robinson. Garnett states that the Kiyuksa warriors rode on the north bank, although the band chief, Little Wound, was evidently with the line of Deciders heading the right-wing column. Eagle Hawk's account assigns to Three Bears the leadership of the scouts but confuses the wing assignments: R. A. Clark, *Killing of Chief Crazy Horse*, 62. No Water was one of the key akicita riding with the right wing.

10. Garnett interview, tablet 2, Ricker Papers; R. A. Clark, *Killing of Chief Crazy Horse*, 62 (with corrections to wing assignments).

11. *Army and Navy Journal*, Sept. 15, 1877. On Crazy Bear, of the Siksicela band, see R. A. Clark, *Killing of Chief Crazy Horse*, 62.

12. Bradley stated that "when the command got out to the [camp]ground, there were but few lodges to be seen and those making for the bluffs": Bradley to Crook, Sept. 4, 1877 (telegram).

13. Clark to Crook, Sept. 4, 1877 (telegram). Red Feather stated that: "When the soldiers were coming I went out to meet them," indicating his status as messenger. Red Feather, in Riley, "Oglala Sources," 24.

14. Garnett interview, tablet 2, Ricker Papers, shows that Crazy Horse and Black Shawl left with Kicking Bear and Shell Boy minutes ahead of the troops and scouts, who probably approached the village soon after 10:00 A.M. On Black Shawl's family at Spotted Tail, see Red Feather, in Riley, "Oglala Sources," 24.

15. On the surrender of Shedding Bear and Low Dog, see J. M. Lee, "Capture and Death," 330–31; Lee interview, Oct. 17, 1912. "List of Indians transferred from other Agencys [sic]," Spotted Tail Agency 1877 census, 63–64, tallies the group, naming all heads of families and adult males.

16. R. A. Clark, *Killing of Chief Crazy Horse*, 81.

17. Ibid., 81–82. Looking Horse belonged to the Cheyenne River Agency, according to Garnett. Not enumerated in the roll of Lakotas surrendering at Red Cloud, he perhaps surrendered with the Miniconjous at Spotted Tail Agency. Nevertheless, he was one of the scouts first enrolled with Crazy Horse on May 12. He may have been the Looking Horse living as one of five unmarried men in Roman Nose's Miniconjou lodge at the time of the June-July census (see Spotted Tail Agency 1877 census, 46) and thus one of Roman Nose's "sons."

18. R. A. Clark, *Killing of Chief Crazy Horse*, 62–63, 82, identifies Buffalo Dance, rather than Woman Dress, as the shooter of Looking Horse's mount. White Cow Killer (born 1831) belonged to the Oglala Spleen band and was keeper of the band's winter count.

19. R. A. Clark, *Killing of Chief Crazy Horse*, 82.

20. Ibid.; Garnett interview, tablet 2, Ricker Papers; *Army and Navy Journal*, Sept. 15, 1877.

21. R. A. Clark, *Killing of Chief Crazy Horse*, 82–83; Garnett interview, tablet 2, Ricker Papers; R. A. Clark, *Killing of Chief Crazy Horse*, 62–63, identifies the youth. As "Crawfish," he appears among the Sans Arcs on the roll of Lakotas "[s]tampeded from Red Cloud Agency" in the aftermath of Crazy Horse's death: Spotted Tail Agency 1877 census, 70.

22. R. A. Clark, *Killing of Chief Crazy Horse*, 82–83; Garnett interview, Ricker Papers; R. A. Clark, *Killing of Chief Crazy Horse*, 62–63: Black Fox's speech from Garnett interview, tablet 2, Ricker Papers; American Horse's quotation from R. A. Clark, *Killing of Chief Crazy Horse*, 83.

23. R. A. Clark, *Killing of Chief Crazy Horse*, 62–63, 82–83; Garnett interview, Ricker Papers. Black Fox's quotation from Garnett interview, tablet 2, Ricker Papers.

24. R. A. Clark, *Killing of Chief Crazy Horse*, 62–63, 82–83; Garnett interview, Ricker Papers. Black Fox's quotations synthesized from the two Garnett accounts. For Garnett's assessment of Black Fox's leadership (with quotation), see R. A. Clark, *Killing of Chief Crazy Horse*, 84.

25. Bradley to Crook, Sept. 4, 1877 (telegram); and Clark to Crook, Sept. 4, 1877 (telegram), Bourke diary, vol. 24, 59–60, which indicate that Clark initially ordered both No Flesh and No Water to lead ten-man details in pursuit. Garnett told Ricker that thirty Scouts followed No Flesh and twenty-five followed No Water. On No Flesh's intent to kill Crazy Horse, see Finerty, *War-Path and Bivouac*, 222.

26. Clark to Crook, Sept. 4, 1877 (includes quotation); Bradley to Crook, Sept. 4, 1877 (telegram); AAG, Dept. of the Platte to AAG, Div. of the Missouri, Sept. 5, 1877 (telegram); Clark to "Dear Lee" [Sept. 4, 1877], in J. M. Lee, "Capture and Death," 334. The latter report was received at Spotted Tail Agency about 4:15 P.M. In it Clark states that Crazy Horse's village "is just [now] going into camp" at Red Cloud Agency, at about 12:15 P.M., four hours (the standard express rate between the agencies) before the note reached Lee.

27. Spotted Tail Agency 1877 census, 1–61, lists all families at the Brule agency in June–July.

28. Lee to CoIA, Sept. 30, 1877, LS, STA, NACPR; J. M. Lee, "Capture and Death," 331–32; Lee, interview, Oct. 17, 1912. Lee's contemporary report states that he arrived at his agency at noon; his reminiscent accounts place it earlier, at 10:00 A.M.

29. Lee to CoIA, Sept. 30, 1877, LS, STA, NACPR; J. M. Lee, "Capture and Death," 331–32; Lee, interview, Oct. 17, 1912 (includes quotation).

30. Lee to CoIA, Sept. 30, 1877, LS, STA, NACPR; J. M. Lee, "Capture and Death," 331–32; Lee, interview, Oct. 17, 1912 (includes quotation); also Bordeaux interview, tablet 11, Ricker Papers.

31. Bordeaux interview, tablet 11, Ricker Papers; J. M. Lee, "Capture and Death," 332 (includes quotation); Lee interview, Oct. 17, 1912.

32. Lee interview, Oct. 17, 1912 (includes Black Crow's quotation); and J. M. Lee, "Capture and Death," 334 (includes transcript of Clark's message). The Lee interview states that Black Crow brought word of Crazy Horse's arrival at about 4:00 P.M., an important chronological crosscheck for the events of the late afternoon.

33. J. M. Lee, "Capture and Death," 334; Bordeaux interview, tablet 11; Garnett interview, tablet 2, Ricker Papers. Garnett claims that the No Flesh party was chased into Camp Sheridan by angry northern Lakotas; Bordeaux denies it, and, unlike Garnett, he was present at Spotted Tail Agency. However, rumor was immediately rife of such an incident. Possibly the No Flesh party scouted the northern village and was chased off.

34. Bordeaux interview, tablet 11, Ricker Papers; *Cheyenne Daily Leader*, Sept. 18, 1877; Col. Thomas Anderson, "Army Episodes and Anecdotes," 37 (includes quotation). Writing about 1890, Anderson was not an eyewitness, but he interviewed and corresponded with many officers involved in the death of Crazy Horse, including Bradley and Lee. Touch the Clouds was at the agency at noon and ordered back to his village by Lee. He left again early in the afternoon to counsel with Spotted Tail, from where he appeared at Camp Sheridan.

35. T. Anderson, "Army Episodes and Anecdotes," 37; Bordeaux interview, tablet 11, Ricker Papers. Merrivale and Tackett, Camp Sheridan post guide and interpreter respectively, had heard of Clark's reward and gone to scout the northern village.

36. Garnett interview, tablet 2, Ricker Papers; Clark to CoIA, Sept. 10, 1877.

37. Red Feather, in Riley, "Oglala Sources," 28; Horn Chips interview, tablet 18, Ricker Papers.

38. J. M. Lee, "Capture and Death," 332.

39. Ibid. Lee's account is obviously derived from eyewitnesses, but he telescopes events, indicating that the northern village began to flee immediately after Crazy Horse's arrival. The chronology of the afternoon, reconstructible from the sequence of events at Spotted Tail Agency and Camp Sheridan, indicates that Crazy Horse arrived in the village about 3:30 P.M., perhaps forty-five minutes before tipis began to be struck.

40. Ibid.

41. Clark to CoIA, Sept. 10, 1877; Lee to CoIA, Sept. 30, 1877. Clark misidentifies the Brule as Big Crow.

42. J. M. Lee, "Capture and Death," 332–33; Bordeaux interview, tablet 11, Ricker Papers.

43. J. M. Lee, "Capture and Death," 333; Lee interview, Oct. 17, 1912; Bordeaux interview, tablet 11, Ricker Papers; Bordeaux affidavit statement, Oct. 9, 1912; T. Anderson, "Army Episodes and Anecdotes," 37.

44. T. Anderson, "Army Episodes and Anecdotes," 37.

45. Lee to CoIA, Sept. 30, 1877; Lee interview, Oct. 17, 1912. Lee's report attributes the first quote to the conversation "in the open air" at Camp Sheridan, but comparison of all accounts suggests that it best fits here.

46. Bordeaux affidavit statement, Oct. 9, 1912; Bordeaux interview, tablet 11, Ricker Papers.

47. Eastman, *Indian Heroes and Great Chieftains*, 103–104; Garnett interview, tablet 2, Ricker Papers. Eastman includes a lengthy and implausible speech attributed to Crazy Horse. Bordeaux is silent on this confrontation, but by his own account, he had hurried ahead of the ambulance.

48. J. M. Lee, "Capture and Death," 333; Bordeaux affidavit; T. Anderson, "Army Episodes and Anecdotes," 37.

49. T. Anderson, "Army Episodes and Anecdotes," 37–38.

50. Ibid., 38; for Spotted Tail's speech, see J. M. Lee, "Capture and Death," 333; and cf. Lee, interview, Oct. 17, 1912; Lee to CoIA, Sept. 30, 1877.

51. J. M. Lee, "Capture and Death," 333; Bordeaux interview, tablet 11, Ricker Papers.

52. T. Anderson, "Army Episodes and Anecdotes," 38; Bordeaux interview, tablet 11, Ricker Papers; J. M. Lee, "Capture and Death," 333–34.

53. T. Anderson, "Army Episodes and Anecdotes," 38; Bordeaux interview, tablet 11, Ricker Papers; J. M. Lee, "Capture and Death," 333–34. Buffalo Chips's performance suggests a heyoka attempt to defuse a tense situation through comedy—a rather dangerous one given the language and culture barrier.

54. J. M. Lee, "Capture and Death," 334; Lee interview, Oct. 17, 1912; Bordeaux interview, tablet 11, Ricker Papers; Bordeaux affidavit; Bordeaux interview, July 6–7, 1910, in Liddic and Harbaugh, *Custer and Company*, 142 ff; T. Anderson, "Army Episodes and Anecdotes," 38–40. These are key eyewitness sources on the talk in Burke's quarters and are used throughout this section. Direct quotations will be cited.

55. Horn Chips interview, tablet 18, Ricker Papers (includes quotation "he should like to keep his country"); Lee, interview, Oct. 17, 1912 (includes second quotation).

56. Bordeaux interview, in Liddic and Harbaugh, *Custer and Company*, 142 ff.

57. Ibid.

58. Ibid.

59. T. Anderson, "Army Episodes and Anecdotes," 39. Anderson writes that Grouard was present at this talk and that Crazy Horse upbraided him, but he confuses this talk with the September 1 talk at Camp Sheridan with Touch the Clouds.

60. Ibid. The correspondence between Burke and Bradley is important in establishing a chronology for the late afternoon and evening. Bradley's first letter was written "about 4 O'clock" in the afternoon; his second, in reply to Burke's note, was datelined "Camp Robinson/ Midnight." The express courier's round trip therefore took eight hours, reaching Burke's quarters at about 8:00 P.M., when the talk with Crazy Horse was already well advanced. Anderson remarks that Burke's reply "was dispatched to Gen. Bradley a little after sunset."

61. Bordeaux interview, in Liddic and Harbaugh, *Custer and Company*, 142 ff.

62. T. Anderson, "Army Episodes and Anecdotes," 39.

63. Lee interview, Oct. 17, 1912.

64. R. A. Clark, *Killing of Chief Crazy Horse*, 64.

65. J. M. Lee, "Capture and Death," 334; Bordeaux interview, in Liddic and Harbaugh, *Custer and Company*, 142 ff.

66. Bordeaux interview, tablet 11, Ricker Papers; Bordeaux affidavit; Bordeaux interview, in Liddic and Harbaugh, *Custer and Company*, 142 ff.; J. M. Lee, "Capture and Death," 334; T. Anderson, "Army Episodes and Anecdotes," 39–40.

67. Standing Bear, *My People the Sioux*, 83–84.

68. For Crazy Horse's vigil, see James M. Chase in Morning, in Kadlecek and Kadlecek, *To Kill an Eagle*, 93. Chase in Morning was born in 1888, the son of Stanley Chase in Morning (born 1860), who was the son of Little Hawk (northern Decider and Crazy Horse's uncle).

Chase in Morning stated that Crazy Horse's prayer for guidance on Beaver Creek took place two days before his death—a clear mistake for one day.

CHAPTER 29

1. T. Anderson, "Army Episodes and Anecdotes," 40, Coe Papers; Bordeaux, *Custer's Conqueror*, 78, and *Conquering the Mighty Sioux*, 92.

2. T. Anderson, "Army Episodes and Anecdotes," 40.

3. Ibid.; Clark to Crook, Sept. 5, 1877 (telegram), in Bourke diary, vol. 24, 61. Burke's original intention seems to have been to escort Crazy Horse personally to Camp Robinson. As the morning progressed, this task devolved on Lee alone.

4. Wounded Horse Woman (Jennie Fast Thunder, a.k.a. Cane), in Standing Bear, *Land of the Spotted Eagle*, 181–82; also Jessie Eagle Heart, in Kadlecek and Kadlecek, *To Kill an Eagle*, 51–52, 98–100.

5. Bordeaux interview, tablet 11, Ricker Papers; Bordeaux interview, July 6–7, 1910, in Liddic and Harbaugh, *Custer and Company*, 145; Bordeaux affidavit, Oct. 9, 1912; T. Anderson, "Army Episodes and Anecdotes," 41; Bordeaux, *Custer's Conqueror*, 81.

6. Bordeaux interview, tablet 11, Ricker Papers; Bordeaux interview, July 6–7, 1910, in Liddic and Harbaugh, *Custer and Company*, 145; Bordeaux affidavit, Oct. 9, 1912; T. Anderson, "Army Episodes and Anecdotes," 41; Bordeaux, *Custer's Conqueror*, 81.

7. Bordeaux interview, tablet 11, Ricker Papers; Bordeaux interview, July 6–7, 1910, in Liddic and Harbaugh, *Custer and Company*, 145; Bordeaux affidavit, Oct. 9, 1912; T. Anderson, "Army Episodes and Anecdotes," 41; Bordeaux, *Custer's Conqueror*, 81.; also J. M. Lee, "Capture and Death," 334–35; Lee interview, Oct. 27, 1912, folder 116, Camp Field Notes, Camp Papers, BYU (includes quotation).

8. Bordeaux interview, tablet 11, Ricker Papers; Bordeaux interview, July 6–7, 1910, in Liddic and Harbaugh, *Custer and Company*, 145; Bordeaux affidavit, Oct. 9, 1912; T. Anderson, "Army Episodes and Anecdotes," 41; Bordeaux, *Custer's Conqueror*, 81; J. M. Lee, "Capture and Death," 334–35 (quotations on 335); Lee interview, Oct. 27, 1912.

9. Bordeaux interview, tablet 11, Ricker Papers.

10. Bordeaux affidavit, Oct. 9, 1912.

11. T. Anderson, "Army Episodes and Anecdotes," 41.

12. *New York Sun*, Sept. 14, 1877. This invaluable newspaper account includes "Whirlwind" among the named Lakotas who prevailed on Crazy Horse to go to Camp Robinson. No leading Brule or Oglala of this name is known at this time, but Whirlwind Soldier's prominence as sergeant in Touch the Clouds's scout Company E, suggests that the reference is to this Brule leader. See also Standing Soldier, interview by Eli S. Ricker, tablet 9, Ricker Papers.

13. Henry Standing Bear, interview by Walter M. Camp, July 1910, in Hardorff, *Surrender and Death of Crazy Horse*, 114–15. Turning Bear belonged to Two Strike's band.

14. Bordeaux interview, tablet 11, Ricker Papers.

15. Ibid.; also Lee interview, Oct. 27, 1912 (includes quotation).

16. Bordeaux, *Conquering the Mighty Sioux*, 92.

17. J. M. Lee, "Capture and Death," 335 (includes quotations); Lucy W. Lee account, in Greencastle (Indiana) *Star*, reprinted in Hardorff, *Surrender and Death of Crazy Horse*, 252.

18. Bordeaux interview, tablet 11, Ricker Papers.

19. Ibid.; Amos Charging First affidavit before Ziebach Co., Oct. 3, 1927, Crazy Horse Biography File; Lucille Runs After statement to the author, Feb. 2, 2004. Charging Eagle was the son of Miniconjou leader Roman Nose. Sixteen-year-old Charging First was enlisted as a scout in Company D, under his nickname Across the Room.

20. Bordeaux interview, tablet 11, Ricker Papers.

21. J. M. Lee, "Capture and Death," 335; Bordeaux interview, tablet 11, Ricker Papers; Bordeaux interview, July 6–7, 1910; Bordeaux affidavit, Oct. 9, 1912; T. Anderson, "Army Episodes and Anecdotes," 41; McGillycuddy, *Blood on the Moon*, 82. Spotted Tail obviously arranged a staggered departure for the various parties of scouts. The last to leave, the Oglalas, caught up with the escort just short of Red Cloud Agency: see Standing Soldier interview, tablet 9, Ricker Papers; and cf. Bordeaux interview, tablet 11, Ricker Papers.

22. T. Anderson, "Army Episodes and Anecdotes," 41.

23. J. M. Lee, "Capture and Death," 335; Lee interview, Oct. 27, 1912; Bordeaux interview, tablet 11, Ricker Papers (includes quotation).

24. J. M. Lee, "Capture and Death," 335; Bordeaux interview, tablet 11, Ricker Papers.

25. J. M. Lee, "Capture and Death," 336; Lee interview, Oct. 27, 1912 (includes quotation); Bordeaux, *Custer's Conqueror*, 82–83.

26. J. M. Lee, "Capture and Death," 336; Lee interview, Oct. 27, 1912; Bordeaux, *Custer's Conqueror*, 83.

27. Bradley to Maj. Gillies, Sept. 5, 1877 (telegram), in Hardorff, *Surrender and Death of Crazy Horse*, 178.

28. Clark to Crook, Sept. 5, 1877 (telegram), Bourke diary, vol. 24, 61.

29. Crook to Bradley, Sept. 5, 1877 (telegram), Bourke diary, vol. 24, 61 (includes quotations); also, for Crook's schedule, see *Chicago Times*, Sept. 6, 1877.

30. Crook to Sheridan, Sept. 5, 1877 (telegram), Bourke diary, vol. 24, 63–64.

31. Sheridan to Gillies, Sept. 5, 1877 (telegram), Bourke diary, vol. 24, 64.

32. Lemly, "Passing of Crazy Horse," 321; Lee interview, Oct. 27, 1912. From Bradley's verbal orders, Wessells and Lt. Lemly, Company E, Third Cavalry, understood that Crazy Horse's ultimate destination was incarceration in Florida. Journalists briefed by Sheridan's Chicago office also reported that, subject to Washington approval, Crazy Horse was to be imprisoned with Kiowa, Comanche, and southern Cheyenne war leaders in Florida. See *Chicago Times*, Sept. 7, 1877. These latter prisoners were held in Fort Marion, at St. Augustine. Although secondary works commonly identify the intended place of Crazy Horse's incarceration as the Dry Tortugas, that island's military post, Fort Jefferson, had been closed in 1874.

33. Red Feather, in, Riley, "Oglala Sources," 28; Pourier interview, tablet 13, Ricker Papers. Following the discharge of Crazy Horse, Little Big Man was promoted to first sergeant of Company C, both changes back dated to August 31.

34. *Chicago Tribune*, Sept. 11, 1877.

35. For Scout and Bad Face–Loafer dispositions, see He Dog, in, Riley, "Oglala Sources," 21; White Calf, ibid., 43.

36. Standing Soldier interview, tablet 9, Ricker Papers; Bordeaux interview, July 6–7, 1910.

37. Charging First affidavit, Oct. 3, 1927, Crazy Horse Biography File; Bordeaux affidavit; Horn Chips interview, tablet 18, Ricker Papers; J. M. Lee, "Capture and Death," 336; *Chicago Tribune*, Sept. 11, 1877.

38. Irwin to CoIA, Sept. 5, 1877 (telegram) RCA, LR, OIA.

39. He Dog, in Riley, "Oglala Sources," 20–21; Joseph Eagle Hawk, in Hardorff, *Surrender and Death of Crazy Horse*, 144.

40. Charging First affidavit, Oct. 3, 1927, Crazy Horse Biography File; Red Feather, Riley, "Oglala Sources," 28.

41. Lemly, "Passing of Crazy Horse," 319; He Dog, Riley, "Oglala Sources," 21. "'Crazy Horse' reached here at 6 o'-clock," Clark to Crook, Sept. 5, 1877 (telegram), Bourke diary, vol. 24, 64. No source openly criticizes Bradley or Clark, but their noninvolvement in a situation demanding hands-on authority seems culpable.

42. He Dog, Riley, "Oglala Sources," 21; White Calf, ibid., 43. Eagle Hawk, in Hardorff, *Surrender and Death of Crazy Horse*, 144.

43. He Dog quotations synthesized from Eagle Hawk, in Hardorff, *Surrender and Death of Crazy Horse*, 144, and R. A. Clark, *Killing of Chief Crazy Horse*, 65; He Dog, Riley, "Oglala Sources," 21.

44. Bordeaux interview, July 6–7, 1910; Bordeaux interview, tablet 11, Ricker Papers; J. M. Lee, "Capture and Death," 336; Lemly, "Passing of Crazy Horse," 319; *New York Sun*, Sept. 14, 1877; Eagle Hawk, in Hardorff, *Surrender and Death of Crazy Horse*, 146.

45. J. M. Lee, "Capture and Death," 336; Lee interview, Oct. 27, 1912 (first quotation); T. Anderson, "Army Episodes and Anecdotes," 42; Lemly, "Passing of Crazy Horse," 319; "Billy Hunter's Account," Bourke diary, vol. 24, 82 (second quotation); *Chicago Times*, Sept. 6, 1877.

46. Red Feather, Riley, "Oglala Sources," 28.

47. J. M. Lee, "Capture and Death," 336–37 (includes quotation); Lee interview, Oct. 27, 1912; T. Anderson, "Army Episodes and Anecdotes," 42.

48. Bordeaux interview, July 6–7, 1910. This statement reveals the extent to which Lee, no less than Agent Irwin, Bradley, and Clark, washed his hands of Crazy Horse. Lee's own accounts, tortured by conscience, and Louis Bordeaux's other statements, do not mention this crucial exchange.

49. J. M. Lee, "Capture and Death," 337; Lee interview, Oct. 27, 1912 (includes quotation).

50. Red Feather, Riley, "Oglala Sources," 28. Red Feather identifies the officer as Clark, but Kennington and Adjutant Calhoun were the only officers present.

51. Bordeaux interview, tablet 11, Ricker Papers; Bordeaux- interview, July 6–7, 1910; J. M. Lee, "Capture and Death," 337; *Chicago Times*, Sept. 6, 1877.

52. Bordeaux interview, tablet 11, Ricker Papers; Bordeaux interview, July 6–7, 1910 (includes quotations); Garnett interview, tablet 2, Ricker Papers; Horn Chips interview, tablet 18, Ricker Papers; J. M. Lee, "Capture and Death," 337; Lemly, "Passing of Crazy Horse," 319–20; *Chicago Times*, Sept. 6, 1877; *New York Sun*, Sept. 14, 1877.

53. Bordeaux, *Custer's Conqueror*, 87.

54. DeBarthe, *Frank Grouard*, 177; Garnett interview, tablet 2, Ricker Papers; He Dog, Riley, "Oglala Sources," 21.

55. He Dog, Red Feather, and White Calf, Riley, "Oglala Sources," 21, 28, 43; Standing Soldier interview, tablet 9, Ricker Papers; Lemly, "Passing of Crazy Horse," 319–20.

56. Bordeaux interview, tablet 11, Ricker Papers; Garnett interview, tablet 2, Ricker Papers; R. A. Clark, *Killing of Chief Crazy Horse*, 93 (includes quotations); *New York Sun*, Sept. 14, 1877; Wounded Horse Woman, in Standing Bear, *Land of the Spotted Eagle*, 182; Charging First affidavit, Oct. 3, 1927, Crazy Horse Biography File.

57. DeBarthe, *Frank Grouard*, 177; He Dog, Riley, "Oglala Sources," 21; J. M. Lee, "Capture and Death," 337–38.

58. Standing Bear interview, July 1910.

59. Horn Chips interview, tablet 18, Ricker Papers.

60. Ibid. Such was Horn Chips' sense of confinement that he believed "the passage led down into the ground."

61. Standing Bear interview, July 1910 (includes Turning Bear quotation); Red Feather, Riley, "Oglala Sources," 28; "Billy Hunter's Account," Bourke diary, vol. 24, 83 (includes Crazy Horse quotation); J. M. Lee, "Capture and Death," 337–38; Lee interview, Oct. 27, 1912; T. Anderson, "Army Episodes and Anecdotes," 42; Lemly, "Passing of Crazy Horse," 320.

62. Lucy W. Lee account, in Hardorff, *Surrender and Death of Crazy Horse*, 253; Eagle Hawk, in Hardorff, *Surrender and Death of Crazy Horse*, 146 (includes quotations); Lee interview, Oct. 27, 1912; Plenty Wolves, in Bad Heart Bull and Blish, *Pictographic History of the Oglala Sioux*, 401–402;

Yellow Horse to John Colhoff, in W. K. Powers [and John Colhoff], *Winter Count of the Oglala*, 33, with additional details from Yellow Horse in John Colhoff to Joseph Balmer, Sept. 6, 1949, transcript in author's collection; He Dog, Riley, "Oglala Sources," 21; Carrie Slow Bear, in ibid., 41; *Chicago Times*, Sept. 6, 1877; *New York Sun*, Sept. 14, 1877; *Chicago Tribune*, Sept. 11, 1877.

63. Lee interview, Oct. 27, 1912; *New York Sun*, Sept. 14, 1877; *Chicago Tribune*, Sept. 11, 1877; Little Big Man's words are derived from Yellow Horse to Colhoff in Colhoff to Balmer, Sept. 6, 1949; Yellow Horse, in R. A. Clark, *Killing of Chief Crazy Horse*, 65.

64. Lee interview, Oct. 27, 1912; T. Anderson, "Army Episodes and Anecdotes," 42; Lemly, "Passing of Crazy Horse," 320; Bordeaux interview, July 6–7, 1910; Garnett interview, tablet 2, Ricker Papers (includes quotation); "Billy Hunter's Account," 83; Standing Soldier interview, tablet 9, Ricker Papers; Pourier interview, tablet 13, Ricker Papers; Little Big Man, Bourke, *On the Border with Crook*, 422–23; Red Feather and White Calf, Riley, "Oglala Sources," 28–29, 43; DeBarthe, *Frank Grouard*, 177–78; *Chicago Times*, Sept. 6, 1877; *New York Sun*, Sept. 14, 1877; *Chicago Tribune*, Sept. 11, 1877; Lucy W. Lee account, in Hardorff, op. cit., 253; Sgt. Wm. Kelly account, *Crawford Tribune* (Nebr.), June 26, 1903.

65. *Chicago Times*, Sept. 6, 1877; *New York Sun*, Sept. 14, 1877; Garnett interview, tablet 2, Ricker Papers; Bordeaux interview, tablet 11, Ricker Papers; J. M. Lee, "Capture and Death," 337–38; DeBarthe, *Frank Grouard*, 177–78; Pvt. Geo. W. McAnulty, in Brininstool, *Crazy Horse*, 86; He Dog, Riley, "Oglala Sources," 21 (includes quotation); American Horse interview, tablet 35, Ricker Papers.

66. *Chicago Times*, Sept. 6, 1877; Sgt. Wm. Kelly account, in *Crawford Tribune*, June 26, 1903; Bordeaux interview, July 6–7, 1910 (first quotation); J. M. Lee, "Capture and Death," 337–38 (second quotation); Lee interview, Oct. 27, 1912; Garnett interview, tablet 2, Ricker Papers; R. A. Clark, *Killing of Chief Crazy Horse*, 93–94; American Horse interview, tablet 35, Ricker Papers.

67. Yellow Horse to Colhoff in Colhoff to Balmer, Sept. 6, 1949; quotation from Powers, *Winter Count of the Oglala*, 33; *Chicago Times*, Sept. 6, 1877; *Chicago Tribune*, Sept. 11, 1877; Private Edwin D. Wood, in *New York Times*, Sept. 28, 1877; Sgt. Wm. Kelly account, in *Crawford Tribune*, June 26, 1903; Garnett interview, tablet 2, Ricker Papers; "Billy Hunter's Account," 83; R. A. Clark, *Killing of Chief Crazy Horse*, 93–94; Bordeaux interview, tablet 11, Ricker Papers; Bordeaux interview, July 6–7, 1910; T. Anderson, "Army Episodes and Anecdotes," 43; J. M. Lee, "Capture and Death," 337–38; Lee interview, Oct. 27, 1912; Lemly, "Passing of Crazy Horse," 320; "Dr. [Valentine T.] McGillycuddy's Story of Crazy Horse," in Brininstool, "Chief Crazy Horse," 38; Charles T. Jordan to Doane W. Robinson, June 26, 1902, Robinson Papers; DeBarthe, *Frank Grouard*, 177–78; Pvt. McAnulty, in Brininstool, *Crazy Horse*, 86–87; American Horse interview, tablet 35, Ricker Papers; Standing Soldier interview, tablet 9, Ricker Papers; Henry Standing Bear interview, July 1910; He Dog, Red Feather, and White Calf, Riley, "Oglala Sources," 21, 29, 43; Eagle Hawk, in Hardorff, *Surrender and Death of Crazy Horse*, 146–48; R. A. Clark, *Killing of Chief Crazy Horse*, 64–65.

For a close analysis of the nature of Crazy Horse's wounds, see the detailed footnotes in Hardorff, *Surrender and Death of Crazy Horse*, 148–49. Although early controversy existed over whether Crazy Horse was killed by one of the guards or by his own knives, deflected in the struggle with Little Big Man, the weight of evidence has always favored the former. For a modern lawyer's application of courtroom techniques to the evidence, see J. N. Gilbert, "Death of Crazy Horse." The exact identity of the sentry who killed Crazy Horse is elusive: for excellent analyses of the evidence, see Hardorff's notes, *Surrender and Death of Crazy Horse,* 146–48, and Dickson, "Crazy Horse." Although not definitive, the balance of evidence suggests that Crazy Horse's killer was Private William Gentles, Company F, Fourteenth Infantry.

68. Garnett interview, tablet 2, Ricker Papers (includes first and third quotations); R. A. Clark, *Killing of Chief Crazy Horse*, 93–94 (second quotation on 94); Bordeaux interview, tablet 11, Ricker Papers; Horn Chips interview, tablet 18, Ricker Papers; Pvt. McAnulty, in Brininstool, *Crazy Horse*, 86–87. The identity of Crazy Horse's uncle is not given in the sources. Since Garnett knew well Oglala relatives such as Little Hawk, it seems most likely that this man was one of the maternal, Miniconjou uncles. From He Dog's testimony, we know that Spotted Crow was at the White River agencies during summer 1877 and was a key anti-American adviser to Crazy Horse. Moreover, Spotted Crow had been present when No Water shot Crazy Horse in 1870, lending significance to his remarks to Little Big Man.

69. R. A. Clark, *Killing of Chief Crazy Horse*, 94.

70. He Dog, Riley, "Oglala Sources," 21; White Calf, ibid., 43; Garnett interview, tablet 2, Ricker Papers; R. A. Clark, *Killing of Chief Crazy Horse*, 94; Bordeaux interview, July 6–7, 1910; Eagle Hawk, in Hardorff, *Surrender and Death of Crazy Horse*, 146–48.

71. DeBarthe, *Frank Grouard*, 178; He Dog, Riley, "Oglala Sources," 21.

72. Charging First affidavit, Oct. 3, 1927, Crazy Horse Biography File; He Dog, Riley, "Oglala Sources," 21 (first quotation); R. A. Clark, *Killing of Chief Crazy Horse*, 66 (second quotation); Eagle Hawk, in Hardorff, *Surrender and Death of Crazy Horse*, 148–50.

73. Red Feather, Riley, "Oglala Sources," 29.

74. R. A. Clark, *Killing of Chief Crazy Horse*, 66; Eagle Hawk, in Hardorff, *Surrender and Death of Crazy Horse*, 150.

75. "Dr. McGillycuddy's Story," in Brininstool, "Chief Crazy Horse," 38–39; V. T. McGillycuddy to William Garnett, June 24, 1927, in R. A. Clark, *Killing of Chief Crazy Horse*, 125–26; *Chicago Times*, Sept. 6, 1877; *New York Sun*, Sept. 14, 1877; *Chicago Tribune*, Sept. 11, 1877; Lucy W. Lee account, in Hardorff, *Surrender and Death of Crazy Horse*, 253; T. Anderson, "Army Episodes and Anecdotes," 43; Lemly, "Passing of Crazy Horse," 320.

76. Lemly, "Passing of Crazy Horse," 320; Bordeaux, *Custer's Conqueror*, 88–89.

77. Lemly, "Passing of Crazy Horse," 320; T. Anderson, "Army Episodes and Anecdotes," 43 (includes quotations); *New York Sun*, Sept. 14, 1877; *Chicago Tribune*, Sept. 11, 1877.

78. "Dr. McGillycuddy's Story," 38–39; McGillycuddy to William Garnett, June 24, 1927, in R. A. Clark, *Killing of Chief Crazy Horse*, 125–26; Ibid., 94–95; Garnett interview, tablet 2, Ricker Papers.

79. R. A. Clark, *Killing of Chief Crazy Horse*, 94–95 (first quotation); ibid., 66 (second quotation); He Dog, Riley, "Oglala Sources," 21–22.

80. R. A. Clark, *Killing of Chief Crazy Horse*, 94–95. Clark's pointed absence from the scene during the most turbulent hour of Camp Robinson's existence did not go entirely unnoticed. Angeline Johnson, wife of Lt. Charles A. Johnson, wrote her sister that a "certain officer . . . took care to keep out of the way of any of them during the fracas": Twitchell, "Camp Robinson Letters," 93.

81. "Dr. McGillycuddy's Story," 38–39.

82. Garnett interview, tablet 2, Ricker Papers; R. A. Clark, *Killing of Chief Crazy Horse*, 94–95; James H. Cook to Neihardt, Mar. 3, 1920, Neihardt Papers (includes quotation).

83. "Dr. McGillycuddy's Story," 38–39; McGillycuddy to Garnett, June 24, 1927, in R. A. Clark, *Killing of Chief Crazy Horse*, 125 (includes quotation); *Chicago Tribune*, Sept. 11, 1877.

84. "Dr. McGillycuddy's Story," 38–39.

85. Ibid.; McGillycuddy, *Blood on the Moon*, 84; Garnett interview, tablet 2, Ricker Papers (includes quotation); R. A. Clark, *Killing of Chief Crazy Horse*, 94–95.

86. Eagle Hawk, in Hardorff, *Surrender and Death of Crazy Horse*, 150; *Chicago Times*, Sept. 6, 1877; Garnett interview, tablet 2, Ricker Papers; R. A. Clark, *Killing of Chief Crazy Horse*, 95;

J. M. Lee, "Capture and Death," 338; t. Anderson, "Army Episodes and Anecdotes," 43; Lemly, "Passing of Crazy Horse," 320.

87. R. A. Clark, *Killing of Chief Crazy Horse*, 95; Garnett interview, tablet 2, Ricker Papers.

88. Lucy W. Lee account, in Hardorff, *Surrender and Death of Crazy Horse*, 253–54; Charging First affidavit, Oct. 3, 1927, Crazy Horse Biography File; He Dog, Riley, "Oglala Sources," 22. Again, Crazy Horse's uncle is not named: it is likely to be Spotted Crow or one of his Miniconjou brothers.

89. Red Feather, Riley, "Oglala Sources," 29.

90. Eagle Hawk, in Hardorff, *Surrender and Death of Crazy Horse*, 150.

91. Lemly, "Passing of Crazy Horse," 320; Red Feather, Riley, "Oglala Sources," 29; J. M. Lee, "Capture and Death," 338; Lee interview, Oct. 27, 1912; Bordeaux interview, tablet 11, Ricker Papers. Spider, a half-brother of Red Cloud married to a sister of Young Man Afraid of His Horse, was the head akicita of the Payabya band; White Bird, his counterpart in the Spleen band.

92. *Chicago Tribune*, Sept. 11, 1877; *New York Sun*, Sept. 14, 1877; "Dr. McGillycuddy's Story," 40; McGillycuddy to Garnett, June 24, 1927, in R. A. Clark, *Killing of Chief Crazy Horse*, 126.

93. R. A. Clark, *Killing of Chief Crazy Horse*, 66–67; Garnett interview, tablet 2, Ricker Papers; R. A. Clark, *Killing of Chief Crazy Horse*, 95; Bordeaux interview, tablet 11, Ricker Papers (includes quotations); Bordeaux interview, July 6–7, 1910.

94. J. M. Lee, "Capture and Death," 338; Lee interview, Oct. 27, 1912; V. T. McGillycuddy to William Garnett, May 10, 1926, in R. A. Clark, *Killing of Chief Crazy Horse*, 117–18; Bordeaux interview, July 6–7, 1910. I have chosen not to credit the extensive verbatim speeches cited in Lee's accounts. They ring too clearly of self-absolution, and in any case are too coherent for the dying, delirious Crazy Horse to have spoken.

95. Bordeaux interview, July 6–7, 1910; Bordeaux interview, tablet 11, Ricker Papers; McGillycuddy, *Blood on the Moon*, 85–86.

96. McGillycuddy, *Blood on the Moon*, 86.

97. Bordeaux interview, tablet 11, Ricker Papers; Pourier interview, tablet 13, Ricker Papers; *New York Sun*, Sept. 14, 1877; *Chicago Tribune*, Sept. 11, 1877.

98. *New York Sun*, Sept. 14, 1877.

99. *Chicago Tribune*, Sept. 11, 1877. Lemly, "Passing of Crazy Horse," 321–22, printed a version of Worm's speech and attributed it to Crazy Horse.

100. Pourier interview, tablet 13, Ricker Papers (includes quotations); *New York Sun*, Sept. 14, 1877. Although estimates of the time of death vary, most fall between 11:30 and 12:00. Clark, in his official report, gave the time as 11:40 P.M. Clark to CoIA, Sept. 10, 1877, STA, LR, OIA.

101. Bradley to AG, Dept. of the Platte, Sept. 7, 1877, SW File. For another translation, with army spin, see *Chicago Tribune*, Sept. 11, 1877.

CHAPTER 30

1. Events of the morning of September 6 are taken from the following sources: *New York Sun*, Sept. 14, 1877; *Chicago Times*, Sept. 7, 1877; *Chicago Tribune*, Sept. 11, 1877; *Army and Navy Journal*, Sept. 15, 1877; Garnett interview, tablet 2, Ricker Papers; Jesse M. Lee Diary, in Brininstool, *Crazy Horse*, 38–39; Lucy W. Lee, dispatch to Greencastle (Indiana) *Star*, datelined Sept. 18, 1877, in ibid., 67; J. M. Lee, "Capture and Death," 339. In the subsequent account, I have footnoted only quotations.

2. *Chicago Times*, Sept. 7, 1877.

3. Ibid.

4. Red Feather, Riley, "Oglala Sources," 30.

5. There is no direct statement that Worm performed the Ghost Owning ceremony in Crazy Horse's memory. However, an albeit garbled memory of Luther Standing Bear strongly suggests that he did: *My People the Sioux*, 91, 100. My account of the rite is generalized from J. E. Brown, *Sacred Pipe*, chap. 2; Densmore, *Teton Sioux Music and Culture*, 77–84; Dorsey, *Study of Siouan Cults*, 487–89; Fletcher, "Indian Ceremonies"; Hassrick, *The Sioux*, 302–305.

6. *Chicago Times*, Sept. 7, 1877.

7. *Chicago Tribune*, Sept. 11, 1877. This paragraph also draws on an illustration in *Frank Leslie's Illustrated Newspaper*, Oct. 13, 1877, depicting Crazy Horse's "Funeral Procession Passing through Camp Sheridan." Although the illustration was drawn in-house in *Frank Leslie's* New York office, it was based on an original sketch by J. H. Hamilton.

8. Burke to Bradley, Sept. 7, 1877; *New York Sun*, Sept. 23, 1877; Jesse M. Lee Diary, Brininstool, *Crazy Horse*, 39. Internal evidence indicates that the scaffold was erected early on September 8.

9. Bradley to AG, Dept. of the Platte, Sept. 7, 1877, SW File; "List of Indians transferred from other Agencys [*sic*]," Spotted Tail Agency 1877 Census, 63–71, NACPR.

10. The political situation is detailed in K. M. Bray, "'We Belong to the North.'"

11. Jesse M. Lee diary, Brininstool, *Crazy Horse*, 39–40; L. W. Lee, "Recollections."

12. Jesse M. Lee diary, Brininstool, *Crazy Horse*, 39.

13. *New York Sun*, Sept. 23, 1877.

14. Ibid.

15. *Sidney Telegraph*, Sept. 15, 1877; Red Feather, Riley, "Oglala Sources," 30.

16. The delegation and the agency departures are covered in K. M. Bray, "'We Belong to the North.'"

17. Clark to Secretary of the Interior, Nov. 7, 1877, STA, LR, OIA.

18. On Worm's journey, see Victoria Conroy (Standing Bear), in Hardorff, *Oglala Lakota Crazy Horse*, 30; Black Elk, in DeMallie, *Sixth Grandfather*, 204; Joseph Eagle Hawk, in John Colhoff to Joseph Balmer, Apr. 25, 1951 (transcript in author's collection); Horn Chips interview, tablet 18, Ricker Papers. Clark to Secretary of the Interior, Nov. 7, 1877, asserts Worm's continued presence with the Red Cloud column as of that date.

19. The statements on the later burial(s) of Crazy Horse are confused and confusing. As far as the second, or November 1877, burial is concerned, the clearest statement is in Walter M. Camp's interview with Horn Chips, ca. July 11, 1910, Camp Papers, BYU. A participant in the burial, Horn Chips stated that he "and Old Man Crazy Horse [Worm] carried [the body] to above the head of Wounded Knee (not on the creek), and buried it in the ground in a box." A contemporary newspaper notice in the *Omaha Daily Bee*, December 3, 1877, reported that Crazy Horse was buried near the mouth of Big White Clay Creek, during the agency removal. The location probably reflects the point at which Worm's party departed the Red Cloud column.

This second burial was not the last for Crazy Horse's restless remains. During the fall 1878 relocations to the present Pine Ridge and Rosebud agencies (probably immediately after the conclusion of the year-long Ghost Owning ceremony), Horn Chips reinterred the body in another place. Although confusion and hearsay continue to confound the record, this interment may have been in a cliff along White Horse Creek (a west tributary of Wounded Knee), about four miles southwest of the modern reservation community of Manderson. Horn Chips seems to have overseen a final reinterment, before the end of the nineteenth century, to an unknown point on Wounded Knee Creek.

20. The final Spotted Tail Agency removal to the present site at Rosebud is detailed in Hyde, *Sioux Chronicle*, chap. 1; and idem, *Spotted Tail's Folk*, 288–94.

21. Breakouts for Canada through January 1878 are detailed in K. M. Bray, "'We Belong to the North.'" For the September 1878 defections, see Captain H. M. Wessells to AAG, Dept. of Dakota, Sept. 27, 1878, Sioux War Papers. Red Eagle was a Miniconjou who married into the Brules, ancestor to today's prominent Leader Charge family at Rosebud. Bad Mustang was a Wazhazha headman considered a trusty by Captain Wessells.

22. The Canadian exile is detailed in Utley, *Lance and the Shield*, chaps. 15–18; and at length in Manzione, *"I Am Looking to the North for My Life."*

23. Although Black Shawl is unnamed in the contemporary census record, she was almost certainly one of the two women in the Red Doe Elk (Woman) family, officially taken up at the new Pine Ridge Agency, fall 1878. The family was subsequently registered with the Oglala Spleen band.

24. On Worm's sojourn at Rosebud, see Hardorff, *Surrender and Death of Crazy Horse*, 128. Standing Bear, *My People the Sioux*, 100, indicates that the Ghost Owning ceremony was held very soon after the arrival at Rosebud. My account of the ceremony is based on J. E. Brown, *Sacred Pipe*, chap. 2; Densmore, *Teton Sioux Music and Culture*, 77–84; Dorsey, *Study of Siouan Cults*, 487–89; Fletcher, "Indian Ceremonies"; Hassrick, *The Sioux*, 302–305.

25. Standing Bear, *My People the Sioux*, 100.

BIBLIOGRAPHY

ARCHIVAL MATERIAL

Adjutant General's Office (AGO), War Department. Records. RG 94. National Archives and Records Service, Washington, D.C.

Appleton Family. Papers. Nebraska State Historical Society, Lincoln.

Bettelyoun, Susan Bordeaux. Papers. Nebraska State Historical Society, Lincoln.

Bourke, John Gregory. Diaries. U.S. Military Academy, West Point, New York.

Bradley, Luther P., Papers. Military History Institute, Carlisle, Pennsylvania.

Bray, Kingsley M., and Jack Meister. Interviews with Lakota informants, 1993–2005. Author's collection.

Bureau of Indian Affairs (BIA). Records. RG 75, National Archives and Records Service (NARS), Washington, D.C.

———. Records. RG 75. National Archives—Central Plains Region (NACPR), Kansas City, Missouri.

Camp, Walter M., Papers. Brigham Young University, Provo, Utah.

———. Papers. Lilly Library, University of Indiana, Indianapolis.

Crazy Horse Biography File. South Dakota Historical Society, Pierre.

Clown Family. Heirship Files. Cheyenne River Tribal Office, Eagle Butte, South Dakota.

Coe, William Robertson. Papers. Yale University, New Haven, Connecticut.

Colhoff, John. Letters to Joseph Balmer, 1948–54. Transcripts in author's collection.

Deloria, Ella. Papers of the American Philosophical Society, Philadelphia. Transcripts at Colorado Historical Society, Denver. Fort Laramie. Post Scout Reports, 1866. Fort Laramie National Historic Site, Wyoming.

Hyde, George E., Research papers in author's collection.

Indian Division, Secretary of the Interior. Records. RG 48. National Archives and Records Service, Washington, D.C.

Mekeel, H. Scudder. Papers. American Museum of Natural History, New York.

Neihardt, John G., Papers. Western History Collections. University of Missouri, Columbia.

Pine Ridge Census Records. RG 75. National Archives and Records Service, Washington, D.C.

Ricker, Eli S., Papers. Nebraska State Historical Society, Lincoln.

Robinson, Doane. Papers. South Dakota Historical Society, Pierre.

Sandoz, Mari. Papers. Love Library, University of Nebraska, Lincoln.

Sheldon, Addison E., Papers. Nebraska State Historical Society, Lincoln.

Spring, Agnes Wright. Papers. University of Wyoming Library, Laramie.

U.S. Army Continental Commands. Records. RG 393. National Archives and Records Service, Washington, D.C.

Waggoner, Josephine F., Papers. Museum of the Fur Trade, Chadron, Nebraska.

Wilson, E. P., Papers. Museum of the Fur Trade, Chadron, Nebraska.

GOVERNMENT PUBLICATIONS

Kappler, Charles J., comp. and ed. *Indian Affairs: Laws and Treaties.* 2 vols. Washington, D.C.: GPO, 1904.

Papers Relating to the Sioux Indians of the United States Who Have Taken Refuge in Canadian Territory: Printed Confidentially for the Use of the Ministers of the Crown. Ottawa: 1879.

Proceedings of a Board of Commissioners to Negotiate a Treaty or Treaties with the Hostile Indians of the Upper Missouri. n.p., n.d. [Washington, D.C., 1866].

Report of the Special Commission Appointed to Investigate the Affairs of the Red Cloud Indian Agency, July 1875, Together with the Testimony and Accompanying Documents. Washington, D.C.: GPO, 1875.

U.S. Bureau of Indian Affairs. *Papers Relating to Talks and Councils Held with the Indians in Dakota and Montana Territories, in the Years 1866–1869.* Washington, D.C.: GPO, 1910.

U.S. Commissioner of Indian Affairs. *Annual Reports* (ARCoIA). Washington, D.C.: Interior Department, 1851–1878.

U.S. Congress. House. *Information Relating to an Engagement between the United States Troops and the Sioux Indians near Fort Laramie.* 33rd Cong., 2nd sess., 1854. H. Rep. 63.

U.S. Congress. Senate. *Senate Executive Documents.* 34th Cong., 1st sess., 1856, S. Doc. 94.

———. *Senate Executive Documents.* 34th Cong., 3rd sess., 1857, S. Doc. 58.

———. *Senate Executive Documents.* 40th Cong., 1st sess., 1867, S. Doc. 13.

———. *Senate Executive Documents.* 40th Cong., 2nd sess., 1868, S. Doc. 77.

———. *Senate Executive Documents.* 44th Cong., 1st sess., S. Doc. 52.

———. *Senate Executive Documents.* 44th Cong., 2nd sess., 1877, S. Doc. 9.

———. *Senate Executive Documents.* 50th Cong., 1st sess., 1888, S. Doc. 33.

U.S. Secretary of the Interior. *Annual Report.* Washington, D.C.: Interior Department, 1875.

U.S. War Department. *The War of the Rebellion: A Compilation of the Official Records of the Union and Confederate Armies.* 130 vols. Washington, D.C.: GPO, 1886–1901.

Warren, Lieutenant G. K. *Preliminary Report of Explorations in Nebraska and Dakota, in the Years 1855–'56–'57.* Washington, D.C.: GPO, 1875.

BOOKS, ARTICLES, AND PAPERS

Adams, Donald K. "The Journal of Ada A. Vogdes, 1868–71." *Montana, The Magazine of Western History,* 13, no. 3 (July 1963).

Ambrose, Stephen E. *Crazy Horse and Custer: The Parallel Lives of Two American Warriors.* Garden City, N.Y.: Doubleday, 1975.

Anderson, Gary Clayton. *Kinsmen of Another Kind: Dakota-White Relations in the Upper Mississippi Valley, 1850–1862.* Lincoln: University of Nebraska Press, 1984.

———. *Little Crow, Spokesman for the Sioux.* St. Paul: Minnesota Historical Society Press, 1986.

———. *Sitting Bull and the Paradox of Lakota Nationhood.* New York: Harper Collins, 1996.

Anderson, Gary Clayton, and Alan R. Woolworth, eds. *Through Dakota Eyes: Narrative Accounts of the Minnesota Indian War of 1862.* St. Paul: Minnesota Historical Society Press, 1988.

Anderson, Harry H. "The Battle of Slim Buttes." *Chicago Westerners Brand Book* 22, no. 7 (Sept. 1965): 49–51, 55–56.

———. "Centennial of Fetterman Fight." *Chicago Westerners Brand Book* 23, no. 10 (Dec. 1966).

———. "A Challenge to Brown's Sioux Indian Wars Thesis." *Montana, the Magazine of Western History,* 12, no. 1 (Winter 1962): 40–49.

———. "Cheyennes at the Little Big Horn: A Study of Statistics." *North Dakota History* 27, no. 2 (Spring 1960): 81–93.

———. "The Controversial Sioux Amendment to the Fort Laramie Treaty of 1851" *Nebraska History* 37, no. 3 (Sept. 1956): 201–20.

———. "From Milwaukee to the California Gold Fields." *Chicago Westerners Brand Book* 26, no. 8 (Oct. 1969).

———. "Fur Traders as Fathers: The Origins of the Mixed-Blooded Community Among the Rosebud Sioux." *South Dakota History* 3, no. 3 (Summer 1973): 233–70.

———. "Harney v. Twiss; Nebraska Territory, 1856" *Chicago Westerners Brand Book* 20, no. 1 (Mar. 1963).

———. "A History of the Cheyenne River Indian Agency and its Military Post, Fort Bennett, 1868–1891" *South Dakota Report and Historical Collections* 28 (1956).

———. "Indian Peace-Talkers and the Conclusion of the Sioux War of 1876" *Nebraska History* 44, no. 4 (Dec. 1963): 233–54.

———. "Nelson Miles and the Sioux War of 1876–77" *Chicago Westerners Brand Book* 16, no. 4 (June 1959): 25–27, 32.

————. "A Sioux Pictorial Account of General Terry's Council at Fort Walsh, October 17, 1877." *North Dakota History* 22, no. 3 (July 1955): 92–116.

————. "With Harney Through the Bad Lands." *The Wi-Iyohi, Monthly Bulletin of the South Dakota Historical Society* 14, no. 6 (Sept. 1960).

Appleman, Roy E. "The Fetterman Fight." In *Great Western Indian Fights*, ed. Members of the Potomac Corral of the Westerners, 117–31. Reprint, Lincoln: University of Nebraska Press, 1966.

————. "The Hayfield Fight." In *Great Western Indian Fights*, ed. Members of the Potomac Corral of the Westerners, 138–39. Reprint, Lincoln: University of Nebraska Press, 1966.

————. "The Wagon Box Fight." In *Great Western Indian Fights*, ed. Members of the Potomac Corral of the Westerners, 152. Reprint, Lincoln: University of Nebraska Press, 1966.

Athearn, Robert G. "The Firewagon Road." In *The Great Sioux War, 1876–77*, ed. Paul L. Hedren, 65–84. Helena: Montana State Historical Society Press, 1991.

————. *William Tecumseh Sherman and the Settlement of the West*. Norman: University of Oklahoma Press, 1956.

Bad Heart Bull, Amos, and Helen H. Blish. *A Pictographic History of the Oglala Sioux*. Lincoln: University of Nebraska Press, 1967.

Bent, George. "Forty Years with the Cheyennes." *The Frontier* 4, no. 7 (Jan. 1906): 4–5.

Berthrong, Donald J. *The Southern Cheyennes*. Norman: University of Oklahoma Press, 1963.

Bettelyoun, Susan Bordeaux, and Josephine Waggoner. *With My Own Eyes: A Lakota Woman Tells Her People's History*. Ed. Emily Levine. Lincoln: University of Nebraska Press, 1998.

Blakeslee, Donald John. "The Plains Interband Trade System: An Ethnohistoric and Archaeological Investigation." PhD dissertation, University of Wisconsin–Milwaukee, 1975.

Bordeaux, William J. *Conquering the Mighty Sioux*. Sioux Falls, S.Dak.: Author, 1929.

————. *Custer's Conqueror*. n.p., n.d. [1944].

Bourke, John Gregory. *On the Border with Crook*. Reprint, Lincoln: University of Nebraska Press, 1971.

Bray, Edmund C., and Martha C. Bray, trans. and ed. *Joseph N. Nicollet on the Plains and Prairies: The Expeditions of 1838–39 with Journals, Letters, and Notes on the Dakota Indians*. St. Paul: Minnesota Historical Society, 1976.

Bray, Kingsley M. "Before Sitting Bull: Interpreting Hunkpapa Political History, 1750–1867." *South Dakota History* (in press).

————. "Crazy Horse and the End of the Great Sioux War." *Nebraska History* 79, no. 3 (Fall 1998): 94–115.

————. "Lone Horn's Peace: A New View of Sioux-Crow Relations." *Nebraska History* 66, no. 1 (Spring 1985): 28–47.

————. "The Oglala Lakota and the Establishment of Fort Laramie." *Museum of the Fur Trade Quarterly* 36, no. 4 (Winter 2000): 3–18.

———. "The Political History of the Oglala Sioux, Part 2: Breaking the Oglala Hoop, 1825–50." *American Indian Studies Series*. London: English Westerners' Society, 1985.

———. "Spotted Tail and the Treaty of 1868" *Nebraska History* 83, no. 1 (Spring 2002): 19–35.

———. "Teton Sioux Population History, 1655–1881." *Nebraska History* 75, no. 2 (Summer 1994): 165–88.

———. "'We Belong to the North': The Flights of the Northern Indians from the White River Agencies, 1877–78" *Montana, the Magazine of Western History* 55, no. 3 (Summer 2005): 28–47.

Brininstool, E. A. *Crazy Horse: The Invincible Ogalalla Sioux Chief.* Los Angeles: Wetzel Publishing, 1949.

———. "Chief Crazy Horse, His Career and Death." *Nebraska History* (special issue) 12, no. 1 (Jan.–Mar. 1929).

———. "How 'Crazy Horse' Died." *Nebraska History* 12, no. 1 (Jan.-Mar. 1929).

Bronson, Edgar Beecher. *Reminiscences of a Ranchman*. Reprint, Lincoln: University of Nebraska Press, 1962.

Brown, Dee. *Bury My Heart At Wounded Knee: An Indian History of the American West*. London: Barrie and Jenkins, 1971.

———. *Fort Phil Kearny: An American Saga*. New York: Putnam's, 1962.

———. *The Galvanized Yankees*. Reprint, Lincoln: University of Nebraska Press, 1986.

Brown, Joseph Epes. *The Sacred Pipe: Black Elk's Account of the Seven Rites of the Oglala Sioux*. Norman: University of Oklahoma Press, 1953.

Brown, Mark H. *The Plainsmen of the Yellowstone: A History of the Yellowstone Basin*. Reprint, Lincoln: University of Nebraska Press, 1969.

Buechel, Eugene. *A Dictionary of Teton Sioux*. Pine Ridge, S.Dak.: Red Cloud Indian School, 1983.

Buechel, Eugene A., and Paul I. Manhart. *Lakota Tales and Texts*. Chamberlain, S.Dak.: Tipi Press, 1998.

Buecker, Thomas R. *Fort Robinson and the American West, 1874–1899*. Lincoln: Nebraska State Historical Society, 1999.

———. "A History of Camp Robinson, Nebraska, 1874–1878." Master's thesis, Chadron State College, 1992.

———. "The Long Summer: Red Cloud Agency and Camp Robinson in 1876." Paper presented at 7th Annual Little Big Horn Symposium, Hardin, Montana, June 25, 1993.

———. "Lt. William Philo Clark's Sioux War Report and Little Big Horn Map." *Greasy Grass* 7 (May 1991): 11–21.

Buecker, Thomas R., and R. Eli Paul, eds. *The Crazy Horse Surrender Ledger*. Lincoln: Nebraska State Historical Society, 1994.

Burdick, Usher L., ed. *David F. Barry's Indian Notes on the Custer Battle*. Baltimore, Md.: The Proof Press, 1937.

Carley, Kenneth. *The Sioux Uprising of 1862*. St. Paul: Minnesota Historical Society, 1976.

Carrington, Frances C. *My Army Life: A Soldier's Wife at Fort Phil Kearny*. Reprint, Boulder, Colo.: Pruett Publishing Co., 1990.

Carrington, Margaret Irvin. *Absaraka: Home of the Crows*. Reprint, Lincoln: University of Nebraska Press, 1983.

Chalfant, William Y. *Cheyennes at Dark Water Creek: The Last Fight of the Red River War*. Norman: University of Oklahoma Press, 1997.

———. *Cheyennes and Horse Soldiers: The 1857 Expedition and the Battle of Solomon's Fork*. Norman: University of Oklahoma Press, 1989.

Chittenden, Hiram Martin, and Alfred Talbot Richardson. *Life, Letters, and Travels of Father Pierre-Jean De Smet, S.J.* 4 vols. New York: F. P. Harper, 1905.

Clark, Robert A., ed. *The Killing of Chief Crazy Horse: Three Eyewitness Views by the Indian, Chief He Dog, the Indian-White, William Garnett, the White Doctor, Valentine McGillycuddy, with Commentary by Carroll Friswold*. Reprint, Lincoln: University of Nebraska Press, 1988.

Clark, W. P. *The Indian Sign Language*. Reprint, Lincoln: University of Nebraska Press, 1982.

Clodfelter, Micheal. *The Dakota War: The United States Versus the Sioux, 1862–1865*. Jefferson, N.C.: McFarland and Co., 1998.

Clow, Richmond L. "Mad Bear: William S. Harney and the Sioux Expedition of 1855–1856." *Nebraska History* 61, no. 2 (Summer 1980): 133–51.

———. "The Whetstone Indian Agency." *South Dakota History* 7 (1977): 291–308.

Clowser, Don C. *Dakota Indian Treaties: The Dakota Indians from Nomad to Reservation*. Deadwood, S.Dak.: Don C. Clowser, 1974.

Coel, Margaret. *Chief Left Hand, Southern Arapaho*. Norman: University of Oklahoma Press, 1981.

Coutant, G. C. *History of Wyoming*. 2 vols. Reprint, New York: 1966.

Culbertson, Thaddeus A. "Journal of an Expedition to the Mauvaises Terres and the Upper Missouri in 1850." Ed. John F. McDermott. *Bureau of American Ethnology Bulletin* 147 (1952): 135–36.

Curtis, Edward S. *The Teton Sioux*. Vol. 3 in *The North American Indian*. Cambridge, Mass.: The University Press, 1908.

Custer, George Armstrong. "Battling with the Sioux on the Yellowstone." In *The Custer Reader*, ed. Paul Andrew Hutton, 201–19. Lincoln: University of Nebraska Press, 1992.

———, ed. *Milo Milton Quaife: My Life on the Plains*. Reprint, Lincoln: University of Nebraska Press, 1966.

D'Azevedo, Warren L., vol. ed. *Great Basin*. Vol. 11 in *Handbook of North American Indians*, series ed. William C. Sturtevant. Washington, D.C.: Government Printing Office, 1986.

DeBarthe, Joe. *The Life and Adventures of Frank Grouard*. Ed. Edgar I. Stewart. Norman: University of Oklahoma Press, 1958.

DeLand, Charles E. *The Sioux Wars*. Pierre: South Dakota Historical Collections 17, 1934.

Deloria, Ella C. *Speaking of Indians*. New York: Friendship Press, 1944.

———. *Waterlily*. Lincoln: University of Nebraska Press, 1988.

DeMallie, Raymond J., vol. ed. *Plains*. Vol. 13, pts. 1 and 2 of *Handbook of North American Indians*, series ed. William C. Sturtevant. Washington, D.C.: Government Printing Office, 2001.

———. "Lakota Belief and Ritual in the Nineteenth Century." In *Sioux Indian Religion*, ed. Raymond J. DeMallie and Douglas R. Parks. Norman: University of Oklahoma Press, 1987.

———. "Sioux Until 1850." In *Handbook of North American Indians,* vol. 13, *Plains*, vol. ed. Raymond J. DeMallie, 718–60. Washington D.C.: Government Printing Office, 2001.

———. *The Sixth Grandfather: Black Elk's Teachings Given to John G. Neihardt*. Lincoln: University of Nebraska Press, 1984.

———. "Teton." In *Handbook of North American Indians,* vol. 13, *Plains*, vol. ed. Raymond J. DeMallie, 794–820. Washington D.C.: Government Printing Office, 2001.

———. "Teton Dakota Kinship and Social Organization." PhD dissertation, University of Chicago, 1971.

———. "Touching the Pen: Plains Indian Treaty Councils in Ethnohistorical Perspective." In *Ethnicity on the Great Plains*, ed. Frederick C. Luebke. Lincoln: University of Nebraska Press, 1980.

DeMallie, Raymond J., and Douglas R. Parks, eds. *Sioux Indian Religion*. Norman: University of Nebraska Press, 1987.

Denig, Edwin Thompson. *Five Indian Tribes of the Upper Missouri: Sioux, Arickaras, Assiniboines, Crees, Crows*. Ed. John C. Ewers. Norman: University of Oklahoma Press, 1961.

———. "Indian Tribes of the Upper Missouri." Ed. J. N. B. Hewitt. *Annual Report of the Bureau of American Ethnology* 46 (1930): n.p.

Densmore, Frances. *Teton Sioux Music and Culture*. Reprint, Lincoln: University of Nebraska Press, 1992.

De Trobriand, Philippe Regis. *Military Life in Dakota: The Journal of Philippe Regis de Trobriand*. Ed. and trans. Lucile M. Kane. Reprint, Lincoln: University of Nebraska Press, 1982.

Dickson, Ephraim D., III. "Crazy Horse: Who really wielded bayonet that killed the Oglala leader?" *Greasy Grass* 12 (May 1996): 2–10.

Diedrich, Mark. *Famous Chiefs of the Eastern Sioux*. Minneapolis, Minn.: Coyote Books, 1987.

———. *The Odyssey of Chief Standing Buffalo and the Northern Sisseton Sioux*. Minneapolis, Minn.: Coyote Books, 1988.

———. *Sitting Bull: The Collected Speeches*. Rochester, Minn.: Coyote Books, 1998.

Dixon, Joseph K. *The Vanishing Race: The Last Great Indian Council*. Garden City, N.Y.: Doubleday, Page and Co., 1913.

Dorsey, James Owen. "Siouan Sociology: A Posthumous Paper." *Annual Report of the Bureau of American Ethnology* 15 (1897): 207–44.

———. *A Study of Siouan Cults*. Reprint, Seattle, Wash.: The Shorey Book Store, 1972.

Drum, Richard C. "Reminiscences of the Indian Fight at Ash Hollow, 1855." *Collections of the Nebraska State Historical Society* 16 (1911): 143–51.

Dunlay, Thomas W. *Wolves for the Blue Soldiers: Indian Scouts and Auxiliaries with the United States Army, 1860–90*. Lincoln: University of Nebraska Press, 1982.

Eastman, Charles A. *Indian Heroes and Great Chieftains*. Reprint, Lincoln: University of Nebraska Press, 1991.

———. "The Story of the Little Big Horn." *The Chautauquan: A Monthly Magazine For Self-Education* 31, no. 4 (July 1900): 353–58.

Ewers, John C. "Military Art of the Plains Indians." In *Military Art, Warfare and Change*, vol. 1 of *The People of the Buffalo: The Plains Indians of North America, Essays in Honor of John C. Ewers*, ed. Taylor, Colin F. and Hugh A. Dempsey, 24–37. Wyk auf Foehr, Germany: Tatanka Press, 2003.

Feraca, Stephen E. *Wakinyan: Lakota Religion in the Twentieth Century*. Lincoln: University of Nebraska Press, 1998.

Finerty, John F. *War-Path and Bivouac, or The Conquest of the Sioux*. Reprint, Norman: University of Oklahoma Press, 1961.

Fletcher, Alice C. "Indian Ceremonies—The Shadow or Ghost Lodge: A Ceremony of the Ogallala Sioux." Report, Peabody Museum of American Archaeology and Ethnology, 16 (1884): 296–307.

Fletcher, Alice C., with James R. Murie. *The Hako: Song, Pipe, and Unity in a Pawnee Calumet Ceremony*. Washington, D.C.: Government Printing Office, 1904.

Fowler, Loretta. *Arapahoe Politics, 1851–1978: Symbols in Crises of Authority*. Lincoln: University of Oklahoma Press, 1982.

Fox, Richard Allan, Jr. *Archaeology, History, and Custer's Last Battle: The Little Big Horn Reexamined*. Norman: University of Oklahoma Press, 1993.

———. "West River History: The Indian Village on Little Bighorn River, June 25–26, 1876." In *Legacy: New Perspectives on the Battle of the Little Bighorn*, ed. Charles E. Rankin. Helena: Montana Historical Society Press, 1996.

Frost, Lawrence A. *Custer's 7th Cav and the Campaign of 1873*. El Segundo, Calif.: Upton and Sons, 1986.

Fugle, Eugene. *The Nature and Function of the Lakota Night Cults*. Reprint, Kendall Park, N.J.: Lakota Books, 1994.

Gibbon, Guy. *The Sioux: The Dakota and Lakota Nations*. Oxford: Blackwell Publishing, 2003.

Gilbert, Hilda. *"Big Bat" Pourier*. Sheridan, Wyo.: Mills Co., 1968.

Gilbert, James N. "The Death of Crazy Horse: A Contemporary Examination of the Homicidal Events of 5 September 1877." *Journal of the West* 34, no. 1 (Jan. 1993): 5–21.

Gilbert, Neil. 1999. "Did Crook Fail Custer?" Lecture given at Hastings Museum, Hastings, U.K., Dec. 4, 1999. Text in author's collection.

Gonzalez, Mario, and Elizabeth Cook-Lynn. *The Politics of Hallowed Ground: Wounded Knee and the Struggle for Indian Sovereignty*. Urbana and Chicago: University of Illinois Press, 1999.

Goodyear, Frank H., III. *Red Cloud: Photographs of a Lakota Chief.* Lincoln: University of Nebraska Press, 2003.

Graham, W. A. *The Custer Myth: A Source Book of Custeriana.* Reprint, Lincoln: University of Nebraska Press, 1986.

———. *The Reno Court of Inquiry: Abstract of the Official Record of Proceedings.* Mechanicsburg, Pa.: Stackpole Books, 1954.

Grange, Roger T., Jr. "Fort Robinson, Outpost on the Plains." *Nebraska History* 39, no. 3 (Sept. 1958): 196–200.

Gray, John S. "Blazing the Bridger and Bozeman Trails." *Annals of Wyoming* 49, no. 1 (Spring 1977): 23–51.

———. *Centennial Campaign: The Sioux War of 1876.* Fort Collins, Colo.: The Old Army Press, 1976.

———. *Custer's Last Campaign: Mitch Boyer and the Little Bighorn Reconstructed.* Lincoln: University of Nebraska Press, 1991.

———. "Frank Grouard: Kanaka Scout or Mulatto Renegade?" *Chicago Westerners Brand Book* 16 (1959): 57–64.

Greene, Jerome A., ed. *Battles and Skirmishes of the Great Sioux War, 1876–1877: The Military View.* Norman: University of Oklahoma Press, 1993.

———. *Evidence and the Custer Enigma: A Reconstruction of Indian-Military History.* Golden, Colo.: Outbooks, 1986.

———., ed. *Lakota and Cheyenne: Indian Views of the Great Sioux War, 1876–1877.* Norman: University of Oklahoma Press, 1994.

———. *Morning Star Dawn: The Powder River Expedition and the Northern Cheyennes, 1876.* Norman: University of Oklahoma Press, 2003.

———. *Nez Perce Summer, 1877: The U.S. Army and the Nee-Me-Poo Crisis.* Helena: Montana Historical Society, 2000.

———. *Slim Buttes, 1876: An Episode of the Great Sioux War.* Norman: University of Oklahoma Press, 1982.

———, ed. "'We do not know what the Government intends to do . . .': Lt. Palmer Writes from the Bozeman Trail, 1867–68." *Montana, The Magazine of Western History,* 28, no. 2 (Summer 1978): 16–35.

———. *Yellowstone Command.* Lincoln: University of Nebraska Press, 1991.

Grinnell, George Bird. *The Fighting Cheyennes.* Norman: University of Oklahoma Press, 1956.

Hackett, Fred B., ed. *Odds and Ends.* [Pamphlet] n.p., n.d. [Chicago, ca. 1955].

Hafen, Leroy R. *Broken Hand, The Life of Thomas Fitzpatrick: Mountain Man, Guide and Indian Agent.* Reprint, Lincoln: University of Nebraska Press, 1981.

Hafen, Leroy R., and Ann W. Hafen. *Powder River Campaigns and Sawyers Expedition of 1865.* Glendale, Calif.: A. H. Clark, 1961.

———. *Relations with the Indians of the Plains, 1857–1861: A Documentary Account of the Military Campaigns, and Negotiations of Indian Agents, etc.* Glendale, Calif.: A. H. Clark, 1959.

Hafen, Leroy R., and Francis Marion Young. *Fort Laramie and the Pageant of the West, 1834–1890*. Reprint, Lincoln: University of Nebraska Press, 1984.

Hall, Robert L. *An Archaeology of the Soul: North American Indian Belief and Ritual*. Urbana: University of Illinois Press, 1997.

Hammer, Kenneth M., ed. *Custer in '76: Walter Camp's Notes on the Custer Fight*. Reprint, Norman: University of Oklahoma Press, 1990.

Hanson, Charles E., Jr. *The David Adams Journals*. Chadron, Neb.: The Museum of the Fur Trade, 1994.

Hanson, James A. *Famous Indians of Northwest Nebraska*. Chadron, Neb.: Chadron Nebraska Centennial, 1983.

———., ed. *Little Chief's Gatherings: The Smithsonian Institution's G. K. Warren 1855–1856 Plains Indian Collection, and the New York State Library's 1855–1857 Warren Expedition Journals*. Crawford, Neb.: The Fur Press, 1996.

———. *Metal Weapons, Tools, and Ornaments of the Teton Dakota Indians*. Lincoln: University of Nebraska Press, 1975.

Hardorff, Richard G., ed. *Cheyenne Memories of the Custer Fight*. Reprint, Lincoln: University of Nebraska Press, 1998.

———., ed. *Hokahey! A Good Day to Die! The Indian Casualties of the Custer Fight*. Spokane, Wash.: A. H. Clark, 1993.

———., ed. *Lakota Recollections of the Custer Fight: New Sources of Indian-Military History*. Spokane, Wash.: A. H. Clark, 1991.

———. *Markers, Artifacts and Indian Testimony: Preliminary Findings on the Custer Battle*. Short Hills, N.J.: Donald Horn, 1985.

———. *The Oglala Lakota Crazy Horse: A Preliminary Genealogical Study and an Annotated Listing of Primary Sources*. Mattituck, N.J.: J. M. Carroll and Co., 1985.

———. "'Stole-One-Hundred-Horses Winter': The Year the Oglala Crazy Horse was Born." *Research Review: The Journal of the Little Big Horn Associates* (June 1987): 44–47.

———., ed. *The Surrender and Death of Crazy Horse: A Source Book about a Tragic Episode in Lakota History*. Spokane, Wash.: A. H. Clark, 1998.

Hassrick, Royal B. *The Sioux: Life and Customs of a Warrior Society*. Norman: University of Oklahoma Press, 1964.

Hayden, Ferdinand V. *Contributions to the Ethnography and Philology of the Indian Tribes of the Missouri Valley*. Philadelphia: Sherman and Son, 1862.

Hebard, Grace Raymond. *Washakie, Chief of the Shoshones*. Reprint, Lincoln: University of Nebraska Press, 1995.

Hebard, Grace Raymond, and E. A. Brininstool. *The Bozeman Trail: Historic Accounts of the Blazing of the Overland Routes into the Northwest and the Fights with Red Cloud's Warriors*. 2 vols. Reprint, Lincoln: University of Nebraska Press, 1990.

Hedren, Paul L. "The Crazy Horse Medal: An Enigma From the Great Sioux War." *Nebraska History* 75, no. 2 (Summer 1994): 195–99.

———. *First Scalp for Custer: The Skirmish at Warbonnet Creek, Nebraska, July 17, 1876*. Reprint, Lincoln: University of Nebraska Press, 1987.

————. *Fort Laramie in 1876: Chronicle of a Frontier Post at War*. Lincoln: University of Nebraska Press, 1988.

————., ed. *The Great Sioux War, 1876–77: The Best from Montana, The Magazine of Western History*. Helena: Montana State Historical Society Press, 1991.

————. *Traveler's Guide to the Great Sioux War: The Battlefields, Forts, and Related Sites of America's Greatest Indian War*. Helena: Montana Historical Society Press, 1996.

Hoig, Stan. *The Sand Creek Massacre*. Norman: University of Oklahoma Press, 1961.

Howard, James H., ed. *The Warrior Who Killed Custer: The Personal Narrative of Chief Joseph White Bull*. Lincoln: University of Nebraska Press, 1968.

Howe, George Frederick. "Expedition to the Yellowstone River in 1873: Letters of a Young Cavalry Officer." In *The Custer Reader*, ed. Paul Andrew Hutton 180–200. Lincoln: University of Nebraska Press, 1992.

Hoxie, Frederick E. *Parading Through History: The Making of the Crow Nation in America, 1805–1935*. Cambridge: Cambridge University Press, 1995.

Hutchins, James S. "Poison in the Pemmican: The Yellowstone Wagon-Road and Prospecting Expedition of 1874." *Montana, the Magazine of Western History* 8 (Summer 1958): 8–15.

Hutton, Paul Andrew, ed. *The Custer Reader*. Lincoln: University of Nebraska Press, 1992.

————. *Phil Sheridan and His Army*. Lincoln: University of Nebraska Press, 1985.

Hyde, George E. *Life of George Bent, Written From His Letters*. Norman: University of Oklahoma Press, 1968.

————. *Red Cloud's Folk: A History of the Oglala Sioux Indians*. Norman: University of Oklahoma Press, 1937.

————. *A Sioux Chronicle*. Norman: University of Oklahoma Press, 1956.

————. *Spotted Tail's Folk: A History of the Brule Sioux*. Norman: University of Oklahoma Press, 1974.

Jackson, Donald. *Custer's Gold: The United States Cavalry Expedition of 1874*. Reprint, Lincoln: University of Nebraska Press, 1972.

Johnson, Barry C., and Francis B. Taunton. *More Sidelights of the Sioux Wars*. London: English Westerners' Society, 2004.

Jones, Brian. "John Richard, Jr. and the Killing at Fetterman." *Annals of Wyoming* 43, no. 2 (Fall 1971).

————. "Those Wild Reshaw Boys." In *Sidelights of the Sioux Wars*, English Westerners' Special Publication No. 2 (1967).

Josephy, Alvin M., Jr. *The Patriot Chiefs: Studies of Nine great leaders of the North American Indians*. London: Eyre and Spottiswoode, 1962.

Kadlecek, Edward, and Mabell Kadlecek. *To Kill an Eagle: Indian Views on the Death of Crazy Horse*. Boulder, Colo.: Johnson Books, 1981.

Keenan, Jerry. *The Wagon Box Fight*. Sheridan, Wyo.: The Fort Phil Kearny/Bozeman Trail Association, 1990.

Kelly, Fanny. *My Captivity Among the Sioux Indians*. Reprint, Secaucus, N.J.: Citadel Press, 1973.

Kime, Wayne R., ed. *The Black Hills Journals of Colonel Richard Irving Dodge*. Norman: University of Oklahoma Press, 1996.

———., ed. *The Powder River Expedition Journals of Colonel Richard Irving Dodge*. Norman: University of Oklahoma Press, 1997.

Knight, Oliver. "War or Peace: The Anxious Wait for Crazy Horse." *Nebraska History* 54, no. 4 (Winter 1973): 521–44.

Krause, Herbert, and Gary D. Olson. *Prelude to Glory: A Newspaper Accounting of Custer's 1874 Expedition to the Black Hills*. Sioux Falls, S.Dak.: Brevet Press, 1974.

Kuhlman, Charles. *Legend Into History, and, Did Custer Disobey Orders at the Battle of the Little Big Horn?* Mechanicsburg, Pa.: Stackpole Books, 1994.

Larson, Robert W. *Red Cloud, Warrior-Statesman of the Lakota Sioux*. Norman: University of Oklahoma Press, 1997.

Lavender, David. *Fort Laramie and the Changing Frontier*. Washington, D.C.: National Park Service, 1983.

Lazarus, Edward. *Black Hills, White Justice: The Sioux Nation Versus the United States, 1775 to the Present*. New York: Harper Collins, 1991.

Lee, Bob. "First Sergeant Crazy Horse." Paper presented at West River History Conference, Sept. 19, 1997.

Lee, Lucy W. "Recollections." *Nebraska History* 12, no. 1 (Jan.–Mar. 1929): 32–34.

Lee, Jesse M. "The Capture and Death of an Indian Chieftain." *Journal of the Military Service Institute of the United States* 54 (1914): 323–40.

Lemly, H. R. "The Passing of Crazy Horse." *Journal of the Military Service Institute of the United States* 54 (1914): 317–22.

Lewis, Thomas H. *The Medicine Men: Oglala Sioux Ceremony and Healing*. Lincoln: University of Nebraska Press, 1990.

Liddic, Bruce R., and Paul Harbaugh, eds. *Camp on Custer: Transcribing the Custer Myth*. Spokane, Wash.: A. H. Clark, 1995.

———. *Custer and Company: Walter Camp's Notes on the Custer Fight*. Reprint, Lincoln: University of Nebraska Press, 1998.

Linderman, Frank B. *Plenty-Coups, Chief of the Crows*. Reprint, Lincoln: University of Nebraska Press, 1962.

Lowe, Percival G. *Five Years A Dragoon ('49 to '54) and other Adventures on the Great Plains*. Kansas City, Mo.: F. Hudson, 1906.

Lowie, Robert H. *The Crow Indians*. Reprint, Lincoln: University of Nebraska Press, 1983.

Mails, Thomas E. *Fools Crow*. New York: Avon Books, 1979.

Mallery, Garrick. *The Dakota and Corbusier Winter Counts*. Reprint, Lincoln, Neb.: J and L Reprint, 1987.

Mangum, Neil C. *Battle of the Rosebud: Prelude to the Little Bighorn*. El Segundo, Calif.: Upton and Sons, 1996.

Manypenny, George W. *Our Indian Wards*. Cincinnati, Ohio: R. Clarke and Co., 1880.

Manzione, Joseph. *"I Am Looking to the North for My Life": Sitting Bull, 1876–1881*. Salt Lake City: University of Utah Press, 1991.

Marquis, Thomas B. *The Cheyennes of Montana*. Algonac, Mich.: Reference Publications, 1978.

————. [Thomas H. Leforge] *Memoirs of a White Crow Indian*. Reprint, Lincoln: University of Nebraska Press, 1974.

————, ed. [Kate Big Head] "She Watched Custer's Last Battle." In *The Custer Reader*, ed. Paul Andrew Hutton. Lincoln: University of Nebraska Press, 1992.

————. *Wooden Leg: A Warrior Who Fought Custer*. Reprint, Lincoln: University of Nebraska Press, n.d.

Masters, J. G. *Shadows Fall Across the Little Horn: Custer's Last Stand*. Laramie: University of Wyoming Library, 1951.

Mattes, Merrill J. *Indians, Infants, and Infantry: Andrew and Elizabeth Burt on the Frontier*. Denver, Colo.: Old West, 1960.

Mattison, Ray H., ed. "The Harney Expedition against the Sioux: The Journal of Capt. John B. S. Todd." *Nebraska History* 43, no. 2 (June 1962): 89–130.

McCann, Lloyd E. "The Grattan Massacre." *Nebraska History* 37, no. 1 (Mar. 1956): 1–25.

McCreight, M. I. *Chief Flying Hawk's Tales: The True Story of Custer's Last Fight*. New York: Alliance Press, 1936.

————. *Firewater and Forked Tongues: A Sioux Chief Interprets U.S. History*. Pasadena, Calif.: Trail's End Publishing, 1947.

McDonnell, Anne, ed. "The Fort Benton Journal, 1854–1856, and the Fort Sarpy Journal, 1855–1856." *Montana State Historical Society Contributions* 10 (1940).

McGillycuddy, Julia B. *Blood on the Moon: Valentine McGillycuddy and the Sioux*. Reprint, Lincoln: University of Nebraska Press, 1990.

McGinnis, Anthony. *Counting Coup and Cutting Horse: Intertribal Warfare on the Great Plains, 1738–1889*. Evergreen, Colo.: Cordillera Press, 1990.

McLaughlin, James L. *My Friend the Indian*. Reprint, Lincoln: University of Nebraska Press, 1989.

McMurtry, Larry. *Crazy Horse*. New York: Lipper/Viking, 1999.

Medicine Crow, Joseph. *From the Heart of the Crow Country: The Crow Indians' Own Stories*. New York: Orion Books, 1992.

Members of the Potomac Corral of Westerners, ed. *Great Western Indian Fights*. Reprint, Lincoln: University of Nebraska Press, 1966.

Michno, Gregory F. "Crazy Horse, Custer, and the Sweep to the North." *Montana, the Magazine of Western History*, 43 (Summer 1993): 42–53.

————. *Lakota Noon: The Indian Narrative of Custer's Defeat*. Missoula, Mont.: Mountain Press, 1997.

————. *The Mystery of E Troop: Custer's Gray Horse Company at the Little Bighorn*. Missoula, Mont.: Mountain Press, 1994.

Miles, Nelson A. *Personal Recollections and Observations of General Nelson A. Miles*. 2 vols. Reprint, Lincoln: University of Nebraska Press, 1992.

Miller, David Humphreys. *Custer's Fall: The Indian Side of the Story*. Reprint, Lincoln: University of Nebraska Press, 1985.

————. *Ghost Dance*. Reprint, Lincoln: University of Nebraska Press, 1985.

Mirsky, Jeanette. "The Dakota." In *Cooperation and Competition Among Primitive Peoples*, ed. Margaret Mead, 382–427. Boston, Mass.: Beacon Press, 1966.

Monnett, John H. *Massacre at Cheyenne Hole: Lieutenant Austin Henely and the Sappa Creek Controversy*. Niwot: University Press of Colorado, 1999.

Murray, Robert A. *Military Posts in the Powder River Country of Wyoming, 1865–1864*. Lincoln: University of Nebraska Press, 1968.

Nadeau, Remi. *Fort Laramie and the Sioux Indians*. Reprint, Lincoln: University of Nebraska Press, 1982.

Neihardt, John G. *Black Elk Speaks, Being the Life Story of a Holy Man of the Oglala Sioux*. Reprint, Lincoln: University of Nebraska Press, 1961.

————. *When the Tree Flowered: The Story of Eagle Voice, a Sioux Indian*. Reprint, Lincoln: University of Nebraska Press, 1991.

"Official Correspondence Pertaining to the War of the Outbreak, 1862–1865." *South Dakota Historical Society Report and Historical Collections* 31 (1962).

Olson, James C. *Red Cloud and the Sioux Problem*. Lincoln: University of Nebraska Press, 1965.

Ostler, Jeffrey. *The Plains Sioux and U.S. Colonialism from Lewis and Clark to Wounded Knee*. Cambridge: Cambridge University Press, 2004.

Panzeri, Peter F. *Little Bighorn 1876*. Oxford: Osprey Publishing, 1995.

Parker, Watson. *Gold in the Black Hills*. Norman: University of Oklahoma Press, 1966.

Paul, R. Eli, ed. *Autobiography of Red Cloud, War Leader of the Oglalas*. Helena: Montana Historical Society Press, 1997.

————. *Blue Water Creek and the First Sioux War, 1854–1856*. Norman: University of Oklahoma Press, 2004.

————. "An Early Reference to Crazy Horse." *Nebraska History* 75, no. 2 (Summer 1994): 189–90.

————., ed. *The Nebraska Indian Wars Reader, 1865–1877*. Lincoln: University of Nebraska Press, 1998.

Pearson, Jeffrey V. "Nelson A. Miles, Crazy Horse, and the Battle of Wolf Mountains." *Montana, the Magazine of Western History* 51, no. 4 (2001): 52–67.

Poole, D. C. *Among the Sioux of Dakota: Eighteen Months' Experience as an Indian Agent, 1869–70*. Reprint, St. Paul: Minnesota Historical Society Press, 1988.

Porter, Joseph C. *Paper Medicine Man: John Gregory Bourke and His American West*. Norman: University of Oklahoma Press, 1986.

Powell, Peter J. *People of the Sacred Mountain: A History of the Northern Cheyenne Chiefs and Warrior Societies, 1830–1879, With an Epilog 1969–1974*. 2 vols. San Francisco: Harper and Row, 1981.

————. *Sweet Medicine: The Continuing Role of the Sacred Arrows, the Sun Dance, and the Sacred Buffalo hat in Northern Cheyenne History*. 2 vols. Norman: University of Oklahoma Press, 1969.

Powers, Marla N. *Oglala Women: Myth, Ritual, and Reality.* Chicago: University of Chicago Press, 1986.

Powers, William K. *Oglala Religion.* Lincoln: University of Nebraska Press, 1977.

———. *Sacred Language: The Nature of Supernatural Discourse in Lakota.* Norman: University of Nebraska Press, 1986.

———. *A Winter Count of the Oglala.* Reprint, Kendall Park, N.J.: Lakota Books, 1994.

———. *Yuwipi: Vision and Experience in Oglala Ritual.* Lincoln: University of Nebraska Press, 1982.

Price, Catherine. *The Oglala People, 1841–1879: A Political History.* Lincoln: University of Nebraska Press, 1996.

Quivey, Addison M. "The Yellowstone Expedition of 1874." *Montana Historical Society Contributions* 1 (1876): 268–84.

Rankin, Charles E., ed. *Legacy: New Perspectives on the Battle of the Little Bighorn.* Helena: Montana Historical Society Press, 1996.

"Red Cloud's Mission to Crazy Horse, 1877: Source Material." *Museum of the Fur Trade Quarterly* 22 (1986): 9–13.

Riggs, Stephen R. *A Dakota-English Dictionary.* Reprint, St. Paul: Minnesota Historical Society Press, 1992.

Riley, Paul D., ed. "Oglala Sources on the Life of Crazy Horse: Interviews given to Eleanor H. Hinman." *Nebraska History* 57, no. 1 (Spring 1976): 1–51.

Robinson, Doane. *A History of the Dakota or Sioux Indians.* Reprint, Minneapolis, Minn.: Ross and Haines, 1967.

Ruby, Robert H. *The Oglala Sioux: Warriors in Transition.* New York: Vantage Press, 1955.

Sajna, Mike. *Crazy Horse: The Life Behind the Legend.* New York: John Wiley and Sons, 2000.

Sandoz, Mari. *Crazy Horse, the Strange Man of the Oglalas: A Biography.* New York: Hastings House, 1944; Reprint, Lincoln: University of Nebraska Press, 1961.

Sarf, Wayne Michael. *The Little Bighorn Campaign, March-September 1876.* Conshohocken, Pa.: Combined Publishing, 2000.

Schmitt, Martin F. *General George Crook, His Autobiography.* Norman: University of Oklahoma Press, 1960.

Schmutterer, Gerhard M. *Tomahawk and Cross: Lutheran Missionaries among the Northern Plains Tribes, 1858–1866.* Sioux Falls, S.Dak.: The Center for Western Studies, Augustana College, 1989.

Scott, Douglas D., and Peter Bleed. *A Good Walk Around the Boundary: Archeological Inventory of the Dyck and Other Properties Adjacent to Little Bighorn Battlefield National Monument.* Lincoln: Nebraska Association of Professional Archeologists and the Nebraska State Historical Society, 1997.

Scott, Douglas D., and Richard A. Fox, Jr. *Archaeological Insights into The Custer Battle: An Assessment of the 1984 Field Season.* Norman: University of Oklahoma Press, 1987.

Simonin, Louis L. *The Rocky Mountain West in 1867.* Trans. Wilson O. Clough. Lincoln: University of Nebraska Press, 1967.

Sklenar, Larry. *To Hell with Honor: Custer and the Little Bighorn.* Norman: University of Oklahoma Press, 2000.

Sneve, Virginia Driving Hawk. *Dakota's Heritage: A Compilation of Indian Place Names in South Dakota.* Sioux Falls, S.Dak.: Brevet Press, 1973.

Spring, Agnes Wright. *Caspar Collins: The Life and Exploits of an Indian Fighter of the Sixties.* Reprint, Lincoln: University of Nebraska Press, 1969.

―――. "Old Letter Book Discloses Economic History of Fort Laramie, 1858–1871." *Annals of Wyoming* 13 (Oct. 1941).

Standing Bear, Luther. *Land of the Spotted Eagle.* Reprint, Lincoln: University of Nebraska Press, 1978.

―――. *My People the Sioux.* Reprint, Lincoln: University of Nebraska Press, 1975.

Stands in Timber, John and Margot Liberty. *Cheyenne Memories.* New Haven, Conn.: Yale University Press, 1967.

Stanley, Henry M. *My Early Travels and Adventures in America.* Reprint, Lincoln: University of Nebraska Press, 1982.

Steinmetz, Paul B. *Pipe, Bible and Peyote among the Oglala Lakota: A Study in Religious Identity.* Syracuse, N.Y.: Syracuse University Press, 1998.

Stewart, Edgar I. *Custer's Luck.* Norman: University of Oklahoma Press, 1955.

―――., ed. *March of the Montana Column.* Norman: University of Oklahoma Press.

Sunder, John E. *The Fur Trade on the Upper Missouri, 1840–1865.* Norman: University of Oklahoma Press, 1965.

Taunton, Francis B. "Yellowstone Interlude: Custer's Earlier Fights with the Sioux." In *More Sidelights of the Sioux Wars*, ed. Barry C. Johnson and Francis B. Taunton, 69–90. London: English Westerners' Society, 2004.

Taunton, Francis B., with Brian C. Pohanka. *Custer's Field: "A Scene of Sickening Ghastly Horror."* London: The Johnson-Taunton Military Press, 1987.

Taylor, Colin F., and Hugh A. Dempsey, eds. *Military Art, Warfare and Change.* Vol. 1 of *The People of the Buffalo: The Plains Indians of North America, Essays in Honor of John C. Ewers.* Wyk auf Foehr, Germany: Tatanka Press, 2003.

Trenholm, Virginia Cole. *The Arapahoes, Our People.* Norman: University of Oklahoma Press, 1970.

Twitchell, Phillip G. "Camp Robinson Letters of Angeline Johnson, 1876–1879." *Nebraska History* 77, no. 2 (Summer 1996).

Unrau, William E., ed. *Tending the Talking Wire: A Buck Soldier's View of Indian Country, 1863–1866.* Salt Lake City: University of Utah Press, 1979.

Utley, Robert M. *Cavalier in Buckskin: George Armstrong Custer and the Western Military Frontier.* Norman: University of Oklahoma Press, 1988.

―――. "Crazy Horse—Will We Ever Know You?" *Montana, the Magazine of Western History*, 49, no. 4 (1999): 72–73.

―――. *Custer and the Great Controversy: The Origin and Development of a Legend.* Reprint, Lincoln: University of Nebraska Press, 1998.

———. *Frontier Regulars: The United States Army and the Indian*. Reprint, Lincoln: University of Nebraska Press, 1984.

———. *Frontiersmen in Blue: The United States Army and the Indian, 1848–1865*. Reprint, Lincoln: University of Nebraska Press, 1981.

———. *The Indian Frontier of the American West, 1846–1890*. Albuquerque: University of New Mexico Press, 1984.

———. *The Lance and the Shield: The Life and Times of Sitting Bull*. New York: Henry Holt and Co., 1993.

———. *Little Bighorn Battlefield*. Washington, D.C.: National Park Service, 1994.

———. "War Houses in the Sioux Country." In *The Great Sioux War, 1876–77*, ed. Paul L. Hedren, 253–63. Helena: Montana State Historical Society Press, 1991.

Vaughn, J. W. *The Battle of Platte Bridge*. Norman: University of Oklahoma Press, 1963.

———. *Indian Fights: New Facts on Seven Encounters*. Norman: University of Oklahoma Press, 1966.

———. *The Reynolds Campaign on Powder River*. Norman: University of Oklahoma Press, 1966.

———. *With Crook at the Rosebud*. Mechanicsburg, Pa.: Stackpole Books, 1956.

Vestal, Stanley. "The Man Who Killed Custer." *American Heritage* 8, no. 2 (Feb. 1957): 6–7.

———. *New Sources of Plains Indian History, 1850–1891*. Norman: University of Oklahoma Press, 1934.

———. *Sitting Bull, Champion of the Sioux*. Reprint, Norman: University of Oklahoma Press, 1957.

———. *Warpath: The True Story of the Fighting Sioux Told in a Biography of Chief White Bull*. Reprint, Lincoln: University of Nebraska Press, 1984.

Viola, Herman J. *Little Bighorn Remembered: The Untold Indian Story of Custer's Last Stand*. New York: Times Books, 1999.

Walker, James R. *Lakota Belief and Ritual*. Ed. Raymond J. DeMallie and Elaine A. Jahner. Lincoln: University of Nebraska Press, 1980.

———. *Lakota Society*. Ed. Raymond J. DeMallie. Lincoln: University of Nebraska Press, 1982.

———. "The Sun Dance and Other Ceremonies of the Oglala Division of the Teton Dakota." *American Museum of Natural History, Anthropological Papers* 16, pt. 2 (1917): 50–221.

Ware, Eugene F. *The Indian War of 1864*. Reprint, Lincoln: University of Nebraska Press, 1994.

"The War on Whiskey in the Fur Trade." *South Dakota Historical Collections* 9 (1918).

Webb, George W. *Chronological List of Engagements Between the Regular Army of the United States and Various Tribes of Hostile Indians Which Occurred During the Years 1790 to 1898, Inclusive*. Reprint, New York: AMS Press, 1976.

White, Richard M. *The Roots of Dependency: Subsistence, Environment, and Social Change among the Choctaws, Pawnees, and Navajos*. Lincoln: University of Nebraska Press, 1983.

———. "The Winning of the West: The Expansion of the Western Sioux in the Eighteenth and Nineteenth Centuries." *Journal of American History* 65, no. 2 (Sept. 1978): 319–43.

Wissler, Clark. "Societies and Ceremonial Associations in the Oglala Division of the Teton-Dakota." *American Museum of Natural History, Anthropological Papers* 11, pt. 1 (1912): 1–99.

Workers of the South Dakota Writers' Project, Work Projects Administration. *Legends of the Mighty Sioux.* Reprint, Interior, S.Dak.: Badlands Natural History Association, 1987.

"Yellow Nose Tells of Custer's Last Stand." *Bighorn Yellowstone Journal* 1, no. 3 (Summer 1992): 14–17.

INDEX

Page numbers for photographs are italicized.